T0201844

THE HANDBOOK OF
MPEG APPLICATIONS

THE HANDBOOK OF MPEG APPLICATIONS

STANDARDS IN PRACTICE

Editors

Marios C. Angelides and Harry Agius
School of Engineering and Design,
Brunel University, UK

A John Wiley and Sons, Ltd., Publication

Library of Congress Cataloguing-in-Publication Data

The handbook of MPEG applications : standards in practice / edited by Marios C. Angelides & Harry Agius.
    p. cm.
  Includes index.
  ISBN 978-0-470-97458-2 (cloth)
  1. MPEG (Video coding standard)–Handbooks, manuals, etc. 2. MP3 (Audio coding standard)–Handbooks, manuals, etc. 3. Application software–Development–Handbooks, manuals, etc. I. Angelides, Marios C.
II. Agius, Harry.
  TK6680.5.H33 2011
  006.6'96–dc22

                                                                            2010024889

A catalogue record for this book is available from the British Library.

Print ISBN 978-0-470-75007-0 (H/B)
ePDF ISBN: 978-0-470-97459-9
oBook ISBN: 978-0-470-97458-2
ePub ISBN: 978-0-470-97474-2

Typeset in 10/12 Times by Laserwords Private Limited, Chennai, India.
Printed and bound in Singapore by Markono Print Media Pte Ltd.

Contents

List of Contributors

Harry Agius
Electronic and Computer Engineering,
School of Engineering and Design,
Brunel University, UK

Rajeev Agrawal
Department of Electronics, Computer and
Information Technology,
North Carolina A&T State University,
Greensboro, NC USA

Samir Amir
Laboratoire d'Informatique Fondamentale
de Lille,
University Lille1, Télécom Lille1,
IRCICA – Parc de la Haute Borne,
Villeneuve d'Ascq, France

Marios C. Angelides
Electronic and Computer Engineering,
School of Engineering and Design,
Brunel University, UK

Wolf-Tilo Balke
L3S Research Center, Hannover, Germany
IFIS, TU Braunschweig,
Braunschweig, Germany

Andrea Basso
Video and Multimedia Technologies and
Services Research Department,
AT&T Labs – Research,
Middletown, NJ, USA

Ioan Marius Bilasco
Laboratoire d'Informatique Fondamentale
de Lille,
University Lille1, Télécom Lille1,
IRCICA – Parc de la Haute Borne,
Villeneuve d'Ascq, France

Yolanda Blanco-Fernández
Department of Telematics Engineering,
University of Vigo,
Vigo, Spain

Alan C. Bovik
Laboratory for Image and Video
Engineering,
Department of Electrical and Computer
Engineering,
The University of Texas at Austin,
Austin, TX, USA

Stavros Christodoulakis
Lab. of Distributed Multimedia
Information Systems & Applications
(TUC/MUSIC),
Department of Electronic & Computer
Engineering,
Technical University of Crete, Chania,
Greece

Damon Daylamani Zad
Electronic and Computer Engineering,
School of Engineering and Design,
Brunel University, UK

Klaus Diepold
Institute of Data Processing,
Technische Universität München,
Munich, Germany

Chabane Djeraba
Laboratoire d'Informatique Fondamentale
de Lille,
University Lille1, Télécom Lille1,
IRCICA – Parc de la Haute Borne,
Villeneuve d'Ascq, France

Mario Döller
Department of Informatics and
Mathematics,
University of Passau, Passau, Germany

Jian Feng
Department of Computer Science,
Hong Kong Baptist University,
Hong Kong

Farshad Fotouhi
Department of Computer Science,
Wayne State University,
Detroit, MI, USA

David Gibbon
Video and Multimedia Technologies and
Services Research Department,
AT&T Labs – Research,
Middletown, NJ, USA

Alberto Gil-Solla
Department of Telematics Engineering,
University of Vigo, Vigo, Spain

Dan Grois
Communication Systems Engineering
Department,
Ben-Gurion University of the Negev,
Beer-Sheva, Israel

William I. Grosky
Department of Computer and Information
Science,
University of Michigan-Dearborn,
Dearborn, MI, USA

Ofer Hadar
Communication Systems Engineering
Department,
Ben-Gurion University of the Negev,
Beer-Sheva, Israel

Hermann Hellwagner
Institute of Information Technology,
Klagenfurt University, Klagenfurt,
Austria

Luis Herranz
Escuela Politécnica Superior,
Universidad Autónoma de Madrid,
Madrid, Spain

Razib Iqbal
Distributed and Collaborative Virtual
Environments Research Laboratory
(DISCOVER Lab),
School of Information Technology and
Engineering,
University of Ottawa, Ontario, Canada

Evgeny Kaminsky
Electrical and Computer Engineering
Department,
Ben-Gurion University of the Negev,
Beer-Sheva, Israel

Benjamin Köhncke
L3S Research Center,
Hannover, Germany

Harald Kosch
Department of Informatics and
Mathematics,
University of Passau, Passau,
Germany

Bai-Ying Lei
Department of Electronic and Information
Engineering,
The Hong Kong Polytechnic University,
Kowloon, Hong Kong

Xiaomin Liu
School of Computing,
National University of Singapore,
Singapore

Zhu Liu
Video and Multimedia Technologies and
Services Research Department,
AT&T Labs – Research,
Middletown, NJ, USA

Kwok-Tung Lo
Department of Electronic and Information
Engineering,
The Hong Kong Polytechnic University,
Kowloon, Hong Kong

Martín López-Nores
Department of Telematics Engineering,
University of Vigo, Vigo, Spain

Jianhua Ma
Faculty of Computer and Information
Sciences,
Hosei University, Tokyo, Japan

Jean Martinet
Laboratoire d'Informatique Fondamentale
de Lille,
University Lille1, Télécom Lille1,
IRCICA – Parc de la Haute Borne,
Villeneuve d'Ascq, France

José M. Martínez
Escuela Politécnica Superior,
Universidad Autónoma de Madrid,
Madrid, Spain

Andreas U. Mauthe
School of Computing and
Communications, Lancaster University,
Lancaster, UK

Anush K. Moorthy
Laboratory for Image and Video
Engineering,
Department of Electrical and Computer
Engineering,
The University of Texas at Austin,
Austin, TX, USA

José J. Pazos-Arias
Department of Telematics Engineering,
University of Vigo, Vigo, Spain

Chris Poppe
Ghent University – IBBT,
Department of Electronics and Information
Systems – Multimedia Lab, Belgium

Manuel Ramos-Cabrer
Department of Telematics Engineering,
University of Vigo, Vigo, Spain

Florian Schreiner
Institute of Data Processing,
Technische Universität München,
Munich, Germany

Beomjoo Seo
School of Computing,
National University of Singapore,
Singapore

Behzad Shahraray
Video and Multimedia Technologies and
Services Research Department,
AT&T Labs – Research,
Middletown, NJ, USA

Nicholas Paul Sheppard
Library eServices,
Queensland University of Technology,
Australia

Shervin Shirmohammadi
School of Information Technology and
Engineering,
University of Ottawa, Ontario, Canada

Anastasis A. Sofokleous
Electronic and Computer Engineering,
School of Engineering and Design,
Brunel University, UK

Florian Stegmaier
Department of Informatics and
Mathematics,
University of Passau, Passau, Germany

Peter Thomas
AVID Development GmbH,
Kaiserslautern, Germany

Christian Timmerer
Institute of Information Technology,
Klagenfurt University,
Klagenfurt, Austria

Chrisa Tsinaraki
Department of Information Engineering
and Computer Science (DISI),
University of Trento,
Povo (TN), Italy

Thierry Urruty
Laboratoire d'Informatique Fondamentale
de Lille,
University Lille1, Télécom Lille1,
IRCICA – Parc de la Haute Borne,
Villeneuve d'Ascq, France

Rik Van de Walle
Ghent University – IBBT,
Department of Electronics and Information
Systems – Multimedia Lab, Belgium

Davy Van Deursen
Ghent University – IBBT,
Department of Electronics and Information
Systems – Multimedia Lab, Belgium

Wim Van Lancker
Ghent University – IBBT,
Department of Electronics and Information
Systems – Multimedia Lab, Belgium

Lei Ye
School of Computer Science and Software
Engineering,
University of Wollongong, Wollongong,
NSW, Australia

Jun Zhang
School of Computer Science and Software
Engineering,
University of Wollongong, Wollongong,
NSW, Australia

Roger Zimmermann
School of Computing,
National University of Singapore,
Singapore

MPEG Standards in Practice

Marios C. Angelides and Harry Agius, Editors

Electronic and Computer Engineering, School of Engineering and Design, Brunel University, UK

The need for compressed and coded representation and transmission of multimedia data has not rescinded as computer processing power, storage, and network bandwidth have increased. They have merely served to increase the demand for greater quality and increased functionality from all elements in the multimedia delivery and consumption chain, from content creators through to end users. For example, whereas we once had VHS-like resolution of digital video, we now have high-definition 1080p, and whereas a user once had just a few digital media files, they now have hundreds or thousands, which require some kind of metadata just for the required file to be found on the user's storage medium in a reasonable amount of time, let alone for any other functionality such as creating playlists. Consequently, the number of multimedia applications and services penetrating home, education, and work has increased exponentially in recent years, and the emergence of multimedia standards has similarly proliferated.

MPEG, the Moving Picture Coding Experts Group, formally Working Group 11 (WG11) of Subcommittee 29 (SC29) of the Joint Technical Committee (JTC 1) of ISO/IEC, was established in January 1988 with the mandate to develop standards for digital audio-visual media. Since then, MPEG has been seminal in enabling widespread penetration of multimedia, bringing new terms to our everyday vernacular such as 'MP3', and it continues to be important to the development of existing and new multimedia applications. For example, even though MPEG-1 has been largely superseded by MPEG-2 for similar video applications, MPEG-1 Audio Layer 3 (MP3) is still the digital music format of choice for a large number of users; when we watch a DVD or digital TV, we most probably use MPEG-2; when we use an iPod, we engage with MPEG-4 (advanced audio coding (AAC) audio); when watching HDTV or a Blu-ray Disc, we most probably use MPEG-4 Part 10 and ITU-T H.264/advanced video coding (AVC); when we tag web content, we probably use MPEG-7; and when we obtain permission to browse content that is only available to subscribers, we probably achieve this through MPEG-21 Digital Rights Management (DRM). Applications have also begun to emerge that make integrated

The Handbook of MPEG Applications: Standards in Practice   Edited by Marios C. Angelides and Harry Agius
© 2011 John Wiley & Sons, Ltd

use of several MPEG standards, and MPEG-A has recently been developed to cater to application formats through the combination of multiple MPEG standards.

The details of the MPEG standards and how they prescribe encoding, decoding, representation formats, and so forth, have been published widely, and anyone may purchase the full standards documents themselves through the ISO website [http://www.iso.org/]. Consequently, it is not the objective of this handbook to provide in-depth coverage of the details of these standards. Instead, the aim of this handbook is to concentrate on the *application* of the MPEG standards; that is, how they may be used, the context of their use, and how supporting and complementary technologies and the standards interact and add value to each other. Hence, the chapters cover application domains as diverse as multimedia collaboration, personalized multimedia such as advertising and news, video summarization, digital home systems, research applications, broadcasting media, media production, enterprise multimedia, domain knowledge representation and reasoning, quality assessment, encryption, digital rights management, optimized video encoding, image retrieval, multimedia metadata, the multimedia life cycle and resource adaptation, allocation and delivery. The handbook is aimed at researchers and professionals who are working with MPEG standards and should also prove suitable for use on specialist postgraduate/research-based university courses.

In the subsequent sections, we provide an overview of the key MPEG standards that form the focus of the chapters in the handbook, namely: MPEG-2, MPEG-4, H.264/AVC (MPEG-4 Part 10), MPEG-7, MPEG-21 and MPEG-A. We then introduce each of the 21 chapters by summarizing their contribution.

MPEG-2

MPEG-1 was the first MPEG standard, providing simple audio-visual synchronization that is robust enough to cope with errors occurring from digital storage devices, such as CD-ROMs, but is less suited to network transmission. MPEG-2 is very similar to MPEG-1 in terms of compression and is thus effectively an extension of MPEG-1 that also provides support for higher resolutions, frame rates and bit rates, and efficient compression of and support for interlaced video. Consequently, MPEG-2 streams are used for DVD-Video and are better suited to network transmission making them suitable for digital TV.

MPEG-2 compression of progressive video is achieved through the encoding of three different types of *pictures* within a media stream:

- *I-pictures (intra-pictures)* are *intra-coded* that is, they are coded *without* reference to other pictures. Pixels are represented using 8 bits. I-pictures group 8×8 luminance or chrominance pixels into blocks, which are transformed using the discrete cosine transform (DCT). Each set of 64 (12-bit) DCT coefficients is then quantized using a quantization matrix. Scaling of the quantization matrix enables both constant bit rate (CBR) and variable bit rate (VBR) streams to be encoded. The human visual system is highly sensitive at low-frequency levels, but less sensitive at high-frequency levels, hence the quantization matrix reflects the importance attached to low spatial frequencies such that quantums are lower for low frequencies and higher for high frequencies. The coefficients are then ordered according to a *zigzag sequence* so that similar values are kept adjacent. DC coefficients are encoded using differential pulse code modulation

(DPCM), while run length encoding (RLE) is applied to the AC coefficients (mainly zeroes), which are encoded as {*run*, *amplitude*} pairs where *run* is the number of zeros before this non-zero coefficient, up to a previous non-zero coefficient, and *amplitude* is the value of this non-zero coefficient. A Huffman coding variant is then used to replace those pairs having high probabilities of occurrence with variable-length codes. Any remaining pairs are then each coded with an escape symbol followed by a fixed-length code with a 6-bit *run* and an 8-bit *amplitude*.

- *P-pictures (predicted pictures)* are *inter-coded*, that is, they are coded *with* reference to other pictures. P-pictures use block-based motion-compensated prediction, where the reference frame is a previous I-picture or P-picture (whichever immediately precedes the P-picture). The blocks used are termed *macroblocks*. Each macroblock is composed of four 8×8 luminance blocks (i.e. 16×16 pixels) and two 8×8 chrominance blocks (4:2:0). However, motion estimation is only carried out for the luminance part of the macroblock as MPEG assumes that the chrominance motion can be adequately represented based on this. MPEG does not specify any algorithm for determining best matching blocks, so any algorithm may be used. The error term records the difference in content of all six 8×8 blocks from the best matching macroblock. Error terms are compressed by transforming using the DCT and then quantization, as was the case with I-pictures, although the quantization is coarser here and the quantization matrix is uniform (although other matrices may be used instead). To achieve greater compression, blocks that are composed entirely of zeros (i.e. all DCT coefficients are zero) are encoded using a special 6-bit code. Other blocks are zigzag ordered and then RLE and Huffman-like encoding is applied. However, unlike I-pictures, *all* DCT coefficients, that is, both DC and AC coefficients, are treated in the same way. Thus, the DC coefficients are not separately DPCM encoded. Motion vectors will often differ only slightly between adjacent macroblocks. Therefore, the motion vectors are encoded using DPCM. Again, RLE and Huffman-like encoding is then applied. Motion estimation may not always find a suitable matching block in the reference frame (note that this threshold is dependent on the motion estimation algorithm that is used). Therefore, in these cases, a P-picture macroblock may be intra-coded. In this way, the macroblock is coded in exactly the same manner as it would be if it were part of an I-picture. Thus, a P-picture can contain intra- and inter-coded macroblocks. Note that this implies that the codec must determine when a macroblock is to be intra- or inter-coded.
- *B-pictures (bidirectionally predicted pictures)* are also inter-coded and have the highest compression ratio of all pictures. They are never used as reference frames. They are inter-coded using interpolative motion-compensated prediction, taking into account the nearest past I- or P-picture and the nearest future I- or P-picture. Consequently, *two* motion vectors are required: one from the best matching macroblock from the nearest past frame and one from the best matching macroblock from the nearest future frame. Both matching macroblocks are then averaged and the error term is thus the difference between the target macroblock and the interpolated macroblock. The remaining encoding of B-pictures is as it was for P-pictures. Where interpolation is inappropriate, a B-picture macroblock may be encoded using bi-directional motion-compensated prediction, that is, a reference macroblock from a future *or* past I- or P-picture will be used (not both) and therefore, only one motion vector is required. If this too is inappropriate, then the B-picture macroblock will be intra-coded as an I-picture macroblock.

D-pictures (*DC-coded pictures*), which were used for fast searching in MPEG-1, are not permitted in MPEG-2. Instead, an appropriate distribution of I-pictures within the sequence is used.

Within the MPEG-2 video stream, a *group of pictures* (*GOP*) consists of I-, B- and P-pictures, and commences with an I-picture. No more than one I-picture is permitted in any one GOP. Typically, IBBPBBPBB would be a GOP for PAL/SECAM video and IBBPBBPBBPBB would be a GOP for NTSC video (the GOPs would be repeated throughout the sequence).

MPEG-2 compression of interlaced video, particularly from a television source, is achieved as above but with the use of two types of pictures and prediction, both of which may be used in the same sequence. *Field pictures* code the odd and even fields of a frame separately using *motion-compensated field prediction* or *inter-field prediction*. The DCT is applied to a block drawn from 8×8 consecutive pixels within the same field. Motion-compensated field prediction predicts a field from a field of another frame, for example, an odd field may be predicted from a previous odd field. Inter-field prediction predicts from the other field of the same frame, for example, an odd field may be predicted from the even field of the same frame. Generally, the latter is preferred if there is no motion between fields. *Frame pictures* code the two fields of a frame together as a single picture. Each macroblock in a frame picture may be encoded in one of the following three ways: using intra-coding or motion-compensated prediction (*frame prediction*) as described above, or by intra-coding using a field-based DCT, or by coding using field prediction with the field-based DCT. Note that this can lead to up to four motion vectors being needed per macroblock in B-frame-pictures: one from a previous even field, one from a previous odd field, one from a future even field, and one from a future odd field.

MPEG-2 also defines an additional alternative zigzag ordering of DCT coefficients, which can be more effective for field-based DCTs. Furthermore, additional motion-compensated prediction based on 16×8-pixel blocks and a form of prediction known as *dual prime* prediction are also specified.

MPEG-2 specifies several profiles and levels, the combination of which enable different resolutions, frame rates, and bit rates suitable for different applications. Table 1 outlines the characteristics of key MPEG-2 profiles, while Table 2 shows the maximum parameters at each MPEG-2 level. It is common to denote a profile at a particular level by using the '*Profile@Level*' notation, for example, Main Profile @ Main Level (or simply MP@ML).

Audio in MPEG-2 is compressed in one of two ways. *MPEG-2 BC* (*backward compatible*) is an extension to MPEG-1 Audio and is fully backward and mostly forward compatible with it. It supports 16, 22.05, 24 kHz, 32, 44.1 and 48 kHz sampling rates and

Table 1   Characteristics of key MPEG-2 profiles

Characteristic	Profile					
	Simple	Main	SNR scalable	Spatially scalable	High	4:2:2
B-frames		X	X	X	X	X
SNR scalable			X	X	X	X
Spatially scalable				X	X	X
4:2:0	X	X	X	X	X	
4:2:2					X	X

Table 2 Maximum parameters of key MPEG-2 levels

	Level			
Parameter	Low	Main	High-1440	High
Maximum horizontal resolution	352	720	1440	1920
Maximum vertical resolution	288	576	1152	1152
Maximum fps	30	30	60	60

uses perceptual audio coding (i.e. sub-band coding). The bit stream may be encoded in mono, dual mono, stereo or joint stereo. The audio stream is encoded as a set of frames, each of which contains a number of samples and other data (e.g. header and error check bits). The way in which the encoding takes place depends on which of three *layers* of compression are used. *Layer III* is the most complex layer and also provides the best quality. It is known popularly as 'MP3'. When compressing audio, the *polyphase filter bank* maps input pulse code modulation (PCM) samples from the time to the frequency domain and divides the domain into sub-bands. The *psychoacoustical model* calculates the masking effects for the audio samples within the sub-bands. The *encoding* stage compresses the samples output from the polyphase filter bank according to the masking effects output from the psychoacoustical model. In essence, as few bits as possible are allocated, while keeping the resultant quantization noise masked, although Layer III actually allocates noise rather than bits. *Frame packing* takes the quantized samples and formats them into frames, together with any optional *ancillary data*, which contains either additional channels (e.g. for 5.1 surround sound), or data that is not directly related to the audio stream, for example, lyrics.

MPEG-2 AAC is not compatible with MPEG-1 and provides very high-quality audio with a twofold increase in compression over BC. AAC includes higher sampling rates up to 96 kHz, the encoding of up to 16 programmes, and uses profiles instead of layers, which offer greater compression ratios and scalable encoding. AAC improves on the core encoding principles of Layer III through the use of a filter bank with a higher frequency resolution, the use of temporal noise shaping (which improves the quality of speech at low bit rates), more efficient entropy encoding, and improved stereo encoding.

An MPEG-2 stream is a synchronization of *elementary streams* (*ESs*). An ES may be an encoded video, audio or data stream. Each ES is split into packets to form a *packetized elementary stream* (*PES*). Packets are then grouped into *packs* to form the stream. A stream may be multiplexed as a *program stream* (e.g. a single movie) or a *transport stream* (e.g. a TV channel broadcast).

MPEG-4

Initially aimed primarily at low bit rate video communications, MPEG-4 is now efficient across a variety of bit rates ranging from a few kilobits per second to tens of megabits per second. MPEG-4 absorbs many of the features of MPEG-1 and MPEG-2 and other related standards, adding new features such as (extended) Virtual Reality Modelling Language (VRML) support for 3D rendering, object-oriented composite files (including audio, video and VRML objects), support for externally specified DRM and various types of interactivity. MPEG-4 provides improved coding efficiency; the ability to encode mixed media data, for example, video, audio and speech; error resilience to enable robust transmission of data associated with media objects and the ability to interact with the audio-visual scene generated at the receiver. Conformance testing, that is, checking whether MPEG-4 devices comply with the standard, is a standard part. Some MPEG-4 parts have been successfully deployed across industry. For example, Part 2 is used by codecs such as DivX, Xvid, Nero Digital, 3ivx and by QuickTime 6 and Part 10 is used by the x264 encoder, Nero Digital AVC, QuickTime 7 and in high-definition video media like the Blu-ray Disc.

MPEG-4 provides a large and rich set of tools for the coding of Audio-Visual Objects (AVOs). Profiles, or subsets, of the MPEG-4 Systems, Visual, and Audio tool sets allow effective application implementations of the standard at pre-set levels by limiting the tool set a decoder has to implement, and thus reducing computing complexity while maintaining interworking with other MPEG-4 devices that implement the same combination. The approach is similar to MPEG-2's Profile@Level combination.

Visual Profiles

Visual objects can be either of natural or of synthetic origin. The tools for representing natural video in the MPEG-4 visual standard provide standardized core technologies allowing efficient storage, transmission and manipulation of textures, images and video data for multimedia environments. These tools allow the decoding and representation of atomic units of image and video content, called Video Objects (VOs). An example of a VO could be a talking person (without background), which can then be composed with other AVOs to create a scene. Functionalities common to several applications are clustered: compression of images and video; compression of textures for texture mapping on 2D and 3D meshes; compression of implicit 2D meshes; compression of time-varying geometry streams that animate meshes; random access to all types of visual objects; extended manipulation functionality for images and video sequences; content-based coding of images and video; content-based scalability of textures, images and video; spatial, temporal and quality scalability; and error robustness and resilience in error prone environments. The coding of conventional images and video is similar to conventional MPEG-1/2 coding. It involves motion prediction/compensation followed by texture coding. For the content-based functionalities, where the image sequence input may be of arbitrary shape and location, this approach is extended by also coding shape and transparency information. Shape may be represented either by a bit transparency component if one VO is composed with other objects, or by a binary mask. The extended MPEG-4 content-based approach is a logical extension of the conventional MPEG-4 Very-Low Bit Rate Video (VLBV) Core or high bit rate tools towards input of arbitrary shape. There are several scalable coding schemes in MPEG-4 Visual for natural video: spatial scalability, temporal scalability, fine granularity scalability and object-based spatial scalability. Spatial scalability supports changing the spatial resolution. Object-based spatial scalability extends the 'conventional' types of scalability towards arbitrarily shaped objects, so that it can be used in conjunction with other object-based capabilities. Thus, a very flexible content-based scaling of video information can be achieved. This makes it possible to enhance Signal-to-Noise Ratio (SNR), spatial resolution and shape accuracy only for objects of interest or for a particular region, which can be done dynamically at play time. Fine granularity scalability was developed in response to the growing need for a video coding standard for streaming video over the Internet. Fine granularity scalability and its combination with temporal scalability addresses a variety of challenging problems in delivering video over the Internet. It allows the content creator to code a video sequence once, to be delivered through channels with a wide range of bit rates. It provides the best user experience under varying channel conditions.

MPEG-4 supports parametric descriptions of a synthetic face and body animation, and static and dynamic mesh coding with texture mapping and texture coding for view-dependent applications. Object-based mesh representation is able to model the shape and motion of a VO plane in augmented reality, that is, merging virtual with real moving objects, in synthetic object transfiguration/animation, that is, replacing a natural VO in a video clip by another VO, in spatio-temporal interpolation, in object compression and in content-based video indexing.

These profiles accommodate the coding of natural, synthetic, and hybrid visual content. There are several profiles for natural video content. The *Simple Visual Profile* provides efficient, Error Resilient (ER) coding of rectangular VOs. It is suitable for mobile network applications. The *Simple Scalable Visual Profile* adds support for coding of temporal and spatial scalable objects to the Simple Visual Profile. It is useful for applications that provide services at more than one level of quality due to bit rate or decoder resource limitations. The *Core Visual Profile* adds support for coding of arbitrarily shaped and temporally scalable objects to the Simple Visual Profile. It is useful for applications such as those providing relatively simple content interactivity. The *Main Visual Profile* adds support for coding of interlaced, semi-transparent and sprite objects to the Core Visual Profile. It is useful for interactive and entertainment quality broadcast and DVD applications. The *N-Bit Visual Profile* adds support for coding VOs of varying pixel-depths to the Core Visual Profile. It is suitable for use in surveillance applications. The *Advanced Real-Time Simple Profile* provides advanced ER coding techniques of rectangular VOs using a back channel and improved temporal resolution stability with low buffering delay. It is suitable for real-time coding applications, such as videoconferencing. The *Core Scalable Profile* adds support for coding of temporal and spatially scalable arbitrarily shaped objects to the Core Profile. The main functionality of this profile is object-based SNR and spatial/temporal scalability for regions or objects of interest. It is useful for applications such as mobile broadcasting. The *Advanced Coding Efficiency Profile* improves the coding efficiency for both rectangular and arbitrarily shaped objects. It is suitable for applications such as mobile broadcasting, and applications where high coding efficiency is requested and small footprint is not the prime concern.

There are several profiles for synthetic and hybrid visual content. The *Simple Facial Animation Visual Profile* provides a simple means to animate a face model. This is suitable for applications such as audio/video presentation for the hearing impaired. The *Scalable Texture Visual Profile* provides spatial scalable coding of still image objects. It is useful for applications needing multiple scalability levels, such as mapping texture onto objects in games. The *Basic Animated 2D Texture Visual Profile* provides spatial scalability, SNR scalability and mesh-based animation for still image objects and also simple face object animation. The *Hybrid Visual Profile* combines the ability to decode arbitrarily shaped and temporally scalable natural VOs (as in the Core Visual Profile) with the ability to decode several synthetic and hybrid objects, including simple face and animated still image objects. The *Advanced Scalable Texture Profile* supports decoding of arbitrarily shaped texture and still images including scalable shape coding, wavelet tiling and error resilience. It is useful for applications that require fast random access as well as multiple scalability levels and arbitrarily shaped coding of still objects. The *Advanced Core Profile* combines the ability to decode arbitrarily shaped VOs (as in the Core Visual Profile) with the ability to decode arbitrarily shaped scalable still image objects (as in the Advanced Scalable Texture Profile). It is suitable for various content-rich multimedia applications such as interactive multimedia streaming over the Internet. The *Simple Face and Body Animation Profile* is a superset of the Simple Face Animation Profile, adding body animation.

Also, the *Advanced Simple Profile* looks like *Simple* in that it has only rectangular objects, but it has a few extra tools that make it more efficient: B-frames, ¼ pel motion compensation, extra quantization tables and global motion compensation. The *Fine Granularity Scalability Profile* allows truncation of the enhancement layer bitstream at any bit position so that delivery quality can easily adapt to transmission and decoding circumstances. It can be used with *Simple* or *Advanced Simple* as a base layer. The *Simple Studio Profile* is a profile with very high quality for usage in studio editing applications. It only has I-frames, but it does support arbitrary shape and multiple alpha channels. The *Core Studio Profile* adds P-frames to *Simple Studio*, making it more efficient but also requiring more complex implementations.

Audio Profiles

MPEG-4 coding of audio objects provides tools for representing both natural sounds such as speech and music and for synthesizing sounds based on structured descriptions. The representation for synthesized sound can be derived from text data or so-called instrument descriptions and by coding parameters to provide effects, such as reverberation and spatialization. The representations provide compression and other functionalities, such as scalability and effects processing. The MPEG-4 standard defines the bitstream syntax and the decoding processes in terms of a set of tools. The presence of the MPEG-2 AAC standard within the MPEG-4 tool set provides for general compression of high bit rate audio. MPEG-4 defines decoders for generating sound based on several kinds of 'structured' inputs. MPEG-4 does not standardize 'a single method' of synthesis, but rather a way to describe methods of synthesis. The MPEG-4 Audio transport stream defines a mechanism to transport MPEG-4 Audio streams without using MPEG-4 Systems and is dedicated for audio-only applications.

The *Speech Profile* provides Harmonic Vector Excitation Coding (HVXC), which is a very-low bit rate parametric speech coder, a Code-Excited Linear Prediction (CELP) narrowband/wideband speech coder and a Text-To-Speech Interface (TTSI). The *Synthesis Profile* provides score driven synthesis using Structured Audio Orchestra Language (SAOL) and wavetables and a TTSI to generate sound and speech at very low bit rates. The *Scalable Profile*, a superset of the Speech Profile, is suitable for scalable coding of speech and music for networks, such as the Internet and Narrowband Audio DIgital Broadcasting (NADIB). The *Main Profile* is a rich superset of all the other Profiles, containing tools for natural and synthetic audio. The *High Quality Audio Profile* contains the CELP speech coder and the Low Complexity AAC coder including Long

Term Prediction. Scalable coding can be performed by the AAC Scalable object type. Optionally, the new ER bitstream syntax may be used. The *Low Delay Audio Profile* contains the HVXC and CELP speech coders (optionally using the ER bitstream syntax), the low-delay AAC coder and the TTSI. The *Natural Audio Profile* contains all natural audio coding tools available in MPEG-4, but not the synthetic ones. The *Mobile Audio Internetworking Profile* contains the low-delay and scalable AAC object types including Transform-domain weighted interleaved Vector Quantization (TwinVQ) and Bit Sliced Arithmetic Coding (BSAC).

Systems (Graphics and Scene Graph) Profiles

MPEG-4 provides facilities to compose a set of such objects into a scene. The necessary composition information forms the scene description, which is coded and transmitted together with the media objects. MPEG has developed a binary language for scene description called BIFS (BInary Format for Scenes). In order to facilitate the development of authoring, manipulation and interaction tools, scene descriptions are coded independently from streams related to primitive media objects. Special care is devoted to the identification of the parameters belonging to the scene description. This is done by differentiating parameters that are used to improve the coding efficiency of an object, for example, motion vectors in video coding algorithms, and the ones that are used as modifiers of an object, for example, the position of the object in the scene. Since MPEG-4 allows the modification of this latter set of parameters without having to decode the primitive media objects themselves, these parameters are placed in the scene description and not in primitive media objects.

An MPEG-4 scene follows a hierarchical structure, which can be represented as a directed acyclic graph. Each node of the graph is a media object. The tree structure is not necessarily static; node attributes, such as positioning parameters, can be changed while nodes can be added, replaced or removed. In the MPEG-4 model, AVOs have both a spatial and a temporal extent. Each media object has a local coordinate system. A local coordinate system for an object is one in which the object has a fixed spatio-temporal location and scale. The local coordinate system serves as a handle for manipulating the media object in space and time. Media objects are positioned in a scene by specifying a coordinate transformation from the object's local coordinate system into a global coordinate system defined by one more parent scene description nodes in the tree. Individual media objects and scene description nodes expose a set of parameters to the composition layer through which part of their behaviour can be controlled. Examples include the pitch of a sound, the colour for a synthetic object and activation or deactivation of enhancement information for scalable coding. The scene description structure and node semantics are heavily influenced by VRML, including its event model. This provides MPEG-4 with a very rich set of scene construction operators, including graphics primitives that can be used to construct sophisticated scenes.

MPEG-4 defines a syntactic description language to describe the exact binary syntax for bitstreams carrying media objects and for bitstreams with scene description information. This is a departure from MPEG's past approach of utilizing pseudo C. This language is an extension of C++, and is used to describe the syntactic representation of objects and the overall media object class definitions and scene description information in an integrated way. This provides a consistent and uniform way of describing the syntax in a very precise form, while at the same time simplifying bitstream compliance testing.

The systems profiles for graphics define which graphical and textual elements can be used in a scene. The *Simple 2D Graphics Profile* provides for only those graphics elements of the BIFS tool that are necessary to place one or more visual objects in a scene. The *Complete 2D Graphics Profile* provides 2D graphics functionalities and supports features such as arbitrary 2D graphics and text, possibly in conjunction with visual objects. The *Complete Graphics Profile* provides advanced graphical elements such as elevation grids and extrusions and allows creating content with sophisticated lighting. The Complete Graphics profile enables applications such as complex virtual worlds that exhibit a high degree of realism. The *3D Audio Graphics Profile* provides tools that help define the acoustical properties of the scene, that is, geometry, acoustics absorption, diffusion and transparency of the material. This profile is used for applications that perform environmental spatialization of audio signals. The *Core 2D Profile* supports fairly simple 2D graphics and text. Used in set tops and similar devices, it supports picture-in-picture, video warping for animated advertisements, logos. The *Advanced 2D profile* contains tools for advanced 2D graphics such as cartoons, games, advanced graphical user interfaces, and complex, streamed graphics animations. The *X3-D Core profile* gives a rich environment for games, virtual worlds and other 3D applications.

The system profiles for scene graphs are known as Scene Description Profiles and allow audio-visual scenes with audio-only, 2D, 3D or mixed 2D/3D content. The *Audio Scene Graph Profile* provides for a set of BIFS scene graph elements for usage in audio-only applications. The Audio Scene Graph profile supports applications like broadcast radio. The *Simple 2D Scene Graph Profile* provides for only those BIFS scene graph elements necessary to place one or more AVOs in a scene. The Simple 2D Scene Graph profile allows presentation of audio-visual content with potential update of the complete scene but no interaction capabilities. The Simple 2D Scene Graph profile supports applications like broadcast television. The *Complete 2D Scene Graph Profile* provides for all the 2D scene description elements of the BIFS tool. It supports features such as 2D transformations and alpha blending. The Complete 2D Scene Graph profile enables 2D applications that require extensive and customized interactivity. The *Complete Scene Graph profile* provides the complete set of scene graph elements of the BIFS tool. The Complete Scene Graph profile enables applications like dynamic virtual 3D world and games. The *3D Audio Scene Graph Profile* provides the tools for three-dimensional sound positioning in relation with either the acoustic parameters of the scene or its perceptual attributes. The user can interact with the scene by changing the position of the sound source, by changing the room effect or moving the listening point. This profile is intended for usage in audio-only applications.

The *Basic 2D profile* provides basic 2D composition for very simple scenes with only audio and visual elements. Only basic 2D composition and audio and video node interfaces are included. These nodes are required to put an audio or a VO in the scene. The *Core 2D profile* has tools for creating scenes with visual and audio objects using basic 2D composition. Included are quantization tools, local animation and interaction, 2D texturing, scene tree updates, and the inclusion of subscenes through weblinks. Also included are interactive service tools such as ServerCommand, MediaControl, and MediaSensor, to be used in video-on-demand services. The *Advanced 2D profile* forms a full superset of the basic 2D and core 2D profiles. It adds scripting, the PROTO tool, BIF-Anim for streamed animation, local interaction and local 2D composition as well as advanced audio. The *Main 2D profile* adds the FlexTime model to Core 2D, as well as Layer 2D and WorldInfo nodes and all input sensors. The *X3D core profile* was designed to be a common interworking point with the Web3D specifications and the MPEG-4 standard. It includes the nodes for an implementation of 3D applications on a low footprint engine, reckoning the limitations of software renderers.

The *Object Descriptor Profile* includes the Object Descriptor (OD) tool, the Sync Layer (SL) tool, the Object Content Information (OCI) tool and the Intellectual Property Management and Protection (IPMP) tool.

Animation Framework eXtension

This provides an integrated toolbox for building attractive and powerful synthetic MPEG-4 environments. The framework defines a collection of interoperable tool categories that collaborate to produce a reusable architecture for interactive animated contents. In the context of Animation Framework eXtension (AFX), a tool represents functionality such as a BIFS node, a synthetic stream, or an audio-visual stream. AFX utilizes and enhances existing MPEG-4 tools, while keeping backward-compatibility, by offering higher-level descriptions of animations such as inverse kinematics; enhanced rendering such as multi- and procedural texturing; compact representations such as piecewise curve interpolators and subdivision surfaces; low bit rate animations such as using interpolator compression and dead-reckoning; scalability based on terminal capabilities such as parametric surfaces tessellation; interactivity at user level, scene level and client–server session level; and compression of representations for static and dynamic tools.

The framework defines a hierarchy made of six categories of models that rely on each other. *Geometric models* capture the form and appearance of an object. Many characters in animations and games can be quite efficiently controlled at this low level; familiar tools for generating motion include key framing and motion capture. Owing to the predictable nature of motion, building higher-level models for characters that are controlled at the geometric level is generally much simpler. *Modelling models* are an extension of geometric models and add linear and non-linear deformations to them. They capture the transformation of models without changing its original shape. Animations can be made on changing the deformation parameters independently of the geometric models. *Physical models* capture additional aspects of the world such as an object's mass inertia, and how it responds to forces such as gravity. The use of physical models allows many motions to be created automatically. The cost of simulating the equations of motion may be important in a real-time engine and in games, where a physically plausible approach is often preferred. Applications such as collision restitution, deformable bodies, and rigid articulated bodies use these models intensively. *Biomechanical models* have their roots in control theory. Real animals have muscles that they use to exert forces and torques on their own bodies. If we have built physical models of characters, they can use virtual muscles to move themselves around. *Behavioural models* capture a character's behaviour. A character may expose a reactive behaviour when its behaviour is solely based on its perception of the current situation, that is, with no memory of previous situations. Reactive behaviours can be implemented using stimulus response rules, which are used in games. Finite-States Machines (FSMs) are often used to encode deterministic behaviours based on multiple states. Goal-directed behaviours can be used to define a cognitive character's goals. They can also be used to model flocking behaviours. *Cognitive models* are rooted in artificial intelligence. If the character is able to learn from stimuli in the world, it may be able to adapt its behaviour. The models are hierarchical; each level relies on the next lower one. For example, an autonomous agent (category 5) may respond to stimuli from the environment he/she is in and may decide to adapt their way of walking (category 4) that can modify physics equation, for example, skin modelled with mass-spring-damp properties, or have influence on some underlying deformable models (category 2) or may even modify the geometry (category 1). If the agent is clever enough, it may also learn from the stimuli (category 6) and adapt or modify his behavioural models.

H.264/AVC/MPEG-4 Part 10

H.264/AVC is a block-oriented motion-compensation-based codec standard developed by the ITU-T Video Coding Experts Group (VCEG) together with the ISO/IEC Moving Picture Experts Group (MPEG), and it was the product of a partnership effort known as the Joint Video Team (JVT). The ITU-T H.264 standard and the ISO/IEC MPEG-4 AVC standard (MPEG-4 Part 10, Advanced Video Coding) are jointly maintained so that they have identical technical content. The H.264/AVC video format has a very broad application range that covers all forms of digital compressed video from low bit rate internet streaming applications to HDTV broadcast and Digital Cinema applications with nearly lossless coding. With the use of H.264/AVC, bit rate savings of at least 50% are reported. Digital Satellite TV quality, for example, was reported to be achievable at 1.5 Mbit/s, compared to the current operation point of MPEG 2 video at around 3.5 Mbit/s. In order to ensure compatibility and problem-free adoption of H.264/AVC, many standards bodies have amended or added to their video-related standards so that users of these standards can employ H.264/AVC. H.264/AVC encoding requires significant computing power, and as a result, software encoders that run on a general-purpose CPUs are typically slow, especially when dealing with HD contents. To reduce CPU usage or to do real-time encoding, hardware encoders are usually employed.

The Blu-ray Disc format includes the H.264/AVC High Profile as one of three mandatory video compression formats. Sony also chose this format for their Memory Stick Video format. The Digital Video Broadcast (DVB) project approved the use of H.264/AVC for broadcast television in late 2004. The Advanced Television Systems Committee (ATSC) standards body in the United States approved the use of H.264/AVC for broadcast television in July 2008, although the standard is not yet used for fixed ATSC broadcasts within the United States. It has since been approved for use with the more recent ATSC-M/H (Mobile/Handheld) standard, using the AVC and Scalable Video Coding (SVC) portions of H.264/AVC. Advanced Video Coding High Definition (AVCHD) is a high-definition recording format designed by Sony and Panasonic that uses H.264/AVC. AVC-Intra is an intra frame compression only format, developed by Panasonic. The Closed Circuit TV (CCTV) or video surveillance market has included the technology in many products. With the application of the H.264/AVC compression technology to the video surveillance industry, the quality of the video recordings became substantially improved.

Key Features of H.264/AVC

There are numerous features that define H.264/AVC. In this section, we consider the most significant.

Inter- and Intra-picture Prediction. It uses previously encoded pictures as references, with up to 16 progressive reference frames or 32 interlaced reference fields. This is in contrast to prior standards, where the limit was typically one; or, in the case of conventional 'B-pictures', two. This particular feature usually allows modest improvements in bit rate and quality in most scenes. But in certain types of scenes, such as those with repetitive motion or back-and-forth scene cuts or uncovered background areas, it allows a significant reduction in bit rate while maintaining clarity. It enables variable block-size motion compensation with block sizes as large as 16×16 and as small as 4×4, enabling precise segmentation of moving regions. The supported luma prediction block sizes include 16×16, 16×8, 8×16, 8×8, 8×4, 4×8 and 4×4, many of which can be used together in a single macroblock. Chroma prediction block sizes are correspondingly smaller according to the chroma sub-sampling in use. It has the ability to use multiple motion vectors per macroblock, one or two per partition, with a maximum of 32 in the case of a B-macroblock constructed of 16, 4×4 partitions. The motion vectors for each 8×8 or larger partition region can point to different reference pictures. It has the ability to use any macroblock type in B-frames, including I-macroblocks, resulting in much more efficient encoding when using B-frames. It features six-tap filtering for derivation of half-pel luma sample predictions, for sharper subpixel motion compensation. Quarter-pixel motion is derived by linear interpolation of the half-pel values, to save processing power. Quarter-pixel precision for motion compensation enables precise description of the displacements of moving areas. For chroma, the resolution is typically halved both vertically and horizontally (4:2:0), therefore the motion compensation of chroma uses one-eighth chroma pixel grid units. Weighted prediction allows an encoder to specify the use of a scaling and offset, when performing motion compensation, and providing a significant benefit in performance in special case, such as fade-to-black, fade-in and cross-fade transitions. This includes implicit weighted prediction for B-frames, and explicit weighted prediction for P-frames. In contrast to MPEG-2's DC-only prediction and MPEG-4's transform coefficient prediction, H.264/AVC carries out spatial prediction from the edges of neighbouring blocks for intra-coding. This includes luma prediction block sizes of 16×16, 8×8 and 4×4, of which only one type can be used within each macroblock.

Lossless Macroblock Coding. It features a lossless PCM macroblock representation mode in which video data samples are represented directly, allowing perfect representation of specific regions and allowing a strict limit to be placed on the quantity of coded data for each macroblock.

Flexible Interlaced-Scan Video Coding. This includes Macroblock-Adaptive Frame-Field (MBAFF) coding, using a macroblock pair structure for pictures coded as frames, allowing 16×16 macroblocks in field mode, compared to MPEG-2, where field mode processing in a picture that is coded as a frame results in the processing of 16×8 half-macroblocks. It also includes Picture-Adaptive Frame-Field (PAFF or PicAFF) coding allowing a freely selected mixture of pictures coded as MBAFF frames with pictures coded as individual single fields, that is, half frames of interlaced video.

New Transform Design. This features an exact-match integer 4×4 spatial block transform, allowing precise placement of residual signals with little of the 'ringing' often found with prior codec designs. It also features an exact-match integer 8×8 spatial block transform, allowing highly correlated regions to be compressed more efficiently than with the 4×4 transform. Both of these are conceptually similar to the well-known DCT design, but simplified and made to provide exactly specified decoding. It also features adaptive encoder selection between the 4×4 and 8×8 transform block sizes for the integer transform operation. A secondary Hadamard transform performed on 'DC' coefficients of the primary spatial transform applied to chroma DC coefficients, and luma in a special case, achieves better compression in smooth regions.

Quantization Design. This features logarithmic step size control for easier bit rate management by encoders and simplified inverse-quantization scaling and frequency-customized quantization scaling matrices selected by the encoder for perception-based quantization optimization.

Deblocking Filter. The in-loop filter helps prevent the blocking artefacts common to other DCT-based image compression techniques, resulting in better visual appearance and compression efficiency.

Entropy Coding Design. It includes the Context-Adaptive Binary Arithmetic Coding (CABAC) algorithm that losslessly compresses syntax elements in the video stream knowing the probabilities of syntax elements in a given context. CABAC compresses data more efficiently than Context-Adaptive Variable-Length Coding (CAVLC), but requires considerably more processing to decode. It also includes the CAVLC algorithm, which is a lower-complexity alternative to CABAC for the coding of quantized transform coefficient values. Although of lower complexity than CABAC, CAVLC is more elaborate and more efficient than the methods typically used to code coefficients in other prior designs. It also features Exponential-Golomb coding, or Exp-Golomb, a common simple and highly structured Variable-Length Coding (VLC) technique for many of the syntax elements not coded by CABAC or CAVLC.

Loss Resilience. This includes the Network Abstraction Layer (NAL), which allows the same video syntax to be used in many network environments. One very fundamental design concept of H.264/AVC is to generate self-contained packets, to remove the header duplication as in MPEG-4's Header Extension Code (HEC). This was achieved by decoupling information relevant to more than one slice from the media stream. The combination of the higher-level parameters is called a *parameter set*. The H.264/AVC specification includes two types of parameter sets: Sequence Parameter Set and Picture Parameter Set. An active sequence parameter set remains unchanged throughout a coded video sequence, and an active picture parameter set remains unchanged within a coded picture. The sequence and picture parameter set structures contain information such as picture size, optional coding modes employed, and macroblock to slice group map. It also includes Flexible Macroblock Ordering (FMO), also known as slice groups, and Arbitrary Slice Ordering (ASO), which are techniques for restructuring the ordering of the representation of the fundamental regions in pictures. Typically considered an error/loss robustness feature, FMO and ASO can also be used for other purposes. It features data partitioning, which provides the ability to separate more important and less important syntax elements into different packets of data, enabling the application of unequal error protection and other types of improvement of error/loss robustness. It includes redundant slices, an error/loss robustness feature allowing an encoder to send an extra representation of a picture region, typically at lower fidelity, which can be used if the primary representation is corrupted or lost. Frame numbering is a feature that allows the creation of sub-sequences, which enables temporal scalability by optional inclusion of extra pictures between other pictures, and the detection and concealment of losses of entire pictures, which can occur due to network packet losses or channel errors.

Switching slices. Switching Predicted (SP) and Switching Intra-coded (SI) slices allow an encoder to direct a decoder to jump into an ongoing video stream for video streaming bit rate switching and trick mode operation. When a decoder jumps into the middle of a video stream using the SP/SI feature, it can get an exact match to the decoded pictures at that location in the video stream despite using different pictures, or no pictures at all, as references prior to the switch.

Accidental Emulation of Start Codes. A simple automatic process prevents the accidental emulation of start codes, which are special sequences of bits in the coded data that allow random access into the bitstream and recovery of byte alignment in systems that can lose byte synchronization.

Supplemental Enhancement Information and Video Usability Information. This is additional information that can be inserted into the bitstream to enhance the use of the video for a wide variety of purposes.

Auxiliary Pictures, Monochrome, Bit Depth Precision. It supports auxiliary pictures, for example, for alpha compositing, monochrome, 4:2:0, 4:2:2 and 4:4:4 chroma sub-sampling, sample bit depth precision ranging from 8 to 14 bits per sample.

Encoding Individual Colour Planes. The standard has the ability to encode individual colour planes as distinct pictures with their own slice structures, macroblock modes, and motion vectors, allowing encoders to be designed with a simple parallelization structure.

Picture Order Count. This is a feature that serves to keep the ordering of pictures and values of samples in the decoded pictures isolated from timing information, allowing timing information to be carried and controlled or changed separately by a system without affecting decoded picture content.

Fidelity Range Extensions. These extensions enable higher quality video coding by supporting increased sample bit depth precision and higher-resolution colour information, including sampling structures known as Y'CbCr 4:2:2 and Y'CbCr 4:4:4. Several other features are also included in the Fidelity Range Extensions project, such as adaptive switching between 4×4 and 8×8 integer transforms, encoder-specified perceptual-based quantization weighting matrices, efficient inter-picture lossless coding, and support of additional colour spaces. Further recent extensions of the standard have included adding five new profiles intended primarily for professional applications, adding extended-gamut colour space support, defining additional aspect ratio indicators, defining two additional types of 'supplemental enhancement information' (post-filter hint and tone mapping).

Scalable Video Coding. This allows the construction of bitstreams that contain sub-bitstreams that conform to H.264/AVC. For temporal bitstream scalability, that is, the presence of a sub-bitstream with a smaller temporal sampling rate than the bitstream, complete access units are removed from the bitstream when deriving the sub-bitstream. In this case, high-level syntax and inter-prediction reference pictures in the bitstream are constructed accordingly. For spatial and quality bitstream scalability, that is, the presence of a sub-bitstream with lower spatial resolution or quality than the bitstream, the NAL is removed from the bitstream when deriving the sub-bitstream. In this case, inter-layer prediction, that is, the prediction of the higher spatial resolution or quality signal by data of the lower spatial resolution or quality signal, is typically used for efficient coding.

Profiles

Being used as part of MPEG-4, an H.264/AVC decoder decodes at least one, but not necessarily all profiles. The decoder specification describes which of the profiles can be decoded. The approach is similar to MPEG-2's and MPEG-4's Profile@Level combination.

There are several profiles for non-scalable 2D video applications. The *Constrained Baseline Profile* is intended primarily for low-cost applications, such as videoconferencing and mobile applications. It corresponds to the subset of features that are in common between the Baseline, Main and High Profiles described below. The *Baseline Profile* is intended primarily for low-cost applications that require additional data loss robustness, such as videoconferencing and mobile applications. This profile includes all features that are supported in the Constrained Baseline Profile, plus three additional features that can be used for loss robustness, or other purposes such as low-delay multi-point video stream compositing. The *Main Profile* is used for standard-definition digital TV broadcasts that use the MPEG-4 format as defined in the DVB standard. The *Extended Profile* is intended as the streaming video profile, because it has relatively high compression capability and exhibits robustness to data losses and server stream switching. The *High Profile* is the primary profile for broadcast and disc storage applications, particularly for high-definition television applications. For example, this is the profile adopted by the Blu-ray Disc storage format and the DVB HDTV broadcast service. The *High 10 Profile* builds on top of the High Profile, adding support for up to 10 bits per sample of decoded picture precision. The *High 4:2:2 Profile* targets professional applications that use interlaced video, extending the High 10 Profile and adding support for the 4:2:2 chroma subsampling format, while using up to 10 bits per sample of decoded picture precision. The *High 4:4:4 Predictive Profile* builds on top of the High 4:2:2 Profile, supporting up to 4:4:4 chroma sampling, up to 14 bits per sample, and additionally supporting efficient lossless region coding and the coding of each picture as three separate colour planes.

For camcorders, editing and professional applications, the standard contains four additional *all-Intra profiles*, which are defined as simple subsets of other corresponding profiles. These are mostly for professional applications, for example, camera and editing systems: the *High 10 Intra Profile*, the *High 4:2:2 Intra Profile*, the *High 4:4:4 Intra Profile* and the *CAVLC 4:4:4 Intra Profile*, which also includes CAVLC entropy coding.

As a result of the Scalable Video Coding extension, the standard contains three additional *scalable profiles*, which are defined as a combination of a H.264/AVC profile for the base layer, identified by the second word in the scalable profile name, and tools that achieve the scalable extension. The *Scalable Baseline Profile* targets, primarily, video conferencing, mobile and surveillance applications. The *Scalable High Profile* targets, primarily, broadcast and streaming applications. The *Scalable High Intra Profile* targets, primarily, production applications.

As a result of the Multiview Video Coding (MVC) extension, the standard contains two *multiview profiles*. The *Stereo High Profile* targets two-view stereoscopic 3D video and combines the tools of the High profile with the inter-view prediction capabilities of the MVC extension. The *Multiview High Profile* supports two or more views using both temporal inter-picture and MVC inter-view prediction, but does not support field pictures and MBAFF coding.

MPEG-7

MPEG-7, formally known as the *Multimedia Content Description Interface*, provides a standardized scheme for content-based metadata, termed *descriptions* by the standard. A broad spectrum of multimedia applications and requirements are addressed, and consequently the standard permits both low- and high-level features for all types of multimedia content to be described. The three core elements of the standard are:

- *Description tools*, consisting of *Description Schemes* (*DSs*), which describe entities or relationships pertaining to multimedia content and the structure and semantics of their components, *Descriptors* (*Ds*), which describe features, attributes or groups of attributes of multimedia content, thus defining the syntax and semantics of each feature, and the primitive reusable *datatypes* employed by DSs and Ds.
- *Description Definition Language* (*DDL*), which defines, in XML, the syntax of the description tools and enables the extension and modification of existing DSs and also the creation of new DSs and Ds.
- *System tools*, which support both XML and binary representation formats, with the latter termed *BiM* (Binary Format for MPEG-7). These tools specify transmission mechanisms, description multiplexing, description-content synchronization, and IPMP.

Part 5, which is the Multimedia Description Schemes (MDS), is the main part of the standard since it specifies the bulk of the description tools. The so-called *basic elements* serve as the building blocks of the MDS and include fundamental Ds, DSs and datatypes from which other description tools in the MDS are derived, for example, linking, identification and localization tools used for referencing within descriptions and linking of descriptions to multimedia content, such as in terms of time or Uniform Resource Identifiers (URIs). The schema tools are used to define *top-level types*, each of which contains description tools relevant to a particular media type, for example, image or video, or additional metadata, for example, describing usage or the descriptions themselves. All top-level types are extensions of the abstract *CompleteDescriptionType*, which allows the instantiation of multiple complete descriptions. A *Relationships* element, specified using the *Graph DS*, is used to describe the relationships among the instances, while a *DescriptionMetadata* header element describes the metadata for the descriptions within the complete description instance, which consists of the confidence in the correction of the description, the version, last updated time stamp, comments, public (unique) and private (application-defined) identifiers, the creator of the description, creation location, creation time, instruments and associated settings, rights and any package associated with the description that describes the tools used by the description. An *OrderingKey* element describes an ordering of instances within a description using the *OrderingKey DS* (irrespective of actual order of appearance within the description). The key top-level types are as follows. Multimedia content entities are catered for by the *Image Content Entity* for two-dimensional spatially varying visual data (includes an *Image* element of type *StillRegionType*), the *Video Content Entity* for time-varying two-dimensional spatial data (includes a *Video* element of type *VideoSegmentType*), the *Audio Content Entity* for time-varying one-dimensional audio data (includes an *Audio* element of type *AudioSegmentType*), the *AudioVisual Content Entity* for combined audio and video (includes an *AudioVisual* element of type *AudioVisualSegmentType*), the *Multimedia Content Entity* for multiple modalities or content types, such as 3D models, which are single or composite (includes a *Multimedia* element of type *MultimediaSegmentType*), and other content entity types such as *MultimediaCollection*, *Signal*, *InkContent* and *AnalyticEditedVideo*. The *ContentAbstractionType* is also extended from the *ContentDescriptionType* and is used for describing abstractions of multimedia content through the extended *SemanticDescriptionType*, *ModelDescription-Type*, *SummaryDescriptionType*, *ViewDescriptionType* and *VariationDescriptionType*. Finally, the *ContentManagementType* is an abstract type for describing metadata related to content management from which the following top-level types are extended: *UserDescriptionType*, which describes a multimedia user; *MediaDescriptionType*, which describes media properties; *CreationDescriptionType*, which describes the process of creating multimedia content; *UsageDescriptionType*, which describes multimedia content usage; and *ClassificationSchemeDescriptionType*, which describes collection of terms used when describing multimedia content. The basic description tools are used as the basis for building the higher-level description tools. They include tools to cater for unstructured (free text) or structured textual annotations; the former through the *FreeTextAnnotation* datatype and the latter through the *StructuredAnnotation* (Who, WhatObject, WhatAction, Where, When, Why and How), *KeywordAnnotation*, or *DependencyStructure* (structured by the syntactic dependency of the grammatical elements) datatypes. The *ClassificationScheme DS* is also defined here, which describes a language-independent vocabulary for classifying a domain as a set of terms organized into a hierarchy. It includes both the term and a definition of its meaning. People and organizations are defined using the following DSs: the *Person DS* represents a person, and includes elements such as their affiliation, citizenship address, organization and group; the *PersonGroup DS* represents a group of persons (e.g. a rock group, a project team, a cast) and includes elements such as the name, the kind of group and the group's jurisdiction; and the *Organization DS* represents an organization of people and includes such elements as the name and contact person. The *Place DS* describes real and fictional geographical locations within or related to the multimedia content and includes elements such as the role of the place and its geographic position. Graphs and relations are catered for by the *Relation DS*, used for representing named relations, for example, spatial, between instances of description tools, and the *Graph DS*, used to organize relations into a graph structure. Another key element is the *Affective DS*, which is used to describe an audience's affective response to multimedia content.

The content description tools build on the above tools to describe content-based features of multimedia streams. They consist of the following:

- **Structure Description Tools**. These are based on the concept of a *segment*, which is a spatial and/or temporal unit of multimedia content. Specialized segment description tools are extended from the *Segment DS* to describe the structure of specific types of multimedia content and their segments. Examples include still regions, video segments, audio segments and moving regions. Base segment, segment attribute, visual segment, audio segment, audio-visual segment, multimedia segment, ink segment and video editing segment description tools are included. *Segment attribute description* tools describe the properties of segments such as creation information, media information, masks, matching hints and audio-visual features. *Segment decomposition tools* describe the structural decomposition of segments of multimedia content. Specialized decomposition tools extend the base *SegmentDecomposition DS* to describe the decomposition of specific types of multimedia content and their segments. Examples include spatial, temporal, spatio-temporal and media source decompositions. The two structural relation classification schemes (CSs) should be used to describe the spatial and temporal relations among segments and semantic entities: *TemporalRelation CS* (e.g. *precedes*, *overlaps*, *contains*) and *SpatialRelation CS*. (e.g. *south*, *northwest*, *below*).
- **Semantic Description Tools**. These apply to real-life concepts or narratives and include objects, agent objects, events, concepts, states, places, times and narrative worlds, all of which are depicted by or related to the multimedia content. *Semantic entity description tools* describe semantic entities such as objects, agent objects, events, concepts, states, places, times and narrative worlds. *Abstractions* generalize semantic description instances (a *concrete* description) to a semantic description of a set of instances of multimedia content (a *media* abstraction), or to a semantic description of a set of concrete semantic descriptions (a *formal* abstraction). The *SemanticBase DS* is an abstract tool that is the base of the tools that describe semantic entities. The specialized *semantic entity description tools* extend this tool to describe specific types of semantic entities in narrative worlds and include *SemanticBase DS*, an abstract base tool for describing semantic entities; *SemanticBag DS*, an abstract base tool for describing collections of semantic entities and their relations; *Semantic DS*, for describing narrative worlds depicted by or related to multimedia content; *Object DS*, for describing objects; *AgentObject DS* (which is a specialization of the *Object DS*), for describing objects that are persons, organizations, or groups of persons; *Event DS*, for describing events; *Concept DS*, for describing general concepts (e.g. 'justice'); *SemanticState DS*, for describing states or parametric attributes of semantic entities and semantic relations at a given time or location; *SemanticPlace DS*, for describing locations; and *SemanticTime DS* for describing time. *Semantic attribute description tools* describe attributes of the semantic entities. They include the *AbstractionLevel* datatype, for describing the abstraction performed in the description of a semantic entity; the *Extent* datatype, for the extent or size semantic attribute; and the *Position* datatype, for the position semantic attribute. Finally, the *SemanticRelation CS* describes semantic relations such as the relationships between events or objects in a narrative world or the relationship of an object to multimedia content. The semantic relations include terms such as *part*, *user*, *property*, *substance*, *influences* and *opposite*.

The *content metadata tools* provide description tools for describing metadata related to the content and/or media streams. They consist of *media description tools*, to describe the features of the multimedia stream; *creation and production tools*, to describe the creation and production of the multimedia content, including title, creator, classification, purpose of the creation and so forth; and *usage description tools*, to describe the usage of the multimedia content, including access rights, publication and financial information, which may change over the lifetime of the content. In terms of media description, the *MediaInformation DS* provides an identifier for each content entity (a single reality, such as a baseball game, which can be represented by multiple instances and multiple types of media, e.g. audio, video and images) and provides a set of descriptors for describing its media features. It incorporates the *MediaIdentification DS* (which enables the description of the content entity) and multiple *MediaProfile DS* instances (which enable the description of the different sets of coding parameters available for different coding profiles). The *MediaProfile DS* is composed of a *MediaFormat D*, *MediaTranscodingHints D*, *MediaQuality D* and *MediaInstance DSs*. In terms of creation and production, the *CreationInformation DS* is composed of the *Creation DS*, which contains description tools for author-generated information about the creation process such as places, dates, actions, materials, staff and organizations involved; the *Classification DSs*, which classifies the multimedia content using classification schemes and subjective reviews to facilitate searching and filtering; and the *RelatedMaterial DSs*, which describes additional related material, for example, the lyrics of a song or an extended news report. In terms of usage description, the *UsageInformation DS* describes usage features of the multimedia content. It includes a *Rights D*, which describes information about the rights holders and access privileges. The *Financial datatype* describes the cost of the creation of the multimedia content and the income the multimedia content has generated, which may vary over time. The *Availability DS* describes where, when, how and by whom the multimedia content can be used. Finally, the *UsageRecord DS* describes the historical where, when, how and by whom usage of the multimedia content.

Navigation and access tools describe multimedia summaries, views, partitions and decompositions of image, video and audio signals in space, time and frequency, as well as relationships between different variations of multimedia content. For example, the summarization tools use the *Summarization DS* to specify a set of summaries, where each summary is described using the *HierarchicalSummary DS*, which describes summaries that can be grouped and organized into hierarchies to form multiple summaries, or the *SequentialSummary DS*, which describes a single summary that may contain text and image, video frame or audio clip sequences.

Content organization tools specify the organization and modelling of multimedia content. For example, collections specify unordered groupings of content, segments, descriptors and/or concepts, while probability models specify probabilistic and statistical modelling of multimedia content, descriptors or collections.

Finally, the user interaction tools describe user preferences that a user has with regards to multimedia content and the usage history of users of multimedia content. This enables user personalization of content and access. The *UserPreferences DS* enables a user, identified by a *UserIdentifier* datatype, to specify their likes and dislikes for types of content (e.g. genre, review, dissemination source), ways of browsing content (e.g. summary type, preferred number of key frames) and ways of recording content (e.g.

recording period, recording location) through three DSs, respectively: the *FilteringAnd-SearchPreferences DS*, the *BrowsingPreferences DS* and the *RecordingPreferences DS*. Through an *allowAutomaticUpdate* attribute, users may indicate whether the automatic update of their *UserPreferences DS* is permitted or not, or whether they should be consulted each time. The *UsageHistory DS* represents past user activity through a set of actions. It groups together a set of *UserActionHistory DS*s, each of which consists of a set of *UserActionList DS*s. Each *UserActionList DS* consists of a set of user actions, each specified by the *UserAction DS*. Within the *UserAction DS*, the time of occurrence and, if applicable, duration may be specified as media time, which is relative to the time reference established for the given media and/or general time. Any associated programme is referred to by its identifier, with only one programme being able to be associated with a given action. A reference to related content-based descriptions may optionally be added to each user action, using identifiers, URIs or XPath expressions.

MPEG-21

MPEG-21 aims at defining a normative open framework for multimedia delivery and consumption for use by all the players in the delivery and consumption chain, that is, content creators, producers, distributors, service providers and consumers. This open framework comprises two essential concepts: the unit of distribution and transaction, that is, the Digital Item, and the Users interacting with the Digital Items. Digital Items can be a video or music collection, and Users can be anyone interested in the exchange, access, consumption, trade and otherwise manipulation of Digital Items in an efficient, transparent but most importantly interoperable way. MPEG-21 defines the mechanisms and elements needed to support the multimedia delivery chain and the relationships between and the operations supported by them. These are elaborated within the parts of MPEG-21 by defining the syntax and semantics of their characteristics. The MPEG-21 standard currently comprises numerous parts that can be grouped together, each dealing with a different aspect of Digital Items.

Digital Items Declaration (DID)

Digital Items Declaration (DID) specifies a set of abstract terms and concepts to form a useful model, not a language, for defining Digital Items in three normative sections. First, the DID Model describes a set of abstract terms and concepts to form a useful model for defining Digital Items. Secondly, the DID Representation is a normative description of the syntax and semantics of each of the DID elements, as represented in XML. Thirdly, the Normative XML schema includes the entire grammar of the DID representation in XML. Principle elements of the DID model are:

- a *container*, a structure that allows items and/or containers to be grouped to form logical packages for transport or exchange, or logical shelves for organization;
- an *item*, a grouping of sub-items and/or components that are bound to relevant descriptors, also known as declarative representations of Digital Items;
- a *component*, binding of a resource to all of its relevant descriptors;

- an *anchor*, binding descriptors to a fragment, which corresponds to a specific location or range within a resource;
- a *descriptor*, that associates information with the enclosing element;
- a *condition*, which describes the enclosing element as being optional, and links it to the selection(s) that affect its inclusion;
- a *choice*, a set of related selections that can affect the configuration of an item;
- a *selection*, a specific decision affecting one or more conditions within an item;
- an *annotation*, information about another element without altering or adding to it;
- an *assertion*, a full or partially configured state of a choice;
- a *resource*, an individually identifiable asset such as a video clip, or a physical object;
- a *fragment* unambiguously designates a specific point or range within a resource;
- a *statement*, a literal textual value that contains information, but not an asset and
- a *predicate*, an unambiguously identifiable declaration that can be true, false or undecided.

Digital Items Identification (DII)

Digital Items Identification (DII) includes unique identification of Digital Items and parts thereof (including resources), types, any related IPs, DSs and URI links to related information such as descriptive metadata. The DII does not specify new identification systems for content elements for which identification and description schemes already exist and are in use. Identifiers associated with Digital Items are included in the STATEMENT element in the DID. Likely STATEMENTs include descriptive, control, revision tracking and/or identifying information. A DID may have DESCRIPTORs, each containing one STATEMENT, which may contain one identifier relating to the parent element of the STATEMENT. DII provides a mechanism that allows an MPEG-21 Terminal to distinguish between different Digital Item Types by placing a URI inside a Type tag as the sole child element of a STATEMENT that appears as a child element of a DESCRIPTOR, which in turn appears as a child element of an ITEM.

Digital Rights Management (DRM)

MPEG-21 Part 4 specifies how to include IPMP information and protected parts of Digital Items in a DID document. It does not include protection measures, keys, key management, trust management, encryption algorithms, certification infrastructures or other components required for a complete DRM system. Rights and permissions on digital resources in MPEG-21 can be defined as the action, or activity, or a class of actions that may be carried out using associated resources under certain conditions within a well-structured, extensible dictionary. Part 5 defines a Rights Expression Language (REL), a machine-readable language that can declare rights and permissions using the terms as defined in the Rights Data Dictionary (RDD). The REL provides flexible, interoperable mechanisms to support transparent and augmented use of digital resources in publishing, distribution and consumption of digital movies, digital music, electronic books, broadcasting, interactive games, computer software and other creations in digital form, in a way that protects the digital content and honours the rights, conditions and fees specified for digital contents. It also supports specification of access and use controls for digital content in cases where financial exchange is not part of the terms of use, and to support exchange of sensitive or private digital content. REL also provides a flexible interoperable mechanism to ensure personal data is processed in accordance with individual rights and to meet the requirement for Users to be able to express their rights and interests in a way that addresses issues of privacy and use of personal data. REL supports guaranteed end-to-end interoperability, consistency and reliability between different systems and services. To do so, it offers richness and extensibility in declaring rights, conditions and obligations; ease and persistence in identifying and associating these with digital contents; and flexibility in supporting multiple usage/business models. REL is defined in XML. The RDD is a prescriptive dictionary that supports the MPEG-21 REL. Its structure is specified, alongside a methodology for creating the dictionary.

Digital Items Adaptation (DIA)

Terminals and Networks key element aims to achieve interoperable transparent access to distributed advanced multimedia content by shielding users from network and terminal installation, management and implementation issues. This enables the provision of network and terminal resources on demand to form user communities where multimedia content is created and shared, always with the agreed/contracted quality, reliability and flexibility, allowing the multimedia applications to connect diverse sets of Users, such that the quality of the user experience will be guaranteed. To achieve this goal, the adaptation of Digital Items is required. It is referred to as *Digital Item Adaptation* (DIA) for *Universal Multimedia Access* (UMA), and Part 7 specifies normative descriptions tools to assist with the adaptation of Digital Items. The DIA standard specifies means enabling the construction of a device and coding format-independent adaptation engines. Only tools used to guide the adaptation engine are specified by DIA. A Digital Item is subject to a resource adaptation engine, as well as a descriptor adaptation engine, which produce together the adapted Digital Item. While adaptation engines are non-normative tools, descriptions and format-independent mechanisms that provide support for DIA in terms of resource adaptation, descriptor adaptation and/or Quality of Service management are within the scope of the requirements. Part 7 includes the following description tools:

- *User Characteristics* specify the characteristics of a User, including preferences to particular media resources, preferences regarding the presentation of media resources and the mobility characteristics of a User.
- *Terminal Capabilities* specify the capability of terminals, including media resource encoding and decoding capability, hardware, software and system-related specifications, as well as communication protocols that are supported by the terminal.
- *Network Characteristics* specify the capabilities and conditions of a network, including bandwidth utilization, delay and error characteristics.
- *Natural Environment Characteristics* specify the location and time of a User in a given environment, as well as audio-visual characteristics of the natural environment, such as auditory noise levels and illumination properties.
- *Resource Adaptability* assists with the adaptation of resources, including the adaptation of binary resources in a generic way, and metadata adaptation, resource-complexity trade-offs and making associations between descriptions and resource characteristics for Quality of Service.

• *Session Mobility* specifies how to transfer the state of Digital Items from one User to another, that is, capture, transfer and reconstruction of state information.

Digital Items Processing (DIP)

This includes methods written in ECMAScript and may utilize Digital Item Base Operations (DIBOs), which are similar to the standard library of a programming language.

Digital Items Transport Systems (DITS)

This includes a file format that forms the basis of interoperability of Digital Items. MPEG's binary format for metadata (BiM) has been adopted as an alternative schema-aware XML format, which adds streaming capabilities to XML documents. This defines how to map Digital Items on various transport mechanisms such as MPEG-2 Transport Stream (TS) or Real-Time Protocol (RTP).

Users

Users are identified specifically by their relationship to another User for a certain interaction. MPEG-21 makes no distinction between a content provider and a consumer, for instance, both are Users. A User may use content in many ways, that is, publish, deliver, consume, and so all parties interacting within MPEG-21 are categorized as Users equally. However, a User may assume specific or even unique rights and responsibilities according to their interaction with other Users within MPEG-21. The MPEG-21 framework enables one User to interact with another User and the object of that interaction is a Digital Item commonly called *content*. Some interactions are creating content, some are providing content, archiving content, rating content, enhancing and delivering content, aggregating content, delivering content, syndicating content, retail selling of content, consuming content, subscribing to content, regulating content, facilitating transactions that occur from any of the above, and regulating transactions that occur from any of the above. Any of these are 'uses' of MPEG-21, and the parties involved are Users.

MPEG-A

The MPEG-A standard supports the creation of Multimedia Application Formats (MAFs). MAF specifications integrate elements from MPEG-1, MPEG-2, MPEG-4, MPEG-7 and MPEG-21 into a single specification that is useful for specific but very widely used applications, such as delivering music, pictures or home videos. In this way, it facilitates development of innovative and standards-based multimedia applications and services within particular domains. In the past, MPEG has addressed the problem of providing domain-based solutions by defining profiles, which are subsets of tools from a single MPEG standard, for example, the Main Profile from MPEG-2, which is geared towards digital TV services.

Typically, MAF specifications encapsulate the ISO file format family for storage, MPEG-7 tools for metadata, one or more coding profiles for representing the media, and tools for encoding metadata in either binary or XML form. MAFs may specify the use of the MPEG-21 Digital Item Declaration Language (DIDL) for representing the structure of the media and the metadata, plus other MPEG-21 tools as required. MAFs may also specify the use of non-MPEG coding tools (e.g. JPEG) for representation of 'non-MPEG' media and specify elements from non-MPEG standards that are required to achieve full interoperability.

MAFs have already been specified for a broad range of applications, including music and photo players, musical slide shows, media streaming, open access, digital media broadcasting, professional archiving, video surveillance and stereoscopic applications.

Chapter Summaries

This book draws together chapters from international MPEG researchers, which span the above standards. The chapters focus on the application of the MPEG standards, thereby demonstrating how the standards may be used and the context of their use, as well as providing an appreciation of supporting and complementary technologies that may be used to add value to them (and vice versa). We now summarize each chapter in turn.

Chapter 1: HD Video Remote Collaboration Application

Beomjoo Seo, Xiaomin Liu and Roger Zimmermann
This chapter describes the design, architectural approach, and technical details of the Remote Collaboration System (RCS) prototype. The objectives of the RCS project were to develop and implement advanced communication technologies for videoconferencing and tele-presence that directly target aviation operations and maintenance. RCS supports High-Definition MPEG-2 and MPEG-4/AVC real-time streaming over both wired and wireless networks. The system was implemented on both Linux and Windows platforms and the chapter describes some of the challenges and trade-offs. On the application side, the project focuses on the areas of remote maintenance and training activities for airlines, while targeting specific benefits that can be realized using conferencing technology, un-tethered and distributed inspection and maintenance support, including situation analysis, technical guidance and authorization with the ultimate objective to save cost and time while maximizing user experience.

Chapter 2: MPEG Standards in Media Production, Broadcasting and Content Management

Andreas Mauthe and Peter Thomas
This chapter discusses the application of MPEG standards in the media production and broadcasting industry. MPEG standards used within professional media production, broad-casting and content management can be divided into two areas, that is, coding standards dealing with the encoding of the so-called essence (i.e. the digitized and encoded audio-visual part of the content), and standards dealing with content description and content management. For the former the most relevant standards are MPEG-2 and MPEG-4. The latter is covered by MPEG-7 and MPEG-21. This chapter discusses the requirements of the content industry for these standards; their main features and the relevant parts of these standards are outlined and placed into the context of the specific requirements of the broadcast industry.

Chapter 3: Quality Assessment of MPEG-4 Compressed Videos

Anush K. Moorthy and Alan C. Bovik

This chapter describes an algorithm for real-time quality assessment, developed specifically for MPEG-4 compressed videos. This algorithm leverages the computational simplicity of the structural similarity (SSIM) index for image quality assessment (IQA), and incorporates motion information embedded in the compressed motion vectors from the H.264 compressed stream to evaluate visual quality. *Visual quality* refers to the quality of a video as perceived by a human observer. It is widely agreed that the most commonly used mean squared error (MSE) correlates poorly with the human perception of quality. MSE is a full reference (FR) video quality assessment (VQA) algorithm. FR VQA algorithms are those that require both the original as well as the distorted videos in order to predict the perceived quality of the video. Recent FR VQA algorithms have been shown to correlate well with human perception of quality. The performance of the algorithm this chapter proposes is tested with the popular Video Quality Experts Group (VQEG) FRTV Phase I dataset and compared to the performance of the FR VQA algorithms.

Chapter 4: Exploiting MPEG-4 Capabilities for Personalized Advertising in Digital TV

Martín López-Nores, Yolanda Blanco-Fernández, Alberto Gil-Solla, Manuel Ramos-Cabrer and José J. Pazos-Arias

This chapter considers the application of MPEG-4 in developing personalized advertising on digital TV. The object-oriented vision of multimedia contents enabled by MPEG-4 brings in an opportunity to revolutionize the state-of-the-art in TV advertising. This chapter discusses a model of dynamic product placement that consists of blending TV programs with advertising material selected specifically for each individual viewer, with interaction possibilities to launch e-commerce applications. It reviews the architecture of a system that realizes this, its MPEG-4 modules and associated tools developed for digital TV providers and content producers. It also reports its findings on technical feasibility experiments.

Chapter 5: Using MPEG Tools in Video Summarization

Luis Herranz and José M. Martínez

In this chapter, the combined use of tools from different MPEG standards is described in the context of a video summarization application. The main objective is the efficient generation of summaries, integrated with their adaptation to the user's terminal and network. The recent MPEG-4 Scalable Video Coding specification is used for fast adaptation and summary bitstream generation. MPEG-21 DIA tools are used to describe metadata related to the user terminal and network and MPEG-7 tools are used to describe the summary.

Chapter 6: Encryption Techniques for H.264 Video

Bai-Ying Lei, Kwok-Tung Lo and Jian Feng
This chapter focuses on the encryption techniques for H.264. A major concern in the design of H.264 encryption algorithms is how to achieve a sufficiently high level of security, while maintaining the efficiency of the underlying compression algorithm. This chapter reviews various H.264 video encryption methods and carries out a feasibility study of various techniques meeting specific application criteria. As chaos has intrinsic properties such as sensitivity to initial conditions, deterministic oscillations and noise-like behaviour, it has acquired much attention for video content protection. A novel joint compression and encryption scheme, which is based on the H.264 CABAC module and uses a chaotic stream cipher is presented. The proposed H.264 encryption scheme, which is based on a discrete piecewise linear chaotic map, is secure in perception, efficient and format compliant and suitable for practical video protection.

Chapter 7: Optimization Methods for H.264/AVC Video Coding

Dan Grois, Evgeny Kaminsky and Ofer Hadar
This chapter presents four major video coding optimization issues, namely, rate control optimization, computational complexity control optimization, joint computational complexity and rate control optimization, and transform coding optimization. These optimization methods are especially useful for future internet and 4G applications with limited computational resources, such as videoconferencing between two or more mobile users, video transrating and video transcoding between MPEG-2 and H.264/AVC video coding standards. The presented approaches, such as the computational complexity and bit allocation for optimizing H.264/AVC video compression can be integrated to develop an efficient optimized video encoder, which enables selection of (i) computational load and transmitted bit rate, (ii) quantization parameters, (iii) coding modes, (iv) motion estimation for each type of an input video signal, and (v) appropriate transform coding. Several H.264/AVC video coding methods are independently effective, but they do not solve common video coding problems optimally, since they provide the optimal solution for each video compression part independently and usually do not utilize the two main constraints of video encoding, that is, transmitted bit rate and computational load that vary drastically in modern communications.

Chapter 8: Spatio-Temporal H.264/AVC Video Adaptation with MPEG-21

Razib Iqbal and Shervin Shirmohammadi
This chapter describes compressed-domain spatio-temporal adaptation for video content using MPEG-21 generic Bitstream Syntax Description (gBSD) and considers how this adaptation scheme can be used for on-line video adaptation in a peer-to-peer environment. Ubiquitous computing has brought about a revolution permitting consumers to access rich multimedia content anywhere, anytime and on any multimedia-enabled device such as a

cell phone or a PDA. In order to ensure UMA to the same media content, media adaptation of the encoded media bitstream might be necessary in order to meet resource constraints without having to re-encode the video from scratch. For example, cropping video frames outside an area of interest to suit device screen resolution or network bandwidth.

Chapter 9: Image Clustering and Retrieval using MPEG-7

Rajeev Agrawal, William I. Grosky and Farshad Fotouhi
This chapter focuses on the application of MPEG-7 in image clustering and retrieval. In particular, it presents a multimodal image framework, which uses MPEG-7 colour descriptors as low-level image features and combines text annotations to create multimodal image representations for image clustering and retrieval applications.

Chapter 10: MPEG-7 Visual Descriptors and Discriminant Analysis

Jun Zhang, Lei Ye and Jianhua Ma
This chapter considers the MPEG-7 visual description tools and focusing on colour and texture descriptors, it evaluates their discriminant power in three basic applications, namely, image retrieval, classification and clustering. The chapter presents a number of application-based methods, which have been developed to effectively utilize the MPEG-7 visual descriptors, all of which are evaluated in extensive experiments. In particular, early and later fusion combines multiple MPEG-7 visual descriptors to improve the discriminant power of individual descriptors. The data is useful where discrimination of image content is required.

Chapter 11: An MPEG-7 Profile for Collaborative Multimedia Annotation

Damon Daylamani Zad and Harry Agius
This chapter contributes an MPEG-7 profile that can be used when annotating multimedia collaboratively. The rise of Web 2.0 and services based on wikis, which allow the pages of a web site to be modified by anyone at any time, have proven that global communities of users are not only able to work together effectively to create detailed, useful content, even minutiae, for the benefit of others, but do so voluntarily and without solicitation. Early applications, such as Flickr, YouTube and del.icio.us that are based on simple social tagging, and folksonomies suggest that this is possible for media annotation too and may be able to be extended to more advanced, structured media annotation, such as that based on the comprehensive, extensible MPEG-7 standard. A dearth of empirical research has been carried out to understand how users work with these types of tools, however. This chapter reports the results of an experiment that collected data from users using both folksonomic (Flickr, YouTube and del.icio.us) and MPEG-7 tools (COSMOSIS) to annotate and retrieve media. A conceptual model is developed for each type of tool that illustrates the tag usage, which then informs the development of an MPEG-7 profile for multimedia annotation communities.

Chapter 12: Domain Knowledge Representation in Semantic MPEG-7 Descriptions

Chrisa Tsinaraki and Stavros Christodoulakis
This chapter exploits the application of MPEG-7 in domain knowledge representation and reasoning. Semantic-based multimedia retrieval and filtering services have recently become very popular. This is due to the large amount of digital multimedia content that is produced everyday and the need for locating, within the available content, the multimedia content that is semantically closer to the preferences of the users. Fortunately, the dominant standard for audio-visual content description today, MPEG-7, allows for the structured description of the multimedia content semantics. In addition, the use of domain knowledge in semantic audio-visual content descriptions enhances the functionality and effectiveness of the multimedia applications. However, the MPEG-7 does not describe a formal mechanism for the systematic integration of domain knowledge and reasoning capabilities in the MPEG-7 descriptions. The specification of a formal model for domain knowledge representation and reasoning using the MPEG-7 constructs is of paramount importance for exploiting domain knowledge in order to perform semantic processing of the multimedia content. This chapter presents a formal model that allows the systematic representation of domain knowledge using MPEG-7 constructs and its exploitation in reasoning. The formal model exploits exclusively MPEG-7 constructs, and the descriptions that are structured according to the model are completely within the MPEG-7 standard.

Chapter 13: Survey of MPEG-7 Applications in the Multimedia Life Cycle

Florian Stegmaier, Mario Döller and Harald Kosch
This chapter surveys the application of MPEG-7 in the context of end-to-end search and retrieval. The ever growing increase of digital multimedia content by commercial as well as by user driven content providers necessitates intelligent content description formats supporting efficient navigation, search and retrieval in large multimedia content repositories. The chapter investigates current state-of-the-art applications that support the production of MPEG-7 annotations. On the basis of the extracted metadata, available MPEG-7 database products that enable a standardized navigation and search in a distributed and heterogeneous environment are reviewed. Part 12 of the MPEG-7 standard, the MPEG Query Format and resulting MPEG-7 middleware are discussed. The end-to-end investigation concludes with discussion of MPEG-7 user tools and front-end environments with applications in the mobile domain.

Chapter 14: Using MPEG Standards for Content-Based Indexing of Broadcast Television, Web and Enterprise Content

David Gibbon, Zhu Liu, Andrea Basso and Behzad Shahraray
This chapter examines the application of MPEG-7 and MPEG-21 in content indexing of broadcast TV, web and enterprise context and for representing user preferences using TVAnytime and DLNA specifications. It addresses the key role MPEG standards

play in the evolution of IPTV systems in the context of the emerging ATIS IPTV Interoperability Forum specifications. It then demonstrates how MPEG-7 and MPEG-21 are used for describing and ingesting media in real-world systems, from low-level audio and video features through to higher-level semantics and global metadata, in the context of a large-scale system for metadata augmentation whose content processing includes video segmentation, face detection, automatic speech recognition, speaker segmentation and multimodal processing. Ingested content sources include ATSC MPEG-2, IPTV H.264/MPEG-4 HD and SD transport streams as well as MPEG-4 encoded video files from web sources.

Chapter 15: MPEG-7/21: Structured Metadata for Handling and Personalizing Multimedia Content

Benjamin Köhncke and Wolf-Tilo Balke
This chapter addresses the application of MPEG-7 and MPEG-21 for personalizing multimedia content in order to serve the consumers' individual needs. For this MPEG-7/21 offers a variety of features to describe user preferences, terminal capabilities and transcoding hints within its DIA part. The chapter investigates the shortcoming of the provided user preference model and discusses necessary extensions to provide overarching preference descriptions. It then discusses the three main approaches in the context of media streaming, namely, semantic Web languages and ontologies, XML databases and query languages, and more expressive preference models.

Chapter 16: A Game Approach to Integrating MPEG-7 in MPEG-21 for Dynamic Bandwidth Dealing

Anastasis A. Sofokleous and Marios C. Angelides
This chapter demonstrates the application of MPEG-7 and MPEG-21 in shared resource allocation using games. Optimization of shared resources enables a server to choose which clients to serve, when and how, which in turn should maximize the end user experience. Approaches addressing this challenge are driven by the shared resource environment and the user preferences. This chapter addresses the challenge of optimizing resource allocation through the combined application of game theory and normative tools such MPEG-21 and MPEG-7. Users are treated as game players in a bandwidth dealing game, where the server(s) takes the role of dealer. The chapter formulates the problem of bandwidth allocation as a repetitive game, during which players are served with bandwidth. Each repetition is a new game consisting of a number of rounds during which the current players will have the chance to develop their strategy for securing bandwidth and, if successful, be allocated enough bandwidth to suit their requirements.

Chapter 17: The Usage of MPEG-21 Digital Items in Research and Practice

Hermann Hellwagner and Christian Timmerer
This chapter discusses the adoption of MPEG-21 both in research and practical applications. One of the first adoptions of Digital Items was within the Universal Plug

and Play (UPnP) forum as DIDL-Lite, which is derived from a subset of MPEG-21 DIDL. Recently, the Digital Item model has been adopted within Microsoft's Interactive Media Manager (IMM) and implemented using the Web Ontology Language (OWL). IMM also adopts Part 3 of MPEG-21, DII, which allows for uniquely identifying Digital Items and parts thereof. This chapter focuses on the adoption of MPEG-21 in research applications, discusses the reference applications that evolved as a result and considers representing, storing, managing, and disseminating such complex information assets in a digital library.

Chapter 18: Distributing Sensitive Information in the MPEG-21 Multimedia Framework

Nicholas Paul Sheppard
This chapter describes how the IPMP Components and MPEG REL were used to implement a series of digital rights management applications. While the IPMP Components and MPEG REL were initially designed to facilitate the protection of copyright, the applications also show how the technology can be adapted to the protection of private personal information and sensitive corporate information. MPEG-21 provides for controlled distribution of multimedia works through its IPMP Components and MPEG REL. The IPMP Components provide a framework by which the components of an MPEG-21 Digital Item can be protected from undesired access, while MPEG REL provides a mechanism for describing the conditions under which a component of a Digital Item may be used and distributed.

Chapter 19: Designing Intelligent Content Delivery Frameworks using MPEG-21

Samir Amir, Ioan Marius Bilasco, Thierry Urruty, Jean Martinet and Chabane Djeraba
This chapter illustrates the application of MPEG-21 in the implementation of domain-dependant content aggregation and delivery frameworks. The CAM4Home project has yielded a metadata model, which enhances the aggregation and context-dependent delivery of content and services. Transforming the metadata model into an MPEG-21 model unravels new development areas for MPEG-21 description schemas.

Chapter 20: NinSuna: A Platform for Format-Independent Media Resource Adaptation and Delivery

Davy Van Deursen, Wim Van Lancker, Chris Poppe and Rik Van de Walle
This chapter discusses the design and functioning of a fully integrated platform for multimedia adaptation and delivery, called NinSuna. The multimedia landscape is characterized by heterogeneity in terms of coding and delivery formats, usage environments and user preferences. The NinSuna platform is able to efficiently deal with the heterogeneity in the multimedia ecosystem, courtesy of format-agnostic adaptation engines that are independent of the underlying coding format, and format-agnostic packaging engines that are independent of the underlying delivery format. NinSuna also provides a seamless integration between metadata standards and the adaptation processes.

Both the format-independent adaptation and packaging techniques rely on a model for multimedia streams, describing the structural, semantic and scalability properties of these multimedia streams. The platform is implemented using both W3C technologies, namely, RDF, OWL and SPARQL and MPEG technologies, namely, MPEG-B BSDL, MPEG-21 DIA, MPEG-7 and MPEG-4. News sequences are used as a test case for the platform, enabling the user to select news fragments matching their specific interests and usage environment characteristics.

Chapter 21: MPEG-A and its Open Access Application Format

Florian Schreiner and Klaus Diepold

This chapter presents the MPEG-A standards, also called Application Formats. These are interoperable formats combining selected standards from MPEG and possibly other standards into one integrated solution for a given application scenario. As a result an Application Format is a concise set of selected technologies, which are precisely defined and aligned to each other within the specification. The chapter discusses the concept of the Application Formats, their components and their relation to other standards. It also considers the advantages of MPEG-A for industry and their integration in existing projects. Thereafter, the chapter adopts the ISO/IEC 23000-7 Open Access Application Format as an example for different Application Formats, in order to demonstrate the concept and application areas in greater detail. It presents the components of the format and their link to application-specific use cases and the reference software as a first implementation of the standard and as a basis for prospective integration and extension.

Reference

ISO (2010) JTC1/SC29. *Coding of audio, picture, multimedia and hypermedia information*. Online http://www.iso.org/iso/iso_catalogue/catalogue_tc/catalogue_tc_browse.htm?commid=45316.

1

HD Video Remote Collaboration Application

Beomjoo Seo, Xiaomin Liu, and Roger Zimmermann
School of Computing, National University of Singapore, Singapore

1.1 Introduction

High-quality, interactive collaboration tools increasingly allow remote participants to engage in problem solving scenarios resulting in quicker and improved decision-making processes. With high-resolution displays becoming increasingly common and significant network bandwidth being available, high-quality video streaming has become feasible and innovative applications are possible. Initial work on systems to support high-definition (HD) quality streaming focused on off-line content. Such video-on-demand systems for IPTV (Internet protocol television) applications use elaborate buffering techniques that provide high robustness with commodity IP networks, but introduce long latencies. Recent work has focused on interactive, real-time applications that utilize HD video. A number of technical challenges have to be addressed to make such systems a reality. Ideally, a system would achieve low end-to-end latency, low transmission bandwidth requirements, and high visual quality all at the same time. However, since the pixel stream from an HD camera can reach a raw data rate of 1.4 Gbps, simultaneously achieving low latency while maintaining a low transmission bandwidth – through extensive compression – are conflicting and challenging requirements.

This chapter describes the design, architectural approach, and technical details of the *remote collaboration system* (RCS) prototype developed under the auspices of the Pratt & Whitney, UTC Institute for Collaborative Engineering (PWICE), at the University of Southern California (USC).

The focus of the RCS project was on the acquisition, transmission, and rendering of high-resolution media such as HD quality video for the purpose of building multisite, collaborative applications. The goal of the system is to facilitate and speed up collaborative maintenance procedures between an airline's technical help desk, its personnel

The Handbook of MPEG Applications: Standards in Practice   Edited by Marios C. Angelides and Harry Agius
© 2011 John Wiley & Sons, Ltd

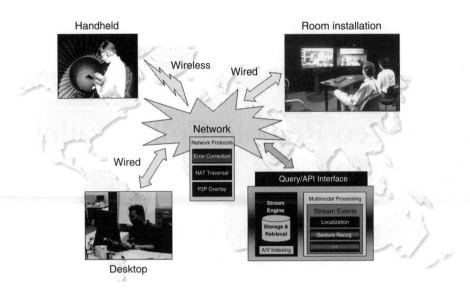

Figure 1.1 RCS collaborative systems architecture.

working on the tarmac on an aircraft engine, and the engine manufacturer. RCS consists of multiple components to achieve its overall functionality and objectives through the following means:

1. Use high fidelity digital audio and high-definition video (HDV) technology (based on MPEG-2 or MPEG-4/AVC compressed video) to deliver a high-presence experience and allow several people in different physical locations to collaborate in a natural way to, for example, discuss a customer request.
2. Provide multipoint connectivity that allows participants to interact with each other from three or more physically distinct locations.
3. Design and investigate acquisition and rendering components in support of the above application to optimize bandwidth usage and provide high-quality service over the existing and future networking infrastructures.

Figure 1.1 illustrates the overall architecture of RCS with different possible end-stations: room installations, desktop and mobile computers.

1.2 Design and Architecture

HD displays have become common in recent years and large network bandwidth is available in many places. As a result, high-quality interactive video streaming has become feasible as an innovative application. One of the challenges is the massive amount of data required for transmitting such streams, and hence simultaneously achieving low latency and keeping the bandwidth low are often contradictory. The RCS project has focused on the design of a system that enables HD quality video and multiple channels of audio to be streamed across an IP based network with commodity equipment. This has been made possible due to the technological advancements in capturing and encoding HD streams with modern, high-quality codecs such as MPEG-4/AVC and MPEG-2. In addition to wired network environments, RCS extends HD live streaming to the wireless networks, where bandwidth is limited and the packet loss rate can be very high.

The system components for one-way streaming from a source (capture device) to a sink (media player) can be divided into four stages: media acquisition, media transmission, media reception, and media rendering. The media acquisition component specifies how to acquire media data from a capture device such as a camera. Media acquisition generally includes a video compression module (though there are systems that use uncompressed video), which reduces the massive amount of raw data into a more manageable quantity. After the acquisition, the media data is split into a number of small data packets that will then be efficiently transmitted to a receiver node over a network (media transmission). Once a data packet is received, it will be reassembled into the original media data stream (media reception). The reconstructed data is then decompressed and played back (media rendering). The client and server streaming architecture divides the above stages naturally into two parts: a server that performs media acquisition and transmission and a client that executes media reception and rendering.

A more general live streaming architecture that allows multipoint communications may be described as an extension of the one-way streaming architecture. Two-way live streaming between two nodes establishes two separate one-way streaming paths between the two entities. To connect more than two sites together, a number of different network topologies may be used. For example, the *full-mesh* topology for multiway live streaming applies two-way live streaming paths among each pair of nodes. Although full-mesh connectivity results in low end-to-end latencies, it is often not suitable for larger installations and systems where the bandwidth between different sites is heterogeneous.

For RCS, we present several design alternatives and we describe the choices made in the creation of a multiway live streaming application. Below are introductory outlines of the different components of RCS which will subsequently be described in turn.

Acquisition. In RCS, MPEG-2-compressed HD camera streams are acquired via a FireWire interface from HDV consumer cameras, which feature a built-in codec module. MPEG-4/AVC streams are obtained from cameras via an external Hauppauge HD-PVR (high-definition personal video recorder) encoder that provides its output through a USB connection. With MPEG-2, any camera that conforms to the HDV standard[1] can be used as a video input device. We have tested multiple models from JVC, Sony, and Canon. As a benefit, cameras can easily be upgraded whenever better models become available. MPEG-2 camera streams are acquired at a data rate of 20–25 Mbps, whereas MPEG-4/AVC streams require a bandwidth of 6.5–13.5 Mbps.

Multipoint Communication. The system is designed to accommodate the setup of many-to-many scenarios via a convenient configuration file. A graphical user interface is available to more easily define and manipulate the configuration file. Because the software is modular, it can naturally take advantage of multiple processors and multiple cores. Furthermore, the software runs on standard Windows PCs and can therefore take advantage of the latest (and fastest) computers.

---

[1] http://www.hdv-info.org/

Compressed Domain Transcoding. This functionality is achieved for our RCS implementation on Microsoft Windows via a commercial DirectShow filter module. It allows for an optional and custom reduction of the bandwidth for each acquired stream. This is especially useful when streaming across low bandwidth and wireless links.

Rendering. MPEG-2 and MPEG-4/AVC decoding is performed via modules that take advantage of motion compensation and iDCT (inverse discreet cosine transform) hardware acceleration operation in modern graphics cards. The number of streams that can be rendered concurrently is only limited by the CPU processing power (and in practice by the size of the screens attached to the computer). We have demonstrated three-way HD communication on dual-core machines.

1.2.1 Media Processing Mechanism

We implemented our RCS package in two different operating system environments, namely, Linux and Windows. Under Linux, every task is implemented as a process and data delivery between two processes uses a pipe, one of the typical interprocess communication (IPC) methods, that transmit the data via standard input and output. In the Linux environment, the pipe mechanism is integrated with the virtual memory management, and so it provides effective input/output (I/O) performance. Figure 1.2a illustrates how a prototypical pipe-based media processing chain handles the received media samples. A packet receiver process receives RTP (real-time transport protocol)-similar packets from a network, reconstructs the original transport stream (TS) by stripping the packet headers, and delivers them to an unnamed standard output pipe. A multiplexer, embedded in a video decoder process, waits on the unnamed pipe, parses incoming transport packets, consumes video elementary streams (ES) internally, and forwards audio ES to its unnamed pipe.

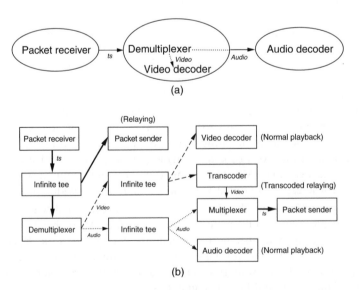

Figure 1.2 Example of delivery paths of received packets, using different media processing mechanisms: (a) pipe-based chaining and (b) DirectShow-based filter chaining.

Lastly, an audio decoder process at the end of the process chain consumes the incoming streams. Alternatively, the demultiplexer may be separated from the video decoder by delivering the video streams to a named pipe, on which the decoder is waiting.

On the Windows platform, our investigative experiments showed that a pipe-based interprocess data delivery mechanism would be very I/O-intensive, causing significant video glitches. As an alternative design to the pipe mechanism, we chose a DirectShow filter pipeline. DirectShow – previously known as ActiveMovie and a part of the DirectX software development kit (SDK) – is a component object model (COM)-based streaming framework for the Microsoft Windows platform. It allows application developers not only to rapidly prototype the control of audio/video data flows through high-level interfaces (APIs, application programming interfaces) but also to customize low-level media processing components (filters).

The DirectShow filters are COM objects that have a custom behavior implemented along filter-specific standard interfaces and then communicate with other filters. User-mode applications are built by connecting such filters. The collection of connected filters is called a *filter graph*, which is managed by a high-level object called the *filter graph manager* (*FGM*). Media data is moved from the source filter to the sink filter (or renderer filter) one by one along the connections defined in the filter graph under the orchestration of the FGM. An application invokes control methods (Play, Pause, Stop, Run, etc.) on an FGM and it may in fact use multiple FGMs. Figure 1.2b depicts one reception filter graph among various filter graphs implemented in our applications. It illustrates how media samples that are delivered from the network are processed along multiple branching paths – that is, a relaying branch, a transcoded relaying branch, and normal playback. The infinite tee in the figure is an SDK provided standard filter, enabling source samples to be transmitted to multiple filters simultaneously.

Unlike the pipe mechanism under Windows, a DirectShow filter chain has several advantages. First, communication between filters is performed in the same address space, meaning that all the filters (which are a set of methods and processing routines) communicate through simple function calls. The data delivery is via passed pointers to data buffers (i.e., a zero-copy mechanism). Compared to IPC, this is much more efficient in terms of I/O overhead. Second, many codecs are available as DirectShow filters, which enables faster prototyping and deployments. During the implementation, however, we observed several problems with the DirectShow filter chaining mechanism. First, the developer has no control over the existing filters other than the methods provided by the vendors, thus leaving little room for any further software optimizations to reduce the acquisition and playback latency. Second, as a rather minor issue, some filter components can cause synchronization problems. We elaborate on this in Section 1.6.1.

1.3   HD Video Acquisition

For HD video acquisition, we relied on solutions that included hardware-implemented MPEG compressors. Such solutions generally generate high-quality output video streams. While hardware-based MPEG encoders that are able to handle HD resolutions used to cost tens of thousands of dollars in the past, they are now affordable due to the proliferation of mass-market consumer products. If video data is desired in the MPEG-2 format, there exist many consumer cameras that can capture and stream HD video in real time. Specifically, the HDV standard commonly implemented in consumer camcorders includes real-time MPEG-2 encoded output via a FireWire (IEEE 1394) interface. Our system can acquire digital video from several types of camera models, which transmit MPEG-2 TS via FireWire interface in HDV format. The HDV compressed data rate is approximately 20–25 Mbps and a large number of manufacturers are supporting this consumer format. Our earliest experiments used a JVC JY-HD10U camera that produces 720p video (1280 × 720 pixels); however, at only 30 frames per second, not the usual 60. More recently, we have used Sony and Canon cameras that implement the 1080i HD standard.

In contrast, the more recent AVCHD (advanced video coding high definition) standard (which utilizes the MPEG-4/AVC codec) that is now common with HD consumer camcorders does not support a FireWire interface. Therefore, these new cameras cannot stream compressed HD video in real time. To overcome this obstacle, we used the stand-alone Hauppauge HD-PVR model 1212 hardware compressor, which can acquire HD uncompressed component signals (YCrCb) and encode them into an MPEG-4/AVC stream. The HD-PVR is officially supported on the Windows platform; however, a Linux driver also exists. Compressed data is streamed from the HD-PVR via a USB connection. Data rates are software selectable between 1 and 13.5 Mbps. A reasonable quality output is produced at 4 Mbps and above, while good quality output requires 6.5–13.5 Mbps. Figure 1.3 illustrates our prototype setup with the HD-PVR.

Figure 1.3 Prototype setup that includes a Canon VIXIA HV30 high-definition camcorder and a Hauppauge HD-PVR MPEG-4/AVC encoder.

1.3.1 MPEG-4/AVC HD System Chain

For HD conferencing an end-to-end chain has to be established, including both the acquisition and rendering facilities. At each end, a combination of suitable hardware and software components must be deployed. Since the objective is to achieve good interactivity, the delay across the complete chain is of crucial importance. Furthermore, video and audio quality must also be taken into consideration. Figure 1.3 illustrates our system setup when utilizing MPEG-4/AVC as the video encoding standard. We will describe each component in more detail.

The end-to-end system chain consists of the following components:

- **HD Video Camcorder**. The acquisition device used to capture the real-time video and audio streams. We utilize the uncompressed component signals that are produced with negligible latency.
- **HD MPEG-4/AVC Encoder**. The Hauppauge HD-PVR is a USB device that encodes the component video and audio outputs of the HD video camcorder. It utilizes the colorspace of YUV 420p at a resolution of 1920 × 1080 pixels and encodes the components inputs in real time using the H.264/MPEG-4 (part 10) video and AAC (advanced audio coding) audio codecs. The audio and video streams are then multiplexed into a slightly modified MPEG-2 TS container format. The bitrate is user selectable from 1 to 13.5 Mbps.
- **Receiver Demultiplexing**. A small library called MPSYS, which includes functions for processing MPEG-2 TS, is used. A tool called ts allows the extraction of ES from the modified MPEG-2 multiplexed stream.
- **Decoding and Rendering**. Tools based on the ffplay library are utilized to decode the streams, render the audio and video data, and play back the output to the users.

1.3.1.1 End-to-End Delay

Video conferencing is very time sensitive and a designer must make many optimization choices. For example, a different target bitrate of the encoder can affect the processing and transmission latencies. End-to-end delays with our implementation at different encoding rates are presented in Figure 1.4.

The results show that with our specific setup at a bitrate of 6.5 Mbps, the latency is lowest. At the same time, the video quality is very good. When the bitrate is below 4 Mbps, the latency is somewhat higher and the video quality is not as good. There are many blocking artifacts. When the bitrate is above 6.5 Mbps, the latency increases while the video quality does not improve very much. Figure 1.5 illustrates the visual quality of a frame when the video is streamed at different bitrates.

Encoding streams with the MPEG-4/AVC codec has several advantages. It offers the potential for a higher compression ratio and much flexibility for compressing, transmitting, and storing video. On the other hand, it demands greater computational resources since MPEG-4/AVC is more sophisticated than earlier compression methods (Figure 1.6).

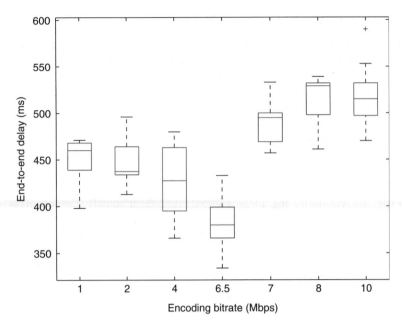

Figure 1.4 End-to-end delay distribution for different encoding bitrates with the hardware and software setup outlined in this chapter. Ten measurements were taken for each bitrate value.

1.4   Network and Topology Considerations

The streams that have been captured from the HD cameras need to be sent via traditional IP networks to one or more receivers. Audio can be transmitted either by connecting microphones to the cameras and multiplexing the data with the same stream as the video or transmitting it as a separate stream. The RCS transmission subsystem uses the RTP on top of the universal datagram protocol (UDP). Since IP networks were not originally designed for isochronous data traffic, packets may sometimes be lost between the sender and the receiver. RCS uses a single-retransmission algorithm (Papadopoulos and Parulkar 1996; Zimmermann *et al.* 2003) to recover lost packets. Buffering in the system is kept to a minimum to maintain a low latency.

To meet flexible requirements, we designed RCS' software architecture to be aware of the underlying network topology. We further reached the design decision that real-time transcoding should be integrated with the architecture to support lower bandwidth links. This requirement becomes especially critical when a system is scaled up to more than a few end user sites. Quite often some of the links may not be able to sustain the high bandwidth required for HD transmissions.

In addition to network bandwidth challenges, we also realized that the rendering quality of the video displayed on today's high-quality LCD and plasma screens suffers when the source camera produces interlaced video. The artifacts were especially noticeable with any fast moving motions. We describe how we addressed this issue in a later section.

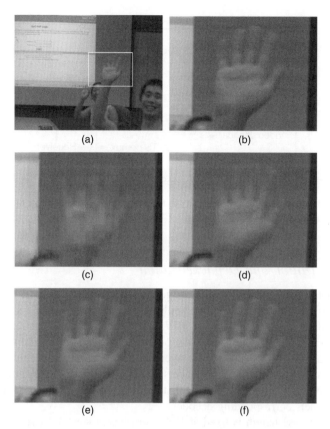

Figure 1.5 Comparison of picture quality at various encoding bitrates: (a) original image; (b) details from the original image; (c) encoded @ 2 Mbps; (d) encoded @ 4 Mbps; (e) encoded @ 6.5 Mbps; (f) encoded @ 10 Mbps.

Figure 1.6 Single end-to-end delay measurement of an MPEG-4/AVC video stream from an HD-PVR encoder at a rate of 6.5 Mbps. The delay is $(887 - 525 = 362)$ ms. The delay is measured by taking snapshot images of both the original display (left) and the transmitted video (right) of a running clock.

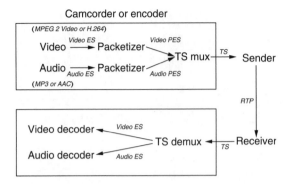

Figure 1.7 Captured media samples (MPEG-2 TS format) are packetized in the RTP format and reconstructed as a sequence of transport stream packets.

1.4.1 Packetization and Depacketization

Figure 1.7 illustrates how RTP packets are generated and delivered in the network. First, camcorders and encoders used for our application generate MPEG-TS packets, whose format is specified in the specification *MPEG-2 Part 1, Systems* (or *ISO/IEC standard 13818-1*) (ISO/IEC 1994). The acquisition process encapsulates a number of TS packets with an RTP header and transmits them over the network. At the receiver side, an RTP reception process recognizes the RTP packets and converts their payload data to a number of TS packets. Next, it separates individual streams by packet identifier (PID) values, and passes them to their corresponding decoders.

A TS packet, whose length is fixed at 188 bytes, has at least a 4-byte header. Each TS header starts with a sync byte (0×47) and contains a 13-bit PID, which enables the TS demultiplexer to efficiently extract individual packetized elementary streams (PES) separately. Every video or audio bitstream or ES cannot be converted to TS packets directly, since the TS format expects PES as input streams. Thus, every ES needs to be converted to a number of PES packets, whose maximum length is limited to 64 KB. Usually, every camcorder vendor assigns a unique PID numbers for each PES. For example, the PID of JVC video ES is 4096, Sony uses 2064, and that of the Hauppauge HD-PVR is 4113. Since identifying the PIDs of individual streams takes a longer time without *a priori* information, we hard-coded such information that is used during the TS demultiplexing in our application.

Once TS packets are acquired via a FireWire or a USB, they need to be aligned at the TS boundary to be transformed into RTP packets. To find the exact offset from the given raw samples, we first attempt to scan the first 188 bytes to locate the position of the sync byte, since the raw data should contain at least one sync byte within the first 188 bytes. Once multiple candidate offsets have been found, the detection continues to check whether their next 188th byte equals to a sync byte. These steps are repeated until only one offset remains. After the aligned offset is detected, the data acquisition software passes 188-byte aligned media samples to the rest of the delivery chain.

A single RTP packet can encapsulate multiple TS packets. To maximally utilize the network bandwidth, we used a maximum transmission unit (MTU) of 1500 bytes; therefore, the RTP packet could encapsulate up to seven TS packets ($\approx 1500/188$). To minimize multiple PES losses from a single RTP packet loss, we separately assign a new RTP packet for each newly arriving PES packet. This condition is detected by examining the payload unit start indicator field in the TS header.

To demultiplex incoming TS packets, we use the MPSYS library[2] by embedding it with the video decoder or running it as a separate process in Linux. The small-footprint library efficiently parses MPEG-TS streams and stores them as either individual PES or ES. In the Windows environment we used an MPEG-2 demultiplexer DirectShow filter when running on the DirectShow platform, or we used the MPSYS library when running the application via the Windows pipe mechanism.

Our packetization scheme, however, has several drawbacks when handling MPEG-4/AVC videos. As specified in RFC 3984 (Wenger *et al.* 2005), the RTP payload scheme for MPEG-4/AVC recommends the use of a network abstraction layer (NAL) unit. The NAL unit that encapsulates a number of slices containing multiple macroblocks is designed for the efficient transmission of the MPEG-4/AVC video over packet networks without any further packetization; therefore, the single loss of an RTP packet does not propagate to adjacent video frames, resulting in better error-resilience. Since the NAL unit works with TS packets, the direct use of the NAL units minimizes the packet overhead. For example, our TS-encapsulated RTP scheme consumes at least the following overhead for headers: 20 (IP) + 8 (UDP) + 12 (RTP) + 7 × 4 (7 TS packet headers) + 8 (PES header, if necessary) = 76 bytes, while the NAL-aware RTP scheme requires the following headers: 20 IP + 8 UDP + 12 RTP = 40 bytes (MacAulay *et al.* 2005). Although we have not implemented this scheme due to its higher parsing complexity to reconstruct the raw MPEG-4/AVC bitstreams, it possesses many undeniable advantages over our TS-aware RTP scheme.

1.4.2   Retransmission-Based Packet Recovery

Our packet recovery algorithm has the following features:

- Reuse of the existing retransmission-based packet recovery solution.
- Reduction of the response time of a retransmission request.

There are many alternative solutions to recover lost packets. One popular solution is to use redundant data such as a forward error correction (FEC)-enabled coding scheme. This approach removes the delay associated with a retransmission request, while somewhat overutilizing the network bandwidth more than the minimally required rate and may require significant on-line processing power.

We validated our single-pass retransmission scheme in a loss-free networking environment by simulating a loss-prone network. For the simulation purposes, we included a probabilistic packet loss model and a deterministic delay model at the receiver side. The packet loss model drops incoming packets probabilistically before delivering them to a receiver application session. The receiver application detects missing packets by examining the sequence numbers in the RTP headers. If the algorithm finds any missing packets,

---

[2] http://www.nenie.org/misc/mpsys/

it immediately issues a retransmission request to the sender. The delay model postpones the delivery of the retransmission requests by a given amount of time. We used a two-state Markov model, widely known as the *Gilbert model*, to emulate a bursty packet loss behavior in the network.

We used a fixed 10 ms delay, since it represents the maximum round trip delay in our target network infrastructure. We varied the packet loss rates as follows: 1, 5, and 10%. For lost packets, our recovery mechanism sends at most a single-retransmission request.

Figure 1.8 reveals that our software recovered a lot of lost packets and maintained a tolerable picture quality with noticeable, but not overwhelming, glitches even in extremely loss-prone network environments such as with a packet loss rate of 10%. This applies as long as the network can utilize more than the required available bandwidth. As seen in the figure, our retransmission scheme recovered lost packets very successfully in a 1% packet loss environment. The retransmission scheme with a 5% packet loss environment also showed a similar trend as for the 1% packet loss environment. Our real-world experiments also confirmed the effectiveness of the retransmission-based recovery mechanism, even with a video conference between cross-continental multisites.

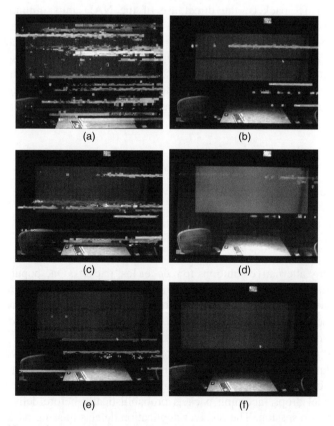

(a)   (b)

(c)   (d)

(e)   (f)

Figure 1.8 Artifacts of retransmission-based packet recovery algorithm: (a, c, and e) show the picture quality without retransmission policy with 10, 5, and 1% loss, respectively. (b, d, and f) show the picture quality with retransmission policy with 10, 5, and 1% loss, respectively.

1.4.3 Network Topology Models

The next step-up in complexity from traditional two-way conferencing is to scale the system to three sites. Unlike in audio conferencing applications where multisite sound data can be mixed together, a three-way video conferencing system requires at least two incoming video channels and one outgoing channel per participating node. This may become a limiting factor in terms of bandwidth and decoding processing resources. Our design also took into consideration real-world factors such as the characteristics of corporate networks which may be asymmetric and heterogeneous and which require optimizations with respect to the underlying available network bandwidth.

Our airline maintenance application involved three sites designated A, B, and C, where A and B are connected via a 1 Gbps dedicated link, while C is connected to other sites via a 25 Mbps public link, thus being limited to one HD stream at a time. In fact, all the video traffic to and from C had to pass through B. Moreover, participants at A are expected to experience all HD quality. This unique situation affected the design of our communication model, and we explored a number of alternative scenarios. To compare these alternatives, we present four possible scenarios, shown in Figure 1.9.

- The *full-mesh model*, illustrated in Figure 1.9a, is a simple three-way communication model, where every site has an individual path with every other site. In its deployment, however, we encountered a fundamental obstacle, as there did not exist enough network bandwidth on the path from C to B. The constraint was largely due to the design of the underlying physical topology. In fact, the path from C to A in the physical network bypasses B, doubling the network utilization of the path from C to A. Without any topology awareness, the logical path would result in intolerable image corruption, resulting from heavy network congestion at the low-bandwidth link.
- The *partial-relay model* in Figure 1.9b tackles the link stress problem of the previous model by relaying the traffic at B. The visual experience at an end user site is the same

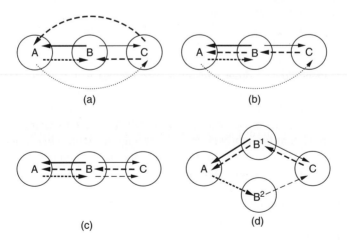

Figure 1.9 Different application-level network topologies for three-way HD conferencing: (a) full-mesh model, (b) partial-relay model, (c) full-relay model, (d) off-loading model. Bold arrows represent an HD path, while normal arrows represent a transcoded SD path.

as that of the conceptual model with a little time shifting due to the newly introduced relay delay. In the meanwhile, the traffic generated from A is still transmitted to B and C, separately. Thus, the outgoing traffic of A will be one HD plus one SD (standard-definition) quality stream.

- The *full-relay model*, shown in Figure 1.9c, additionally minimizes the link stress redundantly imposed on the path from A to C for the logical connection from A to C via relaying at B. This model eventually equals to a centralized model, since B moderates all the traffics. If the required bandwidth for SD video were, however, much smaller than that of HD video and the link capacity of A and B were so high enough to ignore small SD traffics, this optimization would not be benefited any more.

  The two relay models are still exposed to another problem. As shown in Figure 1.9c, B simultaneously captures and delivers one HD video as follows: receives two HD videos from the network, simultaneously renders them in parallel, relays one HD video, and transcodes one captured HD video to SD and delivers the reduced video. These operations are simultaneously executed on a single machine, resulting in significant CPU load. As an improvisational remedy for such a heavy load, we proposed the off-loading solution illustrated in Figure 1.9d.

- The *off-loading model* off-loads the traffic coming from A by redirecting it to B^2, which is geographically located near the B^1 site; thus, a B participant can view two HD videos transmitted from A and C on separate monitors. However, we found that the B^1 machine was still overloaded. Another suggestion to reduce the B^1 load is to move the HD streaming path to B^2.

1.4.4 Relaying

A relay node can play an important role in alleviating bandwidth bottlenecks and in reducing redundant network traffic. However, it may require full knowledge of the underlying physical network topology. In the RCS model, one node may serve as both a regular video participant and as a relay agent.

The relay program is located in the middle of the network, thus being exposed to any occurring network anomalies. To recover from any possible packet losses effectively, the relay host should maintain some small FIFO (first in first out) network buffers that can be used to resequence out-of-order packets and to request lost packets. Packets are then delivered to the destinations after the data cycles through the buffers. It is important to note that a larger buffer size introduces longer delays. Careful selection of the trade-off between the buffer size and the delay is a primary concern of the recovery mechanism. Furthermore, the relay software should be light-weight and not interfere with other programs, because multiple programs may be running on the same machine. In summary, the relay module should satisfy the following requirements:

- recover lost packets (through buffering);
- have an acceptably low relay delay;
- require minimal CPU load.

To implement the relay functionality, we modified the existing network transmission modules. At a traditional receiver, incoming packets sent from another site are temporarily buffered and then pipelined to the video rendering engine as soon as the small local buffer is full. Our relaying mechanism augmented the existing code by writing the full buffer into the user-specified pipe area (or named pipe). The relay sender simply reads data from the pipe and sends the data continuously to the network. Our augmented relay transmission module supports both delivery policies. The relay receiver also included the retransmission-based error recovery algorithm.

However, our experiments showed that the local pipe mechanism, even though it is simple and light-weight, suffered from irregular load fluctuations, resulting in significant quality degradations. Under Linux, it seemed that the pipe mechanism was closely related with the unbalanced CPU load, which made it less useful in some environments. Such oscillations could potentially be a side effect of uneven load scheduling of two separate programs, the receiver and the sender. Thus, the relay operation would probably benefit from running as a single program.

1.4.5 Extension to Wireless Networks

There are numerous challenges when designing and implementing HD streaming over a wireless network. Some existing technologies, for example, 802.11a/g, provide for a maximum sustained bandwidth of approximately 23 Mbps. This is significantly lower than the theoretical and advertised maximum of 54 Mbps. Furthermore, the channel characteristics in wireless networks are very dynamic and variable. As such, packet losses, bandwidth fluctuations, and other adverse effects are a frequent occurrence and require a careful design of the transmission protocol and rendering algorithms. An early prototype of our RCS implementation for wireless networks is shown operational in a laboratory environment in Figure 1.10. In our real-world application, we were able to demonstrate wireless HD streaming in a large aircraft hangar with high visual quality and minimal interference. Figure 1.11 shows the multisite system during a test scenario with the wireless video transmission shown in the upper right corner.

Figure 1.10 HD transmission over a wireless, *ad hoc* link (802.11a) between two laptops in the laboratory.

Figure 1.11 HD multiparty conference with two wired (top left and bottom) and one wireless HD transmission (from an aircraft hangar).

1.5 Real-Time Transcoding

Transcoding refers to a process of converting digital content from one encoding format to another. Owing to its broad definition, it can be interpreted in a number of different ways: conversion from a given video format to another (format conversion); lowering of the bitrate without changing the format (bitrate reduction); reduction of the image resolution to fit to a target display (image scaling); or naively performing complete decoding and re-encoding (cascaded pixel-domain transcoding). Since transcoding allows the adaptation of the video bandwidth to the different requirements of various end users, it is a vital component in the toolkit of a multiway video conference solution, and we narrow the focus of our discussion to three types of bitrate reduction architectures: cascaded pixel-domain transcoding, closed-loop transcoding, and open-loop transcoding.

The cascaded pixel-domain architecture fully decodes compressed bitstreams to reconstruct original signals and then re-encodes them to yield the desired bitstream. While achieving the best performance in terms of video quality, it presents significant computational complexity mainly due to the two iDCT and one DCT processes required. The closed-loop method is the approximation of the cascaded architecture. At the expense of accuracy, and only by using a pair of iDCT and DCT stages, it improves the transcoding complexity significantly.

The open-loop architecture modifies only DCT coefficients in the encoded bitstream by increasing the quantization step size (requantization) or by dropping high-frequency coefficients (data partitioning). In particular, the requantization method converts the encoded bitstream into the DCT domain through variable length decoding (VLD) and then applies coarse-grained quantization to the intermittent signals, which eventually results in more DCT coefficients becoming zero and variable length codes becoming shorter. Since the open-loop approach does not use any DCT/iDCT stages, it achieves minimal processing complexity, but it is exposed to a drift problem. A drift error is caused by the loss of high-frequency information, which damages the reconstruction of reference frames and their successive frames. On the other hand, the cascaded and closed-loop architectures are free from this problem.

In our application, the transcoding component should satisfy the following criteria:

- acceptable video quality;
- acceptable transcoding latency;
- minimal use of local resources.

All three requirements are crucial for a software-driven transcoding component, and it added significant flexibility to our RCS three-way video communication. We started our experiments by customizing an existing transcoding utility, called *mencoder*, which implements the cascaded pixel-domain or the closed-loop system. It is available as one of the utilities for the open-source *MPlayer* video player software package. In the Linux environment, MPlayer is very popular for rendering a multitude of video formats, including the latest video standard such as MPEG-4/AVC. The mencoder was configured to decode incoming MPEG-2 TS packets and then to encode them into a designated video format. We tested two types of transcoded video formats: MPEG-2 program streams (PS) and MPEG-2 TS.

Our earlier experiments in transcoding were a partial success. We were able to successfully transcode MPEG-2 TS into MPEG-2 PS or newly encode an MPEG-2 TS stream. However, two problems were found. First, the transcoding delay was so high that the final end-to-end delay measured about 2 s. Secondly, the machines at one of our sites could not transcode the original HD videos into SD-quality video, due to its underpowered processor. When reproducing the SD-quality video, the transcoder continuously dropped frames, causing frequent video hiccups even without any network retransmissions. Through a series of parameter reconfigurations, we found the optimal video resolution of 300×200 pixels that did not cause any frame drops or video hiccups. Even then, the CPU load was very high, more than 50% on a single core Pentium machine. Thus, we were not able to run two transcoding instances simultaneously on a single machine. The mencoder tended to grab more CPU cycles if any idle time was detected. Such overloads resulted in highly uneven CPU utilization, sometimes causing random program terminations. Transcoding was such an expensive operation that we needed to separate it from other running programs.

Another alternative for software-based transcoding was to use a rather simple, but fast, requantization method, one of the open-loop architectures. Compared to mencoder, this approach does not fully decode and encode the streams, but quantizes pixels at the compressed level. Such a technique would perform much faster and overall be more light-weight.

We experimented with a commercialized DirectShow filter from Solveig Multimedia, called *requantizer*, for our RCS Windows implementation. It was inserted in the middle of several filter chains to convert a 20 Mbps MPEG-2 TS into 10 Mbps MPEG-2 TS in real time. Experimental results showed that the requantizer was able to reduce the bitrate by half while maintaining the same video resolution without any noticeable artifacts caused by drift error. Its CPU utilization was consistently measured to be negligible at less than 1%. It also had no negative effects on any increase in the end-to-end delay from a filter source to a sink. Since the requantization-based transcoding met our criteria, we finally chose the open-loop architecture as our transcoding scheme for the implementation.

One drawback of the requantization scheme was that its bitrate reduction was very limited. Although it met our application needs to some degree, it failed to achieve a bitrate reduction of more than a factor of 2. When reducing the bitrate by more than 50%, we found that the result was a serious deterioration of the picture quality.

1.6 HD Video Rendering

Once a media stream is transmitted over a network, the rendering component requires an MPEG-2 or MPEG-4 HD decoder. While we use specialized hardware assistance for encoding, we considered various hardware and software options for decoding of streams with the goal of achieving the best quality video with minimal latency. With RCS, we tested the following three solutions:

1. *Hardware-Based (MPEG-2).* When improved quality and picture stability are of paramount importance, we experimented with the CineCast HD decoding board from Vela Research. An interesting technical aspect of this card is that it communicates with the host computer through the SCSI (small computer systems interface) protocol. We have written our own Linux device driver as an extension of the generic Linux SCSI support to communicate with this unit. An advantage of this solution is that it provides a digital HD-SDI (high-definition serial digital interface; uncompressed) output for very high picture quality and a genlock input for external synchronization. Other hardware-based decoder cards also exist.

2. *Software-Based (MPEG-2).* Utilizing standard PC hardware, we have used the libmpeg2 library – a highly optimized rendering code that provides hardware-assisted MPEG-2 decoding on current-generation graphics adapters. Through the XvMC extensions of Linux X11 graphical user interface, libmpeg2 utilizes the motion compensation and iDCT hardware capabilities on modern graphics GPUs (graphics processing units; e.g., nVidia). This is a very cost-effective solution. In our earliest experiments, we used a graphics card based on an nVidia FX 5200 GPU, which provides low computational capabilities compared to current-generation GPUs. Even with the FX 5200 GPU, our software setup achieved approximately 70 fps @ 1280×720 with a 3 GHz Pentium 4.

3. *Software-Based (MPEG-4/AVC).* The *ffplay* player is used as the main playback software to decode and render the streams. It is a portable media player based on the *ffmpeg* and the SDL libraries. The player supports many options for users to choose such as to select which kind of video and audio format will be played. For our experiments, the ES extracted by the `ts` tool are input into ffplay while we also specify the input video format using the options.

For MPEG-4/AVC rendering, our prototype system configuration had the following specifications:

- Quad core CPU: Intel(R) Core(TM)2 Extreme CPU X9650 @ 3.00 GHz.
- Video card: nVidia Corporation Quadro FX 1700.

- Sound card: Intel Corporation 82801I (ICH9 Family) HD Audio Controller.
- Operating system: Ubuntu 9.10 with Linux kernel version 2.6.31-17 SMP.
- Main memory: 3.25 GB.

To quantify the image quality of different encoding rates of a Hauppauge HD-PVR box, we use a simple but still widely used performance metric, peak signal-to-noise ratio (PSNR). Especially, the PSNR of the luminance component (Y) for a given image is known to be more suitable for the evaluation of a color image than the normal PSNR. In our experiment, we prerecord a reference video through a Sony HDV camcorder, replay it for the HD-PVR box to re-encode analogous video output with five different encoding rates (1, 2, 4, 8, and 10 Mbps), and obtain the PSNR values of every encoded image from the reference picture. The encoded video resolution was equally configured to that of the reference video – that is, $1920 \times 1080\,i$.

Figure 1.12 depicts the evaluation results of 300 video frames (corresponding to 10 s) for all encoded videos. As shown in the figure, the encoding rate of 4 Mbps could reproduce a very comparable image quality to those of high bitrate videos. Although not shown in this figure, the encoding rate more than 5 Mbps tends to show better treatments on dynamically changing scene. Additionally, we also observe that higher bitrate more than 8 Mbps does no longer improve the picture quality significantly.

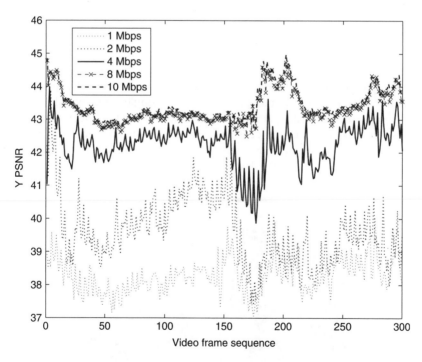

Figure 1.12 The luma PSNR values of different encoding rates by a HD-PVR box are plotted over 300 video frames.

1.6.1 Rendering Multiple Simultaneous HD Video Streams on a Single Machine

In RCS, we performed extensive experiments with a three-way connection topology. Every site was able to watch at least two other participants. Hence, every machine was equipped with the necessary resources to render two HD streams. In our early measurements, one HD decoding process occupied approximately 20% of the CPU load based on our hardware platform. Thus, we naturally expected that every machine could render two simultaneous HD videos locally. Rendering two SD streams was also expected to present a lighter load compared with two HD streams because of the comparatively lower rendering complexity.

We had no problem to display two HD video streams on a single machine. Originally, we were uncertain whether the machines at two sites could support two HD rendering processes simultaneously because of their rather low-end single core CPU architectures. In a slower single core CPU model in our lab, the two HD displays occasionally showed unbalanced CPU loads during tests. We were able to run two HD video renderers and two audio renderers simultaneously on some machines. However, the weaker computers could not run two audio players concurrently while running two video player instances.

In summary, we confirmed that two HD renderings including network transmission modules worked fine at sufficiently powerful sites. However, CPU utilization was a little bit higher than we expected; thus, it was unclear whether the video transcoding utility would be runnable in parallel on a single machine.

1.6.1.1 Display Mode

In order to provide flexibility at each of the end user sites, we implemented a number of display mode presets that a user could easily access in our software. The display mode in RCS specifies how to overlay multiple videos on a single window. The single mode shows only one video at a time (Figure 1.13). The grid mode divides the video screen into multiple equisized rectangular cells and shows one video per grid cell (Figure 1.14). Since we did not plan to support more than eight incoming streams, the maximum number of grid cells was fixed at eight. The last mode, picture-in-picture (PIP) mode, shows two

Figure 1.13 Single display mode.

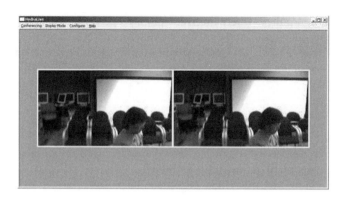

Figure 1.14   Grid display mode (side-by-side).

Figure 1.15   Picture-in-picture display mode.

video streams simultaneously: one main video stream in the background and the other small subvideo screen at the right bottom corner in the foreground (Figure 1.15).

We also provided a navigational method that quickly switches from one video stream to another by pressing the arrow keys. Let us assume an example where there is a need to display three video streams (1, 2, and 3). In single mode, the display order upon any right arrow key stroke is $1 \rightarrow 2 \rightarrow 3 \rightarrow 1$. The left key reverses the display order to $1 \rightarrow 3 \rightarrow 2 \rightarrow 1$. In grid mode, the ordering for the right arrow key is 1,2,3 $\rightarrow$ 3,1,2 $\rightarrow$ 2,3,1 $\rightarrow$ 1,2,3 and for the left key 1,2,3 $\rightarrow$ 2,3,1 $\rightarrow$ 3,1,2 $\rightarrow$ 1,2,3. In PIP mode, the order for a right arrow key press is 1,2 $\rightarrow$ 3,1 $\rightarrow$ 2,3 $\rightarrow$ 1,2 and for the left key 1,2 $\rightarrow$ 2,3 $\rightarrow$ 3,1 $\rightarrow$ 1,2. The up and down arrow keys are assigned to change the display modes. The cycling order of the up key is single $\rightarrow$ grid $\rightarrow$ PIP $\rightarrow$ single. The down key reverses the order: single $\rightarrow$ PIP $\rightarrow$ grid $\rightarrow$ single.

One crucial issue in this display mode is related to the limitation of the DirectShow filter chaining mechanism: synchronized rendering. When all the videos are connected to a single video mixing render (VMR) filter for a unified display on a single video plane, the starting times of individual video renderings are synchronized with the longest start-up latency among all the individual video renderers. This is primarily due to a

VMR implementation policy, where the video mixing operation starts only after all media samples of its input filters are available. On the other hand, as exemplified in Figure 1.12, when video rendering chains are separated and running as different processes, such time synchronization problems do not exist.

1.6.2 Deinterlacing

We tested a number of Sony HD camcorders whose video format is interlaced video output (1080i). As long as the interlaced videos are displayed on an interlaced television and progressive videos are shown on a monitor-like screen, different video modes will not be a problem. However, many new big-screen displays are now progressive in nature and thus they might produce interlacing artifacts during display. Although our test plasma television technically supported interlaced rendering, it turned out to be difficult to enable the computer graphics cards to output interlaced signals, and the autodetection mechanism usually defaulted to a progressive mode. This practical problem may be solvable with further investigations into the compatibility between video drivers and display capabilities. However, even if the interlaced mode can be set successfully, we would be somewhat hesitant to use it because, from our experience, the interlaced display of text output is very unsatisfactory.

In response, we decided to add a deinterlacing routine to the video rendering software. It eliminated the interlacing artifacts produced by alternating odd and even fields of frames. Again, such a module should be light-weight as it will postprocess signals during the last stage of the video rendering process. If its processing load is too heavy, it may result in a failure to display two simultaneous HD renderings.

We implemented the linear blending deinterlacing algorithm at the very end of video rendering pipeline, right before the pixels were displayed on the screen. The approach is to interpolate consecutive even and odd lines. Specifically, the algorithm computes the average values of the pixels of the previous three lines (prioritizing the odd lines or the even lines) and then using them as the final pixel values as follows:

$$i\text{th pixel value of } j\text{th line} = [i\text{th pixel of } (j-3)\text{th line}$$
$$+2 \times (i\text{th pixel of } (j-2)\text{th line}) + i\text{th pixel of } (j-1)\text{th line}]/4$$

Our blending implementation does not use previously rendered video frames. As a result, the artifacts such as "mouse teeth" and "tearing" are noticeably eliminated after applying the averaging mechanism. However, it does have the side effect of blurring the images. Fast motions tend to show less clear images, resulting in poorer video quality. Moreover, interlacing artifacts are still present for fast motions. Our deinterlacing solution did not cause any noticeable performance degradation and its CPU load still remained consistent and stable, similar to the case without it.

In the Windows environment, we tested a hardware supported deinterlacing method, the PureVideo technology available from nVidia Corporation. It performs the motion estimations and compensations through the hardware accelerator on an nVidia graphics card. Surprisingly, its video rendering occupies just about 10% of the CPU load with excellent deinterlaced video output results. We realized that a number of off-the-shelf deinterlacing software libraries available for the Windows environment produced a very decent deinterlaced quality with acceptable CPU load.

As a result, we reached the conclusion to use such off-the-shelf deinterlacing libraries available freely when we moved our development platform to Windows. The only remaining question was whether the video rendering software would still be able to maintain the same degree of low latency that we achieved on the Linux platform.

1.7 Other Challenges

1.7.1 Audio Handling

Multichannel echo cancellation is a largely open research problem. Researchers are pursuing both near-term- and long-term solutions to address the needs of high-quality audio acquisition challenges in conference type environments. Echo cancellation for a single audio channel has been identified as a needed component. Optimal microphone and speaker placements are other design issues. Finally, the output audio quality requirements need to be contrasted and optimized for meeting type environments (as compared to, for example, theater type production environments).

1.7.2 Video Streaming

Optimization of high-quality video in terms of QoS (quality of service)/usability requirements in conjunction with objective performance metrics such as latency is an ongoing research problem. Video streaming issues must be studied in various configurations and settings with new algorithms as well as through usability testing. It should be noted that RCS focuses on HDV quality. As a consequence, a minimum amount of bandwidth must exist in the network, otherwise it is physically impossible to achieve high-quality transmissions. Furthermore, there are constraints on the hardware, which must provide the capabilities and performance required. For example, the RCS rendering system is carefully designed around MPEG-2 and MPEG-4 software decompression modules. To achieve high performance, it is desirable to utilize the hardware capabilities of modern graphics cards. In our current design, a specific combination of graphics hardware, drivers, and software components is necessary to achieve the best possible performance. Further research is required to investigate these trade-offs and to improve performance. It is also important to understand the operating environment in which a remote conferencing system will operate. Public and corporate networks have different characteristics in different parts of the globe.

1.7.3 Stream Format Selection

The RCS software is designed to capture, transmit, and decode MPEG-2 and MPEG-4 bitstreams in the TS format. Although the video rendering software is capable of playing both MPEG-2 formatted TS and PS videos, the software chain was significantly rewritten to optimize the transmission and rendering of TS video streams effectively. The transcoded video output can be either TS or PS formatted.

RCS has also shown the usefulness of a single-pass retransmission mechanism in a lossy network. Some of the retransmitted packets may arrive late or are dropped in the network. The RCS receiver software, aware of the underlying data format, selectively issues a retransmission request for each lost packet. Changes in the software design, for example, as a result of new transcoding modules, may produce data formats other than TS. These are design choices that need to be carefully analyzed in the context of the overall architecture.

1.8   Other HD Streaming Systems

There are several commercial systems available that focus on high-quality video conferencing (i.e., with a visual quality beyond SD). Among them, two popular high-end systems are highlighted here. The TelePresence system from Cisco Systems provides a specially engineered room environment per site, integrating cameras, displays, meeting table, and sound systems (Szigeti *et al.* 2009). The video images taken from custom-designed high-resolution 1080p video cameras are encoded as 720p or 1080p H.264 bitstreams. The encoded bitrates range either from 1 to 2.25 Mbps for 720p or from 3 to 4 Mbps for 1080p. Unlike the usual MPEG-based compression algorithms, reference frames are constructed aperiodically to encode more efficiently. Individual sound samples, acquired from microphones that are positioned at special locations, are encoded with AAC-LD (advanced audio coding low delay). The encoded bitrate and coding delay are 64 kbps and 20 ms, respectively. The encoded media data are then packetized and multiplexed, using the RTP. The system does not employ any packet loss recovery mechanism, but a receiver, after detecting the packet losses, requests a sender to send a reference frame to rebuild the video image, while disposing unusable frames quickly. The end-to-end latency between two systems, excluding the transmission delay, is estimated less than 200 ms. The Halo system from HP[3] features similar room installations with fully assembled hardware communicating over a private, dedicated network. While the cameras used in Halo are SD, the video streams are upconverted to HD at the display side. Each stream requires about 6 Mbps and each room generally supports four streams. The Halo system is turnkey and fully proprietary. While the above two high-end systems are extremely expensive because of their professional setup, several companies offer an affordable solution. For example, LifeSize[4] features 720p cameras and displays. Its proprietary compressor provides very low bandwidth (e.g., 1.1 Mbps for 720p video). While the camera and compressor are proprietary, the display is generic.

A number of research prototypes similar to our solution were implemented in different research communities; they can be classified into two groups. The first group uses uncompressed HD video streams, which are especially useful for very time-sensitive applications such as distributed musical collaborations. Among them is the UltraGrid system, which transmits uncompressed HD at a bandwidth requirement close to or above 1 Gbps (Gharai *et al.* 2006). The Ultra-Videoconferencing project at McGill University[5] was designed especially for low-latency video conferencing applications. It delivers uncompressed 720p HD sources using HD-SDI at 1.5 Gbps and 12 channels of 24-bit raw PCM (pulse code modulation) data with 96 kHz sampling rate.

The second group uses compressed HD videos and audios, captured from commodity MPEG-2 HD camcorders. Kondo *et al.* at Hiroshima University in Japan experimented

---

[3] http://www.hp.com/halo/index.html
[4] http://www.lifesize.com/
[5] http://www.cim.mcgill.ca/sre/projects/rtnm/

with an HD delivery system for multiparty video conferencing applications in Linux environment (Kondo *et al*. 2004). Their prototype system captures MPEG-2 transport bit-streams from hardware encoders such as JVC HD camcorder or Broadcom kfir MPEG-2 encoder card, embeds FEC codes (using the Reed–Solomon method) on the fly, inter-weaves them, and finally shuffles the transmission order of the packets to minimize the effect of burst packet losses. While requiring 10%–50% more transmission bandwidth, its error resilience showed two orders of magnitude packet loss rate reduction. The one-way delay was reported around 600 ms for hardware decoder and 740 ms for software decoder (VLC Client). Audio streams were separately transmitted through a customized RAT (robust audio tool). Similar software packages that were developed for the Windows environment reported much longer latencies (around 1–2 s one-way delay). Compared with these, our system features much lower end-to-end delay with the same capturing setup (due to our software optimization efforts), software-based real-time video transcod-ing capability, and bandwidth-saving packet relaying mechanism.

1.9 Conclusions and Future Directions

We have discussed design challenges for multiway HD video communications and have reported on recent experimental results of specific approaches built into a prototype system called RCS. We implemented real-time transcoding, a relay mechanism, and deinterlaced video rendering, and deployed these mechanisms successfully, including two simultaneous HD renderers per computer. In case of the transcoding output format, we could obtain MPEG-2 TS or PS formatted 300×200 video output from the original MPEG-2 HD TS videos. Both formats could be supported easily, but we found the TS format to be more resilient.

References

Gharai, L., Lehman, T., Saurin, A. and Perkins, C. (2006) Experiences with High Definition Interactive Video Conferencing. IEEE International Conference on Multimedia & Expo (ICME), Toronto, Canada.

ISO/IEC 13818–1 (1994). Information Technology – Generic Coding of Moving Pictures and Associated Audio: Systems Recommendation H.222.0, International Standard, National Organization for Standardiza-tion, ISO/IEC JTC1/SC29/WG11, NO801, 13 November, 1994.

Kondo, T., Nishimura, K. and Aibara, R. (2004) Implementation and evaluation of the robust high-quality video transfer system on the broadband internet. *IEEE/IPSJ International Symposium on Applications and the Internet*, 135.

MacAulay, A., Felts, B. and Fisher, Y. (2005) Whitepaper – IP streaming of MPEG-4: Native RTP vs MPEG-2 transport stream Technical Report, Envivio, Inc.

Papadopoulos, C. and Parulkar, G.M. (1996) *Retransmission-based Error Control for Continuous Media Appli-cations*. Proceedings of the 6th International Workshop on Network and Operating Systems Support for Digital Audio and Video (NOSSDAV 1996), Zushi, Japan.

Szigeti, T., McMenamy, K., Saville, R. and Golwacki, A. (2009) *Cisco TelePresence Fundamentals*, 1st edn, Cisco Press, Indianapolis, Indiana.

Wenger, S., Hannuksela, M., Stockhammer, T., Westerlund, M. and Singer, D. (2005) RTP Payload Format for H.264 Video. RFC 3984.

Zimmermann, R., Fu, K., Nahata, N. and Shahabi, C. (2003) *Retransmission-Based Error Control in a Many-to-Many Client-Server Environment*. SPIE Conference on Multimedia Computing and Networking (MMCN), Santa Clara, CA.

2

MPEG Standards in Media Production, Broadcasting and Content Management

Andreas U. Mauthe[1] and Peter Thomas[2]

[1]*School of Computing and Communications, Lancaster University, Lancaster, UK*
[2]*AVID Development GmbH, Kaiserslautern, Germany*

2.1 Introduction

Content production, broadcasting and content management rely to a large extent on open standards that allow the seamless handling of content throughout the production and distribution life cycle. Moreover, the way content is encoded is also crucial with respect to its conservation and preservation. The first MPEG standard (MPEG-1) [1] was conceived to optimally compress and transmit audio and video in a computerized environment. The basic principles were later adopted by MPEG-2 [2] and in large parts MPEG-4 [3], which represent the next generations in digital encoding standards dealing partially with issues relevant to the broadcast and media production industry, but essentially focusing on the requirements of the computer and content networking domain.

The driving forces behind the Moving Picture Experts Group in the late 1980s were the possibilities that computers, digital storage systems, computer networks and emerging digital multimedia systems offered. It was quickly realized that within the media production and broadcasting domain, digital encoding formats would have to be adopted as well in order to streamline content production and media handling. However, media production and content management in a professional content environment have specific requirements. For instance, encoding formats have to allow production without quality loss, and archiving requires durable formats that preserve the original quality. These requirements have not been at the forefront of the original standardization efforts. Some of the core principles adopted there (e.g. inter-frame compression) are actually suboptimal for specific production and preservation purposes. Nevertheless, MPEG standards have been having

The Handbook of MPEG Applications: Standards in Practice Edited by Marios C. Angelides and Harry Agius
© 2011 John Wiley & Sons, Ltd

a considerable impact on the media and content industry, and the pro-MPEG Forum [4] has been specifically set up to represent these interests within the MPEG world.

Over time, the MPEG standardization efforts also moved towards providing support for content description and a fully digital content life cycle. The relevant MPEG standards in this context are MPEG-7 [5] and MPEG-21 [6]. Despite the fact that these standards have been defined with the input of organizations such as the European Broadcasting Union (EBU) [7], the Society of Motion Pictures Television Engineers (SMPTE) [8] and individual broadcasters, there appears to be a clear difference in the importance between the coding standards and the content description and management-related standards. In content production, broadcasting and content management, MPEG coding standards (i.e. MPEG-1, MPEG-2 and MPEG-4) have driven many new product developments and are underpinning emerging digital television services. In contrast, MPEG-7 and MPEG-21 have not been widely adopted by the industry and play only a minor role in some delivery and content exchange scenarios.

In this chapter, we discuss the requirements of content within media production, broadcasting and content management in order to provide the background for the subsequent discussion on the use of the different MPEG encoding standards in these environments. Following this, MPEG-7 and MPEG-21 and their role within the content industry is analysed. The objective of this chapter is to discuss the relevance of MPEG standards in the context of media production, content management and broadcasting.

2.2   Content in the Context of Production and Management

Content is the central object of operation for broadcasters and media production companies [9]. Over the years, the term content has adopted various meanings referring to ideas and concepts as well as recorded material or archived end-products. At different stages of its life cycle, content is represented in different ways through a multitude of proxies. The entire workflow in a content production, broadcasting and media delivery organization revolves around content in its various forms and representations (as depicted in Figure 2.1) [9]. The content creation process begins with the production process (including commissioning and elaboration), followed by post-production and delivery, and ends in the reception phase. During these stages metadata, as well as encoded program material, is produced, handled and stored. Metadata reflects the various aspects of content from the semantic description of the content, over cataloguing information, broadcasting details, rights-related metadata, to location data and material-related metadata. The encoded program material is available in various copies, versions and different encoding formats.

Since content is an ubiquitous term of which most people have an intuitive understanding, it was deemed necessary by SMPTE and EBU to define it in more detail in order to ensure that there is a common understanding of its constituents and usage. According to the SMPTE and EBU task force definition *content* consists of two elements, namely, *essence* and *metadata* [10]. Essence is the raw program material itself and represents pictures, sound, text, video, and so on, whereas metadata describes all the different aspects and viewpoints of content.

As can be seen in Figure 2.1, both elements are crucial in media production and broadcasting in order to produce high-quality content fast and cost effectively. In such a content-centric operation, the content elements (i.e. metadata and essence, or both) have to

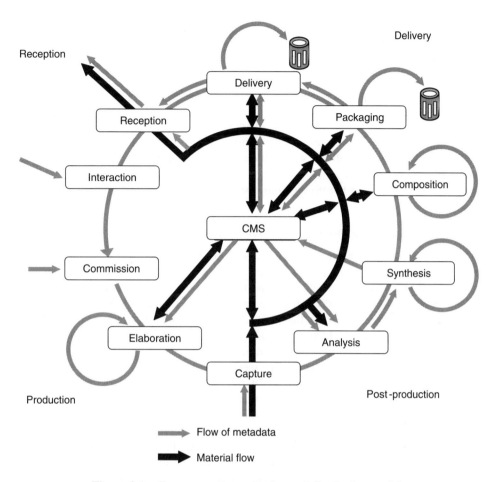

Figure 2.1 Content-centric production and distribution model.

be accessed by everybody included in the content creation process depending on their role in the workflow. For instance, high-quality essence access is required in production, post-production and archives, whereas low-quality browse access can be sufficient for editors, journalists and producers. Metadata accompanies the program material at all stages in the content life cycle. Metadata-only access is sufficient during the early stage (i.e. production stage), and for administrative staff. However, all metadata have to be kept up-to-date in real-time and reflect the status of the content. Thus, in a content-centric organization, essence and metadata have to support the flexible production and handling of content throughout its life cycle.

Another important aspect in the handling of content is its exchange not only within but also across organizations. Consequently, in such a content transfer process, a copy of the essence and a subset of the metadata leave the system. It might be reintroduced later, at which stage any changes have to be recorded and documented.

Thus, not only the requirements on different encoding formats but also metadata schemas and standards originate from the organizational needs, workflow and usage of the content throughout its lifetime. This section looks at the requirements placed onto codec, metadata and framework formats, and discusses the rational behind them and their importance within the content life cycle.

2.2.1 Requirements on Video and Audio Encoding Standards

The choice of codec in media production and content management is governed by specific requirements, some of which may differ considerably between production-oriented and distribution-oriented applications, while others are common across all application domains. An encoding standard used in this environment has to addresses these requirements since they provide the basis for the production, operation and handling of content.

2.2.1.1 General Requirements on Encoding Standards

As expected, a common need in all application domains in media production and distribution is the desire to have the highest possible compression rate achievable while still meeting the specific requirements towards quality, and video and audio fidelity of the respective application domain. On the one hand, a high compression ratio is desirable to save network and storage costs; on the other hand, there should not be any major noticeable artifacts and the quality should stay constant even after a succession of production steps.

Even more important, however, is the requirement for interoperability between systems, different equipment and organizations. The media industry relies on the ability to exchange content. For instance, external producers working for broadcasters, or regional studios contributing to the main program, require that material exchanged between various sites and companies can be readily used in production or distribution at all locations. Format interoperability is the key to avoid unnecessary latencies as well as the additional cost involved in format conversions and normalizations to specific (in-house) formats or format variants. These costs include possible quality deterioration due to transcoding processes.

As a consequence, professional media production and content management require a much more rigid interpretation of standards than other media-related industry domains. For example, MPEG-2 allows selecting from various profiles and levels. Further, it does not specify how content is to be encoded (since only decoding is specified in the standard). The MPEG-2 profiles support different sampling rates (4:2:0, 4:2:2, 4:4:4) and specify a set of coding features that represent a subset of the full MPEG-2 syntax. The MPEG-2 levels specify a subset of spatial and temporal resolutions through which a large set of image formats can be supported. Hence, an MPEG-2 encoded video can in fact have many different formats and even the fact that the decoding is specified rather than the encoding can lead to the incompatibility of certain products. Thus, this level of flexibility and operational freedom has introduced interoperability problems when content is created, edited and distributed by multiple partners using different tools and products that use slight variations, which are, however, still standard conform.

In order to avoid such interoperability problems, the media industry typically agrees upon an unambiguously specified subset of more generic standards. SMPTE has therefore seen it necessary to develop and maintain a set of related standards documents that are more rigid but provide the required level of granularity and detail and thus help to achieve the desired level of interoperability.

2.2.1.2   Specific Requirements in Media Production

In media production the requirements revolve around ease of use of encoded material in production tools such as non-linear editors (NLE), and the ability of the codec to retain excellent picture quality even after multiple edits and content generations. When editing in the compressed domain (which is common for state-of-the-art broadcast editing suites), hard cut editing does not require decoding and re-encoding, as long as the codec used is I-frame only, and is consistent throughout all content used in the edit. However, edit effects that change the image content or combine images from multiple sources (e.g. cross-fades) require re-encoding, and hence introduce a generation loss for the frames affected. When it is required to change the codec of a source clip to match the chosen target codec for the target sequence, all frames of this specific source clip are subjected to a generation loss. Using lossy compression (as specified for MPEG) can, hence, lead to quality deterioration that even after a few editing steps can be quite noticeable. Editing content using inter-frame encoding typically requires recoding of entire groups of pictures (GOPs). Thus the quality of all images that are part of these GOPs is affected.

Content generations are also created due to format changes as part of content preservation processes, especially in long-term archives (i.e. when new formats are introduced and existing content is migrated from the old format to a newer format).

In short, the foremost requirements in media production are as follows:

1. No perceivable loss in picture quality due to compression when compared to the uncompressed signal.
2. Minimum loss in picture quality even after multiple decoding/encoding cycles (minimum generation losses).
3. Ability to perform cuts-only editing without a need to even partially re-encode the pictures.
4. Easy to edit in non-linear editing workstations, including fast navigation in both directions (jog/shuttle forward/backwards) as well as the ability to edit any picture.

The first two requirements typically govern the choice of compression scheme, codec type and, in MPEG-based standards, the layer and profile/level. Usually main or high profile formats are used in combination with main level or high level. The third and fourth requirement typically results in the selection of a scheme where there are no inter-frame dependencies; that is, in MPEG-based standards an I-frame-only codec is the only suitable solution.

2.2.1.3   Specific Requirements in Media Distribution

In conventional television broadcast, content stored as video files is broadcast from the so-called broadcast video servers. The basic functionality of a video server can be compared to a video tape recorder (VTR) where the tape is replaced by a hard disk. Independent of the way the content is stored on the disk of the video server, it is played back to air as an uncompressed stream.

For the first video servers introduced in the mid-1990s, the primary cost driver was the disk storage subsystem. Hence, there was a desire to minimize this cost by using codecs that retained good picture quality at minimum bandwidth. This typically meant using very efficient compression schemes. For MPEG-based compression formats, long GOP codecs have proven to be a suitable option. A long GOP uses a longer sequence of I, P and B frames. Conventionally, a GOP with 9 frames has proven to be suitable. In long GOPs, the group of pictures is extended to 12 or 15 frames, or even beyond. Any quality implication of using a long GOP scheme in this context are minimal, since as long as the material has been only recorded onto the video server by encoding baseband streams (just like a VTR does) this choice has no major impact on the overall picture quality. In this case, the generation losses caused by encoding from baseband to the distribution formats are unavoidable since the studio lines (i.e. SDI, serial digital interface) require the transmission of video in ITU 601 4:2:2 uncompressed format at around 270 Mbit/s.

Nowadays, however, content is primarily "loaded" onto video servers via file transfers. This means that continuing to use long GOP distribution formats would require transcoding from the production format to the distribution format, resulting in an additional generation loss, additional cost for transcoders and additional latencies. The latter is a particularly critical factor in news and sports production. The fact that storage costs have decreased considerably in recent years has resulted in the use of one common format (i.e. suitable for production and transmission of high-quality television content). Still, contribution of news material from agencies to broadcasters uses long GOP formats in order to reduce the data rate, and hence provide faster file transfer. Further, the acquisition of content in the electronic news gathering (ENG) field often applies long GOP compression in order to transmit signals over low-bandwidth connections [11].

In contrast to traditional television, the distribution of content over digital delivery channels has completely different requirements. Here, the single most important requirement is to optimize the picture quality as seen by the viewer versus the bandwidth required to deliver these pictures. For MPEG-based formats, this almost naturally resulted in the use of long GOP formats, both in the distribution of standard-definition (SD) television and high-definition television (HDTV). At present, these formats are typically created through on-the-fly transcoding of the on-air signal, i.e., at the last stage before the signal is transmitted.

For distribution over conventional television distribution channels such as cable, satellite or terrestrial broadcast, the formats to be used are precisely standardized. Other areas of digital distribution, such as Internet streaming or download formats, tend to be less strictly limited. However, at present, an efficient compression scheme is the most stringent requirement. The compression schemes have to adapt to the specific characteristics of the Internet, that is, low and fluctuating bandwidth. Many proprietary schemes have been developed and are currently used in different Internet-based content delivery networks. However, with the emergence of Internet protocol television (IPTV), this might change in future since quality aspects play a much more crucial role for these services. The predominant standards in this context are H.264/MPEG-4 AVC (MPEG-4 Part 10 Advanced Video Coding) [3]. This is deemed a good compromise between the bandwidth and data rates that the network can support and the quality requirements for a TV-like service.

2.2.1.4 Specific Requirements in Content Management

Since the quality requirements are very high in a professional content environment, the media industry tends to use high bit rate formats for most of the application domains representing the different stages of production, post-production, delivery and content management. However, due to bandwidth limitations in the networks of production companies and broadcasters, access to production quality content tends to be restricted to a subset of users with access to actual production systems and production networks, often still based on SDI [12] and SDTI (serial data transfer interface) [13]. Only the latter provides the ability to transmit compressed content. However, the majority of users are only connected to standard local area networks (LANs) such as Ethernet. Owing to these restrictions, a large number of users directly involved in the content life cycle (e.g. more than 75% of all users in a television broadcaster need access to the actual essence in some form) have no easy way to actually see the content they are working with. Thus, modern content management systems (CMS) provide a proxy or browse copy, offering access to frame-accurate, but highly compressed, copies of the available content over the Intranet or even Internet.

The format requirements for such proxies may differ considerably depending on what the users actually want to accomplish. For instance, in news and sports production, it is vital that the proxy is being created in real-time and is fully accessible while incoming content (news feeds or live events) are being recorded. In applications where the proxy is used for offline editing or pre-editing, it is important that the format provides very good user interactivity allowing navigation through the content using trick modes such as jog/shuttle. In quality control, acceptance or the assessment of compliance with standards and practices, the image quality and resolution is more relevant. Thus, depending on the purpose, different proxy formats might be required. However, what they all have in common is the need to transmit them via standard LANs in real-time or faster.

CMS are not only responsible for archiving and managing production content, but more and more have become the hub for all content-related activities. This includes the plethora of new media channels such as Internet portals, VoD (video-on-demand) platforms or mobile content delivery. Therefore, specific formats may have to be generated for the delivery across the different channels. In order to optimize transfer and delivery times for on-demand distribution to such channels, it can be efficient to maintain the content in an additional "mezzanine" format that on the one hand is efficiently compressed so that storage cost and file transfer times to transcoders are of little impact, and on the other hand has good enough picture quality to serve at least as a good source for transcoding to the various lower bit rate target formats. These requirements have been taken into consideration during the MPEG standardization (specifically during the MPEG-4 standardization process).

2.2.2 Requirements on Metadata Standards in CMS and Production

Metadata accompanies all workflow steps and documents all details related to a content item. The data models of many broadcasters and content production companies are very detailed and sophisticated reflecting not only the content creation and production process, the semantic content information, the organizational and management information, but also commercial usage data and rights information. These models are overwhelmingly proprietary and reflect the historical background and specific organizational requirements of a particular organization. However, the use of a standard set of metadata, a metadata description scheme, a metadata dictionary or at least standards for metadata transmission and exchange is required whenever content is exchanged or goes outside the organization. Further, the use of certain products, equipment and tools during the production and transmission process also enforces the use of certain metadata information or prescribes a specific format [14]. Thus, the requirements on metadata can be separated into those that come (i) through the content processes and some general characteristics of content, and (ii) through content exchange.

2.2.2.1 Requirements of Content Representation and Description

The metadata used in content production and content management has to reflect the workflow and gather data and information during the different stages in the production. The data comprises, for instance, identifiers, recording data, technical data, production information, location information, and so on. Further, a semantic description of the content is also necessary, as well as the annotation of rights information (e.g. territorial restrictions, transmission and delivery method and time, and usage period) and business data associated with the content [9]. Thus, the relevant information is mainly concerned with usage and workflow issues, semantic content description and management issues. This information is usually kept in multiple databases that are either based on customized standard products or are entirely proprietary systems. All kinds of databases are encountered and for a large organization the underlying data models as well as the records kept in the database are substantial. Since many databases have been established over decades, their organization, structure and the encoding of the data do not conform to any standard with respect to the representation of content and its underlying concepts. However, what they all have in common is the high complexity and integration of the data models, and a requirement of showing relationships and hierarchies at different levels.

Another important requirement is to describe individual segments of a content object. These segments can be delimited either by time codes or region coordinates. The segments do not adhere to any kind of pre-defined structure and depend entirely on the specific documentation view, that is, shot boundaries or strict time-code delimiters are too prescriptive.

2.2.2.2 Requirements Through Metadata Access and Exchange

Different ways of searching for information in the metadata have to be possible. The common query forms are full text query, query for labels and keywords, query for segments and native database queries [9]. All these different access methods have to be supported by a data repository, and hence have to be considered in any metadata description scheme.

Further, metadata is required when content is exchanged between institutions. Usually a subset of metadata is sufficient. However, there are several steps involved in the exchange as shown in Figure 2.2.

First, the part of the metadata to be exchanged between different institutions has to be transferred into a standard common data model. Before it is transmitted, a common interpretation of the elements and values has to be agreed upon by referencing a common metadata dictionary containing all relevant elements. Thus, there need to be standards to support these processes.

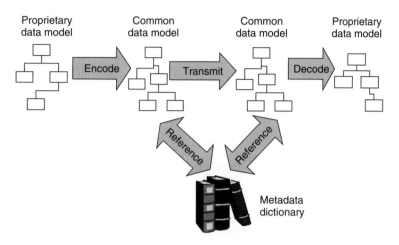

Figure 2.2   Metadata exchange.

Apart from just supporting the metadata and material exchange, the actual process of exchange has to be supported as well. This includes all the commercial transaction details and intellectual property management together with the actual transfer process.

2.3   MPEG Encoding Standards in CMS and Media Production

Since the development of the first MPEG encoding standards in the late 1980, they have been having a large influence on media production, content management and transmission. Despite the fact that MPEG-1's main objective was not related to these domains, the basic ideas and structure have been influencing content formats and products ever since. In this section, the different standards, products and the impact they have within CMS and the media production domain is reviewed. This includes a discussion on the commercial products that are based on MPEG encoding standards.

2.3.1   MPEG-1

MPEG-1, originally developed as a codec for video CD, is still in use in media production as a proxy format, especially in applications related to television news. MPEG-1 has two key advantages:

- First, today's desktop workstations can decode MPEG-1 very fast. Thus the format provides excellent interactivity in proxy editing applications, positioning, jog and shuttle, which allows users to work with the format very intuitively.
- Second, the format can be freely navigated and played back while it is being recorded and written to disk with very little latency. This allows, for instance, encoding incoming news feeds to MPEG-1 and thus providing journalists and producers with browse access to such feeds while they are being received. This is a considerable advantage for these users since it allows production in real-time.

MPEG-1's main features include variable bit rate coding, stereo audio support and an inter-frame coding scheme. Since it was intended for stored media, the MPEG-1 compression scheme is asymmetric; that is, the compression is more processing intensive than the decompression. The inter-frame compression scheme also implies that an entire GOP has to be available in order to decode all frames fully and correctly. The use of discrete cosine transformation (DCT) in conjunction with an 8×8 sampling scheme also has impact on the image and thus the video quality. Mainly the coding artefacts and blockiness of the images can sometimes reduce their value as a browsing format. For instance, MPEG-1 used in a sports scenario does not allow reading the numbers on the back of football players in a wide angle shot. However, this is even possible using analogous VHS (video home system) technology to which MPEG-1 has often been compared in terms of quality. Another issue has been frame and time-code accuracy compared to the original material. However, there are ways how this can be solved and frame and time-code-accurate MPEG-1 encoders exist. Even so, the use of MPEG-1 is declining, especially since most products allow only embedding or using one stereo pair of audio, which is not sufficient for many content production purposes.

2.3.2 MPEG-2-Based Formats and Products

The intention of the MPEG-2 standardization was to satisfy the demands for a high-quality video format that could also be used in a media production and broadcasting context. The standardization work was a joint effort between ISO/IEC, ITU-TS-RS, and representatives of content and broadcasting organizations such as EBU and SMPTE. MPEG-2 shares the basic encoding principles with MPEG-1; that is, it uses inter-frame encoding with four different picture types (I, P, B and D frames), a macroblock size of 8×8, DCT, motion estimation and compensation, run-length coding, and so on. As mentioned above, it also specifies only the video bitstream syntax and decoding semantics and not the actual encoding.

In contrast to MPEG-1, MPEG-2 allows multitrack audio. MPEG-2 Part 3 enhances the MPEG-1 audio part and allows up to 5.1 multichannel audio. MPEG-2 Part 7 even supports 48 audio channels with up to 96 kHz sampling rates. This includes multilingual and multiprogram capabilities.

Owing to the definition of different profiles and levels, MPEG-2 is able to support different qualities for various applications. The supported chrominance sampling modes are 4:2:0, 4:2:2 and 4:4:4. The combination of different profiles and levels defined by the standard are intended for different classes of applications. For instance, MPEG-2 Main Profile was defined for video transmission ranging from 2 to 80 Mbit/s. Very common is the use of Main Profile (with a 4:2:0 sampling using I, P, and B frames in a not scalable mode) at Main Level with a resolution of 720 (pixels/line) $\times$ 572 (line/frame) $\times$ 30 (frames/s). In the television production domain, the MPEG-2 4:2:2 profile is very often used. In news and sports, a GOP of IB and data rate of 18 Mbit/s is common, whereas for feature production I-frame-only schemes with a data rate of 50 Mbit/s and more are used.

In addition to the actual coding features, MPEG-2 also specifies how different components can be combined to form a data stream. The MPEG-2 transport stream has been defined for the transmission of multiple programs, whereas the MPEG-2 program stream has been intended to support system processing in software. The MPEG-2 transport stream has been specified to support a range of different applications such as video telephony and digital television.

There are a large number of MPEG-2-based products since from an early stage vendors and manufacturers have been involved in the standardization process. In 1999 Sony introduced the *Interoperability Material Exchange* (IMX) format, which is composed of MPEG-2 Video 4:2:2 I-frame-only and eight-channel AES3 audio streams. The AES3 audio streams usually contain 24-bit PCM (pulse code modulation) audio samples. The format is specified to support three video bit rates, namely, 30, 40 and 50 Mbit/s.

SMPTE has standardized IMX as "D-10", described in SMPTE 365M [15]. D-10 at 50 Mbit/s is the de facto standard for the production of SD television program in a large number of broadcasters and post-production houses. The most commonly used alternative is DVCPRO50 [12], originally developed by Panasonic. In contrast to MPEG-based formats, DV-based formats (such as DVCPRO50) do not use inter-frame encoding and also have a constant bit rate per frame. This has the perceived advantage that in a (video) tape-based environment, instant access and positioning at a specific frame are possible and that no padding is required.

MPEG-2 is also used in HDTV production. Sony is marketing XDCAM HD and XDCAM HD 422, both using MPEG-2 MP@HL (Main Profile at High Level) as codec. Especially XDCAM HD 422 is popular in the industry as an HD production format, since when using a sampling rate of 4:2:2 (in order to be compliant with the requirements for higher-quality television productions) the format requires only 50 Mbit/s of video bandwidth. Thus, it can readily replace D-10 in a production environment providing superior quality without a need to upgrade storage systems or networks. However, the format employs a long GOP structure and requires editing equipment that supports long GOP editing. Hence, certain generation losses apply when edited GOPs are re-encoded. This is not acceptable for all operations and especially high-value material should use an encoding scheme that prevents generation loss as much as possible. Therefore, XDCAM HD and XDCAM HD 422 are mainly used in a news, sports and current affairs environment.

Apart from production, MPEG-2 has also had considerable impact on the distribution of content in the digital domain. The main digital distribution channels are satellite, cable and digital terrestrial distribution. MPEG-2 MP@ML (i.e. Main Profile at Main Level) has become the de facto standard for SD digital television distribution over satellite using mainly DVB (digital video broadcasting)-S [16, 17] and DVB-S2 [18]. It is also prevalent over cable employing DVB-C [19] or terrestrial using DVB-T [20]. It is interesting to note that DVB-S and DVB-S2 are used both in distribution to the consumer and in contribution. In the latter case, for instance, it is used for feeds from news agencies to broadcasters who then use them for news, sports and other programs. The picture quality of this material is not considered ideal for production purposes, but since the speed, cost effectiveness and ease of transmission are more important for actuality and current affairs programs the quality issue is acceptable.

In order to improve the level of interoperability, the DVB project [16] has imposed restrictions on the implementation of MPEG-2 codecs in DVB-compliant systems [21]. These restrictions are related to the allowable resolutions for SD and HD. This was deemed necessary since despite using standard compliant implementations many products from different vendors could not interoperate and effectively a transcoding process resulting in generation loss was necessary.

In general, MPEG-2 MP@ML has developed into one of the major formats in lower-quality content production and general broadcasting. MPEG-2 MP@ML at approximately 15 Mbit/s, for instance, is also a popular mezzanine format and is frequently used as source for transcoding to various xCast distribution formats. It can be, for instance, transcoded into Web formats as well as suitable mobile formats since it provides a sufficiently high quality while still keeping storage costs at a reasonable level. However, this is not deemed sufficient quality as archiving format since it will quickly suffer from generation loss and will also not be sufficient for high-quality media.

Finally, over the years, MPEG-2 MP@ML at approximately 2 Mbit/s (video bandwidth only) has developed into a useful proxy format for SD content replacing MPEG-1 in this role. Compared to MPEG-1 it has several advantages. For instance, at SD resolution, it provides still adequate interactivity, supports multiple audio tracks, and allows to be navigated and played back while recording is still ongoing. The picture quality and resolution are also better than MPEG-1's, and hence it can also be used as browse format for application areas that MPEG-1 was deemed insufficient. However, at 2 Mbit/s, it is not appropriate for wide area applications since commonly this bit rate is too high for sustainable streaming over the Internet to all areas at all times. In this case it is either necessary to use another lower-quality and lower-bandwidth format or to download the content.

2.3.3 MPEG-4

MPEG-4 (officially called "Coding of Audio-Visual Objects (AVOs)") [3] is the last and latest of the MPEG encoding standards and has a far broader scope than its predecessors. Originally, the intention was to define a standard that can achieve a significantly better compression ratio than current standard encoding and compression schemes. However, during the standardization process it has been realized that not only the emerging multimedia applications such as mobile phones and mobile content devices but also the interactive applications such as computer games require specific support. Hence, the focus of MPEG-4 was changed to encompass not only the needs of a wide variety of multimedia applications but also the needs of media production and broadcasting applications. Effectively, the standard tries to support the convergence of different media and technology sectors (i.e. computing, communication, television and entertainment). Consequently, three functional activity areas that should be covered by the standard have been identified:

1. *Content-based interactivity*, including content-based manipulation, bitstream editing, and hybrid-, natural- and synthetic data coding.
2. *Optimized compression* through improved coding efficiency and coding of multiple data streams.
3. *Universal access* allowing access from various devices over a wide range of networks.

This has resulted in the definition of a toolset reflected in the now 27 parts of the MPEG-4 standard (originally there were 10). Of these 27 parts, Parts 2 and 3 deal with video- and audio coding–related aspects, whereas Part 10 is concerned with AVC issues. Parts 12, 14 and 15 are concerned with media file and wrapper formats for ISO base file formats (Part 12, e.g. JPEG 2000), MP4 file formats (Part 14, replacing the respective definition in Part 1), and AVC file formats (Part 15).

The wide variety of issues covered by the standard can be, for instance, seen in its support for a wide range of video codecs from 5 Kbit/s low-quality, low-bandwidth video for mobile devices to 1 Gbit/s HDTV formats. In MPEG-4, video formats can be progressive or interlaced and the resolution may vary from Quarter Common Intermediate Format (QCIF) to 4K × 4K studio resolution.

Novel aspects in the standard are the content-based coding functionalities, face and body animation and 2D and 3D mesh coding. One way to achieve this was to adopt the object-oriented coding in addition to the traditional rectangular video coding. The idea of object-oriented coding is to compose a video out of AVOs of arbitrary shape and spatial and temporal extent. An AVO is represented by coded data carried separately in an elementary stream. Objects are described by object descriptors (OD), which are carried in a separate OD stream. A scene is composed of multiple AVOs; information about the different AVO is carried separately in an accompanying OD stream. Information on how to compose a scene is carried in the scene descriptor information. This defines the spatial and temporal position of AVOs and the relationships between them. It also describes the kind of interactivity possible within a specific scene.

However, MPEG-4 is downward compatible and also, for instance, specifies "conventional" rectangular video coding and advanced audio coding based on the MPEG-2 audio coding techniques, which are extended to provide better compression performance and error resilience.

Like MPEG-2, MPEG-4 also specifies different profiles and levels in order to reduce the complexity and restrict the set of tools that need to be supported within a decoder. For each profile, a set of tools that have to be supported is defined, whereas levels set complexity bounds (e.g. bit rate and number of supported objects). Thus, a specific profile/level combination defines a well-defined conformance point.

Mainly the following four elements of MPEG-4 have been accepted into mainstream use in the media industry:

1. The MPEG-4 wrapper format (derived from the Quicktime wrapper originally developed by Apple Computer, Inc.).
2. The MPEG-4 Advanced Audio Codec (AAC).
3. The MPEG-4 Part 2 video codec, used in certain proxy formats.
4. The MPEG-2 Part 10 video codec (H.264).

The MPEG-4 wrapper is supported by many video servers and other broadcast and production equipment. Especially products based on technology provided or promoted by Apple, Inc., or equipment and tools that are specifically designed to interoperate with such products have adopted the MPEG-4 wrapper format. However, the preferred approach by other vendors in the content and media domain is to use an MXF (Media eXchange Format) wrapper. The MXF is a family of wrapper formats designed by the pro-MPEG Forum [4] and the Advanced Media Workflow Association (AMWA). These wrapper formats are specified in various standards by SMPTE (the most relevant ones are given in [22–27]). MXF is also applied as a metadata enabler in production and archive workflows [28, 29].

With respect to the coding-specific parts of the MPEG-4 standard, MPEG-4 Part 2 is currently used as video codec for proxy video created by the Sony eVTR and XDCAM families of products. These proxies are directly created by the respective recording devices, and hence are instantaneously available for browsing while recording. Sony uses a custom MXF wrapper that allows for low latency navigation in the proxy. However, the audio tracks are encoded using the A-Law audio codec, and hence are considered by professionals to be of inadequate quality for certain applications. Hence, within this product there is actually a combination of approaches and standards, which is indicative of the selectiveness with which the industry deploys the different parts of the MPEG-4 standard.

For television related applications, MPEG-4 Part 10, or H.264, is the most important part of the MPEG-4 standard as it is widely used to encode HDTV.

Panasonic is promoting a format for HD production called "AVC-Intra". AVC-Intra uses the H.264 codec, but in an I-frame-only configuration. Thus, the format meets the requirements for editing, while, at nominally 100 Mbit/s of video bandwidth with 4:2:2 chroma subsampling, it is still reasonably manageable with respect to storage space and required network bandwidth. AVC-Intra has been widely accepted by large broadcasting organizations and it is expected to have further strong impact in this space.

The H.264 is also the format of choice of the DVB project for digital delivery of HD content via DVB-S, DVB-C and DVB-T, and to deliver content to mobile devices via, for example, DVB-H [30].

Further versions of H.264 are also used as a proxy formats either in applications where minimum bandwidth is crucial or where users require full HD resolution for proxy viewing. This is, for instance, necessary for quality assessment, compliance viewing and high-end offline editing. It is therefore used in a very specific part of the workflow within the content production life cycle. However, owing to the complexity of the codec, today's workstations require a substantial part of their resources to decode H.264. Hence, the format has some deficiencies with respect to interactivity and smoothness in navigation such as jog/shuttle. With increasing performance of workstations, these deficiencies will gradually disappear and an even better acceptance can be expected.

2.3.4 Summary

In CMS and professional media production, the MPEG encoding standards have been having considerable impact over the past 10 years; MPEG-1, MPEG-2 and MPEG-4 are used for low resolution browsing, media production and media contribution and distribution. MPEG-4 Part 10 is primarily used in HDTV, and MPEG-2 is used in SD television.

Production applications prefer I-frame-only codecs for easy frame-accurate editing and rendering with minimum generation losses. In browsing- and distribution-related applications, long GOP structures are preferred, providing minimum bit rates for a desired image quality.

The formats are also used within archives and content libraries. However, owing to the compression scheme there is still an ongoing debate about their suitability in content archiving and preservation. The generation loss that MPEG base formats suffer in production and transcoding is frequently considered as too severe. Thus MPEG-based formats are deemed not appropriate for archiving. On the other hand, due to storage restrictions, the use of a compressed format is inevitable and no format has emerged that would satisfy all the requirements of this domain.

The fact that MPEG-2 and MPEG-4 specify different profiles and levels in conjunction with the fact that only bitstream syntax and decoding semantic are specified provides a level of flexibility that resulted in sometimes incompatible products (despite the fact that they were correctly implementing the MPEG standards). Therefore, in order to achieve the best possible level of interoperability between various products used in the production and delivery chain, encoding and wrapper parameters are precisely specified, thus narrowing the degrees of freedom that the MPEG standards otherwise offer for the implementation of such codecs and wrappers. This work has been carried out under the auspice of SMPTE and EBU as central bodies dealing with broadcast technologies.

It can be noted that only parts of the extensive standard suite is actually used within the content production and broadcasting domain at the moment. The focus here is clearly the coding elements. The MPEG-2 transport stream definition has also been having significant impact. Of the very extensive MPEG-4 standard suite, mainly the encoding parts and, in part, the wrapper format have been subsumed into relevant systems and products. However, in the main areas where wrappers are used (i.e. editing, archiving and file exchange), the industry prefers MXF instead of MPEG wrappers. This is the case since MXF provides better interoperability while also allowing embedding other (especially DV-based) codecs. SMPTE acts as the primary authority for providing the required adapted standards in this context.

2.4 MPEG-7 and Beyond

The relevance of specific parts of the MPEG-based encoding standards in media and content production as well as in content management (and to a lesser extent in archiving) is significant. The role of the non-coding standards (i.e. MPEG-7 and MPEG-21) is more complex, and it is harder to assess what impact they have been having in these domains. In this section, the potential of these standards is reviewed – the role they could play in this domain and the impact they have been having so far. The requirements they have to fulfil in the content management and media production domain are mainly related to metadata, management and content exchange aspects.

2.4.1 MPEG-7 in the Context of Content Management, Broadcasting and Media Production

The focus of the multimedia content description interface specified by MPEG-7 is on providing a comprehensive set of description schemes and tools accompanied by the specification of the necessary description language, reference software, conformance guidelines and extensions [31]. It was one of the main objectives of MPEG-7 to provide a comprehensive and widely applicable set of specification and tools. It has not been limited to any specific domain or content type. At present, MPEG-7 consists of 12 parts (originally 8) that cover systems aspects, language for description and description schemes, the actual visual, audio and multimedia description schemes, and various other aspects related to reference software, conformance testing, query formats, and so on [5]. One of MPEG-7's goals was to provide a standard that allows describing the "main issues" related to content. As such, not only low-level characteristics and information related to content structure but also content models and collections have been identified as central aspects. The low-level characteristics are specified in Parts 3 (Visual) and 4 (Audio) and make up a substantial part of the standard. They also reflect the initial focus of the standardization efforts. The more high-level concepts such as content description, content models and collections are part of Part 5 (Multimedia Description Scheme). One specific focus here also is to provide information about combinations and assembling of parts, for example, scenes in a video or a piece of music. These could be low-level objects of higher-level concepts. The former also relates to the object-oriented coding scheme of MPEG-4.

Another goal was to provide tools for fast and efficient searching, filtering and content identification. These should include direct content searches through advanced methods such as image and audio similarity retrieval. Therefore, the audio-visual information that MPEG-7 deals with includes audio, voice, video, images, graphs and 3D models (besides textual data).

An important aspect of MPEG-7 is the independence between the description and information itself. This is also manifested in the standard through the separation of systems concerns (Part 1) and the language for description scheme and description scheme definition (Part 2), or the schema (Part 10).

Industry bodies such EBU and SMPTE, broadcasters and their related research institutes have been engaged early in the MPEG-7 standardization process. Therefore, there should have been sufficient input about the requirements of the content production and broadcast industry. There have been a number of activities that explored to use of MPEG-7 in different parts of the content life cycle. For instance, the European-funded SAMBITS project looked into the use of MPEG-7 at consumer terminals [32]. Low-level capabilities as well as combination of components were part of the investigation. The objective of the DICEMAN project was to develop an end-to-end chain of technologies for indexing, storage, search and trading of digital audio-visual content [33]. Despite the fact that there have been a number of projects and initiatives similar to this, it is interesting to observe that they did not have any wider impact on the operation within content and broadcasting organizations. Further, these projects and initiatives do not appear to have had major impact on tools or the equipment used within the media industry.

In parallel to MPEG-7, many other metadata-related standardization activities such as SMPTE Metadata Dictionary [34], Dublin Core [35] or the EBU-P/Meta initiative [36] have been taking place. It was recognized by all of these initiatives that it is necessary to coordinate the activities in order to achieve the highest possible impact [37]. However, standardization attempts in the metadata and content description domain all suffered the same fate of being of little practical relevance. The main reason for this is the difficulty in capturing the complexity of content workflows, the vast variety of data and information, and the distinctness of organizational requirements. MPEG-7's initial focus on low-level descriptors also branded it as a description scheme that has been mainly designed for the purpose of automatic content processing. Further, there have been concerns about issues related to fusing the language syntax and schemata semantics, the representation of the semantics of media expressions and the semantic mapping of schemata [38]. This has been partly addressed in the newer parts of the standard (e.g. Part 10 and Part 11). However, the questions regarding the general applicability of MPEG-7 within specific domains such as content production and broadcast still remain.

So far there are not very many products in the broadcasting and content production domain that integrate MPEG-7 or significant parts of it. Usually MPEG-7 integration is an add-on to a specific product; for example, in the UniSay suite that interoperate with Avid post-production products. It is difficult to assess, however, what influence the MPEG-7 integration has on the success of a product.

The largest impact of MPEG-7 has been on TV-Anytime [39]. The metadata working group of TV-Anytime is concerned with the specification of descriptors used in electronic program guides (EPG) and on Web pages. It is mainly concerned with metadata relevant to a transmission context. Although the major part is (segmented) content description, the representation of user preferences, consumption habits, etc., are also important elements in the context of TV-Anytime. TV-Anytime and MPEG-7 share the basic principles and many ideas. However, TV-Anytime uses a much more restricted subset of the MPEG-7 concepts in order to reduce the complexity and focus on the needs of the TV-Anytime application area. The first phase of the TV-Anytime development has focused on unidirectional broadcast and metadata services over bidirectional networks [40]. The main parts of the MPEG-7 suite used in TV applications are the wrapper structure, DDL (description definition language) and the extended description tools. Further, the MPEG-7 content management description tools and the MPEG-7 collection description tools have been considered in the TV-Anytime development.

The impact of MPEG-7 on the content production and broadcasting industry as well as on the equipment manufacturers has been limited. From the rich set of concepts, tools, description languages and descriptors, only a very small subset has actually found its way into products so far. Although it was never anticipated that all standard parts would be equally used and of similar importance, it was an expectation that certain parts would be more widely adopted. At present, MPEG-7's biggest impact has been on the relationship with content exchange and delivery. In general, this is the area where standardization is most required since multiple parties with different equipment from various vendors are involved. However, MPEG-7 suffers from a similar problem than MPEG-2 and MPEG-4 of allowing too large a degree of freedom and flexibility, which has a negative impact on the compatibility of MPEG-7-based products. In general, MPEG-7 is deemed to be too complex and not specific enough. Hence, even though only a small subset of the entire standard is actually required in the context of media production, broadcasting and content management, it is considered as insufficient. Moreover, there are still crucial concepts missing and extensions are necessary. Thus, MPEG-7 suitability in this space is considered as being very limited.

2.4.2 MPEG-21 and its Impact on Content Management and Media Production

One of the main ideas behind MPEG-21 has been to specify a set of standards facilitating interaction, provisioning, and transaction of content in order to provide support for a fully electronic workflow comprising all stages of the content production, management and distribution process. MPEG-21 has been envisaged as providing an open normative framework with the overall objective of facilitating an open market providing equal opportunities to all stake holders. This includes content consumers since an MPEG-21-based system would enable them to access a large variety of content in an interoperable manner. The core concept of MPEG-21 is the digital item. A digital item represents the actual content object, which is the focal point of all interaction. It can be created, enhanced, rated, delivered, archived, and so on. The digital item is specified in Part 2 of the MPEG-21 specification. In this part, a set of abstract terms specify the make-up, structure, organization, etc., of a digital item. This includes concepts such as container, component, anchor, descriptor, etc. Essentially, all the elements required for a digital item are defined. Other parts dealing with digital items are the Digital Item Identification (Part 3) and Digital Item Adaptation (Part 7). One major issue addressed by MPEG-21 is rights-related issues (i.e. in Part 4 Intellectual Property Management and Protection, Part 5 Rights Expression Language and in Part 6 Rights Data Dictionary). The preservation and enforcement of IPR and copyrights are deemed to be one of the major aspects in the digital content workflow and life cycle. Technology issues within MPEG-21 are addressed in Part 1 Vision, Technologies and Strategy, Part 8 Reference Software Reference Software and (partially) in Part 9 File Formats. MPEG-21 places a strong emphasis on (external) transactions such as trading, distribution and handling of content in an open environment. This has been inspired by the success of the World Wide Web as a trading platform and the penetration of the Internet. The strong focus on rights-related issues should facilitate content-related e-commerce interaction in such an open environment. Hence, the MPEG-21 standard is more outward facing, concentrating on the interaction between external organizations and entities.

However, the focus of MPEG-21 reflects part of the transition the media and broadcast industry is currently undertaking. Especially, with the move to digital television and IPTV, it is envisaged that new workflows will emerge where MPEG-21 could provide a framework for a standardized and comprehensive solution, but, nevertheless, open solution [41]. Particularly, the digital broadcast item model (DBIM) has been designed to incorporate relevant metadata standards and provide the basis for a unified life cycle and workflow model. Though, the strong focus of MPEG-21 on digital rights management (DRM) rather than operational or architectural issues gives it less practical relevance. Admittedly, DRM is an integral part of many operations within the content life cycle. However, its main relevance and impact is at the content delivery and reception stage. Thus, DRM is still considered an issue that can be separated from more operational concerns.

A number of European-funded projects such as Visnet [42], ENTHRONE [43] and MediaNet have been addressing different aspects related to the MPEG-21 framework. Broadcasters, media production companies and content providers have engaged themselves in these projects. However, for most of them, this has remained a research activity with limited or no impact on current operations. Even on the strategic level (i.e. the planning of new systems), MPEG-21 does not appear to be a relevant topic at present.

MPEG-21-based products have also not been emerging on the market at the rate originally anticipated. Products with MPEG-21 interoperability are mainly found in the DRM space (e.g. AXIMEDIS DRM). Thus, MPEG-21's impact on content management, broadcasting and media production domain has been minor, and it can be concluded that MPEG-21 is of little relevance on the operational or strategic levels in the content industry.

2.4.3   Summary

MPEG-7 and MPEG-21 appeared to be a further step forward towards more standardized media production. They address important issues in the creation, production and distribution of content. Metadata issues have been hampering a more streamlined production. Also, inter-organizational content exchange has suffered from a lack of common standards. Emerging digital platforms even more require a common and open framework, as envisaged in the MPEG-21 standardization. However, the impact of MPEG-7 as well as MPEG-21 on the content management, broadcasting and media production domain has been very limited. In inter-organizational processes compliance to either standard is not deemed important. MPEG-7 so far has its largest impact in the area of delivery and exchange through the adoption of some of its principles within TV-Anytime. One reason why MPEG-7 has not had a large impact is its perceived emphasis on low-level descriptors and description tools that are still considered largely irrelevant for media production and content management processes. Further, its complexity and the fact that still not all processes can be captured using the MPEG-7 description schemes are further reasons for its failure to be more widely adopted. Also, similar to MPEG-2 and MPEG-4 further specification would be necessary to ensure the interoperability of MPEG-7-compliant systems.

MPEG-21 has even less impact on the content industry than MPEG-7. It has not influenced the processes and workflows in media production and content management in the anticipated manner. With the emphasis on DRM, issues and important problem domain are addressed. However, they are considered to be orthogonal to the production and content management process at present and therefore are addressed as a separate issue. In inter-organizational interaction, it has also not been used so far. However, this would be the area it could be most relevant for.

In general, it can be concluded that MPEG-7 but probably even more so MPEG-21 are trying to tackle too wide a problem space. They are not focused enough and the solutions they provide are considered to be too complex, open and not addressing the central issues of media production, broadcasting and content management.

Further, both standards operate in a space that up to now has seen very little standardization. Workflows in content production and content management are quite individual and differ from organization to organization. Most metadata description schemes and the databases they are documented in are based on proprietary systems or heavily customized products. Thus, standardizing these processes and procedures is very difficult. Further, standardization of data models, content description schemes or even exchange formats has proven difficult. None of the schemes (e.g. SMPTE Metadata Dictionary [34], P-Meta [36] or Dublin Core [35]) that have attempted to do this have succeeded in this space.

2.5   Conclusions

The impact of MPEG standards on the media production, broadcasting and content management domain has been varied. MPEG coding standards are the basis for a number of formats and products used in these domains. The degree of freedom the MPEG standards offer needed to be restricted, and hence further specification was necessary in order to enable better interoperability between different products and vendor formats based on the MPEG coding standards. However, in general, there are at present, only two relevant formats being used in this industry (i.e. DV and MPEG). Hence, they will continue to be important in the foreseeable future. They address an important area where standardization is essential and MPEG-2- and MPEG-4-based formats have proven suitable for many steps within the content life cycle.

In contrast, as of today, MPEG-7 and MPEG-21 are of hardly any importance in this industry space. Their impact has been much less than originally anticipated, and they play only a minor role at the delivery and reception stage of the content life cycle. MPEG-7 has this in common with other metadata description schemes and standardization efforts that have also failed in standardizing the content description or content documentation process. Possible reasons for this are the complexity and the heterogeneity of the requirements and underlying tasks. Also, historically there have always been organization-specific processes and proprietary systems dealing with these aspects. Therefore, there is no tradition and no urgent need to use standards in this area. In the case of essence, standards have always been necessary. Before the emergence of digital video and audio, a number of analogous tape and film formats were used in the production of content. These were always based on standardization efforts of industry bodies or international standardization organizations. Thus, MPEG-based encoding formats presented themselves as one alternative for digital video and audio coding, but there was never a question about the need for standards in general. It is therefore most likely that the MPEG encoding standards will maintain their role in media production, broadcasting and content management. MPEG-7 might become more important if its current use within content delivery would be extended and if it might also be used in content exchange. The future relevance of MPEG-21 ultimately will depend on how the media and broadcast industry engages with digital platforms and if the MPEG-21 frameworks will prove suitable in this context.

References

[1] ISO/IEC (2010) JTC1/SC29. *Programme of Work, MPEG-1 (Coding of Moving Pictures and Associated Audio for Digital Storage Media at up to about 1,5 Mbit/s)*. Online http://www.itscj.ipsj.or.jp/sc29/29w42911.htm#MPEG-1 (accessed January 2010).

[2] ISO/IEC (2010) JTC1/SC29. *Programme of Work, MPEG-2 (Generic Coding of Moving Pictures and Associated Audio Information)*. Online http://www.itscj.ipsj.or.jp/sc29/29w42911.htm#MPEG-2 (accessed January 2010).

[3] ISO/IEC (2010) JTC1/SC29. *Programme of Work, MPEG-4 (Coding of Audio-visual Objects)*. Online http://www.itscj.ipsj.or.jp/sc29/29w42911.htm#MPEG-4 (accessed January 2010).

[4] Pro-MPEG Forum (2010) *The Professional MPEG Forum*. Online http://www.pro-mpeg.org/ (accessed 2010).

[5] ISO/IEC (2010) JTC1/SC29. *Programme of Work, MPEG-7 (Multimedia Content Description Interfaces)*. Online http://www.itscj.ipsj.or.jp/sc29/29w42911.htm#MPEG-7 (accessed January 2010).

[6] ISO/IEC (2010) JTC1/SC29. *Programme of Work, MPEG-21 (Multimedia Framework (MPEG-21))*. Online http://www.itscj.ipsj.or.jp/sc29/29w42911.htm#MPEG-21 (accessed January 2010).

[7] EBU (2010) *European Broadcasting Union*. Online http://www.ebu.ch/ (accessed 2010).

[8] SMPTE (2010) *Society of Motion Picture and Television Engineers*. Online http://www.smpte.org/home/ (accessed 2010).

[9] Mauthe, A. and Thomas, P. (2004) *Professional Content Management Systems – Handling Digital Media Assets*, *Wiley Broadcast Series*, John Wiley & Sons, Ltd, Chichester.

[10] SMPTE/EBU (1998) Task Force for Harmonized Standards for the Exchange of Program Material as Bitstreams – Final Report: Analyses and Results.

[11] Pittas, J.L. (2009) Getting the shot: advanced MPEG-4 AVC encoding and robust COFDM modulation deliver HD-ENG. *SMPTE Motion Picture Image Journal*, 40–49.

[12] SMPTE (1999) Data structure for DV-based audio and compressed video 25 and 50 Mb/s, SMPTE Standard for Television, SMPTE 314M, 1999.

[13] SMPTE (2005) Television Serial Data Transport Interface, SMPTE 305M-2005.

[14] Smith, C. (2008) A user's perspective on MXF and media. *SMPTE Motion Imaging Journal*, **2002**, 24–24.

[15] SMPTE (2004) Digital Television Tape Recording – 12.65-mm Type D-10 Format for MPEG-2 Compressed Video – 525/60 and 625/50, SMPTE 365M-2001 (Archived 2006).

[16] DVB Org (2010) *The Digital Video Broadcasting Project*, Online http://www.dvb.org/ (accessed 2010).

[17] ETSI (1997) DVB-S – Framing Structure, Channel Coding and Modulation for 11/12 GHz Satellite Services, EN 300 421.

[18] ETSI (2005) DVB-S2 – Second Generation Framing Structure, Channel Coding and Modulation Systems for Broadcasting, Interactive Services, News Gathering and Other Broadband Satellite Applications, EN 302 307.

[19] ETSI (1998) DVB-C – Framing Structure, Channel Coding and Modulation for Cable Systems, EN 300 429 V1.2.1.

[20] ETSI (2009) DVB-T – Framing Structure, Channel Coding and Modulation for Digital Terrestrial Television, EN 300 744 V1.6.1.

[21] ETSI (2007) DVB-MPEG – Implementation Guidelines for the Use of MPEG-2 Systems, Video and Audio in Satellite, Cable and Terrestrial Broadcasting Applications, TS 101 154 V1.8.1.

[22] SMPTE (2004) Television – Material Exchange Format (MXF) – Operational Pattern 1a (Single Item, Single Package), SMPTE 378M-2004.

[23] SMPTE (2004) Television – Material Exchange Format (MXF) – Specialized Operational Pattern "Atom" (Simplified Representation of a Single Item), SMPTE 390M-2004.

[24] SMPTE (2004) Television – Material Exchange Format (MXF) – MXF Generic Container, SMPTE 379M-2004.

[25] SMPTE (2004) Television – Material Exchange Format (MXF) – Mapping Type D-10 Essence Data to the MXF Generic Container, SMPTE 386M-2004.

[26] SMPTE (2004) Television – Material Exchange Format (MXF) – Mapping DV-DIF Data to the MXF Generic Container, SMPTE 383M-2004.

[27] SMPTE (2004) Television – Material Exchange Format (MXF) – Descriptive Metadata Scheme-1 (Standard, Dynamic), SMPTE 380M-2004.

[28] Oh, Y., Lee, M. and Park, S. (2008) The CORE project: aiming for production and archive environments with MXF. *SMPTE Motion Imaging Journal*, **117** (5), 30–37.

[29] Devlin, B.F. (2008) Metadata-driven workflows with MXF: a proposal for tagging languages. *SMPTE Motion Imaging Journal*, **117** (5), 38–41.

[30] ETSI (2004) DVB-H – Transmission System for Handheld Terminals, EN 302 304 V1.1.1.

[31] Martínez, J.M. (ed.) (2002) Document ISO/IEC JTC1/SC29/WG11/N4674, *MPEG-7 Overview*, Jeju, March 2002.

[32] Permain, A., Lalmas, M., Moutogianni, E. *et al.* (2002) Using MPEG-7 at the consumer terminal in broadcasting. *Eurasip Journal on Applied Signal Processing*, **2002** (4), 354–361.

[33] Schrooten, R. and van den Maagdenberg, I. (2000) *DICEMAN: Distributed Internet Content Exchange with MPEG-7 and Agent Negotiations, in Agents Technology, ACTS activities*. http://cordis.europa.eu/infowin/acts/analysys/products/thematic/agents/toc.htm (accessed 2000).

[34] SMPTE (2001) SMPTE Metadata Dictionary, RP210.2 (Including RP210.1) Merged Version, Post Trail Publication of RP210.2, White Plains, SMPTE RP210-2. http://www.smpte-ra.org/mdd/RP210v2-1merged-020507b.xls.

[35] Dublin Core Metadata Initiative (DCMI) (2000) *Dublin Core Qualifiers*. http://dublincore.org/documents/2000/07/11/dcmes-qualifiers/ (accessed 2010).

[36] European Broadcasting Union (2001) PMC Project P/META (Metadata Exchange Standards), Geneva, Switzerland. Online http://www.ebu.ch/pmc_meta.html (accessed 2001).

[37] Mulder, P. (2000) The Integration of Metadata from Production to Consumer. EBU Technical Review.

[38] Nack, F. and Hardman, L. (2002) Towards a Syntax for Multimedia Semantics, CWI INS-R0204, ISSN 1386-3681.

[39] TV-Anytime (2010) *TV-Anytime Forum*. Online http://www.tv-anytime.org/ (accessed 2010).

[40] Evain, J.-P. and Martinez, J. (2007) TV-anytime phase 1 and MPEG-7. *Journal of the American Society for Information Science and Technology*, **58** (9), 1367–1373.

[41] Kaneko, I., Lugmayr, A., Kalli, S. *et al*. (2004) MPEG-21 in broadcasting role in the digital transition of broadcasting. Proceedings of ICETE'04.

[42] Visnet NoE (2010) *Visnet II Networked audiovisual media technologies*. Online http://www.visnet-noe.org/ (accessed 2010).

[43] Enthrone (2010) *ENTHRONE – end-to-end QoS Through Integrated Management of Content Networks and Terminals*. Online http://www.enthrone.org/ (accessed 2010).

3

Quality Assessment of MPEG-4 Compressed Videos

Anush K. Moorthy and Alan C. Bovik
Department of Electrical and Computer Engineering, The University of Texas at Austin, TX, USA

3.1 Introduction

As you sit in front of your machine streaming videos from Netflix, you notice that their software judges the level of quality allowed for by your bandwidth (Figure 3.1) and then streams out the video. Unfortunately, if it is a bad day and there is not too much bandwidth allocated to you, you can see those annoying blocks that keep coming up during scenes with high motion. That is not all, some of the colors seem to be off too – color bleeding, as this is called is another impairment that a compressed video suffers from. Blocking, color bleeding, and a host of such distortions [1] affect the perceived quality of the video and, hence, the viewing experience. Ensuring quality of service (QoS) for such content streamed either through the Internet or wireless network is one of the most important considerations when designing video systems. Since almost every video sent over a network is compressed (increasingly with MPEG-4), assessing the quality of (MPEG-4) compressed videos is of utmost importance. One can imagine the different techniques one could use to assess the quality of compressed videos over a network. We could have a set of people coming in to view a large collection of these videos and then rate them on a scale of say 1–10 where 1 is bad and 10 is excellent. Averaging these scores produces a mean opinion score (MOS) or differential mean opinion score (DMOS) which is representative of the perceived quality of the video. Such subjective assessment of quality is time consuming, cumbersome, and impractical, and hence the need for development of objective quality assessment algorithms. The goal behind objective video quality assessment (VQA) is to create algorithms that can predict the quality of a video with high correlation with human perception. Objective VQA forms the core of this chapter.

The Handbook of MPEG Applications: Standards in Practice   Edited by Marios C. Angelides and Harry Agius
© 2011 John Wiley & Sons, Ltd

Figure 3.1 Netflix software judges the level of quality allowed for by your bandwidth and then streams out the video.

Objective VQA algorithms are classified as full reference (FR), reduced reference (RR), and no reference (NR) algorithms. FR algorithms are those that evaluate the quality of a test sequence *relative* to a known original. In this case, both the original/pristine video and the video under test are given and the algorithm is required to predict the subjective quality of the test video. RR algorithms are those in which the original video is not available to the algorithm. However, some additional information – the type of compression used, side-channel information, and so on – is available. The goal of the algorithm is the same as for the FR case. NR algorithms are those that do not receive any additional information about the video under test. Simply put, the algorithm is presented with a video and is expected to produce a score that matches its subjective quality. We note that even though there is a general agreement on the terminology for the FR case, RR and NR algorithms may be defined differently elsewhere. In this chapter, our focus will be on the FR case, and hence any algorithms mentioned henceforth refer to FR algorithms.

The ultimate viewer of a video is a human observer. In humans, information from visual sequences passes through the retinal ganglion cells and is processed by the lateral geniculate nucleus (LGN) – a relay station – before being sent to Area V1 of the primary visual cortex. These cortical cells are known to be orientation-, scale-, and, to some extent, direction selective. They also encode binocular and color information [2]. V1 cells also extract motion information from the visual stimulus. However, further motion processing is hypothesized to occur in visual area MT (middle temporal), whose neurons are driven by the so-called M (magnocellular) pathways, which carry motion information [3]. Little is understood about how MT performs motion computation, but some theories exist [4, 5]. What is known is that area MT, as well as the neighboring area MST (medial superior temporal), is responsible for motion processing and that a significant amount of neural activity is dedicated to motion processing. It is not surprising that motion processing is essential, since it allows us to perform many important tasks, including depth perception, tracking of moving objects, and so on. Humans are extremely good at judging velocities of approaching objects and in discriminating opponent velocities [2]. Given that the human visual system (HVS) is sensitive to motion, it is imperative that objective measures of quality take motion into consideration. In this chapter, we discuss an algorithm that utilizes such motion information to assess the perceived quality.

The H.264 AVC/MPEG-4 Part 10 is the latest standard for video compression [6] and has already begun to be widely used. For example, the World Airline Entertainment Association (WAEA) has standardized the H.264 encoder for delivery of wireless video entertainment [7], for on-board video presentations. Our focus will be the quality assessment of videos compressed using the H.264 standard. Also note that in this chapter, we alternately refer to the coding standard as MPEG-4 or H.264.

Before we go further, we would like to discuss how an algorithm that predicts visual quality is evaluated for its performance. It is obvious that for an objective comparison between various proposed algorithms we need to have a common test bed. For FR VQA algorithms, this test bed must consist of several undistorted pristine reference videos, and their distorted versions. Further, these distorted videos must span a large range of quality – from very bad to excellent – so that the range of quality that a viewer is bound to experience in a real-time situation is encompassed in the database. Given that these videos are obtained, their perceptual quality needs to be ascertained. This is generally done by asking a set of human observers to watch each of the distorted videos and rate them.[1] Since we need a general perception of quality, a large number of such subjects are needed to provide a statistically significant opinion on the quality. Such subjective quality assessment is generally carried out under controlled conditions so that external influences that may affect the perceived quality such as lighting conditions and viewing distance are minimized. On the basis of the scores provided, an MOS or a DMOS[2] is formed. MOS/DMOS is representative of the perceived quality of that video. Such a large-scale study was conducted by the video quality experts group (VQEG) in [9] and the database called *VQEG FR TV Phase-I* is publicly available along with the DMOS scores. The VQEG conducted further studies as well; however, the data was not made public [10].

Given that we now have a database of distorted videos along with their perceived quality scores, the question is how do we evaluate algorithm performance. Most of the proposed algorithms are evaluated using the techniques suggested by the VQEG [9]. The algorithm is run on each of the videos in the dataset and the algorithmic scores are stacked up into a vector. This objective vector is then compared with the subjective vector of MOS/DMOS using statistical criterion. The statistical measures include the Spearman's rank ordered correlation coefficient (SROCC), root mean squared error (RMSE), and linear (Pearson's) correlation coefficient (LCC). While SROCC may be calculated directly between the two vectors, LCC and RMSE are computed after passing the objective vector through a logistic function [9]. This is necessary because the subjective and objective scores need not be linearly related. However, LCC and RMSE are measures that compute the amount of

---

[1] Note that there exist many modalities for such testing. This could include modalities where the subject watches the reference video first and the distorted one next – call double stimulus study. The one we describe here is a single stimulus study. The reader is referred to [8] for a discussion of different modalities for conducting such studies.

[2] DMOS is generally computed when the user has been asked to rate the original reference video with/without his knowledge of its presence. The scores are differences between the scores for the pristine video and the distorted ones.

linear correlation/difference between two vectors. A high value for SROCC and LCC (close to 1) and a low value of RMSE (close to 0) indicate that the algorithm correlates well with human perception of quality. Outlier ratio (OR) is yet another measure proposed by the VQEG that is not used very often. Finally, even though we have discussed the methods used by most researchers to evaluate algorithm performance, recently researchers have proposed different methods for the same [11, 12, 13].

Having discussed the essence of VQA and techniques to evaluate algorithm performance, we now proceed toward describing some previous approaches to VQA and then follow it up with a description of our algorithm designed to assess the quality of videos which utilizes motion estimates computed from MPEG-4 compressed videos. We demonstrate how the described algorithm performs on the VQEG dataset. We then enumerate the drawbacks associated with the VQEG dataset and propose a new dataset to overcome these limitations. This new dataset – the LIVE wireless VQA database [14] – was created at the Laboratory for Image and Video Engineering and along with the LIVE video quality database [15], and is available free-of-cost to researchers in the field of VQA for noncommercial purposes. The LIVE wireless VQA database was specifically created for H.264 AVC compressed videos transmitted over a wireless channel. For wireless applications, H.264 is widely included in relevant technologies as the DVB-H [16, 17] and Mediaflo [17] broadcast standards. After having described our algorithm and the dataset, we conclude this chapter with possible future research directions.

3.2 Previous Work

Mean-squared error (MSE), owing to its simplicity and history of usage in the signal processing community, has been ubiquitous as a measure of difference between two signals, and this is true for image quality assessment (IQA) and VQA as well. Unfortunately, however, the "nice" qualities of MSE as a measure of difference are of little use in IQA/VQA, because, as vision researchers have argued, MSE along with its counterpart – peak signal-to-noise ratio (PSNR) – are poorly correlated with human perception of quality [18, 19]. Hence, researchers have produced a variety of algorithms that seek to assess the quality of videos with high correlation with human perception. Since we are interested in developing an FR VQA algorithm, our focus in this section is on the recently proposed FR VQA algorithms. For MPEG-2, there have been many NR algorithms proposed in the literature [20, 21]. Almost all of these algorithms proceed in the same way. The main distortion that they seek to model is blocking. This is either done in the spatial domain using edge detection (e.g., a Canny filter) or in the frequency domain using the Fourier transform. Most of the proposed algorithms rely on the fact that MPEG-2 uses 8×8 blocks for compression, hence blocking can be detected at these block boundaries (spatially) or using periodicity (Fourier domain). Some of the algorithms also model blur. The rest are simple extensions of this technique, which take into account some motion estimates for example [20]. NR VQA for H.264 compressed videos is obviously a much harder task.

The most obvious way to design a VQA algorithm is by attempting to model HVS mechanisms and many researchers have done exactly that. VQA algorithms, which are based on HVS modeling, include moving pictures quality metric (MPQM) [22], a scalable wavelet-based video distortion index [23], perceptual distortion metric (PDM) [24], digital video quality (DVQ) [25], and the Sarnoff JND (just-noticeable-difference) vision model [26]. Each of these methods used either a combination of a low-pass and band-pass filter along the temporal dimension or simply a single low-pass filter. Although a HVS-based system seems like an ideal route to take, much work is left to be done in understanding human visual processing. Indeed, it has been suggested that at present 80–90% of the V1 functioning remains unclear [27]. Until research in vision science allows for a complete and precise modeling of the HVS, measures of quality based on the HVS are likely to fall short of accurately predicting the quality of videos.

Another approach to VQA is a feature-driven one. The algorithm extracts a set of features from the reference and distorted video and a comparison between these features is undertaken to form a measure of distortion. One such algorithm is the video quality metric (VQM), proposed by [28]. VQM extracts a host of features from the reference and test video sequences that are pooled using various strategies. Although the features extracted and the constants proposed lack justification in terms of correlation with HVS processing, VQM seemingly performs well. Indeed, VQM was the top performer in the VQEG Phase-II studies [10].

The authors in [29] took a slightly different route toward solving the FR IQA problem by proposing the popular single-scale structural similarity index (SS-SSIM). In [30], an information-theoretic measure based on natural scene statistics (NSS) called *visual information fidelity* (*VIF*) was proposed for FR IQA. The excellent performance of SSIM and VIF for image quality was studied in [31].[3] In [34], a relationship between the structure term in SSIM (which is seemingly the most important term, see [35]) and the information-theoretic quality measure VIF was demonstrated. Since VIF is based on an NSS model, and NSS has been hypothesized to be a dual problem to modeling the HVS [31], a relationship between SSIM and the HVS seems to exist. Further research in this area will be of great interest.

After having demonstrated that SSIM performs well for IQA, it was first extended for VQA in [36]. The essential idea was to apply SS-SSIM on a frame-by-frame basis, where the frame was sampled sparsely. The authors also proposed the use of a weighting scheme that took into account some motion estimated using a block motion estimation algorithm. In [37], the authors used an alternate weighting scheme based on human perception of motion information. In both these cases, spatial quality computed using SS-SSIM was weighted based on motion information. However, temporal-based weighting of spatial quality scores does not necessarily account for temporal distortions [38]. As mentioned before, temporal distortions can differ significantly from spatial distortions. Further, vision research has hypothesized that the HVS has (approximately) separate channels for spatial and temporal processing [39–41]. The weighted pooling of spatial scores does not capture this separability.

The space of temporal distortions and its effect on perceived video quality has been recently explored. In [42], temporal distortions such as mosquito noise were modeled as a temporal evolution of a spatial distortion in a scene, and a VQA index based on visual attention mechanisms was proposed. The algorithm was not evaluated on a publicly available dataset, however. In work closest in concept to ours, the authors of [43] used a motion estimation algorithm to track image errors over time. These authors also chose to use a dataset that is not publicly available.

---

[3] Note that the SSIM scores in [31] are actually for multiscale structural similarity index (MS-SSIM) [32]. SS-SSIM does well on the LIVE image database as well, see [33].

Most of the above-mentioned algorithms [42, 43] use a variety of prefixed thresholds and constants that are not intuitive. Even though some of the algorithms work well, the relationship of these algorithms to human vision processing is not well understood. In a radically different approach, the authors in [44] sought to model the motion processing in the HVS areas by the use of a linear decomposition of the video. By utilizing the properties of the neurons in the visual cortex including spatial frequency and orientation selectivity, the proposed index, named motion-based video integrity evaluation (MOVIE), was shown to perform well. However, the computational complexity of the algorithm makes practical implementation difficult as it relies on three-dimensional optical flow computation.

We have omitted from this discussion several VQA algorithms. The interested reader is referred to [45, 46] for a review.

3.3 Quality Assessment of MPEG-4 Compressed Video

In this section, we describe our algorithm – motion-compensated structural similarity index (MC-SSIM). The proposed algorithm can be used without MPEG-4 compression, by using motion vectors extracted from a block motion estimation process. However, since MPEG-4 compressed videos already possess motion vectors in the transmitted bitstream, it is computationally efficient to extract these vectors instead of recomputing them during the quality assessment stage. The algorithm is first described, followed by an explanation of how MPEG-4 motion vectors are used for the purpose of temporal quality assessment.

Consider two videos that have been spatiotemporally aligned. We denote the reference video as $R(x, y, t)$ and the test video as $D(x, y, t)$ where the tuple (x, y, t) defines the location in space (x, y) and time t. Since the algorithm is defined for digital videos, the space coordinates are pixel locations and the temporal coordinate is indicative of the frame number. The test video is the sequence whose quality we wish to assess. Our algorithm is designed such that if $D = R$, that is, if the reference and test videos are the same, then the score produced by the algorithm is 1. Any reduction from this perfect score is indicative of distortion in D. Also, the algorithm is symmetric, that is, MC-SSIM(R, D) = MC-SSIM(D, R). We assume that each video has a total of N frames and a duration of T seconds. We also assume that each frame has dimensions $P \times Q$.

3.3.1 Spatial Quality Assessment

The SS-SSIM [36], which correlates well with human perception [33], is used for assessing spatial quality as well as moving "block quality" (Section 3.3.2).

Spatial quality is evaluated in the following way. For each frame t from R and D and each pixel (x, y), the following spatial statistics are computed:

$$\mu_{R(x,y,t)} = \frac{1}{N^2} \sum_{i=1}^{N} \sum_{j=1}^{N} w_{ij} R(i, j, t)$$

$$\mu_{D(x,y,t)} = \frac{1}{N^2} \sum_{i=1}^{N} \sum_{j=1}^{N} w_{ij} D(i, j, t)$$

$$\sigma^2_{R(x,y,t)} = \frac{1}{N^2 - 1} \sum_{i=1}^{N} \sum_{j=1}^{N} w_{ij} (R(i, j, t) - \mu_{R(x,y,t)})^2$$

$$\sigma^2_{D(x,y,t)} = \frac{1}{N^2 - 1} \sum_{i=1}^{N} \sum_{j=1}^{N} w_{ij} (D(i, j, t) - \mu_{D(x,y,t)})^2$$

$$\sigma_{RD(x,y,t)} = \frac{1}{N^2 - 1} \sum_{i=1}^{N} \sum_{j=1}^{N} w_{ij} (R(i, j, t) - \mu_{R(x,y,t)})(D(i, j, t) - \mu_{D(x,y,t)})$$

For spatial quality computation, w_{ij} is an $N \times N$ circular-symmetric Gaussian weighting function with standard deviation of 1.5 samples, normalized to sum to unity with $N = 11$ [29]. Finally,

$$S(x, y, t) = \text{SSIM}(R(x, y, t), D(x, y, t)) \tag{3.1}$$

$$= \frac{(2\mu_{R(x,y,t)}\mu_{D(x,y,t)} + C_1)(2\sigma_{RD(x,y,t)} + C_2)}{\left(\mu^2_{R(x,y,t)} + \mu^2_{D(x,y,t)} + C_1\right)\left(\sigma^2_{R(x,y,t)} + \sigma^2_{D(x,y,t)} + C_2\right)} \tag{3.2}$$

where $C_1 = (K_1 L)^2$, $C_2 = (K_2 L)^2$ are small constants; L is the dynamic range of the pixel values, and $K_1 \ll 1$ and $K_2 \ll 1$ are scalar constants with $K_1 = 0.01$ and $K_2 = 0.03$. The constants C_1, C_2, and C_3 prevent instabilities from arising when the denominator is close to zero.

This computation yields a map of SSIM scores for each frame of the video sequence. The scores so obtained are denoted as $S(x, y, t)$, $(x = \{1 \ldots P\}$, $y = \{1 \ldots Q\}$, $t = \{1 \ldots N - 1\})$.

3.3.2 Temporal Quality Assessment

Our algorithm proceeds as follows. Motion vectors for frame i are obtained from its preceding frame $i - 1$ from the encoded reference video bitstream. This strategy was previously explored in [37, 38]. We have a map of motion vectors of size $(P/b, Q/b, N - 1)$ where b is the block size, since vectors cannot be calculated for the first frame. For simplicity, assume that P and Q are multiples of the block size.

For a frame i and for block (m_R, n_R) $(m_R = \{1, 2, \ldots P/b\}, n_R = \{1, 2, \ldots Q/b\})$, in video R, we compute the motion-compensated block (m'_R, n'_R) in frame $i - 1$ by displacing the (m_R, n_R)th block by an amount indicated by the motion vector. A similar computation was performed for the corresponding (m_D, n_D)th block in D, thus obtaining the motion-compensated block (m'_D, n'_D). We then performed a quality computation between the blocks $B_R = (m'_R, n'_R)$ and $B_D = (m'_D, n'_D)$ using the Single SS-SSIM. Although SS-SSIM does not have as good a performance as MS-SSIM, a much simpler implementation was obtained with very good performance, as is shown later. Hence, for each block we obtained a quality index corresponding to the perceived quality of that block, and for each frame we obtained a quality map of dimension $(P/b, Q/b)$. We denote the temporal quality map thus obtained as $T(x, y, t)$, $(x = \{1 \ldots P/b\}$, $y = \{1 \ldots Q/b\}$, $t = \{1 \ldots N - 1\})$. A schematic diagram explaining the algorithm is shown in Figure 3.2.

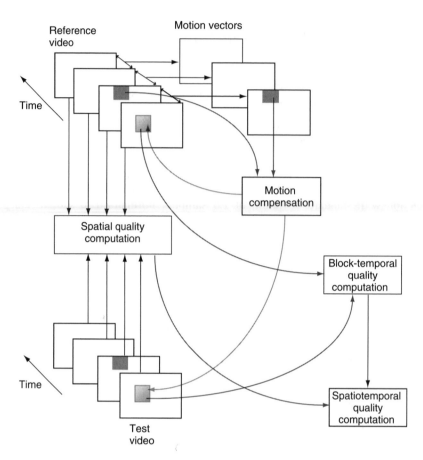

Figure 3.2 Motion-compensated SSIM. Spatial quality computation is done on a frame-by-frame basis. Temporal quality computation: for the current block (dark gray) in frame i, the motion-compensated block from frame $i - 1$ (light gray) is recovered for both the reference and test video sequences using motion vectors computed from the reference sequence. Each set of blocks so obtained is evaluated for their quality. Spatial and temporal quality scores are combined to produce a final score for the test video sequence. See text for details.

3.3.3 Pooling Strategy

The original SS-SSIM proposed for IQA used the mean of the local quality scores to form a single score for the image. When applied on a frame-by-frame basis on a video, the score for the video was defined as the mean value of the scores obtained from each of the frames. Researchers have argued that the simple mean does not effectively capture the overall quality of the image [47, 48]. Our algorithm employs the strategy based on percentile pooling proposed in [33]. Specifically, for each frame t, we compute

$$T(t) = \frac{1}{|\xi|} \sum_{x,y \in \xi} T(x, y, t)$$

and

$$S(t) = \frac{1}{|\xi|} \sum_{x,y \in \xi} S(x, y, t)$$

where ξ denotes the set consisting of the lowest 6% of the quality scores of each frame and $|\cdot|$ denotes the cardinality of the set [48]. $S(t)$ and $T(t)$ are then averaged across frames to produce the spatial and temporal quality scores for the sequence – S and T. We note that this method is similar to the approach proposed in [28].

Quality is assessed not only on the "Y" component, but also on the color channels "Cb" and "Cr". The final temporal quality score for the video is computed as

$$T^{\text{final}} = 0.8 \times T^{\text{Y}} + 0.1 \times T^{\text{Cb}} + 0.1 \times T^{\text{Cr}}$$

where T^{Y}, T^{Cb} and T^{Cr} are the temporal quality scores on each of the three color channels.

A similar quality computation is undertaken for each of the three channels to assess the spatial quality as well. The final spatial quality is computed as

$$S^{\text{final}} = 0.8 \times S^{\text{Y}} + 0.1 \times S^{\text{Cb}} + 0.1 \times S^{\text{Cr}}$$

where S^{Y}, S^{Cb}, and S^{Cr} are the spatial quality scores on each of the three color channels. The weights assigned to each of the channels are exactly as in [36] and are reused here, though incorporating color in VQA remains an interesting avenue of research.

3.3.4 MPEG-4 Specific Quality Assessment

Assume that we have the pristine reference video for quality assessment. In a practical scenario, we envisage a system where the available reference video is itself a compressed version. The "black-box" (which may be MPEG-4 compression to smaller bit rates or an actual transmission channel) induces distortion in this video when the video passes through it. The goal then is to assess the quality of the video at the output of the channel with respect to the original video. Most FR quality assessment algorithms (except those that operate in the compressed domain) will decompress the source and distorted video and then assess the quality. If the algorithms are designed such that they require motion estimates, then optical flow/block motion estimation computation ensues. It is at this point that using MC-SSIM provides a tremendous benefit in terms of computational complexity as well as performance.

MPEG-4 utilizes a motion-compensated frame differencing approach to compression in order to compress a video, which in many cases has high spatial and temporal redundancy, where motion vectors are computed using a block-based approach between adjacent frames. These motion vectors are then used to perform frame/block differencing, so that only the change in information between blocks separated by the motion vectors in adjacent frames needs to be encoded (along with the motion vectors). At the decoder, the process is reversed, where the encoded motion vectors are used to reconstruct the encoded frame. Note that this description is overly simplified. MPEG-4 allows for multiple reference frames to be used for motion estimation, each frame need not be encoded using a motion-compensated approach; it also allows for using both past and future frames for motion estimation [49].

Since MC-SSIM performs a computation mimicking the decompression process, the easiest solution to VQA using MC-SSIM is to reuse the motion vectors computed by the compression algorithm. Specifically, the motion vectors that we use for motion-compensated quality assessment will be the same as those used by the algorithm for motion-compensated decompression. By reutilizing motion vectors from the compression process,[4] we have effectively eliminated a major bottleneck for VQA algorithms – that of computing motion. This coupled with the fact that we use the simple SSIM for quality assessment will reduce overhead, and will allow for practical deployment of the algorithm.

In the implementation of MC-SSIM that we test here, we allow for motion compensation using only one previously decoded frame. The block size for motion estimates is fixed at 16×16 and subpixel motion estimates are disabled. This overly simplistic compression process will allow us to set an approximate lower bound. It should be clear that improved motion estimates will provide improved performance. The group-of-pictures (GOP) setting is such that only the first frame is encoded as an intra-frame and all other frames are P-frames (IPPPPP...). The quantization parameter is set at 16 (so as to allow for visually lossless compression) and the JM reference encoder is used to perform compression and decompression of the reference video [50].

At this stage, we are in the situation described at the beginning of this section. We have with us a set of compressed reference videos (which we created artificially for the purpose of evaluation here) and we have a "black-box". We also have the (decompressed) videos at the output of this black-box (distorted videos from the VQEG dataset). So, all that remains to be done is decompress the compressed originals and perform quality assessment on the corresponding input–output video pairs. The only addition here, as we described before, is the extraction of motion vectors from the original video. Specifically, as we decompress the original video prior to quality computation, we also extract and save corresponding motion vectors from the decompression algorithm.

After having extracted motion vectors from the MPEG-4 compressed videos, MC-SSIM is applied as described before on the decompressed reference and test videos. For the chroma channels, we follow the recommendations of the MPEG-4 standard, where the chroma motion vectors are extracted by multiplying the luma motion vectors by a factor of 2 [51]. We use the VQEG database described before [9] as a test bed for evaluating performance. In this case, the reference videos are compressed as described here and then decompressed to produce the motion vectors, in order to emulate the scenario described before. The distorted videos are used as they are, since our main goal was motion vector extraction.

The results of using MC-SSIM using MPEG-4 motion vectors on the VQEG database are shown in Table 3.1, where we also list the performance of MOVIE [38] for a comparison. The algorithm performance is evaluated in terms of the above-mentioned measures – SROCC and LCC. Even though MC-SSIM does not seek to explicitly model the HVS, it is based on SSIM, and it was shown in [34] that SSIM relates to the NSS model for quality proposed in [52]. The statistics of natural scenes differ significantly from those for artificial scenes. The VQEG dataset consists of four artificial sequences

---

[4] We utilize motion vectors from the compressed reference videos for MC-SSIM. However such a technique could be extended for NR VQA using motion estimates at the decoder for the distorted video.

Table 3.1 Evaluation of MC-SSIM when applied to videos from the VQEG dataset (natural videos only)

Algorithm	SROCC	LCC
MOVIE (Y only) [38]	0.860	0.858
MC-SSIM	0.872	0.879

(src4, src6, src16, src17), including scrolling text. In these cases, judging quality through an algorithm that has been developed for VQA may not be completely fair. Hence, we test the performance on only natural sequences.

3.3.5 Relationship to Human Visual System

After having demonstrated that our algorithm functions well on the VQEG dataset, the most pertinent question to ask is how the proposed technique is related to the HVS. Even though we have not actively modeled the HVS, the fact that the algorithm performs well in terms of its correlation with human perception demands that we try and understand how the proposed technique may be related to the HVS.

The efficient coding hypothesis states that the purpose of the early sensory processing is to recode the incoming signals, so as to reduce the redundancy in representation [53]. Time-varying natural scenes – videos – possess high spatial and temporal correlation. The reader will immediately notice that video compression algorithms utilize this high correlation to efficiently compress the signal. Motion-compensated frame differencing allows one to transmit only the change in the video being processed, thereby reducing the amount of information sent. Given the redundancy in videos and the efficient coding hypothesis, the principle that the visual pathway tries to improve the efficiency of representation is compelling. It has been hypothesized that the LGN performs such a temporal decorrelation [54].

In our description of the HVS and its visual processing, we dismissed the LGN – which lies in an area called the *thalamus* – as a relay center. However, the amount of feedback that the thalamus receives from the visual cortex leads one to the conclusion that the LGN may perform significant tasks as well [55]. The hypothesis is that the thalamus does not send raw stimuli to the higher areas for processing, but instead performs some processing before such a relay in order that irrelevant information from the stimulus is reduced. In [55], the authors propose an *active blackboard* analogy, which in the case of motion computation allows for feedback about the motion estimates to the thalamus (to compute figure-ground cues, for example). Such a feedback system has many advantages for visual processing. For example, a feedback system would allow for rapid computation of motion estimates, since only the difference between the previously relayed signal and the new stimuli needs to be computed. Some of the so-called "extraclassical" receptive field effects have been modeled by the authors in [56] using predictive coding. We hypothesize that by assessing quality after temporal decorrelation using motion compensation, we are emulating some of these functions of the early visual system.

Further, the quality index that we use for spatiotemporal quality estimates is SS-SSIM. The relationship between the structure term in SSIM and the information-theoretic VIF was studied in [34]. It was demonstrated that the structure term in SSIM when applied between subband coefficients in a filtered image is equivalent to VIF. This is interesting, since VIF is based on an NSS model. NSS have been used to understand the human visual processing [57, 58], and it has been hypothesized that NSS and HVS modeling are essentially dual problems [52]. Further, the authors in [34] also demonstrated that the structure term in SSIM can be interpreted as a divisive normalization model for control gain mechanisms in HVS. Thus, even in its simplicity, MC-SSIM, which is based on SSIM, mirrors various features of the HVS.

The essence of the proposed algorithm is SS-SSIM. It can easily be shown that the computational complexity of SS-SSIM is $O(PQ)$. Since we use percentile pooling, there is a need to sort the SSIM scores and this can be performed with a worst-case complexity of $O(PQ \log(PQ))$. The major bottleneck in MC-SSIM is this motion estimation phase. However, as we have discussed, we can completely avoid this bottleneck by reutilizing motion vectors computed for compressed videos. In this case, the complexity of MC-SSIM is not much greater than that for SS-SSIM. Further, as shown in [35], the SSIM index can be simplified without sacrificing performance. Finally, MC-SSIM correlates extremely well with human perception of quality thus making MC-SSIM an attractive VQA algorithm.

3.4   MPEG-4 Compressed Videos in Wireless Environments

Even though we have utilized the VQEG Phase-I dataset to test our algorithm, the dataset is not without is drawbacks. The video database from the VQEG is dated – the report was published in 2000, and was made specifically for TV and hence contains inter-laced videos. Even though the VQEG conducted other studies, data from these studies have not been made public, and hence any comparison of algorithm performance is impossible [10, 59]. The deinterlacing process used by a VQA algorithm complicates the prediction of quality, since it is unclear if the deinterlacing algorithm has produced the measured impairments in quality or if it was part of the video. Further, the VQEG study included distortions only from old-generation encoders such as the H.263 [60] and MPEG-2 [61], which exhibit different error patterns compared to present-generation encoders like the H.264 AVC/MPEG-4 Part 10 [6]. Finally, the VQEG Phase-I database of distorted videos suffers from problems with poor perceptual separation. Both humans and algorithms have difficulty in producing consistent judgments that distinguish many of the videos, lowering the correlations between humans and algorithms and the statistical con-fidence of the results. Figure 3.3 shows a histogram of DMOS across the videos from the VQEG dataset. It is clear that the quality range that the VQEG set spans is not uniform. Hence, there exists a need for a publicly available dataset that uses present-generation encoders – MPEG-4 – and encompasses a wide range of distortions.

To address this need, we conducted a large-scale human and algorithm study using H.264 compressed videos and simulated wireless transmission errors as distortions. An effort has been made to include a wide variety of distortion types having good perceptual separations. In this section, we present some details of this study.

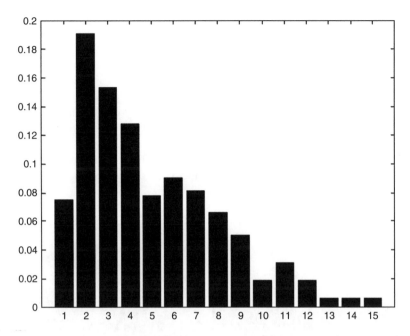

Figure 3.3 Histogram (normalized) of differential mean opinion scores from the entire VQEG dataset [9]. Notice how the distribution of scores is highly skewed.

3.4.1 Videos for the Study

The source videos were in RAW uncompressed progressive scan YUV420 format with a resolution of 768 × 480 and a frame rate of 30 frames per second (fps). They were provided by Boeing. From a large collection, the chosen videos were those which incorporated a diverse range of interesting motions, objects, and people. Some of the videos were night sequences. Many of the videos chosen contained scene cuts – in order to include as much of the space of videos as possible. There were 10 source sequences, each 10 s long and hence containing 300 frames. Figure 3.4 shows frames from the various videos used in the study.

Further, in order to emulate the situation that we described previously, we did not use the raw YUV videos as the pristine videos, but instead converted the videos first into H.264 compressed videos, which are visually lossless (i.e., having a PSNR >40 dB). There are multiple reasons to do this. One of the main reasons is that the visually lossless reference videos have available quality motion vectors that can be used to develop VQA algorithms that use motion, like MC-SSIM. By making available quality motion vectors, we make it possible for the developers to focus their efforts on other aspects of VQA algorithm development. Further, the overall compressed test set is enormously smaller in size than the original raw video dataset, making it highly convenient for delivering the video set electronically. Finally, we repeat that such a situation is more practical. The user is likely to never see the pristine uncompressed YUV video and these videos are not going to be used as a reference in practical scenarios.

Perceptually lossless MPEG-4 videos were created using the following parameters:

- quantization parameters $(Q_p, Q_i) = 18$;
- I-frame period $= 14$.

Although the I-frame period does not influence the perceived quality, we code at a period of 14 frames in order to reduce the time complexity of the encoding process. We also note that with the quantization parameters set as above, the average PSNR is greater than 45 dB, exceeding the 40 dB level.

A total of 160 distorted videos were created from these 10 reference videos – 4 bit rates $\times$ 4 packet loss rates $\times$ 10 reference videos. In order to compress the video, we

Figure 3.4 Example frames of the videos used. (a)–(j) correspond to videos (see text for description).

(g)   (h)

(i)   (j)

Figure 3.4   (*continued*).

used the JM reference software (Version 13.1) [50, 62] made available by the Joint Video Team (JVT) for H.264 encoding. The bit rates chosen were 500 kbps, 1 Mbps, 1.5 Mbps, and 2 Mbps according to the WAEA Recommendation [7]. The number of slice groups were set at 3.

All videos were created using the same value of the I-frame period (96). We also enabled *RD* optimization, and used RTP as the output file mode. We used the baseline profile for encoding, and hence did not include B-frames. We aimed for wireless transmission of the videos and hence restricted the packet size to between 100 and 300 bytes [63]. We set the flexible macroblock ordering (FMO) mode as "dispersed" and used three slices per frame.

Once the videos were compressed, we simulated a wireless channel over which these videos are sent. We used the software provided by ITU [64] documented in [65] to simulate wireless channel errors of packet loss. The software allows for six different error patterns and hence for six different bit-error rates of 9.3×10^{-3}, 2.9×10^{-3}, 5.1×10^{-4}, 1.7×10^{-4}, 5.0×10^{-4}, and 2.0×10^{-4}. The bit-error patterns used are captured from different real or emulated mobile radio channels. For the packet sizes we simulated, these bit-error rates correspond, on an average, to packet loss rates around 0.4, 0.5, 1.7–2, 2, 5, and 17–18%. We assumed that a packet containing an erroneous bit is an erroneous packet [63]. The simulated packet loss rates indicated that the rates can be divided into four groups instead of six. Hence, we simulated a wireless channel with packet loss rates of 0.5, 2, 5, and 17, respectively.

Thus, we now have 10 H.264 pristine reference videos, and associated 160 distorted videos which are versions of these 10 reference videos, compressed and sent over a wireless channel with varying compression rates and channel packet loss rates. In order to quantify the perceived visual quality, we then conducted a subjective study.

3.4.2 The Study

The study conducted was a single stimulus continuous quality evaluation (SSCQE), as detailed in [8]. The only difference in our study was the use of a "hidden-reference". In a recent literature [66], this model is used in order to "equalize" the scores. Specifically, in the set of videos that the subject is shown, the original reference videos are displayed as well. The subject is unaware of its presence or its location in the displayed video set. The score that the subject gives this reference is representative of the supposed bias that the subject carries, and when the scores for the distorted videos are subtracted from this bias, a compensation is achieved, giving us the difference score for that distorted video sequence.

The user interface on which these videos were displayed and ratings were collected were developed using the XGL toolbox for MATLAB which was developed at The University of Texas at Austin [67]. It is obvious that any errors in displaying the videos, such as latencies, must be avoided when conducting such a study, since these artifacts affect the perceived quality of a video. In order that display issues do not factor into the quality score provided by a subject, all the distorted videos were first completely loaded into the memory before their presentation. The XGL toolbox interfaces with the ATI Radeon X600 graphics card in the PC and utilizes its ability to play out the YUV videos. There exist many arguments for and against the use of CRTs/LCDs [68, 69]. There is evidence that effects such as motion blur are amplified on an LCD screen [70], hence we chose to use a CRT monitor. The monitor was calibrated using the Monaco Optix XR Pro device. The same monitor was used for the entire course of the study. The monitor refresh rate was set at 60 Hz, and each frame of the 30 Hz video was displayed for two-monitor refresh cycles. The screen was set at a resolution of 1024×768 pixels and the videos were displayed at their native resolution; the remaining areas of the display were black.

The videos were shown at the center of the CRT monitor with a bar at the bottom of the screen, calibrated – "Bad", "Poor", "Fair", "Good", and "Excellent", equally spaced across the scale. Although the scale was continuous, the calibrations served to guide the subject. The rating bar was controlled using a mouse and was displayed at the end of the video, where the subject was asked to rate the quality of the video sequence. Once the score was entered, the subject was not allowed to go back and change the score. Further, we also collected "continuous" scores. The subjects were asked to rate the quality of the video as the video was being played out. Even though we do not use this data in our analysis, future work can utilize this data to understand how temporal pooling of quality leads to a final judgment of video quality.

The study consisted of the set of videos shown in random order and was conducted over two sessions each lasting less than 30 min and spread over at least 24 h. The order was randomized for each subject as well as for each session. Care was taken to ensure that two consecutive sequences did not belong to the same reference, to minimize memory effects [8]. A short training was undertaken before each session in order for the subject to get a feel for the task and to acquaint him/her with the range of quality that he/she is bound to see during the course of the study. A snapshot of the screen as seen by the subject is shown in Figure 3.5.

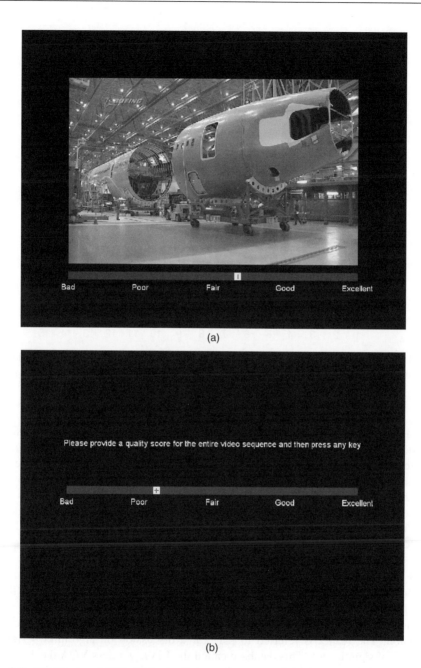

(a)

(b)

Figure 3.5 Study setup: (a) The video is shown at the center of the screen and a bar at the bottom is provided to rate the videos as a function of time. The pointer on the bar is controlled by using the mouse. (b) At the end of the presentation, a similar bar is shown on the screen so that the subject may rate the entire video. This score is used for further processing.

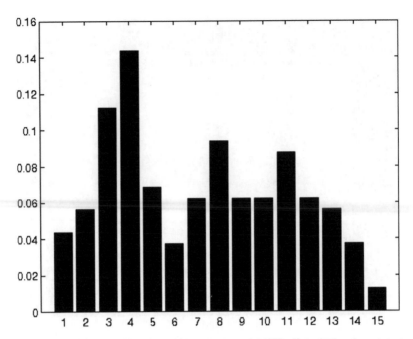

Figure 3.6 Histogram (normalized) of differential mean opinion scores from our wireless video quality study. Notice how the distribution of scores is uniform compared to that from the VQEG – Figure 3.3.

A total of 31 subjects participated in the study. The score that each subject assigned to a distorted sequence in a session was subtracted from the score that the subject assigned to the reference sequence in that session, thus forming a difference score. The quality rating obtained from the subjects was converted into a score between 0 and 100. A subject rejection procedure as described in [8] followed and a DMOS representative of the perceived quality of the video was obtained. This DMOS was used to evaluate a host of FR VQA algorithms. In Figure 3.6, we plot the histogram of scores obtained from our study. Notice how uniform the scores are compared to the DMOS scores in the VQEG study 3.3.

The FR VQA algorithms that we evaluated are described in [71] and include PSNR, SS-SSIM [36], MS-SSIM [32], VQM [28], visual signal-to-noise ratio (VSNR) [72], video VIF [30], speed-weighted structural similarity index (SW-SSIM) [37], and P-SSIM [48]. The algorithms were evaluated on the statistical measures that we discussed in the introduction. The reader is referred to [71] for a discussion on algorithm performance and statistical significance. This database called the LIVE wireless VQA database can be found online at [14], available to researchers at no-cost for noncommercial use.

3.5 Conclusion

In this chapter, we discussed FR VQA for MPEG-4 compressed videos. We demonstrated how the proposed algorithm (MC-SSIM) functions and we evaluated its performance on the popular VQEG dataset. Using motion vectors from the MPEG-4 compression process we demonstrated how we could achieve superior performance at low computational cost. Further, we described the drawbacks associated with the VQEG dataset and then went on to discuss a subjective study conducted at LIVE for assessing the quality of H.264 compressed videos transmitted over a wireless channel. The discussion of the study involved how we created the videos for the study and how subjective quality assessment of videos was undertaken. The LIVE wireless VQA database and its associated DMOS are available for research purposes [14].

We focused our attention on FR VQA algorithms in this chapter. However, it must be obvious by now that the original reference video may not be available in many practical applications of VQA. It is therefore that areas of NR and RR VQA have seen a lot of activity in the recent past [20, 21]. Even though some of the proposed techniques seem to function well, a thorough analysis of these techniques on public datasets such as those seen in this chapter is essential. Further, the area of RR/NR image and VQA will benefit from incorporating techniques such as visual attention and foveation.

References

[1] Yuen, M. and Wu, H. (1998) A survey of hybrid MC/DPCM/DCT video coding distortions. *Signal Processing*, **70** (3), 247–278.
[2] Sekuler, R. and Blake, R. (1988) *Perception*, Random House USA Inc.
[3] Wandell, B. (1995) *Foundations of Vision*, Sinauer Associates.
[4] Born, R. and Bradley, D. (2005) Structure and function of visual area MT. *Annual Review of Neuroscience*, **28**, 157–189.
[5] Rust, N.C., Mante, V., Simoncelli, E.P., and Movshon, J.A. (2006) How MT cells analyze the motion of visual patterns. *Nature Neuroscience*, **9** (11), 1421–1431.
[6] ISO/IEC (2003) 14496–10 and ITU-T Rec. H.264. *Advanced Video Coding*, International Telecommunications Union.
[7] World Airline Entertainment Association (2003) Digital Content Delivery Methodology for Airline In-flight Entertainment Systems, Std.
[8] International Telecommunication Union (2002) BT-500–11: Methodology for the Subjective Assessment of the Quality of Television Pictures, Std.
[9] V.Q.E. Group (2000) *Final Report from the Video Quality Experts Group on the Validation of Objective Quality Metrics for Video Quality Assessment*. http://www.its.bldrdoc.gov/vqeg/projects/frtv_phasei (accessed 2010).
[10] V.Q.E. Group (2003) *Final Report from the Video Quality Experts Group on the Validation of Objective Quality Metrics for Video Quality Assessment*. http://www.its.bldrdoc.gov/vqeg/projects/frtv_phaseii (accessed 2010).
[11] Charrier C., Knoblauch, K., Moorthy, A.K. *et al.* (2010) Comparison of image quality assessment algorithms on compressed images. SPIE Conference on Image Quality and System Performance.
[12] Wang, Z. and Simoncelli, E.P. (2008) Maximum differentiation (MAD) competition: a methodology for comparing computational models of perceptual quantities. *Journal of Vision*, **8** (12), 1–13.
[13] Charrier, C., Maloney, L.T., Cheri, H., and Knoblauch, K. (2007) Maximum likelihood difference scaling of image quality in compression-degraded images. *Journal of the Optical Society of America*, **24** (11), 3418–3426.
[14] Moorthy, A.K. and Bovik, A. *LIVE Wireless Video Quality Assessment Database*. http://live.ece.utexas.edu/research/quality/live_wireless_video.html (accessed 2010).
[15] Seshadrinathan, K., Soundararajan, R., Bovik A., and Cormack, L.K. (2007) *LIVE Video Quality Assessment Database*. http://live.ece.utexas.edu/research/quality/live_video.html (accessed 2010).
[16] ETSI E. (2004) 302 304V1. 1.1. Digital Video Broadcasting (DVB): Transmission System for Handheld Terminals (DVB-H), ETSI Standard Std.
[17] Furht, B. and Ahson, S. (2008) *Handbook of Mobile Broadcasting: DVB-H, DMB, ISDB-T, and MediaFLO*, Auerbach Publications.

[18] Girod, B. (1993) What's wrong with mean-squared error? in *Digital Images and Human Vision* (ed. A.B. Watson), European Telecommunications Standards Institute, pp. 207–220.

[19] Wang, Z. and Bovik, A.C. (2009) Mean squared error: love it or leave it? – a new look at fidelity measures. *IEEE Signal Processing Magazine*, **33** (13), 1765–1771.

[20] Tan, K.T. and Ghanbari, M. (2000) Blockiness detection for MPEG2-coded video. *IEEE Signal Processing Letters*, **7** (8), 213–215.

[21] Vlachos, T. (2000) Detection of blocking artifacts in compressed video. *Electronics Letters*, **36** (13), 1106–1108.

[22] Van den Branden Lambrecht, C. and Verscheure, O. (1996) Perceptual quality measure using a spatiotemporal model of the human visual system. Proceedings of the SPIE, pp. 450–461.

[23] Masry, M., Hemami, S., and Sermadevi, Y. (2006) A scalable wavelet-based video distortion metric and applications. *IEEE Transactions on Circuits and Systems for Video Technology*, **16** (2), 260–273.

[24] Winkler, S. (1999) A perceptual distortion metric for digital color video. *Proceedings of the SPIE*, **3644** (1), 175–184.

[25] Watson, A., Hu, J., and McGowan, J. III. (2001) Digital video quality metric based on human vision. *Journal of Electronic Imaging*, **10**, 20.

[26] Lubin, J. and Fibush, D. (1997) Sarnoff JND Vision Model. T1A1.5 Working Group Document, pp. 97–612.

[27] Olshausen, B.A. and Field, D.J. (2005) How close are we to understanding V1? *Neural Computation*, **17** (8), 1665–1699.

[28] Pinson, M.H. and Wolf, S. (2004) A new standardized method for objectively measuring video quality. *IEEE Transactions on Broadcasting*, (3), 312–313.

[29] Wang, Z., Bovik, A.C., Sheikh, H.R., and Simoncelli, E.P. (2004) Image quality assessment: from error measurement to structural similarity. *IEEE Signal Processing Letters*, **13** (4), 600–612.

[30] Sheikh, H.R. and Bovik, A.C. (2005) A visual information fidelity approach to video quality assessment. The 1st International Workshop on Video Processing and Quality Metrics for Conumser Electronics, January, 2005.

[31] Sheikh, H.R., Sabir, M.F., and Bovik, A.C. (2006) A statistical evaluation of recent full reference image quality assessment algorithms. *IEEE Transactions on Image Processing*, **15** (11), 3440–3451.

[32] Wang, Z., Simoncelli, E.P., and Bovik, A.C. (2003) Multi-scale structural similarity for image quality assessment. Proceedings IEEE Asilomar Conference on Signals, Systems, and Computers, (Asilomar), November, 2003.

[33] Moorthy, A.K. and Bovik, A.C. (2009) Perceptually significant spatial pooling techniques for image quality assessment. SPIE Conference on Human Vision and Electronic Imaging, January, 2009.

[34] Seshadrinathan, K. and Bovik, A.C. (2008) Unifying analysis of full reference image quality assessment. Proceedings of the 15th IEEE International Conference on Image Processing, ICIP 2008, pp. 1200–1203.

[35] Rouse, D. and Hemami, S. (2008) Understanding and simplifying the structural similarity metric. Proceedings of the 15th IEEE International Conference on Image Processing, ICIP 2008, pp. 1188–1191.

[36] Wang, Z., Lu, L., and Bovik, A.C. (2004) Video quality assesssment based on structural distortion measurement. *Signal Processing-Image communication*, (2), 121–132.

[37] Wang, Z. and Li, Q. (2007) Video quality assessment using a statistical model of human visual speed perception. *Journal of the Optical Society of America*, **24** (12), B61–B69.

[38] Seshadrinathan, K. (2008) Video quality assessment based on motion models. PhD dissertation, The University of Texas at Austin.

[39] Tolhurst, D. and Movshon, J. (1975) Spatial and temporal contrast sensitivity of striate cortical neurones. *Nature*, **257** (5528), 674–675.

[40] Friend, S. and Baker, C. (1993) Spatio-temporal frequency separability in area 18 neurons of the cat. *Vision Research(Oxford)*, **33** (13), 1765–1771.

[41] Morrone, M.C., Di Stefano, M., and Burr, D.C. (1986) Spatial and temporal properties of neurons of the lateral suprasylvian cortex of the cat. *Journal of Neurophysiology*, **56** (4), 969–986.

[42] Ninassi, A., Meur, O.L., Callet, P.L., and Barba, D. (2009) Considering temporal variations of spatial visual distortions in video quality assessment. *IEEE Journal of Selected Topics in Signal Processing, Issue on Visual Media Quality Assessment*, **3** (2), 253–265.

[43] Barkowsky, M., Bialkowski, B.E.J., Bitto, R., and Kaup, A. (2009) Temporal trajectory aware video quality measure. *IEEE Journal of Selected Topics in Signal Processing, Issue on Visual Media Quality Assessment*, **3** (2), 266–279.

[44] Seshadrinathan, K. and Bovik, A.C. (2007) A structural similarity metric for video based on motion models. IEEE International Conference on Acoustics, Speech and Signal Processing, ICASSP, April 2007, pp. 869–872.

[45] Seshadrinathan, K. and Bovik, A.C. (2009) Video quality assessment, in *The Essential Guide to Video Processing* (ed. A.C. Bovik), Academic Press, 417–436.

[46] Moorthy, A.K., Seshadrinathan, K., and Bovik, A.C. (2009) *Digital video quality assessment algorithms, Handbook of Digital Media in Entertainment and Arts*, Springer.

[47] Wang, Z. and Shang, X. (2006) Spatial pooling strategies for perceptual image quality assessment. IEEE International Conference on Image Processing, September 2006.

[48] Moorthy, A.K. and Bovik, A.C. (2009) Visual importance pooling for image quality assessment. *IEEE Journal of Selected Topics in Signal Processing, Issue on Visual Media Quality Assessment*, **3** (2), 193–201.

[49] Richardson, I. (2003) H. 264 and MPEG-4 Video Compression.

[50] Encoder, J.R. (2007) *H.264/Avc Software Coordination*. Online http://iphome.hhi.de/suehring/tml/ (accessed 2010).

[51] AVC, Joint Video Team (JVT) of ISO/IEC MPEG and ITU-T VCEG (2003) ITU-T Recommendation H.264/ISO/IEC 14 496–10, JVT-G050 Std. *Draft ITU-T Recommendation and Final Draft International Standard of Joint Video Specification*.

[52] Sheikh, H.R. and Bovik, A.C. (2006) Image information and visual quality. *IEEE Transactions on Image Processing*, **15** (2), 430–444.

[53] Atick, J. (1992) Could information theory provide an ecological theory of sensory processing? *Network-Computation in Neural Systems*, **3** (2), 213–251.

[54] Dong, D. and Atick, J. (1995) Temporal decorrelation: a theory of lagged and nonlagged responses in the lateral geniculate nucleus. *Network-Computation in Neural Systems*, **6** (2), 159–178.

[55] Mumford, D. (1992) On the computational architecture of the neocortex. *Biological Cybernetics*, **66** (3), 241–251.

[56] Rao, R. and Ballard, D. (1999) Predictive coding in the visual cortex: a functional interpretation of some extra-classical receptive-field effects. *Nature Neuroscience*, **2**, 79–87.

[57] Olshausen, B.A. and Field, D.J. (1996) Natural image statistics and efficient coding. *Network-Computation in Neural Systems*, **7**, 333–339.

[58] Simoncelli, E. and Olshausen, B. (2001) Natural image statistics and neural representation. *Annual Review of Neuroscience*, **24** (1), 1193–1216.

[59] ITU Study Group 9 (2008) Final Report of Video Quality Experts Group Multimedia Phase I Validation Test, TD 923.

[60] Rijkse, K. (1996) H. 263: video coding for low-bit-rate communication. *IEEE Communications Magazine*, **34** (12), 42–45.

[61] ITU-T and ISO/IEC JTC 1 (1994) ITU-T Recommendation H.262 and ISO/IEC 13 818–2 (MPEG-2). *Generic Coding of Moving Pictures and Associated Audio Information – Part 2: Video*.

[62] Wandell, B.A. (2007) *H.264/mpeg-4 avc Reference Software Manual, JM Reference Encoder*. Online http://iphome.hhi.de/suehring/tml/JM(JVT-X072).pdf (accessed 1995).

[63] Stockhammer, T., Hannuksela, M., and Wiegand, T. (2003) H.264/avc in wireless environments. *IEEE Transactions on Circuits and Systems for Video Technology*, **13** (7), 657–673.

[64] International Telecommunications Union (2001) *Common Test Conditions for RTP/IP Over 3GPP/3GPP2*. Online http://ftp3.itu.ch/av-arch/videosite/ 0109 San/VCEG-N80 software.zip (accessed 2010).

[65] Roth, G., Sjoberg, R., Liebl, G. *et al.* (2001) Common Test Conditions for RTP/IP over 3GPP/3GPP2. ITU-T SG16 Doc. VCEG-M77.

[66] Pinson, M.H. and Wolf, S. (2003) Comparing subjective video quality testing methodologies. *Visual Communications and Image Processing, SPIE*, **5150**, 573–582.

[67] Perry, J. (2008) *The XGL Toolbox*. Online http://128.83.207.86/jsp/software/xgltoolbox-1.0.5.zip (accessed 2010).

[68] Pinson, M. and Wolf, S. (2004) The Impact of Monitor Resolution and Type on Subjective Video Quality Testing. Technical Report TM-04-412, NTIA.

[69] Tourancheau, S., Callet, P.L., and Barba, D. (2007) Impact of the resolution on the difference of perceptual video quality between CRT and LCD. IEEE International Conference on Image Processing, ICIP 2007, vol. 3, pp. III-441–III-444.

[70] Pan, H., Feng, X.F., and Daly, S. (2005) Lcd motion blur modeling and analysis. IEEE International Conference on Image Processing, pp. II-21–4.

[71] Moorthy, A.K. and Bovik, A.C. (2010) Wireless video quality assessment: a study of subjective scores and objective algorithms. *IEEE Transactions on Circuits and Systems for Video Technology*, **20** (4), 513–516.

[72] Chandler, D.M. and Hemami, S.S. (2007) VSNR: a wavelet-based visual signal-to-noise ratio for natural images. *IEEE Transactions on Image Processing*, **16** (9), 2284–2298.

4

Exploiting MPEG-4 Capabilities for Personalized Advertising in Digital TV

Martín López-Nores, Yolanda Blanco-Fernández, Alberto Gil-Solla, Manuel Ramos-Cabrer, and José J. Pazos-Arias
Department of Telematics Engineering, University of Vigo, Vigo, Spain

4.1 Introduction

The potential of the television to sell products was already in mind by the time of its invention, around the early 1930s. Several decades of broadcasting consolidated TV advertising as the most effective method of mass promotion, allowing TV providers to charge very high prices for commercial airtime. In the increasingly competitive market of digital television (DTV) technologies, however, the advertising revenues have been steadily decreasing for some years now, pointing out the need to somehow reinvent the publicity business [1, 2]. In fact, numerous studies have revealed a significant drop in the effectiveness of the advertising techniques in use, due to limitations that stem from presenting the same products to all the TV viewers in a way that interferes with their enjoyment of the audiovisual contents. The classical *spots* that interrupt the TV programs from time to time to display commercials are often criticized for disappointing the viewers (e.g., by spoiling important action, like the scoring of a goal in the fictitious example given in Figure 4.1a) and for promoting *channel surfing*. This implies that the advertising material does not reach the viewers or does so with the background of a negative sensation [3]. The situation worsens with the proliferation of *digital video recorders* (DVRs) that enable viewers to fast-forward and skip over the advertisements [4, 5].

The drop in the effectiveness of the spots has encouraged the search for alternative techniques. Currently, one common practice consists of occupying a region of the screen with advertising material, either laying banners or promotional logo bugs (also named *secondary events* by media companies) directly over the programs (Figure 4.1b) or pushing

The Handbook of MPEG Applications: Standards in Practice Edited by Marios C. Angelides and Harry Agius
© 2011 John Wiley & Sons, Ltd

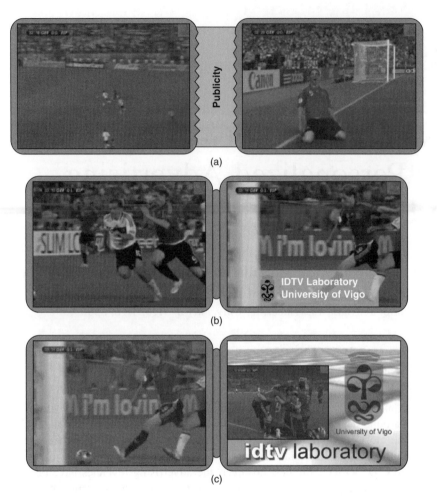

Figure 4.1 Examples of invasive advertising techniques. Reproduced from Alemania 0-1 España (Torres) Carrusel Deportivo, user: diegovshenry http://www.youtube.com/watch?v=6JRaUnTSKSo.

the programs to a smaller part of the screen (Figure 4.1c). This form of *spatial invasiveness* (as opposed to the *temporal invasiveness* of the spots) is also frowned upon by the viewers [6], because the ads may hide interesting parts of the action and hamper the viewing in devices with small screens.

A long-known alternative to invasive techniques is the so-called *product placement*, which consists in intentionally inserting advertising material into the audiovisual contents in diverse ways, ranging from the inclusion of visual imagery with embedded publicity in a scene (e.g., the classical billboards around a football pitch, as in Figure 4.2) to the use of a specific product by the people involved in it (e.g., an actor accessing the internet via a popular network operator). Product placement is gaining momentum, as several market studies have shown that it improves the viewers' perception of publicity and reinforces brand images [7, 8]. On the negative side, since the advertisements are introduced one

Figure 4.2 A sample product placement. Reproduced from Alemania 0-1 España (Torres) Carrusel Deportivo, user: diegovshenry http://www.youtube.com/watch?v=6JRaUnTSKSo.

and for all at production time, the approach suffers from lack of temporal and spatial *locality*. For example, it usually happens with internationally distributed movies, when some products advertised are not sold in the regions where many viewers live (at least under the same brand). Similarly, it is common in the case of several-year-old contents where the products are no longer manufactured, or that they have been rebranded, or that the manufacturer has undergone an aesthetics change.

As a common flaw of all the aforementioned techniques, there is currently no way to tailor the publicity to the specific interests and needs of the viewers, which, according to Graves [9], holds the key to turning advertising into a source of useful information for the viewers. In this chapter, we describe the MiSPOT system, which harnesses the object-oriented vision of multimedia contents enabled by the MPEG-4 standard to support a noninvasive and personalized advertising model that we call *dynamic product placement*. Basically, this model consists in (i) delivering ad-free TV programs along with pieces of advertising material that may be suitable to embed in their scenes, and (ii) selecting which pieces to embed at viewing time, taking into account the interests and preferences of each individual viewer. Thus, the viewers enjoy a publicity that does not interfere with their viewing of the TV programs, while solving the problems that arise from inserting all the advertising material at production time. Additionally, we exploit the possibilities of MPEG-4 and interactive DTV technologies to link the publicity with commercial applications (*i-spots*) that let the viewer navigate for detailed information about the advertised items, buy/hire on-line, subscribe to the notification of novelties, and so on.

The chapter is organized as follows. First, Section 4.2 provides a survey of related work in noninvasive, personalized and interactive advertising. Next, Section 4.3 describes the modules that enable the model of personalized and dynamic product placement, along with the different MiSPOT features. An example of the whole approach is given in Section 4.4. Finally, Section 4.5 includes a report of the experiments we have carried out to assess the technical feasibility of the proposal, and Section 4.6 summarizes our conclusions.

4.2 Related Work

Attempts to minimize the invasiveness of advertising have been traditionally limited by the transmission of multimedia contents as binary flows, with hardly more structure than *frames* (for video sequences) and *samples* (for audio). With such constraints, the best one

Figure 4.3 Viewing-time product placement exploiting information about cameras and bill-boards. Reproduced from Alemania 0-1 España (Torres) Carrusel Deportivo, user: diegovshenry http://www.youtube.com/watch?v=6JRaUnTSKSo.

can do is to insert advertisements in the boundaries between two scenes or to play out some recording during periods of silence, as in [10, 11]. Dynamic product placement is only possible in very specific settings, such as sports events. For example, in [12–14], advertisements are implanted in locations like billboards, the central ellipse, or the region above the goal-mouth, which are automatically delimited by recognizing the pitch lines, aided by information about the cameras' locations and perspectives. A fictitious example is given in Figure 4.3, placing the logo of our research group instead of the original advertiser in one of the billboards.

The aforementioned limitations are bound to disappear with the consolidation of the MPEG-4 standard, in which frames and samples give way to a language called XMT-A (*eXtensible MPEG-4 Textual format*) that can separate different objects in an audiovisual scene (people, furniture, sound sources, etc.) and allows to combine arbitrarily shaped video sequences, recorded or synthetic audio tracks, 3D objects and text, among others. Besides, it is possible to attach spatial, temporal, and shape information to apply advanced effects of illumination, warping, echo, pitch modulation, and so on. These features have been already exploited for noninvasive advertising [15], though leaving aside the aspects of personalization and interactivity that we do address in the MiSPOT system.

To date, research in personalized advertising for TV has focused on invasive techniques [16–21]. As regards the personalization logic, the first systems merely looked at demographic data (e.g., age or gender) to locate products that had interested other viewers with similar information. The results so obtained often fail to reflect changes of the viewer preferences over time, inasmuch as personal data are stable for long periods. This problem was solved with *content-based filtering*, which considers the products that gained the viewers' interest in the recent past [22, 23]. Unfortunately, this approach leads to repetitive suggestions, and the minimal data available about new viewers makes the first results highly inaccurate. As an alternative, *collaborative filtering* makes recommendations for one viewer by analyzing the preferences of viewers with similar profiles (*neighbors*) [24, 25]. This approach is generally more precise than the aforementioned ones, but is at the expense of scalability problems: the algorithms are comparatively costlier, and it may be difficult to delimit neighborhoods when the number of items considered becomes large. Knowing this, the current trend (and the MiSPOT approach) is to develop *hybrid filtering*, combining several strategies to gather their advantages and neutralize their shortcomings [26].

Whichever the approach to filtering may be, it is noticeable that most of the personalization systems have relied on *syntactic matching* techniques, which depend too much on describing products and viewer preferences using exactly the same words. Inspired by the philosophy of the *Semantic Web*, the MiSPOT system relies on techniques to discover *semantic* relationships between metadata documents, thus gaining much insight into the objects and the subjects of the recommendations (so that, for example, *"Golden Retriever"* and *"Boxer"* can be automatically recognized as two breeds of dogs, the latter having nothing to do with a combat sport). A taste of recent advances in this area can be found in [27].

In what concerns the interactivity features, MiSPOT differs from previous proposals like those of Young and Ryu [28, 29], which could merely link the advertisements to URLs that would be opened in a web navigator. As explained in [30], it is not a suitable approach to link the TV programs to the same resources available to personal computers through the Internet, due to the limited interaction and presentation capabilities of the DTV receivers – factors like the low resolution and flickering of a TV screen or the input through the remote control render a classical web navigator unusable. Indeed, there are many receivers nowadays in the market that do not incorporate web navigators, and several mainstream manufacturers do not plan to do so in the short-to-medium term [31]. Knowing this, the MiSPOT approach is to deliver interactive commercial functionalities through specialized applications (the i-spots) triggered by the MPEG-J (*MPEG-4 Java*) APIs and written with the libraries of the MHP (*Multimedia Home Platform*) standard [32]. Given a set of i-spots for the same item, the personalization logic of MiSPOT serves to automatically decide which is the most suitable one for each individual viewer. For example, if the viewer's profile indicates that he/she watches automobile programs quite frequently, the system would choose one i-spot that describes a car focusing on the technical data of its mechanics and equipment, rather than another one that deals exclusively with aspects of its cabin and styling. Furthermore, for the cases in which there are no i-spots available, MiSPOT can automatically generate one by bringing together multimedia contents from various sources of information, selected according to the viewer's preferences. To the best of our knowledge, there are no precedents to these ideas in literature.

For the purposes of this chapter, it is worth noting that there already exist DTV receivers in the market that claim to support MPEG-4, but this is only true for the features that the standard absorbs from previous technologies like MPEG-1 and MPEG-2. Notwithstanding, the object-oriented approach and the advanced interaction capabilities of MPEG-4 have already been demonstrated [33]. Interestingly, many features of MPEG-4 are optional, so it is possible to define subsets for different types of receivers, fitting a range of computational, representation, and interaction capabilities. Adaptability also embraces the communication networks, from modem connections with low transmission rates to broadcast networks with enormous bandwidth. Detailed reports of the evolution and the current state of the DTV technologies can be found in [34, 35].

4.3 Enabling the New Advertising Model

The model of dynamic product placement enabled by the MiSPOT system involves four major tasks, that will be explained in the following sections along with the modules of the system architecture, depicted in Figure 4.4.

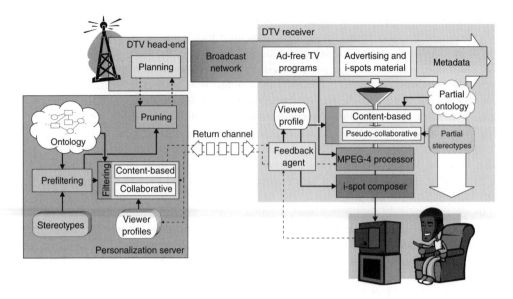

Figure 4.4   Architecture of the MiSPOT system.

- Broadcasting ad-free TV programs and potentially suitable advertising material separately.
- Identifying the most suitable items according to the preferences of each viewer and the program he/she is watching.
- Integrating advertising material of the selected items in the scenes of the TV programs.
- Launching i-spots that provide the viewer with personalized commercial functionalities if he/she interacts with the publicity.

4.3.1   Broadcasting Ad-Free TV Programs and Advertising Material

The concept of dynamic product placement starts out with the identification of elements prepared to lodge advertising material within the TV programs. These elements, that we shall refer to as *hooks*, may vary from simple time stamps (e.g., to insert a selected tune when an actor of a movie switches on his car radio) to plain areas and meshes (e.g., to render selected logos over a billboard on a roadside) or arbitrarily shaped 3D objects.

4.3.1.1   Defining Hooks

In order to define hooks, we have developed a tool called *HookTool* that can work with compositions packed in MP4 format and AVI or MPEG-2 plain videos. Using this tool, the hooks can be defined in three different ways:

- When working with compositions of multimedia objects, we can designate any of those objects or any of its facets as a hook, so that the advertising material can be placed over it just by modifying its filling properties.

Figure 4.5   A snapshot of *HookTool*.

- In the case of plain videos, we can delimit regions by drawing polygons over different frames (as in the snapshot of Figure 4.5) and relate their vertices. *HookTool* interpolates those vertices lineally over the different frames, allowing the user to work with intermediate ones in order to ensure that the hook moves and deforms coherently with the objects on the scene. There are also several features to adjust the visibility of the hook in successive shots of the same scene, with regard to the interposition of other objects, and so on.
- Finally, in all cases, we can select time instants or periods to insert pieces of audio, controlling the evolution of volume, echo, and pitch.

We save the XMT-A scene and hook definitions in such a way that, when compiling to the corresponding binary format (called BIFS), each hook includes commands that allow to dynamically embed the advertising material selected for each viewer, as well as the logic needed to add interactive elements suited to the input capabilities of the receivers. Everything is finally packed in the MP4 format.

Finally, the *HookTool* allows to characterize the hooks defined in the TV programs and the advertising material available for any item using MPEG-7 metadata. Additionally, it automatically matches the low-level features of the hooks against each piece of advertising material, considering questions of format (sound, still image, video, etc.) and any requirements on background noise, minimum/maximum size on screen, aspect ratio, time of visibility, contrast, and so on. As a result, we get an index of possible advertisements per hook, removing from subsequent phases the items that cannot be effectively publicized within the TV program broadcast at any given moment.

4.3.1.2   Reasoning about Hooks and Advertisements

Clearly, not all the advertisements that match the format and low-level features of a hook would make an effective product placement. As a first measure to ensure good targeting, the MiSPOT system relies on the assumption that any TV program watched by a viewer is related to his/her interests at the time (otherwise, he/she would not be watching it). Those interests should be taken into account to decide what publicity to insert, so that, for instance, a nature documentary is automatically recognized as a more propitious context to advertise items related to animals or climate change than pop music compilations or do-it-yourself home improvements. According to this observation, the selection driven by low-level features is followed by another one driven by higher-level aspects, to measure the strength of the relations between (i) the topics of the TV program in question, (ii) the context of the scene that contains a given hook, (iii) the use/purpose of the items that may be advertised, and (iv) the preferences of the potential audiences of the program. To this aim, we run a *semantic similarity* metric presented in [36] over two sources of information:

- First, there is an ontology – written in the OWL language [37] – that contains metadata from various standards: TV-Anytime for TV programs, MPEG-7 for individual scenes, and eCl@ss[1] for commercial products and services. The audiovisual scenes inherit and extend the characterization of the corresponding programs, and the advertisements inherit and extend the characterization of the corresponding items.
- Second, to characterize the preferences of potential audiences, we use a set of *stereotypes* that quantify the interests of different groups of viewers by means of numerical indices called DOIs (*degrees Of interest*) attached to specific items. DOIs take values in the range $[-1, 1]$, with -1 representing the greatest disliking and 1 representing the greatest liking. Besides, the stereotypes may contain values for a list of demographic features defined by TV-Anytime: age, gender, job, income, and so on.

Using the similarity metric, we can sort out the advertisements that may fit in a given scene by decreasing relevance in terms of semantics and interest for the potential audiences. This can be done off-line as soon as the TV schedule is known, with no pressing time requirements. The resulting ordered list can serve two different purposes:

- On the one hand, it allows to begin the computations of subsequent stages of the personalization process with pieces of advertising material that are likely to be effective, just in case it were necessary to return suboptimal results for lack of time (obviously, it would be unfeasible to identify off-line, the most suitable pieces for each viewer in each hook of each possible TV program).
- On the other, since it is not possible to broadcast all the pieces of advertising material at the same time, the ordered list allows to deliver only the ones that are potentially most interesting for the expected audiences. This way, for example, when a nature documentary is being broadcast, it will more likely go along with hypermedia about animals or climate change than with pop music compilations or do-it-yourself home improvements.

---

[1] We chose eCl@ss instead of other products-and-services categorization standards for the reasons of completeness, balance, and maintenance discussed in [38].

4.3.2   Identifying the Most Suitable Items for Each Viewer

In order to decide what items will be publicized during the TV programs, it is necessary to match the advertisements available against *profiles* that store demographic data plus information about the interests and preferences of individual viewers.[2] To this aim, the MiSPOT system incorporates algorithms we had presented in [36] to support the two main strategies in the literature: content-based filtering and collaborative filtering. Depending on technical settings such as the computational power of the receivers or the availability of return channels for bidirectional communication, the system can work according to two different schemes (see Figure 4.4):

- In the *server-side personalization* procedure, the filtering algorithms run in dedicated servers, which may be powerful enough to apply complex reasoning processes over the whole ontology of TV programs, audiovisual scenes, items, and advertisements. This scheme is intended for scenarios with permanently enabled return channels (e.g., with cable networks) and when the legal conditions are met to store the viewers' profiles in a centralized repository, according to a service-level agreement that defines the viewers' consent and the providers' commitment to privacy.
- In the *receiver-side personalization* procedure, the algorithms run in the viewers' receivers, with some preprocessing (in servers) and planning (in the DTV head end) to provide them with *partial ontologies* of a manageable size. These ontologies include only the most relevant concepts about the TV program broadcast at any given moment, and about the items that correspond to the pieces of advertising material that have been found to be potentially most interesting (see above). Since there is no need to store any personal information remotely, the collaborative filtering strategy has to look for a viewer's neighbors among *partial stereotypes* (also delivered through broadcast) that capture the relevant information of average viewers about the concepts included in the partial ontologies. The details of this *pruning* can be found in [39], where it is shown that this approach still helps overcome the problem of overspecialization that is typical of content-based strategies.

Closely linked to the filtering algorithms, a *feedback agent* (Figure 4.4) is in charge of gathering information to update the viewers' profiles over time, either locally or remotely. This module considers implicit and explicit forms of feedback to add DOI entries for new items and to recompute the DOIs of existing ones.

- The implicit forms gather information from whether the viewer browses the advertisements inserted in the TV programs, whether he/she launches i-spots, how long he/she takes to learn about the items, whether he/she decides to buy or hire on-line, and so on.
- The explicit forms rely on questionnaires that may ask the viewer to rate certain items or to indicate topics of interest.

---

[2] The stereotypes and the profiles of individual viewers use exactly the same data structures.

In the server-based personalization procedure, the feedback agent acts as a centralized point for communication with the servers, providing them with the context information that indicates what the viewer is watching, retrieving filtering results, and even downloading advertising material on demand. For the first task, to increase the likelihood that the recommendations will arrive in time, the agent issues pieces of context information as soon as the viewer has been watching a given TV program for a few seconds (just to filter out zapping), labeling each piece with an expected deadline.

4.3.3 Integrating the Selected Material in the Scenes of the TV Programs

Once the personalization mechanisms have selected certain advertisements and i-spots, it is time for a module called the *MPEG-4 processor* to integrate them with the corresponding scenes of the TV programs. As shown in Figure 4.6, this is done by manipulating the BIFS binaries of the scene descriptions using the MPEG-J APIs. Specifically, we act on the nodes that characterize the hooks as follows:

- Regarding the integration of advertising material, the MPEG-4 processor links the properties of the hooks to the resources (sound files, images, etc.) selected by the personalization logic. As for any ordinary scene, the actual composition and rendering are left to the hardware resources of the DTV receiver.
- As regards the launching of i-spots, the MPEG-4 processor inserts sensor elements and simple logic linked to the MHP APIs (specifically, with JavaTV). If the receiver is operated with an ordinary remote control, the viewer can use its arrow buttons (or the 2, 4, 6, and 8 buttons) to highlight one advertisement, and then press OK (or 5) to flag the associated i-spot. Alternatively, the viewer can click directly on an advertisement if it is possible to move a mouse cursor over the screen. Finally, the i-spots linked to audio-only advertisements can be flagged by pressing OK when no visual advertisement is highlighted, or by clicking over any ad-free region of the screen.

Whichever the flagging method, the i-spots can be started immediately, or marked to be executed later (most commonly, when the current program finishes). In the former case, if the receiver allows operation as a DVR, it is even possible to do *time shift*, that is, to pause the programs while the viewer explores the i-spot, and then resume the viewing.

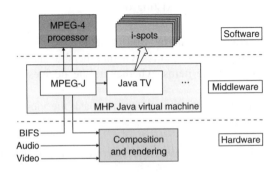

Figure 4.6 Situation of the MPEG-4 processor.

4.3.4 Delivering Personalized Commercial Functionalities

As we mentioned at the end of Section 4.2, the i-spots linked to the advertisements integrated in the audiovisual scenes may have been either developed manually or composed automatically. To support the manual approach, we have been using a tool called *ATLAS*, first presented in [40] as an environment for the development of t-learning applications (i.e., interactive educational services tailored to the social and technical peculiarities of the DTV medium). The latest version of *ATLAS* allows to characterize the i-spots with semantic concepts from the ontology of Section 4.3.1, so that the same personalization logic of Section 4.3.2 can identify which is the most suitable application for a given viewer at any time.

While manual development worked well in the first stages of our research, we soon noticed that no workforce would suffice to write specific applications for all the different viewers, items, and devices in an open scenario of e-commerce through television (see [41] for an analysis of the reasons), and so we started to work in automatic composition mechanisms. In this line, we conceived the i-spots as a sort of specialized *mashups* that bring together multimedia content from various sources of information and deliver functionality through pieces of software characterized as web services. The services may be realized over different *templates*, which differ from each other in the interactive elements shown to the viewer and the supported model of interactivity, which may be one of the following three:

- *local interactivity*, dealing exclusively with contents delivered in the broadcast stream and relying on alternative media for communication with commercial providers;
- *deferred interactivity*, storing information to forward when a return channel becomes available; or
- *full interactivity*, accessing information on demand through a permanently available return channel.

Just like the selection of items, the i-spot composition procedure relies on profiles and semantic similarity metrics to identify the most suitable services and sources of information for each viewer. Furthermore, we have added an engine of SWRL (*Semantic Web Rule Language*) rules to enable reasoning about the viewer's levels of familiarity with (or fondness for) semantic concepts. Thus, for example, if the item advertised in an i-spot were a sports car, a viewer who has scarce knowledge about mechanics would be faced with vague descriptions about motor components retrieved from *Wikipedia*, whereas an expert in mechanics and motor-related issues would see more detailed information from specialized sites like www.autoguide.com. As regards the selection of templates, the goal is to identify the most suitable interactive elements to assemble an i-spot about the item in question. This decision is driven by user preferences (e.g., the kind of elements the viewer has accessed in previous i-spots, monitored by the feedback agent of Section 4.3.2) and parameters like the computational power of the receiver, its input/output capabilities or the availability of a return channel. Thus, for example, we refrain from using templates with maps in the case of viewers who have never fiddled with such artifacts in previous i-spots, while we limit the amount of text to be shown in the case of small screen devices or with users who have never fully read lengthy descriptions of other items. Further details can be found in [41, 42].

4.4   An Example

To illustrate the reasoning and the functionalities enabled by the MiSPOT system, we shall consider the case of a childless man from London in his early 20s, with significant income and subscribed to the *Racing Sports* magazine. This viewer has opted to receive publicity following the server-side personalization procedure of MiSPOT; he is currently watching a documentary about Italy, using a high-end DTV receiver permanently connected to a cable network. The provider's repository of advertising material contains logos and videos for a range of cars and tourist resorts worldwide.

Assume that, as shown in the top left corner of Figure 4.7, the current scene of the movie is set in a noisy city street, and that the producers have identified the banner on the bus as a suitable hook to render static images with an aspect ratio nearing 4:1. As the first step in the MiSPOT operation, the low-level matching performed by the *HookTool* discards audio and video advertisements for this hook, and the same happens with nonfitting static images. Then, the semantic similarity metric identifies cars as the most suitable items to advertise within this scene, because cars are commonly found in city streets and the semantic characterization of the tourist resorts makes them more suitable for relaxing scenes.

When it comes to reasoning about the viewer's preferences, the data in his profile lead to finding a sports car as a potentially interesting item, for several reasons: (i) the explicit interest in motor sports reinforces the relevance of cars over tourist resorts, as we do not know anything about the viewer's fondness for traveling; (ii) the viewer's high economic power does not disregard him as a potential client for expensive items; and (iii) the viewer does not need space for children, which could promote other types of cars instead of sports ones. The specific brand selected in this example was found more relevant than others in this context because it has its headquarters in the Italian city of Modena. Thus, the car's logo ends up rendered within the hook as shown in the bottom right corner of Figure 4.7.

Figure 4.7   Warping the sports car logo over a bus.

We assume that the viewer feels curious about the sports car and activates the advertisement using his remote control, which tells the system to compose an i-spot about it. In doing so, the high level of income first leads the SWRL engine to select a car selling service instead of one that would simply provide information about the car. Next, the computing and communication capabilities of the viewer's high-end receiver makes it possible to use a template with demanding interactive elements like maps and video players. Finally, the viewer's preference for motor-related issues suggests getting information from specialized sites like www.autoguide.com. Figure 4.8 shows a few snapshots of the resulting i-spot. The first one displays information about the car's specifications retrieved from the aforementioned web site. Another tab provides a collection of pictures from Flickr and videos from *Youtube*. The last one provides an interactive map to locate dealers of the car brand around the region where the viewer lives, plus a calendar to arrange an appointment for a test drive.

4.5   Experimental Evaluation

We have conducted preliminary experiments in laboratory to assess the interest and viability of the MiSPOT system in practice. Next, we describe the technical settings of the experiments, followed by the evaluation methodology and results.

4.5.1   Technical Settings

On the technical side, we have analyzed the requirements imposed on the DTV receivers. Owing to the yet incipient development of receivers with MPEG-4 capabilities, we have built a prototype receiver that follows the essentials of the MHP architecture, though including enhancements proposed in [43] for MPEG-4 support. Regarding the latter, we considered two configurations:

- The first configuration supported only audio and 2D composition features, following the *Complete 2D Graphics* profile of the *MPEG-4 Systems* specification [44]. For the composition and rendering mechanisms, we used the open-source tools from the GPAC project [45], introducing new means for 2D mesh texture mapping and support for the MPEG-J APIs.
- The second configuration supported 3D composition features, incorporating most of the *X3D Core* profile of *MPEG-4 Systems*. On top of the same GPAC basis as before, the 3D composition and rendering mechanisms were implemented *ad hoc* using OpenGL libraries.

Through our experiments, we found that the first configuration above (used in the example of Section 4.4) can readily operate with little more than the computational power of the current DTV receivers. Indeed, a processor speed of 200 MHz and 128 MB of RAM memory – which can be considered standard for domestic receivers nowadays – achieved 21.8 frames per second when blending static images and 18.9 when blending videos in the resolution supported by MHP (720×576 pixels). On the contrary, the second configuration turned out to be significantly costlier, since we estimated that the processor speed should be at least 1.2 GHz to ensure real-time operation.

Figure 4.8 Snapshots of the i-spot assembled for the sports car.

Apart from the MPEG-4 features, all the code for the receiver-side modules of MiSPOT was written using the Java APIs provided by MHP – specifically, the filtering mechanisms were adapted from the implementation of the AVATAR recommender system of Blanco-Fernández *et al.* [46]. For the broadcasting infrastructure, we implemented the *planning* module in C++, and simulated DVB-T networks with a bit rate of 256 kbps to deliver advertising material and resources for i-spots. As return channels for the server-side personalization scheme, we considered 56 kbps dial-up connections. Finally, we deployed one server over a 2.0 GHz, 4096 MB RAM machine, with all the MiSPOT modules implemented in Java.

Our experiments involved episodes of two TV series, in which we defined a minimum of 10 hooks using the *HookTool*. The ontology stored in the server had a size of more than 20,000 nodes, while the partial ontologies were limited to 1000 nodes, which yields an average time of 7 s for the receivers to compute recommendations. Regarding the interactive offerings, we did not provide any manually developed i-spots, but rather relied entirely on the automatic composition mechanisms.

4.5.2 Evaluation Methodology and Results

Within the aforementioned settings, we conducted experiments to assess the personalization quality achieved by the MiSPOT system in terms of *precision* (% of advertised items that the viewers rate positively), *recall* (% of interesting items advertised), and overall perception of our proposal. The experiments involved 60 viewers recruited among our graduate/undergraduate students and their relatives or friends. They made up a diverse audience, with disparate demographic data and educational backgrounds; there were nearly as many men as women (54% vs 46%), with ages ranging from 12 to 55 years.

Prior to making any recommendations, we defined a set of 15 stereotypes by clustering the viewer profiles that had built up during previous experiments with the AVATAR recommender system [40]. Specifically, 14 clusters contained the profiles that had comparatively high (close to 1) or comparatively low (close to −1) DOIs for items classified under *Sports*, *Nature*, *Technology*, *Science*, *Health*, *Culture*, or *Traveling*. One final cluster gathered the profiles that did not meet any of those conditions. From each cluster, one stereotype was computed by averaging the DOIs of the profiles they contained. Having done this, we asked each viewer to rate his/her interest in topics related to *Sports*, *Nature*, *Technology*, *Science*, *Health*, *Culture*, and *Traveling* with a number between 0 and 9, and their individual profiles were then initialized by weighing the DOIs of the corresponding stereotypes. Those profiles were stored in the server's repository, together with 20 profiles previously elaborated by members of our research group.

The viewers interacted with our prototype system during at least 6 h over a period of three months. That time was distributed so that each viewer would receive more or less the same number of recommendations from the server-side and the receiver-side personalization schemes. After each session, the viewers were faced with a list of the items that had been advertised to them, which they had to rate between 0 and 9. At the end, we collected the log files and analyzed the data, getting to the precision and recall charts of Figure 4.9:

- For the estimation of precision, we divided the number of advertisements that the viewers had liked (i.e., rated greater than 5) by the number of advertisements recommended to them. As a result, we got a value nearing 72% for the server-side personalization scheme, which is 10% higher than the value achieved by the receiver-side counterpart. The lower performance of the latter is due to the fact that the partial ontologies do not always include all the attributes that may relate different items, so the semantic similarity metric becomes somewhat less effective (the smaller the ontologies, the worse). Also, there is an issue with viewers who happen not to be adequately represented by any of the stereotypes, implying that the advertisements most suited to their preferences are not included in the broadcast emissions. Nevertheless, it is worth noting that the 62% we achieve in the worst case remains much greater than the precision of syntactic approaches to receiver-side personalization in DTV (e.g., in [40] we had measured the approach of [47] to reach barely above 20%).

- For the estimation of recall, we examined the logs of 17 viewers who had previously agreed to classify the available items as *potentially interesting* or *potentially uninteresting*, and measured the percentage of the former that were ever advertised to them (obviously, on a per-viewer basis).[3] The values represented in Figure 4.9 are not meaningful in absolute terms: 30% in the best case may seem a very low recall, but this is because we do not provide the viewers with a list of potentially interesting items per hook, but rather only one. The important point is the significant difference between the values achieved by server-side and the receiver-side schemes. The lower recall of the latter is due to the fact that, in the absence of return channels, the viewers can only be faced with advertisements delivered through broadcast, which hardly ever include all the material of interest for any given individual.

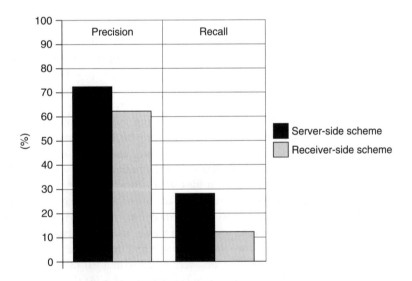

Figure 4.9 Experimental results: precision and recall.

---

[3] A posteriori, we could check that the ratings given by the viewers to items they had classified as *potentially appealing* were lower than 5 only in 8% of the cases, which undoubtedly supports the validity of our estimations.

Table 4.1 Experimental results: Viewers' opinions

	Very positive (%)	Positive (%)	Neutral (%)	Negative (%)
Opinion about the personalized offerings	29	39	23	9
Opinion about the advertising model	36	31	18	15
Interest in the i-spot concept	29	39	21	11
Opinion about the functionalities delivered	19	46	23	12
Quality and coherence of the contents displayed	12	28	33	27

It is worth noting that the reductions in precision and recall in the receiver-side personalization scheme can be tuned by modifying parameters like the bandwidth available to broadcasting data and the limit size of the partial ontologies, which directly affect loading times and the computational cost of the recommendations, respectively.

In order to appraise the viewers' perceptions, we ran a poll off-line asking them to rate the personalization service, the new advertising model of dynamic product placement, and the interest of enhancing the traditional TV publicity with interactive commercial functionalities. The results are shown in Table 4.1.

To begin with, it is noticeable that the viewers' satisfaction with the personalized offerings was quite high, with 68% of the viewers rating the experience positively or very positively. Many of the test subjects noticed that the quality of the recommendations increased as they interacted with the system (obviously, thanks to the relevance feedback), but they agreed that the targeting of the publicity was not any worse than usual even during the first sessions. In what concerns the advertising model, the viewers' appreciation was just as good, with 67% of positive or very positive ratings. Here, almost 15% of the viewers considered the product placements a nuisance, but this was often due to cases in which the integration of the advertisements within the TV programs was not always as smooth as desired – a question of technical refinements and finer definition of the hooks. Finally, regarding the i-spot concept, a significant number of viewers (more than 35%) admitted that they do not yet think of using the TV receivers for anything else than TV watching. Anyway, nearly 65% of them gave positive or very positive ratings to the functionalities delivered, which confirms the interest of the local and deferred interactivity modes. The bad news has to do with the quality and coherence of the contents displayed, because the i-spots sometimes failed to make a cohesive whole out of pieces of information retrieved from diverse sources. This fact reveals that it is necessary to develop more fine-grained reasoning about the contents, or to restrict the possible sources by requiring greater amounts of metadata. We leave this question to be the subject of future research.

4.6 Conclusions

The MiSPOT system described in this paper proposes a complement to the advertising techniques currently employed on TV, betting on personalization as the only means to achieve better targeting and exploiting recent advances in multimedia (most of them enabled by the MPEG-4 standard) to render the advertisements in a way that does not interfere with what the viewers are watching. MiSPOT introduces novel engineering solutions (like the existence of local and remote personalization engines, and the management of partial ontologies at the receivers' side) that serve to cater to the peculiarities of the DTV medium, and which have no precedents in literature.

In such a competitive market as envisioned for the future of DTV (characterized by the great diversity of users, providers and contents), the approach of MiSPOT has the potential to benefit all the stakeholders involved in the publicity business:

- Thanks to the personalization and interaction features, the DTV providers will be able to offer a more effective advertising medium, sustaining their traditional main source of income and opening new forms of making money. The MiSPOT architecture is flexible enough to support diverse deployments, fitting different network types, availability requirements, and receiver capabilities. Likewise, it is possible to switch between server-side and receiver-side personalization to meet legal aspects such as the necessary levels of viewer's consent, the limits to the exchange and aggregation of data from different sources, the limits to granting access to third parties or to trade information, and so on.[4] The charging mechanisms may combine different measures of visibility, such as the actual number of advertisement insertions or the number of i-spot launches. With server-side personalization, such measures can be collected from the material downloaded on demand, whereas a receiver-side scheme must rely on the same kind of audience studies that drive charging mechanisms nowadays (statistical analyses of data gathered from a representative sample of viewers, provided with specialized receiver equipment). Interestingly, for both approaches, it would be easy to modify the personalization logic so as to consider not only semantics and viewer preferences, but also the advertisers' investment and interest for specific programs, specific groups of viewers, or specific time frames.
- The advertisers will be provided with better and more accessible/affordable means to reach consumers potentially interested in their products or services, with possibilities to trade directly through the TV. Focusing on the model of product placement, we lower the barriers for small- and medium-sized enterprises to earn visibility in mainstream TV channels in their areas of influence, because they are no longer forced to buying expensive airtime for expensive spots. In the simplest case, it suffices to provide a number of properly characterized multimedia resources (pieces of audio, static images, or videos) and rely on the automatic i-spot composition mechanisms.
- The viewers will enjoy a better TV experience, watching the programs they choose without (or, at least, with fewer) breaks or invasions of the screen due to advertisement insertions. In pay-per-view scenarios, it would be possible to tailor the amount of publicity delivered to the cost of the fee. In any case, the personalization features make it likely that the viewers will start to regard publicity as a valuable information service instead of a nuisance.
- Finally, content creators will find an important added value in the possibility of preparing the material they produce for viewing-time integration with different pieces of

---

[4] In-depth details about the legal context for personalization can be found in [48, 49].

advertising, thus overcoming the limitations of traditional product placement in terms of temporal and spatial locality. In principle, the definition and characterization of hooks and scenes appears as a manual task, but it can be supported by a wealth of solutions for the automatic recognition of low-level and high-level features in images [50, 51].

Obviously, implementing the approach of MiSPOT requires updating the production and broadcasting chains according to the MPEG-4, TV-Anytime, and MPEG-7 standards. However, this seems to be the industry's next step anyway, due to the well-known advantages of improving the use of bandwidth, suiting a wide range of consumer devices, enabling better electronic programming guides, and so on. It may also require more expensive receivers than the ones available nowadays, but the possibility to increase the revenues of publicity may well take advertisers and content creators to bear part of the expenses.

Acknowledgments

This work has been supported by the Ministerio de Educación y Ciencia (Gobierno de España) research project TSI2007-61599 and by the Consellería de Educación e Ordenación Universitaria (Xunta de Galicia) incentives file 2007/000016-0.

References

[1] Berman, S.J., Shipnuck, L.A., and Duffy, N. (2006) The End of Television as We Know It. IBM Business Consulting Services.

[2] ScreenDigest (2008) *Europe's TV Broadcasters Trapped in a Downward Spiral as Advertising Revenues Plummet*. Online http://www.goldmedia.com/uploads/media/Pressemeldung_TV_Werbemarkt.pdf (accessed 2009).

[3] Kim, P. (2006) Advertisers face TV reality. *Business View Trends*, Forrester Research: Cambridge, MA.

[4] Pearson, S. and Barwise, P. (2007) PVRs and advertising exposure: a video ethnographic study. *International Journal of Internet Marketing and Advertising*, **4** (1), 93–113.

[5] Wilbur, K.C. (2008) How the Digital Video Recorder (DVR) changes traditional television. *Journal of Advertising*, **37** (1), 143–149.

[6] Chodhury, R., Finn, A., and Douglas Olsen, G. (2007) Investigating the simultaneous presentation of advertising and TV programming. *Journal of Advertising*, **39** (1), 95–101.

[7] iTVx (2007) *Measuring the Quality of Product Placement*, http://www.itvx.com (accessed 2009).

[8] Russell, C. (2002) Investigating the effectiveness of product placements in television shows: the role of modality and plot connection congruence on brand memory and attitude. *Journal of Consumer Research*, **29**, 306–318.

[9] Graves, D. (2008) *Personal TV: the reinvention of television, Business View Trends*, Forrester Research: Cambridge, MA.

[10] Mei, T., Hua, X.-S., Yang, L., and Li, S. (2007) VideoSense: towards effective online video advertising. Proceedings of the ACM International Multimedia Conference and Exhibition, Augsburg, Germany, September.

[11] Sengamedu, S.H., Sawant, N., and Wadhwa, S. (2007) VADeo: video advertising system. Proceedings of the ACM International Multimedia Conference and Exhibition, Augsburg, Germany, September.

[12] Li, Y., Wah Wan, K., Yan, X., and Xu, C. (2005) Real time advertisement insertion in baseball video based on advertisement effect. Proceedings of the 13th Annual ACM International Conference on Multimedia, Singapore, November.

[13] Wan, K. and Yan, X. (2007) Advertising insertion in sports webcasts. *IEEE Multimedia*, **14** (2), 78–82.

[14] Xu, C., Wan, K.W., Bui, S.H., and Tian, Q. (2004) Implanting virtual advertisement into broadcast soccer video. *Lecture Notes in Computer Science*, **3332**, 264–271.

[15] Roger, J., Nguyen, H., and Mishra, D.O. (2007) Automatic generation of explicitly embedded advertisement for interactive TV: concept and system architecture. Proceedings of the 4th International Conference on Mobile Technology, Applications and Systems (Mobility), Singapore, September.

[16] Bozios, T., Lekakos, G., Skoularidou, V., and Chorianopoulos, K. (2001) Advanced techniques for personalized advertising in a digital TV environment: the iMEDIA system. Proceedings of the eBusiness and eWork Conference, Venice, Italy, October.

[17] de Pessemier, T., Deryckere, T., Vanhecke, K., and Martens, L. (2008) Proposed architecture and algorithm for personalized advertising on iDTV and mobile devices. *IEEE Transactions on Consumer Electronics*, **54** (2), 709–713.

[18] Kastidou, G. and Cohen, R. (2006) An approach for delivering personalized ads in interactive TV customized to both users and advertisers. Proceedings of the 4th European Conference on Interactive Television, Athens, Greece, May.

[19] Kim, M., Kang, S., Kim, M., and Kim, J. (2005) Target advertisement service using tv viewers' profile inference. *Lecture Notes in Computer Science*, **3767**, 202–211.

[20] Lekakos, G. and Giaglis, G. (2004) A lifestyle-based approach for delivering personalised advertisements in digital interactive television. *Journal of Computer-Mediated Communication*, **9** (2).

[21] Thawani, A., Gopalan, S., and Sridhar, V. (2004) Context-aware personalized ad insertion in an Interactive TV environment. Proceedings of the 4th Workshop on Personalization in Future TV, Eindhoven, The Netherlands, August.

[22] Ricci, F., Arslan, B., Mirzadeh, N., and Venturini, A. (2002) ITR: a case-based travel advisory system. *Lecture Notes in Computer Science*, **2416**, 613–627.

[23] Shimazu, H. (2002) ExpertClerk: a conversational case-based reasoning tool for developing salesclerk agents in e-commerce webshops. *Artificial Intelligence Review*, **18** (3), 223–244.

[24] Cho, Y. and Kim, J. (2004) Application of Web usage mining and product taxonomy to collaborative recommendations in e-commerce. *Expert Systems with Applications*, **26**, 233–246.

[25] Cho, Y., Kim, W., Kim, J. *et al.* (2002) A personalized recommendation procedure for Internet shopping support. *Electronic Commerce Research and Applications*, **1** (3), 301–313.

[26] Burke, R. (2002) Hybrid recommender systems: survey and experiments. *User Model User Adapted Interaction*, **12** (4), 331–370.

[27] Anyanwu, K. and Sheth, A. (2003) ρ-queries: enabling querying for semantic associations on the Semantic Web. Proceedings of the 12th International World Wide Web Conference, Budapest, Hungary, May.

[28] Cho, J., Young, J.S., and Ryu, J. (2008) A new content-related advertising model for interactive television. Proceedings of the IEEE International Symposium on Broadband Multimedia Systems and Broadcasting, Las Vegas (NV), USA, March.

[29] Jong, W.K. and Stephen, D. (2006) Design for an interactive television advertising system. Proceedings of the 39th Annual Hawaii International Conference on System Sciences, Honolulu (HI), USA, January.

[30] Klein, J.A., Karger, S.A., and Sinclair, K.A. (2003) *Digital Television for All: A Report on Usability and Accessible Design*, http://www.acessibilidade.net/tdt/Digital_TV_for_all.pdf (accessed 2009).

[31] Digital Tech Consulting, Inc. (2006) *Digital TV Receivers: Worldwide History and Forecasts (2000–2010)*, http://www.dtcreports.com/report_dtvr.aspx (accessed 2009).

[32] DVB (2003) ETSI Standard TS 102 812. The Multimedia Home Platform, ETSI: Sophia Antipolis, France, http://www.mhp.org.

[33] Creutzburg, R., Takala, J., and Chen, C. (2006) *Multimedia on Mobile Devices II*, International Society for Optical Engineering: San Jose, CA.

[34] Alencar, M.S. (2009) *Digital Television Systems*, Cambridge University Press, Cambridge, UK.

[35] Benoit, H. (2008) *Digital Television*, Focal Press, Oxford.

[36] López-Nores, M., Pazos-Arias, J.J., García-Duque, J. *et al.* (2010) MiSPOT: dynamic product placement for digital TV through MPEG-4 processing and semantic reasoning. *Knowledge and Information Systems*, **22** (1), 101–128.

[37] McGuinness, D. and van Harmelen, F. (2004) OWL Web Ontology Language Overview, W3C Recommendation.

[38] Hepp, M., Leukel, J., and Schmitz, V. (2007) A quantitative analysis of product categorization standards: content, coverage and maintenance of eCl@ss, UNSPSC, eOTD, and the RosettaNet Technical Dictionary. *Knowledge and Information Systems*, **13** (1), 77–114.

[39] López-Nores, M., Blanco-Fernández, Y., Pazos-Arias, J. *et al.* (2009) Receiver-side semantic reasoning for Digital TV personalization in the absence of return channels. *Multimedia Tools And Applications*, **41** (3), 407–436.

[40] Pazos-Arias, J., López-Nores, M., García-Duque, J. *et al.* (2008) Provision of distance learning services over Interactive Digital TV with MHP. *Computers & Education*, **50** (3), 927–949.

[41] Blanco-Fernández, Y., López-Nores, M., Pazos-Arias, J., and Martín-Vicente, M. (2009) Automatic generation of mashups for personalized commerce in Digital TV by semantic reasoning. *Lecture Notes in Computer Science*, **5692**, 132–143.

[42] Blanco-Fernández, Y., López-Nores, M., Gil-Solla, A. *et al.* (2009) Semantic reasoning and mashups: an innovative approach to personalized e-commerce in Digital TV. Proceedings of the 4th International Workshop on Semantic Media Adaptation and Personalization, Bilbao, Spain, December.

[43] Illgner, K. and Cosmas, J. (2001) System concept for interactive broadcasting consumer terminals. Proceedings of the International Broadcast Convention, Amsterdam, The Netherlands, September, http://www.irt.de/sambits (accessed 2009).

[44] Ebrahimi, T. and Pereira, F. (2002) *The MPEG-4 Book*, Prentice Hall, Upper Saddle River, NJ.

[45] GPAC (2007) *GPAC Project on Advanced Content*, http://gpac.sourceforge.net (accessed 2009).

[46] Blanco-Fernández, Y., Pazos-Arias, J.J., Gil-Solla, A. *et al.* (2008) An MHP framework to provide intelligent personalized recommendations about Digital TV contents. *Software-Practice and Experience*, **38** (9), 925–960.

[47] Ghaneh, M. (2004) System model for t-learning application based on home servers (PDR). *Broadcast Technology*, **19**, http://www.nhk.or.jp/strl/publica/bt/en/rep0019.pdf.

[48] Rodríguez de las Heras Ballell, T. (2009) *Personalization of Interactive Multimedia Services: A Research and Development Perspective*, Nova Science Publishers, Hauppauge, NY. Legal framework for personalization-based business models.

[49] Wang, Y., Zhaoqi, C., and Kobsa, A. (2007) *A Collection and Systematization of International Privacy Laws*. Online http://www.ics.uci.edu/~kobsa/privacy/intlprivlawsurvey.html (accessed 2009).

[50] Athanasiadis, T., Mylonas, P., Avrithis, Y.S., and Kollias, S.D. (2007) Semantic image segmentation and object labeling. *IEEE Transactions on Circuits and Systems for Video Technology*, **17** (3), 298–312.

[51] Pinheiro, A.M.G. (2007) Image description using scale-space edge pixel directions histogram. Proceedings of the 2nd International Workshop on Semantic Media Adaptation and Personalization, Uxbridge, United Kingdom, December.

5

Using MPEG Tools in Video Summarization

Luis Herranz and José M. Martínez

Escuela Politécnica Superior, Universidad Autónoma de Madrid, Madrid, Spain

5.1 Introduction

Owing to the huge amount of content available in multimedia repositories, abstractions are essential for efficient access and navigation [1, 2]. Video summarization includes a number of techniques exploiting the temporal redundancy of video frames in terms of content understanding. Besides, in modern multimedia systems, there are many possible ways to search, browse, retrieve, and access multimedia content through different networks and using a wide variety of heterogeneous terminals. Content is often adapted to the specific requirements of the usage environment (e.g., terminal and network), performing adaptation operations such as spatial downsampling or bitrate reduction in order to accommodate the bitstream to the available screen size or network bandwidth. This adaptation is often addressed using technologies such as transcoding or scalable coding.

This chapter describes a framework that uses scalable video coding (SVC) for the generation of the bitstreams of summaries, which are also adapted to the usage environment. The whole summarization–adaptation framework uses several coding and metadata tools from different MPEG standards. The main advantage is the simplicity and efficiency of the process, especially when it is compared to the conventional approaches such as transcoding. The framework and results are gathered mainly from works published in [3, 4].

This chapter is organized as follows. Section 5.2 briefly describes the related technologies and works. Section 5.3 overviews the use of MPEG standards in the summarization framework. Section 5.4 describes the summarization framework using MPEG-4 AVC (advanced video coding). Section 5.5 shows how MPEG-7 can be used to describe summaries. In Section 5.6, the framework is extended to include adaptation using MPEG-4 SVC. Experimental results are presented in Section 5.7 while Section 5.8 concludes the chapter.

The Handbook of MPEG Applications: Standards in Practice   Edited by Marios C. Angelides and Harry Agius
© 2011 John Wiley & Sons, Ltd

5.2 Related Work

5.2.1 Video Summarization

Video summarization techniques provide the user with a compact but informative representation of the sequence, usually in the form of a set of key images or short video sequences [5–8]. In general, a summarized sequence is built from the source sequence selecting frames according to some kind of semantic analysis of the content. Many algorithms have been proposed for keyframe selection and video summarization, using different criteria and abstraction levels. Recent surveys [9, 10] provide comprehensive classifications and reviews of summarization techniques.

Important examples of systems using video abstractions or summaries are digital video libraries, such as YouTube,[1] the Internet Archive[2] or the OpenVideo project[3] [11]. Search and browsing are much easier and efficient using abstracts than browsing actual video sequences. Usually, a single key image, the title, and a short description are used to represent a specific piece of content. However, other modalities of visual abstractions have also been proposed, in order to include more (audio)visual information. A widely used representation is the image storyboard, which abstracts the content into a set of key images that are presented simultaneously. Figure 5.1 shows an example of the web interface of the Open Video project. It depicts a storyboard summary in addition to the conventional textual description of the sequence.

However, when dealing with video content, it is often more useful and meaningful to present the summary as a short video sequence, instead of independent frames. Segments provide information about the temporal evolution of the sequence, which isolated images cannot provide. This representation is often known as *video skim*, composed of significant segments extracted from the source sequence. Several approaches have been used in video skimming, including visual attention [12], image and audio analysis [13, 14], and high level semantics [2].

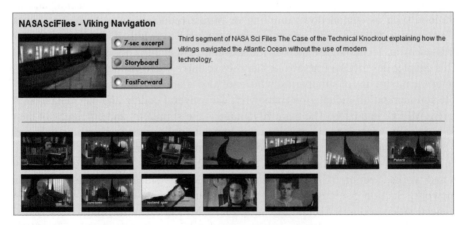

Figure 5.1 Example of summary (storyboard) in a digital library. Reproduced with permission of © the Open Video project.

[1] http://www.youtube.com
[2] http://www.archive.org
[3] http://www.open-video.org

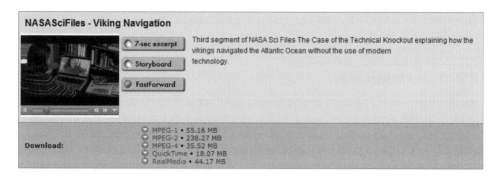

Figure 5.2 Fast-forward summary and adapted versions of the content. Reproduced with permission of © the Open Video project.

Between selecting single frames and selecting whole segments, there is still the possibility of selecting a variable amount of frames per segment. Fast-forwarding the sequence at a constant rate can provide the user with a preview of the content (see Figure 5.2), which will be useful to browse it in a shorter time [15]. However, there are often less important parts that can be sped up, while more significant parts can be played at normal rate. Thus, a content-based fast-forward can be obtained if the skimming of frames is done in a frame basis guided by a semantic clue. Motion activity and camera motion have been used as clues to drive the selection of frames [16, 17]. A related technique is frame dropping driven by some low level features, where less important frames are discarded during the transmission of the sequence in case of network congestion. Reference [18] uses MPEG-7 intensity motion descriptor to guide the frame dropping and [19] uses the perceived motion energy.

Besides these widely extended representations, there is an increasing interest on the development of more intuitive abstractions. In this direction, comics and posters have inspired several works [1, 20, 21], where the key images are presented with variable size in a layout where temporal order is replaced by a spatial scan order. Edited video is structured into more abstract units such as shots and then scenes, which typically contain several related shots. This hierarchical structure can also be exploited for summarization [22] and browsing [6, 7].

In order to obtain better results, the domain of the content has been exploited by the algorithms. Thus, sports video summarization tries to exploit prior knowledge, such as the structure and characteristics of a specific sport game for better results. Usually, these approaches are based on the detection of some important events that must be included in the summary (e.g., goals and end of game). Other typical scenarios are news [23–26], which is a highly structured and edited video content, surveillance [24], and home videos [27]. Additionally, metadata can be provided for higher level understanding of the content [28].

Recently, an intense research in rushes summarization has been motivated by the TRECVid rushes summarization task [29, 30]. This content is significantly different compared to other video sources, as rushes are unedited footage containing retakes and much more redundant compared to other sources. This content also contains undesirable junk segments containing blank frames, clapboards, and so on. Participants in TRECVid rushes summarization task have developed systems designed to summarize this specific content [29–31].

5.2.2   Video Adaptation

Content adaptation [32] is a main requirement to effectively bring the content from service providers to the actual users, using different terminals and networks and enabling the so-called universal multimedia access (UMA) [33]. Especially important is the case of mobile devices, such as personal digital assistants (PDAs) and mobile phones, where other issues such as limited computational resources and low power consumption requirements become very important.

In contrast to content-blind adaptation (e.g., resolution downsampling and bitrate adaptation), which does not consider the content itself, content-based adaptation takes advantage of a certain knowledge of what is happening (semantics) in the content to perform a better adaptation. In [32], video summarization is even considered a special type of structural adaptation, in which the summary is an adapted version of the original content. Content-based adaptation is often known as *semantic adaptation*, which also includes personalization [23, 34] and object-based adaptation [35, 36]. Knowledge about the content that semantic adaptation needs can be automatically extracted or provided as metadata [37, 38] from previous automatic analysis or manual annotation. This knowledge ranges from very low level (shot changes, color and motion features, etc.) to high level (events, objects, actions, etc.).

The generation of the adapted bitstream often implies decoding, adaptation to the target usage environment, and encoding of the adapted content. This approach to adaptation is known as *transcoding* [39], and it can be computationally very demanding, although efficient architectures have been developed [40]. An alternative to transcoding is the use of (off-line) variations [41, 42] – covering a number of predefined versions of the content which are generated and stored prior to their use in the system. Figure 5.2 shows an example of adapted versions available as off-line variations (e.g., MPEG-1 and MPEG-2). The user can then decide which version is most suitable according to codec capabilities, display resolution, network capacity, or storage requirements.

5.2.2.1   Scalable Video Coding

SVC tackles the problem of adaptation at the encoding stage, in a way that simplifies the adaptation process. A scalable video stream contains embedded versions of the source content that can be decoded at different resolutions, frame rates, and qualities, by simply selecting the required parts of the bitstream. Thus, SVC enables simple, fast, and flexible adaptation to a variety of heterogeneous terminals and networks. The numerous advantages of this coding paradigm have motivated an intense research activity in the last years [43–45].

Recently, the Joint Video Team (JVT) has standardized a scalable extension of the successful H.264/MPEG-4 AVC [46] standard, supporting multiple scalabilities, notably temporal, spatial, and quality scalabilities. This new specification is known as *MPEG-4 SVC* [45]. In this chapter, the term AVC is used to refer to the H.264/MPEG-4 AVC specification and SVC to the scalable extension.

5.2.2.2 Bitstream Modification

As video is usually distributed in a compressed format, the coding structure can also be exploited for lightweight customization of the bitstream, directly operating with the compressed data. For example, scalable bitstreams are adapted with minimum processing directly on the compressed bitstream. Bitstream syntax description (BSD) tools [47] of MPEG-21 digital item adaptation (DIA) [33, 48] were developed for generic adaptation of coded sequences directly manipulating the bitstream.

In some cases, bitstream modification can be used for other content-based structural adaptations, such as summarization. In that case, the summary is created operating with the syntax elements in the bitstream. Specifically, for H.264/MPEG-4 AVC, in the framework of MPEG-21 DIA, [49] proposes a content-based adaptation system using a shot-based approach, while [19] uses a similar approach for frame dropping based on the perceived motion energy. A generic model based on bitstream extraction, integrating both adaptation and summarization, is proposed in [4] and described in this chapter.

5.3 A Summarization Framework Using MPEG Standards

Over the last years, MPEG specifications have tackled different aspects and requirements of multimedia systems, initially focusing on efficient and flexible coding of audio and video. Later, MPEG specifications broadened to include not only standardized descriptions of bitstreams but also standardized descriptions of the content itself and other elements and agents involved in multimedia systems. Several of these MPEG tools are combined in the application described in this chapter to provide standard syntax for bitstreams, content, and usage context (Figure 5.3).

In the proposed framework, summaries are stored as metadata along with the bitstream. They are described following the MPEG-7 multimedia description schemes (MDS) specification [50], which provides metadata tools for summarization.

A key for the success of video applications is the coding format used to compress the huge amount of data into bitstreams that can be handled by telecommunication networks. The bitstream syntax (BS) and the coding structure can be used for lightweight customization of the bitstream, directly operating with the compressed data. The only requirement is that the output sequence should be still compliant with the standard. In our case, the coding format is MPEG-4 AVC for nonscalable bitstreams, extended to MPEG-4 SVC for scalable bitstreams.

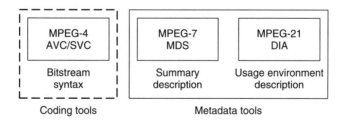

Figure 5.3 Use of MPEG standards in the application.

Finally, The MPEG-21 standard specifies a number of tools and concepts in a standard framework to enable advanced multimedia applications in heterogeneous usage environments. Particularly, MPEG-21 DIA [33, 48] tackles the adaptation for universal access, with metadata tools, to describe the usage environment, including terminal capabilities, network, and user characteristics.

5.4 Generation of Summaries Using MPEG-4 AVC

In general, the term video summarization is used to refer to a number of techniques that analyze the semantics of the source sequence and then create a summary according to this analysis. For convenience, we separate the whole summarization process into two stages: analysis of the input bitstream and generation of the summarized bitstream. Actually, analysis is completely detached from generation and it can be performed in a previous stage and stored as metadata. Analysis consists of either manual annotation or an automatic summarization algorithm.

A summary is usually generated by the concatenation of frames. Here, the basic unit for summarization is the frame. In the case of uncompressed video (e.g., in YUV format), it is possible to select each frame independently and build a new sequence just concatenating the values of the samples of each selected frame. Thus, a summary can be described with the indices of the frames of the source sequence that must be included. The analysis stage only needs to provide these indices to the generation stage.

5.4.1 Coding Units and Summarization Units

AVC specifies two conceptual layers: a video coding layer (VCL), which deals with the efficient representation of the video content, and a network abstraction layer (NAL), which deals with the format and header information in a suitable manner to be used by a variety of network environments and storage media. The bitstream is composed of a succession of NAL units, each of them containing payload and header with several syntax elements. An access unit (AU) is a set of consecutive NAL units which results in exactly one decoded picture.

For simplicity, we will consider that each frame is coded into one slice and one NAL unit, and it corresponds to a single AU. However, concatenating the NAL units of the frames belonging to the summary will probably generate a nondecodable bitstream, as most of them are encoded predictively with respect to previous frames in the source bitstream. If these reference frames are removed from the output bitstream, predicted frames will not be decodable. For this reason it is more convenient to refer the results of the analysis to coding-oriented structures rather than to single frames, taking into account the prediction dependencies between them.

If we consider a sequence with N frames, coded with T temporal decompositions (that means $T + 1$ temporal levels), then the frame index can be notated as $n \in \{0, 1, \ldots, N - 1\}$ and the temporal level as $t \in \{0, 1, \ldots, T\}$. For each temporal level, a subsampled version in the temporal axis can be decoded, as there are no breaks in the prediction chain. In this case, we use an alternative representation that describes the summary using groups of frames related by prediction rather than frame indices. In

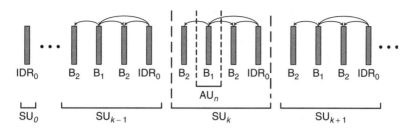

Figure 5.4 Coding structures and summarization units in H.264/AVC.

this alternative representation, the basic unit for summarization is the summarization unit (SU). We define the SU as a set of consecutive AUs at certain temporal level related by the prediction structure and that can be decoded independently from the other AUs in the sequence. The sequence is then partitioned into M SUs. Figure 5.4 shows an example of a hierarchical coding structure and its corresponding SUs. The SU at the highest temporal level is the one formed by an instant decoding refresh (IDR) frame and three B frames, which are coded predictively. Obviously, it is not possible to include a B frame in the summary without including its reference frames, as it would not be decoded by the user's decoder. However, there are more SUs in the bitstream, at different temporal levels, as the one composed by the IDR and B frames at the first temporal level, and the one composed only by the IDR frame. The only requirement for these groups of NAL units is that they must be decodable independent of the rest of the bitstream (except other required non-VCL NAL units such as parameter sets) and that their decoding results exactly in a set of consecutive frames at a certain temporal level.

Within this framework, the summaries are built by concatenating SUs, resulting directly in the output bitstream. All the frames in the bitstream can be decoded with a suitable AVC or SVC decoder. Each SU must be decoded independently from other SUs, as the summarization process could eventually remove some of them. In order to guarantee that each SU can be decoded independently, it is important to provide each of them with a random access point. In AVC, the simplest method is the use of an IDR AU for each SU, as an IDR AU signals that the IDR AU and all the following AUs can be decoded without decoding any previous picture. An additional advantage of using IDR AUs is the limited error propagation. An eventual transmission error would propagate only until the next IDR AU. Although the use of IDR AUs is simple and convenient, it is still possible to provide the same functionality using I slices if the SUs are independently decodable [51].

The selection based on SUs has the drawback of losing some accuracy in the selection of frames. This accuracy depends on the length of the SU and it is given by the coding structure (e.g., the SU of Figure 5.4 has a precision of four frames).

Besides the concept of SUs, we define the summarization constraint $tlevel\,(m)$ as the maximum temporal level for each SU_m. This function describes how to generate the summaries, as the indices of the frames do in the case of uncompressed bitstreams. If the value of $tlevel\,(m)$ is set to -1 for a certain m it means that SU_m is not included in the summary. The objective of the analysis stage of a summarization algorithm in this framework is to determine the summarization constraint for each video sequence, based on certain content analysis.

5.4.2   Modalities of Video Summaries

There are different video summarization modalities that can be easily adapted to the proposed scheme. Depending on the values that $tlevel\,(m)$ takes for the SUs, we distinguish the following modalities of video summaries (Figure 5.5):

- Storyboard. It is built by selecting a few independent and separated frames to represent the content as a collection of images. Within the proposed model, for convenience, we restrict the potential selected frames to be I frames belonging to the lowest temporal level. We also assume that the lower temporal resolution has only one I frame. In practice, there is no noticeable difference for practical applications, and actually most storyboard summarization algorithms use temporal subsampling to speed up the analysis. With these assumptions, the storyboard is characterized as follows:

$$tlevel\,(m) = \begin{cases} 0 & \text{keyframe} \in SU_m \\ -1 & \text{otherwise} \end{cases}$$

- Video Skim. The adapted sequence is shorter than the input sequence, obtained by selecting certain segments of the input sequence. In this case, the valid options for each SU are either not constraining its temporal level or skipping it. Thus, if the maximum temporal level is t_{max}, the video skim can be characterized as follows:

$$tlevel\,(m) = \begin{cases} t_{max} & SU_m \in \text{skim} \\ -1 & \text{otherwise} \end{cases}$$

- Content-Based Fast-forward or Fast-playback. This summarization modality is based on the acceleration and deceleration of the sequence controlled by a certain content-based criteria, in order to visualize it in a shorter time. In this case, the number of frames of each SU is variable depending on the required frame rate at each SU.

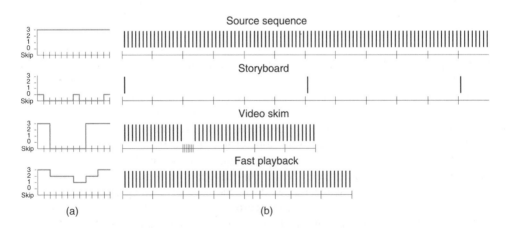

Figure 5.5   Examples of the function $tlevel\,(m)$ (a) and frames selected (b).

5.5   Description of Summaries in MPEG-7

In contrast to previous MPEG standards, MPEG-7 focuses on the description of multimedia content, from low level features to high level concepts, providing description tools with standarized syntax and semantics. It has been designed as a generic standard, which can be used in a broad range of applications. The MPEG-7 Part 5 covers the MPEG MDS [50], which deals with generic and multimedia entities.

5.5.1   MPEG-7 Summarization Tools

The description tools in MPEG-7 MDS are grouped into six areas. One of these areas is *navigation and access*, including tools for summarization. These tools can be used to specify summaries of time-varying audiovisual data that support hierarchical and sequential navigations. The former uses the *HierarchicalSummary* description scheme to specify summaries used in hierarchical navigation, with several related summaries including different levels of detail. Each level can support also sequential navigation. The *SequentialSummary* description scheme specifies summaries of data that support sequential navigation. Examples of such summaries are content-based fast-forward and video slideshows.

A *SequentialSummary* consists of a list of elements describing the video, audio, and textual components of the summary. These elements can be synchronized using *SyncTime* elements. Each component of the summary is specified by a *VisualSummaryComponent*, *AudioSummaryComponent*, or *TextualSummaryComponent* with the location of a particular frame, video segment, audio clip, or textual annotation.

5.5.2   Examples of Descriptions

In our framework, we use storyboards, content-based fast-forwards and video skims, which can be described as sequential summaries. No audio is included so there is no need to include synchronization information. As we explained earlier, the summaries are described using the function $tlevel(m)$, which is referred to SUs. This information must be converted to a suitable representation for MPEG-7 description tools, specifying which frames must be included rather than the temporal level of an SU. Therefore, when a description is read to generate the summary, it must be converted back to $tlevel(m)$, in order to be used by the summarization framework.

The following is an example of storyboard description in MPEG-7. A *SourceLocator* element specifies the source video, and several *ImageLocator* elements specify the frames selected for the storyboard. The reference of the frames in the description is relative to the source video.

```
<SequentialSummary id="StoryboardSummary" components="visual">
    <SourceLocator><!--Location of the source content -->
        <MediaUri>file://video.264</MediaUri>
    </SourceLocator>
    <VisualSummaryComponent>
```

```
      <ImageLocator><!--Locates summary keyframe in the original video -->
         <MediaRelIncrTimePoint mediaTimeUnit="PT1N25F" mediaTimeBase="
            ../../../SourceLocator[1]">801</MediaRelIncrTimePoint>
      </ImageLocator>
   </VisualSummaryComponent>
   <VisualSummaryComponent>
      <ImageLocator>
         <MediaRelIncrTimePoint mediaTimeUnit="PT1N30F" mediaTimeBase="
            ../../../SourceLocator[1]">961</MediaRelIncrTimePoint>
      </ImageLocator>
   </VisualSummaryComponent>
   ...
</SequentialSummary>
```

Similarly, video skims can be easily described using the SequentialSummary tool, as in the following example. In this case, several *VideoSourceLocator* elements specify the start time and the duration of each video segment.

```
<SequentialSummary id="VideoSkimSummary" components="visual">
   <SourceLocator><!--Location of the source content -->
      <MediaUri>file://video.264</MediaUri>
   </SourceLocator>
   <VisualSummaryComponent>
      <VideoSourceLocator><!--Locates a temporal segment in the
         original video -->
         <MediaRelIncrTimePoint mediaTimeUnit="PT1N25F" mediaTimeBase="
            ../../../SourceLocator[1]">793</MediaRelIncrTimePoint>
         <MediaDuration>PT32N25F</MediaDuration>
      </VideoSourceLocator>
   </VisualSummaryComponent>
   <VisualSummaryComponent>
      <VideoSourceLocator>
         <MediaRelIncrTimePoint mediaTimeUnit="PT1N25F" mediaTimeBase="
            ../../../SourceLocator[1]">954</MediaRelIncrTimePoint>
         <MediaDuration>PT32N25F</MediaDuration>
      </VideoSourceLocator>
   </VisualSummaryComponent>
   ...
</SequentialSummary>
```

5.6 Integrated Summarization and Adaptation Framework in MPEG-4 SVC

Most video summarization techniques can be formulated as a special case of video adaptation, where the adaptation is performed in the temporal axis, and the adapted version is composed by the selection and concatenation of frames from the original sequence. For this reason, it is very convenient to describe the summarization process using tools similar to those used for video adaptation.

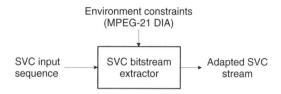

Figure 5.6 Adaptation in the SVC framework.

The advantage of SVC relies on its efficient adaptation scheme. With SVC, the adaptation engine is a simple module, known as extractor, which modifies the bitstream selecting only the parts required according to some constraints (Figure 5.6). The constraints (resolution, bitrate, etc.) are imposed by the usage environment. The extractor selects the appropriate layers of the input bitstream satisfying the constraints. The output bitstream is also conforming to the SVC standard so it can be decoded with a suitable SVC decoder.

5.6.1 MPEG-21 Tools for Usage Environment Description

The MPEG-21 standard aims at developing a normative open framework for multimedia delivery and consumption, based on the concepts of digital item (DI) as a basic unit of transaction and users as entities who interact with DIs. The objective is to enable a transparent and augmented use of multimedia data across a wide range of networks and devices. The description of the usage environment in which the multimedia content is consumed is essential to be able to adapt the content to each case in the UMA paradigm.

The usage environment description (UED) tools of MPEG-21 DIA can be used to describe, among others, the terminal capabilities and network characteristics with a standardized specification. The following example shows how some basic, but important, characteristics of the terminal and the network can be described using the *TerminalCapability* and *NetworkCharacteristics* elements. It describes the context of a user who accesses the multimedia using a PDA (with resolution 480 × 352) through a 384 kbps network.

```
<DIA>
    <Description xsi:type="UsageEnvironmentPropertyType">
        <!-- Network description -->
        <UsageEnvironmentProperty xsi:type="NetworksType">
            <Network xsi:type="NetworkType">
                <NetworkCharacteristic xsi:type="NetworkConditionType"
                    maxCapacity="384000"/>
            </Network>
        </UsageEnvironmentProperty>
        <!-- Terminal description -->
        <UsageEnvironmentProperty xsi:type="TerminalsType">
            <Terminal id="pda">
                <TerminalCapability xsi:type="DisplaysType">
                    <Display>
                        <DisplayCapability xsi:type="DisplayCapabilityType">
                            <Mode>
                                <Resolution horizontal="480" vertical="320"/>
```

```
                </Mode>
              </DisplayCapability>
            </Display>
          </TerminalCapability>
        </Terminal>
    </UsageEnvironmentProperty>
  </Description>
</DIA>
```

In the application, each user is linked at least to one UED. Each user may use different terminals or networks depending on the situation. The summarization and adaptation engine must know this information in order to deliver an appropriate version of the sequence or the summary.

5.6.2 Summarization Units in MPEG-4 SVC

The SVC standard [45] is built as an extension of AVC, including new coding tools for scalable bitstreams. SVC is based on a layered scheme, in which the bitstream is encoded into a base layer, which is AVC compliant, and one or more enhancement layers. Each enhancement layer improves the video sequence in one or more of the scalability types. There are different types of scalability, with temporal, spatial, and quality being the most important.

Spatial scalability is achieved by using interlayer prediction from a lower spatial layer, in addition to intralayer prediction mechanisms such as motion-compensated prediction and intraprediction. The same mechanism of interlayer prediction for spatial scalability can provide also coarse grain scalability (CGS) for quality scalability. It can also be achieved using medium grain scalability (MGS), which provides quality refinements inside the same spatial or CGS layer. Temporal scalability in SVC is provided using hierarchical prediction structures, already present in AVC. Each temporal enhancement layer increases the frame rate of the decoded sequence.

In SVC, the versions at different spatial and quality resolutions for a given instant form an AU, which can contain NAL units from both base and enhancement layers. Each NAL unit belongs to a specific spatial, temporal, and quality layer. This information is stored in the header of the NAL unit in the syntax elements $dependency\_id$, $temporal\_id$, and $quality\_id$. The length of the NAL unit header in AVC is extended to include this information. In SVC, the base layer is always AVC compatible. However, the extended NAL unit header would make the bitstream noncompliant with AVC. For this reason, each base layer NAL unit has a nonextended header, but it is preceded by an additional NAL unit containing the SVC-related information. These units are called *prefix NAL units*. If the stream is processed by an AVC decoder, these prefix NAL units and the other enhancement layer NAL units are simply ignored, and the base layer can still be decoded.

In SVC, the concept of SU can be extended, in order to include the additional versions given by spatial and quality scalabilities. Thus, it is possible to define more SUs with only the NAL units from the base layer, or including also NAL units from enhancement layers, having versions of each SU with different spatial resolutions and qualities. Figure 5.7 shows an example of coding structures and SUs in SVC. Discarding the enhancement layer, it is still possible to find more SUs in the base layer, as shown earlier in Figure 5.4.

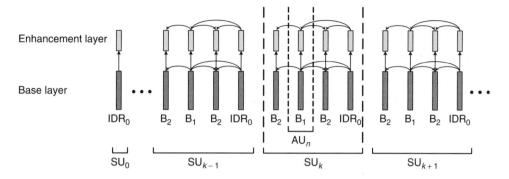

Figure 5.7   Coding structures and summarization units in SVC.

5.6.3   Extraction Process in MPEG-4 SVC

The extraction process in SVC is nonnormative, with the only constraint that the output bitstream obtained from discarding enhancement layers must be compliant with the SVC standard. The JVT provides the joint scalable video model (JSVM), including a software implementation of SVC. In this section, we briefly describe the basic extraction process of SVC in the JSVM.

The extractor processes NAL units using the syntax elements *dependency_id*, *temporal_id*, and *quality_id* to decide which must be included in the output bitstream. Each adaptation decision is then taken for each AU AU_n, where n is the temporal instant. Each layer (base or enhancement) in AU_n can be denoted as $L(d, t, q; n)$. An operation point $OP_n = (d_n, t_n, q_n)$ is a specific coordinate (d, t, q) at temporal instant n, representing a particular resolution (spatial and temporal) and quality, related, respectively, to the syntax elements *dependency_id*, *temporal_id*, and *quality_id*. If we denote the extraction process as $\mathcal{E}(OP, AU)$, the result of adapting an AU_n with a particular OP_n can be defined as the adapted $A\tilde{U}_n = \mathcal{E}(OP_n, AU_n)$, containing all the layers and data necessary to decode the sequence at this particular resolution and quality. For each AU_n, the extractor must find OP_n satisfying the constraints and maximizing the utility of the adaptation. In a typical adaptation scenario, the terminal and the network impose constraints that can be fixed (*display_width*, *display_height*, and *display_supported_rate*) or variable (*available_bits* (n) with respect to the instantaneous network bitrate at instant n). Thus, the adaptation via bitstream extraction can be formulated as an optimization problem:

for each instant n find $OP_n^* = \left(d_n^*, t_n^*, q_n^*\right)$ maximizing $utility\left(A\tilde{U}_n\right)$

subject to

$$frame\_width\,(d) \leq display\_width$$

$$frame\_height\,(d) \leq display\_height$$

$$frame\_rate\,(t) \leq display\_frame\_rate$$

$$bitsize\left(A\tilde{U}_n\right) \leq available\_bits\,(n)$$

In this formulation, $utility\left(\tilde{AU}_n\right)$ is a generic measure of utility or quality of the resulting adaptation. It should be computed or estimated for all the possible adapted AUs, in order to select the most appropriate. The actual values of resolution and frame rate can be obtained indirectly from d and t, and the size of any AU can be obtained just parsing the bitstream.

The JSVM extractor solves the problem using a prioritization approach. The NAL units in an AU are ordered in a predefined order and selected in this order until the target bitrate or size is achieved. In Figure 5.8, each block represents an NAL unit containing a layer $L(d, t, q; n)$. The base quality layer ($q = 0$) of each spatial and temporal level is placed first in the priority order. Then, NAL units including quality refinements are placed in the increasing order of their temporal level. Spatial enhancement layers are placed next. The extractor just drops the NAL units with a priority lower than the required one.

However, this prioritization scheme does not ensure the optimality of the extraction path in terms of utility. For this reason, besides the basic extraction method, SVC provides additional tools for improved extraction, namely, the optional syntax element *priority_id*, which signals explicitly the priority of each NAL unit, based on any other (nonnormative) criteria [52].

5.6.4 Including Summarization in the Framework

In the previous framework, the constraints imposed to the adaptation engine are external, due to the presence of a constrained usage environment (*environment constraints*). Adaptation modifies the resolution and quality of the bitstream, but the information in the content itself does not change. However, there is no restriction on the nature of the constraints. Summarization can be seen as a modification of the structure of the bitstream based on the

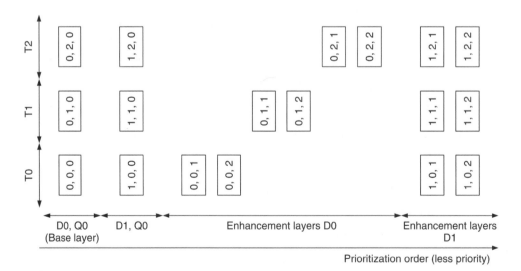

Figure 5.8 Prioritization of NAL units in the JSVM extractor (adapted from [52]).

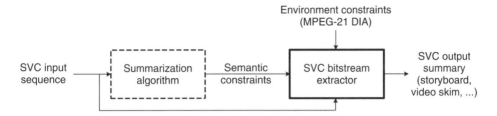

Figure 5.9 Integrated summarization and adaptation of SVC.

information in the content itself, in order to remove semantic redundancies in the temporal axis, in a constrained situation where the number of frames must be reduced considerably. For this reason, we reformulate the video summarization problem (typically, the selection of a suitable set of keyframes or segments) into the problem of finding the appropriate constraints such that the extractor generates a suitable summary. In this context, we call them *summarization constraints*. These constraints can modify the value of the temporal resolution. If both environment and summarization constraints are used together in the extraction, the result is an integrated summarization and adaptation engine, which can generate summaries adapted to the usage environment using only SVC tools (Figure 5.9).

The adaptation process, as described earlier, is performed on an AU basis. However, in the proposed summarization model, the summaries are referred to the SU index with the summarization constraint $tlevel\,(m)$, so it must be harmonized with the adaptation process. When a sequence is partitioned into SUs, each of them contains one or more AUs and, for simplicity, we assume that each AU belongs only to a single SU. Then, we define a new summarization constraint $\widetilde{tlevel}\,(n)$ for each AU_n associated to a certain SU_m:

$$\widetilde{tlevel}\,(n) \equiv tlevel\,(m)\,, \quad \mathrm{AU}_n \in \mathrm{SU}_m, \quad \forall n \in \{0, \ldots, N-1\}$$

Note that the MPEG-7 descriptions of summaries are referred to frames rather than SUs, so it is straightforward to obtain $\widetilde{tlevel}\,(n)$ from these descriptions. The problem of adaptation in the extractor, including the new summarization constraint, can now be expressed as

for each instant n find $\mathrm{OP}_n^* = \left(d_n^*, t_n^*, q_n^*\right)$ maximizing $utility\,(\mathcal{E}\,(\mathrm{OP}_n, \mathrm{AU}_n))$

subject to

$frame\_width\,(d) \le display\_width$

$frame\_height\,(d) \le display\_height$

$frame\_rate\,(t) \le display\_frame\_rate$

$bitsize\,(\mathcal{E}\,(\mathrm{OP}_n, \mathrm{AU}_n)) \le available\_bits\,(n)$

$t \le \widetilde{tlevel}\,(n)$

The last constraint makes the extraction process content-based, constraining directly the temporal level. The problem can be solved using the same tools described in the previous section, including the prioritization scheme of the JSVM. Implicitly, d, t, and q are assumed to be positive (or zero). Thus, if $\widetilde{tlevel}\,(n)$ takes a negative value for a certain n, the problem has no solution, as the new summarization constraint cannot be satisfied. In that case, we assume that the extractor will skip that AU not including any of its NAL units in the output bitstream. The summarization algorithm can take advantage of this fact to signal when a certain SU must not appear in the output bitstream.

As in the model for AVC, all the SUs must be independently decodable for all the possible adapted versions. Again, the simplest solution is the use of IDR AUs. In SVC, IDR AUs only provide random access points for a specific dependency layer. For this reason, enhancement layers must also have an IDR AU at the beginning of each SU, in order to guarantee the independence of the SUs for all layers.

5.6.5   Further Use of MPEG-21 Tools

Apart from tools to describe the usage environment, MPEG-21 provides more tools to address the challenge of developing an interoperable framework, including the adaptation of DI. Particularly, MPEG-21 DIA specifies tools to describe the adaptation decision taking and the bitstream adaptation itself. The adaptation engine has two main modules: the adaptation decision taking engine (ADTE) and the bitstream adaptation engine (BAE). The ADTE uses the context information and the constraints to make appropriate decisions, while the BAE performs the actual bitstream adaptation, according to the decisions provided by the ADTE.

The proposed framework does not follow any specific standard in these two aspects, and are dependent on the coding format used (MPEG-4 AVC/SVC). In this section, we describe how the decision taking can be done using MPEG-21 tools. In addition, we briefly describe the MPEG-21 bitstream adaptation framework, which is independent of the coding format.

5.6.5.1   Assisted Decision Taking

MPEG-21 DIA provides tools to assist the adaptation engine to take the appropriate adaptation decisions. In addition to the UED tool, the adaptation quality of service (AQoS) and universal constraints description (UCD) tools provide the required information and mechanism to steer the decision taking [53]. The AQoS tool describes what types of adaptation can be applied to a given adaptation unit (in our case, an AU), while the UCD tool declares the constraints between resources and usage environment involved in the decision taking.

The same optimization problem described earlier can be stated using AQoS and UCD tools (Figure 5.10). We used an utility-based framework, in which the ADTE selects the option that maximizes the utility given a set of constraints. In the extractor described in the previous section, the utility is not stated explicitly, but it is related to the predefined prioritization scheme following the values of the syntax elements *dependency_id*, *temporal_id*, and *quality_id* of each AU, or the more flexible approach using *priority_id*. However, depending on the application, it can be estimated by the extractor, the encoder,

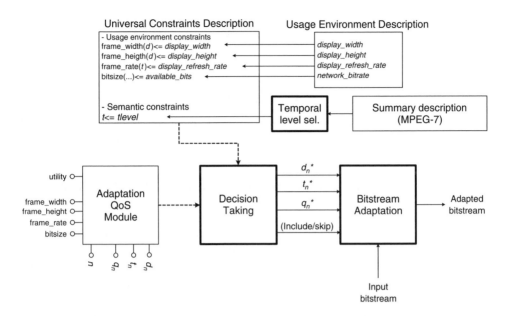

Figure 5.10   Summarization and adaptation engine using MPEG-21 DIA tools.

or any other module and can be available as external metadata, using the MPEG-21 AQoS description tool [53].

The AQoS description contains two main components: modules and IOPins. The IOPins are input and/or output parameters corresponding to fixed values and/or variables. These IOPins can be dependent or independent from other IOPins. In Figure 5.10, there are some independent IOPins that correspond to the variables d_n, t_n, and q_n. Other IOPins such as *frame_width* and *frame_rate* depend directly on single IOPins (e.g., d_n and t_n respectively), while others, such as *utility*, depend on the combination of all these variables. The value of the utility can be specified using one of the three available modules: lookup table, utility function and stack function. Depending on the application, a suitable module must be used.

The UCD declares constraints between the characteristics of the usage environment (described in the UED) and the feasible values of the IOPins. For instance, *frame_width* cannot be greater than the value of *display_width* specified in the UED.

As explained earlier, the summarization process is included as additional constraints in the UCD [3]. If usage environment constraints are obtained from the UED, summarization constraints are obtained from the MPEG-7 description of the summary. In order to follow the same summarization model used in the previous sections, we propose the conversion of the description of the summary to the temporal level *tlevel* of each SU, which is used in the constraint $t \leq tlevel$, declared also in the UCD. However, it is possible to use different mechanisms to link the value of the frames and segments in the summary to the UCD.

For each adaptation unit, the ADTE parses both UCD and AQoS descriptions and tries to find a feasible solution, given the constraints. If there is no feasible solution, the decision is to skip the adaptation unit, which means that it is not included in the summary. If there are feasible solutions, the ADTE looks for that with the maximum utility, as stated in the AQoS, and obtains the solution (d_n^*, t_n^*, q_n^*). Then, the BAE selects the appropriate packets from the bitstream according to the solution, and includes these packets into the bitstream of the adapted summary.

5.6.5.2 Bitstream Syntax Description Framework

In our framework, the BAE corresponds to the SVC bitstream extractor of the JSVM. However, the extractor is a nonstandard module. Different coding formats need specific BAEs according to their syntax. To solve this dependence on the coding format, MPEG-21 DIA defines a generic framework for bitstream adaptation, independent of the coding format. This framework is based on XML and the concept of BSD [47]. A BSD is an XML document describing, in a standard way, the high level structure of a bitstream. The adapted bitstream is described by another BSD. The adaptation process consists of the transformation of the first BSD into the second one. Any XML transformation language, such as XSLT or STX, can be used to describe this transformation.

The syntax of a coding format is also described in BS schema, and it is used by a specific processor called *BintoBSD* to generate the BSD from the input bitstream. Once the output BSD is obtained, the output bitstream is generated by another processor called *BSDtoBin*. Along with the BSD, MPEG-21 DIA also defines the generic bitstream syntax description (gBSD), which is a generic version of BSD.

Scalable formats are organized in such a way that it is easy to obtain adapted versions using few operations such as data truncation and simple header modifications. BSD-based adaptation is very suitable for these formats. For instance, SVC can be adapted using BSDs, so the JSVM extractor could be replaced by an extractor based on BSDs, as described in [54].

5.7 Experimental Evaluation

This section describes some experiments to evaluate the main advantage of the framework, which is the efficient generation of the bitstream of adapted summaries. Thus, experiments were directed to evaluate the performance in terms of efficiency. For comparison, we also provide experimental results with an alternative approach based on transcoding.

5.7.1 Test Scenario

We assume a test usage scenario with users using two types of terminals capable of decoding AVC and SVC: (i) a PDA with a display of 480×320 pixels in a medium capacity network and (ii) a mobile phone with a display of 174×144 in a low capacity network. We also assume that the mobile phone cannot render sequences at a rate greater than 15 frames per second.

We used the reference software JSVM 9.8 in the simulations. The test sequence is an excerpt of 10001 frames from the sequence *news12* (CIF (common intermediate format, 352×288 pixels) resolution and 25 frames per second) from the MPEG-7 content set [55]. The sequence was encoded in SVC with two spatial levels and two quality levels, using CGS for quality scalability, with one base layer and three enhancement layers. The details of these layers are shown in Table 5.1. Dyadic hierarchical structures were used

Table 5.1 Settings of the layers for SVC encoding

Layer number	Spatial resolution	Temporal resolution (Hz)	Quality resolution (QP)
0	QCIF[a]	25	38
1	QCIF[a]	25	32
2	CIF[b]	25	38
3	CIF[b]	25	32

[a]QCIF - quarter common intermediate format.
[b]CIF - common intermediate format.

for temporal scalability with GOP (group of pictures) lengths from 1 to 32 frames (1 to 6 temporal levels). In order to compare the approach with a nonscalable approach, the sequence was also encoded with AVC with the same settings of the layer 3 in Table 5.1.

Given the test scenario, we considered two target conditions to test the performance of the framework:

- **CIF@25**. Both spatial and temporal resolutions do not change with respect to the original bitstream. Therefore, neither spatial nor temporal adaptation will be required, and only efficiency in the generation of summaries is studied. This is the adaptation path for the PDA case.
- **QCIF@12.5**. In this scenario, there is adaptation in both spatial and temporal resolutions. Both generation of the summary and adaptation to the target conditions are studied. This is the adaptation path for the mobile case.

The main advantage of the proposed framework is the efficient generation of adapted summaries. Thus, the experiments are directed to evaluate the performance in terms of efficiency. For comparison, we also provided experimental results with an alternative approach based on transcoding. The summaries were generated and adapted to the test conditions with the following methods (Table 5.2):

- **AVC Transcoding**. In this approach, the sequence is first decoded to YUV format. The summary is generated and adapted (if required) into another YUV sequence, which is finally encoded to H.264/AVC.
- **SVC Extraction**. It uses the SVC bitstream extractor to select the required packets and to generate the adapted summary.
- **AVC Extraction**. The same bitstream extractor is used for this case. This method can be used only when neither spatial nor quality adaptation is required.
- **AVC Hybrid**. This method complements the previous one, as the summary is first generated using AVC extraction, and then it is transcoded. Note that, compared to transcoding, only a few frames (depending on the length of the summary) are transcoded, as most of them were discarded during extraction.

For AVC transcoding and AVC hybrid methods, the settings of the encoder were modified to significantly reduce the computational burden due to encoding and, specifically, due to motion estimation. Thus, a fast search method was used with a smaller search range (8 pixels).

Table 5.2 Methods and cases used in the experiments

Method (resolution)	Spatial resolution (input/output)	Temporal resolution (input/output) (Hz)
AVC transcoding (CIF@25)	CIF/CIF	25/25
AVC transcoding (QCIF@12.5)	CIF/QCIF	25/12.5
AVC extraction (CIF@25)	CIF/CIF	25/25
AVC hybrid (QCIF@12.5)	CIF/QCIF	25/12.5
SVC extraction (CIF@25)	CIF/CIF	25/25
SVC extraction (QCIF@12.5)	CIF/QCIF	25/12.5
SVC extraction (CIF@25 low)	CIF/CIF	25/25
SVC extraction (QCIF@12.5 low)	CIF/QCIF	25/12.5

5.7.2 Summarization Algorithm

The summarization algorithm itself, in terms of analysis, is out of the scope of this chapter. Most conventional summarization algorithms [9] could be used in this framework, adapted to its requirements. For instance, analysis results must be referred to SUs rather than frames, in order to match the units used in the generation of the bitstream. In these experiments, we considered two modalities of summaries: storyboards and video skims, computed using the algorithm described in [4]. This algorithm uses spectral clustering [56] to group similar information into clusters. Then, keyframes or segments are selected to represent the clusters in the summary.

For each summary, we first computed the summarization constraint to be used. For a given summary, the same summarization constraint was used for every method tested, in order to have the same selected frames. Figure 5.11 shows the summarization constraints, for both storyboard and video skim, in the test sequence encoded with a GOP length of 8 frames.

The algorithm described in [4] does not generate fast-forward summaries. An example of summarization constraint for this case is shown in Figure 5.12. It was obtained using a different approach described in [3]. In this approach, a measure of activity is computed for every SU, obtaining an activity curve that eventually drives the playback. This curve is then quantized to obtain the summarization constraint, according to the number of temporal scales. Static and low active segments are temporally subsampled so these segments are sped up, while segments with high activity are played at the original rate. Figure 5.13 shows the frames of the resulting fast-forward summary after constraining the extraction with the summarization constraint shown in Figure 5.12. The original sequence was created by concatenating three sequences of 300 frames each. In this example, few frames are selected from the first sequence as it is much more static compared to the other two sequences. Note that this alternative method is presented only as a complement to the previous summarization algorithm, and is not considered in the experimental results described in the next section.

5.7.3 Experimental Results

In the first experiment, the different methods were compared for several modalities and summary lengths, ranging from the empty to the whole sequence. The test sequence was

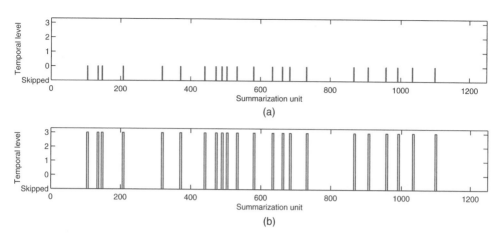

Figure 5.11   Examples of summarization constraint $tlevel(m)$ for the test sequence: (a) storyboard and (b) video skim.

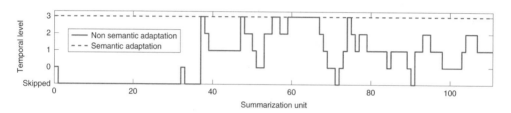

Figure 5.12   Example of summarization constraint $tlevel(m)$ in fast-forward summary using motion activity.

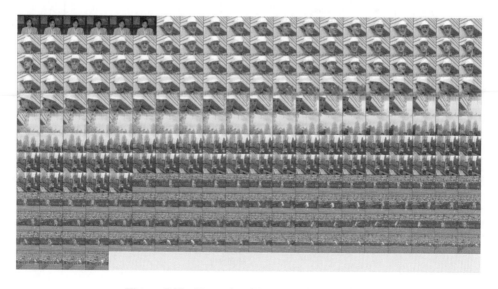

Figure 5.13   Example of fast-forward summary.

encoded with a GOP of 8 frames. As expected, transcoding is much slower than methods based on extraction. As expected, SVC- and AVC extractions have good performance. The latter is about two times faster, as the extractor needs to parse and process packets from a single layer, instead of the four layers as in SVC extraction.

Methods based on extraction also have an almost constant performance for all the summary lengths. Methods based on transcoding are more sensitive, but still very constant, with the length of the summary. Most of the processing time in transcoding is due to decoding, as encoding complexity is reduced and only a few frames are encoded in contrast to the decoding of all frames. However, a significant increment of the processing time can be noticed for longer summaries. The hybrid method performs very fast for storyboards with few frames, but the processing time increases rapidly for longer summaries, because of transcoding.

The generation of a summary with the 0% of the frames in the sequence (an empty summary) is very useful to have a reference of the time used in initialization and other processes independent of the length of the summary. In transcoding, this time is due to the decoding of all frames, and it is the most important contribution to the overall processing time. In the case of extraction, the JSVM extractor performs the extraction in two passes. In the first pass, all the NAL headers are parsed in order to obtain a description of the bitstream, which is then used to perform the actual extraction. As it can be seen in Figure 5.14, most of the extraction time is used in this first pass.

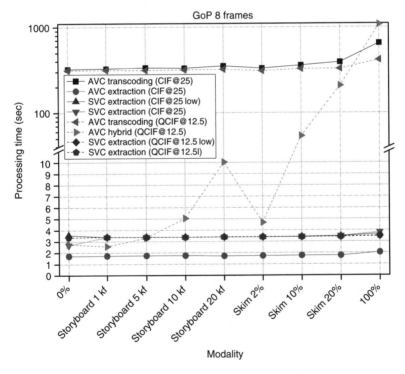

Figure 5.14 Processing time for different modalities. Note that half of the vertical scale is linear and the rest is logarithmic.

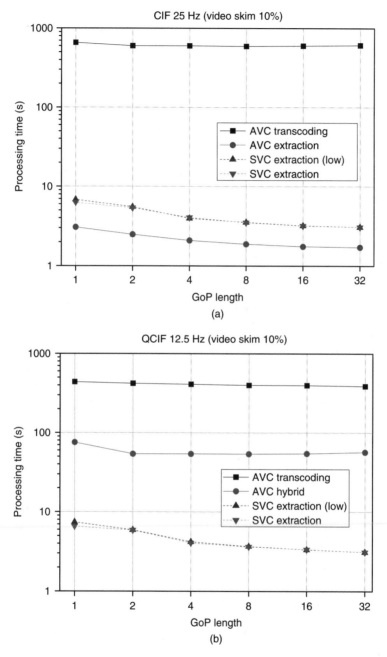

Figure 5.15 Dependency of the processing time with the GOP length: (a) CIF 25 Hz and (b) QCIF 12.5 Hz.

An important parameter in the framework is the SU length (GOP length in the experiments), as it is related to the precision in analysis, coding efficiency, and also processing time in the generation of the bitstream. Figure 5.15 shows the results for a video skim (10% of the total length) with the different methods tested. It shows that the processing time is almost constant with the GOP length, for both transcoding and extraction.

As experiments have shown, a simple solution based on extraction has a better performance than others based on transcoding, for the purpose of video summarization. A hybrid solution based on both extraction and transcoding can also be useful when no spatial or quality scalability are available, especially for short summaries such as storyboards.

5.8 Conclusions

In this chapter, we described an application using tools from three MPEG standards in the context of video summarization. Summaries are described using MPEG-7 MDS summarization tools, while the information about the usage environment, mainly terminal and network characteristics, is described using the UED tool specified in MPEG-21 DIA. The main advantage of having public and standarized syntax is the possibility of reusing the same descriptions in other applications and systems with MPEG-7 and MPEG-21-compliant devices, capable of parsing them.

The chapter also describes the use of MPEG-4 AVC and its extension MPEG-4 SVC for summarization purposes. The use of an integrated approach has several advantages. One is that the generation of the summary has all the advantages of bitstream extraction in terms of efficiency. Another advantage is the adaptation, in the same process, of summaries to a specific usage environment, using the layered approach of SVC.

References

[1] Yeung, M. and Yeo, B.-L. (1997) Video visualization for compact presentation and fast browsing of pictorial content. *IEEE Transactions on Circuits and Systems for Video Technology*, **7** (5), 771–785.

[2] Pfeiffer, S., Lienhart, R., Fischer, S., and Effelsberg, W. (1996) Abstracting digital movies automatically. *Journal of Visual Communication And Image Representation*, **7** (4), 345–353.

[3] Herranz, L. (2007) Integrating semantic analysis and scalable video coding for efficient content-based adaptation. *Multimedia Systems*, **13** (2), 103–118.

[4] Herranz, L. and Martínez, J.M. (2009) An integrated approach to summarization and adaptation using H.264/MPEG-4 SVC. *Signal Processing-Image Communication*, **24** (6), 499–509. scalable Coded Media beyond Compression.

[5] Chang, H.S., Sull, S., and Lee, S.U. (1999) Efficient video indexing scheme for content-based retrieval. *IEEE Transactions on Circuits and Systems for Video Technology*, **9** (8), 1269–1279.

[6] Dimitrova, N., Zhang, H.-J., Shahraray, B. *et al.* (2002) Applications of video-content analysis and retrieval. *IEEE Multimedia*, **9** (3), 42–55.

[7] Zhu, X., Elmagarmid, A., Xue, X. *et al.* (2005) InsightVideo: toward hierarchical video content organization for efficient browsing, summarization and retrieval. *IEEE Transactions on Multimedia*, **7** (4), 648–666.

[8] Li, Z., Schuster, G., Katsaggelos, A., and Gandhi, B. (2005) Rate-distortion optimal video summary generation. *IEEE Transactions on Image Processing*, **14** (10), 1550–1560.

[9] Truong, B.T. and Venkatesh, S. (2007) Video abstraction: a systematic review and classification. *ACM Transactions on Multimedia Computing, Communications and Applications*, **3** (1), 3.

[10] Money, A.G. and Agius, H. (2008) Video summarisation: a conceptual framework and survey of the state of the art. *Journal of Visual Communication and Image Representation*, **19** (2), 121–143.

[11] Marchionini, G., Wildemuth, B.M., and Geisler, G. (2006) The Open Video digital library: a Möbius strip of research and practice. *Journal of the American Society for Information Science and Technology*, **57** (12), 1629–1643.

[12] Ma, Y.-F., Hua, X.-S., Lu, L., and Zhang, H.-J. (2005) A generic framework of user attention model and its application in video summarization. *IEEE Transactions on Multimedia*, **7** (5), 907–919.

[13] Smith, M. and Kanade, T. (1998) Video skimming and characterization through the combination of image and language understanding. Proceedings of the IEEE International Workshop on Content-based Access of Image and Video Database, January 3, pp. 61–70.

[14] Li, Y., Lee, S.-H., Yeh, C.-H., and Kuo, C.-C. (2006) Techniques for movie content analysis and skimming: tutorial and overview on video abstraction techniques. *IEEE Signal Processing Magazine*, **23** (2), 79–89.

[15] Wildemuth, B., Marchionini, G., Yang, M., *et al.* (2003) How fast is too fast? Evaluating fast forward surrogates for digital video. Proceedings of the Joint Conference on Digital Libraries, May 27–31, pp. 221–230.

[16] Peker, K., Divakaran, A., and Sun, H. (2001) Constant pace skimming and temporal sub-sampling of video using motion activity. Proceedings of the International Conference on Image Processing, **3**, 414–417.

[17] Bescos, J., Martinez, J.M., Herranz, L., and Tiburzi, F. (2007) Content-driven adaptation of on-line video. *Signal Processing-Image Communication*, **22**, 651–668.

[18] Lotfallah, O.A., Reisslein, M., and Panchanathan, S. (2006) Adaptive video transmission schemes using MPEG-7 motion intensity descriptor. *IEEE Transactions on Circuits and Systems for Video Technology*, **16** (8), 929–946.

[19] Gang, Z., Chia, L.-T., and Zongkai, Y. (2004) MPEG-21 digital item adaptation by applying perceived motion energy to H.264 video. *International Conference on Image Processing*, **4**, 2777–2780.

[20] Calic, J., Gibson, D., and Campbell, N. (2007) Efficient layout of comic-like video summaries. *IEEE Transactions on Circuits and Systems for Video Technology*, **17** (7), 931–936.

[21] Mrak, M., Calic, J., and Kondoz, A. (2009) Fast analysis of scalable video for adaptive browsing interfaces. *Computer Vision and Image Understanding*, **113** (3), 425–4434. Special Issue on Video Analysis.

[22] Ngo, C.-W., Ma, Y.-F., and Zhang, H.-J. (2003) Automatic video summarization by graph modeling. Proceedings of the 19th IEEE International Conference on Computer Vision, vol. 1, pp. 104–109.

[23] Maybury, M., Greiff, W., Boykin, S. *et al.* (2004) Personalcasting: tailored broadcast news. *User Modeling and User-Adapted Interaction*, **14** (1), 119–144.

[24] Damnjanovic, U., Piatrik, T., Djordjevic, D., and Izquierdo, E. (2007) Video summarisation for surveillance and news domain, *Semantic Multimedia*, series Lecture Notes in Computer Science, vol. 4816, Springer-Verlag, Berlin, pp. 99–112.

[25] Lie, W.-N. and Lai, C.-M. (2005) News video summarization based on spatial and motion feature analysis, *Advances in Multimedia Information Processing – PCM 2004*, Series Lecture Notes in Computer Science, vol. 3332, Springer-Verlag, Berlin, pp. 246–255.

[26] Zhang, H.J., Wu, J., Zhong, D., and Smoliar, S.W. (1997) An integrated system for content-based video retrieval and browsing. *Pattern Recognition*, **30** (4), 643–658. Image Databases.

[27] Peng, W.-T., Huang, W.-J., Chu, W.-T. *et al.* (2008) A user experience model for home video summarization, *Semantic Multimedia*, Series Lecture Notes in Computer Science, vol. 5371, Springer-Verlag, Berlin, pp. 484–495.

[28] Fonseca, P.M. and Pereira, F. (2004) Automatic video summarization based on MPEG-7 descriptions. *Signal Processing-Image Communication*, **19** (8), 685–699.

[29] Over, P., Smeaton, A.F., and Kelly, P. (2007) The TRECVid 2007 BBC rushes summarization evaluation pilot, *TVS '07: Proceedings of the International Workshop on TRECVID Video Summarization*, ACM, New York, pp. 1–15.

[30] Over, P., Smeaton, A.F., and Awad, G. (2008) The TRECVid 2008 BBC rushes summarization evaluation, *TVS '08: Proceedings of the 2nd ACM TRECVid Video Summarization Workshop*, ACM, New York, pp. 1–20.

[31] Ren, J. and Jiang, J. (2009) Hierarchical modeling and adaptive clustering for real-time summarization of rush videos. *Transactions on Multimedia IEEE*, **11** (5), 906–917.

[32] Chang, S.-F. and Vetro, A. (2005) Video adaptation: concepts, technologies, and open issues. *Proceedings of the IEEE*, **93** (1), 148–158.

[33] Vetro, A. (2004) MPEG-21 digital item adaptation: enabling universal multimedia access. *IEEE Multimedia*, **11** (1), 84–87.

[34] Tseng, B., Lin, C.-Y., and Smith, J. (2004) Using MPEG-7 and MPEG-21 for personalizing video. *IEEE Multimedia*, **11** (1), 42–52.

[35] Cavallaro, A., Steiger, O., and Ebrahimi, T. (2005) Semantic video analysis for adaptive content delivery and automatic description. *IEEE Transactions on Circuits and Systems for Video Technology*, **15** (10), 1200–1209.

[36] Cheng, W.-H., Wang, C.-W., and Wu, J.-L. (2007) Video adaptation for small display based on content recomposition. *IEEE Transactions on Circuits and Systems for Video Technology*, **17** (1), 43–58.

[37] van Beek, P., Smith, J., Ebrahimi, T. *et al.* (2003) Metadata-driven multimedia access. *IEEE Signal Processing Magazine*, **20** (2), 40–52.

[38] Magalhaes, J. and Pereira, F. (2004) Using MPEG standards for multimedia customization. *Signal Processing-Image Communication*, **19** (5), 437–456.

[39] Ahmad, I., Wei, X., Sun, Y., and Zhang, Y.-Q. (2005) Video transcoding: an overview of various techniques and research issues. *IEEE Transactions on Multimedia*, **7** (5), 793–804.

[40] Xin, J., Lin, C.-W., and Sun, M.-T. (2005) Digital video transcoding. *Proceedings of the IEEE*, **93** (1), 84–97.

[41] Böszörményi, L., Hellwagner, H., Kosch, H. *et al.* (2003) Metadata driven adaptation in the ADMITS project. *Signal Processing-Image Communication*, **18** (8), 749–766. Special Issue on Multimedia Adaptation.

[42] Libsie, M. and Kosch, H. (2004) Video adaptation using the variation factory. Proceedings of the IEEE 6th Workshop on Multimedia Signal Processing, pp. 403–406.

[43] Adami, N., Signoroni, A., and Leonardi, R. (2007) State-of-the-art and trends in scalable video compression with wavelet-based approaches. *IEEE Transactions on Circuits and Systems for Video Technology*, **17** (9), 1238–1255.

[44] Ohm, J.-R. (2005) Advances in scalable video coding. *Proceedings of the IEEE*, **93** (1), 42–56.

[45] Schwarz, H., Marpe, D., and Wiegand, T. (2007) Overview of the scalable video coding extension of the H.264/AVC standard. *IEEE Transactions on Circuits and Systems for Video Technology*, **17** (9), 1103–1120.

[46] Sullivan, G.J. and Wiegand, T. (2005) Video compression – from concepts to the H.264/AVC standard. *Proceedings of the IEEE*, **93** (1), 18–31.

[47] Devillers, S., Timmerer, C., Heuer, J., and Hellwagner, H. (2005) Bitstream syntax description-based adaptation in streaming and constrained environments. *IEEE Transactions on Multimedia*, **7** (3), 463–470.

[48] ITU-T,ISO/IEC (2003) 21000-7. Information Technology – Multimedia Framework (MPEG-21) – Part 7: Digital Item Adaptation.

[49] De Bruyne, S., De Schrijver, D., De Neve, W. *et al.* (2007) Enhanced shot-based video adaptation using mpeg-21 generic bitstream syntax schema. IEEE Symposium on Computational Intelligence in Image and Signal Processing, CIISP 2007, April 1–5, 2007, pp. 380–385.

[50] ITU-T, ISO/IEC (2001) 15938-5. *Information Technology – Multimedia Content Description Interface – Part 5: Multimedia Description Schemes*.

[51] Herranz, L. and Martínez, J.M. (2009) On the use of hierarchical prediction structures for efficient summary generation of H.264/AVC bitstreams. *Signal Processing-Image Communication*, **24** (8), 615–629.

[52] Amonou, I., Cammas, N., Kervadec, S., and Pateux, S. (2007) Optimized rate-distortion extraction with quality layers in the scalable extension of H.264/AVC. *IEEE Transactions on Circuits and Systems for Video Technology*, **17** (9), 1186–1193.

[53] Mukherjee, D., Delfosse, E., Kim, J.G., and Wang, Y. (2005) Optimal adaptation decision-taking for terminal and network quality-of-service. *IEEE Transactions on Multimedia*, **7** (3), 454–462.

[54] De Schrijver, D., De Neve, W., Van de Walle, R. *et al.* (2006) MPEG-21 bitstream syntax descriptions for scalable video codecs. *Multimedia Systems*, **11** (5), 403–421.

[55] Paek, S. (1998) Description of MPEG-7 Content Set. Tech. Rep. N2467 ISO/IEC JTC1/SC29/WG11N2467, ISO/IEC JTC1/SC29/WG11. Atlantic City.

[56] Ng, A.Y., Jordan, M.I., and Weiss, Y. (2001) On spectral clustering: analysis and an algorithm, in *Advances in Neural Information Processing Systems*, vol. 14 (eds T.G. Dietterich, S. Becker and Z. Ghahramani), Neural Information Processing Systems (NIPS) Foundation, Vancouver, Canada.

6

Encryption Techniques for H.264 Video

Bai-Ying Lei[1], Kwok-Tung Lo[1], and Jian Feng[2]
[1]*Department of Electronic and Information Engineering, The Hong Kong Polytechnic University, Hong Kong*
[2]*Department of Computer Science, Hong Kong Baptist University, Hong Kong*

6.1 Introduction

With the rapid development of information technology, multimedia data are transmitted over all kinds of wired/wireless networks more and more frequently. A number of information servers are available for people to access various multimedia contents such as digital images, video, and audio through the network. Consequently, the security of multimedia data becomes a serious concern of many people. However, the traditional text encryption schemes cannot be used in a naive way to protect multimedia data efficiently in some applications, mainly due to the big differences between textual and multimedia data and some special requirements of the entire multimedia system. This challenge stirs the design of special multimedia encryption schemes to become a hot research topic in multimedia signal processing area in the past decade.

Data encryption is one of the key information security technologies used for safeguarding multimedia content from unauthorized access. The simplest way of video encryption is to use a textual cipher, such as Advanced Encryption Standard (AES) and Data Encryption Standard (DES), to encrypt the digital video as an 1D bitstream, which is called *naive encryption* in the literature. However, naive encryption is not suitable for some security applications of video encryption, due to the following special considerations on video encryption: (i) the trade-off between bulky data and slow speed; (ii) the trade-off between compression efficiency and encryption performance; (iii) dependence of encryption on details of compression algorithms; (iv) incapability of lossy compression in some conditions; (v) some special features of video encryption, such as format compliance,

The Handbook of MPEG Applications: Standards in Practice   Edited by Marios C. Angelides and Harry Agius
© 2011 John Wiley & Sons, Ltd

scalability, perceptibility, error tolerability, and so on. To fulfill the special demands on video encryption, recently, many specific video encryption schemes have been proposed.

As the latest video coding standard, H.264/MPEG-4 advanced video coding (AVC) [1, 2] has become the most promising technique for future video communications. This chapter will focus on the encryption techniques for H.264 video. A major concern in the design of H.264 encryption algorithms is how to achieve a sufficiently high level of security, while maintaining the efficiency of the underlying compression algorithm. H.264 encryption in the compressed domain should take into account not only serving sensitive digital contents but also offering security to ensure digital rights management and confidentiality. In this chapter, a review on various video encryption techniques will be given. Feasibility study on various techniques meeting application specific criteria will be carried out and some problems of these existing techniques will be pointed out. A novel joint compression and encryption scheme based on the context-based adaptive binary arithmetic coding (CABAC) module of H.264 video codec is presented using a chaotic stream cipher. The proposed encryption scheme provides an efficient way to scramble the video streams and the feasibility for H.264 video content protection, which would serve rapidly increasing demands of multimedia security and copyright protection in some typical applications and to prevent illegal users from plagiarizing. Some possible directions on H.264 encryption will be also discussed in this chapter.

6.2   Demands for Video Security

The proliferation of digital video products and Internet technology enables the widespread use of digital video for many distributed multimedia applications such as video-on-demand (VoD), videoconferencing, and IPTV. However, the challenging issues such as unauthorized access, copying and/or redistributing the digital video data, forgeries of video data, and copyright violation have caused serious legal, social, and economic effects. Consequently, the content protection issue of multimedia data, especially for video from device manufacturers, content creators, artwork creators as well as end users of video applications, has gained much attention. Hence, multimedia data security is becoming an important focus of the multimedia business and industrial realization. For example, it is expected that only those persons who paid for the services can view the videos in a VoD system, while we hope that only the specific groups of people can watch the video in videoconferencing. Obviously, it is desirable to provide a secure way to distribute and deliver video data, which is of great significance for digital video applications. Currently, there are mainly two technologies for protection of video content as follows:

- encryption technology to provide end-to-end security;
- watermarking technology to achieve copyright protection.

Multimedia encryption [3] encrypts media data into incomprehensible and not clearly understood ones with their own ciphers, which can protect media content's confidentiality efficiently. The encrypted videos are often too complicated and difficult to be understood. Different from other data encryption schemes such as text and images, video encryption should be format compliant and time efficient to satisfy the real-time requirement of lots of applications such as videoconferencing, pay-TV services, distribution of commercial, medical, governmental, and military videos, and sharing of private videos (e.g., multimedia short messages via mobile phones and PDAs) [4]. Indeed, due to the high computational cost, it is not feasible and practical to adopt the traditional ciphers such as DES or AES completely and blindly in video data encryption [5]. Meanwhile, by modifying the data slightly and adaptively, watermarking is another method to embed hidden content protection information into digital media to protect the video data and achieve security.

6.3 Issues on Digital Video Encryption

With the development of information technology, distribution of digital video contents over various channels becomes more and more frequent. Meanwhile, security of video data becomes more and more important. Therefore, the demand for secure and fast encryption schemes for digital video has greatly increased in the recent few years. Unlike plain text, encryption of digital video has its own unique properties. First, the size of video data is very large although compression is employed. The video coding system, storage systems, and network communications have to bear a great burden when processing the huge volume of data. Second, video encryption needs to be done in real-time in many applications. Heavy-weight encryption algorithms (during or after the encoding phase) will aggregate the problem and increase the latency, and are likely to become a performance bottleneck for multimedia applications. Third, video data is time dependent and must be well synchronized. Encryption must be done within time restrictions and keep temporal relations among multimedia streams intact. Such characteristics make video encryption more difficult. In the following text, we highlight some of the major concerns for the design of video encryption process.

6.3.1 Security Issue

A lot of cryptanalysis work has been done for many existing video encryption schemes [6–8]. On the basis of the results of their work, the security of those schemes that do not use standard cryptographic algorithms is not very high. Even for those using standard cryptographic algorithms such as DES and AES, many security problems still exist. The encryption schemes using standard encryption algorithms are easier to be proven secure, but they may not satisfy other requirements such as time constraints. The video encryption scheme should take different applications into consideration with different security levels. Generally, some important things should be considered when designing a video encryption scheme and the most important aspect is security for video encryption schemes. The video encryption algorithms (VEAs) should be able to resist different attacks such as chosen-plaintext attacks, ciphertext-only attacks, known-plaintext attacks, cryptanalytic attacks, and perceptual attacks. In order to design an efficient video encryption scheme with high security for video data, the characteristics of digital video data should be utilized sufficiently.

6.3.2 Complexity Issue

As video contains huge amount of data, computational complexity is another main concern for video encryption. Some methods can provide substantial security for video data.

However, the computational overhead and data overhead become worse. Some special considerations and designs are needed to alleviate the large processing burden. Another important consideration of video encryption scheme design is the processing overhead generated in encryption process. In order to decrease the processing overhead, it is necessary to encrypt only a portion of video data; as a result, the selection of object data becomes a key job, which is known as *selective encryption*. On the other hand, it is important to adopt some light-weight encryption algorithms [9], which have low computational complexity to relieve the computation problem.

6.3.3 Feasibility Issue

Feasibility is another problem existing in many schemes of VEAs [10]. A lot of existing schemes are the so-called integrated video compression and encryption system [11–13]. It means that the video encryption module must be integrated into video compression system and can be conducted in one single step. In other words, the encryption is integrated with compression by introducing randomness into the compressor. For example, permutation of AC, DC coefficients should be done before entropy coding. In this way, the encryption should break the procedure of video compression, and the encryption module must be integrated into video compression system. That is why the standard decoder cannot work when applying encrypted video data. The corresponding decoder to this kind of encoder should be an integrated video decompression and decryption decoder. This causes such kind of schemes that are very hard to be really used in a commercial application. More specifically, this problem is investigated in the entropy coding stage due to the following reasons:

- It is easy to identify which components contribute most to the overall image/video quality in the entropy coding stage. This is very desirable for designing a selective encryption method to achieve security with small number of resources.
- The bit stream after entropy coding is compressed compared with the original content. Therefore, the number of coefficients to be encrypted is less than the original content. This is helpful to reduce the system complexity.
- Entropy coding and encryption have many similarities, such as, random-like bit stream. By introducing randomness into the entropy coding, we can obtain a system having many cryptographically nice properties.

6.4 Previous Work on Video Encryption

In the past two decades, a number of encryption algorithms have been proposed to protect video contents [3, 14–34]. A major concern in the design of these VEAs is how to achieve a sufficiently high level of security, while maintaining the efficiency of the underlying compression algorithm. A commonality that can be found from the previous work [18, 21, 22] is that, to achieve both of the effective encryption, all the encryption methods have to make good use of the features of video encoding schemes. Actually, the purpose of the encryption process is to encrypt the extremely small portions of the entire video stream in order to reduce the computations in the encryption/decryption process, and to make it secure against known attacks. According to where the encryption operations are performed with respect to multimedia compression, there are three possible approaches of realizing multimedia encryption:

1. precompression encryption: encryption before compression;
2. postcompression encryption: encryption after compression;
3. joint compression and encryption: the compression followed by encryption with a partial decompression–recompression process.

The first approach is the most direct and simplest one. One consideration in this approach is that the encryption scheme should not provide adverse impact to the compression efficiency of video compression tools. That means the encryption schemes should introduce as few bit overhead to video bitstream as possible. A large amount of bit overhead will increase the processing time and power consumption of video codec. Qiao and Nahrstedt [14] presented an encryption method called *video encryption algorithm* (VEA) for MPEG video by making use of the statistical features of the compressed data. The VEA algorithm divides the video streams into chunks, which are further separated into lists. Light-weight operation, the exclusive OR (XOR) operation, and highly efficient encryption algorithm, the DES algorithm, are used to encrypt certain parts of the lists. Tang [23] proposed four levels of encryptions for MPEG video: (i) encrypting all headers, (ii) encrypting all headers and I frames, (iii) encrypting all I frames and all I blocks in P and B frames, and (iv) encrypting all frames. Another method for encrypting MPEG video was proposed by Shi and Bhargava [15], whose basic idea is to use a secret key to randomly change the sign bits of all the discrete cosine transform (DCT) coefficients of MPEG video. Although, using very light-weight encryption, these methods do not provide high security; however, the algorithm is highly efficient for scrambling the video stream in real-time. Zhu *et al*. [24], discussed the scalable protection for MPEG-4. By making use of the mechanism of fine granularity scalability (FGS), the authors proposed two novel encryption algorithms to adapt to the varying network traffic conditions. The first algorithm encrypts an FGS stream into a single access layer and preserves the original scalability and error resilience performance. The second algorithm encrypts an FGS stream into multiple quality layers divided according to peak signal to noise ratio (PSNR) and bit rates. Both the algorithms enable intermediate stages to process encrypted data directly without decryption. Therefore, the algorithm preserves most adaptation capabilities of FGS.

By simply employing a traditional cipher to the output of the video coder, the syntax format of the compressed multimedia data will be destroyed, and any further multimedia processing on the encrypted data will not be possible. However, format compliance of encrypted multimedia data is very useful in a lot of real applications, such as the following ones:

- Postprocessing of encrypted multimedia data without decryption: watermark embedding, rescrambling, transcoding, bitrate control, repacketization, and so on.
- Perceptual encryption [35]: encryption is used to degrade the visual quality of the target multimedia data and the encrypted data is still decodable and replayable by any standard-compliant decoder, which is useful for preview-before-pay multimedia services.
- Scalable encryption (or multilayer encryption): different resolutions of the same multimedia data have different encryption configurations.

- Region-of-interest (ROI) encryption: only part of the whole multimedia data needs to be kept secret, for example, human faces of criminals and witnesses in a court video.
- Error-resilient encryption: the error-resilient mechanism embedded in the multimedia syntax format is exploited to make the multimedia encryption system insensitive to transmission errors.

To achieve format compliance, it is obvious that the multimedia data cannot be fully encrypted. Hence, selective (partial) encryption has to be adopted to exclude some syntax elements from being encrypted. This means joint compression-encryption.

The second approach for performing encryption after compression, will be quite difficult as encryption generally leads to a random output with very high entropy that cannot be further compressed effectively. A recent work based on distributed source coding was proposed by Bose and Pathak [36], taking the encryption key as useful side information available at the decoder side. However, decoding is generally impossible without the knowledge of the key. Therefore, decryption and decoding have to be carried out simultaneously, which is not desirable in some real applications. Also, this scheme adds some requirements on the encryption algorithm involved such that not all available ciphers can be freely chosen and deployed. Another problem is that too many modifications have to be made on existing standards, which makes it very difficult to be adopted in future standards.

Different from the first two approaches, the joint encryption and compression approach is more promising and has attracted much more attention in recent years. Since the early 1990s, a large number of joint compression-encryption schemes have been proposed, most of which were designed based on one of the following basic encryption techniques or their combinations:

- Secret permutations of various syntax elements, which include pixels, bitplanes, transform coefficients, blocks (group of pixels), macroblocks (MBs, group of blocks), slices (group of MBs), packets, and so forth.
- Fixed-length codeword (FLC) encryption, where FLC denotes syntax elements that have fixed bit sizes predefined by the standards or other syntax elements.
- Variable-length codeword (VLC) index encryption [29], which encrypts the index of a VLC and output a new VLC according to the cipher-index.
- Secret entropy coding, which achieves the goal of VLC encryption by keeping the underlying probability model and/or some related parameters secret.
- "Virtual full encryption" working with adaptive entropy coding, which encrypts selective leading bits of the compressed data to conceal the context that is required for the decoding of other unencrypted data.
- Header encryption, which encrypts some syntax elements in the headers of multimedia data.

While each of the above multimedia encryption techniques can provide good performance in some cases, there exist trade-offs between security, format compliance, and influence on compression efficiency for all of them. The following is a list of some known trade-offs.

- Secret permutation can be easily implemented to ensure format compliance, but it is not secure against plaintext attack [37].

- FLC encryption can be used to realize perceptual encryption, but is unable to provide high confidentiality because some visual information can be leaked from unencrypted VLC data elements and other information embedded in the standard itself [35].
- VLC encryption can ensure format compliance and security when used properly. But it can also cause a negative and uncontrollable influence on compression efficiency. By constraining the index encryption in a small number of VLCs, such an influence will not be very serious, but the security level is also compromised [38].
- Secret entropy coding may not be able to keep format compliance, and many of the designs are insecure against chosen-plaintext attack [39].
- "Virtual full encryption" and header encryption cannot ensure format compliance for some multimedia coding standards.
- Some encryption algorithms can only work with a pseudorandom keystream generated by a stream cipher, which makes them sensitive to plaintext attack if the key is reused.

For an ideal video encryption scheme, it is expected to have at least the following properties, simultaneously:

- Strict format compliance (every smallest syntax element can still be decoded).
- Strict size preservation.
- Offering high confidentiality when configured properly.
- Very light-weight selective encryption (less than 10% data encrypted).
- Capability to support perceptual/transparent encryption.
- Be able to work with any traditional cipher (either block cipher or stream cipher).

According to the differences between H.264 and MPEG, the encryption algorithms used in MPEG 1/2 are difficult to be used in H.264 directly. For example, encrypting only the DCT coefficients may be not secure enough because the residue DCT coefficients produced by scalable interprediction and intraprediction are often near zeros. As mentioned before, partial encryption is the most common method for video encryption [40, 41]. However, it has been found that selective encryption cannot ensure high-level security due to the following features of most video coding standards based on orthogonal transforms [42, 43].

1. In most video coding standards, different transform coefficients are independent of each other, so encrypting partial coefficients does nothing to other coefficients. So error-concealment-based attack can be used to get some visual information of the plain video.
2. Although the energy of a compressed image concentrates on lower transform coefficients, the visible information does not concentrate on partial coefficients, but scatters over all transform coefficients.
3. The scattering effect of visible information also exists in different bits of transform coefficients, which makes it insecure to partially encrypt significant bits of transform coefficients.
4. Only encrypting intraencoded pictures of a video cannot provide sufficient security against ciphertext-only attack.
5. Because all intraencoded pictures occupy about 30–60% or even more of a video [7, 12], the reduction of computation load of encrypting intraencoded pictures alone is not significant.

6. If selective encryption is exerted before the entropy coding stage, the compression performance will decrease, whereas if it is exerted after the entropy coding stage, format compliance will be impossible.

The above facts hold for H.264 video standard and most transform-based video coding standards. Fortunately, with the use of adaptive entropy encoding algorithm, correlation can be introduced between different transform coefficients in the same block, which may make selective encryption much more useful. This requires more future study. In addition, a possible improvement of selective encryption is to combine a fast (but less secure) cipher and a slow (but securer) cipher to encrypt the plain video.

6.5 H.264 Video Encryption Techniques

As the most recent video compression standard, H.264 has become the most promising technique for future video communications. H.264 video encryption techniques [3, 4, 6–8, 23, 24, 44–51] involve the problem of how to design a fast and secure H.264 incorporated encryption-and-encoding system, in which the encryption algorithm is incorporated into the encoding process and does not bring much additional computational burden with an acceptable high-level security. An important feature of the incorporated system is that it is able to generate totally syntax-compliant H.264 videos. This is generally impossible in naive encryption schemes of H.264 videos, in which a video stream is simply encrypted bit by bit with a textual cipher, such as DES or AES. In digital video encryption, the trade-offs between security and speed, encryption, compression and format compliance are of great importance in designing and implementing an encryption framework or algorithm. For commercial video encryption, if strict confidentiality needs to be maintained, then the technique should involve operations where content will not be revealed unless proper decryption key is used. On the other hand, in transparent encryption, full quality is restricted to the legitimate user only.

Without some classification schemes, it is usually difficult to determine the features of VEAs as in previous survey papers [3, 5]. Therefore, some distinct classifications are needed on the design of H.264 encryption techniques. To uniquely identify the features of the H.264 VEAs, we classify the encryption algorithms referring to the H.264 encoding process as illustrated in Figure 6.1. As mentioned in the previous section, depending on where the encryption operations are performed with respect to multimedia compression, there are three different approaches: precompression, postcompression, and joint compression and encryption. In Figure 6.1, different selective encryption methods according to different H.264 coding components are also highlighted.

Entropy coding encryption algorithm encrypts the codeword index or map before encoding or prediction; the encryption space is the encrypting codeword index or map with different keys. DCT coefficient signs and the motion vector difference (MVD) signs encryption algorithms have small encryption space, therefore, the security is not very high. Zig-zag scanning scrambling algorithm and intraprediction mode encryption algorithms have the lowest security level. Furht et al. [3] have presented a comprehensive classification to include most of the presented selective VEAs.

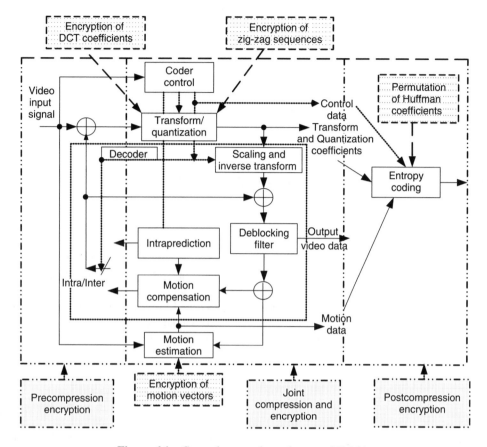

Figure 6.1   General encryption schemes of H.264.

6.5.1   Complete Encryption Technique

Complete encryption algorithm performs XOR operation on video data as ordinary binary bitstreams with secret keys. It can use the stream cipher algorithm or block cipher algorithm such as AES, DES to enhance its security. VEA and the chaotic encryption algorithm are two improved methods [14]. VEA [14] divides plaintexts into odd and even parts. This algorithm has reduced the complexity to half of the original. In chaotic encryption algorithm [14], the chaotic data generated by chaotic sequence generator XOR with video data and become ciphertexts [35, 38, 39, 42]. This algorithm is faster than block cipher algorithms such as DES. The complete encryption algorithm encrypts data after compression and encoding, it does not change the compression ratio; however, it does not have data operability because of header data encryption. Meanwhile, huge amount of encrypted data and time cost reduce its speed. Methods relying on fast chaotic maps are promising due to their fast performance. An excellent overview of these approaches, along with their comparative security analysis is presented in [52].

6.5.2 Partial Encryption Technique

The partial encryption algorithms encrypt only a fraction of video data during the process of video coding, such as only I frame encryption, I blocks in P/B frames encryption [14], and scrambling intraprediction mode [53]. Typical partial encryption algorithms include header data encryption algorithm, I frames encryption algorithm, I blocks complete encryption algorithm, I blocks and P frames encryption algorithm.

6.5.3 DCT Coefficients Scrambling Encryption Technique

DCT coefficient encryption technique encrypts videos by scrambling DCT coefficients after compression [18, 23, 25]. There are DCT coefficients selective encryption algorithm and DCT coefficient signs encryption algorithm. DCT coefficients selective encryption algorithm chooses appropriate DC, AC coefficients to encrypt. Its security is high, but selecting data and encrypting operation will reduce its speed. Typical encryption algorithms include complete and subsection scrambling algorithm, high-low-frequency scrambling algorithm, and subblocks scrambling algorithm. Bhargava *et al.* [18] proposed to encrypt only the sign bits of the DCT coefficients and differential values of motion vectors in P and B frames of MPEG video. Wang *et al.* [25] scrambled DCT coefficient values, whereas compression efficiency can also obviously degrade due to destroying energy distribution in DCT transform, and introduce rate fluctuation.

6.5.4 MVD Encryption Technique

DCT coefficients and MVDs (motion vector) are the important data in H.264 encoding process; DC coefficients contain main information of a video, AC coefficients contain detail information, and MVD contains dynamic temporal information. The MVD encryption techniques mainly modify the MVD signs to carry out encryption algorithm [29, 49]. Zeng and Lei [49] proposed selective bit scrambling, block permutation, and block rotation for wavelet-based compression, and also DCT coefficient and motion vector scrambling for DCT-based compression. The compression efficiency may be also degraded greatly for incomprehensible pictures due to a global permutation of spatially disjoint transform coefficient blocks. Wen *et al.* [29] proposed format-compliant selective encryption and permutation of codewords in MPEG-4 visual standard for wireless video applications, whereas the compression efficiency may be degraded due to the encryption of MVD. Although [29, 49] showed that encryption of DCT coefficients and MV signs have no effect on compression efficiency, information leakage always exists due to error concealment tools.

6.5.5 Entropy Coding Encryption Technique

Two entropy coding methods in H.264 are context-adaptive variable length codeword (CAVLC) encoding and CABAC. CAVLC-based entropy coding encryption algorithm encrypts the codeword index with stream cipher algorithm to get a new index, then searches new codeword according to the encrypted index from the codeword table; thus it is secure. Encryption operation and encoding occur at the same time so that it does not affect the encoding time. The cost time is only dependant on controlling keys, thus, the encryption is very fast. Entropy coding encrypts before packing, it has date operability and small compression ratio changes.

6.5.6 Zig-Zag Scanning Encryption Technique

Zig-zag scanning maps the 4*4 DCT coefficients in an MB into 16*16 vectors. The nonzero AC coefficients stand before a number of 0 after scanning. It has changed DCT coefficients' original sequence, and reduced the number of continuous 0s. Because DCT coefficients' sequence has a strong orderliness after zig-zag scanning and easy to restore, and it has poor security. Zig-zag scanning sequence scrambling algorithm is rarely applied in practice.

6.5.7 Flexible Macroblock Ordering (FMO) Encryption Technique

Flexible macroblock ordering (FMO) is advanced for resisting bit errors. It arranges the blocks into different slices according to the MB. In this way, the image can also be restored after a slice lost. FMO encryption algorithm scans blocks according to the encrypted FMO map. It uses high-strength encryption algorithms or arranges the MBs into many slices to improve security. As the FMO map alone is encrypted, its speed is high. And it does not change the compression ratio and date operability. In the approach proposed by Li *et al.* [35], only the fixed-length coded data elements of a video stream are encrypted; therefore, the encryption speed is very high.

6.5.8 Intraprediction Mode Encryption Technique

H.264 intraprediction produces the predicted blocks from current blocks and rebuilds blocks according to different prediction models. The encryption algorithm XORs the codewords of prediction models with secret keys. Owing to the prediction mode words being only 3 bits, its security is low. It encrypts before compression and encoding, so it does not change the compression ratio and data operability.

6.6 A H.264 Encryption Scheme Based on CABAC and Chaotic Stream Cipher

6.6.1 Related Work

Video encryption has been an active research topic for the past decades due to its potentially wide usages. Motivated by the specific requirements of video encryption, a variety of encryption algorithms have been proposed [25, 36–38, 52, 54]. In recent years, the need for the secure copyright protection of H.264 video keeps increasing. This has lead to a growing interest in the investigation of a joint compression and encryption scheme for H.264, simultaneously. There have been some research efforts devoted to the development of specific H.264 video encryption methods on the use of chaos in the joint operation of video compression and encryption. For example, Bose and Pathak [1], proposed an adaptive arithmetic coding technique based on chaos. A pseudorandom bitstream is generated by coupled chaotic systems and the coder's statistical model varied with it adaptively. The chaotic key stream generated from the logistic map and plaintext is utilized in [36] that maps intervals of the arithmetic coder. A chaotic stream cipher for the selective encryption of video streams was proposed in [37]. Besides, another generic encryption concept with scalable bitstreams is presented in [38]. This method has some shortcomings when dealing with the scalability features of the H.264 standard. Ahn *et al.* [25] presents a H.264 encryption method, which utilizes the intraprediction mode to scramble original video on the condition that there is no code size increase and the code method remains unchanged to protect video data to some extent. The advantages of this method are the high data operation efficiency and keeping the original compression rate; however, it is limited to protect the video information according to the experimental results. Some work has been done on secure transcoders for H.264 bitstreams [54] that can be modified for H.264 encryption. A selective encryption approach that encrypts only important parts of a quad-tree wavelet-type encoder is presented in [52]. While these papers utilize chaos in their schemes, they are just built on the framework of compression such as entropy coding or transform coding, but actually not based on H.264 video codec to realize joint compression and encryption simultaneously. In our proposed scheme, chaotic systems can act as pseudorandom bitstream generators and achieve the joint compression and encryption in the CABAC model at the same time.

6.6.2 New H.264 Encryption Scheme

The proposed H.264 encryption scheme is shown in Figure 6.2. The new scheme is integrated into the H.264 standard with format compliance. It could even become a part of the standard, simply by employing a reserved encrypted data. As shown, chaos-based encryption techniques are integrated into the H.264 standard. They encrypt video data using fast chaotic maps to carry out secret permutations of the video frames independent to the compression process. The efficient format-compliant encryption is transparent as well. In this work, we focus on video blocks of size 4*4. It is a selective encryption algorithm that only operates on H.264 compressed video.

For the chaos-based H.264 encryption schemes, the following factors should be taken into account:

1. Regression problem; when the chaotic system is implemented by discrete sequences on the computer with limited precision, there will be some regression problem such as worse correlation characteristics and shorter period. In fact, most of existing chaotic systems ignore this fact. The security of these algorithms should be improved.
2. Complexity problem; the speed of some chaotic systems is too slow to realize real-time information protection and confidentiality. In limited precision, integer data structure has priority over floating data structure as integer structure is much faster than floating data structure. Therefore, the simpler chaotic system should be preferred such as section linear chaotic systems, which only need few data operations. Some encryption methods improve confidentiality with a number of iterations, which sacrifice the encryption efficiency; however, the number of iterations should be avoided to improve encryption speed.

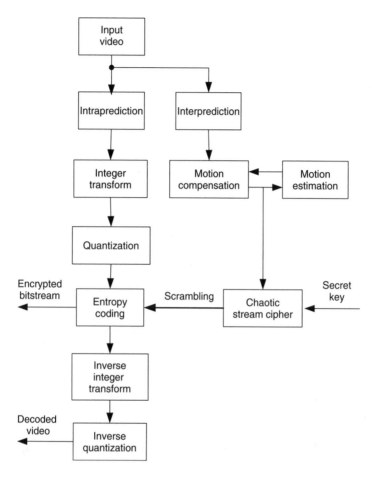

Figure 6.2   Diagram of H.264 encryption scheme based on chaotic stream cipher.

3. Confidentiality problem; with the development of chaos theory, multitudes of chaotic analysis techniques have been developed. As chaotic system is a nonlinear system with certainty. If the intruders know the related chaotic trajectory information, they can break the code with the analysis of the chaotic structure. Therefore, the chaotic system should be designed without information leak, besides, complicated or a combination of chaotic systems can be adopted to enhance the security and confidentiality.
4. Hardware and software codesign feasibility problem; for a good algorithm, it is important for it to be implemented by hardware or software easily with less resource occupation. If the data structure of the chaotic system is simple, it is easier to be implemented by integrated circuits, which indicate good feasibility.

6.6.3   Chaotic Stream Cipher

The chaotic stream cipher is widely used in the video encryption. The speedy and secure chaotic stream cipher should satisfy basic video encryption requirements. That is, the integer operation replaces the floating operation. In our H.264 encryption scheme, the pseudorandom sequence generator is based on the discrete piecewise linear chaotic map due to its unique characteristics such as good correlation property and randomness and sensitivity to initial seed and parameters. The original and parameter-controllable chaotic map is denoted as

$$x(k+1) = f(x(k), p) = \begin{cases} x(k)/p, & 0 \le x(k) < p, \\ (x(k) - p)/(1/2 - p), & p \le x(k) < 1/2 \\ (1 - p - x(k))/(1/2 - p), & 1/2 \le x(k) < 1 - p \\ (1 - x(k))/p, & 1 - p \le x(k) < 1 \end{cases} \quad (6.1)$$

The chaotic sequence has the property of randomness and security, which can be shown in the correlation tests. The auto- and cross-correlation characteristics shown in Figure 6.3 confirm the good performance of the chaotic map as a stream cipher.

From the auto-correlation and cross-correlation of the random sequences, it can be noted that the autocorrelation is like the δ function, and the cross-correlation curve is very close to zero, though there is only a slight difference between the parameters. It can be also observed that the random sequence is of long period and proper order of correlation immunity. From the correlation results, we can know that the results are desirable for encryption. The change of different parameters, initial values can get the desirable characteristics too, which confirm the sensitivity of the chaotic sequence's parameters. All these properties make it suitable for stream cipher construction.

Chaotic stream cipher encrypts the video data of finite length. The feedback cipher mode can counteract the plaintext attack. The cipher feedback is adopted to increase security, and the detailed encryption feedback process is computed by

$$C(i) = XOR(s(i), C(i - 1 - s(i))) \quad (6.2)$$

where $s(i)$ is the chaotic stream cipher, XOR represents exclusive OR operation, and $C(i)$ is current cipher text.

The block is scrambled with each frame differently using chaotic stream cipher. This method is easy and speedy. For each frame with N blocks, four scrambling steps based on chaos describe the specific scrambling process.

Step 1. Extract sequence $a = \{a_1, a_2 \ldots a_N\}$ from the integer chaotic sequence.
Step 2. Reorder the sequences with increase or decrease order to produce a new sequence $\tilde{a} = \{\tilde{a}_1, \tilde{a}_2 \ldots \tilde{a}_N\}$. As there is no same element in the chaotic sequence, this method is feasible.
Step 3. Record the position of each element in sequence $\tilde{a} = \{\tilde{a}_1, \tilde{a}_2, \ldots, \tilde{a}_N\}$ from the corresponding sequence $a = \{a_1, a_2, \ldots, a_N\}$. The scrambled position is recorded as $p = \{p_1, p_2, \ldots, p_N\}$.
Step 4. Scramble the block in the current scanned frame with $p = \{p_1, p_2, \ldots, p_N\}$.

This method does not increase the number of iterations; thus, it makes the whole process easy and convenient.

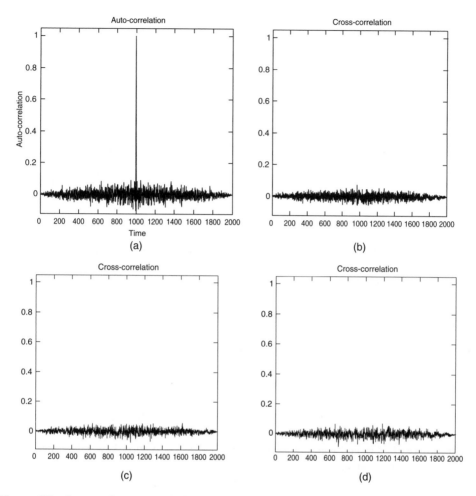

Figure 6.3 Auto- and cross-correlation test of chaotic sequence; (a) auto-correlation of chaotic sequence; (b) cross-correlation of chaotic sequence with different initial value; (c) cross-correlation of chaotic sequence with a different parameter p; (d) cross-correlation of the chaotic sequence with a different key.

6.6.4 CABAC Encryption

CABAC consists of four basic code trees for the binarization step, that is, the unary code, the truncated unary (TU) code, the kth-order Exp-Golomb (KEG) code, and the fixed-length (FL) codes. CABAC utilizes 399 context models, and one direct encryption method is to encrypt the context index, but cipher space of this method is only 399 which are too easy to be broken. On the other hand, the CABAC model can be scrambled, which increases the space to 399. However, the syntax element of CABAC context model is limited, and a different syntax element is assigned to different context indexes; in this way, the cipher space is reduced significantly. Meanwhile, the combination of the context index and the encryption model is feasible and compatible to the H.264 standard. In our proposed scheme, the unitary, TU, KEG, and FL codes are encrypted differently with different encryption functions, which are described as follows.

6.6.4.1 Unary Code Encryption

The unary code is mainly used in the *ref_idx_10* and *ref_idx_11*, which represent the reference frame index in the motion estimation respectively; therefore, the unary code encryption affects the interprediction of blocks. The method to encrypt unary code is expressed by

$$C_i' = E_u(C_{i-1}', C_i, Key_i) \tag{6.3}$$

where C_i is the syntax value of unary code, $E_u(\bullet)$ is the unitary code encryption function, and C_{i-1}' and C_i' are the previous and current cipher values respectively. C_i' is lower than the max value of the reference frame. Key_i is the encryption key.

6.6.4.2 TU Code Encryption

The TU code is mainly adopted in syntax *intra_chroma_pred_mode*. The TU encryption influences the luma prediction mode, and then has an effect on luma prediction. TU sets a *cMax* value based on unary code and the encryption algorithm is computed by

$$C_i' = E_{TU}(C_{i-1}', C_i, Key_i), 0 \le C_i \le cMax \tag{6.4}$$

where $E_{TU}(\bullet)$ is TU encryption function. Key_i is the encryption key. C_i' is the current cipher value which satisfies $0 \le C_i' \le cMax$.

6.6.4.3 KEG Code Encryption

The KEG code is utilized in the MVD of binary syntax *(mvd_lx)* and the absolute value of the residue coefficient minus one *(coeff_abs_level_minus1)*. The binary code contains suffix and prefix. The prefix adopts the TU code, that is, $M = floor(\log_2(S/2^k + 1))$, where S is the syntax element value. The suffix *INFO* includes M bits and $INFO = S - 2^k(2^M - 1)$. In the motion vector code, the *cMax* value of TU code equals 9 and the exponential k is 3. While in the residue code, the *cMax* value is 14 and k is 0. This encryption only affects the motion vector and residue coefficients. When the syntax is lower than cMax, the TU encryption method is used, otherwise, the suffix is encrypted by

$$INFO_i' = E_{KEG}(INFO_{i-1}', INFO_i, Key_i) \tag{6.5}$$

where $E_{KEG}(\bullet)$ is encryption function, $INFO_{i-1}'$ and $INFO_i'$ are the previous and current cipher streams respectively, and Key_i is the secret key.

6.6.4.4 FL Code Encryption

The encryption of the finite length code is calculated by

$$bitStr'_i = E_{FL}(bitStr'_{i-1}, bitStr_i, Key_i) \tag{6.6}$$

where $E_{FL}(\bullet)$ is the encryption function, $bitStr'_{i-1}$ and $bitStr'_i$ are the previous and current encrypted cipher, and Key_i is the secret key.

Note that the four above-mentioned encryption functions take advantage of the cipher feedback, that is, the function can be adapted according to the specific application. For example, bitwise XOR can be used to carry out encryption algorithm. Besides, Key_i is bitstream key. The keys are generated by the chaotic stream cipher. Each function has its unique key generation method to increase the key space and security.

The four encryption methods are related to different H.264 syntaxes with different significance levels. Thus the encryption is scalable for different requirements. The unary and KEG encryption affect the motion vectors and residue coefficients in the highest important level. As human eyes are not sensitive to chrominance elements, the chroma prediction mode encryption will have less significance.

6.6.5 Experimental Results and Analysis

For the simulation of the proposed video scrambling, all sequences are simulated based on Joint Model (JM) 12.0 test model, which runs on the Windows XP operation system with Visual Studio Software. The standard QCIF test sequences with 30 f/s frame rate, including foreman (middle motion sequence), news (mixture motion sequence), mobile, coastguard, akiyo, and mother and daughter frame rates are used to test the system performance. Actually, encrypting different data will achieve different results. For example, the effects of the motion vector encryption are obvious as more motion involved. To further increase security, the high- and low-frequency coefficients are scrambled based on 4×4 blocks. The macroblock is scrambled too; however, the compression ratio and encryption speed are sacrificed. The detailed analysis is carried out as follows.

6.6.5.1 Complexity Analysis

If the test sequence is $W*H$, then each has $W*H/(16*16)$ luma blocks and $1/2*W*H/(8*8)$ chroma blocks. All I frames adopt intraprediction; thus, there are $W*H / (16*16)*16$ luma prediction, $1/2*W*H/(8*8)*4$ chroma prediction and $W*H/(16*16)*256 + 1/2 W*H/(8*8)*64$ residue coefficient times encryption. For P and B frames, there are $W*H/(16*16) *16$ times motion vector encryption. If only XOR encryption method is used, the speed is very fast. As shown in Table 6.1, there is rarely a change of the compression after the encryption.

In fact, the computing complexity of the proposed encryption scheme depends on the complexity of the stream cipher and the data volumes to be encrypted. In the chaos-based cipher, it needs 11 times of multiplication, 6 times of addition, and 6 times of bitwise to encrypt N bits, where N is the stream cipher's word length (no smaller than 32). If once multiplication equals to twice addition or four times of bitwise, then each cipher-bit needs about $15/N$ times of multiplication. According to DCT transformation,

Table 6.1 Compression and encryption efficiency test

Sequence	Resolution	Time ratio between encryption and compression (%)
Akiyo	176*144	2.22
Carphone	176*144	1.86
Foreman	176*144	2.16
Mobile	176*144	1.78
News	176*144	2.45
Suize	176*144	2.86

each pixel needs more than 64 times of multiplication and 63 times of addition. Thus, the operation time ratio between the stream cipher and the encoding process is smaller than 15/(6N)*100%. Since there are some other operations besides DCT transformation and motion estimation, the operation time ratio between the stream cipher and the compression process is much lower than 10%.

6.6.5.2 Security Analysis

In this encryption scheme, the security is determined by the chaos-based stream cipher and the selective encryption scheme. For the chaos-based stream cipher, the key space, key sensitivity, and ciphertext statistics are in relation with the security. The slight change of the chaotic parameters leads to totally different sequences. Obviously, the secret key space is big enough to stand brute force attack. At the same time, the iteration times and initial value of the chaos change in real-time to resist plaintext attacks. For the selective encryption scheme, the selected data streams are in relation with video data's intelligibility.

For the secret keys, the highly secure chaotic stream cipher is used to ensure security. Besides, the cipher feedback mode is used for encryption, which increases the ability to resist analysis attacks. For the brute force attack, as there are 9 prediction modes in the luma block and 4 chroma blocks, it needs $9*W*H/(16*16)*16 + 4*1/2*W*H/(8*8)$ times in total for the exhaustive search, which is too computation intensive to attack exhaustively. Therefore, the technique proposed is highly secure and can resist emulative and other attacks.

6.6.5.3 Compression Performance

According to the analysis of different encryption modes, the unary, FL, and KEG encryptions do not increase the code length while the TU encryption will increase or decrease the code length, but the change is too small to be noticed. Therefore, the proposed method rarely affects the compression ratio and format. It can be observed that joint compression and encryption algorithms influence the compression efficiency of a video coder slightly.

6.6.5.4 H.264 Video Codec Compliance

The modifications for encryption are based on H.264 standard, and therefore, the encrypted bitstream are compatible with the H.264 video stream and can be decoded accordingly. Actually, joint compression and encryption algorithms require modifications to be integrated into an existing system. Certainly, the chaos-based H.264 video streams encrypted with joint compression and encryption algorithms are inherently compliant to the standardized syntax because the syntax is formatted in the last step of the compression process.

6.6.5.5 Encryption Efficiency

The proposed joint compression and encryption algorithms are, in general, more efficient than the traditional compression-independent ones as they add very little computational overhead to the original video codec. This method simply modifies the original coding process by shuffling or encrypting coefficients selectively. Actually, the encryption time depends on the generation time of chaotic stream cipher and encrypted data volume. The proposed method only encrypts the video data that affect the visual effect significantly and only involve the syntax symbol. For example, as most AC coefficients are zero, the DC chroma coefficient is chosen to be ciphered. The computational complexity of these operations is generally negligible compared to that of the naive algorithm, so that the proposed joint compression and encryption algorithms, usually, have a relatively high encryption speed. Meanwhile, the synchronization information stays unchanged during the data operation.

6.6.5.6 Applicability for Perceptual Encryption

Not all algorithms support perceptual encryption. But, in general, a joint compression and encryption algorithm can be easily adapted for the perceptual encryption purpose because perceptual encryption requires the syntax of the encrypted video stream to be compliant with the standardized syntax so that an ordinary video player can play the perceptually encrypted video stream without crashing.

On the basis of the above analysis, we compare our proposed H.264 encryption scheme and chaotic stream cipher with other typical schemes, and the results are shown in Table 6.2. It can be observed that the proposed scheme has relatively high security level, and has almost no effect on compression ratio as joint compression and encryption are implemented in our scheme.

6.7 Concluding Remarks and Future Works

The most secure way of protecting video data is through a naive algorithm, which encrypts the entire video data by a standard cryptosystem. However, larger computational overhead makes it inefficient or impossible in lots of applications. As a result, selective encryption becomes popular in most of the video encryption researches. In this chapter, we surveyed

Table 6.2 Comparison with other schemes

	Security	Speed	Data operation
Traditional technique	Very high	High demanding	Has data operation
DCT coefficient scrambling based on chaos	Relatively high, depending on the security of chaos	Relatively low	Has data operation and effect on compression ratio
DCT coefficient scrambling	Relatively high, depending on the security of the scrambling algorithm	Medium	Has data operation and high effect on compression
Our proposed	Relatively high, depending on the security of stream cipher	Low, easier for hardware realization	Has data operation and hardly any effect on compression

some H.264 video encryption techniques to facilitate the design of the new H.264 video techniques. The special characteristics of H.264 can be explored to design joint H.264 compression and encoding schemes perceptually, which can resist a lot of cryptanalytic and other typical attacks.

In this chapter, the piecewise linear chaotic map is used to construct an efficient stream cipher with random feedback mode. The H.264 encryption scheme based on chaos increases the security with the introduction of the chaotic cipher. Only limited data is encrypted, which addresses the speed problem. The proposed encryption scheme is low in complexity and has data compatibility with original data encryption. These properties make it a suitable choice for H.264 video protection, such as secure video transmission, especially for IPTV or mobile media transmission scheme.

Some guidelines to design new H.264 video encryption techniques for further improvement are also provided in this chapter. Most of the H.264 video encryption methods are based on frequency domain while spatial domain schemes make use of spatial information in video data. Entropy coding schemes use special entropy codecs to do encryption. With respect to the joint compression-encryption, some interesting problems are as follows:

- Designing a light-weight encryption scheme satisfying the format compliance requirement.
- Investigating the error tolerance of the light-weight encryption schemes.
- Designing joint compression-encryption schemes robust to channel errors.
- Jointly considering the channel coding and encryption.

Some possible future works for H.264 video encryption are listed as follows.

1. To investigate which encryption configuration can produce totally format-compliant H.264 videos.
2. To investigate which encryption configuration can maintain the video size in which level (block, sub-MB, MB, slice, slice group, picture, frame, layer, and stream).
3. To study the idea of selective encryption on different sets of selective data elements. The results will be used to optimize the encryption speed of related configurations.

4. For encryption techniques that cannot maintain the video size, the compression efficiency will be studied, with different encoding parameters of H.264 videos.
5. To investigate which configurations can be used to realize perceptual encryption and scalable encryption of H.264 video. One or more criteria will be introduced to measure the visual quality degradation of the encrypted H.264 videos.
6. To investigate whether or not one can encrypt some data elements in various headers to benefit the encryption.

Acknowledgments

This work was supported by the Research Grant Council of the Hong Kong SAR Government under Project 523206 (PolyU 5232/06E).

References

[1] Lian, S.G., Sun, J.S., Wang, J.W., and Wang, Z.Q. (2007) A chaotic stream cipher and the usage in video protection. *Chaos Solitons & Fractals*, **34**, 851–859.
[2] Wiegand, T., Sullivan, G.J., Bjntegaard, G., and Luthra, A. (2003) Overview of the H.264/AVC video coding standard. *IEEE Transactions on Circuits and Systems for Video Technology*, **13**, 560–576.
[3] Fuhrt, B. and Kirovski, D. (2004) *MultimediaSecurity Handbook*, CRC Press, Inc. Boca Raton, FL, USA.
[4] Socek, D., Kalva, H., Magliveras, S. *et al.* (2007) New approaches to encryption and steganography for digital videos. *Multimedia Systems*, **13**, 191–204.
[5] Uhl, A., Pommer, A. (2005) *Image and Video Encryption – From Digital Rights Management to Secured Personal Communication*, Springer Science+Business Media, Inc., New York, USA, 45–134.
[6] Lian, S.G., Liu, Z.X., Ren, Z., and Wang, H.L. (2006) Secure advanced video coding based on selective encryption algorithms. *IEEE Transactions on Consumer Electronics*, **52**, 621–629.
[7] Shin, S., Sim, K., and Rhee, K. (1999) A secrecy scheme for MPEG video data using the joint of compression and encryption. Information Security, pp. 774–774.
[8] Wu, C.-P. and Kuo, C.-C.J. (2005) Design of integrated multimedia compression and encryption systems. *IEEE Transactions on Multimedia*, **7**, 828–839.
[9] Lian, S.G., Cao, Y.J., Sun, J.S., and Wang, Z.Q. (2004) Lightweight MPEG4 video encryption algorithm suitable for network transmission. Proceeding of the SPIE – the International Society for Optical Engineering, pp. 320–329.
[10] Iqbal, R., Shirmohammadi, S., and El Saddik, A. (2006) Secured MPEG-21 digital item adaptation for H.264 video. Proceeding of IEEE International Conference on Multimedia and Expo, pp. 2181–2184.
[11] Iqbal, R., Shirmohammadi, S., and El Saddik, A. (2006) Compressed-domain encryption of adapted H.264 video. Proceedings of 8th IEEE International Symposium on Multimedia, pp. 979–984.
[12] Lian, S.G. (2007) Commutative encryption and watermarking in video compression. *IEEE Transactions on Circuits and Systems for Video Technology*, **17**, 774–778.
[13] Zhou, J.T. and Au, O.C. (2008) Comments on a novel compression and encryption scheme using variable model arithmetic coding and coupled chaotic system. *IEEE Transactions on Circuits and Systems I: Regular Papers*, **55**, 3368–3369.
[14] Qiao, L. and Nahrstedt, K. (1998) Comparison of MPEG encryption algorithms. *Computers & Graphics*, **22**, 437–448.
[15] Shi, C.G. and Bhargava, B. (1998) An efficient MPEG video encryption algorithm. Proceedings of 7th IEEE Symposium on Reliable Distributed Systems, pp. 381–386.
[16] Hosseini, H.M.M. and Tan, P.M. (2007) Encryption of MPEG video streams. Proceedings of TENCON.
[17] Alattar, A.M., Al-Regib, G.I., and Al-Semari, S.A. (1999) Improved selective encryption techniques for secure transmission of MPEG video bit-streams. Proceedings of International Conference on Image Processing, pp. 256–260.
[18] Bhargava, B., Changgui, S., and Sheng-Yih, W. (2004) MPEG video encryption algorithms. *Multimedia Tools and Applications*, **24**, 57–79.

[19] Wu, X.L. and Moo, P.W. (1999) Joint image/video compression and encryption via high-order conditional entropy coding of wavelet coefficients. Proceedings of IEEE International Conference on Multimedia Computing and Systems, pp. 908–912.

[20] Kankanhalli, M.S. and Guan, T.T. (2002) Compressed-domain scrambler /descrambler for digital video. *IEEE Transactions on Consumer Electronics*, **48**, 356–365.

[21] Gang, L., Ikenaga, T., Goto, S., and Baba, T. (2006) A selective video encryption scheme for MPEG compression standard. *IEICE Transactions on Fundamentals of Electronics Communications and Computer Sciences*, **E89-A**, 194–202.

[22] Iqbal, R. (2008) Compressed-domain video processing for adaptation, encryption, and authentication. *IEEE Multimedia*, **15**, 38–50.

[23] Tang, L. (1996) Methods for encrypting and decrypting MPEG video data efficiently. Proceedings of the ACM International Conference on Multimedia.

[24] Zhu, B.B., Chun, Y., Yidong, W., and Shipeng, L. (2005) Scalable protection for MPEG-4 fine granularity scalability. *IEEE Transactions on Multimedia*, **7**, 222–233.

[25] Ahn, J., Shim, H., Jeon, B., and Choi, I. (2005) Digital video scrambling method using intra prediction mode. Advances in Multimedia Information Processing – PCM 2004, pp. 386–393.

[26] Changgui, S. and Bharat, B. (1998) A fast MPEG video encryption algorithm. Proceedings of the 6th ACM International Conference on Multimedia.

[27] Chiaraluce, F., Ciccarelli, L., Gambi, E. *et al*. (2002) A new chaotic algorithm for video encryption. *IEEE Transactions on Consumer Electronics*, **48**, 838–844.

[28] Yen, J.-C. and Guo, J.-I. (2002) Design of a new signal security system. Proceeding of IEEE International Symposium on Circuits and Systems, pp. 121–124.

[29] Tosun, A.S. and Feng, W.C. (2000) Efficient multi-layer coding and encryption of MPEG video streams. Proceedings of IEEE International Conference on Multimedia and Expo, pp. 119–122.

[30] Wen, J.G., Severa, M., Zeng, W. *et al*. (2002) A format- compliant configurable encryption framework for access control of video. *IEEE Transactions on Circuits and Systems for Video Technology*, **12**, 545–557.

[31] Agi, I. and Gong, L. (1996) An empirical study of secure MPEG video transmissions. Proceedings of the Symposium on Network and Distributed System Security, pp. 137–144.

[32] Shubo, L., Zhengquan, X., Jin, L., and Wei, L. (2008) A novel format-compliant video encryption scheme for H.264/AVC stream in wireless network. Proceedings of 4th International Conference on Wireless Communications, Networking and Mobile Computing.

[33] Li, C.Q., Li, S.J., Chen, G.R., and Halang, W.A. (2009) Cryptanalysis of an image encryption scheme based on a compound chaotic sequence. *Image and Vision Computing*, **27**, 1035–1039.

[34] Li, C.Q., Li, X.X., Li, S.J., and Chen, G.R. (2005) Cryptanalysis of a multistage encryption system. Proceedings of IEEE International Symposium on Circuits and System, vol. 882, pp. 880–883.

[35] Li, S.J., Chen, G.R., Albert, C. *et al*. (2007) On the design of perceptual MPEG-Video encryption algorithms. *IEEE Transactions on Circuits and Systems for Video Technology*, **17**, 214–223.

[36] Bose, R. and Pathak, S. (2006) A novel compression and encryption scheme using variable model arithmetic coding and coupled chaotic system. *IEEE Transactions on Circuits and Systems I-Fundamental Theory and Applications*, **53**, 848–857.

[37] Mi, B., Liao, X., and Chen, Y. (2008) A novel chaotic encryption scheme based on arithmetic coding. *Chaos Solitons & Fractals*, **38**, 1523–1531.

[38] Stutz, T. and Uhl, A. (2008) Format-compliant encryption of H.264/AVC and SVC. Proceedings of IEEE International Symposium on Multimedia, pp. 446–445.

[39] Li, S.J., Chen, G.R., Cheung, A. *et al*. (2009) On the security of an MPEG-video encryption scheme based on secret huffman tables. Advances in Image and Video Technology – PSIVT 2009, pp. 898–909.

[40] Ho-Jae, L. and Jeho, N. (2006) Low complexity controllable scrambler/descrambler for H.264/AVC in compressed domain. Proceedings of the 14th Annual ACM International Conference on Multimedia.

[41] Hong, G.-M., Yuan, C., Wang, Y., and Zhong, Y.-Z. (2006) A quality-controllable encryption for H.264/AVC video coding. Advances in Multimedia Information Processing – PCM 2006, **1270**, pp. 510–517.

[42] Li, S.J., Li, C.Q., Chen, G.R., and Lo, K.-T. (2008) Cryptanalysis of the RCES/RSES image encryption scheme. *Journal of Systems and Software*, **81**, 1130–1143.

[43] Arachchi, H.K., Perramon, X., Dogan, S., and Kondoz, A.M. (2009) Adaptation -aware encryption of scalable H.264/AVC video for content security. *Signal Processing-Image Communication*, **24**, 468–483.

[44] Jakimoski, G. and Subbalakshmi, K.P. (2008) Cryptanalysis of some multimedia encryption schemes. *IEEE Transactions on Multimedia*, **10**, 330–338.

[45] Zou, Y. (2006) H.264 video encryption scheme adaptive to DRM. *IEEE Transactions on Consumer Electronics*, **52**, 1289–1297.

[46] Stutz, T. and Uhl, A. (2008) Format-compliant encryption of H.264/AVC and SVC. Proceedings of 10th IEEE International Symposium on Multimedia, pp. 446–451.

[47] Yang, L., Chun, Y., and Yuzhuo, Z. (2007) A new digital rights management system in mobile applications using H.264 encryption. Proceedings of International Conference on Advanced Communication Technology, pp. 583–586.

[48] Wang, Y., Cai, M., and Tang, F. (2007) Design of a new selective video encryption scheme based on H.264. Proceedings of International Conference on Computational Intelligence and Security, pp. 883–887.

[49] Zeng, W. and Lei, S. (2003) Efficient frequency domain selective scrambling of digital video. *IEEE Transactions on Multimedia*, **5**, 118–129.

[50] Zhou, Y., Panetta, K., and Aagaian, S. (2008) Partial multimedia encryption with different security levels. Proceedings of IEEE International Conference on Technologies for Homeland Security, pp. 513–518.

[51] Zhou, J.T., Liang, Z.Q., Chen, Y., and Au, O.C. (2007) Security analysis of multimedia encryption schemes based on multiple huffman table. *IEEE Signal Processing Letters*, **14**, 201–204.

[52] Cheng, H. (2000) Partial encryption of compressed images and videos. *IEEE Transactions on Signal Processing*, **48**, 2439–2451.

[53] Dittmann, J. and Steinmetz, A. (1997) Enabling technology for the trading of MPEG-encoded Video. *InformationSecurity and Privacy*, **1270**, 314–324.

[54] Thomas, N.M., Lefol, D., Bull, D.R., and Redmill, D. (2006) A novel secure H.264 transcoder using selective encryption. Proceedings of International Conference on Image Processing, pp. IV85–IV88.

7

Optimization Methods for H.264/AVC Video Coding

Dan Grois[1], Evgeny Kaminsky[2], and Ofer Hadar[1]
[1]*Communication Systems Engineering Department, Ben-Gurion University of the Negev, Beer-Sheva, Israel*
[2]*Electrical and Computer Engineering Department, Ben-Gurion University of the Negev, Beer-Sheva, Israel*

7.1 Introduction to Video Coding Optimization Methods

Video compression is, in general, divided into four main parts: (i) spatial and temporal prediction, (ii) data transform, (iii) quantization of transform coefficients, and (iv) entropy coding. Spatial and temporal predictions are often referred to as *intra*prediction and *inter*prediction (or motion estimation), respectively. Spatial and temporal predictions are lossless methods that dramatically improve coding efficiency, but usually require a high computational load of total encoder computational consumption. Entropy coding compresses data without loss of information but, in many cases, its achievable compression is insufficient by itself for the purpose of low rate coding. In contrast, data transform and quantization can provide flexible compression for a wide range of encoding bit rates but at the cost of quantization errors or information loss.

In generic encoding, prediction is followed by data transform and quantization, which is then followed by entropy coding, the purpose of which is to achieve the desired compression rate with minimum loss of information. In Figure 7.1, the components of a generic source coding system are shown. Many well-established methods are available in various coding applications for intra/interprediction, data transform, quantization, and entropy coding of quantized data. For example, in image and video coding systems, the discrete cosine transform (DCT) and discrete wavelet transform (DWT) are used for data transform, and Huffman coding and arithmetic coding are used for entropy coding of quantized data [1–3].

The Handbook of MPEG Applications: Standards in Practice   Edited by Marios C. Angelides and Harry Agius
© 2011 John Wiley & Sons, Ltd

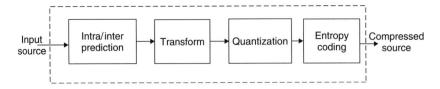

Figure 7.1 Block diagram of a generic encoding system.

Until recently, uniform quantization, which is not optimal if the input data is not uniformly distributed, has been used in most practical compression systems. For example, both the Joint Photographic Experts Group (JPEG) [1] and the Motion Pictures Experts Group (MPEG) [2, 4], which emerged during the last decade, use uniform quantization to quantize DCT block coefficients. Although a uniform quantizer does not provide the best available compression quality owing to its simplicity, it is preferred over other quantizers. In other words, the high complexity of more advanced quantizers outweighs their potential performance advantage, and thus limits their use in practice.

Owing to the advancement in high speed circuits, many sophisticated source coding techniques have become affordable. Consequently, advanced quantization algorithms, for example, code excited linear prediction (CELP) coder, that have long been employed in standards for digital speech coding systems have been able to employ an adaptive vector quantization technique for a low rate (4.8 Kbits) speech coding standard [5]. In the case of still image compression, the emerging ISO/ITU standard JPEG 2000 [6, 7] uses a wavelet transform coder based on a trellis coded quantizer (W/TCQ) [8] as a possible baseline algorithm. In addition, many adaptive arithmetic coders with complicated source modeling techniques have been proposed to enhance entropy coding in various image coding applications [9, 10].

The second major research problem is that most of the overall video encoding computational load (60% or more [11]) is required for the prediction operations (such as "inter" and "intra" predictions). Numerous prediction algorithms (e.g., fast motion estimation (FME) algorithms) have recently been suggested for performing these operations [12]. However, no single prediction algorithm can operate with the best efficiency with respect to input parameters such as numerous input video sequences, various channel conditions (e.g., bit rates), and different computational loads. Thus, one of the major research topics in the area of video coding optimization is the reduction of computational complexity. This problem is solved in [13] by developing an effective and generic optimization coding control methodology for any given channel conditions with the lowest possible computational load (such as the total number of CPU clocks per overall video coding task) and with any given computational loads. Thus, in [13], the quality video coding is provided under various transmission channel conditions with the lowest possible computational load (such as the total number of CPU clocks per overall video coding task).

7.2 Rate Control Optimization

7.2.1 Rate–Distortion Theory

The two most important parameters in video coding and communications are the coding bit rate (R) and the picture quality. The communication channel bandwidth determines the output bit rate needed to transfer the coded visual data. The most commonly used measure for picture/video quality is the mean square error (MSE) between the coded image/video and the source image/video [11], which can be formulated as

$$\text{MSE} = \frac{1}{MN} \sum_{m=1}^{M} \sum_{n=1}^{N} [I_c(m, n) - I_o(m, n)]^2 \tag{7.1}$$

where I_c is the decoded image; I_o, the original image; M, the horizontal resolution of a frame; N, the vertical resolution of a frame; and m and n, the corresponding horizontal and vertical coordinates.

A reconstruction error introduced by compression is often referred to as *distortion (D)*. In transform coding, both R and D are controlled by the quantizer step-size (q). The most important task of bit allocation is how to determine the value of q to achieve the target coding bit rate, or video/picture presentation quality. Therefore, it is required to analyze and estimate the *R-D* behavior of the image/video encoder. This behavior is characterized by its rate-quantization $(R\text{-}Q)$ and distortion-quantization $(D\text{-}Q)$ functions, denoted by $R(q)$ and $D(q)$, respectively [14, 15]. The quantizer step-size parameter q has to be resolved to achieve the target bit rate R_T or picture quality D_T, as shown in Figure 7.2. Rate–distortion analysis and estimation have potential applications in visual coding and communication [16]. An adaptive rate–distortion estimation can change the quantization setting of the encoder and control the output bit rate or picture quality according to the channel condition, the storage capacity, or the user's requirements [17–19]. On the other hand, optimum bit allocation as well as other rate–distortion optimization (RDO) procedures can be performed based on *R-D* estimation to improve coding efficiency, and, as a result, to improve video presentation quality [20–22].

7.2.2 Rate Control Algorithms

A rate control algorithm dynamically adjusts encoder parameters to achieve a target bit rate. It allocates a budget of bits to each group of pictures (GOP), individual picture, and/or subpicture in a video sequence. Rate control is not a part of the standard. Block-based hybrid video encoding algorithms, such as the MPEG [2] and H.26x [3, 23, 24] families,

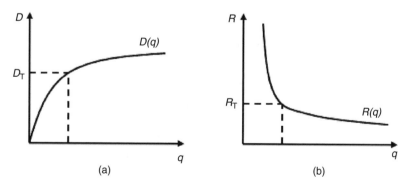

Figure 7.2   (a) Rate-quantization $(R\text{-}Q)$ curve and (b) distortion-quantization $(D\text{-}Q)$ curve.

are inherently lossy processes. They achieve compression not only by removing truly redundant information from the bit stream but also by making small quality compromises in ways that are intended to be minimally perceptible. In particular, the quantization scale q regulates how much spatial detail is saved. When q is very small, almost all that detail is retained. When q increases, some of that detail aggregates so that the bit rate drops, but at the expense of some increase in distortion and some loss of quality. Figure 7.3 shows this relationship for a particular input picture; one can lower the bit rate by increasing q at the cost of increased distortion. Figure 7.4 suggests that as source complexity varies during a sequence, one can move from one such curve to another.

In Figure 7.5, an open-loop (or VBR (variable bit rate)) operation of a video encoder is illustrated. A user supplies two key inputs – the uncompressed video source and a value for q. As the source sequence progresses, one gets compressed video of fairly constant quality, but the bit rate may dramatically vary. As the complexity of pictures is continually changing in a real video sequence, it is not so obvious what value of q to pick. If one fixes q for an "easy" part of the sequence having slow motion and uniform areas, then the bit rate will dramatically increase when one reaches the "hard" (i.e., more complex) parts.

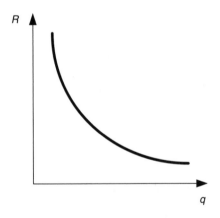

Figure 7.3   Particular source frame [22], where quality is decreased.

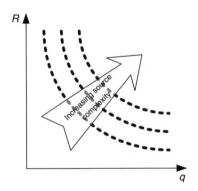

Figure 7.4   Various source complexities.

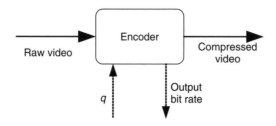

Figure 7.5 Open-loop rate control (VBR).

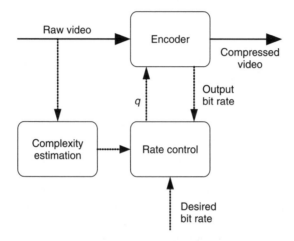

Figure 7.6 Closed-loop rate control (CBR).

In reality, constraints imposed by decoder buffer size and network bandwidth force to encode video at a more nearly constant bit rate (CBR). In order to do this, as shown in Figure 7.6, value of q must be dynamically varied based on the estimates of the source complexity, so that each picture (or GOP) gets an appropriate allocation of bits to work with. Rather than specifying q as an input, the user should specify demanded bit rate instead.

A real-time video encoding requires a relatively low-complexity bit rate control algorithm. The choice of rate control can have significant effect on video presentation quality and on total video encoder complexity. The choice of rate control algorithm is not straightforward because a number of aspects are involved, including:

- The computational complexity of the algorithm.
- Where the rate control algorithm is implemented (e.g., software or power limited video encoder).
- The type of the video content to be encoded (e.g., static videoconferencing scenes or fast-action movies).
- The constraints of the transmission channel (e.g., low-delay real-time communication or off-line storage).

7.2.3   Rate–Distortion Optimization

Several rate control and bit allocation methods have been proposed for minimizing distortion in video compression standards, preceding the H.264/AVC standard. Conventional optimal encoding methods [25, 26] decrease a video sequence distortion by optimizing the bit allocation, as illustrated in Figure 7.7, which schematically illustrates a set of operating R-D points, while each point represents the mean bit rate and distortion achieved for a specific set of coding parameters. In turn, by performing the RDO, a set of coding parameters, which achieves an operating R-D point as close as possible to the optimal R-D curve, is determined.

As seen in Figure 7.7, the distortion D decreases as the rate R increases. The operating R-D points that represent the best R-D performance are located in proximity to the dotted curve (according to the R-D theory, this dotted curve is a convex hull).

In [26], a theoretical study has been presented to achieve an optimal bit allocation with minimized distortion by considering a relationship between rate and distortion and determining an optimal set of quantizers for a given information source. In [25], another solution is proposed to achieve an optimal bit allocation with minimizing distortion by implementing the Viterbi algorithm. These solutions are relatively complicated, as they use dynamic programming for updating the settings of quantizer. More recent papers, such as [27], propose a feedback rate control scheme for minimizing distortion in MPEG-2 and MPEG-4 by calculating the target bit rate for each frame based on a quadratic equation of a rate–distortion function. In addition, [27] proposes a method for determining a set of optimal coding modes for encoding each macroblock in the H.264/AVC standard. According to this method, the RDO for each macroblock is performed to select an optimal coding mode by minimizing a Lagrange function.

It should be noted that the Lagrange function enables to determine a set of coding parameters for the best R-D performance, which is schematically presented in Figure 7.8. Two values of λ are shown: λ_a and λ_b. In each case, the solution to the cost function $J = D + \lambda R$ is a straight line with a slope. The points (R, D) that lead to obtaining the smallest cost function are shown as filled circles. It should be noted that these points

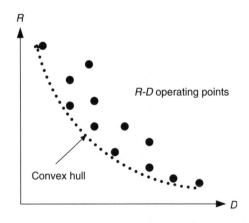

Figure 7.7 R-D convex hull.

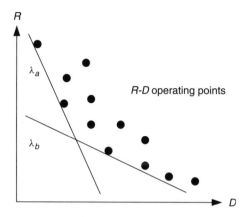

Figure 7.8 Lagrangian optimization for determining optimal R-D points.

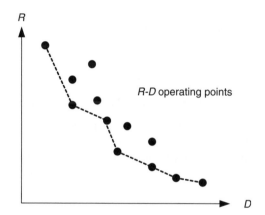

Figure 7.9 Optimized operational R-D curve.

occur in proximity to the convex hull of all R-D points. Thus, the optimal operating R-D points, which lead to the smallest cost function J, can be determined.

It should be noted that the computing of R-D points, thereby obtaining an optimized operational R-D curve as shown in Figure 7.9, is usually more complex than the optimization process itself, and, in such a case, the complexity of the RDO technique can be neglected.

According to [27], the coding mode selection is relatively complicated since all coding modes are considered for selecting the optimal coding mode. Further, in [28], the quadratic rate control scheme was implemented for the H.264/AVC standard. However, [28] considers only the quantization settings and optimal mode selection and not the computational complexity. Thus, similar to [27], the method used in [28] provides an optimal solution only if all coding modes are examined.

There were several attempts to provide an algorithm for controlling video stream complexity in order to save encoder computational resources. For example, in [29], a complexity control algorithm is proposed for the H.264/AVC encoder. Computational savings are achieved by the early prediction of skipped macroblocks prior to motion estimation through the estimation of a Lagrange rate–distortion–complexity cost function. A feedback control algorithm ensures that the encoder maintains a predefined target computational complexity. According to [29], each macroblock is either skipped (not coded) or coded by considering all coding modes, leading to relatively high complexity because of a large number of possible coding modes, and leading (especially for low bit rates) to significant fluctuations of distortions between each skipped and coded macroblock.

In the recent paper [30], a power–rate–distortion (P-R-D) analysis framework is proposed, extending the traditional R-D analysis by including the power consumption as an additional dimension. According to [30], power consumption is considered for determining an overall constant complexity level according to the average P-R-D model. Further, [31] proposes a generic rate–distortion–complexity model that can generate DIA (digital item adaptation) descriptions for image and video decoding algorithms running on various hardware architectures.

In a more recent work, such as [13], an approach for optimizing H.264/AVC video compression by dynamically allocating computational complexity (such as the number of CPU clocks) and bits for each basic unit within a video sequence, according to its predicted activity, is presented. The approach is based on computational complexity–rate–distortion (C-R-D) analysis and is discussed in detail in Section 7.4.

7.3 Computational Complexity Control Optimization

In Section 7.2, the trade-off between bit rate and distortion was considered. However, it has to be noted that there is another trade-off between computational complexity and the quality of a video sequence. It is possible to achieve higher quality of a video sequence by increasing computational resources, as described below in the view of the following issues.

7.3.1 Motion Estimation Algorithm

The block matching motion estimation (BMME) [32] is the simplest and most widely used method for motion estimation in video compression. In this method, each frame in a sequence is divided into a fixed number of square blocks. For every block in an "inter" frame, BMME performs a search in the reference frame over a search area (SA). The goal of the search is to find the best matching block that will minimize the prediction error. BMME uses different distance criteria for best matching block calculation (usually MSE or sum absolute difference (SAD) which is easier to compute) in order to achieve the least prediction error. The block sizes that are commonly used are 16×16 pixels, and the maximum SA can be ± 64 pixels (SA64) from the block's position.

In order to achieve higher video quality at the expense of increased computation, several search strategies may be adopted, all of which usually use some kind of sampling mechanism. The simplest approach is a full search (FS) motion estimation algorithm, which may be employed for the selection of the best motion vector (MV) position according to the minimum distance criteria by iterating over all candidate MVs of the SA [11]. This motion estimation algorithm can outperform most reduced-complexity motion estimation algorithms in terms of visual quality. However, considering all possible candidate MVs and calculating a distortion measure at every search position result in high computational consumption of the computational load of the video encoder. A good match during the search means that a good prediction can be made, but improvement in prediction must outweigh the cost of transmitting the MV. A good match requires that the whole block undergoes the same translation, and that the block does not overlap objects that have different degrees of motion, including the background. Small and numerous blocks used for motion estimation can give a good representation of complex motion, but may also increase the cost of transmission as the number of MVs increases. Texture and "inter"-frame noise may also affect the choice of block size [33]. MV distributions are, in general, center-based, but the horizontal motion is the often preferred motion direction [11]. Thus, the motion estimation algorithms, which are based on these observations, provide better results than their competitors.

On the other hand, many FME techniques have been proposed in the literature. Two popular approaches can be chosen to reduce computation in BMME. The first approach reduces the number of candidate blocks in the search window (fast searching techniques). Well-known examples [32] are two-dimensional logarithmic (TDL) search, three-step search (TSS) [34], block-based gradient descent search (BBGDS) [35], new three-step search (NTSS) [36], diamond search (DS) [37, 38], and hexagon-based search (HEXBS) [39]. These methods usually show good speed gain but have relatively larger rate–distortion (R-D) performance degradation.

The schematic shown in Figure 7.10 illustrates a DS [37, 38], which uses a small DS pattern for all search steps. The algorithm starts in the co-located (shown in Figure 7.10 by horizontal and vertical dashed lines) macroblock in the reference frame and performs eight additional SADs around the diamond center. It should be noted that in the FS all possible overlapping SADs are calculated, which is contrary to the DS. The DS pattern is moved horizontally and vertically in pixel steps toward the minimum SAD location. Upon determining the minimum SAD location, the diamond center is displaced to the optimum location, and a new DS is executed. The search is terminated once the position of the minimum SAD is determined in the center of the diamond. Generally, the best matching block is determined upon executing a few iterations, thus requiring only fewer SAD calculations per macroblock compared to the FS algorithm. The DS extends the SA, thereby allowing more reference frame coverage by using fewer computations; however, there is a possibility of missing an optimal matched block near the center. For this purpose,

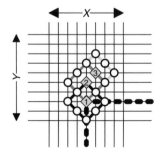

Figure 7.10   Diamond search motion estimation algorithm.

a number of algorithms, based on the DS, have been proposed in the literature to perform a hierarchical search [40] in order that when the best matching macroblock is determined an inner DS should be performed for covering points that are located inside the diamond (excluding the center point).

The second approach reduces the complexity of block distortion measure computation such as SAD or MSE [11]. Important work includes subsampling [41], partial distortion search (PDS) [42], normalized PDS [43, 44], and successive elimination algorithm (SEA) [1, 45]. These methods often achieve good coding efficiency, but have limited speedup gain. Other techniques include predicted spatial–temporal search, adaptive early termination [46–48], and dynamic search range adjustment [49]. For example, the enhanced predictive zonal search (EPZS) [50] FME algorithm improves the prediction accuracy by considering more elaborate and reliable search patterns, and a larger adaptive set of temporal (e.g., MVs of the collocated block in the previous frame) and spatial (e.g., MVs of adjacent blocks in the current frame) initial predictors. Unfortunately, the larger adaptive set of initial predictors implemented in EPZS implies a rather significant overhead increase in terms of checked points compared to previous FME algorithms [51].

7.3.2 Motion Estimation Search Area

In this regard, in order to achieve higher video quality at the expense of increased computation, it should be noted that a good match, and hence better rate–distortion performance, is more likely if the motion estimation SA is large. However, usually video encoders limit the SA to keep computation to controllable levels [11].

7.3.3 Rate–Distortion Optimization

Obtaining optimal (or near-optimal) R-D performance requires relatively high computational resources and appropriate optimization of encoding parameters; that is, the video presentation quality for a given bit rate is achieved in a trade-off of a relatively high complexity [15].

7.3.4 DCT Block Size

With a larger DCT block size, usually a better decorrelation can be achieved. However, higher complexity will be required. The 8×8 block size, as presented in Figure 7.11, is popular since it achieves good performance with relatively low computational complexity. It should be noted that increasing the block size beyond 8×8 size may also reduce performance, since using a larger DCT block size may lead to signal (image) nonstationarity.

7.3.5 Frame Rate

Owing to the computational complexity constraints, it may be required to use a relatively low frame rate, since the encoding (and decoding) computational complexity increases with the frame rate.

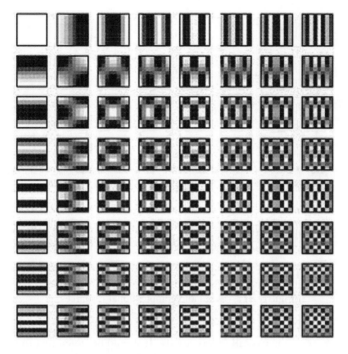

Figure 7.11   DCT typical basic patterns.

7.3.6   Constant Computational Complexity

Conventional hardware video encoders are designed with a constant computational complexity. The video encoder architecture and clock rate determine the maximum achievable video processing rate. Motion estimation algorithm, motion estimation SA, DCT block size, and maximum frame rate are fixed by their design, and place a predetermined setting on rate–distortion performance of the video encoder. However, the recently developed video coding standards, such as H.264/AVC, and novel video coding applications based on these standards require more flexible trade-offs between complexity and visual quality. The examples of such trade-off are presented in the following section.

7.4   Joint Computational Complexity and Rate Control Optimization

The computational complexity issue is critical for the present and future real-time video applications using the H.264/AVC standard, which has a large number of coding modes. In conventional advanced video coding applications, these coding modes are not fully selected at the time of video sequence encoding, since selecting all possible coding modes leads to a significant increase of the overall computational complexity. The greater the computational complexity, the larger the processing (power) resources required; the power issue becomes critical for wireless applications. On the other hand, not selecting all possible coding modes leads to an increase of the encoded video sequence distortion, and

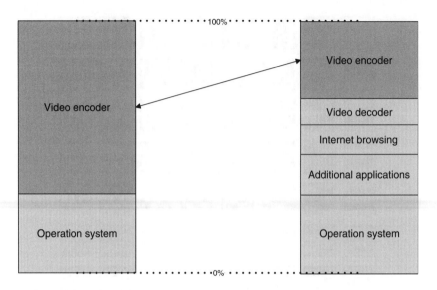

Figure 7.12   Available computational resources.

in turn to a decrease of the overall video quality. It should be noted that in order to change the overall computational constraints, the method needs to be robust. The difference in the overall video sequence quality, related to an optimal and constant computational complexity and bit allocations, defines the level of robustness.

The two schematic illustrations presented in Figure 7.12 present the need for a generic coding control methodology for any given coded bit rate and computational complexity in a video encoder, according to which computation can no longer be considered to be fixed. Generally, the video encoder performance can be considered as a function of three variables: computational complexity, coded bit rate, and video presentation quality. However, the maximum achievable video quality depends on the available coded bit rate and processing resources. Optimizing the complexity, rate, and distortion performance of a video encoder requires flexible allocation of complexity and bits for each coded element (i.e., a macroblock, slice, or frame), leading to the development of effective rate–complexity control algorithms and models for video encoding [12, 52].

Reference [13] suggests an approach for optimizing H.264/AVC video compression, thereby providing high quality video coding for H.264/AVC applications, by dynamically allocating computational complexity (such as a number of CPU clocks) and bits of each basic unit within a video sequence, according to its predicted MAD (mean absolute difference). According to this method, the overall encoding process can be performed at different levels of video quality. Higher quality levels require more computational complexity (in terms of CPU clocks). When setting the quality levels, the computational constraints of the system; the characteristics of the input, such as video sequence statistics; and the characteristics of the output, such as the distortion and the number of CPU clocks that are required for encoding each element, are taken into account. Further, a basic unit is defined as a group of adjacent macroblocks (MBs). A basic unit can be macroblock (MB), slice, field, or frame [53]. The approach suggested in [13] is based on a computational complexity–rate–distortion (*C-R-D*) analysis, which adds a complexity dimension to the conventional rate–distortion (*R-D*) analysis, and in [13] it is proved that the optimal computational complexity allocation along with optimal bit allocation is better than the constant computational complexity allocation along with optimal bit allocation. Further, the maximal processing resources usage, such as the CPU usage for a predetermined period, is achieved. As a result, the method suggested in [13] is computationally efficient.

7.4.1 Computational Complexity and Bit Allocation Problems

There are two main problems related to computational complexity and bit allocation in conventional video encoding and decoding system (Figure 7.13). The first problem is that according to the conventional *R-D* analysis, a user or a system is unable to define (manually or automatically) the computational complexity (such as the number of CPU clocks, memory bandwidth usage, and power consumption) for the overall encoding process (e.g., for encoding and storing a number of various video sequences on a server for a predetermined period). This issue becomes critical for video applications used on mobile/wireless devices due to waste of power recourses [54–56]. The second is that the computational complexity resources, such as the CPU processing resources, are not fully used during real-time encoding and transmission, since CPU processing usage depends on the encoder buffer occupancy. If the CPU has high processing resources, then the encoder buffer (having a limited memory size) is loaded too quickly under a constant quantization. One of the conventional solutions for this problem in real-time video transmission is to pause (idle) the CPU processing by sending a "wait cycle" command to CPU. However, this wastes CPU resources and impedes the CPU from operating with its maximal available power. Still another conventional solution is to decrease the CPU clock frequency (if the CPU is implemented to operate with variable clock cycles). However,

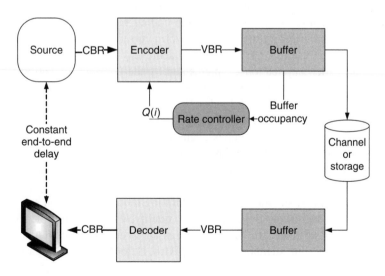

Figure 7.13   Conventional video encoding and decoding system.

by decreasing the CPU clock frequency, the available CPU resources are also wasted. Still another conventional solution is to increase the quantization settings. However, an increase of quantization settings leads to a decrease of video quality.

Most traditional video applications do not enable a user or a system to define (manually or automatically) an overall computational complexity, which can be critical for mobile/wireless devices (because of the power constraint). In these applications, the encoder receives an uncompressed CBR video sequence from any kind of source (such as a video camera or a storage device), processes it, and outputs a compressed video sequence in the form of a VBR by using entropy coding. Since almost all existing applications such as satellite broadcasting or CD-ROM playbacks use the CBR channel, a buffer between the encoder and the CBR channel is used for smoothing bit rate fluctuations. In addition, an additional buffer between the CBR channel and a decoder is used for restoring the original VBR format. As shown in Figure 7.13, which depicts the conventional video encoding and decoding system and process, a user (while off-line) cannot determine the overall computational complexity, since he/she cannot control the encoder and buffer operations during the video encoding process. For real-time applications, the system is calibrated to the worst-case video sequence, implying that it is calibrated to a video sequence having the highest complexity (the greatest video scene changes and the highest objects movements). In turn, the coding modes are selected concerning this highest complexity. As a result, if a video sequence has a low complexity, then the CPU processing recourses are not fully used, causing a waste of processing recourses. In this case, in conventional real-time transmission applications, the CPU receives the "wait cycle" command or starts operating with the decreased clock frequency.

In traditional video applications, the CPU can perform the overall encoding process of a given video sequence faster than the corresponding video presentation time of this video sequence. In addition, a better video sequence quality can be achieved if more coding modes are initially allocated for each transmitted video sequence. However, for both real-time and off-line conventional applications, achieving the best video sequence quality is usually an impossible task, since the coding modes are selected only for the worst case, without considering the complexity of a currently transmitted or stored video sequence. The optimal use of CPU recourses to achieve the best possible video quality is critical for many video applications implemented by the constant allocation H.264/AVC standard (especially for the use on mobile/wireless devices because of power constraints), which has a large number of coding modes.

Further, in conventional video applications, the encoder performs a predefined constant allocation of limited coding modes even before starting the encoding process, and therefore they cannot achieve the minimal distortion for a CBR or VBR, and for limited computational complexity. In conventional off-line applications, before starting the encoding process the user decides about the output video quality by selecting an appropriate number of coding modes, such as SAs for performing motion estimation and macroblock partition modes. By decreasing the output video quality, while keeping the same bit rate, frame rate, and GOP structure, the user decreases the overall computational complexity. The advanced video coding standards (e.g., MPEG-4, H.264/AVC) have a large number of coding modes, which significantly complicate the overall encoding process compared to previous standards, such as MPEG-2. In H.264/AVC, for example, the full coding mode selection allocates all processing and computational resources. Therefore, conventional bit allocation methods [57], employing the H.264/AVC video coding standard, usually do not use the full set of coding modes for providing real-time conditions or performing fast off-line storage encoding, which leads to lower video quality.

In Section 7.4.2, the optimal coding mode selection for the H.264/AVC video compression is considered. The optimal coding mode selection is required for achieving optimal computational complexity and optimal bit allocation.

7.4.2 Optimal Coding Modes Selection

For each given basic unit i, a full set of coding modes $m_{\text{Full}} = \{1, \ldots, M\}$ can be defined. In order to decrease the complexity of the encoding process, the number of coding modes can be reduced to a partial set of coding modes $m(i) = \{M_1 \ldots M_n\}$ and $m(i) \in m_{\text{Full}}$ (for example, 1100100100001, where ones relate to the selected coding modes and zeros to the nonselected modes). Further, by performing the RDO [58] (for encoding each macroblock k), the best (optimal) coding modes $\tilde{m}_k(i)$, which are within the above partial set of the coding modes ($\tilde{m}_k(i) \in m(i)$), are selected from $m(i)$. The partial set $m(i)$ can be different for each basic unit and can comprise any combination of different available coding modes within the above full set of coding modes m_{Full}. The better the partial set of the coding modes for a given basic unit is estimated, the smaller this set is, and the lower the computational complexity of the overall encoding process is. However, it should be noted that the computational complexity for encoding different basic units can depend not only on a set of selected coding modes but also on the activity of these basic units (e.g., if the fast mode decision and/or FME is implemented), because when performing the RDO different coding modes $\tilde{m}_k(i)$ can be allocated from the partial set of the coding modes $m(i)$ for encoding each macroblock within each basic unit i.

If the partial set of coding modes $m(i)$ is selected as a single coding mode, then the smallest possible encoding computational complexity is obtained. Therefore, if this single coding mode is the best (optimal) after performing the RDO, the same distortion is obtained, as for the full set of coding modes m_{Full}.

The performance index S_{FP} is defined by the following expression:

$$S_{\text{FP}} = \frac{\sum_{i=1}^{N} D(best(m_{\text{Full}}, \text{QP}(i)))}{\sum_{i=1}^{N} D(best(m(i), \text{QP}(i)))} = \frac{D_{\text{F}}}{D_{\text{P}}} \leq 1 \qquad (7.2)$$

where $i = 1, \ldots, N$ is a basic unit within a given video sequence; D_{F} is the sum of distortions of the full set of coding modes for the whole video sequence; D_{P} is the sum of distortions of the partial set of coding modes for the whole video sequence; $best(m_{\text{Full}}, \text{QP}(i))$ is the best set of coding modes for each basic unit selected from the full set of coding modes after performing RDO; and $best(m(i), \text{QP}(i))$ is the best set of coding modes for each basic unit selected from the estimated partial set of coding modes after performing RDO. The quantization parameter $\text{QP}(i)$ can be constant (leading

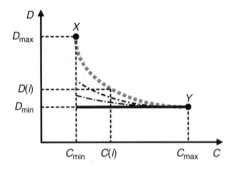

Figure 7.14   Computational complexity (C-D) curve. The solid line indicates the optimal solution.

to a VBR) or it can depend on a rate control algorithm (leading to a CBR). At the same bit rate, it is desirable to obtain the smallest computational complexity by selecting the optimal partial sets of coding modes, with respect to the computational complexity of the full set of coding modes, while the distortion of the partial set of coding modes is as close as possible to the optimal distortion of the full set of coding modes (see the wide solid line in Figure 7.14). It is obvious that the smaller the overall encoding computational complexity, the faster the overall encoding process.

Figure 7.14 presents an encoding computational complexity (C-D) curve. D_{max} is the maximal distortion and D_{min} is the minimum distortion. C_{max} is the maximal encoding computational complexity for the full set m_{Full} of coding modes. C_{min} is the minimum encoding computational complexity for the minimal set $m(i)$ of coding modes (the minimal set of coding modes can have only single mode, if a basic unit size is equal to a macroblock size). The wide dashed curve is a complexity–distortion representation of the encoding computational complexity allocation for a constant number of coding modes (the set of coding modes and the number of coding modes for each basic unit remains constant). Point X relates to the minimal set of coding modes, and therefore has the minimal encoding computational complexity and the maximal distortion. On the other hand, point Y relates to the full set of coding modes m_{Full}, and therefore it has the maximal encoding computational complexity and the minimal distortion.

Figure 7.15 presents experimental results for ''News'' video sequence under CBR encoding with a target bit rate of 28.14 Kbits/s (the bit rate is derived from VBR encoding of JM9.5 with a constant quantization parameter 32). The dashed line (convex hull of JM9.5) in Figure 7.15 represents best results of the test platform JM9.5. The Y axis of the figure represents the PSNR (peak signal-to-noise ratio) of Y component (luminance) in decibels and the X axis represents the encoding computational complexity in percents. There are total $2^{12} = 4096$ test results (12 coding modes are varied) for encoding each video sequence. Each result is shown as a single dot in Figures 7.10 and 7.11 representing different set of coding modes (from 1000000111111 to 1111111000000). The solid line on the figure represents experimental data results) for the encoding computational complexity and bit allocation method. As seen in Figure 7.15, a clear improvement in PSNR gain for the same encoding computational complexity and bit rate is obtained.

In the following section, an analysis of the computational complexity and bit allocation problems, based on the C-R-D analysis, is presented.

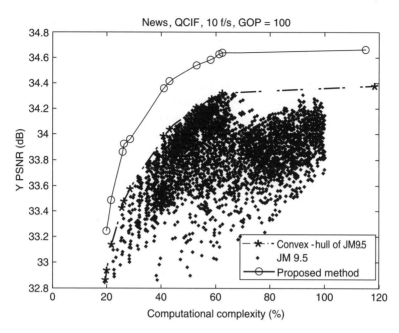

Figure 7.15 Experimental results for "News" under CBR encoding with a target bit rate of 28.14 Kbits/s.

7.4.3 C-R-D Approach for Solving Encoding Computational Complexity and Bit Allocation Problems

For a video sequence $\{x(i)\}_{i=1}^{N}$ (where $i = 1, \ldots, N$ is used to index the basic units $x(i)$, each of which can be a macroblock, slice, field, or frame), the following may be defined: a distortion function $D(x) = \sum_{i=1}^{N} e(x(i))$, the number of bits required for sequence encoding $R(x) = \sum_{i=1}^{N} r(x(i))$, and the encoding computational complexity $C(x) = \sum_{i=1}^{N} c(x(i))$, where $\{e(x(i)), c(x(i)), r(x(i))\}$ is the distortion, encoding computational complexity, and rate of the basic unit $x(i)$, respectively. An encoding computational complexity and bit allocation problem is a constrained optimization problem [26]. The cost function is a distortion function, and the constraints are encoding computational complexity and the number of bits required for video sequence encoding.

For convenience, $\{e(x(i)), c(x(i)), r(x(i))\}$ may be notated as $\{e(i), c(i), r(i)\}$. The distortion is related to the encoding computational complexity and rate, such that when $c(i)$ and/or $r(i)$ become smaller, their corresponding distortion $e(i)$ becomes larger, and vice versa. Furthermore, if the sequence of the encoding computational complexity $\{c(i)\}$ and the sequence of the rate $\{r(i)\}$ are determined, then the corresponding sequence of the distortion can be obtained. To obtain an optimal encoding computational complexity and bit allocation for each basic unit for a given rate and for a given encoding computational complexity for the overall video sequence, a sequence of the encoding computational complexity and a sequence of bits, which minimize the distortion $D(x)$ with the constraints $C(x) \leq C$ and $R(x) \leq R$, have to be found. The equation of the encoding computational complexity and bit allocation problem can be modified by using other limitations, besides the above limitation of minimizing the distortion $D(x)$. For example, it is supposed that it is given a sequence $\{x(i)\}_{i=1}^{N}$, and it is assumed that P is the number of total available combinations of quantizers and coding modes that can be selected for encoding each basic unit. Then, the problem of obtaining the optimal encoding computational complexity and bit allocation can be solved by selecting the optimal set of coding modes (and the optimal quantizers) from a set of available combinations of coding modes (and quantizers). Therefore, a sequence of optimal sets of coding modes (and quantizers) have to be found, denoted by $m(i) \in P, i = 1, 2, \ldots, N$, which minimizes the distortion function $D(x)$ with constraints $C(x) \leq C$ and $R(x) \leq R$.

$e_{im(i)}$, $r_{im(i)}$, and $c_{im(i)}$ are denoted as the distortion, rate and encoding computational complexity of the basic unit i, respectively, while using the optimal set of coding modes (and quantizers) $m(i)$. The encoding computational complexity and bit allocation problem can be defined by

$$\min_{\{m(i)\}} \left\{ \sum_{i=1}^{N} e_{im(i)} \right\} \text{ subject to:}$$

$$\sum_{i=1}^{N} r_{im(i)} \leq R \text{ and } \sum_{i=1}^{N} c_{im(i)} \leq C \tag{7.3}$$

where C is the encoding computational complexity and R is the total number of bits allocated for encoding the video sequence $\{x(i)\}_{i=1}^{N}$.

The encoding computational complexity and bit allocation problem is defined as

$$\min_{\{c(i), r(i)\}} \left\{ \sum_{i=1}^{N} e(i) \right\} \text{ subject to:}$$

$$\sum_{i=1}^{N} c(i) \leq C \text{ and } \sum_{i=1}^{N} r(i) \leq R \tag{7.4}$$

where $e(i)$, $r(i)$, and $c(i)$ are distortion, rate, and encoding computational complexity of the basic unit i, respectively. In Equation 7.4, it is assumed that there is a clear relationship between the distortion, encoding computational complexity, and bit rate. From this equation, an optimal set of coding modes (and quantizers) can be found. Of course, the computational cost of Equation 7.3 is greater than that of Equation 7.4, because for each solution (for each C, R) according to Equation 7.4, the set of modes $m(i)$ is not updated and remains constant, as initially selected. If the number of coding modes and quantizers of Equation 7.3 is large, the computational costs of Equations 7.3 and 7.4 are almost the same because (according to Equation 7.4) the optimal solutions C and R are selected based on the full (or almost the full) set of modes. Thus, in this case, the solutions of Equations 7.3 and 7.4 are both optimal. Since Equation 7.4 is much simpler to analyze than Equation 7.3, a solution to Equation 7.4 may be determined. Thus, for simplicity, the dependence between the basic units may not be considered. For solving the encoding computational complexity and bit allocation problems, expressed in Equations 7.3 and 7.4, the Lagrange multiplier method [59] can be used.

If the following sequences $\{c(i)\}_{i=1}^{N}$ and $\{r(i)\}_{i=1}^{N}$ minimize the cost function J, formulated by

$$J = \sum_{i=1}^{N} \{e(i) + \lambda_C \cdot c(i) + \lambda_R \cdot r(i)\} \tag{7.5}$$

then for some values of λ_C and λ_R, which are the computational complexity and rate Lagrange multipliers ($\lambda_C > 0$ and $\lambda_R > 0$), the optimal solution to Equation 7.3 is equivalent to the optimal solution to Equation 7.4 when $C(x) = C$ and $R(x) = R$. The Lagrange multipliers λ_C and λ_R in Equation 7.5, which ensure $R(x) = R$ and $C(x) = C$, cannot be obtained directly from Equation 7.5, but can be found iteratively. Some updating methods of 1D (one-dimensional) λ can be found in [25]. According to these methods, the number of iterations for updating λ is not significant. However, the encoding computational complexity in these methods increases with the increase of the length of the video source N. It should be noted that there are other alternative methods for searching in the 2D space of Lagrange multipliers (e.g., approximation methods [60]); however, these methods do not provide optimal results.

As known from the literature, for example, from [61, 62], most distortion–complexity–rate (D-C-R) surfaces are actually exponential distortion–complexity–rate (ED-C-R) surfaces. The average D-C-R surface of the video sequence is an ED-C-R surface. The following model can represent the ED-C-R surface:

$$D(C, R) = A\alpha^{-R}\beta^{-C}, \text{ for } C > 0, R > 0 \tag{7.6}$$

where $A > 0, \beta > 0$, and $\alpha > 1$. From Equation 7.6, the corresponding average complexity–rate–distortion (C-R-D) and rate–complexity–distortion (R-C-D) surfaces are given by

$$C(R, D) = \log_\beta \left(A\alpha^{-R}/D \right), \text{ for } A\beta^{-R} > D > 0 \tag{7.7}$$

and

$$R(C, D) = \log_\alpha \left(A\beta^{-C}/D \right), \text{ for } A\beta^{-C} > D > 0 \tag{7.8}$$

Equations 7.6–7.8 can be used in various video applications for solving encoding computational complexity and bit allocation problems.

7.4.4 Allocation of Computational Complexity and Bits

As described above, while selecting the minimal encoding computational complexity, an optimal set of coding modes for encoding each basic unit cannot be obtained, thus resulting in the maximal distortion. In other words, the minimal encoding computational complexity relates to a single coding mode, thus resulting in the maximal distortion.

The H.264/AVC standard adopt a conventional method [27, 53] for determining an optimal coding mode for encoding each macroblock. According to [53], the RDO for each macroblock is performed for selecting an optimal coding mode by minimizing the Lagrangian function as follows:

$$J\ (orig, rec, MODE \mid \lambda_{MODE})$$

$$= D\ (orig, rec, MODE \mid QP) + \lambda_{MODE}\ R\ (orig, rec, MODE \mid QP) \qquad (7.9)$$

where the distortion $D\ (orig, rec, MODE \mid QP)$ is the sum of squared differences (SSD) between the original block ($orig$) and the reconstructed block (rec); QP is the macroblock quantization parameter; $MODE$ is the mode selected from the set of available prediction modes; $R\ (orig, rec, MODE \mid QP)$ is the number of bits associated with the selected $MODE$; and λ_{MODE} is the Lagrangian multiplier for the mode decision.

However (if not enabling all available modes), after performing the high-complexity RDO and using FS motion estimation, the computational complexity allocation required for encoding each macroblock within each frame type (I, P, or B) is constant and not optimal. When implementing the FME, the computational complexity allocation is variable, but is still not optimal.

The conventional encoder rate control may try to code each frame of the same type (I, P, and B) with the same number of bits as presented in Figure 7.16, where the dashed line represents an average bit rate. But then the video quality would be poor for I frames or for scenes with high complexity. Thus, by adding the computational complexity dimension, higher video quality can be achieved by dynamically allocating the encoding computational complexity and bits; that is, for complicated video scenes, higher computational complexity should be allocated.

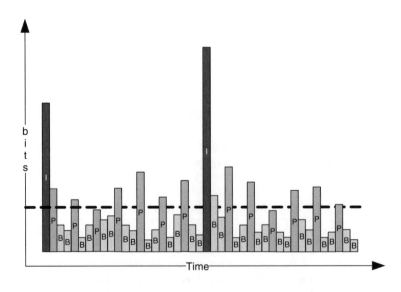

Figure 7.16 Conventional bit allocation.

In this section, a system for dynamic allocation of the encoding computational complexity and bits, according to the predicted MAD of each basic unit, based on both encoding computational complexity allocation and bit allocation is presented. A set of best groups of coding modes is determined for further rate-constrained mode selection (for performing the RDO). According to this method, the computational complexity and bit rate required for encoding each basic unit within each frame type (I, P, or B) are varied depending on the number of selected coding modes and depending on the quantization parameter QP (or depending on the quantization step-size Q). The QP is calculated to determine λ_R [53] to further perform RDO, and Q is used for quantizing the "intra" or "inter" compensation image residual between the original block and the predicted block (after performing the H.264/AVC integer DCT) [29].

In Figure 7.17, the system for dynamic allocation of the encoding computational complexity and bits, based on the $C\text{-}R\text{-}D$ analysis [13] is presented. For solving the problem related to the off-line storage encoding process (Section 7.4.1), at the first stage the user or system determines (manually or automatically) an overall computational complexity for the storage encoding process. The encoding computational complexity controller receives the predetermined overall encoding computational complexity and allocates the corresponding set of coding modes $m(i)$ for each frame and/or for each basic unit in

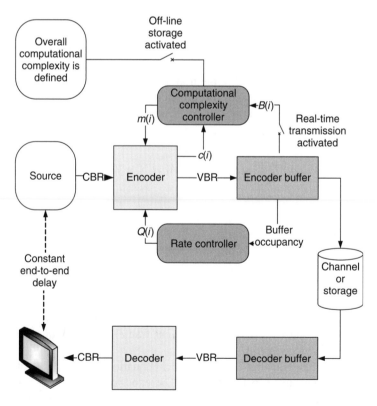

Figure 7.17   The video encoding and decoding system, according to [13].

order to minimize the overall distortion at a CBR or VBR. According to Figure 7.17, the user also predetermines the size of a storage file or predetermines a bit rate of the output video sequence. $B(i)$ expresses the encoder buffer occupancy for each basic unit i. The encoder transfers to the encoding computational complexity controller the actual encoding computational complexity $c(i)$ for each encoded basic unit i. $m(i)$ is selected by the computational complexity controller in accordance with the user's predetermined overall encoding computational complexity. The greater the user's predetermined overall computational complexity, the larger the set of coding modes $m(i)$. If there is a real-time operation, then the real-time transmission switch is activated for enabling the usage of the encoder buffer in order to prevent the loss of synchronization between the encoder and the decoder. This leads to quality degradation and frames dropping, causing the video sequence playback to be unsmooth. In real-time, a hypothetical reference decoder (HRD) of a given encoder buffer size should decode a video bit stream without suffering from buffer overflow or underflow. The reasons for desynchronization are usually not in the decoder, but in the encoder. If the encoder buffer is almost overloaded, then additional encoding computational complexity can be allocated for each basic unit. It should be noted that the method relates to both real-time and off-line encoding.

7.4.4.1 Frame Level Encoding Computational Complexity and Bit Rate Control

On the basis of Equations 7.6–7.8, the average R-Q-C and C-I-R models for determining the quantization step-size Q and the complexity step I for selecting a corresponding group of coding modes (e.g., $I = 1, \ldots, M$; where M is the number of coding modes) are presented as follows. These models can be formulated by the following equations (analogous to [22, 27], which are related to the traditional quadratic R-Q model). In Equation 7.10, the distortion D is represented, for simplicity [27], by the average computational complexity step I, and in Equation 7.11, it is represented by the average quantization step-size Q:

$$C(I, R) = A_{C_1} I^{-1} + A_{C_2} I^{-2} + A_{C_3} R \tag{7.10}$$

and

$$R(Q, C) = A_{R_1} Q^{-1} + A_{R_2} Q^{-2} + A_{R_3} C \tag{7.11}$$

where A_{C_1}, A_{C_2}, A_{C_3} and A_{R_1}, A_{R_2}, A_{R_3} are the corresponding coefficients that are calculated regressively; I is the complexity step for selecting a corresponding group of coding modes; and Q is the corresponding quantization step-size for performing RDO for each macroblock in each basic unit in the current frame by using Equation 7.9 and by using the method provided in [63].

Experimental and fitted quadratic R-Q-C model (Equation 7.11) surfaces of the "News" video sequence are presented in Figure 7.18. The experimental surface is based on the experimental data, and the fitted surface is represented by Equation 7.11. An average error between the experimental and fitted surfaces is 2.84%.

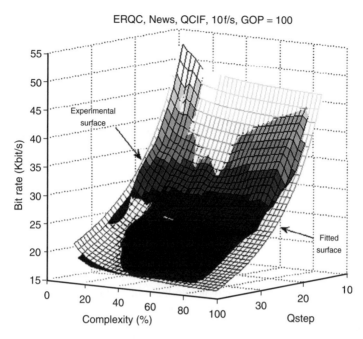

Figure 7.18 The experimental and the fitted with quadratic R-Q-C model surfaces of the "News" video sequence (QCIF, 10 fps; GOP, 100 (IPPP...); QP range, 28–36). The experimental surface is based on the experimental data, and the fitted surface is represented by Equation (7.11).

7.4.4.2 Basic Unit Level Encoding Computational Complexity and Bit Rate Control

The concept of a basic unit is defined in [53]. Each basic unit can be an MB, a slice, a field, or a frame. For example, a QCIF video sequence may be considered, wherein the number of MBs in each frame is 99. Therefore, according to [53], the number of basic units per frame can be 1, 3, 9, 11, 33, or 99.

It should be noted that by employing a large basic unit size, a higher visual quality is achieved; however, bit fluctuations are also increased, since greater bit rate variations are required to obtain the target bit rate. On the other hand, by using a small basic unit size, bit fluctuations are less drastic, but they usually decrease the visual quality [28]. Therefore, there is a trade-off between the visual quality and bit fluctuations, when the basic unit size is varied. Similarly, the same analogy is used for the encoding computational complexity trade-off. As more encoding computational complexity is allocated for each basic unit, the higher is the visual quality and the more drastic are the variations that are required for obtaining the target encoding computational complexity.

Similar to the frame level encoding computational complexity control described in Section 7.4.4.1, the target computational complexity for each basic unit, according to its predicted MAD [28, 53] is determined. For each basic unit in each frame, a set of groups of coding modes is selected so that the overall complexity for encoding each basic unit is close to its target encoding computational complexity. For the bit rate control, a method described in [13] can be applied, except for the following quadratic model (Equation 7.12), which can be used for calculating the quantization step-size Q:

$$R(Q, C) = (A_{R_1} Q^{-1} + A_{R_2} Q^{-2} + A_{R_3} C)\sigma(i) \tag{7.12}$$

where A_{R_1}, A_{R_2}, A_{R_3} are the corresponding coefficients that are calculated regressively and $\sigma(i)$ is the predicted MAD of the current basic unit. Equation 7.12 is similar to Equation 7.11, as presented in Section 7.4.4.1.

It should be noted that the complexity step I should be computed by using the following quadratic model, which is similar to Equation 7.10:

$$C(I, R) = \left(A_{C_1} I^{-1} + A_{C_2} I^{-2} + A_{C_3} R\right) \sigma(i) \tag{7.13}$$

where A_{C_1}, A_{C_2}, A_{C_3} are the corresponding coefficients that are calculated regressively; I is the complexity step for selecting a corresponding group of coding modes; and $\sigma(i)$ is the predicted MAD of the current basic unit i.

7.5 Transform Coding Optimization

Advances in telecommunications and networking have facilitated the next broadband revolution which focuses on home networking. Services such as PVRs (personal video recorders), next-generation game consoles, video-on-demand, and HDTV have created a sophisticated home entertainment environment. To reduce transmission rates and to utilize the bandwidth of communication systems, data compression techniques need to be implemented. There are various methods to compress video data. These methods are dependent on application and system requirements. Sometimes, compression of video data without losses (lossless compression [64]) is required, but most of the time, in order to achieve high compression ratios, only partial data is processed and coded without actual image quality degradation. Frequently, the compression process by the video encoder requires special real-time manipulations such as insertion of the objects, change of frame properties, quantization, filtering, and motion compensation. Incorporation of these manipulation techniques in conventional digital video encoders requires their implementation in the pixel domain (e.g., motion estimation and filtering) before forward DCT or in the DCT domain (e.g., quantization and dequantization) before inverse discrete cosine transform (IDCT). The implementation of these manipulation techniques increases the number of DCT/IDCT and thereby requires increased computational resources.

According to [65], the two-dimensional (2D) DCT (and its inverse, the IDCT) can be described in terms of transform matrix A. The forward DCT of $N \times N$ sample block is given by

$$AXA^T \tag{7.14}$$

The IDCT is given by

$$A^T YA \tag{7.15}$$

where X is a matrix of samples, Y is a matrix of coefficients, and A is an $N \times N$ transform matrix. The elements of A are

$$A_{ij} = C_i \cos \frac{(2j + 1)i\pi}{2N}$$

where

$$
C_i = \begin{cases} \sqrt{\dfrac{1}{N}}, \text{ for } i = 0 \\[2ex] \sqrt{\dfrac{2}{N}}, \text{ for } i > 0 \end{cases}
\tag{7.16}
$$

Therefore, the transform matrix A for a 2×2 DCT is

$$
\begin{pmatrix} \sqrt{\dfrac{1}{2}}\cos(0) & \sqrt{\dfrac{1}{2}}\cos(0) \\[2ex] \sqrt{1}\cos\dfrac{\pi}{4} & \sqrt{1}\cos\dfrac{3\pi}{4} \end{pmatrix} = \begin{pmatrix} \sqrt{\dfrac{1}{2}} & \sqrt{\dfrac{1}{2}} \\[2ex] \sqrt{\dfrac{1}{2}} & -\sqrt{\dfrac{1}{2}} \end{pmatrix}
\tag{7.17}
$$

As each 2×2 block consists of four pixels, only four DCT coefficients are required for the DCT domain representation. As a result of the DCT transform, the four equations for the four DCT coefficients can be derived by substituting Equation 7.15 in Equation 7.17:

$$
\begin{aligned}
Y(0,0) &= \frac{1}{2} \times (X(0,0) + X(1,0) + X(0,1) + X(1,1)) \\[1ex]
Y(0,1) &= \frac{1}{2} \times (X(0,0) + X(1,0) - X(0,1) - X(1,1)) \\[1ex]
Y(1,0) &= \frac{1}{2} \times (X(0,0) - X(1,0) + X(0,1) - X(1,1)) \\[1ex]
Y(1,1) &= \frac{1}{2} \times (X(0,0) - X(1,0) - X(0,1) + X(1,1))
\end{aligned}
\tag{7.18}
$$

On the basis of Equation 7.18, a 2×2 forward/inverse DCT can be extracted with only eight summations and four right-shifting operations. An illustrative schematic block diagram for the transform's implementation is shown in Figure 7.19, which presents the implementation of eight summation units and four right-shift operation units without using any multiplications.

In Figure 7.19, the following notations are adopted, as further presented in Figure 7.20.

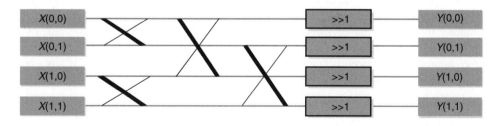

Figure 7.19   Signal flow graph for 2×2 DCT computation.

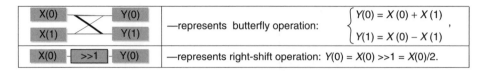

Figure 7.20 Signal flow graph for butterfly and right-shift operations.

On the basis of Equation 7.18, the forward 2×2 DCT in matrix form (Equation 7.14) can be written as

$$Y = \frac{1}{2}AXA^T = \frac{1}{2}\begin{pmatrix} 1 & 1 \\ 1 & -1 \end{pmatrix}\begin{pmatrix} x_{00} & x_{01} \\ x_{10} & x_{11} \end{pmatrix}\begin{pmatrix} 1 & 1 \\ 1 & -1 \end{pmatrix} \tag{7.19}$$

It should be noted that no actual multiplications or right shifts are necessary to compute the transform, since the transform matrix elements are all equal to ± 1, and the final scaling by a factor of 1/2 can be absorbed by the quantization operation. Also, it should be noted that the smaller DCT (such as 2×2 forward/inverse DCT, which is presented in Figure 7.19) matrices can be more easily implemented, but they are less efficient due to undesired artifacts (e.g., blocking effects), which appear after performing the quantization process. Therefore, a larger DCT is usually used, but such a transform has to be optimized for reducing computational complexity.

Further, numerous fast DCTs/IDCTs have been proposed in the literature. Loeffler *et al*. [66] have presented an 11-multiplication – a 29 summations algorithm that appears to be the most efficient one for 8-point 1D DCTs [67]. 1D DCTs are, in general, used to compute 2D DCTs. For example, 1D DCT can be applied on each row, and then on each column of the row transform result. This approach is called the *row–column method*, and would require $2N$ 1D transforms of size N to realize an $N \times N$ 2D transform. The alternative to the row–column method is the direct 2D method of computing the transform from the N^2 input numbers. The paper by Kamangar *et al*. [68] is the first work on the 2D transforms to reduce the computational complexity. There are also techniques proposed to convert a 2D $N \times N$ transform into an N 1D transform plus some pre/postprocessing. Cho and Lee's paper [69] was followed by Feig *et al*. [70]. All two proposals require the same number of multiplications, half of what the row–column method [66] requires, while Feig *et al*.'s [70] has slightly lower summation count than Cho and Lee's [69]. Compared to applying $2N$ instances of 1D DCT, 2D $N \times N$ DCT/IDCT algorithms generally require fewer multiplications, yet have larger flow graphs, which translate to implementation as more temporary storage and/or larger data path. To reduce computational complexity of fast-fixed complexity forward DCT, two major approaches have been proposed in the literature. In the first, namely, *frequency selection*, only a subset of DCT coefficients is computed [71, 72], and in the second, namely *accuracy selection*, all the DCT coefficients are computed with reduced accuracy [73, 74]. For example, Docef *et al*. [73] have proposed quantizer-dependent variable complexity approximate DCT algorithm based on the *accuracy selection*. Its performance shows saving of up to 70% complexity as compared to the fast-fixed complexity forward DCT implementations, with 0.3 dB PSNR degradation. The variable complexity hybrid forward DCT algorithm that combines both frequency and accuracy selection approaches was proposed by Lengwehasatit *et al*. [75]. Its performance shows saving of up to 73% complexity as compared to the fast-fixed complexity forward DCT implementations, with 0.2 dB PSNR degradation.

7.6 Summary

In this chapter, four major video coding optimization issues have been presented in detail: rate control optimization, computational complexity control optimization, joint computational complexity and rate control optimization, and transform coding optimization. The presented approaches, such as the computational complexity and bit allocation for optimizing H.264/AVC video compression can be integrated to develop an efficient video encoder. While being controlled by an efficient computational and bit rate control algorithm, the video encoder will enable (i) selecting computational load and transmitted bit rate, (ii) selecting quantization parameters, (iii) selecting coding modes, (iv) selecting motion estimation algorithm for each type of an input video signal, and (v) selecting appropriate transform coding.

The presented optimization methods might be especially useful for future Internet and 4G applications with limited computational resources, such as videoconferencing (between two or more mobile users), video transrating, video transcoding between MPEG-2 and H.264/AVC video coding standards, and the like.

References

[1] Pennebaker, W.B. and Mitchell, J.L. (1993) *JPEG Still Image Data Compression Standard*, Van Nostrand Reinhold, New York.
[2] Sikora, T. (1997) The MPEG-4 video standard verification model. *IEEE Transactions on Circuits and Systems for Video Technology*, **7**, 19–31.
[3] Wiegand, T. and Sullivan, G. (2003) Final draft ITU-T Recommendation and Final Draft International Standard of Joint Video Specification, ITU-T Rec. H.264/ISO/IEC 14496-10 AVC, Pattaya, Thailand, March 7–15.
[4] Richardson, I.E.G. (2005) *H.264 and MPEG-4 Video Compression: Video Coding for Next-generation Multimedia*, John Wiley & Sons, Ltd, Chichester.
[5] Spanias, S. (1994) Speech coding: a tutorial review. Proceedings of the IEEE, pp. 1541–1582.
[6] VM ad-hoc (1999) JPEG-2000 verification model version 5.2. ISO/IEC JTC1/SC29/WG01 Ad-hoc Group on JPEG-2000 Verification Model, WG1 N1422, August.
[7] Marcellin, M.W., Gormish, M.J., Bilgin, A., and Boliek, M.P. (2000) An overview of JPEG-2000. Proceedings of the IEEE Data Compression Conference, pp. 523–541.
[8] Marcellin, M. and Rountree, J. (1997) Wavelet/TCQ Technical Details. ISO/IEC JTC1/SC29/WG1 N632, November.
[9] Wu, X. (1997) High-order context modeling and embedded conditional entropy coding of wavelet coefficients for image compression. Presented at the in 31st Asilomar Conference on Signals Systems Computers, Pacific Grove, CA, November.
[10] Wu, X. and Memon, N. (1997) Context-based, adaptive, lossless image codec. *IEEE Transactions on Communications*, **45**, 437–444.
[11] Kuhn, P. (1999) *Algorithms, Complexity Analysis and VLSI Architectures for MPEG-4 Motion Estimation*, Kluwer Academic Publishers, Boston, MA, pp. 29–33.
[12] Vanam, R., Riskin, E.A., and Ladner, R.E. (2009) H.264/MPEG-4 AVC encoder parameter selection algorithms for complexity distortion tradeoff. Proceedings of the IEEE Data Compression Conference, pp. 372–381.
[13] Kaminsky, E., Grois, D., and Hadar, O. (2008) Dynamic computational complexity and bit allocation for optimizing H.264/AVC video compression. *Journal of Visual Communication and Image Representation – Elsevier*, **19**, 56–74.

[14] Gish, H. and Pierce, J.N. (1968) Asymptotically efficient quantizing. *IEEE Transactions on Information Theory*, **IT-14**, 676–683.

[15] Berger, T. (1984) *Rate Distortion Theory*, Prentice Hall, Englewood Cliffs, NJ.

[16] He, Z. (2001) ρ-domain rate distortion analysis and rate control for visual coding and communications. PhD thesis. University of California, Santa Barbara.

[17] Chiang, T. and Zhang, Y. (1997) A new rate control scheme using quadratic rate-distortion modeling. *IEEE Transactions on Circuits and Systems for Video Technology*, **7**, 246–250.

[18] Lin, C.W., Liou, T.J., and Chen, Y.C. (2000) Dynamic rate control in multipoint video transcoding. Proceedings IEEE International Symposium Circuits and Systems, pp. 28–31.

[19] Wang, L. (2000) Rate control for MPEG video coding. *Signal Processing-Image Communication*, **15**, 493–511.

[20] Shoham, Y. and Gersho, A. (1988) Efficient bit allocation for an arbitrary set of quantizers. *IEEE Transactions on Acoustics Speech and Signal Processing*, **36**, 1445–1453.

[21] Shen, J. and Chen, W.Y. (2000) Fast rate-distortion optimization algorithm for motion-compensated coding of video. *IEE Electronics Letters*, **36**, 305–306.

[22] Wiegand, T. (2002) Working Draft Number 2, Revision 2 (WD-2). Joint Video Team (JVT) of ISO/IEC MPEG and ITU-T VCEG, Doc. JVT-B118R2, March.

[23] Kwon, D.-K., Shen, M.-Y., and Kuo, C.-C.J. (2007) Rate control for H.264 video with enhanced rate and distortion models. *IEEE Transactions on Circuits and Systems for Video Technology*, **17** (5), 517–529.

[24] Wu, S., Huang, Y., and Ikenaga, T. (2009) A macroblock-level rate control algorithm for H.264/AVC video coding with context-adaptive MAD prediction model. Proceedings of the International Conference on Computer Modeling and Simulation, pp. 124–128.

[25] Ortega, A., Ramchandran, K., and Vetterli, M. (1994) Optimal trellis-based buffered compression and fast approximations. *IEEE Transactions on Image Processing*, **3**, 26–40.

[26] Choi, J. and Park, D. (1994) A stable feedback control of the buffer state using the controlled Lagrange multiplier method. *IEEE Transactions on Image Processing*, **3** (5), 546–557.

[27] Chiang, T. and Zhang, Y.-Q. (1997) A new rate control scheme using quadratic rate distortion model. *IEEE Transactions on Circuits and Systems for Video Technology*, **7** (1), 246–250.

[28] Li, Z., Pan, F., Lim, K.P. *et al.* (2003) Adaptive Basic Unit Layer Rate Control for JVT. Joint Video Team (JVT) of ISO/IEC MPEG and ITU-T VCEG (ISO/IEC JTC1/SC29/WG11 and ITU-T SG16 Q.6), Doc. JVT-G012, Pattaya, Thailand, March.

[29] Kannangara, C.S. and Richardson, I.E.G. (2005) Computational control of an h.264 encoder through Lagrangian cost function estimation. Proceedings of VLBV 2005 Conference, Glasgow, UK, pp. 379–384.

[30] He, Z., Liang, Y., Chen, L. *et al.* (2005) Power-rate-distortion analysis for wireless video communication under energy constraints. *IEEE Transactions on Circuits and Systems for Video Technology*, **15** (5), 645–658.

[31] Schaar, M. and Andreopoulos, Y. (2005) Rate-distortion-complexity modeling for network and receiver aware adaptation. *IEEE Transactions on Multimedia*, **7** (3), 471–479.

[32] Kaminsky, E. and Hadar, O. (2008) Multiparameter method for analysis and selection of motion estimation algorithm for video compression. *Springer Multimedia Tools and Applications*, **38**, 119–146.

[33] Ribas-Corbera, J. and Neuhoff, D.L. (1997) On the optimal block size for block-based, motion compensated video coders. *SPIE Proceedings of Visual Communications and Image Processing*, **3024**, 1132–1143.

[34] Koga, T., Iinuma, K., Hirano, A. *et al.* (1981) Motion compensated interframe coding for video conferencing. Proceedings of National Telecommunication Conference, pp. G5.3.1–G5.3.5.

[35] Liu, L.K. and Feig, E. (1996) A block-based gradient descent search algorithm for block motion estimation in video coding. *IEEE Transactions on Circuits and Systems for Video Technology*, **6**, 419–423.

[36] Li, R., Zeng, B., and Liou, M.L. (1994) A new three-step search algorithm for block motion estimation. *IEEE Transactions on Circuits and Systems for Video Technology*, **4**, 438–442.

[37] Tham, J.Y., Ranganath, S., Ranganth, M., and Kassim, A.A. (1998) A novel unrestricted center-biased diamond search algorithm for block motion estimation. *IEEE Transactions on Circuits and Systems for Video Technology*, **8**, 369–377.

[38] Zhu, S. and Ma, K.-K. (2000) A new diamond search algorithm for fast block-matching motion estimation. *IEEE Transactions on Image Processing*, **9**, 287–290.

[39] Zhu, C., Lin, X., and Chau, L.-P. (2002) Hexagon-based search pattern for fast block motion estimation. *IEEE Transactions on Circuits and Systems for Video Technology*, **12**, 349–355.

[40] Bergen, J.R., Anandan, P., Hanna, K.J., and Hingorani, R. (1992) Hierarchical model-based motion estimation. Proceedings of Computer Vision – ECCV, pp. 237–252.

[41] Lin, Y.-L.S., Kao, C.-Y., Chen, J.-W., and Kuo, H.-C. (2010) *Vlsi Design for Video Coding: H.264/Avc Encoding from Standard Specification*, Springer, New York.

[42] Eckart, S. and Fogg, C. (1995) ISO/IEC MPEG-2 software video codec. Proceedings of SPIE, vol. 2419, pp. 100–118.

[43] Cheung, C.K. and Po, L.M. (2000) Normalized partial distortion search algorithm for block motion estimation. *IEEE Transactions on Circuits and Systems for Video Technology*, 10, 417–422.

[44] Lengwehasatit, K. and Orgega, A. (2001) Probabilistic partial-distance fast matching algorithms for motion estimation. *IEEE Transactions on Circuits and Systems for Video Technology*, 11, 139–152.

[45] Li, W. and Salari, E. (1995) Successive elimination algorithm for motion estimation. *IEEE Transactions on Image Processing*, 4, 105–107.

[46] Gao, X.Q., Duanmu, C.J., and Zou, C.R. (2000) A multilevel successive elimination algorithm for block matching motion estimation. Proceedings of the International Conference on Image Processing, vol. 9, pp. 501–504.

[47] Tourapis, A.M., Au, O.C., and Liou, M.L. (2002) Highly efficient predictive zonal algorithm for fast block-matching motion estimation. *IEEE Transactions on Circuits and Systems for Video Technology*, 12, 934–947.

[48] Chen, Z., Zhou, P., and He, Y. (2002) Fast Integer and Fractional Pel Motion Estimation for JVT. JVT-F017r.doc, Joint Video Team (JVT) of ISO/IEC MPEG & ITU-T VCEG. 6th Meeting, Awaji, Island, Japan, December 5–13.

[49] Hong, M.-C. and Park, Y.M. (2001) Dynamic search range decision for motion estimation. VCEG-N33, September.

[50] Tourapis, A.M. (2002) Enhanced predictive zonal search for single and multiple frame motion estimation. Proceedings of Visual Communications and Image Processing, pp. 1069–1079.

[51] Lu, X., Tourapis, A.M., Yin, P., and Boyce, J. (2005) Fast mode decision and motion estimation for H.264 with a focus on MPEG-2/H.264 transcoding. Presented at the IEEE International Symposium on Circuits and Systems (ISCAS), Kobe, Japan, May.

[52] Foo, B., Andreopoulos, Y., and van der Schaar, M. (2008) Analytical rate-distortion-complexity modeling of wavelet-based video coders. *IEEE Transactions on Signal Processing*, 56, 797–815.

[53] Lim, K.-P., Sullivan, G., and Wiegand, T. (2005) Text description of joint model reference encoding methods and decoding concealment methods. Study of ISO/IEC 14496-10 and ISO/IEC 14496-5/ AMD6 and Study of ITU-T Rec. H.264 and ITU-T Rec. H.264.2, in Joint Video Team (JVT) of ISO/IEC MPEG and ITU-T VCEG, Busan, Korea, April, Doc. JVT-O079.

[54] Kannangara, C.S., Richardson, I.E.G., and Miller, A.J. (2008) Computational complexity management of a real-time H.264/AVC encoder. *IEEE Transactions on Circuits and Systems for Video Technology*, 18 (9), 1191–1200.

[55] He, Z., Cheng, W., and Chen, X. (2008) Energy minimization of portable video communication devices based on power-rate-distortion optimization. *IEEE Transactions on Circuits and Systems for Video Technology*, 18, 596–608.

[56] Su, L., Lu, Y., Wu, F. *et al*. (2009) Complexity-constrained H.264 video encoding. *IEEE Transactions on Circuits and Systems for Video Technology*, 19, 477–490.

[57] Ma, S., Gao, W., Gao, P., and Lu, Y. (2003) Rate control for advanced video coding (AVC) standard. Proceedings of International Symposium Circuits and Systems (ISCAS), pp. 892–895.

[58] Zeng, H., Cai, C., and Ma, K.-K. (2009) Fast mode decision for H.264/AVC based on macroblock motion activity. *IEEE Transactions on Circuits and Systems for Video Technology*, 19 (4), 1–10.

[59] Everett, H. (1963) Generalized lagrange multiplier method for solving problems of optimum allocation of resources. *Operations Research*, 11, 399–417.

[60] Jiang, M. and Ling, N. (2006) Lagrange multiplier and quantizer adjustment for H.264 frame-layer video rate control. *IEEE Transactions on Circuits and Systems for Video Technology*, 16 (5), 663–668.

[61] Grecos, C. and Jiang, J. (2003) On-line improvements of the rate-distortion performance in MPEG-2 rate control. *IEEE Transactions on Circuits and Systems for Video Technology*, 13 (6), 519–528.

[62] Lengwehasatit, K. and Ortega, A. (2003) Rate-complexity-distortion optimization for quadtree-based DCT coding. Proceedings of International Conference on Image Processing (ICIP), vol. 3, Vancouver, BC, Canada, September 2003, pp. 821–824.

[63] Wiegand, T. and Girod, B. (2001) Parameter selection in Lagrangian hybrid video coder control. Proceedings of the International Conference on Image Processing, vol. 3, Thessaloniki, Greece, pp. 542–545.

[64] Salomon, D. (2007) *Data Compression: The Complete Reference*, Springer-Verlag, London.

[65] Rao, K.R. and Yip, P. (1990) *Discrete Cosine Transform: Algorithms, Advantages, Applications*, Academic Press, Boston, MA.

[66] Parhi, K.K. and Nishitani, T. (1999) *Digital Signal Processing for Multimedia Systems*, Marcel Dekker, New York, pp. 355–369.

[67] Loeffler, C., Ligtenberg, A., and Moschytz, G.S. (1989) Practical fast 1-D DCT algorithms with 11 multiplications. Proceedings of ICASSP, pp. 988–991.

[68] Kamangar, F.A. and Rao, K.R. (1985) Fast algorithms for the 2-D discrete cosine transform. *IEEE Transactions on Computer*, **ASSP-33**, 1532–1539.

[69] Fetweis, G. and Meyr, H. (1990) Cascaded feed forward architectures for parallel Viterbi decoding. Proceedings of IEEE International Symposium on Circuits and Systems, pp. 978–981.

[70] Feig, E. and Winograd, S. (1992) Fast algorithms for the discrete cosine transform. *IEEE Transactions on Signal Processing*, **40**, 2174–2193.

[71] Girod, B. and Stuhlmüller, K.W. (1998) A content-dependent fast DCT for low bit-rate video coding. Proceedings of ICIP, pp. 80–84.

[72] Pao, I.-M. and Sun, M.-T. (1999) Modeling DCT coefficients for fast video encoding. *IEEE Transactions on Circuits and Systems for Video Technology*, **9**, 608–616.

[73] Docef, A., Kossentini, F., Nguuyen-Phi, K., and Ismaeil, I.R. (2002) The quantized DCT and its application to DCT-based video coding. *IEEE Transactions on Image Processing*, **11**, 177–187.

[74] Lengwehasatit, K. and Ortega, A. (1998) DCT computation based on variable complexity fast approximations. Proceedings of International Conference of Image (ICIP), Chicago, IL, October. 1998.

[75] Lengwehasatit, K. and Ortega, A. (2004) Scalable variable complexity approximate forward DCT. *IEEE Transactions on Circuits and Systems for Video Technology*, **14**, 1236–1248.

8

Spatiotemporal H.264/AVC Video Adaptation with MPEG-21

Razib Iqbal and Shervin Shirmohammadi
School of Information Technology and Engineering, University of Ottawa, Ontario, Canada

8.1 Introduction

Over the last decade, internet-based multimedia applications, such as video streaming and video-on-demand (VOD), have grown tremendously and have become part of people's daily lives. Rich media distribution has become very useful for massively distributed content delivery systems, such as file sharing, VOD, and live video broadcasting applications. But, the variety of video coding formats necessitates a methodology to enable the processing of video contents in a format-independent way. Smart handheld devices with built-in Wi-Fi and multimedia capabilities are also making it easier to accessing on-line multimedia resources and video streams. Some on-line video portals are already offering high-definition video for mass public viewers. However, considering the unavoidable limitations of small handhelds, there exist intricacies to render even standard-definition videos to multimedia-enabled handheld devices mainly because of their resource limitations in terms of screen resolution, processing power, battery life, and bandwidth. Now, "video" in general is used as an ordinary expression albeit there is a broad application space that deals with different types of video. For example, video for conferencing, surveillance systems, Web-based streaming to a desktop or mobile device, e-learning videos, and entertainment services are just a few to mention. Each of these applications has different characteristics and performance requirements as do the respective video. From the consumer's viewpoint, the end user is not interested in the details of the video coding format as she/he is interested only in the video itself, for example, a movie. On the other hand, from the content/service providers' viewpoint, it will be convenient to store only one format of the content (probably the highest quality version), and to adapt the content according to the end user's requirement on demand and in real time, avoiding the burden of maintaining multiple versions of the same content.

The Handbook of MPEG Applications: Standards in Practice   Edited by Marios C. Angelides and Harry Agius
© 2011 John Wiley & Sons, Ltd

To address different applications and to encompass device heterogeneity, traditional video delivery solutions today incorporate cascaded operations involving dedicated media adaptation and streaming servers. These solutions, however, eventually suffer from high workload due to frequent user requests and limited capacity. For example, the most common and straightforward solution, which is used by most content providers (e.g., Apple movie trailers, http://www.apple.com/trailers/), is to store multiple versions of the same content taking into consideration different end user capabilities: one version for desktop/laptop users with high bandwidth internet access (high quality version), another one for desktop/laptop users but with slower DSL (digital subscriber line) access (normal quality version), and one for iPod users with mobile access (iPod version). This obviously is not very scalable given the numerous device types entering the market each day. Therefore, adaptation of video contents, on the fly and according to the capabilities of the receiver, is a more realistic approach. In this chapter, we cover a metadata-based real-time compressed-domain spatial and temporal adaptation scheme that makes this possible.

8.2 Background

The H.264 video coding standard is becoming popular and widely deployed due to its advanced compression technique, improved perceptual quality, network friendliness, and versatility. For compressed-domain spatial and temporal adaptation, the sliced architecture and the multiple frame dependency features can be exploited, as we shall see below.

To make an adaptation decision, one needs to first identify the adaptation entities (e.g., pixel, frame, and group of pictures); second, identify the adaptation technique (e.g., requantization and cropping); and finally, develop a method to estimate the resource and the utility values associated with the video entities undergoing adaptation. Now to ensure interoperability, it is advantageous to have an adaptation scheme that is not dependant on any specific video codec. For this reason, the MPEG-21 framework has set out an XML-based generic approach for directly manipulating bitstreams in the compressed domain. XML is used to describe the high-level structure of the bitstream, and with such a description, it is straightforward for a resource adaptation engine to transform the bitstream, and then generate an adapted bitstream. All of this is done without decoding and re-encoding. Adaptation operations usually take place on some intermediary nodes such as gateways and proxies. They can be done on the server, although this will not scale beyond a certain population of receivers as the server becomes the bottleneck. To perform the adaptation operations in an intermediary node, we emphasize on structured metadata-based adaptation utilizing MPEG-21 generic bitstream syntax description (gBSD). gBSD-based adaptation ensures codec independence, where any MPEG-21-compliant host can adapt any video format instantaneously. It also helps to avoid the conventional adaptation procedures (e.g., cascaded decoding and re-encoding scheme) that substantially increase the speed of video adaptation operations [1]. Practically, gBSD is a metadata representation of the actual video bitstream in the form of an XML which describes syntactical and semantic levels (e.g., headers, layers, units, and segments) of its corresponding video bitstream. Organization of the gBSD depends on the requirements of the actual application. Please note that gBSD does not replace the actual bitstream but provides additional metadata regarding bit/byte positions of syntactical and semantic levels of a video. Eventually, gBSD does not necessarily provide any information on the actual coding format.

The benefits of gBSD are manifold, which includes, but is not limited to, the following: (i) it enables coding format independence, and the description represents arbitrary bitstream segments and parameters; (ii) the bitstream segments may be grouped in a hierarchical way allowing for efficient, hierarchical adaptation; (iii) a flexible addressing scheme supports various application requirements, and it also allows random access into a bitstream.

8.2.1 Spatial Adaptation

The goal of spatial adaptation is to adapt video frames for a target resolution or screen size. It can be done in two ways: (i) downscaling the video for a particular display resolution and (ii) cropping a particular region form the video stream. In this chapter, we introduce a cropping scheme for compressed videos, which enables an intermediary node to serve different regions of video frames based on client demands from a single encoded high-resolution video stream. Cropping can be done in several ways. One way is to transcode the video; that is, decompressing the video first, cropping the desired regions, and then recompressing it before transmitting to the client. No doubt, this approach requires significant computational overhead and time, which makes it less suitable for real-time applications. Another approach is to create many smaller regions of the video and compress them separately. In this approach, it is easier to select particular regions from the video. However, it requires the client-side application to synchronize and merge together multiple video streams for display, which eventually leads to added complexities.

8.2.2 Temporal Adaptation

Temporal adaptation allows meeting end user requirements when an end system supports only a lower frame rate due to limited processing power or low bandwidth availability. Frame dropping is a well-known technique for temporal adaptation. It tries to meet the desired frame rate by dropping or skipping frames in a video bitstream. A major concern in frame dropping is that if an anchor/reference frame is dropped, subsequent frames may need to be re-encoded to avoid error propagation. Moreover, when frames are skipped, the motion vectors cannot directly be reused because the motion vectors from the incoming video frame point to the immediately previous frame. If the previous frame is dropped in the transcoder, the link between two frames is broken and the end decoder will not be able to reconstruct the picture using these motion vectors. To avoid such problems, the H.264 video codec offers multiple reference frames for motion compensation. This allows the video codec to choose from more than one previously encoded frame on which to base each macroblock in the next frame.

8.3 Literature Review

In the past decades, there have been many research activities and advancements in video adaptation techniques. A comprehensive overview of digital video transcoding in terms of architecture, techniques, quality optimization, complexity reduction, and watermark insertion is presented by Xin et al. [2]. Cascaded transcoding schemes for downscaling videos are quite established. Until very recently, most of the video adaptation schemes applied cascaded transcoding operations for temporal and spatial adaptation [3–5], and, as time progressed, these schemes happened to be suitable only for off-line applications. Cascaded schemes provide high quality output video but at the cost of high transcoding time; for example, Zhang *et al*. proposed a method [4], where the video is first decoded and then downscaled in the pixel domain. During re-encoding, a mode-mapping method is employed to speed up the process where mode information of the pre-encoded mac-roblocks is used to estimate the mode of the corresponding macroblock in the transcoded bitstream. Cock *et al*. [5] proposed a similar downscaling scheme that uses transcoding. In addition to applying mode-mapping strategy, this scheme reduces re-encoding complexity by performing motion compensation only in the reduced resolution domain.

Spatial adaptation by cropping is discussed by Wang *et al*. [6] and Arachchi *et al*. [7]. In [6], authors employ a set of transcoding techniques based on the H.264 standard to crop the region of interest in each frame. In this process, compressed H.264 bitstream is first decoded to extract the region of interest. The cropped video stream is then re-encoded. The region of interest is determined by using an attention-based modeling method. In [7], authors use a similar transcoding process for cropping H.264 videos. Additionally, this scheme reduces transcoding complexity by using a special process for encoding SKIP mode macroblocks in the original video. When re-encoding these macroblocks in the cropped video, the transcoder compares the motion vector predictors (MVPs) for the macroblock in the original video with the computed MVPs in the cropped video. If the MVPs are the same, then SKIP mode is selected for the macroblock. Thus, the transcoding complexity is reduced by avoiding the expensive rate–distortion optimization process to detect the macroblock modes for SKIP mode macroblocks in the input video.

Bonuccellit *et al*. [8] have introduced buffer-based strategies for temporal video transcoding adding a fixed transmission delay for buffer occupancy in frame skipping. A frame is skipped if the buffer occupancy is greater than some upper value, and it is always transcoded if the buffer occupancy is lower than some lower value, provided the first frame, which is I-frame, is always transcoded. In his paper [9], Deshpande proposed adaptive frame scheduling for video streaming using a fixed frame drop set. Sender adjusts the deadline of an important frame, which is estimated to miss its deadline by dropping less important next frame(s), and sends the deadline-adjusted/postponed frame to be displayed in place of the next dropped frame(s). However, the visual quality of the reconstructed video stream on the receiver side may not be acceptable for those videos having high motion or frequent scene change. To overcome this issue, the technique described in this chapter uses individual frame importance. In addition, frames are managed in groups, naming *frameset*, so that after transmission and adaptation, every *frameset* is self-contained.

Overview of digital item adaptation (DIA), its use and importance in multimedia applications, and report on some of the ongoing activities in MPEG on extending DIA for use in rights-governed environments is well discussed by Vetro and Timmerer [10] and Rong and Burnett [11]. Devillers *et al*. proposed bitstream syntax description (BSD)-based adaptation in streaming and constrained environments [12]. In their framework, authors emphasized on BSD-based adaptation applying BS schema and BSDtoBin processors. Compared to BSD-based adaptation, gBSD provides an abstract view on the structure of the bitstream, which is useful for bitstream transformation, in particular, when the availability of a specific BS schema is not ensured.

Most recently, scalable video coding (SVC) is in the center of interest to achieve adaptability of the coded video sequence where the compressed video is coded into layers – the base layer is coded at low quality and then one or more enhancement layers are coded to gain high quality. Thereby, the adaptability of the coded sequence is obtained by changing the number of enhancement layers transmitted from the sender side. In the literature, there are several papers summarizing the above concept (e.g., [13, 14]), and extending it for different scenarios such as in-network adaptation with encryption [15] and adaptation of the SVC stream on a network device [16]. However, concern with the SVC is that it can only achieve bitrates in a limited set, usually decided at coding time.

8.4 Compressed-Domain Adaptation of H.264/AVC Video

In Figure 8.1, we summarize the concept of the compressed-domain video adaptation scheme from video preparation to adapted video generation. As can be seen, part 1 comprises compressed video and metadata generation, which is performed during the encoding phase. Part 2, adaptation, is performed in some intermediary node which can be logically divided into two subprocesses, namely, the metadata transformation and the adapted video generation. To perform adaptation in a trusted intermediary node requires the digital item (DI; video bitstream along with its gBSD) to be available. This DI performs as original content for resource server or content provider on the delivery path. Therefore, the generation of DI is one of the important tasks in the initial stage. gBSD can be generated during the encoding process of the raw video by adding a gBSD generation module to the encoder, which requires the H.264 encoder in use to be modified with the gBSD generation mechanism.

8.4.1 Compressed Video and Metadata Generation

To facilitate temporal and spatial adaptation in the compressed domain, gBSD containing the information (e.g., starting byte and length of each frame, and slice size) pertaining to an encoded bitstream is written while encoding that video. A modified H.264 encoder capable of generating gBSD is needed so that it can generate the metadata representing the compressed bitstream while performing compression from the uncompressed video, that is, the YUV input.

For spatial adaptation, each video frame is divided into slices. The video frame slices are encoded in a fixed size and in a self-contained manner. To achieve a target resolution,

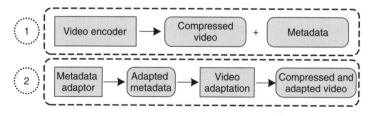

Figure 8.1 Compressed-domain video adaptation: step 1, in video source; step 2, in an intermediary node.

the adaptation engine serves only the slices that belong to the requested region of the clients. In gBSD, the "marker" attribute provides semantically meaningful marking of syntactical elements. While encoding, some slices are marked as *essential* so that they are always included in the served video to the client. The rest of the slices are marked as *disposable*. Only the disposable slices are considered for removal when adapting the video stream. No macroblock in a disposable slice is used as a reference for any macroblock in the essential slices. This results in fewer choices for prediction for the macroblocks along the edges of the slice. The slices in different regions of the video frame are designed to be of the same size in each frame, allowing the user to select a region for cropping from a wide range of croppable regions. In the gBSD, the hierarchical structure of the encoded video (e.g., frame numbers along with their starting byte number), length of the frame, and frame type are written. For temporal adaptation, in gBSD, frame *"importance"* level is set in the marker attribute based on the following: (i) reference frame, (ii) motion in the frame, and (iii) frame size. As a part of hierarchical information organization, for each frame, the slice data information is also included in the gBSD. The metadata for a slice includes the starting byte number of the slice, the length of the slice in bytes, and a marker *"essential"* or *"disposable"* for each slice. In Figure 8.2, a block diagram of the gBSD generation is shown, and in Box 8.1 a sample gBSD file is shown.

Box 8.1 Sample gBSD of a compressed bitstream

```
<?xml version="1.0" encoding="UTF-8" ?>
<dia:DIA xmlns="urn:mpeg:mpeg21:2003:01-DIA-gBSD-NS"
xmlns:dia="urn:mpeg:mpeg21:2003:01-DIA-NS"
xmlns:xs="http://www.w3.org/2001/XMLSchema"
xmlns:xsi="http://www.w3.org/2001/XMLSchema-instance">
    <dia:Description xsi:type="gBSDType">
        <Header>
         <ClassificationAlias alias="MV4"
         href="urn:mpeg:mpeg4:video:cs:syntacticalLabels"/>
         <!-- ...and so on.. -->
        </Header>
        <gBSDUnit syntacticalLabel="Frame-1" start="21"
        length="1553" marker="importance-1">
        <Parameter name="Slice-0" length="148"
        marker="disposable"></Parameter>
        <!-- ...and so on.. -->
        <Parameter name="Slice-2" length="85"
        marker="essential"></Parameter>
        </gBSDUnit>
        <gBSDUnit syntacticalLabel="Frame-2" start="1574"
        length="1077" marker="importance-1">
        <!-- ...and so on.. -->
        </gBSDUnit>
    </dia:Description>
</dia:DIA>
```

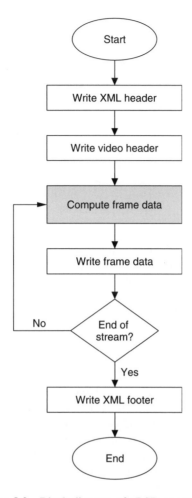

Figure 8.2 Block diagram of gBSD generation.

For each gBSD, XML header specifies the XML version number and the character encodings followed by uniform resource identifiers (URIs) to identify MPEG-21 descriptions. For video header in gBSD, `dia:Description` element is used with the `xsi:type="gBSDType"` to define the default values for address mode, address unit, and bitstream URI for the entire gBSD. In frame data, `gBSDUnit` describes individual sections of the bitstream. At the end of writing all frame data in the gBSD, gBSD output buffer is ended by closing `"dia:Description"`.

8.4.2 Adapting the Video

Adaptation of DI is performed in the following two steps: first, the metadata characterizing adaptation goal is transformed, and, second, the adapted bitstream using the transformed metadata is generated. The adaptation steps are illustrated in Figure 8.3.

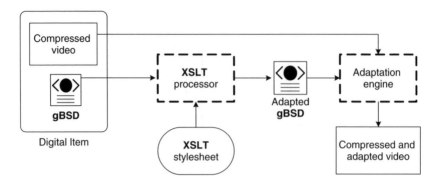

Figure 8.3   Adaptation steps using MPEG-21 gBSD.

End user's preference or device requirement is the input to the transformation decision making mechanism. The MPEG-21 usage environment description (UED) tool may be used to gather this information. To achieve the target bitstream, the adaptation module parses the frame and/or slice data information from the adapted gBSD. gBSD is transformed to an adapted gBSD by means of XSLT (http://www.w3.org/TR/xslt). The transformation rules are predisposed in the XSL style sheet. The metadata transformation module receives as an input the gBSD of the original compressed video bitstream and a style sheet that transforms the gBSD according to the context information, for example, the device capabilities. The output of this process is a transformed gBSD, which reflects the bitstream segments of the target (i.e., adapted) bitstream. However, the transformed gBSD still refers to the bit/byte positions of the original compressed video bitstream that needs to be parsed in order to generate the adapted bitstream within the second step of the adaptation process, that is, adapted video generation.

For spatiotemporal adaptation, the encoded bitstream is adapted by discarding the portions to achieve the target resolution or frame rate. For temporal adaptation, frames are usually discarded based on their importance level; for example, frames used as a reference frame, or with high motion, have higher priority than others. Otherwise, frames with low priority or same priority are dropped randomly based on the total size of the discarded frames to achieve the target rate. For low target frame rate, to maintain the visual quality, the first frame of a frameset (*frameset refers to the number of frames in a one-second video/clip before adaptation*) is always considered as the base frame while decoding on the receiver side. For spatial adaptation, within the encoded bitstream, only the slice(s) belonging to the desired region of interest need to be served to the clients. Offsets of the slices are first parsed from the gBSD. This is used to extract the desired region from the compressed video in the serving nodes. Once the slices have been extracted, this adaptation module removes the disposable slices from the compressed video stream. In the next section, we briefly introduce some slicing strategies.

8.4.3   Slicing Strategies

In general, it is preferable to have smaller number of slices for each frame. The reason is that if we increase the number of slices, then it will eventually increase the overhead due

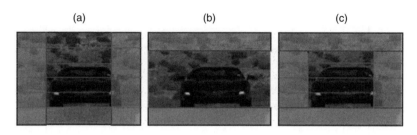

Figure 8.4   Slicing strategies: (a) block strategy (b) wide strategy, and (c) o-strategy.

to the added number of slice headers, and simultaneously due to the reduced number of macroblocks available for use as references. On the positive side, using a large number of slices in each frame gives more region-based cropping options to the clients. To facilitate spatial adaptation by means of dropping slices, a slicing strategy needs to be decided at the time of encoding the video [17]. The strategy should be chosen in a way such that the number of slices required for each frame is optimized, while allowing maximum flexibility for slice dropping. Example of some slicing strategies (*block strategy*, *wide strategy* and *o-strategy*) are illustrated in Figure 8.4, where shaded slices represent the disposable slices, that is, an adaptation server can drop these slices to achieve the requested resolution, and the rest of the slices represent the essential slices. Slicing strategies are selected based on the characteristic of the input video stream. For example, the block strategy or wide strategy is appropriate for a video with a large area of interest, whereas the o-strategy may suffice for a video with a smaller area of interest, for example, a newsreader reading the news.

Table 8.1 presents sample adapted video frames after spatial adaptation. As we can see from the results, some of the videos are very well suited for the o-strategy, for example, "coastguard". However, some videos have a larger region of interest than is possible to retain using the o-strategy. For example, using o-strategy, too much of the video gets cropped for "silent", The block strategy is appropriate in this case. For some videos, the wide strategy is more appropriate, for example, "flower". The enforced slicing of the video frames may cause an increased file size of the encoded video compared to the single sliced per frame videos. The amount of this increment depends on the slicing strategy selected. From experiments, we have found that the block strategy causes the most increase in the file size because there is less number of available macroblocks to be used as reference due to the small self-contained slices created by the block strategy. The o-strategy has fewer slices, and it is better in terms of overall file size increase compared to the block strategy. Finally, the wide strategy uses only three slices per frame, and the resultant file size is the smallest compared to the block strategy and o-strategy.

8.4.4   Performance Evaluation

In this section, we provide DI generation and spatiotemporal adaptation performance in an ordinary computer, for example, an Intel P4 3.4-GHz processor running Windows XP Pro SP2 and 1-Gbyte of RAM. Table 8.2 shows the average DI generation performance for the precoded video adaptation of three test sequences – coastguard, silent, and flower.

Table 8.1 Spatial adaptation: sample adapted videos

Video	Original video (352 × 288)	Block strategy (160 × 288)	Wide strategy (352 × 160)	o-Strategy (160 × 160)
Flower (250 frames)	 a	 b	 c	 d
Coastguard (300 frames)	 e	 f	 g	 h
Silent (300 frames)	 i	 j	 k	 l

Table 8.2 Digital Item generation performance

Video resolution	Elapsed time	Encoding rate
SQCIF (128×96)	11.61 s	25 frames/s
QCIF (176×144)	23.35 s	12 frames/s
CIF (352×288)	95.07 s	4 frames/s

Target frame rate: 30 frames per second; quantization parameter: 28.

For temporal adaptation, the adaptation time varies from 0.6 to 1 s to achieve new frame rate between 1 and 20 frames per second. For spatial adaptation (i.e., CIF to QCIF and CIF to SQCIF), irrespective of the slicing strategies, average adaptation time is 0.06 s.

Spatiotemporal adaptation in the compressed domain has a larger footprint than the cascaded approach in terms of the encoding, that is, DI generation and adaptation procedures. However, it is considerably faster during the actual adaptation process. From a cost-benefit standpoint, compressed-domain approach is efficient because encoding will occur only once in a certain video's lifetime and adaptation will occur many times for different user contexts.

8.5 On-line Video Adaptation for P2P Overlays

Centrally managed systems such as VOD applications, user-generated content (UGC) web sites, Push VOD applications, and IP video surveillance systems lack support for heterogeneous devices; they already suffer from scaling issues as the user base continues to grow due to bandwidth and storage space bottleneck of the servers. Therefore, a solution is needed to take away some of the load from the servers to other nodes. The peer-to-peer (P2P) paradigm has been proven to be efficient for large-scale multimedia systems to replicate the contents more cheaply and flexibly. If we combine the P2P content distribution concept and metadata-driven adaptation of videos in the compressed domain, it will not only shift the bandwidth burden to participating peers but also move the computation load for adapting video contents away from dedicated media-streaming/adaptation servers. It can be seen as an initiative to merge the adaptation operations and the P2P streaming basics to support the expansion of context-aware P2P systems. Federated video adaptation design will enable peers to contribute both CPU and bandwidth requiring no dedicated adaptation server and/or streaming server. A rendezvous point may be needed for the video stream originators and the peers in the overlay. For universal multimedia access (UMA) and mass-scale distribution, it is better to create a video once in its lifetime along with its metadata in the form of MPEG-21 gBSD. Utilizing the gBSD and an adaptation engine, intermediary nodes can perform adaptation operations in a format-independent way. Thus, the gBSD-based approach can enable support for dynamic and distributed adaptation.

Considering the spatiotemporal adaptation technique described earlier in this chapter as a utility tool, in this section we briefly explain how, using this tool, peers can adapt, transmit, and buffer video streams to match the varying network conditions in a P2P environment. We also describe a combination of infrastructure-centric and application end-point architecture for P2P video delivery applications. The infrastructure-centric architecture refers to a tree controller which will be responsible for tree/overlay administering and maintenance. Therefore, no control message needs to be exchanged among peers for overlay maintenance. The application end-point architecture refers to video sharing, streaming, and adaptation by the participating resourceful peers.

Given global knowledge of the participating nodes and abundance of bandwidth and computing power, designing the overlays would be relatively straightforward. However, in a real scenario, designs are constrained by the limited bandwidth and computing power available with the peers. In this design, receivers are organized into multiple subtrees based on a hierarchy of adaptation and streaming requirements following a set of rules. The design enables a separate overlay for each video and a common rendezvous point, named *Controller*, as shown in Figure 8.5.

The tree controller is responsible for node joining and maintaining the multicast tree for each video stream. In this system, either a media server or a participating peer can be the stream source, denoted as *Originator*. Originator initiates streaming and forms an overlay with the help of the controller. In addition to the desired content, the *originator* should be able to adapt the content and provide overall streaming service to the immediate receiver peers in the tree. All the streamed content should have the corresponding metadata component in the form of MPEG-21 gBSD. The success and efficiency of a particular overlay will directly depend on users' contributing bandwidth and CPU power.

8.5.1 Adaptation/Streaming Capability of Peers

To determine the adaptation/streaming capability of peers, available computing power (CPU power) can be mapped to adaptation time. For example, during the client-side application installation, a small video clip may be adapted for different spatiotemporal requirements and the adaptation timing profile can be recorded. On the basis of this timing profile, the controller will be able to decide on the number of adaptations this peer can perform in a certain time frame. On the basis of this information and the available bandwidth, the controller may assign a particular peer *adaptation and streaming peer* role or just *streaming peer* role. Devices with limited resources may join as *free riders*.

8.5.2 Peer Joining

An incoming peer will register with the controller, and eventually it will receive a list of available video streams. It also passes the video adaptation preferences in the form

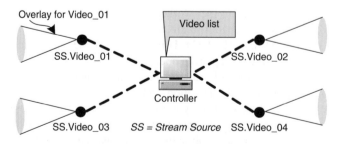

Figure 8.5   Overlay generation.

of UED descriptions. The controller attempts to connect an incoming node requesting certain video quality directly to one of the existing subtrees (if any). If it fails, then a suitable node is chosen, which can perform the necessary adaptation, to serve the new peer. The tree controller usually stores the peer information and sends a copy of the graph to the video originators. Therefore, the video originator is the secondary administrative point of contact if the tree controller fails.

8.5.3   Peer Departure

A peer can depart gracefully or ungracefully by hanging. If the originator has departed, then that overlay will be dissolved gradually. If a root node/serving node has departed, then the controller attempts to assign a parent from the sorted availability list preferably from the same level or the ancestors of the disconnected node. Otherwise, the controller simply updates the list of available peers for an overlay and informs the originator accordingly once reported by a neighboring node or a tracker. A peer failure can be detected by monitoring the TCP control channel established between the receiver and each of the sending peers. If a connection reset is detected, then either the receiver peer or the parent of the departed node informs the controller and/or stream originator.

8.5.4   Video Buffering, Adaptation, and Transmission

The video stream to be served by the originator is divided into segments/clips (e.g., 2 s video, i.e., two framesets), so that the clips can be better exchanged among peers without any long processing delays. For continuous playback, an initial buffering enables the receivers to fill up with the received video frames for immediate and future playback, and retransmissions to another node (as shown in Figure 8.6). The size of the buffer depends on the average frame size, number of frames in each frameset, available memory, and delay. Clearly, a large buffer size can better accommodate streaming dynamics, but it costs a longer start-up delay. Now, if a node requires adapted video, then its parent node adapts the video parts based on gBSD before transmitting those parts. Intermediary nodes may discard the received video segments right after retransmitting and/or adapting.

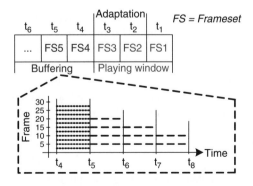

Figure 8.6   Client-side video buffering, adaptation, and playing.

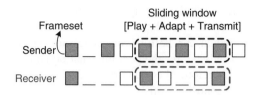

Figure 8.7   Sliding window for simultaneous adaptation and forwarding.

On the receiver side, framesets occupy the buffer and use a sliding window protocol. In Figure 8.7, a sliding window represents the active buffer portion of each peer. While viewing, a sender peer forwards the framesets from the active buffer portion to its immediate receiver peer(s) (and also adapts before transmission, if required). For a peer, if the sliding window detects too many missing framesets in the active buffer portion (up to a predetermined limit), then either the administrative tasks (e.g., checking existence of the parent) start or the video is paused and buffering continues until the number of missing framesets drop to the acceptable limit.

8.6   Quality of Experience (QoE)

Spatiotemporal adaptation requirements are usually computed and set at the beginning of each streaming sessions. However, network fluctuations can happen due to network congestion in the network. In such a case, the tree controller recomputes the adaptation and/or bandwidth requirements. From the experimental results [1, 17], we have observed that both spatial and temporal adaptation can be performed in real time depending on the available computing power of each ordinary node. This is a remarkable improvement over the methods that use cascaded methods at the intermediary nodes. For live videos, end users will experience a fixed waiting time at the beginning for video capture, encoding, adaptation, and transmission operations. In the case of high adaptation ratio (e.g., 30 to 2 frames per second), if a key frame cannot be reconstructed due to packet loss during transmission, then instead of retransmitting that frame it is reasonable to skip that frameset and go to the next frameset on the receiver side. From the viewpoint of quality of experience (QoE), the end user will experience freezing of video for those framesets that were supposed to be forwarded by the departed parent. If multiple parents are assigned to serve a single node, then the missing frameset problem will cause comparatively less annoyance to the end user since the frameset drop will occur after a couple of seconds, and until a new parent has been assigned. In order to get optimal resource utilization and to increase reliability, peers with higher aptitude and stability (can be decided from peer history) should be placed in the upper layer of the tree as a part of tree refinement operation. The tree refinement procedure may be called when end-to-end delay of certain percentage of receiving peers exceeds the predetermined value for an overlay.

8.7   Conclusion

As we steer toward digital video broadcasting for handhelds and pervasive computing appliances, multimedia content transmission through 3G and beyond 3G networks requires suitable adaptation tools to accommodate various end user requirements. The variation of devices emerging on a regular basis is inevitable, causing service providers to look for solutions to increase their revenue by providing mobile video streaming and downloads to these devices. Metadata support for video adaptation seems to be a promising solution because it allows adaptation of video contents in a format-independent way. Real-time adaptation architecture for H.264 video, conforming to MPEG-21 DIA described in this chapter is a feasible solution for commercial deployment since any MPEG-21-compliant host can adapt the video on-line. An alternative solution – hierarchical multilayer encoding of video – divides the video into multiple layers where there is a base layer with a given quality that can be improved by adding more layers depending on the bandwidth and processing capability of a receiver. However, it requires a rather powerful decoder at the receiver; not many handheld devices are capable of decoding such streams. Moreover, layer encoding does not enable fine-grained adaptation since the more the number of layers, the less the coding efficiency. In P2P systems, with the help of the metadata-based compressed-domain adaptation tools, CPU-rich peers can serve those peers which require adapted video stream. In addition, it is very convenient to handle latecomers and early leavers since videos are processed in small segments. On the negative side, a P2P system could suffer from churn: nondeterministic leaving of peers causing disruptions in the parent–child relationship in the P2P tree. Also, it might be possible that, due to a shortage in CPU-rich peers, the scheme might not be able to serve all end user devices. However, experimental results [18] are promising, and show that along with the bandwidth, idle computing power of the participating peers can also be utilized, which does not exhaust a serving peer's own resource entirely.

While many advances have been made to play rich media contents in small handhelds, we are still at the stage of learning and discovering how we can apply the UMA concept to give best viewing experience to the end users. What we need is feasible techniques to accommodate new user/device requirements effectively and efficiently. Toward this, spatiotemporal adaptation using MPEG-21 gBSD is a positive step toward addressing the device heterogeneity and UMA.

References

[1] Iqbal, R., Shirmohammadi, S., El Saddik, A., and Zhao, J. (2008) Compressed domain video processing for adaptation, encryption, and authentication. *IEEE Multimedia*, **15** (2), 38–50.

[2] Xin, J., Lin, C.W., and Sun, M.T. (2005) Digital video transcoding. *Proceedings of the IEEE*, **93** (1), 84–97.

[3] Shin, I., Lee, Y., and Park, H. (2005) Motion estimation for frame-rate reduction in H.264 transcoding. Proceedings of the 2nd IEEE Workshop on Software Technologies for Future Embedded and Ubiquitous Systems, pp. 63–67.

[4] Zhang, P., Lu, Y., Huang, Q., and Gao, W. (2004) Mode mapping method for H.264/AVC spatial downscaling transcoding. Proceedings of the IEEE ICIP, vol. 4, pp. 2781–2784.

[5] Cock, J., Notebaert, S., Vermeirsch, K. *et al.* (2008) Efficient spatial resolution reduction transcoding for H.264/AVC. Proceedings of the IEEE ICIP, pp. 1208–1211.

[6] Wang, Y., Fan, X., Li, H. *et al.* (2006) An attention based spatial adaptation scheme for H.264 videos on mobiles. Proceedings of MMM.

[7] Arachchi, H.K., Dogan, S., Uzuner, H., and Kondoz, A.M. (2007) Utilizing macroblock SKIP mode information to accelerate cropping of an H.264/AVC encoded video sequence for user centric content adaptation. Proceedings of International Conference on Automated Production of Cross Media Content for Multi-Channel Distribution.

[8] Bonuccellit, M.A., Lonetti, F., and Martelli, F. (2005) Temporal transcoding for mobile video communication. Proceedings of the MobiQuitous, pp. 502–506.

[9] Deshpande, S.G. (2008) High quality video streaming using content-aware adaptive frame scheduling with explicit deadline adjustment. Proceedings of the ACM Multimedia, pp. 777–780.

[10] Vetro, A. and Timmerer, C. (2005) Digital item adaptation: overview of standardization and research activities. *IEEE Transactions on Multimedia*, **7** (3), 418–426.

[11] Rong, L. and Burnett, I. (2004) Dynamic multimedia adaptation and updating of media streams with MPEG-21. Proceedings of the CCNC, pp. 436–441.

[12] Devillers, S., Timmerer, C., Heuer, J., and Hellwagner, H. (2005) Bitstream syntax description-based adaptation in streaming and constrained environments. *IEEE Transactions on Multimedia*, **7** (3), 463–470.

[13] Ahmed, T., Mehaoua, A., Boutaba, R., and Iraqi, Y. (2005) Adaptive packet video streaming over ip networks: a cross-layer approach. *IEEE Journal on Selected Areas in Communications*, **23** (2), 385–401.

[14] Li, B. and Liu, J. (2003) Multirate video multicast over the internet: an overview. *IEEE Network*, **17** (1), 24–29.

[15] Hellwagner, H., Kuschnig, R., Stutz, T., and Uhl, A. (2009) Efficient in-network adaptation of encrypted H.264/SVC content. *Image Communication*, **24** (9), 740–758.

[16] Kofler, I., Prangl, M., Kuschnig, R., and Hellwagner, H. (2008) An H.264/SVC-based adaptation proxy on a WiFi router. Proceedings of the NOSSDAV, pp. 63–68.

[17] Shahabuddin, S., Iqbal, R., Nazari, A., and Shirmohammadi, S. (2009) Compressed domain spatial adaptation for H.264 video. Proceedings of the ACM Multimedia, pp. 797–800.

[18] Iqbal, R. and Shirmohammadi, S. (2009) DAg-stream: distributed video adaptation for overlay streaming to heterogeneous devices. *Springer's Peer-to-Peer Networking and Applications*, **3** (2), 202–216.

9

Image Clustering and Retrieval Using MPEG-7

Rajeev Agrawal[1], William I. Grosky[2], and Farshad Fotouhi[3]

[1]*Department of Electronics, Computer and Information Technology, North Carolina A&T State University, Greensboro, NC USA*
[2]*Department of Computer and Information Science, University of Michigan-Dearborn, Dearborn, Michigan, USA*
[3]*Department of Computer Science, Wayne State University, Detroit, MI, USA*

9.1 Introduction

There is an increasing demand for efficient image clustering and retrieval solutions, due to the increasing amount of digital image data being produced every day. To represent a huge amount of digital media data, we need a format that is compact, effective, and reasonably invariant to scaling, rotation, noise, change in illumination, and minor changes in viewing direction. It is also highly desirable that the features used are highly distinctive, to allow for correct object identification with low probability of incorrect mismatches. The algorithms to extract these features should be fast enough to calculate them in almost real-time, given a query image for a match in a large image database. Broadly, we can divide these descriptors into two categories: one which first detects some salient points in the images, such as corners, high entropy regions, and scale-space maxima and then construct from each region or its surroundings a discriminative description [1]; the other, a more global approach, which calculates the features of an image considering the entire image as a region, such as a color histogram. Even though color histograms have been found to be useful in many applications [2], the problem with a global characterization is in distinguishing between a red car and an apple, since it does not incorporate any spatial information. Therefore, it is important to have some notion of the local distribution of features.

Image features have been represented using many different approaches, starting from simple color histograms to more complex scale-invariant feature transforms (SIFT)

The Handbook of MPEG Applications: Standards in Practice Edited by Marios C. Angelides and Harry Agius
© 2011 John Wiley & Sons, Ltd

descriptors in image clustering and retrieval applications. The MPEG-7 standard has not been designed to target any one application in particular. This standard provides support to a broad range of applications; for example, it can define still pictures, graphics, 3D models, audio, speech, video, and composition information about how these elements are combined in a multimedia presentation. The MPEG-7 color descriptors have the ability to characterize perceptual color similarity and need relatively low complexity operations to extract them, besides being scalable and interoperable. We propose an approach for efficient image clustering and retrieval operations using low-level image features (content) and the human interpretation of the image (context). To take the cue from text-based retrieval techniques, we construct *visual keywords* using vector quantization of small-sized image tiles. Each tile's features are represented using three MPEG-7 color descriptors, namely, scalable color, color structure, and color layout. Both visual and text keywords are combined and used to represent an image as a single multimodal vector. We present a diffusion kernel-based graph-theoretic nonlinear approach to reduce the high dimensionality of multimodal image representation, which also identifies the modality relationship between visual and text modalities. By comparing the performance of this approach with the low-level feature-based approach, we demonstrate that visual keywords, when combined with textual keywords, significantly improve the image clustering and retrieval results.

9.2   Usage of MPEG-7 in Image Clustering and Retrieval

9.2.1   Representation of Image Data

The color histogram has been the most commonly used representation technique [3, 4], statistically describing combined probabilistic properties of the various color channels (such as the (R)ed, (G)reen, and (B)lue channels), by capturing the number of pixels having particular properties. For example, a color histogram might describe the number of pixels of each red channel value in the range [0, 255]. It is well known that histograms lose information related to the spatial distribution of colors and that two very different images can have very similar histograms. It is important to observe that the captured color varies considerably depending on the orientation of the surface, angle of the camera, position of the illumination, spectrum of the illuminant, and the way that the light interacts with the object [5]. Therefore, this variability has to be taken into account.

There has been much work done in extending histograms to capture spatial information. Two well-known approaches involve the use of correlograms [6] and anglograms [7]. Correlograms capture the distribution of colors of pixels in particular areas around pixels of particular colors, while anglograms capture a particular signature of the spatial arrangement of areas (single pixels or blocks of pixels) having common properties, such as similar colors. The RGB color space is not very efficient for image search and retrieval applications. MPEG-7 has approved the following color spaces: monochrome, RGB, HSV, YCrCb, and HMMD. Table 9.1 shows the color spaces used by different color descriptors.

We briefly describe here only those descriptors that are used in our framework. The details of visual descriptors are from [8–10].

Table 9.1　Color spaces used by MPEG-7 color descriptors

Color descriptor	Color space
SCD	HSV
CSD	HMMD
CLD	YCrCb
DCD	Any color space approved by MPEG-7

9.2.1.1　Scalable Color Descriptor (SCD)

The scalable color descriptor (SCD) is a global color histogram, encoded by a Haar transform in HSV color space. The histogram values are extracted, normalized, and nonlinearly mapped into a four-bit integer representation. It has been found to be useful for image-to-image matching and retrieval based on color features. Retrieval accuracy increases with the number of bits used in its representation. The number of bins can be 16, 32, 64, 128 or 256, where, for most applications, it has been found that 64 bits are good enough to use.

9.2.1.2　Color Layout Descriptor (CLD)

The color layout descriptor (CLD) is obtained by applying the discrete cosine transform (DCT) transformation on a 2D array of local representative colors in Y or Cb or Cr color space, producing 12 coefficients: 6 for luminance and 3 for each chrominance. This descriptor effectively represents the spatial distribution of color of visual signals in a very compact form. This compactness allows visual signal matching functionality with high retrieval efficiency at very small computational costs. CLD is not dependent on image format, resolutions, and bit-depths. It can be applied to a whole image or to any arbitrary part of the image. This feature is represented in the frequency domain and supports a scalable representation of the feature by controlling the number of coefficients enclosed in the descriptor. The user can choose any representation granularity, depending on their objectives, without interoperability problems in measuring the similarity among the descriptors with different granularities. It also provides for a very friendly user interface using hand-written sketch queries, since these descriptors capture the layout information of color features.

9.2.1.3　Color Structure Descriptor (CSD)

The color structure descriptor (CSD) captures both, color content and the structure of this content. The CSD is extracted as a 256-bin color structure histogram from an image represented in the 256 cell-quantized HMMD color space. It is used for image-to-image matching and for still image retrieval. An 8 × 8 structuring element is used to extract color structure information instead of using each pixel individually. This descriptor can distinguish two images in which a given color is present in identical amounts but where the structure of the groups of pixels having that color is different in the two images. The color values are represented in HMMD color space. The number of bins can be 32, 64,

128 or 256. The CSD provides improved similarity-based image retrieval performance compared to ordinary color histograms.

9.2.2 State of the Art in Image Clustering and Retrieval

In the last two decades, many image clustering and retrieval applications have been developed based on various representations of image data. Swain and Ballard [11] use color for high-speed image location and identification. Color histograms of multicolored objects are used, providing a robust and efficient representation for indexing the images. In [12], an image is represented by three 1D color histograms in the red, green, and blue channels, while a histogram of the directions of edge points is used to represent general shape information. A blobworld representation [13] has been used to retrieve images. This approach recognizes the images as a combination of objects, making both query and learning in the blobworld more meaningful to the user. In all these works, color is the fundamental unit used to represent an image, which is very similar to the keywords in a text document. The Qbic system [14] stores color, texture, shape, sketch, and object information of each image and uses techniques similar to information retrieval techniques. In this system, it is possible to integrate all of these in one single query. The user can specify the color proportion, select regions of relevant texture, and draw a sketch of the query image. In Photobook [15], principal component analysis (PCA) is used to create eigenimages, which are small sets of perceptually significant coefficients. This technique is referred to as *semantics-preserving image compression*. These low-level features have been used as terms, over which to apply standard information retrieval techniques.

In other approaches, images have been divided into blocks of pixels and then each block is described using low-level features. Various text retrieval techniques, such as inverted files, term weighting, and relevance feedback (RF) are then applied on the blocks of an image [16]. In [17], image contents are combined with textual contents. The low-level image features used are HSV color space and Gabor texture filters. The retrieval results for the text and image features are better than image-only and text-only results. Similar results are achieved in [18].

Recently, there has been attempt to develop systems that incorporate human behavior and their needs, as any multimedia system is closely tied to human perception. These types of systems extend the scope from a data-centric approach to a more human-centric approach. Human-centered multimedia systems take the advantage of the research from multiple disciplines such as computer vision, multimedia, psychology, pattern recognition, artificial intelligence (AI), and so on. In [19], an object-based image retrieval (OBIR) scheme is introduced, which is based on how humans perceive color. The MultiMatch system has been designed specifically for the access, organization, and personalized presentation of cultural heritage information [20]. The users can formulate queries using different modalities, such as free text, similarity matching, or metadata. It also provides browsing capability to navigate the collection, using a web directory-like structure based on the MultiMatch ontology. People do not observe all parts of an image with the same interest. It is possible that some parts of an image are more prominent than the other parts, for example, regions with vivid colors or regions where important information would be found based on past experience. In [21], first the saliency features of intensity, color, and texture are calculated, and then an integrated global saliency map is synthesized and its histogram is used as a new feature for image retrieval.

While searching information on the Web, one big challenge is the selection of the appropriate keywords, as different terms can represent the same meaning. A solution to this problem is to use an ontology, which is a formal representation of a set of concepts in a certain domain. This ontology may consist of classes, relations, functions, and whatever else is relevant to that representation. Metadata ontologies like Dublin Core [22] provide a vocabulary for describing the contents of on-line information resources on the Web. There are several systems developed using ontologies. In [23], the object ontology is used to allow the qualitative definition of the high-level concepts the user queries for, in a human-centered approach. After applying segmentation to divide images into regions, the low-level features describing color, position, size and shape of the regions are extracted and mapped onto the defined ontology. The core ontology on multimedia (COMM) is proposed in [24] for storing and processing low-level image features, based on current semantic web technologies. It claims to address the limitations of MPEG-7, but is still largely compliant to it, containing all MPEG-7 descriptors formalized using the same naming convention as defined in the standard. A LEGO-like metadata architecture for image search and retrieval is proposed in [25], which is designed on top of the latest standards ISO/IEC 15938-12 (MPEG Query Format) and ISO/IEC 24800 (JPSearch). The word LEGO comes from its metadata annotations as an assembly of LEGO pieces, each one of the pieces an individual metadata statement.

9.2.3   Image Clustering and Retrieval Systems Based on MPEG-7

The image representation of images using the MPEG-7 standard is still in its infancy. In this section, we will focus on the systems that have used MPEG-7 to represent the images. The PicSOM system uses the following MPEG-7 descriptors to represent the images: dominant color, scalable color, color layout, color structure, edge histogram, and region shape [26]. The system is based on pictorial examples and RF. The name stems from "picture" and the self-organizing map (SOM). The PicSOM system is implemented by using tree-structured SOMs. The efficacy of using MPEG-7 descriptors in conjunction with XML database technology for region labeling and retrieval in aerial image databases is demonstrated in [27]. MPEG-7 descriptors are associated with aerial images and their derived features at each stage of the image insertion process, producing a multifaceted integrated representation that can be used to give the database administrator an indication as to when this representation should be rebuilt, so as to result in improved retrieval behavior. An aggregated feature approach to combining text and visual features from MPEG-7 descriptions of video is used for video retrieval [28]. It is based on the assumption that the shots within the same cluster are not only similar visually but also semantically, to a certain extent. This is useful when each video in a collection contains a high proportion of shots that have visual and semantic similarity. The MPEG-7 descriptions in Caliph are used to represent metadata description, creation information, media information, textual annotation, semantics, and visual descriptors [29]. Emir supports retrieval in file system-based photo repositories created with Caliph. Different types of retrieval mechanisms are supported, such as content-based image retrieval (CBIR) using the MPEG-7 descriptors color layout, edge histogram, and scalable color, keyword-based searching, graph-based retrieval, and 2D data repository and result set visualization based on FastMap and force-directed placement (FDP) algorithms. A framework based on service-oriented architectures for mapping semantic descriptions and MPEG-7 visual descriptors into a pure-relational model is proposed in [30]. The Fuzzy C-Means (FCM) clustering algorithm on a large set of images, represented by MPEG-7 low-level descriptors, has been used for an image classification system. The original space was reduced using standard PCA, which significantly increases the accuracy of classification [31].

There are various types of descriptors provided by MPEG-7. In most MPEG-7 frameworks, the descriptors have been selected by the researchers arbitrarily, based on their subjective view. It is suggested in [32] that selecting the same set of descriptors for different classes of images may not be reasonable. An MPEG-7 descriptor selection method that selects different MPEG-7 descriptors for different image classes in an image classification problem is better suited for a set of heterogeneous images. The proposed method L-GEMIM combines the Localized Generalization Error Model (L-GEM) and mutual information to assess the relevance of MPEG-7 descriptors for a particular image class. The L-GEMIM model assesses the relevance based on the generalization capability of an MPEG-7 descriptor using L-GEM and prevents redundant descriptors being selected, by mutual information. A prototype has been developed as a proof of concept, showing how to access MPEG-7-based multimedia services from a mobile host and how to provide multimedia services in the form of web services from the mobile host to other mobile devices [33]. In the biomedical domain, the usage of the two MPEG-7 textual features, edge histogram descriptor (EHD), and homogeneous texture descriptor (HTD) has been studied in [34] to improve the detection of masses in screening mammograms. The detection scheme was originally based on morphological directional neighborhood features extracted from mammographic regions of interest (ROIs).

The MPEG standardization group has identified a need for a set of visual signature tools supporting ultrafast search and robust detection at very low false-positive rates. These are necessary for a wide range of applications, including usage monitoring, copyright management, and content linking and identification [35]. A set of nine common requirements, uniqueness, robustness, independence, fast matching, fast extraction, compactness, nonalteration, self-containment, and coding independence, for both image and video signature tools have been identified. The explanation of these requirements is given in [36]. The group has recently completed standardization of the MPEG-7 image signature tools and work on video signature tools is under progress.

The SAPIR system (search in audio visual content using peer-to-peer image retrieval) measures the image similarity by a combination of MPEG-7 features [37]. The similarity of images is measured using five MPEG-7 features (scalable color, color layout, color structure, edge histogram, homogeneous texture) extracted from the images. These features are combined into a single metric function by a weighted sum of the individual feature distances. Eptascape (http://www.eptascape.com/), has launched several products, which use MPEG-7 to store video data. The video analytics software platform is composed of server-side detection engine software to provide behavioral analysis and event detection from MPEG-7 streams acquired from connected IP cameras. This product is intended to be a plug-in integration with DVR and camera products. The video content analysis hardware includes an embedded MPEG-7 real-time encoder, but it can only be used with Texas Instruments' DSP processors. The Eptavision Intelligent Video Management Software Suite is an end-to-end solution that is fully integrated with server-side and client-side operations. UniSay (http://www.unisay.com/) has a suite of automated solutions for media professionals for track reading and translation, closed captioning, subtitling, and dubbing. Customers can upload media files for processing and download the results using its automated web services. Of course, there are many tools and products developed as research prototypes.

9.2.4   Evaluation of MPEG-7 Features

In [38], a detailed quantitative analysis of the performance of the features, color histogram, Tamura textures features, Gabor features, spatial autocorrelation features, SIFT descriptors, and patches including three MPEG-7 features (color layout, scalable color, edge histogram) for various CBIR tasks, has been done on the following five databases:

- WANG database, a subset from the Corel stock photo collection.
- University of Washington database and the UCID database mainly including vacation pictures.
- IRMA-10000 database of medical radiographs.
- ZuBud (Zurich buildings database for image-based recognition) database of buildings, where pictures are taken from different viewpoints and under different weather conditions.

The above analysis groups the commonly used image features into four categories; color representation, texture representation, local features, and shape representation. The authors have tried to answer the question about the suitability of features in CBIR using mean average precision and classification error rate parameters. The results show that color histograms can still be considered as a reasonably good baseline for general color photographs. However, local image descriptors outperform color histograms with additional computational cost. It is also concluded that none of the texture features presented can convey a complete description of the texture properties of an image [38; Tables 3, 4].

A feature evaluation procedure based on statistical data analysis is suggested in [39], which is not based on the usual precision-recall metric. The precision-recall method requires execution of hundreds of queries to guarantee the statistical validity of the quality indicators, and this process is very time consuming, as it has to be repeated on every change in the feature transformation. The following three statistical methods are used for evaluation: (i) univariate description (e.g. moments), (ii) identification of similarities between feature elements (e.g., cluster analysis) and (iii) identification of dependencies between variables (e.g., factor analysis). All four color descriptors, two texture descriptors (edge histogram, homogeneous texture), and one shape descriptor (region-based) are used for the statistical evaluation. The texture browsing descriptor is not used, due to the nonavailability of a stable implementation. Contour-based shape is not used because it depends on the employed segmentation algorithm and does not generate feature vectors of fixed length. There are a total of 306 features created after summing up all the extracted visual descriptors. It is found that most of the visual MPEG-7 features are highly robust against transformation and quality changes.

The MPEG-7 CLD along with SIFT descriptors [40] are found to yield better object re-detection results than the use of only SIFT or only MPEG-7 descriptors [41]. The SIFT and MPEG-7 color descriptors are extracted around the same interest points. This method takes advantage of using the structural information extracted as SIFT and the color information as MPEG-7 descriptors. In MPEG-7, the curvature scale-space descriptor (CSSD) and Zernike moment descriptor (ZMD) have been adopted as the contour-based shape descriptor (CBSD) and region-based shape descriptor (RBSD), respectively. The CBSD is evaluated against Fourier descriptor (FD) and RBSD is compared against FD, geometric moment descriptor (GMD) and grid descriptor (GD) [42]. The FD is better than CBSD in terms of computation complexity, robustness, hierarchical coarse-to-fine representation, and retrieval accuracy, but RBSD is found to be better than the other three descriptors as it captures spectral shape features, which are more robust than spatial shape features. It is also found that RBSD outperforms CBSD and therefore, can be replaced with it.

9.3   Multimodal Vector Representation of an Image Using MPEG-7 Color Descriptors

In this section, we describe an approach to create a multimodal vector representation of an image using the visual keywords and text annotation available with an image. The visual keywords are generated after extracting low-level MPEG-7 color descriptors of an image.

9.3.1   Visual Keyword Generation

Let $\{I_i | i = 1 : n\}$ be a set of n images. Each image is divided into nonoverlapping tiles, after which we extract various features from each tile, resulting in T, k-element feature vectors, where T is the total number of tiles in all images I. Let V be the desired number of visual keywords. We then cluster this set of feature vectors into V clusters, each cluster corresponding to one of the V visual keywords. Our approach treats each tile as a word in a text document, counting the number of times tiles from each bin appear in an image. Tile-feature vector can be formed using simple low-level features, such as color histograms and textures, or more sophisticated features such as SIFT [40] and MPEG-7 descriptors [43]. SIFT is a transformation that transforms images into scale-invariant coordinates relative to local features. SIFT generates a large number of features that densely cover the image over the full range of scales and locations. In SIFT, keypoints are detected by checking the scale-space extrema. The descriptor of each keypoint is based on the gradient magnitude and orientation in a region around the keypoint.

Figure 9.1 shows our approach to generating visual keywords from the low-level features. We start with a set of full-size images and divide them into tiles as described above; in the next step, MPEG-7 descriptors of each tile are generated and concatenated to form a tile-feature matrix. This matrix is passed through a clustering algorithm to create clusters of similar tiles. These clusters are then considered to be visual keywords, as all the tiles in each cluster are considered to belong to the same semantic category.

The procedure to create visual keywords is completely unsupervised and does not involve any image segmentation. Another important parameter to consider is the selection of template size to create tiles, since this size has a direct effect on the computation costs.

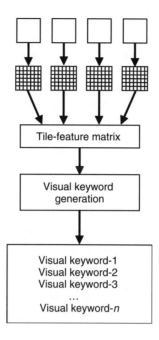

Figure 9.1 Visual keyword generation process.

A small template size will result in a large number of tiles and, hence, higher computation costs. We find that a template size of 32×32 pixels is appropriate [44], which extracts important information from an image and still does not create a very large number of tiles. We use the SCD with 64 coefficients, which are good enough to provide reasonably good performance; the CLD with 12 coefficients, found to be the best trade-off between the storage cost and retrieval efficiency; and the CSD with 64 coefficients, sufficient to capture the important features of a tile. Hence, a tile vector has 140 coefficients. We note that all three MPEG-7 descriptors have different sizes in different feature spaces as described in Section 9.3.1; therefore, they are normalized within their own feature space using the following simple normalization technique:

$$f_i' = \frac{f_i - \min_i}{\max_i - \min_i}$$

where f_i represents the ith feature in the feature space, $\min_i$ is the minimum possible value of the ith feature, $\max_i$ is the maximum possible value of the ith feature, and f_i' is the normalized feature value. The tile matrix is then created using the normalized tile vectors as its column vectors.

After obtaining the normalized MPEG-7 descriptors, we use the high-dimensional clustering algorithm, *vcluster* [45], to cluster all the tile vectors into the desired number of clusters. Each cluster will represent a visual keyword. The *vcluster* routine uses a method called *repeated bisections*. In this method, the desired k-way clustering solution is computed by performing a sequence of $k - 1$ repeated bisections. In this approach, the matrix is first clustered into two groups, and then one of these groups is selected and bisected further. This process continues until the desired number of clusters is found. During each step, a cluster is bisected so that the resulting two-way clustering solution optimizes a particular clustering criterion function. Note that this approach ensures that the criterion function is locally optimized within each bisection, but in general, it is not globally optimized. The cluster that is selected for further partitioning is the cluster whose bisection will optimize the value of the overall clustering criterion function. The following criterion function is used to find the membership of a tile with a cluster:

$$\text{maximize} \sum_{i=1}^{k} \sqrt{\sum_{v,u \in s_i} \text{sim}(v, u)}$$

where $\text{sim}(v, u)$ is the similarity between vector v and u, and it can be computed by the dot product of v and u. The above criterion function is used by many popular vector space variants of the k-means algorithm. In this method, each cluster is represented by its centroid vector and the goal is to find the clustering solution that maximizes the similarity between each vector and the centroid of the cluster to which it is assigned.

After this step, an image is then described by a vector, whose size is equal to the number of clusters (visual keywords). The jth element of this vector is equal to the number of tiles from the given image that belongs to the jth cluster. The visual keyword-image matrix is then formed, using the image vectors as columns. Finally, we normalize each column vector to unit length and generate the normalized visual keyword-image matrix. Normalization is basically a scaling operation to keep the many visual keywords in an image from overwhelming few visual keywords in other images. This process makes sure that every image is given equal importance in an image database.

9.3.2   Text Keyword Generation

The metadata available with images has been used in the past for image retrieval. This metadata may be in the form of text annotations or any information associated with the image. In social networking environments, users are encouraged to annotate images in the form of tags, which can be used later to search or browse images. Many techniques have been proposed to automatically annotate images using the available text annotations. There is a variety of information associated with images in addition to low-level features. They may be in the form of content-independent metadata, such as a time stamp, location, image format, or content-bearing metadata, which describes the higher-level concepts of an image, such as *animal*, *pet*, *male* to describe a dog image. This semantic information, however, cannot be extracted directly from visual contents, but represents the relatively more important meanings of the objects that are perceived by human beings. These conceptual aspects are more closely related to users' preferences and subjectivity. Concepts may vary significantly in different circumstances. Subtle changes in the semantics may lead to dramatic conceptual differences.

In practice, the text associated with images has been found to be very useful for image retrieval; for example, newspaper archivists index largely on captions [46]. Smeaton and Quigley [47] use hierarchical concept graphs (HCG) derived from Wordnet [48] to estimate the semantic distance between caption words. The algorithm for this step is very straightforward. We first create an initial term–document matrix using the available text keywords associated with each image. To control for the morphological variations of words, we use Porter's stemming algorithm [49]. The minimum and maximum term (word) length thresholds are set as 2 and 30, respectively, which are reasonable for our experiments. The term-document matrix is then normalized to unit length.

9.3.3   Combining Visual and Text Keywords to Create a Multimodal Vector Representation

The visual and text keywords generated in previous steps are combined to form a multimodal image vector representation before setting up image clustering and retrieval experiments. The visual keyword matrix and text keyword matrices are concatenated together to create a single multimodal matrix. This operation results in the creation of a high-dimensional vector representation. Next, a diffusion kernel is applied on this multimodal image representation to reduce the dimension and at the same time, to learn the co-occurrence relation between visual keywords and text keywords.

9.4   Dimensionality Reduction of Multimodal Vector Representation Using a Nonlinear Diffusion Kernel

There are several different approaches to dimensionality reduction, such as *feature selection*, which involves finding a subset of features by means of a filter, and *feature extraction*, which involves using a mapping of the multidimensional space to fewer dimensions. In some applications, it is possible to use new representations in which there has been some information loss. There is a trade-off between preserving important aspects of original data and the dimensions desired. In feature selection, an appropriate subset of the original features is found to represent the data. The criteria to select appropriate features are dependent on the application domain. This method is useful when a limited amount of data is present, but represented with a large number of features. In feature extraction, new features are computed using the original features, without losing any important information. Feature extraction methods can be divided into linear and nonlinear techniques. Linear techniques are based on getting the resultant feature set Y, which are derived using a linear combination of the original feature set X. The linear feature extraction process generally uses a weight vector w to optimize a criterion, which is also considered a quality parameter.

In this section, we introduce the nonlinear dimensional reduction technique using a *diffusion kernel*. This technique provides a framework based on diffusion processes that allow one to obtain a multiscale description of the geometric structures of the data, as well as of spaces of functions defined on the data. This approach uses the ideas from spectral graph theory, harmonic analysis, and potential theory [50]. We obtain a large number of modalities (features) in the form of visual and textual keywords. These modalities are not completely independent of each other; we need to find an effective strategy to fuse them.

We are given a multimodality matrix $T_{\text{vis-text}}$, obtained after concatenating the visual keywords–image matrix T_{vis} and the textual keyword–image matrix T_{text}. Let Ω represent the set of columns in $T_{\text{vis-tex}}$ and x, y be any two vectors in Ω. Then we can define a finite graph $G = (\Omega, W_\sigma)$ with n nodes, where the weight matrix $W_\sigma(x, y)$ is defined as follows:

$$W_\sigma(x, y) = \exp\left(-\left(\frac{|x - y|}{\sigma}\right)^2\right)$$

where $|x - y|$ is the $L2$ distance between vector x and y. Let

$$q_\sigma(x) = \sum_{y \in \Omega} W_\sigma(x, y)$$

Then we can have a new kernel, called a *diffusion kernel*:

$$W_\sigma^\alpha(x, y) = \frac{W_\sigma(x, y)}{q_\sigma^\alpha(x) q_\sigma^\alpha(y)}$$

The parameter α is used to specify the amount of influence density has in the infinitesimal transitions of the diffusion. We can obtain the anisotropic transition kernel $p_\sigma(x, y)$ after applying the normalized graph Laplacian construction to $W_\sigma^\alpha(x, y)$:

$$d_\sigma(x) = \sum_{y \in \Omega} W_\sigma^\alpha(x, y)$$

and

$$p_\sigma(x, y) = \frac{W_\sigma^\alpha(x, y)}{d_\sigma(x)}$$

Matrix $p_\sigma(x, y)$ can be viewed as the transitional kernel of a Markov chain on Ω. The diffusion distance D_t between x and y at time t of a random walk is defined as

$$D_t^2(x, y) = \|p_t(x, .) - p_t(y, .)\|_{1/\phi_0}^2$$

$$= \sum_{z \in \Omega} \frac{(p_t(x, z) - p_t(y, z))^2}{\phi_0(z)}$$

where ϕ_0 is the stationary distribution of the Markov chain.

The diffusion distance can be represented by the right eigenvectors and eigenvalues of matrix $p_\sigma(x, y)$:

$$D_t^2(x, y) \cong \sum_{j \geq 1} \lambda_j^{2t} \left(\psi_j(x) - \psi_j(y)\right)^2$$

ψ_0 does not show up because it is a constant. Since the eigenvalues tend to be zero and have a modulus strictly less than one, the above sum can be computed to a preset accuracy $\delta > 0$ with a finite number of terms. If we define $s(\delta, t) = \max\{j \in N, \text{ such that } |\lambda_j|^t > \delta|\lambda_1|^t\}$, up to relative precision δ, then we have

$$D_t^2(x, y) \cong \sum_{j=1}^{s(\delta,t)} \lambda_j^{2t} \left(\psi_j(x) - \psi_j(y)\right)^2$$

Therefore, we can have a family of diffusion maps $\psi_\tau, \tau \in N$, given by

$$\psi_t : x \to \left(\lambda_1^t \psi_1(x), \lambda_2^t \psi_2(x), \ldots, \lambda_{s(\delta,t)}^t \psi_{s(\delta,t)}(x)\right)^T$$

The mapping $\psi_t \colon \Omega \to \mathcal{R}^{s(\delta,t)}$ provides a parameterization (fusion) of the dataset Ω; in other words, a parameterization of the graph G in a lower-dimensional space $\mathcal{R}^{s(\delta,t)}$, where the rescaled eigenvectors are the coordinates. The dimensionality reduction and the weight of the relevant eigenvectors are dictated by both, the time t of the random walk and the spectral fall-off of the eigenvalues. This diffusion mapping represents an effective fusion of visual and textual keywords and is a low-dimensional representation of the image set. The values of σ and α in the diffusion kernel are set to 10 and 1 respectively, for all of our experiments.

9.5 Experiments

9.5.1 Image Dataset

In this section, we discuss various experiments conducted to investigate the effectiveness of using visual and text keyword model on the well-known Corel image dataset and the LabelMe collection, available through the MIT AI Lab [51]. We selected 10 categories (*playing cards, college buildings, cats, bonsai plants, bird art, buses, mushrooms, perennial plants, pyramids, and sail boats*) of images from the Corel dataset, each category having almost 100 images. Figure 9.2 shows two images from each of the following four categories in the Corel dataset: *bonsai, playing cards, mushrooms*, and *pyramids* starting from the first row and proceeding left to right.

From the LabelMe dataset, we selected 658 images belonging to 15 categories. The categories with the number of images in them are listed here: *Boston street scene* (152), *cars parked in the underground garage* (39), *kitchen* (14), *office* (24), *rocks* (41), *pumpkins* (58), *apples* (11), *oranges* (18), *conference room* (28), *bedroom* (14), *dining* (63), *indoor home* (59), *home office* (19), *silverware* (81), and *speaker* (37). This collection has been annotated by on-line users, and therefore has a wide variety of annotations. They do not conform to any fixed annotation list. In this collection, many classes have very few

Figure 9.2   Images from the categories *bonsai, playing card, mushroom*, and *pyramid*.

Figure 9.3 Images from the categories *office*, *bedroom*, *indoor home*, and *home office*.

training samples; on the other hand, there are classes with many training samples. In addition to this, we have to deal with partially labeled training images. Figure 9.3 has two images from each of the following four categories: *office*, *bedroom*, *indoor home*, and *home office*, starting from the first row and then proceeding left to right.

The MILOS software [52], which is based on the MPEG-7 XM model, is used to extract the color descriptors SCD, CSD, and CLD. The total number of descriptors used is 140, in which we have 64 of SCD, 64 of CSD, and 12 of CLD. The details of the image database are given in Table 9.2.

9.5.2 Image Clustering Experiments

We use a metric called the *silhouette value* [53] to measure the quality of the clusters. The silhouette value for each point is a measure of how similar a point is to other points in its own cluster versus points in other clusters, and ranges from -1 to $+1$. It is defined as

$$S(i) = (\min(d_1(i, k)) - d_2(i))/ \max(d_2(i), \min(d_1(i, k))),$$

where $d_2(i)$ is the average distance from the ith point to the other points in its own cluster, and $d_1(i, k)$ is the average distance from the ith point to points in another cluster k. The silhouette uses the squared Euclidean distance between points in the matrix. We maximize the average silhouette values over all the values considered for the possible number of clusters.

Table 9.2 Details of LabelMe and Corel datasets including number of tiles, visual keywords, and text keywords

Dataset	Number of images	Number of tiles	Number of visual keywords	Number of text keywords
LabelMe	658	165,750	1500	506
Corel	999	95,904	900	924

In all the experiments, we select the number of dimensions after dimensionality reduction, in such a manner that not more than 0.1% information is lost in the reconstructed data matrix representation. After that, we apply the k-means clustering technique. We then compare the results of the nonlinear diffusion kernel dimensionality reduction technique with the popular *singular value decomposition* (SVD). The different approaches we use are as follows:

- tiles of each image, using SVD (*tssvd*);
- tiles of each image (*tsdk*): we apply the diffusion kernel on the visual keyword-image matrix and find that only the first 20 dimensions are needed to keep the information loss the same as before;
- tiles of each image + text keywords, using SVD (*tssvdtk*);
- tiles of each image + text keywords, using diffusion kernel (*tstktk*);
- true-k (forcing the number of tile clusters to be the known correct number) for tiles of each image + text keywords, using the diffusion kernel (*tsdktk*).

To find the appropriate number of clusters, we vary the value of k from 3 to 30 in the k-means algorithm and calculate the silhouette value for each point/image and maximize the average value. Table 9.3 shows the result of applying the k-means algorithm over different sets of data, as described earlier. As we can see in this table, the diffusion kernel can be applied not only to reduce the dimensions of a large dataset, but it can also be used to improve the clustering results. In both datasets, the mean of the silhouette value is more when we use the diffusion kernel instead of directly applying the SVD. We also note that the dimensionality of the resulting space is lower when we use the diffusion kernel rather than the SVD. Also, we use a fewer number of dimensions and this results in faster computation.

In any unsupervised learning based on low-level image features, it is difficult to match any solution with the true class labels. We compare the results of our approach with the true class labels; the k in k-means is 15 and 10, respectively, for the LabelMe and Corel datasets. When we examine the image clusters of the Corel dataset, we observe that for *tsdktk*, some of the classes *bird art*, *bonsai*, *buses*, *cards*, *perennial*, and *sailboat* are reasonably discovered. We also notice that some of the classes are being split; the reason is that low-level MPEG-7 features extracted from the images not only consider the colors, but also the structure of the images. There are 9 out of 10 classes which

Table 9.3 Clustering results after applying SVD and diffusion kernel with and without text keywords

Data	Mean silhouette		Number of clusters	
	LabelMe	Corel	LabelMe	Corel
tssvd	0.14	0.16	28	16
tsdk	0.44	0.57	22	5
tssvdtk	0.17	0.23	24	3
tsdktk	0.64	0.47	10	19
true-k (tsdktk)	0.56	0.46	15	10

Table 9.4 Precision results

Data	10% recall		30% recall		Average precision	
	LabelMe	Corel	LabelMe	Corel	LabelMe	Corel
tssvd	0.69	0.72	0.54	0.57	0.44	0.45
tsdk	0.69	0.75	0.57	0.61	0.45	0.50
tstksvd	0.80	0.87	0.68	0.76	0.56	0.62
tstkdk	0.81	0.86	0.69	0.77	0.59	0.63
txt only	0.77	0.81	0.68	0.69	0.52	0.51

have more than 50 images correctly classified into the same clusters. There are three classes – *colleges, mushrooms*, and *pyramids* – which are not classified very well, but the results are consistent with the type of images in these categories. Upon closer inspection, we find that many *colleges* images are put into the *pyramid* category, which in fact has similar low-level features; both of them have "concrete" structure in the images. A similar argument can be applied to the classification results of the classes *bonsai* and *perennial*.

The important observation is that if we let the k-means algorithm find the value of k, the clusters discovered are much more natural. For example, *bonsai* images and *perennial* plants are very similar from a low-level feature perspective. At the same time, the *colleges* and *pyramids* classes have large variations in their image collection. A similar explanation holds true for the LabelMe dataset.

9.5.3 Image Retrieval Experiments

For image retrieval experiments, we measure the precision at 10% and 30% recall and the average precision at 10%, 20%, ..., and 100% recall. The values vary between zero and one. We consider the entire collection of images in our database as the query dataset to avoid favoring certain query results.

The results in Table 9.4 show that multimodal keywords give the best results at average precision level. In most cases, they also show improved performance at the 10% recall level. As we increase the recall level, multimodal keywords consistently show better performance, but using only low-level image features provides results worse than those provided by multimodal keywords. However, using text keywords alone is better than using of low-level features, which indicates that at a higher recall value, the utility of low-level features diminishes. These results are consistent for both the datasets used in the experiments. The diffusion kernel saves computation cost, avoids high dimensionality, and finds the modalities that are the most representative of a large feature set.

9.6 Conclusion

In this chapter, we have described a diffusion kernel-based approach for image clustering and retrieval. In our experiments, we have established the usefulness of MPEG-7 color descriptors. MPEG-7 not only deals with the low-level encoding of a multimedia element, but is also used to store metadata to describe it in words or sentences. This metadata, being in XML format, can be used effectively for storage, search, and retrieval applications. In the future, we expect to see more and more MPEG-7-based commercial products that will drive its popularity.

References

[1] Grabner, M., Grabner, H., and Bischof, H. (2006) Fast approximated SIFT. Proceedings of the ACCV, pp. 918–927.
[2] Flickner, M., Sawhney, H., Niblack, W. *et al*. (1995) Query by image and video content: the QBIC system. *IEEE Computer*, **28**, 23–32.
[3] Ogle, V. and Stonebraker, M. (1995) Chabot: retrieval from a relational database of images. *IEEE Computer*, **28** (9) 40–48.
[4] Niblack, C.W., Barber, R.J., Equitz, W.R. *et al*. (1993) The QBIC project: querying images by content using color, texture, and shape. Proceedings of Storage and Retrieval for Image and Video Databases, pp. 173–187.
[5] Smeulders, W.M.A., Worring, M., Santini, S. *et al*. (2000) Content-based image retrieval at the end of the early years. *IEEE Transactions on Pattern Analysis and Machine Intelligence*, **22**, 1349–1380.
[6] Huang, J., Kumar, S.R., Mitra, M. *et al*. (1997) Image indexing using color correlograms. Proceedings of Conference on Computer Vision and Pattern Recognition, pp. 762–768.
[7] Tao, Y. and Grosky, W.I. (2001) Spatial color indexing using rotation, translation, and scale-invariant anglograms. *Multimedia Tools and Applications*, **15** (3), 247–268.
[8] Martinez, J.M. (2002) MPEG-7, Part 1. *IEEE Multimedia*, **9** (2), 78–87.
[9] Miroslaw, B. (2001) MPEG-7 visual shape descriptors. *IEEE Transactions on Circuits and Systems for Video Technology*, **11**, 716–719.
[10] Martinez, J.M. (2002) MPEG-7, Part 2. *IEEE Multimedia*, **9** (3), 83–93.
[11] Swain, M. and Ballard, D. (1991) Color indexing. *Journal of Computer Vision*, **7**, 11–32.
[12] Jain, A.K. and Vailaya, A. (1996) Image retrieval using color and shape. *Journal of Pattern Recognition*, **29** (8), 1233–1244.
[13] Carson, C., Belonge, S., Greenspan, H., and Malik, J. (2002) Blobworld: image segmentation using expectation-maximization and its application to image querying. *IEEE Transactions on Pattern Analysis and Machine Intelligence*, **24** (8), 1026–1038.
[14] Faloutsos, C., Barber, R., Flickner, M. *et al*. (1994) Efficient and effective querying by image content. *Journal of Intelligent Information Systems*, **3** (3/4), 231–262.
[15] Pentland, A., Picard, R.W., and Sclaroff, S. (1996) Photobook: tools for content-based manipulation of image databases. *Journal of Computer Vision*, **18** (3), 233–254.
[16] Squire, D.M., Muller, W., Muller, H., and Pun, T. (2000) Content-based query of image databases: inspirations from text retrieval. *Pattern Recognition Letters*, **21**, 13–14.
[17] Westerveld, T. (2000) Image retrieval: content versus context. Proceedings of Content-based Multimedia Information Access, RIAO Conference, pp. 276–284.
[18] Grosky, W.I. and Zhao, R. (2002) Negotiating the semantic gap: from feature maps to semantic landscapes. *Journal of Pattern Recognition*, **35** (3), 593–600.
[19] Broek, E.L., van Rikxoort, E.M., and Schouten, T.E. (2005) Human-centered object-based image retrieval, *Lecture Notes in Computer Science (Advances in Pattern Recognition)*, vol. 3687, SpringerLink, Berlin, pp. 492–501.
[20] Amato, G., Debole, F., Peters, C., and Savino, P. (2008) The multimatch prototype: multilingual/ multimedia search for cultural heritage objects. Proceedings of ECDL, pp. 385–387.
[21] Wan, S., Jin, P., and Yue, L. (2009) An approach for image retrieval based on visual saliency. Proceedings of the IASP, pp. 172–175.
[22] Haslhofer, B. and Klas, W. (2010) A Survey of Techniques for Achieving Metadata Interoperability. *ACM Surveys*, **42** (2), 1–37.
[23] Mezaris, V., Kompatsiaris, I., and Strintzis, M.G. (2003) An ontology approach to object-based image retrieval. Proceedings of the ICIP, vol. 2, pp. 511–514.
[24] Arndt, R., Troncy, R., Staab, S. *et al*. (2007) COMM: designing a well-founded multimedia ontology for the web. Proceedings of the ISWC/ASWC, pp. 30–43.

[25] Tous, R. and Delgado, J. (2009) A LEGO-like metadata architecture for image search & retrieval. Proceedings of the DEXA, pp. 246–250.
[26] Laaksonen, J., Koskela, M., Laakso, S., and Oja, E. (2000) PicSOM – content-based image retrieval with self-organizing maps. *Pattern Recognition Letters*, **21**, 1199–1207.
[27] Grosky, W.I., Patel, N., Li, X., and Fotouhi, F. (2005) Dynamically emerging semantics in an MPEG-7 image database. *Computer Journal*, **48** (5), 536–544.
[28] Ye, J. and Smeaton, A.F. (2004) Aggregated feature retrieval for MPEG-7 via clustering. Proceedings of the ACM SIGIR Conference on Research and Development in Information Retrieval, pp. 514–515.
[29] Lux, M., Becker, J., and Krottmaier, H. (2003) Semantic annotation and retrieval of digital photos. Proceedings of the CAiSE, pp. 85–88.
[30] Florian, M. and Trujillo, M. (2008) MPEG-7 service oriented system – MPEG-7 SOS. Proceedings of the Content-Based Multimedia Indexing, pp. 476–483.
[31] Kaczmarzyk, T. and Pedrycz, W. (2006) Content-based image retrieval: an application of MPEG-7 Standard and Fuzzy C-Means. Annual Meeting of the North American Fuzzy Information Processing Society, pp. 172–177.
[32] Wang, J., Ng, W.W.Y., Tsang, E.C.C. *et al*. (2008) MPEG-7 descriptor selection using Localized Generalization Error Model with mutual information. Proceedings of the Machine Learning and Cybernetics, pp. 454–459.
[33] Yiwei, C., Jarke, M., Klamma, R. *et al*. (2009) Mobile access to MPEG-7 based multimedia services. Proceedings of the Mobile Data Management: Systems, Services, and Middleware, pp. 102–111.
[34] Tourassi, G.D., Elmaghraby, A.S., Eltonsy, N.H., and Fadeev, A. (2006) Significance of MPEG-7 textural features for improved mass detection in mammography. Proceedings of the IEEE International Conference of Engineering in Medicine and Biology Society, pp. 4779–4782.
[35] MPEG Video Subgroup (2008) Updated Call for Proposals on Video Signature Tools. MPEG Doc. No. W10154, October 2008.
[36] Bober, M. and Brasnett, P. (2009) MPEG-7 visual signature tools. Proceedings of the ICME, pp. 1540–1543.
[37] Novak, D., Batko, M., and Zezula, P. (2008) Web-scale system for image similarity search: when the dreams are coming true. Proceedings of the Content-Based Multimedia Indexing, pp. 446–453.
[38] Deselaers, T., Keysers, D., and Ney, H. (2008) Features for image retrieval: an experimental comparison. *Journal of Information Retrieval*, **11** (2), 77–107.
[39] Eidenberger, H. (2007) Evaluation of content-based image descriptors by statistical methods. *Multimedia Tools and Applications*, **35** (3), 241–258.
[40] Lowe, D.G. (1999) Object recognition from local scale invariant features. Proceedings of the ICCV, pp. 1150–1157.
[41] Schgerl, P., Sorschag, R., Bailer, W., and Thallinger, G. (2007) Object re-detection using SIFT and MPEG-7 color descriptors. Proceedings of the Multimedia Content Analysis and Mining, vol. 4577, pp. 305–314.
[42] Zhang, D. and Lu, G. (2003) Evaluation of MPEG-7 shape descriptors against other shape descriptors. Proceedings of the Multimedia Systems, vol. 9, pp. 15–30.
[43] Manjunath, B.S., Salembier, P., and Sikor, T. (eds) (2002) *Introduction to MPEG-7 Multimedia Content Description Interface*, John Wiley & Sons, Inc., Indianapolis, IN.
[44] Agrawal, R., Grosky, W.I., and Fotouhi, F. (2009) Searching an appropriate template size for multimodal image clustering. Proceedings of the ICMCS, pp. 113–123.
[45] Karypis, G. (2003) Cluto: A Clustering Toolkit, Release 2.1.1. *Tech. Rep*. 02-017. University of Minnesota, Department of Computer Science.
[46] Markkula, M. and Sormunen, E. (1998) Searching for photos – Journalists' practices in pictorial IR. Proceedings of the Challenge of Image Retrieval, pp. 1–13.
[47] Smeaton, A.F. and Quigley, I. (1996) Experiments on using semantic distances between words in image caption retrieval. Proceedings of the SIGIR, pp. 174–180.
[48] Fellbaum, C. (ed.) (1998) *WorldNet: An Electronic Lexical Database*, MIT Press, Cambridge, MA.
[49] van Rijsbergen, C.J., Robertson, S.E., and Porter, M.F. (1980) New Models in Probabilistic Information Retrieval. *Tech. Rep*. 5587, British Library Research and Development, Cambridge, Eng.
[50] Coifman, R.R. and Lafon, S. (2006) Diffusion maps. *Applied and Computational Harmonic Analysis, Special Issue on Diffusion Maps and Wavelets*, **21** (1), 5–30.

[51] Russell, B.C., Torralba, A., Murphy, K.P., and Freeman, W.T. (2008) LabelMe: a database and web based tool for image annotation. *Journal of Computer Vision*, **77**, 157–173.
[52] Amato, G., Gennaro, C., Savino, P., and Rabitti, F. (2004) Milos: a multimedia content management system for digital library applications. Proceedings of the European Conference on Research and Advanced Technology for Digital Libraries, vol. 3232, pp. 14–25.
[53] Kaufman, L. and Rousseeuw, P.J. (1990) Finding groups in data, *An Introduction to Cluster Analysis*, John Wiley & Sons, Inc., Indianapolis (IN).

10

MPEG-7 Visual Descriptors and Discriminant Analysis

Jun Zhang[1], Lei Ye[1], and Jianhua Ma[2]
[1]*School of Computer Science and Software Engineering, University of Wollongong, Wollongong, NSW, Australia*
[2]*Faculty of Computer and Information Sciences, Hosei University, Tokyo, Japan*

10.1 Introduction

The MPEG-7 standards defines a set of descriptors to characterize the content of visual media [1, 2]. These visual descriptors, such as color and texture descriptors, have undergone extensive evaluation and development based on the application of retrieval ranking. Specifically, under query-by-example (QBE) paradigm, average normalized modified retrieval rank (ANMRR), a rate-accuracy like performance measure, is adopted to test these descriptors on image collection and predefined ground truth datasets. The experimental results show that each descriptor has good retrieval performance. However, there are some questions left to be answered in practice. How to apply visual descriptors in various applications? Does each visual descriptor have good performance in the applications besides retrieval ranking? How to combine multiple visual descriptors for a specific application? What is the performance of the aggregated visual descriptors?

It would be generally accepted that a good visual descriptor should have excellent ability to separate distinct visual media content, named *discriminant power*. In various applications, the discriminant power of visual descriptors would be evaluated by the application-dependent performance criteria. Since the core experiments applied for the MPEG-7 standards concentrate on single visual descriptor and retrieval ranking, the discriminant power of visual descriptors has not been sufficiently evaluated. Particularly, the applications and technologies should be taken into account for evaluating the discriminant power of visual descriptors. This chapter answers the above questions from the perspective of discriminant power.

The Handbook of MPEG Applications: Standards in Practice   Edited by Marios C. Angelides and Harry Agius
© 2011 John Wiley & Sons, Ltd

Three basic applications are considered in this chapter, which are image clustering [3], image classification [4], and image retrieval [5, 6]. These applications are related to each other and have different features. Image clustering aims to discover the meaningful categories in an unorganized image collection without any supervising information. Image classification, compared to image clustering, holds different assumptions that the image categories have been predefined and a set of training samples are available for each category. The goal of image classification is to assign the unlabeled images into the predefined image categories. Most of traditional clustering and classification algorithms can be applied to address the problems of image clustering and image classification. The problem of image retrieval is more complex due to the user's intention. The retrieval methods should adapt to the user's query. In detail, single query image, multiple query image, and relevance feedback are three situations that we consider in the application of visual descriptors. Furthermore, in practice, different methods will be applied to utilize visual descriptors. For instance, given a color descriptor, we can apply support vector machine (SVM) [7] or k nearest neighbors (k-NN) [8] to design the image classifiers. The selected classification algorithm may dramatically effect the performance of a visual descriptor. In summary, the performance of a visual descriptor with a certain method in a specific application may not effectively demonstrate its discriminant power.

In the case of multiple visual descriptors, it is an important topic of combining these descriptors to obtain stronger discriminant power. From the information theory point of view, multiple descriptors have stronger discriminant power than single descriptor. However, it is well known that this conclusion may not always be true in practice. The combination of multiple visual descriptors, named *feature aggregation*, is a critical problem. In the literature, there are two main approaches [9], one is early fusion and the other is later fusion. Given a designed visual descriptor, an image is normally represented as a vector. Early fusion first combines multiple descriptor vectors into a single aggregated vector. Then, the image similarity is measured by the distance between the aggregated vectors. Later fusion applies another strategy. It first measures image similarity, such as feature distance, in multiple individual feature spaces. Then, the final image similarity is obtained by combining these feature distances. These two approaches have their own advantages. With early fusion, the theoretical analysis can be easily conducted in the aggregated feature space. It is feasible to incorporate meaningful distance metrics in later fusion. In practice, there are two important tasks: (i) designing of feature aggregation methods for a specific application and (ii) evaluating the discriminant power of the aggregated visual descriptors.

In this chapter, the technologies for utilizing the MPEG-7 visual descriptors in various situations are explored, as well as a number of experimental results to demonstrate the discriminant power of the descriptors are reported. The following two sections focus on single visual descriptor and multiple visual descriptors, separately. For single visual descriptor, the MPEG-7 standards have done a lot of significant work. The recommended distance metrics are briefly reviewed, which are the basis of some methods presented in this chapter. A number of methods are presented for practical applications using either single visual descriptor or multiple visual descriptors. Some methods use the recommended distance metrics, which are able to keep the semantic of visual descriptors, and some other methods perform in the original feature space or aggregated feature space, which can directly apply all traditional clustering or classification algorithms. We demonstrate the discriminant power of the aggregated visual descriptors using the corresponding performance criteria in various applications.

The remainder of this chapter is organized as follows: a short literature review is provided in Section 10.2; Section 10.3 reports single visual descriptor–based methods and the discriminant power of each visual descriptor; Section 10.4 presents feature aggregation methods and the discriminant power of the aggregated visual descriptors; finally, Section 10.5 draws conclusions.

10.2 Literature Review

This section provides a short review on the study and application of the MPEG-7 visual descriptors. During the design process, the MPEG-7 visual descriptors were evaluated with a specific performance measure, named ANMRR, which is similar to precision and recall [1]. All retrieval experiments were conducted on large image datasets and predefined ground truth information. These evaluation represented well the performance of single descriptors in retrieval application, but they can demonstrate neither the performance of visual descriptors in other applications nor the performance of combined visual descriptors. In [10], a study was presented to analyze the MPEG-7 visual descriptors from a statistical point of view, which revealed the properties and qualities (redundancies, sensitivity to media content, etc.) of the descriptors used. A recent experimental comparison of features for image retrieval was provided in [11], which also included the MPEG-7 visual descriptors. That study analyzed the correlation of the features, which provided a way to find suitable features for a specific task.

In various applications of the MPEG-7 visual descriptors, fusing visual descriptors is normally preferred because it may obtain better performance than using single descriptor. For image retrieval (ranking), PicSOM [12] combined relevance feedback mechanism and self-organizing map (SOM) technique to fuse MPEG-7 visual descriptors, which showed better retrieval performance than a vector quantization (VQ)-based retrieval scheme. In [13], a decision fusion framework was proposed for content-based image retrieval of art images based on the combination of MPEG-7 visual descriptors. This framework obtained image similarities by fusing feature distances using fuzzy theory. We also proposed a feature dissimilarity space–based method [14] to combine MPEG-7 visual descriptors, in which the feature distances can be aggregated by SVM technique to achieve a nonlinear combination. For image classification, three techniques were proposed to fuse MPEG-7 visual descriptors in [15], which were based on SVM, k-NN, and fuzzy neural network, respectively. The reported experimental results showed that the fuzzy neural network–based fusion technique was superior. Another work [16] used radial basis function neural networks (RBFNN) to combine MPEG-7 visual descriptors, which showed RBFNN-based scheme has the preferred results compared to SVM-based image classification scheme. For image clustering, MPEG-7 visual descriptors were used to describe the image content, and a graph-based method was applied to automatically organize similar images in a photo display system [17]. An image clustering model was proposed [18] to use MPEG-7 color descriptors to represent temple-based visual keywords, which were then combined with any text keyword annotations. Moreover, MPEG-7 visual descriptors can be used for automated feature extraction in capsule endoscopy [19]. In that application, a methodology was presented for measuring the potential of selected visual MPEG-7 descriptors for the task of specific medical event detection such as blood and ulcers. In [20], MPEG-7 visual descriptors were combined with SURF to effectively retrieve the events from visual lifelogs, which showed an improvement on using either of those sources or SIFT individually.

Although the study and application of MPEG-7 visual descriptors are extensive, the discriminant powers of these descriptors have not been sufficiently investigated. In particular, it is not clear how to combine multiple MPEG-7 visual descriptors and about the discriminant ability of the aggregated descriptors in different applications, such as retrieval, classification, and clustering. These issues are the objectives of this chapter.

10.3 Discriminant Power of Single Visual Descriptor

This chapter focuses on five standardized MPEG-7 visual descriptors [1] including the color structure descriptor (CSD), dominant color descriptor (DCD), color layout descriptor (CLD), edge histogram descriptor (EHD), and homogeneous texture descriptor (HTD). Taking practical applications into account, various methods of utilizing single visual descriptor are presented and summarized in this section. In addition, we evaluate the discriminant power of these descriptors based on both applications and methods.

10.3.1 Feature Distance

The MPEG-7 standards provide a recommended distance metric for each descriptor based on the core experiments [1]. In other words, the recommended metrics are good choice to match feature distances and visual similarity. Since a number of methods presented in this chapter are based on these metrics, a short summary on visual descriptors and recommended distance metrics is provided in this section.

CSD provides information regarding color distribution as well as localized spatial color structure in the image. The image is represented by a modified color histogram. The distance between two CSD histograms for two images is calculated using L_1-norm metric as follows:

$$D_{\text{CSD}}(X, Y) = \sum_{i=0}^{255} |H_{X,i} - H_{Y,i}| \tag{10.1}$$

where $H_{X,i}$ and $H_{Y,i}$ represent the ith bin of the color structure histogram for two images, respectively. DCD compactly conveys global information regarding the dominant colors present in the image. An image is represented as a set of color vectors, c_i, together with their percentages, p_i. The recommended distance measure applied for DCD is

$$D_{\text{DCD}}(X, Y) = \left(\sum_{i=1}^{N_Y} p_{Yi}^2 + \sum_{j=1}^{N_X} p_{Xj}^2 - \sum_{i=1}^{N_Y} \sum_{j=1}^{N_X} 2a_{Yi,Xj} \, p_{Yi} \, p_{Xj} \right)^{\frac{1}{2}} \tag{10.2}$$

$a_{k,l}$ denotes the similarity coefficient between c_k and c_l, which is calculated as

$$a_{k,l} = \begin{cases} 1 - \dfrac{d_{k,l}}{d_{\max}}, & d_{k,l} \le T \\ 0, & d_{k,l} > T \end{cases} \tag{10.3}$$

In Equation 10.3, $d_{k,l} = \|c_k, c_l\|$ represents the Euclidean distance between two color vectors, and T and $d_{\max}$ are empirical values. CLD provides information about the spatial color distribution within images. After an image is divided into 64 blocks, CLD descriptor is extracted from each of the blocks based on the discrete cosine transform. The distance between two CLD vectors can be calculated as

$$D_{\text{CLD}}(X, Y) = \sqrt{\sum_i w_{yi}(Y_{Xi} - Y_{Yi})^2} + \sqrt{\sum_i w_{Cbi}(Cb_{Xi} - Cb_{Yi})^2}$$

$$+ \sqrt{\sum_i w_{Cri}(Cr_{Xi} - Cr_{Yi})^2} \qquad (10.4)$$

where w_i represents the weight associated with ith coefficient.

EHD captures the edge distribution within an image. The image similarity based on EHD descriptors is determined by calculating the L_1-norm of the 80-dimensional feature vectors H_X and H_Y:

$$D_{\text{EHD}}(X, Y) = \sum_{i=0}^{79} \left| H_{X,i} - H_{Y,i} \right| . \qquad (10.5)$$

HTD characterizes the mean and energy deviation of 30 frequency channels modeled by Gabor functions. The distance between two vectors T_X and T_Y is calculated as

$$D_{\text{HTD}}(X, Y) = \sum_k \left| \frac{T_{X,i} - T_{Y,i}}{\alpha(k)} \right| \qquad (10.6)$$

where $\alpha(k)$ is determined experimentally.

10.3.2 Applications Using Single Visual Descriptor

In this section, we consider three applications – image clustering, image classification, and image retrieval. Several methods using single visual descriptor are presented to achieve the goals of these applications.

Image clustering aims to discover the meaningful structure of an image collection, which normally applies unsupervised learning technologies. In image clustering, it assumes that an image collection has N images, $\Omega_i = \{I_1, \ldots, I_N\}$. Given a selected visual descriptor, the image collection can be described as $\Omega_f = \{F_1, \ldots, F_N\}$, where F_i is a feature vector for the ith image. Specifically, the goal of image clustering is to discover k meaningful clusters in Ω_f. The number of categories, k, can be predefined or predicted automatically in the clustering procedure. The distance calculation between images in a feature space is important for the results of image clustering. In this chapter, the recommended metrics are used to calculate the image distance to single visual descriptor. Then, the problem of image clustering is solved. To illustrate this method, an example implementation that utilizes k-medoids algorithm [21] and the CLD descriptor is provided. The most common realization of k-medoid clustering is the partitioning around medoids (PAM) algorithm. PAM is based on the search for k representative images (medoids) among the images of the collection. After finding a set of k representative objects, the k clusters are constructed

Table 10.1 Example method using PAM algorithm and CLD descriptor

Step	Description
1	Randomly select k of the N images as the medoids, $\{F_1^o, \ldots, F_k^o\}$.
2	Associate each image to the closet medoid based on the distance of CLD descriptors. For instance, the distance of an image F_i to a medoid F_j^o can be calculated using Equation 10.4, which can described as $d_{ij} = D_{\text{CLD}}(F_i, F_j^o)$
3	For each medoid F_j^o and for each nonmedoid image F_i, swap F_i and F_j^o and compute the total cost of the configuration
4	Select the configuration with the lowest cost
5	Repeat Steps 1 to 4 until there is no change in the medoid.

by assigning each image of the collection to the nearest medoid. The PAM algorithm for image clustering is listed in detail in Table 10.1. Since the recommended distance metric can well match people's visual similarity, it is hopeful that this image clustering method can construct some meaningful image clusters based on visual similarity.

In contrast to image clustering, image classification assigns unlabeled images to the predefined image categories, which is usually achieved by applying supervised learning technologies. In image classification, there are k predefined image categories and a set of training samples is available for each category, $\Gamma = \{I_1', \ldots, I_S'\}$. Given a selected visual descriptor, the training set can be described as $\Gamma = \{F_1', \ldots, F_S'\}$, where F_i' is a feature vector for the ith training sample. There are two kinds of methods to design image classifiers, one utilizes the recommended distance metrics and the other does not. For example, k-NN algorithm classifies images based on the closest training samples in the feature space. An image is classified based on the majority vote of its neighbors, with the image being assigned to the category most common amongst its k-NN. The distance of two images in a feature space can be computed using the recommended distance metrics presented in Section 10.3.1. However, it is not very clear whether the recommended distance metrics can guarantee the good classification performance of visual descriptors. In contrast, SVM algorithm is an example in which case the recommended distance metrics are not necessary. SVM aims to find a set of maximum-margin hyperplane in a high-dimensional space which is able to well separate the image categories, normally in which Euclidean distance function is used to measure the feature distance. It should be pointed out that DCDs cannot be used in this method because DCDs of two images may have different number of components.

Image retrieval is a more specific application, which searches images relevant to a user's query from an image collection. The visual descriptors are used to characterize the content of images and a user's intention is described by some example images. In image retrieval, we discuss some situations featured by the number of example images provided by the user. In the case of single query image, the conventional way of image ranking is based on the distance between an image and the query image. The image distance can be computed using the recommended distance metrics. And, top k images in the ranked list will be returned as retrieval results. The retrieval performance depends on the discriminant power of a selected visual descriptor. In the case of multiple query images, the relevance of an image to the user's query can be obtained by combining the distances of the image to multiple query images in a feature space. Assume that a query consists of L example images, $Q = \{Q_1, \ldots, Q_L\}$, and the selected visual descriptor is CLD. The image relevance between an image X and Q can be calculated as

$$d_{xq} = \odot D_{\text{CLD}}(F_x, F_{qj}) \forall j \tag{10.7}$$

where F_x is the feature vector of CLD for image X and $\odot$ represents a combination rule. In this chapter, three simple and effective combination rules, min, max, and sum, which have different meanings and are usually adopted in practice, are evaluated.

In the last decade, much effort has been made on relevance feedback–based image retrieval [22, 23, 24]. The idea of relevance feedback is to involve the user in the retrieval process so as to improve the final retrieval results. First, the user supplies an image as a query and the system returns an initial set of retrieved results. After that, the user labels some returned images as relevant or irrelevant and the system adjusts the retrieval parameters based on the user's feedback. Then, the system displays the revised retrieval results. Relevance feedback can go through one or more iterations until the user is satisfied with the results. In this case, image retrieval can be formulated as a classification problem. Positive and negative example images provided by the user during multiple feedback iterations are used to train a classifier. Then, the images are ranked according to the decisions produced by the classifier. For instance, SVM can address a specified binary classification problem derived from relevance feedback–based image retrieval. However, DCD cannot be used in this method because of unfixed number of components. Another interesting method is based on the dissimilarity space [13, 25], which can be applied to all kinds of visual descriptors. First, some positive examples are selected as the prototypes, $P = \{P_1, \ldots, P_M\}$. Then, an image is represented using the distances of that image to the prototypes on a visual descriptor, which becomes a point in a new space, named *dissimilarity space*. For example, if CLD is selected to describe the image content, an image X will be represented as $\{D_{\text{CLD}}(F_x, F_{p1}), \ldots, D_{\text{CLD}}(F_x, F_{pM})\}$. The number of prototypes decides the dimension of a dissimilarity space. Finally, image retrieval can be formulated as a classification problem in the dissimilarity space and can be solved by the traditional classification algorithms. The advantage of this method is that a dissimilarity space can be constructed using the visual descriptors and the recommended distance metrics that are independent of the internal structure of the visual descriptors.

All the above methods using single visual descriptor are summarized in Table 10.2 for an easy check.

10.3.3 Evaluation of Single Visual Descriptor

This section reports on the experiments carried out and the results obtained for single MPEG-7 visual descriptor. The objective is to empirically evaluate the discriminant power of each visual descriptor. In detail, a number of experiments are carried out on a Corel image dataset [26]. There are ten real-world image categories in the dataset and each category includes 100 images. The images in each category are associated to a visual concept, so the ground truth dataset can be image categories–based. Several methods have been implemented to utilize single visual descriptor in the applications of image clustering, classification, and retrieval. The application-dependent evaluation criteria are applied to measure the discriminant power of each visual descriptor.

Table 10.2 Applications and methods using single visual descriptor

			Applicable descriptor
1	Image clustering	Recommended distance metric + clustering algorithm	Any descriptor
2	Image classification	Recommended distance metric + classification algorithm (e.g., k-NN)	Any descriptor
3	Image classification	Classification algorithm (e.g., SVM)	Except DCD
4	Image retrieval (single query image)	Recommended distance metric	Any descriptor
5	Image retrieval (multiple query image)	Recommended distance metric + combination rules	Any descriptor
6	Image retrieval (relevance feedback)	Classification algorithm (e.g., SVM)	Except DCD
7	Image retrieval (relevance feedback)	Dissimilarity space + classification algorithm	Any descriptor

For image clustering, we use Macro F1 measure to evaluate the clustering results. F1 measure is based on traditional information retrieval measures – precision and recall. For an image cluster constructed by a clustering algorithm, we predict a ground truth category to which most images in the target cluster belong.

$$Precision = \frac{\#GroundTruthImagesInTargetCluster}{\#ImagesInTargetCluster} \qquad (10.8)$$

$$Recall = \frac{\#GroundTruthImagesInTargetCluster}{\#ImagesInGroundTruthCategory} \qquad (10.9)$$

$$\text{F1} = \frac{2 \times Precision \times Recall}{Precision + Recall} \qquad (10.10)$$

The Macro F1 measure is defined as the average of F1 measures on all image clusters. The higher the Macro F1, the better the clustering performance. In the experiments, k-medoids algorithm is implemented to perform image clustering and the MPEG-7 recommended distance metrics are adapted to compute the feature distances. Table 10.3 shows the clustering performance of each visual descriptor. In this experiment, HTD has much weaker discriminant power than other descriptors.

Table 10.3 Clustering with single descriptor

	CSD	DCD	CLD	EHD	HTD
Macro F1	0.58	0.45	0.51	0.49	0.29

For image classification, we use error rate to evaluate the classification results. The error rate is defined as

$$Error\ Rate = \frac{\#ImagesClassifiedIncorrectly}{\#TestingImages} \tag{10.11}$$

The smaller the error rate, the better the classification performance. In the experiments, 30% images in each category are randomly selected as the training samples and the left images are used for testing, following the conventional experimental design. Two classification algorithms, k-NN and SVM, are implemented to perform image classification. k-NN utilizes the MPEG-7 recommended distance metrics to compute feature distance, while SVM does not. Table 10.4 shows the classification performance of visual descriptors. In this experiment, DCD cannot be applied to the SVM algorithm. The classification performance of k-NN is comparable to that of SVM. HTD shows much weaker discriminant power than other descriptors.

For image retrieval, we use precision–recall curve [27] to evaluate the retrieval results. Average precision–recall curve on 100 random queries is reported in the experiment. Figure 10.1 shows the retrieval performance of each visual descriptor in the case of

Table 10.4 Classification with single descriptor

	Error rate on CSD	Error rate on DCD	Error rate on CLD	Error rate on EHD	Error rate on HTD
k-NN	0.23	0.36	0.39	0.38	0.54
SVM	0.21	–	0.44	0.32	0.49

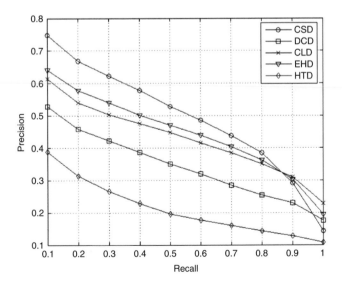

Figure 10.1 Retrieval with single query image.

single query image. CSD, CLD, and EHD have much stronger discriminant powers than DCD and HTD. Moreover, CSD is significantly better than CLD and EHD before recall reaches 0.5.

For the case of multiple query images, three combination rules, min, max, and sum, are evaluated. In the experiment, each query consists of three example images, and multiple distances on visual descriptor are combined for ranking. Figures 10.2–10.6 show the

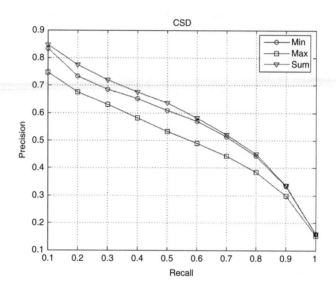

Figure 10.2 Combination rules for multiple query images using CSD.

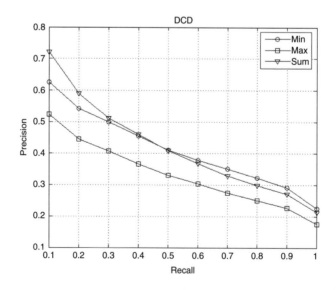

Figure 10.3 Combination rules for multiple query images using DCD.

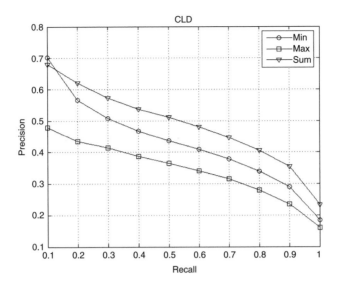

Figure 10.4 Combination rules for multiple query images using CLD.

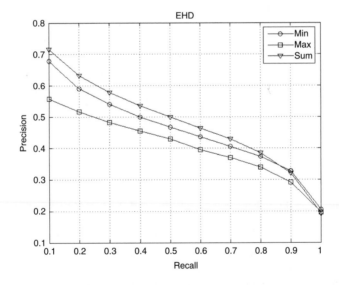

Figure 10.5 Combination rules for multiple query images using EHD.

retrieval performance of each single visual descriptor using the combination rules. From the experimental results, we can see that the sum combination rule is slightly better than the min combination rule and both of them are superior than max. HTD has much weaker discriminant power than other descriptors.

In relevance feedback–based methods, we assume that the initial query includes only one image. First, the retrieval results based on the recommended distance metrics are

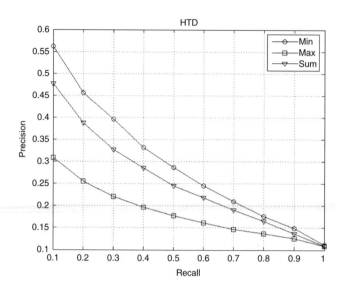

Figure 10.6 Combination rules for multiple query images using HTD.

returned. Then, the system automatically labels some positive and negative example images as feedback, which are used to train a classifier. Finally, all images are ranked according to their decision values produced by the classifier. Figure 10.7 shows the retrieval results of SVM-based method, in which DCD is not used. In this method, sufficient feedback can guarantee that the discriminant power of the visual descriptor can be demonstrated effectively, especially for CSD and EHD. Figure 10.8 shows the retrieval results of dissimilarity space–based method, in which the dimension of dissimilarity space is fixed to 5. The experimental results demonstrate that this method does not work well for the visual descriptors.

10.4 Discriminant Power of the Aggregated Visual Descriptors

It is, in general, accepted that each visual descriptor characterizes an aspect of image content, and the discriminant power can be improved by combining multiple visual descriptors. For example, the MPEG-7 visual descriptors extract different kinds of information to describe the image content from their own perspectives. In this section, we discuss how to combine the MPEG-7 visual descriptors in practice and report the discriminant power of the aggregated visual descriptors as well.

10.4.1 Feature Aggregation

Feature aggregation is a technology of combining multiple features to obtain the stronger discriminant power than single feature. In this chapter, we focus on feature aggregation methods using the MPEG-7 visual descriptors. Since the relationship between the discriminant power of visual descriptors is unknown, it is difficult to find a proper feature aggregation method for a specific application.

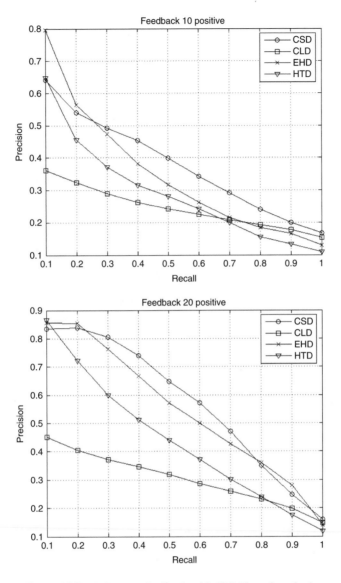

Figure 10.7　Relevance feedback with SVM-based method.

There are two popular feature aggregation approaches, early fusion and later fusion. In early fusion, multiple visual descriptors are connected into a single feature vector and all images can be represented as vectors in a high-dimensional feature space. Then, image relevance can be measured in the combined feature space, such as feature distance. The advantage of early fusion is that it is possible to perform theoretical analysis in the new feature space. However, the semantics of each visual descriptor will be lost. In later fusion, an image is represented using multiple vectors on visual descriptors, and multiple distances between a pair of images can be computed in various feature spaces. Then,

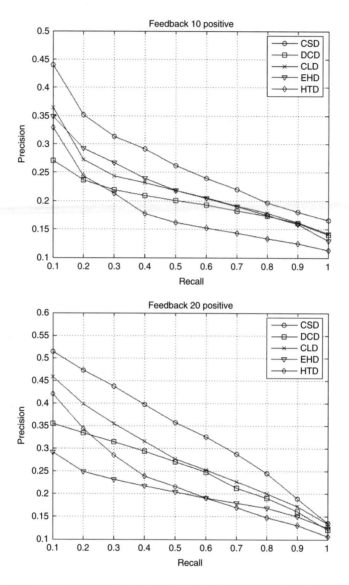

Figure 10.8   Relevance feedback with dissimilarity space–based method.

these image distances are combined to obtain the final image relevance. The advantage of later fusion is that the semantics of visual descriptors is not lost. But most of the practical later fusion methods are heuristic [14].

Figure 10.9 shows an example of feature aggregation, in which two visual descriptors, CLD and HTD, are selected to characterize the image content. The problem with early fusion is measuring the image relevance in the combined feature space, which is similar to the case of measuring in the single visual descriptor. In the case of later fusion, it has to combine multiple relevances measured in different feature spaces. Generally speaking,

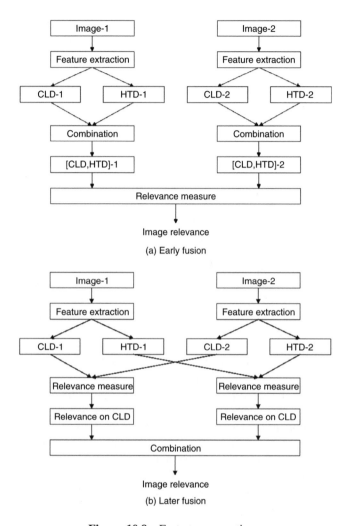

Figure 10.9 Feature aggregation.

either early fusion or later fusion method should be application-dependent. If the training samples are available, the supervised learning technologies should be the first choice. Or, some heuristic methods can be considered for the applications.

10.4.2   Applications Using the Aggregated Visual Descriptors

In this section, we explore the feature aggregation methods for image clustering, image classification, and image retrieval. Although these feature aggregation methods are basically independent of the visual descriptors, we still concentrate on how to combine the MPEG-7 visual descriptors in this chapter.

First, we consider image clustering. On the basis of the idea of early fusion, the vectors for the MPEG-7 visual descriptors are connected into a single feature vector. All images become the points in a new high-dimensional feature space. Then, the traditional clustering algorithms can be applied to perform image clustering. However, DCD cannot be applied in this method as mentioned above. This method will lose the semantic of visual descriptors and it is hard to find an effective distance metric for the high-dimensional feature space. With the approach of later fusion, there are two different image clustering methods. In the first method, feature distance is calculated using the recommended metrics, and multiple feature distances are combined to obtain the final image distance for the clustering algorithms. The feature distances combination can be described as

$$D_{xy} = \odot(D_{\mathrm{CSD}}(F_x, F_y), D_{\mathrm{DCD}}(F_x, F_y), D_{\mathrm{CLD}}(F_x, F_y), D_{\mathrm{EHD}}(F_x, F_y), D_{\mathrm{HTD}}(F_x, F_y))$$
(10.12)

where $\odot$ is a combination rule, such as min, max, or sum. In addition, k-medoids algorithm can use the aggregated distance to perform image clustering. In the second method, image clustering is performed based on multiple pairs of visual descriptor and the recommended distance metric. Then, multiple clustering results are combined to get the final results, which is a special case of ensemble clustering [28]. Basically, ensemble clustering is motivated by the classifier combination. A more robust and accurate clustering result may be obtained by combining multiple weak partitions of an image collection. Figure 10.10 presents an example of this method in which two visual descriptors, CLD and HTD, and their recommended distance metrics are selected for the k-medoids algorithm.

Secondly, we consider image classification. As mentioned above, early fusion can make it easy to perform theoretical analysis. In other words, traditional classification algorithms, such as SVM, can be applied in a new high-dimensional feature space directly. One of its disadvantages is that some descriptors, such as DCD, cannot be connected with others. Let us investigate the approach of later fusion. A natural way is to combine multiple feature distances to obtain an aggregated image distance. Then, k-NN algorithm can use the aggregated distances to perform image classification. The other way is to perform ensemble of image classification based on multiple pairs of visual descriptor and the recommended distance metric. Then, classifier combination method can be applied to obtain the final classification results. In this chapter, multiple classification results are combined using the strategy of majority vote.

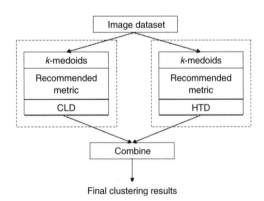

Figure 10.10   Ensemble clustering with multiple visual descriptors.

Table 10.5 Applications and methods using multiple visual descriptors

Number	Application	Method	Applicable descriptor
1	Image clustering	Early fusion + clustering algorithm	Except DCD
2	Image clustering	Feature distance combination + clustering algorithm	Any descriptor
3	Image clustering	Recommended distance metric + ensemble clustering	Any descriptor
4	Image classification	Early fusion + classification algorithm (e.g., SVM)	Except DCD
5	Image classification	Feature distance combination + classification algorithm (e.g., k-NN)	Any descriptor
6	Image classification	Recommended distance metric + classifier combination	Any descriptor
7	Image retrieval (single query image)	Recommended distance metric + combination rules	Any descriptor
8	Image retrieval (multiple query image)	Recommended distance metric + combination rules	Any descriptor
9	Image retrieval (relevance feedback)	Early fusion + classification algorithm	Except DCD

Finally, we consider image retrieval. Since the user may query the content-based image retrieval (CBIR) system using different strategy, it may be more complex than image clustering and image classification. In the case of single query image, the role of feature aggregation is to combine multiple feature distances and obtain final distance between an image and the query image. Then, all images can be ranked according to the aggregated distance. With multiple query images, there are two levels of distance combination. In the first level, multiple distance on visual descriptors are combined to obtain the distance between an image and a query image. In the second level, multiple distance of an image to the query images are combined to obtain the relevance of the image to the query. The key point is to select a proper combination rule. Relevance feedback can provide more example images to explain the user's intention. These example images make it possible to formulate the image retrieval as a classification problem. With early fusion, the classification problem can be addressed directly by traditional classification algorithm in a new high-dimensional feature space.

All the above methods using multiple visual descriptors are summarized in Table 10.5 for an easy check.

10.4.3 Evaluation of the Aggregated Visual Descriptors

This section reports on the experiments carried out and the results obtained for multiple visual descriptors. The objective is to empirically evaluate the discriminant power of the aggregated visual descriptors. For this purpose, several feature aggregation methods are

Table 10.6 Clustering with multiple visual descriptors

	Early fusion	Combination			Ensemble
		Min	Max	Sum	
Macro F1	0.53	0.44	0.53	0.59	0.63

Table 10.7 Classification with multiple visual descriptors

	Early fusion	Combination			Ensemble
	SVM	Min + k-NN	Max + k-NN	Sum + k-NN	k-NN
Error rate	0.18	0.25	0.23	0.16	0.23

implemented and a number of experiments are carried out on the Corel image dataset. Different applications adopt their own evaluation criteria.

Table 10.6 shows the clustering performance in terms of Macro F1 measure. In the experiment, all methods employ k-medoids algorithm. The ensemble clustering has the best performance among these methods. For the feature distance combination method, the sum combination rule is better than max, while the min combination rule cannot be applied at all.

In the image classification experiment, 30% images in each category are randomly selected as the training samples and the left images are used for testing. Table 10.7 shows the classification performance in terms of error rate. The method based on early fusion and

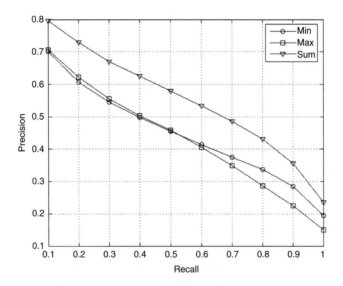

Figure 10.11 Single query image with feature distance combination.

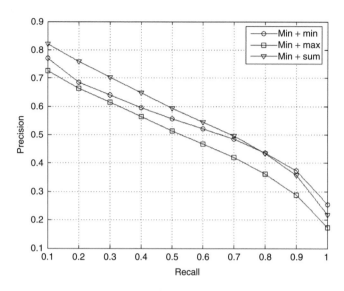

Figure 10.12 Multiple query images and two levels combination min $+x$.

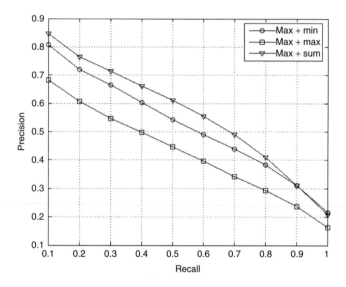

Figure 10.13 Multiple query images and two levels combination max $+x$.

SVM has a comparable performance to the method based on feature distance combination and k-NN. Both are better than other methods.

Three sets of experiments are performed for single query image, multiple query image, and relevance feedback. Figure 10.11 shows the retrieval performance of single query image. Among the combination rules for combining feature distances, sum has the best performance. Figures 10.12–10.14 show the retrieval performance of multiple query

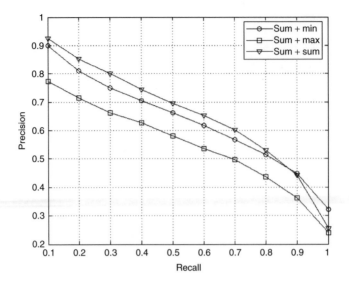

Figure 10.14 Multiple query images and two levels combination sum $+ x$.

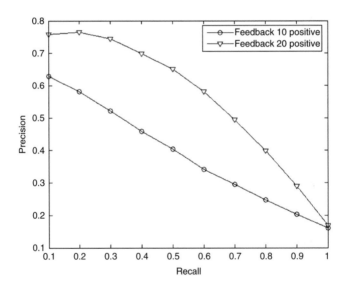

Figure 10.15 Relevance feedback with SVM.

images using two levels combination strategy. On the basis of the experimental results, for practical purpose, a good choice is to use the sum combination rule in both levels. Finally, retrieval performance of relevance feedback is shown in Figure 10.15. The experimental results also prove the observation that sufficient feedback is necessary to effectively improve the retrieval performance.

10.5   Conclusions

This chapter focused on the applications of the MPEG-7 visual descriptors. Three basic applications were considered including image clustering, image classification, and image retrieval. From the perspective of discriminant power, we answered the important questions, that is, how good are these visual descriptors and how to utilize them in practice. Specifically, 16 methods have been explored for using single visual descriptor and the aggregated visual descriptors. The discriminant power of visual descriptors are evaluated in various situations using the corresponding performance criteria. The presented methods and reported experimental results can be used as reference for future applications of visual descriptors.

References

[1] Manjunath, B.S., Ohm, J.R., Vasudevan, V.V., and Yamada, A. (2001) Color and texture descriptors. *IEEE Transactions on Circuits and Systems for Video Technology*, **11** (6), 703–715.

[2] Chang, S.-F., Sikora, T., and Puri, A. (2001) Overview of the mpeg-7 standard. *IEEE Transactions on Circuits and Systems for Video Technology*, **11** (6), 688–695.

[3] Chen, Y., Wang, J.Z., and Krovetz, R. (2005) Clue: cluster-based retrieval of images by unsupervised learning. *IEEE Transactions on Image Processing*, **14** (8), 1187–1201.

[4] Vailaya, A., Figueiredo, M.A.T., Jain, A.K., and Zhang, H.-J. (2001) Image classification for content-based indexing. *IEEE Transactions on Image Processing*, **10** (1), 117–130.

[5] Smeulders, A.W.M., Worring, M., Santini, S. *et al.* (2000) Content-based image retrieval at the end of the early years. *IEEE Transactions on Pattern Analysis and Machine Intelligence*, **22** (12), 1349–1380.

[6] Datta, R., Joshi, D., Li, J., and Wang, J.Z. (2008) Image retrieval: Ideas, influences, and trends of the new age. *ACM Computing Surveys*, **40** (2), 5:1–5:60.

[7] Vapnik, V. (1995) *The Nature of Statistical Learning Theory*, Springer-Verlag, New York.

[8] Duda, R.O., Hart, P.E., and Stork, D.G. (2001) *Pattern Classification*, Wiley, New York.

[9] Snoek, C.G.M., Worring, M., and Smeulders, A.W.M. (2005) Early versus late fusion in semantic video analysis. Proceedings of the ACM International Conference on Multimedia, Hilton, Singapore, November, pp. 399–402.

[10] Eidenberger, H. (2004) Statistical analysis of content-based mpeg-7 descriptors for image retrieval. *Multimedia Systems*, **10** (2), 84–97.

[11] Deselaers, T., Keysers, D., and Ney, H. (2008) Features for image retrieval: an experimental comparison. *Information Retrieval*, **11** (2), 77–107.

[12] Laaksonen, J., Koskela, M., and Oja, E. (2002) Picsom – self-organizing image retrieval with mpeg-7 content descriptors. *IEEE Transactions on Neural Networks*, **13** (4), 841–853.

[13] Kushki, A., Androutsos, P., Plataniotis, K.N., and Venetsanopoulos, A.N. (2004) Retrieval of images from artistic repositories using a decision fusion framework. *IEEE Transactions on Image Processing*, **13** (3), 277–292.

[14] Zhang, J. and Ye, L. (2009) Content based image retrieval using unclean positive examples. *IEEE Transactions on Image Processing*, **18** (10), 2370–2375.

[15] Spyrou, E., Borgne, H.L., Mailis, T. *et al.* Fusing mpeg-7 visual descriptors for image classification. Proceedings of International Conference on Artificial Neural Networks, Part II: Formal Models and Their Applications, 2005, vol. 3697, Warsaw, Poland, pp. 847–852.

[16] Nga, W.W., Dorado, A., Yeung, D.S. *et al.* (2007) Image classification with the use of radial basis function neural networks and the minimization of the localized generalization error. *Pattern Recognition*, **40** (1), 19–32.

[17] Chen, J.-C., Chu, W.-T., Kuo, J.-H. *et al.* (2006) Tiling slideshow. Proceedings of the 14th Annual ACM International Conference on Multimedia, pp. 25–34.

[18] Agrawal, R., Grosky, W., and Fotouhi, F. (2006) Image clustering using multimodal keywords. The 1st International Conference on Semantics and Digital Media Technology, pp. 113–123.

[19] Coimbra, M.T. and Cunha, J.P.S. (2006) Mpeg-7 visual descriptors-contributions for automated feature extraction in capsule endoscopy. *IEEE Transactions on Circuits and Systems for Video Technology*, **16** (5), 628–637.

[20] Doherty, A.R., OConaire, C., Blighe, M. *et al.* Combining image descriptors to effectively retrieve events from visual lifelogs. Proceedings of the 1st ACM International Conference on Multimedia Information Retrieval, 2008, pp. 10–17.

[21] Kaufman, L. and Rousseeuw, P. (1990) *Finding Groups in Data: An Introduction to Cluster Analysis*, John Wiley & Sons, Inc, New York.

[22] Rui, Y., Huang, T.S., Ortega, M., and Mehrotra, S. (1998) Relevance feedback: a power tool for interactive content-based image retrieval. *IEEE Transactions on Circuits and Systems for Video Technology*, **8** (5), 644–655.

[23] Zhou, X.S. and Huang, T.S. (2003) Relevance feedback in image retrieval: a comprehensive review. *Multimedia Systems*, **8** (6), 536–544.

[24] Tao, D., Tang, X., Li, X., and Wu, X. (2006) Asymmetric bagging and random subspace for support vector machines-based relevance feedback in image retrieval. *IEEE Transactions on Pattern Analysis and Machine Intelligence*, **28** (7), 1088–1099.

[25] Pezkalska, E. and Duin, R.P.W. (2002) Dissimilarity representations allow for building good classifiers. *Pattern Recognition Letters*, **23** (8), 943–956.

[26] Wang, J., Li, J., and Wiederhold, G. (2001) Simplicity: semantics-sensitive integrated matching for picture libraries. *IEEE Transactions on Pattern Analysis and Machine Intelligence*, **23** (9), 947–963.

[27] Muller, H., Muller, W., Squire, D.M. *et al.* (2001) Performance evaluation in content-based image retrieval: overview and proposals. *Pattern Recognition Letters*, **22** (5), 593–601.

[28] Strehl, A. and Ghosh, J. (2002) Cluster ensembles – a knowledge reuse framework for combining multiple partitions. *Journal of Machine Learning Research*, **3**, 583–617.

11

An MPEG-7 Profile for Collaborative Multimedia Annotation

Damon Daylamani Zad and Harry Agius
Electronic and Computer Engineering, School of Engineering and Design, Brunel University, UK

11.1 Introduction

The use of multimedia on the web has grown massively in recent years. Internet traffic to video websites in the United Kingdom alone increased by 40% in 2009, with YouTube being the most popular, followed by the BBC iPlayer and Google Video [1]. Thus, the need to annotate multimedia content has become ever more imperative for users to be able to access these multimedia resources effectively [2]. Web 2.0 has brought with it increasing use of multimedia content on the web and many collaborative multimedia environments have emerged such as Flickr, YouTube and del.icio.us, where users are able to share and view multimedia content in a community. These so-called folksonomic or social tagging applications allow users within the community to describe the multimedia content using simple, flat metadata such as titles, categories and tags. In the social networks and collaborative environments based on Web 2.0, the most popular method for creating and maintaining multimedia content metadata is tagging, where tags are used to identify content features, such as objects and events, within the media stream. Folksonomies are user-generated taxonomies where such tags are collaboratively created and managed to annotate and categorize content. In contrast to traditional subject indexing, metadata in folksonomies is generated not only by experts but also by creators and consumers of the content. Figure 11.1 depicts a typical folksonomic environment where users who are members of the community can view and edit the metadata, whereas users who are not part of the community can only view the metadata and associated content. These folksonomic applications suggest that it may be possible to extend this approach to more advanced,

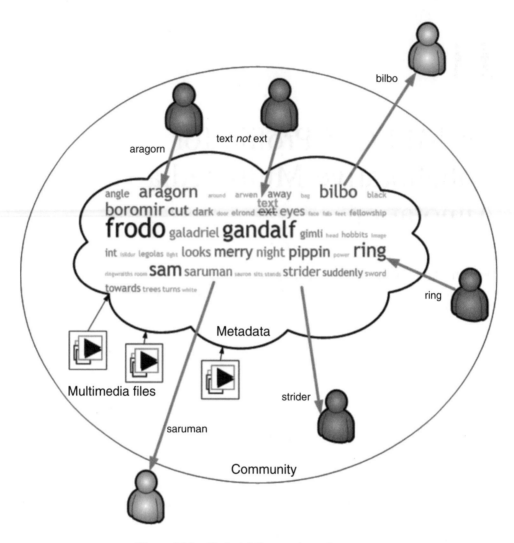

Figure 11.1 Typical folksonomic environment.

structured media annotation, such as that based on the comprehensive, extensible MPEG-7 standard. In this way, the power of web communities would be harnessed to overcome what is otherwise an intensely time-consuming task for single users of creating, updating and maintaining annotations for multimedia resources. However, very little empirical research has been reported in the literature to understand how users annotate multimedia collaboratively. Consequently, we have undertaken an experiment that collected data from users using both folksonomic (Flickr, YouTube and del.icio.us) and MPEG-7 tools (COSMOSIS) to annotate and retrieve media. From the experiment, we contribute a conceptual model for each type of tool that illustrates the usage characteristics and identifies their relative merits and inhibitors. Our results reveal that users are ready to engage in more advanced collaborative multimedia annotation if appropriate means are provided. The most popular tags used in our experiment were those describing inanimate objects, people and events. We also report results demonstrating how users relate tags to each other. In addition, the results show that users tend to add time points for the elements they annotate when appropriate means are provided. The proposed conceptual models are then used to design an MPEG-7 profile for use in collaborative multimedia annotation environments.

The organization of the rest of this chapter is as follows: In Section 11.2, we discuss the suitability of the MPEG-7 standard for collaborative multimedia annotation. In Sections 11.3–11.5, we present our experiment design, research method and results, respectively. In Section 11.6, we contribute our MPEG-7 profile and discuss the implications. A review of related research work in multimedia annotation communities is presented in Section 11.7, while Section 11.8 presents a brief concluding discussion.

11.2 MPEG-7 as a Means for Collaborative Multimedia Annotation

The MPEG-7 multimedia description schemes (MDS) [3–5] provide a standardized set of XML schemes for describing multimedia content and users in a structured fashion. One of the problems in collaborative content modelling is that tags are highly individualistic and different users often use a variety of terms to describe the same concept. This makes searching problematic since users may only search for one synonym but require results for the entire group of synonyms. Synonym control can help to mitigate these issues. MPEG-7 enables the definition of terms used during annotation within a classification scheme (CS) through the use of the TermDefinition DS, thereby assisting with the implementation of synonym control solutions. The TermDefinition DS incorporates an identifier for a term, a set of human-readable names, and a textual definition of the term's meaning. Also, by using the termRelationQualifierType, one can define the relationship between different terms. The options that may be specified by the termRelationQualifierType are as follows:

- BT, to signify a broader term, such that the related term is more general in meaning than the current term.
- NT, to signify a narrower term, such that the related term is more specific in meaning than the current term.
- US, to signify 'use instead' when the related term is (nearly) synonymous with the current term but the related term is preferred to the current term.
- UF for 'use for', to indicate that the related term is (nearly) synonymous with the current term but the current term is preferred to the related term.
- RT, to signify a related term that is not a synonym, quasi-synonym, broader or narrower term, but is associated with the current term.

In this way, not only may synonyms and related terms be defined, but they may also be created and updated collaboratively by the user community.

Since MPEG-7 provides a scheme whereby description tools are defined for specific uses and may be combined and related to each other as required, the metadata exhibits a well-defined structure, both in terms of tag expressiveness and connectedness. Tag expressiveness refers to issues caused by the ambiguity in the meanings of tags. Users have become so comfortable with tagging that they do not give it much thought; their tags might lack clarity and structure and, therefore, be unusable to anyone but the author [6, 7]. For example, unstructured text in tags results in having many tags that are difficult to interpret and relate to other tags by anyone other than the tag author [8]. Similarly, incorrectly spelled keywords within the tags can cause retrieval problems and lead to orphaned content that can only be retrieved when the query also happens to contain the same misspellings. Acronyms also prove problematic and can reduce the usability of the tags when they are not commonly accepted and are decided by the content author alone. Consequently, users may search for different acronyms or search for the full phrase instead, both of which would fail to retrieve the required content. On the other hand, the full semantic meaning and extents of relationships between tags that make sense to users are difficult to develop within tag-based systems and thus are often not implemented. Hence, the connectedness of the tags is not fully exploited.

The identification of patterns found within the tags that are created by the users can help to enhance the retrieval process. For example, for a photo, users tend to specify the date taken, location and the visible people or landmarks. Recognizing such pattern stability and encouraging users to conform to these patterns through, for example, suggested or mandatory fields can help to better direct the tagging process, subsequently producing well-formed tags. While there may be some loss of creativity and comprehensiveness in the annotation process, the usability of the tags within the retrieval process is improved. Consequently, defined structures can be enforced to ensure pattern stability across the community such that tag creation is controlled. Research has shown that although users demonstrate great variety regarding what keywords and phrases they use within tags and how frequently they use them, stable, aggregate patterns are emerging that can be used to help structure the tagging process [8]. The text annotation description tools that are used mainly in the various content entity types of MPEG-7 (e.g. multimedia content, image, video, audio, audiovisual, multimedia) support the use of both unstructured (free text) and structured textual annotations, with the latter helping to improve pattern stability. The StructuredAnnotation datatype incorporates fields such as Who, WhatObject, What-Action, Where, When, Why and How, while the KeywordAnnotation datatype enables annotations to be expressed as a set of single words or phrases, each of which may be specified as primary, secondary or 'other' to denote their importance. In this way, the KeywordAnnotation datatype proves helpful in specifying acronyms. Using the MPEG-7 description tools in this way, as defined in the standard, enables users to comprehend the structure of multimedia metadata that they have not participated in the creation of, since all MPEG-7 multimedia metadata will exhibit a core structure that is reflected by the description tools. For example, all objects will be defined using the Object DS where the user will have defined an object name, definition, location and spatiotemporal link to the media stream. Consequently, a great deal of pattern stability is exhibited but since elements of the description tools are optional, a great deal of flexibility is also possible. In this way, metadata are readily understandable and thus broadly useful, while also making re-use feasible. Moreover, while MPEG-7 does not provide spell checking tools since it specifies the metadata representation only, there are many external tools that will spell check the tags and can be easily deployed in conjunction, thereby further helping to improve tag expressiveness.

MPEG-7 can be used to group multimedia streams and multimedia metadata together through the use of collections and models, thereby enabling metadata propagation. Metadata propagation refers to issues caused by annotating a group of media streams when they share specific tags. For example, consider the situation where all the videos of a holiday contain the same people in them; consequently, tagging may incur many repetitions and redundancies. The ability to tag the whole group of media streams as opposed to tagging them one by one is the concern of metadata propagation. This problem is exacerbated in collaborative annotation systems where there are multiple users carrying out the tagging. For example, photos of a certain occasion will often be taken by many users who were present and these photos will contain common content features, such as the people present and the location. If the metadata could be propagated or inherited by all related photos once a single (or a small number of) user(s) had tagged them, user effort would be greatly reduced while also greatly improving the consistency of the tags [9].

The content organization tools describe the organization and annotation of multimedia content. For example, the ContentCollection DS describes collections of multimedia data, such as images, videos and audio tracks, providing the basic functionality for describing a grouping of multimedia content, including aggregated audio and visual features, into an unordered, unbounded nested collection. Similarly, the SegmentCollection DS is used for describing collections of segments, the DescriptorCollection DS is used for describing collections of descriptors of multimedia content, the ConceptCollection DS is used for describing a collection of semantic concepts related to multimedia content, such as objects and events, while the MixedCollection DS is used for describing mixed collections of multimedia content, descriptors and semantic concepts related to multimedia content. The StructuredCollection DS is used to describe association relationships among collections. These content organization tools can be used to specify metadata common to a group of multimedia streams. For example, if a group of photos taken at a birthday party are being modelled, the Collection DS can include various features such as the people, locations and events, which can then be inherited by all or a subset of photos. The metadata for each photo may then define spatial, temporal and semantic relationships between these features.

A large body of research tackles various aspects of MPEG-7-based retrieval, such as image retrieval [10], video retrieval [11] and video object extraction [12]. Tag-based ranking refers to providing means to rank the search results based on the tags that are used to annotate the media and the strength of these tags in each media. Using MPEG-7 element attributes such as preferenceValue and relation strength can help to provide tag-based rankings [13] when used in conjunction with the MPEG-7 query format (MPQF) specified in Part 12 of the standard [14]. The MPQF provides a standardized interface for multimedia content retrieval systems, which enables users to describe their search criteria with a set of precise input parameters and also allows them to specify a set of preferred output parameters to depict the return result sets. Furthermore, the MPQF specifies query management tools that are provided in order to support service discovery and service capability querying and description [14]. Various query types are defined, such as QueryByFeatureRange, which is a query based on given descriptions denoting start and end ranges, and a Join operation is specified which enables filtering conditions to be defined over multiple sets of multimedia objects. In this way, separate filtered sets may be retrieved and then combined.

11.3 Experiment Design

While many (typically isolated) approaches have been proposed to support collaborative media annotation, very little empirical research exists which seeks to understand how users actually annotate multimedia collaboratively. Consequently, we undertook an experiment with 51 users. This section describes the experiment design; results are presented in the subsequent section.

In the experiment, users were asked to undertake a series of tasks using four existing multimedia metadata tools (three folksonomy tools and one structured annotation tool) and their interactions were tracked. The users were chosen from a diverse population, similar to the ZoneTag average user approach [15]. The users were unsupervised, but were communicating with other users via an instant messaging application such as Windows Live Messenger. The communication transcripts contain information on user behaviour in collaborative communities and also contain metadata information if they are considered to be comments on the content. This is similar to the approach of Yamamoto *et al*. [16] who tried to utilize user comments and blog entries as sources for annotations. Users were also interviewed after they completed all tasks.

The four tools used during the experiment are summarized in Table 11.1. The visual content used in the experiment was categorized according to the most popular types of multimedia content, which are summarized in Table 11.2. In addition, the content exhibits certain features and thus Table 11.3 presents the key content features in this experiment. The AV content used in this experiment was chosen for its ability to richly exhibit one or more of these features within one or more of the content categories. Each segment of AV content can contain one or more of these features. For example, one video might be object-rich while another is people-rich and another is both object- and event-rich.

Users were given a series of tasks, requiring them to tag and model the content of the AV content using the tools above. Users were assigned to groups of 12–13 participants, one group for each of the four different content categories above, but were not informed of this. Within each category, users worked in smaller experiment groups of 3–6 to ease the logistics of the users collaborating together at the same time. Members of the same group were instructed to communicate with other group members while they were undertaking

Table 11.1 Tools used during the experiment

Tool	Content	Description
YouTube	Videos	Users can upload, set age ratings for, and enter descriptions and keywords for videos. Missing aggregate front end common to folksonomy tools
Flickr	Images	Photos may be shared in original quality with tools provided for tagging and simple manipulations, such as rotating and cropping
del.icio.us	Website-based AV content	Users can bookmark, tag, comment on and describe web pages for sharing with other users
COSMOSIS	AV content	Using MPEG-7, users can annotate video content according to four semantic categories: objects, events, temporal relations and spatial relations [17, 18]

Table 11.2 Content categories of the experiment

Category	Description
Personal	Personal to users; for example, videos of family, friends and work colleagues, and typically based around the people, occasion or location
Business	Created and used for commercial purposes, mainly including videos created for advertising and promotion, such as video virals
Academic	Serves academic purposes, such as teaching and learning or research
Recreational	Created and used for purposes other than personal, business or academic, such as faith, hobbies, amusement or filling free time

Table 11.3 Key content features in the experiment

Tool	Description
Objects	People, animals, inanimate objects and properties of these objects
Events	Visual or aural occurrences within the video; for example, a car chase, a fight, an explosion, a gunshot, a type of music. Aural occurrences include music, noises and conversations
Relationships	Temporal, spatial, causer (causes another event or object to occur), user (uses another object or event), part (is part of another object or event), specializes (a sub-classification of an object or event) and location (occurs or is present in a certain location)

the tasks, using an instant messaging application such as Windows Live Messenger. The collaborative communication transcripts were returned for analysis using grounded theory [19]. The importance of user communication during the experiment was stressed to users. Table 11.4 summarizes the relationships between the content categories, user category groups and content-rich features.

Each user was required to tag and model the content of 15 images in Flickr, 10 web pages containing AV content in del.icio.us, and 3–5 min worth of videos (one 5 min long video or a number of videos that total up to 5 min) in YouTube and COSMOSIS. This ensured that users need not take more than about an hour to complete the tasks, since more time than this would greatly discourage them from participating, either initially or in completing all tasks. At the same time, the video duration, number of images and web pages are sufficient to accommodate meaningful semantics. Users did not have to complete all the tasks in one session and were given a two week period to do so. YouTube tags, Flickr tags, del.icio.us tags and COSMOSIS metadata and collaborative communication transcripts were collected post-experiment.

After the users had undertaken the required tasks, a short, semi-structured interview was performed with each user. The focus of the interviews was the users' experiences with, and opinions regarding, the tools. Typical questions included which tool the users found easiest and most functional to use, which tags were used most when tagging and describing the AV content, which aspects the users felt were important when tagging and if they felt certain aspects were more important for different types of content, and additional features the users would have liked to have seen in the tools.

Table 11.4   Mapping of content categories to user category groups to content features

	Personal User group 1	Business User group 2	Academic User group 3	Recreation User group 4
People	X	X	X	X
Inanimate objects	X	X	X	X
Animals	X	X	X	X
Properties	X	X	X	X
Events	X	X	X	X
Music[a]	X	–	–	X
Noise[a]	X	–	X	X
Conversation[a]	–	X	–	X
Temporal relations[a]	–	–	X	–
Spatial relations	X	–	X	–
Causer relations	–	–	X	X
User relations	–	X	X	–
Part relations	–	X	X	X
Specializes relations	–	X	X	–
Location relations	X	–	–	X

[a]Applies only to video, not images.

11.4   Research Method

This section presents the research method for analysing the data from the experiment described in the previous section. The experiment produced three types of data from four different sources: the metadata from tagging AV content in the folksonomy tools (YouTube, Flickr and del.icio.us), the MPEG-7 metadata created by COSMOSIS, the collaborative communication transcripts, and the interview transcripts. The vast amount of textual data generated by these sources called for the use of a suitable qualitative research method to enable a thorough but manageable analysis of all the data to be performed.

A grounded theory is defined as theory which has been 'systematically obtained through social research and is grounded in data' [20]. Grounded theory methodology comprises systematic techniques for the collection and analysis of data, exploring ideas and concepts that emerge through analytical writing [21]. Grounded theorists develop concepts directly from data through its simultaneous collection and analysis [22]. The process of using this method starts with *open coding* which includes theoretical comparison and constant comparison of the data, up to the point where conceptual saturation is reached. This provides the *concepts*, otherwise known as *codes*, which will build the means to tag the data in order to properly treat it as a *memo* and thus, provide meaningful data (dimensions, properties, relationships) to form a theory. Conceptual saturation is reached when no more codes can be assigned to the data and all the data can be categorized under one of the codes already available, with no room for more codes. In our approach, we include an additional visualization stage after memoing in order to assist with the analysis and deduction of the grounded theory. Figure 11.2 illustrates the steps taken in our data analysis approach.

As can be seen in the figure, the MPEG-7 metadata and the metadata gathered from folksonomy tools tagging, along with the collaborative communication transcripts and interviews, form the basis of the open coding process. The memoing process is then

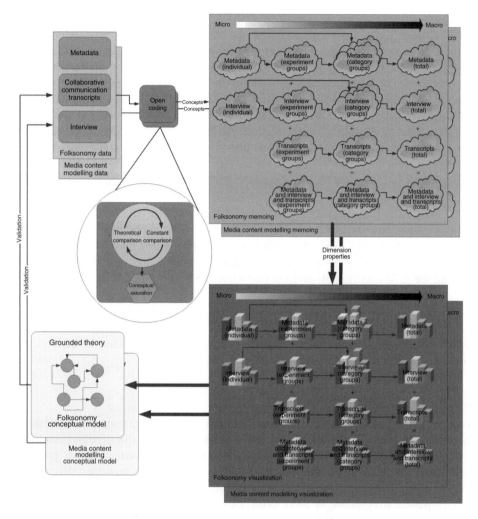

Figure 11.2   Grounded theory as applied to the collected data in this experiment.

performed on a number of levels. The process commences at the individual level where the metadata from individual users is processed independently. Then the metadata from users within the same experiment group are memoed. Following this, the metadata from the entire user category group (personal, academic, business and recreational) is considered so that the metadata from all the users who were assigned to the same category are together memoed to allow further groupings to emerge. Finally, all the metadata generated is considered as a whole. The same process is applied to the data from the interviews. Then, the transcripts are considered on an experiment group level, followed by the transcript data from all the users in the same category groups and, finally, all the transcript data is processed as a whole.

The data from each level of the memo process is combined with the data from processing other inputs at the same level; that is, the data from processing the metadata, interviews and transcripts are combined at the experiment group level, then once again at the category group level and finally at the total level. Then by processing the data produced from this procedure, we acquire the final data. All of the dimensions, properties and relationships that emerge from the above memoing stages are then combined together and visualised. The visualization stage follows the same procedure as the memoing stage, where the data is processed through different levels. Finally, the visualised data is analysed to provide a grounded theory in the form of a conceptual model for the MPEG-7 data. The same procedure is performed on the folksonomy data (YouTube, Flickr and del.icio.us) to produce another grounded theory in the form of a conceptual model for folksonomy tools.

11.5   Results

Figure 11.3 presents the conceptual model resulting from applying grounded theory to the raw data. As can be seen, the model is vertically divided into two areas: effect of time and tag usage. The model is also horizontally divided into two areas: the top area affecting the folksonomy tools and the bottom area affecting the MPEG-7 tool.

11.5.1   Tag Usage

This section presents a detailed description of the tag usage area and its effects on the tools used in the experiment.

11.5.1.1   Most Commonly Used Tags

According to Li and Lu [23], recognizing the most common tags used by different users when modelling any AV content can assist with combining the ontology and social networking approaches (described earlier) when designing a collaborative annotation system. Our results indicate that the differences in the use of tags for AV content in different content categories are inconsiderable and, overall, the popularity of tags remains fairly consistent irrespective of these categories.

The most commonly used tags in the folksonomy tools concerned inanimate objects, events and people. Consequently, a collaborative content modelling system should fully support these commonly used tags and prioritize their accessibility. Inanimate objects were the most popular type of tag used in the folksonomy tools. As can be seen in Figure 11.4–Figure 11.7, tags concerning inanimate objects were used 2637 times altogether by users. We found that this ranged from a minimum of 7 times to a maximum of 112 times for a single user. On average, these types of tags were used 52 times per user, with an average deviation of 20.57. Considering these figures, we can conclude that not only were inanimate objects the most used type of tags overall but were a popular tag among individual users as well. This is no doubt due to the vast number of inanimate objects reflected within AV content which users wish to give primacy to within the metadata.

Events were the second most popular type of tag used within the folksonomy tools, being used 1384 times in total, with a minimum usage of 8 and a maximum usage of 49 occurrences for an individual user, and an average usage of 28 per user with an average

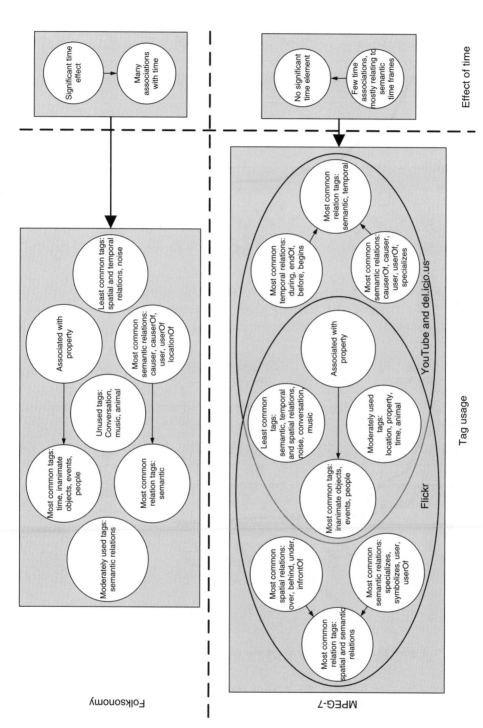

Figure 11.3   Conceptual model.

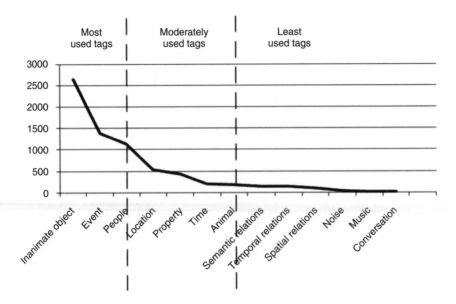

Figure 11.4 Total tag usage in folksonomy tools.

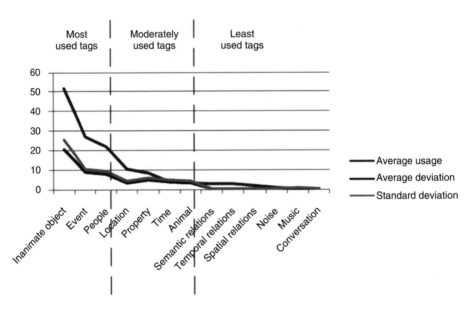

Figure 11.5 Average tag usage and deviation in folksonomy tools.

deviation of 8.67. The fact that any type of occurrence within the AV content can be considered to be an event means that events are highly likely to be identified and thus annotated by users. The high prominence of events also means that they are generally considered by users to be important content.

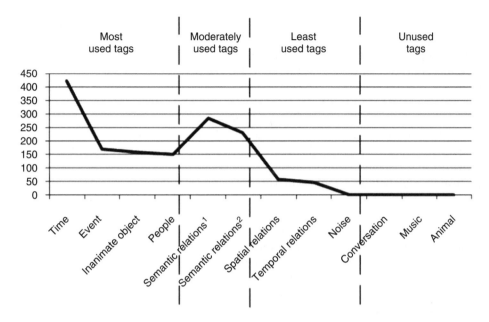

Figure 11.6   Total tag usage in MPEG-7 tool ([1]full, [2]without locationOf and propertyOf).

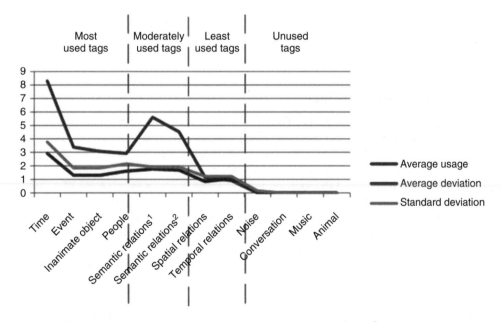

Figure 11.7   Average tag usage and deviation in MPEG-7 tool ([1]full, [2]without locationOf and propertyOf).

People tags were also used extensively by the participants, ranking third overall. Tags concerning people were used 1134 times by users in the experiment, with an average use of 23 times per user and an average deviation of 7.67. While all content categories featured a significant number of people within the video and images, people tags were used most within the Personal category, since the content included users and people known to them, such as their friends and family.

As with the folksonomy tools, although there are differences in the use of tags for AV content in different content categories, the popularity of tags remains fairly consistent irrespective of these categories for COSMOSIS. The most commonly used tags by users related to time, events, inanimate objects and people. Time was the most popular tag employed in the MPEG-7 tool, being used 423 times with an average use of 9 times per user and an average deviation of 2.9. Unlike the folksonomy tools, the MPEG-7 tool considers time an integral feature of the media stream and therefore primacy is given to its support during annotation. Consequently, not only are facilities provided for adding one or more time points for each content feature, but users are also prompted to do so. These are, therefore, the key reasons for the considerable difference between the usage of time in the folksonomy tools and the MPEG-7 tool. The other three most commonly used tags are the same as the folksonomy tools for the same reasons, but the ranking differs slightly with events being used somewhat more than inanimate objects. Event tags occurred 170 times in total with an average of 4 occurrences per user and an average deviation of 1.32, whereas inanimate objects were used 156 times in total, with an average use of 4 times per user and an average deviation of 1.29. The slightly higher prominence of event tags may be because of their temporal quality and the support afforded this by COSMOSIS. Tags concerning people were the next most popular, having been used 148 times with an average use of 3 times per user and an average deviation of 1.59.

11.5.1.2 Moderately Used Tags

The tag types presented in this part of Figure 11.3 are those that were not used significantly enough to be amongst the most used tags since a significant drop in usage was observed, but there were still ample instances of use of these types of tags for them to be considered important. The moderately used tags in the folksonomy tools are location, property, time and animal. Participants used the location tag 535 times, with an average use of 11 times per user and average deviation of 3.44 which demonstrates the usefulness of this tag despite it having significantly less usage than the most used tags. This is likely due to the fact that most AV streams depict content occurring in one or more locations; for example, even a short 3 min personal video could depict many different rooms within a house and therefore necessitate several location tags. Property tags normally accompany the most used tags. Users used property tags 430 times when using the folksonomy tools, with an average of 9 uses per user. While this is not as significant as other tags, this is still considerable, especially given that property tags cannot be used on their own as they are used to further describe another content feature, such as an inanimate object (e.g., its colour) or an event (e.g., its status). Due to this associative use, properties are generally not well supported within folksonomy tools. Property tags are discussed further at the end of this section. Time tags were the next moderately used, with an average of one use per user and a total of 206 occurrences. There is a very clear reason for the relatively low usage: folksonomy tools do not provide any means for specifying start and end points of different content features, only general (semantic) time tags can be used. The fact that, in spite of this, time was still moderately used by users during the experiment is an indicator of the importance of time when modelling AV content. Lastly, animal tags were used 174 times with an average use of 4 instances per user, which is explained by both the relatively low occurrence of animal content compared to other types of content and the relative importance that users attach to animal annotations.

The semantic relations are a collection of tags concerned with semantic relationships between other content features. When considered in aggregate, they were the second most used type of tag by users of COSMOSIS, ranking above events but below time tags, and also the most commonly used relation type. However, given that semantic relations are a set of individual tags being considered together, where some of the semantic relations were not used at all while others were used more frequently, it seems unreasonable for the aggregate total to carry the same weight as the other tags ranked as most commonly used. However, their use is significant and therefore we consider them to be moderately used. Given that the MPEG-7 MDS includes propertyOf and locationOf tags within the set of semantic relations, we analysed the usage of the semantic relations both with and without these tags. When considered with these tags, semantic relations were used 284 times in total, with an average of 4 times per user; when considered without these tags, semantic relations were used 231 times, with an average of 5 times per user.

11.5.1.3   Least Common Tags

On the basis of the data gathered by our experiment, semantic relations, temporal relations, spatial relations, noise, music and conversation were the least used tags by users when using the folksonomy tools. Usage of all of these tags was very low compared to the other tags, but the most used were the various semantic and temporal relations, while noise tags were rarely used at all. While the low use of noise and music can be considered to be because of the deemed lack of significance of noise and music by annotating users and the low use of conversation can be because of its complexity to annotate, the low use of semantic, temporal and spatial relation tags is that they tend to be considered complex and are not well understood by users. As with the property tags, they are also associative since they indicate a relationship between other content features. Similarly, they are thus not well supported within folksonomy tools. We consider the relation tags further in the next section.

On the basis of the data gained from our experiment, the following are the least used tags by the participants when using the MPEG-7 tool: spatial relations, temporal relations and noise. Spatial relations were used 59 times in total for this single tool, which is much higher than the figure per tool for the folksonomy tools (30.33) although the average per user is approximately the same. Similarly, temporal relations have slightly higher usage when considered against the average per tool figure for folksonomies. In both cases, this is no doubt due to the facilities provided within COSMOSIS to support the annotation of spatial relations. Noise was barely used at all, being used only once by the participants. It is believed that this is due to both the nature of the content and the deemed importance of this tag for video content by the users.

11.5.1.4   Most Common Relation Tags

There were some differences in the use of relations between the different folksonomy tools used in the experiment (Table 11.5). While the use of relation tags in del.icio.us and YouTube were very similar, this was not the case for the use of relations in Flickr. In Flickr, participants used spatial and semantic relations considerably more than temporal relations, since still images do not present temporal relations as clearly as video. The most used spatial relations were *over*, *behind*, *under* and *infrontOf* and spatial relations were used 83 times in total in Flickr with an average close to 2 instances of use per user. There were 9 instances in all of the semantic relations being used, the most common being *specializes*, *symbolizes*, *user* and *userOf*. In YouTube and del.icio.us the story is notably different with the most used relations being semantic and temporal. Semantic relations were used 130 times in total, the most popular being *causer*, *causerOf*, *user*, *userOf* and *specializes*. Thus, there is some commonality here with the most popular semantic relations used with Flickr. Temporal relations were used 135 times in total, with the most common being *during*, *endOf*, *before* and *begins*.

As stated above, semantic relations were the second most used type of tag by users of COSMOSIS. Table 11.6 presents the most commonly used types of semantic relations.

11.5.1.5   Unused Tags

There were no tags left unused by the users in the folksonomy tools. However, based on the data gained from our experiment, the following are the tags left unused in COSMOSIS by the participants: conversation, music and animal. These tags were not used at all. There was no clear option provided for the user to use these tags. Conversation is a complex tag as the user needs to add the text of a conversation and define who the speaker was for each part of that text. It may also be necessary for the users to add time points for each part of the conversation, making it clear when the conversation is occurring in the stream. Therefore, without such facilities, or at least a free-text option, it is impossible to annotate conversations. Annotating music requires similar supporting facilities: to annotate music a user may need to enter a name of a song, its composer, its performer, year of release, and so on. (S)he may also need to represent lower level features such as tempo, key, and notes. As none of these facilities were provided, it is clear why this tag was left unused in COSMOSIS. There are also no facilities to tag animals specifically in COSMOSIS, except through specifying them as objects, and users did not recognize this option.

11.5.1.6   Relationships Between Tags

Another set of key results from the experiment concerned relationships between the tags; that is, which tags were used with which other tags most often; for example, if an object is tagged in a scene, which other tags tend to be used in conjunction with it. As users are not able to provide time points in folksonomy tools, the relation between time and

Table 11.5 The most common relations in folksonomy tools

Tool	Relation type	Relation	Usage	Average	Average deviation	Standard deviation
	Spatial relations	over	45	0.88	0.968858131	1.47847298
		behind	21	0.41	0.678200692	1.061630267
		under	6	0.12	0.207612457	0.325395687
Flickr		infrontOf	5	0.10	0.180699731	0.360826937
	Semantic relations	specializes	3	0.06	0.038431373	0.196039212
		symbolizes	2	0.04	0.078431373	0.280056017
		user	2	0.04	0.078431373	0.280056017
		userOf	2	0.04	0.038431373	0.196039212
	Semantic relations	causerOf	38	0.75	0.455209535	0.532106432
		causer	31	0.61	0.572087659	0.634930906
		user	30	0.59	0.548250673	0.602608708
YouTube and del.icio.us		userOf	26	0.51	0.561314879	0.62329989
		specializes	1	0.2	0.038446751	0.140028008
	Temporal relations	during	49	0.96	0.414455978	0.662141505
		endOf	31	0.61	0.548250673	0.602608708
		before	28	0.55	0.581314879	0.64229979
		begins	14	0.28	0.419838524	0.532106432

Table 11.6 Most used semantic relations in the MPEG-7 tool

Semantic relation	Usage	Average usage	Average deviation	Standard deviation
causer	87	1.71	1.727797001	1.910959106
causerOf	52	1.10	0.813533256	1.191472972
userOf	46	0.90	1.061130334	1.25307465
user	27	0.53	0.788927336	1.046000787
propertyOf	27	0.53	0.378316032	0.513351158
locationOf	26	0.51	0.719723183	0.85726423

other tags is considerably low. Overall, the most common relationships between tags in folksonomy tools discovered from the experiment data were as follows:

Inanimate object – property   Inanimate object – people
Event – property   Event – inanimate object
People – property   People – event

As users are able to provide time points in COSMOSIS, which was not the case with the folksonomy tools, the relation between time and other tags is extremely high. Overall, the most common relationships between tags in the MPEG-7 tool discovered from the experiment data were as follows:

Inanimate Object – time   Inanimate object – people
Event – time   Event – inanimate object
People – time   People – event

11.5.1.7   Associated with Property

Finally, we consider those tags that have high associated usage with properties. Our data revealed that property tags were generally used by users to further describe the most common tags identified previously. As can been seen in Figure 11.8, in folksonomy tools, inanimate object tags were the most likely to be accompanied by property annotations (41%), followed by event tags (40%) and people tags (38%). Location (26%), animal (18%) and time (17%) tags had associated property descriptions for significantly less times.

As was the case with the folksonomy tools, the most commonly used tags had high associated usage with properties in the MPEG-7 tool. As can be seen in Figure 11.9, people were the most likely to be accompanied by property annotations (28%), followed by inanimate objects (25%), then events (22%) and finally, time (10%).

11.5.2   Effect of Time

As stated previously, time tags were not used considerably in the folksonomy tools. The time tags that were used related predominantly to semantic time frames, such as morning, afternoon, summer, as well as to absolute dates, for example a particular year. The lack of time tags and the inability to associate start and end points (or start points and duration)

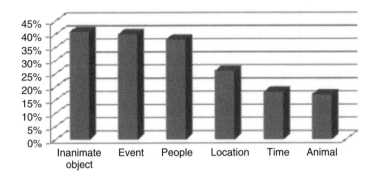

Figure 11.8   Percentage used with property for folksonomy tools.

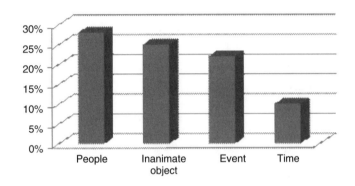

Figure 11.9   Percentage used with property for the MPEG-7 tool.

with tags for given AV streams within the folksonomy tools is the key reason for this. Users who are interested in annotating time cannot do this easily and are thus discouraged from doing so.

Users employed time tags significantly when using the MPEG-7 tool. As stated previously, COSMOSIS supports temporal annotation through features that prompt the user to associate one or more time points with each content feature. In this way, tags may be associated with specific segments of the media stream, enabling content to be pinpointed precisely when searching. The convenience of this for users caused a great increase in the use of time tags compared with the folksonomy tools. In addition, users also incorporate semantic time frames within their tags, for example, morning, afternoon, summer, and absolute dates such as particular years.

11.6   MPEG-7 Profile

An MPEG-7 profile [24] is a subset of tools defined in MPEG-7, providing a particular set of functionalities for one or more classes of applications. The keyword to define profiles is *functionality*; profiles are a set of tools providing a set of functionalities for a certain class of applications. A new profile should be defined if it provides a significantly different set of functionalities. Figure 11.10 presents a sample profile and illustrates the

```
<?xml version="1.0" encoding="utf-8"?>
<!-- ############################################## -->
<!-- Collaborative Multimedia Annotation Profile    -->
<!-- ############################################## -->
<schema xmlns:mpeg7="urn:mpeg:mpeg7:schema:2001"
        xmlns="http://www.w3.org/2001/XMLSchema"
        targetNamespace="urn:mpeg:mpeg7:schema:2001"
        elementFormDefault="qualified"
        attributeFormDefault="unqualified">
  <import namespace="http://www.w3.org/XML/1998/namespace"
          schemaLocation="http://www.w3.org/2001/03/xml.xsd"/>
  <!-- Mpeg7BaseType -->
  <complexType ...
  <!-- DType -->
  <complexType ...
  <!-- DSType -->
  <complexType ...
  <!-- HeaderType -->
  <complexType ...
  <!-- Mpeg7Type -->
  <complexType ...
  <!-- DescriptionProfileType -->
  <complexType ...
  <!-- Mpeg7 -->
  <element ...

     :
     :

  <!-- SemanticType -->
  <complexType ...
  <!-- ObjectType -->
  <complexType name="ObjectType">
    <complexContent>
      <extension base="mpeg7:SemanticBaseType">
        <choice minOccurs="0" maxOccurs="unbounded">
          <element name="Object" type="mpeg7:ObjectType"/>
          <element name="ObjectRef" type="mpeg7:ReferenceType"/>
        </choice>
      </extension>
    </complexContent>
  </complexType>
  <!-- AgentObjectType -->
  <complexType ...
  <!-- PersonType -->
  <complexType ...
  <!-- PersonGroupType -->
  <complexType ...

    :
    :

  <!-- RelationType -->
  <complexType ...

  <!-- Definition of UserDescription Top-level Type -->
  <complexType ...
  <!-- Definition of UserPreferences DS -->
  <complexType ...
  <!-- Definition of UsageHistory DS -->
  <complexType ...
</schema>
```

Wrapper

Basic description tools

Semantic description tools

Usage description tools

Figure 11.10   A sample MPEG-7 profile.

different sections that a profile could encapsulate. The set of functionalities that are the focus in this paper are the functionalities derived from the experiment results that are needed in a collaborative multimedia annotation system. The proposed profile is shown in Figure 11.11. The profile contains the definition of all the tools that are used wrapped in the *scheme* element. Definitions are consistent with the standard documentation, thus a profile may be considered as a subset of the full description tools available in MPEG-7.

As can be seen in Figure 11.11, the profile consists of three components: *content model*, which represents all the semantic annotations relating to the content of the multimedia stream, *user details* which represents all the user profile information and actions, and *archives* that represents the various states of the model due to changes made by users. Each component is now discussed in detail.

11.6.1 The Content Model

This part of the profile is based on the results gained from the experiments described in the previous sections. It represents all the semantic annotations relating to the content of the multimedia stream. The Semantic DS is used to represent various content features as it can incorporate many semantic concepts. The AgentObject DS is used to represent people in different forms as Person DS, PersonGroup DS or Organization DS. The users in the experiment used all three of these forms. The Event DS is used for defining events, while the Object DS is used to define objects. AgentObject DS, Event DS and Object DS can include SemanticState DS for the representation of associated properties, SemanticTime DS for the representation of associated semantic time, and SemanticPlace DS for the representation of associated location, since users demonstrated a desire to associate these with the most used tags. Noise can be represented using the Event DS while music can be represented using the Object DS. Further music details can be represented using the CreationInformation DS, which provides the Creation DS and RelatedMaterial DS tools. The CreationInformation DS and the Object DS can be linked using the Reference type.

There is no native DS to cater for conversations. Therefore, they are represented using the SemanticState DS, with the text of the conversation represented by AttributeValuePair elements (there is no limit on the number of AttributeValuePair elements that can be included). The conversations can be linked to AgentObject DSs (speakers) using the Agent semantic relation. This enables the speaker of each part of a conversation to be identified.

All semantic, spatial and temporal relations are represented by the Graph DS which can be nested in the Semantic DS. These relations add further structure to the model and allow individual features to be associated.

11.6.2 User Details

This component of the MPEG-7 profile represents metadata regarding a user's profile and actions. All the data is stored under the top-level type, UserDescriptionType, which encapsulates the profile and login info of the user as User from AgentType and all the user's actions under the UsageHistory DS. The UsageHistory DS is used to describe a set of UserActionHistory elements. The UserActionHistory DS is used to describe a set of UserActionList elements. UserActionList DS represents metadata regarding

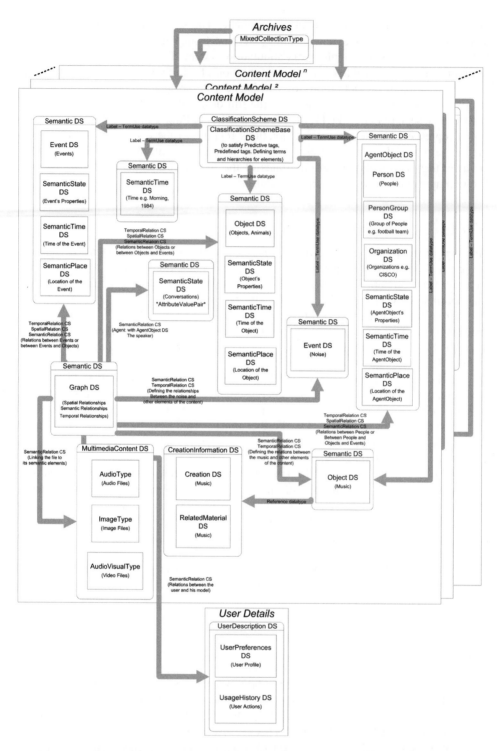

Figure 11.11 MPEG-7 profile for collaborative multimedia annotation communities.

action type, time of action, name of stream and describes a link to the element that has been modelled using the XPath format. These are stored respectively in ActionType, ActionTime, ProgramIdentifier and ActionDataItem. We have defined new ActionTypes for this framework in MPEG-7 that are: Comment, Create, Remove, Update and Upload, that respectively represent the action of commenting on a media, creating a new tag, removing a tag, updating an existing tag and uploading a new media.

11.6.3   Archives

This component of the MPEG-7 profile represents the information regarding changes to the content model and effectively represents the different states of the system. The Archives are formed by Collection DSs. Each Collection DS is from the MixedCollectionType and can contain a SemanticBase DS or Relation DS under the Content element and a reference to the user who has performed an action in the ContentRef element. This structure will represent any tag that has been added, removed or updated in its new form with a reference to the user who has made the change, therefore representing the various states of the model and also simplifying version control and rollback operations.

11.6.4   Implications

The profile proposed above can support collaborative multimedia annotation communities in a number of ways. The use of ClassificationScheme DS as the parent DS of the semantics stored in the MPEG-7 profile allows us to link and relate synonym tags through the TermDefinition DS. Tags that are derived from the same root, for example *shadow* and *shade*, can be connected to each other and defined with US (used instead), therefore creating a structure and controlling the synonyms in the system. Having such capability in the MPEG-7 profile allows any application or system using this profile to control the synonym tags added to the system and manage them so that the users can avoid duplicate tagging and confusion. It allows better querying of the metadata as by adding this relation, users can query the system with derived tags, for example querying with *shadow* and content matching either *shadow* or *shade* being included in the results set, thereby making the results set more inclusive.

The proposed profile has a stable pattern for tagging which makes the content model readable; for example, all Objects are represented with the same pattern. The fact that MPEG-7 is an XML-based tool makes it platform-independent and thus its content patterns can persist, with tools customized to work with it.

The TermDefinition DS also allows other relationships between tags that are obvious to users but not to an automated system to be defined. As mentioned previously, TermDefinition DS allows us to define more complex relations between tags such as narrower or broader term, used for, and so on. The use of these relations between tags allows for richer metadata and, subsequently, retrieval results. For example, in this way it is possible to connect terms such as *olympics*, *medal* and *pool* to *swimming*. This has a wide-reaching impact since the connection list can be used for other searches and, ultimately, can be incorporated into search engines, thereby expanding the results set.

The TermDefinition DS also provides tools for defining keywords and acronyms. These acronyms help users to identify meaning, since one acronym can have different meanings in different contexts. By attaching a definition to the acronym, the proposed MPEG-7 profile reduces the confusion that acronyms can create in the metadata, while also serving to make the tags more expressive and allowing users to be able to choose what they mean by the acronyms they have entered or are searching for.

The MediaOccurrence tag in the SemanticBase DS allows multiple occurrences such that one tag can be assigned to many streams or many segments of a stream. This means that the user can define a tag once and then assign it to as many streams as (s)he wants. Consequently, this supports the concept of metadata propagation, limiting metadata redundancy within the community.

Furthermore, as user actions are recorded and users connect to the models using these relations, they can use the preferenceValue for each tag and give a value to the tag. This will be described within their user profile and can be used to measure and rank different tags, based on their behaviour and preference. This will allow the users to rank the tags they use, facilitating their tagging process by providing them with better access to the tags they like to use most.

By adding conversation-tagging functionality to the profile, users are able to annotate a conversation, time-stamp it and connect each sentence to its speaker. Not only does this enable a very rich representation of metadata, but it also enables further functionality to be derived, such as easily adding subtitles to videos, where each subtitle is tagged with start point and duration. In this way, all tagging and preference information along with the subtitles of the video may be included in a single metadata file.

The archives component supports strong version control where any change to a tag is logged with the original state and the new state, allowing swift rollbacks to any previous state, as well as being related to the users undertaking the change, allowing users to backtrack their steps and, where necessary, communicate with other users if a change is not acceptable to one party.

11.7 Related Research Work

In this section, we consider the research literature to examine approaches that have been hitherto proposed for collaborative multimedia annotation. Usually, freely chosen keywords are used for tagging in social networks instead of a controlled vocabulary [25]. Consequently, the tags are highly individualistic and different users often use a variety of terms to describe the same concept [7]. Begelman, Keller and Smadja [26] have investigated different factors in the formation of folksonomy and tag use. Their research, which studied frequency of use and co-word clustering, showed that tagging actually mimics the behaviours observed in conventional classification systems. Bentley, Metcalf and Harboe [27] performed two separate experiments: one asking users to socially share and tag their personal photos and one asking users to share and tag their purchased music. They discovered multiple similarities between the two in terms of how users interacted and annotated the media, which has implications for the design of future music and photo applications. Kwon and Kim [28] propose a novel methodology that increases user performance in terms of costs associated with building consensus and successful negotiation rates. To do so, they have developed a two-step approach: joint learning and negotiation to consensus building.

At the same time, tagging is so widely used now that users have become comfortable with it to the point where they do not give it much conscious thought and therefore do not consider the clarity, structure and subsequent usability of the tags they create [7]. Tag expressiveness is another area that has been explored in collaborative annotation. Elliot and Ozsoyoglu [29] present a system that targets this problem through the use of suggestive tags. It shows how semantic metadata about social networks and family relationships can be used to improve semantic annotation suggestions. This includes up to 82% recall for people annotations as well as recall improvements of 20–26% in tag annotation recall when no annotation history is available. In addition, utilizing relationships among people, while searching, can provide at least 28% higher recall and 55% higher precision than keyword search, while still being up to 12 times faster. Their approach to speeding up the annotation process is to build a real-time suggestion system that uses the available multimedia object metadata such as captions, time, an incomplete set of related concepts and additional semantic knowledge such as people and their relationships. Approaches such as Cloudalicious [30] illustrate the tag clouds or folksonomies as they develop over time for a given URL. Other studies have begun to incorporate the tag and entity relationships, including displaying related entities as hints to assist the user in finding the appropriate tags as those tags are being entered.

One of the most popular tools used to deal with connectedness is WordNet [31], which is an English semantic lexicon. It groups English words into sets of synonyms, provides general definitions and acronyms, and records the various semantic relations between terms. It has been used to solve tagging issues and develop retrieval systems that utilize folksonomies; for example, TagPlus [7] retrieves from Flickr by using WordNet to correct, identify and group tags generated by users to improve the relevance of the presented results. However, such systems are add-ons to existing systems and not integrated into the community, which limits the breadth and depth of their functionality. Mika [32] built various ontologies from tags on the basis of concepts and communities. It was found that although concept-oriented ontologies conform much more closely to a formal structure, they tend to lose track of the relevance of the tag or resource. Ohmukai, Hamasaki and Takeda [33] present a community-based ontology using both, the metadata generated by users and their personal social networks. Cloudalicious [30] is an approach that is trying to target this problem as well. Aurnhammer, Hanappe and Steels [34] introduce an approach that combines social tagging and visual features to extend the navigation possibilities of image archives. The user interface makes use of an editable navigation map to give the users control over how the entities are related to each other and to the tags. Maleewong, Anutariya and Wuwongse [35] present a collective intelligence approach to collaborative knowledge creation which enables multiple users to collaboratively create knowledge in a systematic and dynamic process. It encourages members to collaboratively express ideas or solutions regarding the complex or challenging issues and submit arguments to support or oppose other members' ideas. In order to semantically capture and describe the community deliberation and maintain it as a community knowledge-base, a collective argumentation ontology is proposed. Moreover, degrees of argument, individual preference, position, and expertise are calculated based on the deliberation for evaluating the acceptance level of each position to create temporary power users. A position accepted by most members will be selectively integrated as collective knowledge, which is collaboratively developed until the final knowledge is obtained.

Ontologies help provide pattern stability and one way to use a formal ontology with collaborative tagging is to derive it from the tags deployed within the system through data mining [6]. Ulges *et al*. [36] present a system that automatically tags videos by detecting high-level semantic concepts, such as objects or actions. They use videos from online portals like YouTube as a source of training data, while tags provided by users during upload serve as ground truth annotations. Another method is to employ ontology seeding, which embeds an ontology into the system before the users commence tagging and typically asks the users for additional semantic information to ensure that the tags they contribute follow the conventions of the ontology [6]. FolksAnnotation [37], a system that extracts tags from del.ici.ous and maps them to various ontological concepts, has helped to demonstrate that semantics can be derived from tags. However, before any ontological mapping can occur, the vocabulary must usually be converted to a consistent format for string comparison.

Another key aspect that has attracted considerable research focus is metadata propagation. CONFOTO [38] is a browsing and annotation service for conference photos which exploits sharing and collaborative tagging through RDF (resource description framework) to gain advantages such as unrestricted aggregation and ontology re-use. Figure 11.12 presents the architecture of CONFOTO.

Zonetag [15] is a prototype mobile application that uploads camera phone photos to Flickr and assists users with context-based tag suggestions derived from multiple sources. A key source of suggestions is the collaborative tagging activity on Flickr, based on the user's own tagging history and the tags associated with the location of the user. A prioritized suggested tag list is generated from these two sources. Several heuristics are used to take into account the tags' social and temporal context, and other measures that weight the tag frequency to create a final score. These heuristics are spatial, social and temporal characteristics: all tags used in a certain location regardless of the exact location are gathered, tags the users themselves applied in a given context are considered more likely to apply to their current photo than tags used by others, and finally, tags are considered to more likely to apply to a photo if they have been used recently.

A final key area of investigation is how to use the tags to help improve the ranking of retrieved results, for example by making them more personalized to individual users. Studies show that tag-based rankings produce more relevant results than traditional rankings and clusterings [39] as demonstrated by the recommendations of online music sites and communities such as Yahoo Launch and Last.fm. Zhang *et al*. [40] propose a video blog management model which comprises automatic video blog annotation and user-oriented video blog search. For video blog annotation, they extract informative keywords from both, the target video blog itself and relevant external resources. As well as this semantic annotation, they perform sentiment analysis on comments to obtain an overall evaluation. For video blog search, they present saliency-based matching to simulate human perception of similarity, and organize the results by personalized ranking and category-based clustering. An evaluation criterion is also proposed for video blog annotation, which assigns a score to an annotation according to its accuracy and completeness in representing the video blog's semantics.

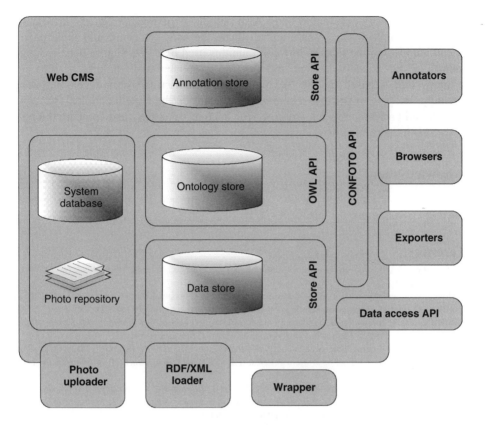

Figure 11.12 CONFOTO architecture. *Source*: [38].

11.8 Concluding Discussion

This paper has presented an MPEG-7 profile for use in multimedia annotation communities. We started by considering the suitability of the MPEG-7 standard for such communities. Then, an experiment to observe users' behaviour while annotating multimedia content when using both folksonomic (Flickr, YouTube and del.icio.us) and MPEG-7 (COSMOSIS) tools was described and the results presented. These results were used in the design of an MPEG-7 profile, which was introduced and explained, and the implications discussed. Finally, we considered research work from the literature, related to collaborative multimedia annotation communities.

The results presented here have many research implications and opportunities. These results can be used to design and implement multimedia collaborative communities for content modelling that better support user behaviour. For example, this approach can be applied to perform experiments in audio communities such as Last.fm to evaluate and analyse user behaviour and preferences in audio-based communities and compare the results with results presented here. Also, similar experiments can be performed on specialist communities to compare and evaluate the user behaviour and preferences in such communities to the folksonomy communities used here. We plan to use the findings presented in this paper to design and develop a collaborative multimedia annotation community that is based on user behaviour and preferences. After developing such a community, we plan to perform a similar experiment on the system and analyse the user behaviour and preferences when working with such a community and compare the results with the results presented here.

Acknowledgment

This research was supported by the UK Engineering and Physical Sciences Research Council (EPSRC), grant no. EP/E034578/1.

References

[1] BBC News (2009) *Surge in Demand for Online Video*, http://news.bbc.co.uk/1/hi/technology/7954941.stm (accessed 2009).

[2] Money, A.G. and Agius, H. (2008) Video summarisation: a conceptual framework and survey of the state of the art. *Journal of Visual Communication and Image Representation*, **19** (2), 121–143.

[3] ISO/IEC (2003) International Standard 15938-5. *Information Technology – Multimedia Content Description Interface – Part 5: Multimedia Description Schemes*, Geneva, Switzerland.

[4] ISO/IEC (2004) International Standard 15938-5/Amd.2. *Information Technology – Multimedia Content Description Interface – Part 5: Multimedia Description Schemes: Amendment 2: Multimedia Description Schemes Extensions*, Geneva, Switzerland.

[5] ISO/IEC (2005) International Standard 15938-5/Amd.2. *Information Technology – Multimedia Content Description Interface – Part 5: Multimedia Description Schemes: Amendment 2: Multimedia Description Schemes User Preference Extensions*, Geneva, Switzerland.

[6] Golder, S.A. and Huberman, B.A. (2006) Usage patterns of collaborative tagging systems. *Journal of Information Science*, **32** (2), 198–208.

[7] Lee, S.-S. and Yong, H.-S. (2007) TagPlus: a retrieval system using synonym tag in folksonomy. Proceedings of the International Conference on Multimedia and Ubiquitous Engineering (MUE '07), April 26–28, 2007, Seoul, Korea, pp. 294–298.

[8] Golder, S. and Huberman, B.A. (2006) The structure of collaborative tagging systems. *Journal of Information Science*, **32** (2), 198–208.

[9] William, K. (2006) Exploiting "The World is Flat" syndrome in digital photo collections for contextual metadata. Proceedings of the 8th IEEE International Symposium on Multimedia (ISM'06), December 11–13, 2006, San Diego, CA, pp. 341–347.

[10] Hejazi, M.R. and Ho, Y.-S. (2007) An efficient approach to texture-based image retrieval. *International Journal of Imaging Systems and Technology*, **17** (5), 295–302.

[11] Tjondronegoro, D. and Chen, Y.-P.P. (2002) Content-based indexing and retrieval using MPEG-7 and X-query in video data management systems. *World Wide Web Journal*, **5** (3), 207–227.

[12] Lu, Y. and Li, Z.-N. (2008) Automatic object extraction and reconstruction in active video. *Pattern Recognition*, **41** (3), 1159–1172.

[13] Mallik, A., Chaudhury, S., Jain, A. *et al.* (2007) Content based re-ranking scheme for video queries on the web. Proceedings of the 2007 IEEE/WIC/ACM International Conferences on Web Intelligence and Intelligent Agent Technology – Workshops, November 2–5, 2007, Silicon Valley, pp. 119–122.

[14] ISO/IEC (2007) Final Committee Draft 15938-12. *Information Technology – Multimedia Content Description Interface – Part 12: Query Format*, Shenzhen, China, October.

[15] Naaman, M. and Nair, R. (2008) ZoneTag's collaborative tag suggestions: what is this person doing in my phone?. *IEEE Multimedia*, **15** (3), 34–40.

[16] Yamamoto, D., Masuda, T., Ohira, S. and Nagao, K. (2008) Video scene annotation based on web social activities. *IEEE Multimedia*, **15** (3), 22–32.

[17] Agius, H. and Angelides, M. (2006) MPEG-7 in action: end user experiences with COSMOS-7 front end systems. Proceedings of the 21st Annual ACM Symposium on Applied Computing (SAC '06), vol. 2, 23–27 April, 2006, Dijon, France, pp. 1348–1355.

[18] Angelides, M. and Agius, H. (2006) An MPEG-7 scheme for semantic content modelling and filtering of digital video. *Multimedia Systems*, **11** (4), 320–339.

[19] Corbin, J. and Strauss, A. (2008) *Basics of Qualitative Research: Techniques and Procedures for Developing Grounded Theory*, 3rd edn, Sage Publications, Thousand Oaks, California, USA.

[20] Goulding, C. (1998) Grounded theory: the missing methodology on the interpretivist agenda. *Qualitative Market Research*, **1** (1), 50–57.

[21] Charmaz, K. (2006) *Constructing Grounded Theory: A Practical Guide through Qualitative Analysis*, Sage Publications, Thousand Oaks, California, USA.

[22] Matavire, R. and Brown, I. (2008) Investigating the use of "Grounded Theory" in information systems research. Proceedings of the 2008 Annual Research Conference of the South African Institute of Computer Scientists and Information Technologists on IT Research in Developing Countries: Riding the Wave of Technology, Wilderness, South Africa, pp. 139–147.

[23] Li, Q. and Lu, S.C.Y. (2008) Collaborative tagging applications and approaches. *IEEE Multimedia*, **15** (3), 14–21.

[24] ISO/IEC (2005) International Standard 15938-11. *Information Technology – Multimedia Content Description Interface – Part 11: MPEG-7 Profile Schemas*, Geneva, Switzerland.

[25] Voss, J. (2007) Tagging, folksonomy and co-renaissance of manual indexing? Proceedings of 10th International Symposium for Information Science, Cologne, Germany, pp. 234–254.

[26] Begelman, G., Keller, P. and Smadja, F. (2006) Automated Tag Clustering: Improving search and exploration in the tag space. Proceedings of Workshop on Collaborative Web Tagging Workshop, Edinburgh.

[27] Bentley, F., Metcalf, C. and Harboe, G. (2006) Personal vs. commercial content: the similarities between consumer use of photos and music. Proceedings of SIGCHI Conference on Human Factors in Computing Systems, Montreal, Quebec, Canada, pp. 667–676.

[28] Kwon, O. and Kim, J. (2009) A two-step approach to building bilateral consensus between agents based on relationship learning theory. *Expert Systems with Applications*, **36** (9), 11957–11965.

[29] Elliott, B. and Ozsoyoglu, Z.M. (2008) Annotation suggestion and search for personal multimedia objects on the web, *Proceedings of the 2008 International Conference on Content-based Image and Video Retrieval*, ACM, Niagara Falls, Canada, pp. 75–84.

[30] Russell, T. (2006) Cloudalicious: folksonomy over time, *Proceedings of the 6th ACM/IEEE-CS Joint Conference on Digital Libraries*, ACM, Chapel Hill, NC.

[31] Fellbaum, C. (1998) *WordNet: An Electronic Lexical Database*, MIT Press, Cambridge, MA.

[32] Mika, P. (2007) Ontologies are us: a unified model of social networks and semantics. *Web Semantics: Science, Services and Agents on the World Wide Web*, **5** (1), 5–15.

[33] Ohmukai, I., Hamasaki, M. and Takeda, H. (2005) A proposal of community-based folksonomy with RDF metadata. Proceedings of the 4th International Semantic Web Conference (ISWC), Galaway, Ireland.

[34] Aurnhammer, M., Hanappe, P. and Steels, L. (2006) Augmenting navigation for collaborative tagging with emergent semantics, *Lecture Notes in Computer Science*, vol. 4273/2006, Springer, Berlin/Heidelberg, pp. 58–71.

[35] Maleewong, K., Anutariya, C. and Wuwongse, V. (2008) A collective intelligence approach to collaborative knowledge creation, *Proceedings of the 2008 4th International Conference on Semantics, Knowledge and Grid*, IEEE Computer Society, Beijing, China, pp. 64–70.

[36] Ulges, A., Schulze, C., Keysers, D. and Breuel, T. (2008) A system that learns to tag videos by Watching Youtube. International Conference on Computer Vision Systems, pp. 415–424.

[37] Al-Khalifa, H.S. and Davis, H.C. (2006) FolksAnnotation: a semantic metadata tool for annotating learning resources using folksonomies and domain ontologies. Proceedings of the Innovations in Information Technology, 2006, pp. 1–5.

[38] Nowack, B. (2006) CONFOTO: browsing and annotating conference photos on the Semantic web. *Web Semantics: Science, Services and Agents on the World Wide Web*, **4** (4), 263–266.

[39] Firan, C.S., Nejdl, W. and Paiu, R. (2007) The benefit of using tag-based profiles. Proceedings of the Latin American Web Congress (LA-WEB 2007), October 31-November 2, 2007, Santiago, Chile, pp. 32–41.

[40] Zhang, X., Xu, C., Cheng, J. *et al*. (2009) Effective annotation and search for video blogs with integration of context and content analysis. *IEEE Transactions on Multimedia*, **11** (2), 272–285.

12

Domain Knowledge Representation in Semantic MPEG-7 Descriptions

Chrisa Tsinaraki[1] and Stavros Christodoulakis[2]
[1]*Department of Information Engineering and Computer Science (DISI),*
University of Trento, Povo (TN), Italy
[2]*Department of Electronic and Computer Engineering,*
Technical University of Crete, Chania, Greece

12.1 Introduction

Some important developments in the area of multimedia applications lead to an open, internet-based environment for multimedia. These developments include (i) the popularity of the audiovisual content and its associated services (including the traditional TV and video services); (ii) the advent of the digital media; (iii) the availability of low-cost audiovisual content management devices; and (iv) the development of advanced network infrastructures.

In such an open environment, the syntactic interoperability provided by the standards (such as the MPEG standards) is necessary for the services offered by different vendors to interoperate. However, since the amount of the available audiovisual content grows exponentially, efficient semantic-based retrieval services should be offered, in order to allow the users to effectively manage the audiovisual content. Such services can be built on top of the semantic-based MPEG-7 audiovisual content descriptions.

The *MPEG-7* standard [1], which is the dominant standard for audiovisual content description, provides interoperability at the syntactic level and, at the same time, allows for the semantic description of the audiovisual content. There is, though, a serious limitation of the MPEG-7 standard: The MPEG-7 constructs intended for the semantic description of the audiovisual content are general-purpose constructs and the standard does not describe

The Handbook of MPEG Applications: Standards in Practice   Edited by Marios C. Angelides and Harry Agius
© 2011 John Wiley & Sons, Ltd

a formal mechanism for the systematic integration of domain knowledge in the MPEG-7 descriptions. Thus, the utilization of the MPEG-7 semantic description constructs, even in conjunction with textual or keyword-based descriptions of the audiovisual content, has serious limitations [2]. Consider, as an example, a query asking for the audiovisual content containing the goals of a soccer game. This approach would return, in addition to the requested material, audiovisual content that contains, in its description, the word "goal" (e.g., "shot-on-goal" and "near-goal") while it does not contain goal.

It is well accepted today that the utilization of domain knowledge can improve the functionality and effectiveness of the information system applications. It can, for example, allow for reasoning on top of the content metadata descriptions and improve the efficiency of the content retrieval and filtering. The integration of domain knowledge in the metadata descriptions allows more precise querying on a semantic vocabulary which is well understood by the domain communities [3, 4].

A straightforward solution for the systematic representation of domain knowledge in the MPEG-7 framework is the definition of XML Schema types that extend the general-purpose MPEG-7 types in order to represent domain-specific entities (e.g., goals in the soccer domain). Such an approach, though, causes a serious interoperability problem, since the extended types are not part of the MPEG-7 standard and the standard-based software will not be able to process them.

The domain knowledge is usually expressed today in the form of domain ontologies and, since the OWL (Web ontology language) [5] is the dominant standard in domain knowledge description and the Semantic Web environment offers tools (e.g., reasoners) for OWL ontology processing, several domain ontologies have been expressed (and more are expected to be expressed) in OWL syntax. A Semantic Web–based methodology for the specification of audiovisual content descriptions that exploit domain knowledge includes the following steps: (i) the expression of the MPEG-7 semantics in OWL/RDF syntax, resulting in MPEG-7 ontologies [6–9]; (ii) the integration of the OWL/RDF MPEG-7 ontologies with the OWL domain ontologies [10, 11]; and (iii) the specification of OWL/RDF audiovisual content descriptions based on the integrated MPEG-7 and domain ontologies. Unfortunately, these descriptions cannot be exploited by the MPEG-7 community, since the MPEG-7-based software cannot interpret them. Furthermore, the MPEG-7-based search and filtering services cannot take into account such descriptions.

It is therefore clear from the above paragraphs that the systematic integration of domain knowledge in the MPEG-7 descriptions is necessary for the support of efficient, semantic-based audiovisual content retrieval and filtering in the open environment formed in the Internet today. The specification of a formal model for domain knowledge representation using the MPEG-7 constructs is of paramount importance for exploiting domain knowledge in order to perform semantic processing of the audiovisual content. Without such a formal model the complete semantics of the descriptions will not be unambiguously understood and automatically processible by software across organizations.

In this chapter, we present a formal model for domain knowledge representation within MPEG-7. The proposed model allows for the systematic integration of domain knowledge in the MPEG-7 descriptions using MPEG-7 constructs, thus maintaining interoperability with existing MPEG-7–based software. In particular, the proposed formal model for domain knowledge representation using MPEG-7 constructs achieves the following objectives:

- It presents clearly and unambiguously a way to integrate domain knowledge in MPEG-7 using exclusively the MPEG-7 constructs. Therefore, all the descriptions produced are completely within the MPEG-7 standard.
- It describes clearly and formally the axioms that hold, and therefore it allows reasoning to be performed by distributed applications that utilize these axioms. This allows advanced functionality (such as for retrieval) for multimedia applications to be implemented and exploited in distributed environments.
- The representations and axioms of the formal model clearly map to corresponding representations and axioms of OWL. The subset of the OWL axioms that hold for the domain knowledge representation is clearly specified. This allows the transformation of the domain knowledge in OWL syntax, its integration in MPEG-7–based ontological infrastructures such as the one of the DS-MIRF framework [7, 10, 11], and the use of the existing OWL reasoners for semantic processing.

The model for domain knowledge representation using MPEG-7 constructs that we present here is a formal logic-based extension of the informal model we have developed in our previous research [12, 13], which essentially allowed only the representation of taxonomies using MPEG-7 syntax.

The rest of the chapter is organized as follows: The proposed MPEG-7–based domain knowledge representation model is introduced in Section 12.2 and is detailed in Sections 12.3–12.7. The exploitation of the domain knowledge that is represented according to the proposed model is presented in Section 12.8 and the chapter is concluded in Section 12.9.

12.2 MPEG-7-Based Domain Knowledge Representation

In this section, we describe our formal model for domain knowledge representation using MPEG-7 constructs. In our model, domain knowledge is usually represented by domain ontologies. Every domain ontology DO may be expressed, in MPEG-7 syntax, as a domain ontology MP7DO. To do this, the domain expert utilizes the general-purpose MPEG-7 semantic description constructs, which are a set of general-purpose XML Schema types, rooted at the *SemanticBaseType* of MPEG-7, that allow for the description of the audiovisual content semantics.

Our formal model utilizes exclusively the MPEG-7 constructs to describe domain knowledge, and therefore it remains strictly within the MPEG-7 standard.

The model, depicted in Figure 12.1, is based on the MPEG-7 relationships and on the capability of defining both abstract and concrete MPEG-7 semantic entities (essentially agents, objects, concepts, events, places, times, and states). As shown in Figure 12.1, in our model the general-purpose classes are represented by the standard MPEG-7 types, the domain-specific classes are represented by abstract MPEG-7 semantic entities, and the individuals are represented by concrete MPEG-7 semantic entities. The MPEG-7 descriptions may utilize the domain knowledge structured according to the proposed model through references to the (abstract and concrete) semantic entities comprising it. Notice that both the abstract and the concrete semantic entities are defined at the MPEG-7/XML document level and not at the XML Schema level. Thus, the domain knowledge can be systematically represented and, at the same time, full compatibility with the MPEG-7 standard is maintained.

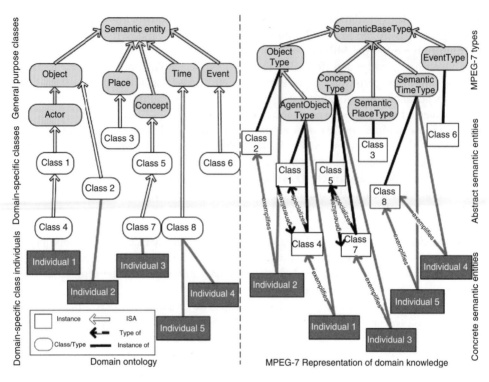

Figure 12.1 The domain knowledge representation model.

Table 12.1 provides an overview of the proposed model for domain knowledge representation using MPEG-7 constructs. In particular, the first column contains the ontology constructs modeled and the second column shows the MPEG-7 constructs used for their representation.

As is shown in Table 12.1, the proposed model describes clearly and formally the axioms that hold, essentially a subset of the semantics of OWL. Thus, the semantics of the proposed model are mapped to the OWL semantics. As a consequence, every domain ontology MP7DO, expressed according to our model, can also be expressed in OWL syntax as an OWL ontology ODO. Thus, the existing OWL reasoners can be used with ODO, making this way possible the semantic processing of the semantics of MP7DO. This allows the transformation of the domain knowledge in OWL syntax, its integration in MPEG-7-based ontological infrastructures such as the one of the DS-MIRF framework [7, 10, 11], and the use of the existing OWL reasoners for semantic processing.

The domain knowledge representation model that utilizes MPEG-7 constructs is detailed in the following sections: the domain ontology representation is described in Section 12.3, the representation of properties is described in Section 12.4, the representation of classes is described in Section 12.5, the representation of individuals is described in Section 12.6, and the representation of axioms is described in Section 12.7.

Table 12.1 Overview of the domain knowledge representation model

Ontology construct	MPEG-7 representation
Ontology declaration	"Description" element of type "SemanticDescriptionType"
Property	"Property" element/pair of "Relation" elements of type "property"–"propertyOf"/"AttributeValuePair" Element
Class	"SemanticBase" element with "AbstractionLevel /@dimension" $= 1$
Individual	"SemanticBase" Element with "AbstractionLevel/@dimension" $= 0$
Subsumption	Pair of "Relation" elements of type "exemplifies"–"exemplifiedBy"
Class generalization/ specialization	Pair of "Relation" elements of type "specializes"–"generalizes"
Property value restriction	"Term" element/pair of "Relation" elements of type "Relation" of type "property"–"propertyOf"
Class equivalence	"Relation" element of type "equivalent"
Disjointness	"Relation" element of type "disjoint"
Equivalence of individuals	"Relation" element of type "equals"
Separation of individuals	"Relation" element of type "separated"
Class union	"Relation" element of type "union"
Class intersection	"Relation" element of type "intersection"

12.3 Domain Ontology Representation

In this section, we describe the representation of domain ontologies using MPEG-7 constructs. Let DO be a domain ontology. We describe DO in a regular expression form, independent of the knowledge representation language in which it may have been expressed (thus allowing the application of the proposed model to domain ontologies expressed using different syntax):

$$DO(do\_name, label, comment, imported\_ontologies, classes, properties, \quad (12.1)$$
$$individuals, relationships)$$

where

- do_name is the name of DO.
- label is the (optional) label of DO.
- comment is an (optional) comment describing DO.
- imported_ontologies is a set comprising of the ontologies imported in DO.
- classes are the classes of DO.
- properties are the properties of DO.
- individuals are the individuals of DO.
- relationships are the relationships defined in DO.
- axioms are the axioms defined in DO. Such axioms may specify class and property hierarchies, equivalence and difference relationships for classes, properties and individuals as well as value, type, and cardinality restrictions (details on axioms are provided in Section 12.7).

The domain ontology DO is represented in MPEG-7 syntax by an MPEG-7 domain ontology MP7DO that is implemented by a "Description" element D, of type "SemanticDescriptionType". The D element has a "Semantics" element S, of type "SemanticType", formally described in the regular expression 12.2:

$$S(id, alevel, l, d, iop, sop, p, sb, r) \qquad (12.2)$$

where

- id is the identity of S, is represented by the "id" attribute and has do_name as value.
- alevel is the value of the "dimension" attribute of the "AbstractionLevel" element of S and has 1 as value, in order to express that the current description is abstract.
- l is the label of S and is represented by the value of the "Name" subelement of the "Label" element of S. If DO has a label, l has label as value and if it does not l has do_name as value.
- d is the (optional) description of S. d is defined if a comment describing DO exists, and is represented by the value of the "FreeTextAnnotation" element of a "Definition" element defined in S and has comment as value.
- iop is the set of the declarations of the ontologies imported in DO.
- sop is the declaration of DO.
- p is the set of the "Property" elements of S, which represent properties of DO.
- sb is the set of the "SemanticBase" elements of S, which represent the classes and the individuals of DO (see Sections 12.5 and 12.6 for details).
- r is the set of the "Relation" elements of S, which represent properties and relationships of DO.

As an example, consider a soccer ontology having the "soccer" identity. This ontology is represented by the "Description" element, of type "SemanticDescriptionType", shown in Box 12.1.

Box 12.1 Soccer ontology representation in MPEG

```
<Description xsi:type="SemanticDescriptionType">
  <Semantics id="soccer">
    <AbstractionLevel dimension="1"/>
    <Label>
      <Name>Soccer Ontology</Name>
    </Label>
    <Definition>
      <FreeTextAnnotation>OWL Ontology for Soccer</FreeTextAnnotation>
    </Definition>
    <Property>
      <Name>Ontology Self</Name>
      <Definition>socceragents</Definition>
      <Term>
        <Name>href</Name>
```

```
        <Definition>"http://soccer.org/socceragents#"</Definition>
      </Term>
    </Property>
                              ...
  </Semantics>
</Description>
```

12.3.1   Ontology Declaration Representation

A domain ontology DO contains a domain ontology declaration that refers to itself and a set of domain ontology declarations for the domain ontologies imported in DO. Every domain ontology declaration OD contained in DO is represented by a "Property" element, which is defined in the S element of D (where D is the representation of DO) and is formally described by the regular expression 12.3:

$$OD(name, def, uri) \qquad (12.3)$$

where

- name is the value of the "Name" element of OD and its value is "Ontology" if OD is an ontology imported in DO and "Ontology Self" if OD is the declaration of DO.
- def is the value of the (optional) "Definition" element defined in OD and has as value the name of the (optional) XML entity that represents the ontology declared in OD.
- uri is a "Term" element that represents the URI of the ontology declared in OD and is formally described by regular expression 12.4

$$uri(tname, tdef) \qquad (12.4)$$

where

- tname is the value of the "Name" element defined in uri and has "href" as value.
- tdef is the value of the "Definition" element defined in uri and has as value the URI of the ontology declared by OD.

For example, the declaration of the soccer ontology of Box 12.1 is represented by the "Property" element that has as value of its "Name" element "Ontology Self".

12.4   Property Representation

The representation of the properties defined in a domain ontology DO using MPEG-7 constructs is detailed in this section. The domain-specific properties of a domain ontology DO are represented in MPEG-7 syntax by the following: (i) "Property" elements, if they are simple type properties or are of type "InlineTermDefinitionType" (or of an MPEG-7 type extending it); (ii) "Relation" elements, if they are complex type properties; and (iii) "AttributeValuePair" elements, if they have as domains classes that represent states and either are simple type properties or have as range one of the types "IntegerMatrixType", "FloatMatrixType", "TextualType" (or an

MPEG-7 type extending it), "`TextAnnotationType`" (or an MPEG-7 type extending it), "`ControlledTermUseType`" (or an MPEG-7 type extending it), and "`DType`" (or an MPEG-7 type extending it).

Let P be a property defined in the domain ontology DO that is described in the regular expression 12.5:

$$P(p\_id, range, domain, value, label, comment) \tag{12.5}$$

where

- `p_id` is the identity of P.
- `domain` is the domain of P.
- `range` is the range of P.
- `value` is the (optional) fixed value of P.
- `label` is the (optional) label of P.
- `comment` is the (optional) description of P.

Property Representation by "`Property`" Elements. Let `prop` be a "`Property`" element, which represents the P property of DO. `prop` is formally described by the regular expression 12.6:

$$prop(name, type, fixed) \tag{12.6}$$

where

- `name` is the name of P, and is represented by the "`Name`" element of `prop` and has `p_id` as value.
- `type` is the type of P, and is represented by the "`Definition`" element of `prop`.
- `fixed` is the representation of a fixed value axiom on P so that it has `value` as value.

Consider as an example that, in the soccer ontology of Box 12.1, a "`DateOfBirth`" property, of type "`Date`", has been defined for the soccer players. The MPEG-7 representation of the "`DateOfBirth`" property is shown in Box 12.2.

Box 12.2 Representation of the "`DateOfBirth`" property

```
<Property>
  <Name>DateOfBirth</Name>
  <Definition>Date</Definition>
</Property>
```

Property Representation by "`Relation`" Elements. Let P be a property defined in the domain ontology DO, which is represented by "`Relation`" elements. P is represented by a pair of "`Relation`" elements for each of its domains, the elements `pr_relationship` and `prOf_relationship`, which are described by the regular expressions 12.7 and 12.8:

$$pr\_relationship(pr\_type, pr\_source, pr\_target, pr\_name) \tag{12.7}$$

$$prOf\_relationship(por\_type, por\_source, por\_target, por\_name) \tag{12.8}$$

The following hold for the `pr_relationship` element, which is formally described in the regular expression 12.7:

- `pr_type` is the type of `pr_relationship` and has "property" as value.
- `pr_source` is the source of `pr_relationship` and has "domain" as value.
- `pr_target` is the target of `pr_relationship` and has "range" as value.
- `pr_name` is the name of P and has p_id as value.

The following hold for the `prOf_relationship` element, which is formally described in the regular expression 12.8:

- `por_type` is the type of `prOf_relationship` and has "propertyOf" as value.
- `por_source` is the source of `prOf_relationship` and has "range" as value.
- `por_target` is the target of `prOf_relationship` and has "domain" as value.
- `por_name` is the name of P and has p_id as value.

Consider as an example that, in the soccer ontology of Box 12.1, a "PlaceOfBirth" property has been defined for the soccer players (who are represented by the "Soccer-Player" class), which associates them with the places they were born in (such places are represented by the "City" class). The MPEG-7 representation of the "PlaceOfBirth" property is shown in Box 12.3.

Box 12.3 Representation of the "PlaceOfBirth" property

```
<Relation type="property" source="#SoccerPlayer" target="#City">
  <Header xsi:type="DescriptionMetadataType">
    <Comment>
      <FreeTextAnnotation>PlaceOfBirth</FreeTextAnnotation>
    </Comment>
  </Header>
</Relation>
<Relation type="propertyOf" source="#City"target="#SoccerPlayer">
  <Header xsi:type="DescriptionMetadataType">
    <Comment>
      <FreeTextAnnotation>PlaceOfBirth</FreeTextAnnotation>
    </Comment>
  </Header>
</Relation>
```

Property Representation by "AttributeValuePair" Elements. Let AVOP be an instance of the "AttributeValuePair" element that represents the P property of the domain ontology DO and is formally described in the regular expression 12.9:

$$AVOP(name,\ def,\ type,\ fixed) \tag{12.9}$$

where

- name is the value of the "Name" element of the "Attribute" element of AVOP and has p_id as value.
- def is the value of the (optional) "Definition" element of the "Attribute" element of AVOP and has comment as value.
- type is the value of an instance of the "TextValue" element of AVOP and has as value the identity of the domain of P.
- fixed is an (optional) element defined in AVOP, which represents a fixed value axiom on P so that P has value as value.

Consider as an example that in a soccer tournament every soccer team must start the game with 11 players and that the initial number of players is represented by the "InitialNumOfPlayers" property, of value 11, of the "TournamentSoc-cerTeamGameState" class, which represents the state of a soccer team that participates in the tournament. The MPEG-7 representation of the "InitialNumOfPlayers" property is shown in Box 12.4

Box 12.4 Representation of the "InitialNumOfPlayers" property

```
<AttributeValuePair>
  <Attribute>
    <Name>InitialNumOfPlayers</Name>
  </Attribute>
  <TextValue>integer</TextValue>
  <IntegerValue>11</IntegerValue>
</AttributeValuePair>
```

12.4.1 Property Value Representation

The property values of the individuals that are defined in a domain ontology DO are represented, in accordance with the representation of the corresponding properties, by "Property" elements, "Relation" elements, and "AttributeValuePair" elements.

Property Value Representation by "Property" Elements. Let pr be a "Property" element that represents a property value defined in the domain ontology DO, which is described in the regular expression 12.10:

$$pr(name, value) \qquad (12.10)$$

where

- name is the property name and is represented by the value of the "Name" element of pr.
- value is the property value and is represented by the value of the "Definition" element of pr.

Consider as an example that the "Ronaldinho" individual, which represents the soccer player Ronaldinho, exists in the soccer ontology of Box 12.1 and that the value of its "DateOfBirth" property is "21/03/1980". The MPEG-7 representation of the property value is shown in Box 12.5.

Box 12.5 Representation of the value of the "DateOfBirth" property

```
<Property>
  <Name>DateOfBirth</Name>
  <Definition>21/03/1980</Definition>
</Property>
```

Property Value Representation by "Relation" Elements. Let Ind be an individual having a property P defined in the domain ontology DO and that the value of P is represented by a pair of "Relation" elements. The property value is represented by the pair of "Relation" elements pr_relationship and prOf_relationship, which are formally described by the regular expressions 12.11 and 12.12:

$$pr\_relationship(pr\_type, pr\_source, pr\_target, pr\_name) \qquad (12.11)$$

$$prOf\_relationship(por\_type, por\_source, por\_target, por\_name) \qquad (12.12)$$

The following hold for the pr_relationship element, which is formally described in regular expression 12.11:

- pr_type is the type of pr_relationship and has "property" as value.
- pr_source is the source of pr_relationship and has the identity of Ind as value.
- pr_target is the target of pr_relationship and has as value the identity of the property value.
- pr_name is the name of P.

The following hold for the prOf_relationship element, which is formally defined in regular expression 12.12:

- por_type is the type of prOf_relationship and has "propertyOf" as value.
- por_source is the source of prOf_relationship and has as value the identity of the property value.
- por_target is the target of prOf_relationship and has the identity of Ind as value.
- por_name is the name of P.

Consider as an example that the "Ronaldinho" individual has the "PortoAllegre" as value of its "PlaceOfBirth" property. The MPEG-7 representation of the property value is shown in Box 12.6.

Box 12.6 Representation of the value of the "PlaceOfBirth" property

```
<Relation type="property" source="#Ronaldinho"target="#PortoAllegre">
  <Header xsi:type="DescriptionMetadataType">
    <Comment>
      <FreeTextAnnotation>PlaceOfBirth</FreeTextAnnotation>
```

```
     </Comment>
   </Header>
 </Relation>
 <Relation type="propertyOf" source="#PortoAllegre"target="#Ronaldinho">
   <Header xsi:type="DescriptionMetadataType">
     <Comment>
       <FreeTextAnnotation>PlaceOfBirth</FreeTextAnnotation>
     </Comment>
   </Header>
 </Relation>
```

Property Value Representation by "`AttributeValuePair`" Elements. Let `Ind` be an individual having a property `P` defined in the domain ontology `DO` and that the value of `P` is `V` and is represented by an "`AttributeValuePair`" element. `V` is represented by the value of the appropriate element of "`AttributeValuePair`" (according to its type) and in particular by the following: (i) the value of the element "`BooleanValue`" if `V` is a boolean value; (ii) the value of the element "`IntegerValue`" if `V` is an integer value; (iii) the value of the element "`FloatValue`" if `V` is a float number value; (iv) the value of the element "`TextValue`" if `V` is a string value or a value of type "`TextualType`" (or of an MPEG-7 type that extends it); (v) the value of the element "`IntegerMatrixValue`" if `V` is of type "`IntegerMatrixType`"; (vi) the value of the element "`FloatMatrixValue`" if `V` is of type "`FloatMatrixType`"; (vii) the value of the element "`TextAnnotationValue`" if `V` is of type "`TextAnnotationType`" (or of an MPEG-7 type that extends it); (viii) the value of the element "`ControlledTermUseValue`" if `V` is of type "`ControlledTermUseType`" (or of an MPEG-7 type that extends it); and (ix) the value of the element "`DescriptorValue`" if `V` is of type "`DType`" (or of an MPEG-7 type that extends it).

Consider as an example that every soccer team has a status, which expresses its professionalism level. The soccer team status is represented in the soccer ontology of Box 12.1 by the "`Status`" property of the "`SoccerTeamState`" class, which represents the soccer team state. The "`Status`" property may have the value "`professional`" if it refers to a professional soccer team, the value "`semiprofessional`" if it refers to a semiprofessional soccer team, or the value "`amateur`" if it refers to an amateur soccer team. The MPEG-7 representation of the value of the "`Status`" property of a professional soccer team is shown in Box 12.7.

Box 12.7 Representation of the value of the "`Status`" property of a professional soccer team

```
<AttributeValuePair>
  <Attribute>
    <Name>Status</Name>
  </Attribute>
  <TextAnnotationValue id="professional">
    <FreeTextAnnotation id="profFTA">
```

```
        Professional
      </FreeTextAnnotation>
    </TextAnnotationValue>
  </AttributeValuePair>
```

12.5   Class Representation

We present in this section the MPEG-7 representation of the classes defined in domain ontologies. The domain ontology classes are represented, according to our formal model, by abstract MPEG-7 semantic entities.

Consider as an example that the "SoccerPlayer" and "Goalkeeper" classes represent, respectively, the soccer players and the goalkeepers in the soccer ontology of Box 12.1 and that "Goalkeeper" is a subclass of "SoccerPlayer". Figure 12.2 shows the representation of the ontology classes using MPEG-7 constructs. As shown in Figure 12.2, both "SoccerPlayer" and "Goalkeeper" are represented by the abstract semantic entities of type "AgentObjectType", associated by a pair of "generalizes"/"specializes" relationships. These relationships express that "Goalkeeper" is a subclass of "SoccerPlayer".

The MPEG-7 representation of the "SoccerPlayer" and "Goalkeeper" classes is shown in Box 12.8.

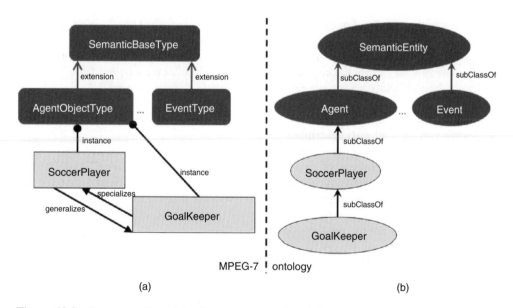

(a)   (b)

Figure 12.2   Representation of the "SoccerPlayer" and "Goalkeeper" classes according to the domain knowledge representation model using MPEG-7 constructs (a) and in the original ontology (b).

Box 12.8 Representation of the "`SoccerPlayer`" and "`Goalkeeper`" classes

```
<SemanticBase xsi:type="AgentObjectType" id="SoccerPlayer">
  <AbstractionLevel dimension="1"/>
  <Label>
    <Name>Soccer Player</Name>
  </Label>
                                     . . .
</SemanticBase>
<SemanticBase xsi:type="AgentObjectType" id="Goalkeeper">
  <AbstractionLevel dimension="1"/>
  <Label>
    <Name>Goalkeeper Object</Name>
  </Label>
  <Relation type="specializes" source="#Goalkeeper"
  target="#SoccerPlayer"/>
  <Relation type="generalizes" source="#SoccerPlayer"
  target="#Goalkeeper"/>
</SemanticBase>
```

Let C be a class defined in a domain ontology DO that is described in the regular expression 12.13:

$$C(cid, superclass, subclasses, label, comment, MPEG7\_type, properties, relationships)$$
(12.13)

where

- cid is the identity of C. For example, the "`SoccerPlayer`" class has "`SoccerPlayer`" as identity.
- superclass is the MPEG-7 representation of the superclass of C. For example, the "`SoccerPlayer`" class has as superclass the value "`AgentObjectType`" and the "`Goalkeeper`" class has as superclass the value "`SoccerPlayer`".
- subclasses is the set of the subclasses of C.
- label is the (optional) label of C.
- comment is an (optional) description of C.
- MPEG7_type is the identity of the MPEG-7 type that represents the closest general-purpose MPEG-7 concept of C. For example, both "`SoccerPlayer`" and "`Goalkeeper`" have as MPEG7_type the type "`AgentObjectType`". Notice that for the classes extending a general-purpose MPEG-7 concept superclass = MPEG7_type.
- properties are the properties of C.
- relationships are the relationships of C.

C is represented by the abstract semantic entity AI, formally described in the regular expression 12.14:

$$AI(ai\_id, label, type, abstraction\_level, spec\_relationship, gen\_relationships, property\_$$

$$elements, pr\_relationships, prOf\_relationships, exBy\_relationships, relationships)$$
(12.14)

where

- `ai_id` is the identity of the abstract semantic entity `AI`, is represented by the "id" attribute and has `cid` as value. For example, the abstract semantic entity "`Soccer-Player`" defined in Box 12.8 has "`SoccerPlayer`" as identity.
- `label` is a label that describes `AI`, and is represented by the "`Label`" element. For example, the abstract semantic entity "`SoccerPlayer`" defined in Box 12.8 has "`Soccer Player`" as label.
- `type` is the MPEG-7 type having `AI` as an instance, and is represented by the "`type`" attribute and has `MPEG7_type` as value. For example, the abstract semantic entities "`SoccerPlayer`" and "`Goalkeeper`" defined in Box 12.8 have "`AgentObjectType`" as type.
- `abstraction_level` expresses that `AI` is an abstract semantic entity and is represented by the "`dimension`" attribute of the "`AbstractionLevel`" element, which has a value greater than 0. For example, the abstract semantic entities "`SoccerPlayer`" and "`Goalkeeper`" defined in Box 12.8 have `AbstractionLevel.dimension=1`.
- `spec_relationship` is an MPEG-7 relationship of type "`specializes`", which is defined only if `superclass` $\neq$ `MPEG7_type` and associates the abstract semantic entity `AI` with its superclass if the latter is a domain-specific class.
- `gen_relationships` is the set of the MPEG-7 relationships, of type "`generalizes`", which associate the abstract semantic entity `AI` with the abstract semantic entities that represent its subclasses.
- `property_elements` is the set of the "`Property`" elements of `AI`, which represent properties of `C`.
- `pr_relationships` is the set of the MPEG-7 relationships, of type "`property`", which represent complex type properties of `C`.
- `prOf_relationships` is the set of the MPEG-7 relationships, of type "`propertyOf`", which associate the abstract semantic entity `AI` with the abstract semantic entities that represent classes with properties having `C` as domain.
- `exBy_relationships` is the set of the MPEG-7 relationships, of type "`exempli-fiedBy`", which associate the abstract semantic entity `AI` with the concrete semantic entities that represent the individuals belonging to `C`.
- `relationships` is the set of the relationships of `C`.

12.6   Representation of Individuals

We describe in this section the representation of individuals defined in domain ontologies using MPEG-7 constructs. The domain ontology individuals are represented, according to our formal model, by concrete MPEG-7 semantic entities.

Consider as an example the "`Ronaldinho`" individual, which represents the soccer player Ronaldinho. The representations of the "`Ronaldinho`" individual, according to the domain knowledge representation model using MPEG-7 constructs and in the original ontology, are depicted in Figure 12.3. Notice that the "`Ronaldinho`" individual is represented by a concrete semantic entity of type "`AgentObjectType`", which is associated with the abstract semantic entity "`SoccerPlayer`" that represents the class of the soccer players through a pair of "`exemplifies`"/"`exemplifiedBy`" relationships.

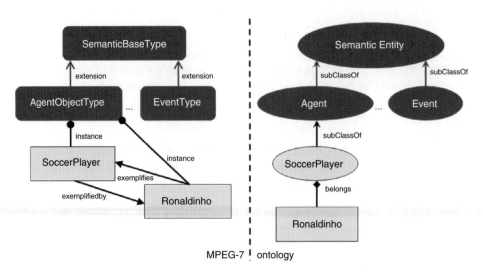

Figure 12.3 Representation of the individual "Ronaldinho" according to the domain knowledge representation model using MPEG-7 constructs (a) and in the original ontology (b).

The representation of the "Ronaldinho" individual in MPEG-7 syntax is shown in Box 12.9.

Box 12.9 Representation of the individual "Ronaldinho"

```
<SemanticBase xsi:type="AgentObjectType" id="Ronaldinho">
  <AbstractionLevel dimension="0"/>
  <Label>
    <Name>Ronaldinho</Name>
  </Label>
  <Definition>
    <FreeTextAnnotation>Ronaldinho</FreeTextAnnotation>
  </Definition>
  <Property>
    <Name>DateOfBirth</Name>
    <Definition>21/03/1980</Definition>
  </Property>
  <Relation type="exemplifies" source="#Ronaldinho"
  target="#SoccerPlayer"/>
  <Relation type="exemplifiedBy" source="#Goalkeeper"
  target="#SoccerPlayer"/>
  <Agent xsi:type="PersonType" id="RonaldinhoPerson">
    <Name>
      <GivenName>Ronaldinho</GivenName>
    </Name>
  </Agent>
</SemanticBase>
```

Let `Ind` be an individual that belongs to `C` and `C` be a domain-specific class defined in the domain ontology `DO`. `Ind` is formally described in the regular expression 12.15:

$$Ind(ind\_id, class, MPEG7\_type, properties, relationships, label, comment) \quad (12.15)$$

where

- `ind_id` is the identity of the `Ind` individual.
- `class` is the identity of `C`.
- `MPEG7_type` is the identity of the MPEG-7 type that represents the closest general-purpose MPEG-7 concept of the class `C` where `Ind` belongs.
- `properties` are the properties of `Ind`.
- `relationships` are the relationships of `Ind`.
- `label` is the (optional) label of `Ind`.
- `comment` is an (optional) description of `Ind`.

The `Ind` individual is represented by the concrete semantic entity `CI`, formally described in the regular expression 12.16:

$$CI(ci\_id, label, type, abstraction\_level, property\_elements, pr\_relationships,$$

$$prOf\_relationships, ex\_relationship, relationships) \quad (12.16)$$

where

- `ci_id` is the identity of `CI` and has `ind_id` as value.
- `label` is a label that describes `CI`.
- `type` is the MPEG-7 type, having `CI` as an instance, and is represented by the "`type`" attribute and has `MPEG7_type` as value.
- `abstraction_level` has a value of 0 and expresses that `CI` is a concrete semantic entity.
- `property_elements` is the set of the "`Property`" elements of `CI`, which represent properties of `Ind`.
- `pr_relationships` is the set of the MPEG-7 relationships, of type "`property`", which represent complex type properties of `Ind`.
- `prOf_relationships` is the set of the MPEG-7 relationships, of type "`propertyOf`", which associate the concrete semantic entity `CI` with the concrete semantic entities having a property with `Ind` as value.
- `ex_relationship` is an MPEG-7 relationship, of type "`exemplifies`", which associates the concrete semantic entity `CI` with the abstract semantic entity that represents `C`. `ex_relationship` is defined only if class $\neq$ `MPEG7_type`.
- `relationships` is the set of the relationships of `Ind`.

12.7 Representation of Axioms

We describe in this section the representation of ontology axioms using MPEG-7 constructs. The axioms supported are class generalization and specialization, subsumption, property value restriction specification, equivalence and disjointness of classes, equivalence and separation of individuals, and class union and class intersection.

Class Generalization and Specialization. The axioms of class generalization and specialization are represented by MPEG-7 relationships of type "specializes" and "generalizes", respectively.

Let spec_relationship be a "Relation" element that represents an MPEG-7 relationship expressing that the subclass abstract semantic entity specializes the class represented by the superclass abstract semantic entity. spec_relationship is formally described in the regular expression 12.17:

$$spec\_relationship(sr\_type, sr\_source, sr\_target) \qquad (12.17)$$

where

- sr_type is the type of spec_relationship and has "specializes" as value.
- sr_source is the source of spec_relationship and has as value the identity of subclass.
- sr_target is the target of spec_relationship and has as value the identity of superclass.

Let gen_relationship be a "Relation" element that represents an MPEG-7 relationship expressing that the superclass abstract semantic entity generalizes the class represented by the subclass abstract semantic entity. gen_relationship is formally described in the regular expression 12.18:

$$gen\_relationship(gr\_type, gr\_source, gr\_target) \qquad (12.18)$$

where

- gr_type is the type of gen_relationship and has "generalizes" as value.
- gr_source is the source of gen_relationship and has as value the identity of superclass.
- gr_target is the target of gen_relationship and has as value the identity of subclass.

Consider as an example the "specializes"/"generalizes" pair of relationships between the "SoccerPlayer" and the "Goalkeeper" classes, shown in Box 12.8.

Subsumption. The subsumption of an individual Ind to a class C is represented by the pair of MPEG-7 relationships ex_relationship and exBy_relationship, of type "exemplifies" and "exemplifiedBy", respectively.

exBy_relationship is represented by a "Relation" element that is formally described in the regular expression 12.19:

$$exBy\_relationship(ebr\_type, ebr\_source, ebr\_target) \qquad (12.19)$$

where

- ebr_type is the type of exBy_relationship and has "exemplifiedBy" as value.
- ebr_source is the source of exBy_relationship and has as value the identity of the abstract semantic entity that represents C.

- `ebr_target` is the target of `exBy_relationship` and has the identity of `Ind` as value.

`ex_relationship` is represented by a "`Relation`" element that is formally described in the regular expression 12.20:

$$ex\_relationship(er\_type,\ er\_source,\ er\_target) \tag{12.20}$$

where

- `er_type` is the type of `ex_relationship` and has "`exemplifies`" as value.
- `er_source` is the source of `ex_relationship` and has as value the identity of `Ind`.
- `er_target` is the target of `ex_relationship` and has as value the identity of the abstract semantic entity that represents `C`.

Consider as an example the "`exemplifies`"/"`exemplifiedBy`" pair of relationships between the "`Ronaldinho`" and the "`SoccerPlayer`" semantic entities, shown in Box 12.1.

Value Restrictions. The specification of a fixed value for a property `P` is specified in a different way, depending on the representation of `P`.

If `P` is represented by a "`Property`" element, the value restriction is represented by the `fixed` "`Term`" element that is formally described in the regular expression 12.21:

$$fixed(fname,\ (fdef\,|\,fhref)) \tag{12.21}$$

where

- `fname` is the value of the "`Name`" element of `fixed` and has "`fixed`" as value.
- `fdef` is the value of the "`Definition`" element of `fixed` and defines the fixed value of `P`.
- `fhref` is the value of the "`href`" element of `fixed` and has as value a reference to the fixed value of `P`.

If `P` is represented by "`Relation`" elements, the value restriction is represented for each class `D` that belongs to the domain of `P` by a pair of MPEG-7 relationships of type "`property`"/"`propertyOf`" that associate `D` with the concrete semantic entity `V`, representing the fixed value.

If `P` is represented by an "`AttributeValuePair`" element, the value restriction is represented according to the type of the fixed value `V` by the value of the appropriate element of "`AttributeValuePair`" and in particular by the following: (i) the value of the element "`BooleanValue`" if `V` is a boolean value; (ii) the value of the element "`IntegerValue`" if `V` is an integer value; (iii) the value of the element "`FloatValue`" if `V` is a float number value; (iv) the value of the element "`TextValue`" if `V` is a string value or a value of type "`TextualType`" (or a type that extends it); (v) the value of the element "`IntegerMatrixValue`" if `V` is of type "`IntegerMatrixType`"; (vi) the value of the element "`FloatMatrixValue`" if `V` is of type "`FloatMatrixType`"; (vii) the value of the element "`TextAnnotationValue`" if `V` is of type "`TextAnnotationType`" (or a type that extends it); (viii) the value of the element "`ControlledTermUseValue`" if `V` is of type "`ControlledTermUseType`" (or a type that extends it); and (ix) the value of the element "`DescriptorValue`" if V is of type "`DType`" (or a type that extends it).

Consider as an example the fixed value of the "`InitialNumOfPlayers`" property, which is represented by the "`IntegerValue`" element shown in Box 12.4.

Equivalence of Classes. The specification of a class A as equivalent to a class B is represented by the "`Relation`" element `eq_relationship` that is formally described in regular expression 12.22:

$$eq\_relationship(eq\_type, eq\_source, eq\_target) \qquad (12.22)$$

where

- `eq_type` is the type of `eq_relationship` and has "`equivalent`" as value.
- `eq_source` is the source of `eq_relationship` and has the identity of A as value.
- `eq_target` is the target of `eq_relationship` and has the identity of B as value.

Consider as an example that the class "`Goalie`" of an ontology "`O1`" is equivalent with the class "`Goalkeeper`" of the ontology of Box 12.1. The MPEG-7 representation of the equivalence of the classes "`Goalie`" and "`Goalkeeper`" is shown in Box 12.10.

Box 12.10 Representation of the equivalence of the class "`Goalie`" of the ontology "`O1`" with the class "`Goalkeeper`" of the ontology of Box 12.1

```
<Relation type="equivalent" source="O1#Goalie" target="#Goalkeeper"/>
```

Disjointness. The specification of a class A as disjoint with a class A is represented by a "`Relation`" element `disjoint_relationship` that is formally described in the regular expression 12.23:

$$disjoint\_relationship(d\_type, d\_source, d\_target) \qquad (12.23)$$

where

- `d_type` is the type of `disjoint_relationship` and has "`disjoint`" as value.
- `d_source` is the source of `disjoint_relationship` and has the identity of A as value.
- `d_target` is the target of `disjoint_relationship` and has the identity of B as value.

Equivalence of Individuals. The specification of an individual A as equivalent to an individual B is represented by a "`Relation`" element `equals_relationship` that is formally described in the regular expression 12.24:

$$equals\_relationship(eq\_type, eq\_source, eq\_target) \qquad (12.24)$$

where

- `eq_type` is the type of `equals_relationship` and has "`equals`" as value.

- `eq_source` is the source of `equals_relationship` and has the identity of A as value.
- `eq_target` is the target of `equals_relationship` and has the identity of B as value.

Separation of Individuals. The specification of an individual A as separated from an individual B is represented by a "Relation" element `sep_relationship` that is formally described in the regular expression 12.25:

$$sep\_relationship(eq\_type,\ eq\_source,\ eq\_target) \qquad (12.25)$$

where

- `eq_type` is the type of `sep_relationship` and has "separated" as value.
- `eq_source` is the source of `sep_relationship` and has the identity of A as value.
- `eq_target` is the target of `sep_relationship` and has the identity of B as value.

Consider as an example that the individual "Ronaldo" of an ontology "O1" is separated from the individual "Ronaldinho" of the ontology of Box 12.1 since the two individuals represent different soccer players. The MPEG-7 representation of the separation of the individuals "Ronaldo" and "Ronaldinho" is shown in Box 12.11.

Box 12.11 Representation of the separation of the individual "Ronaldo" of the ontology "O1" with the individual "Ronaldinho" of the ontology of Box 12.1

```
<Relation type="separated" source="O1#Ronaldo" target="#Ronaldinho"/>
```

Class Union. The definition of a class A as the union of the N (N>0) classes A_1, A_2, ..., A_N is represented by a "Relation" element `union_relationship` of type "union".

Let S be an MPEG-7 semantic entity S of type "SemanticType" that represents a collection comprising of the abstract semantic entities that represent the classes A_1, A_2, ..., A_N. The `union_relationship` "Relation" element is formally described in the regular expression 12.26:

$$union\_relationship(u\_type,\ u\_source,\ u\_target) \qquad (12.26)$$

where

- `u_type` is the type of `union_relationship` and has "union" as value.
- `u_source` is the source of `union_relationship` and has the identity of A as value.
- `u_target` is the target of `union_relationship` and has the identity of S as value.

Class Intersection. The definition of a class A as the intersection of the N (N>0) classes A_1, A_2, ..., A_N is represented by a "Relation" element `union_relationship` of type "intersection".

Let s be an MPEG-7 semantic entity s of type "SemanticType" that represents a collection comprising of the abstract semantic entities that represent the classes A_1, A_2, ..., A_N. The in_relationship "Relation" element is formally described in the regular expression 12.27:

$$in\_relationship(i\_type, i\_source, i\_target) \qquad (12.27)$$

where

- i_type is the type of in_relationship and has "intersection" as value.
- i_source is the source of in_relationship and has the identity of A as value.
- i_target is the target of in_relationship and has the identity of s as value.

12.8 Exploitation of the Domain Knowledge Representation in Multimedia Applications and Services

Once the domain knowledge regarding the multimedia semantics has been captured and systematically represented, it can be exploited by semantic-based applications and services. In this section, we present how the domain knowledge that has been represented according to the proposed model can be exploited both for reasoning support (in Section 12.8.1) and in the context of the semantic-based multimedia content retrieval (in Section 12.8.2), and filtering (in Section 12.8.3).

12.8.1 Reasoning Support

Since the representations and axioms of the formal model clearly map to the corresponding representations and axioms of OWL, the subset of the OWL axioms that hold for the domain knowledge representation are clearly specified. This allows the transformation of the domain knowledge in OWL syntax, its integration in MPEG-7-based ontological infrastructures such as the one of the DS-MIRF framework [7, 10, 11], and the use of the existing OWL reasoners for semantic processing. In order to support this scenario in the DS-MIRF framework, we have developed an MPEG-7 to OWL mapping model that allows us to automatically transform domain ontologies expressed in MPEG-7 syntax, according to our formal model, into OWL ontologies. In addition, the audiovisual content descriptions that have been defined according to these ontologies can also be transformed into OWL/RDF descriptions and then be used and exploited in the Semantic Web environment. In particular, the OWL/RDF descriptions may be enriched through reasoning that will be performed on both the descriptions and the ontologies. Then, the enriched descriptions can be transformed back to the MPEG-7 syntax and be used in the MPEG-7 working environment.

12.8.2 Semantic-Based Multimedia Content Retrieval

The MPEG-7 descriptions that utilize the domain knowledge that is systematically represented according to our formal model allow for the development of advanced semantic-based retrieval capabilities on top of them. In particular, semantic-based queries that cannot be accurately answered if the domain knowledge is not systematically integrated in the MPEG-7 descriptions can now be supported.

Consider, as an example, the query "give me the goals scored by the national team of Greece." If the domain knowledge is not systematically integrated in the MPEG-7 descriptions, the query results will include, in addition to the goals scored by Greece, other events caused by the national team of Greece that contain the word "goal" in their descriptions ("shot-on-goal," "near-goal," etc.). The false drops are not included in the query results if the domain knowledge has been systematically integrated and the query language allows the accurate specification of the query conditions. This can be achieved using expressive query languages such as the MP7QL query language [14] that we have developed. The MP7QL is a powerful query language that has the MPEG-7 as data model and allows for querying every aspect of an MPEG-7 multimedia content description, while it fully supports the exploitation of domain knowledge in semantic-based queries.

12.8.3 Semantic-Based Multimedia Content Filtering

In addition to the support of advanced semantic-based queries, our formal model also allows the support of advanced semantic-based multimedia content filtering. This can be achieved if, instead of the MPEG-7 user preferences that have limited expressive power, user preference descriptions that are isomorphic with the MPEG-7 content descriptions are supported [14–17]. Thus, a user preference description model that is isomorphic with the MPEG-7 content description model allows the retrieval of audiovisual content that has been described according to the proposed domain knowledge description model and contains "the goals scored by Greece" (instead of the audiovisual content that contains in its description the keywords "goal" and "Greece," that will also retrieve the goals scored against Greece). Such a user preference model is the MP7QL filtering and search preferences (FASP) model [14, 17] that we have developed, which is compatible with the MP7QL query language. The MP7QL FASP model allows multimedia content filtering based on every aspect of an MPEG-7 multimedia content description as well as the exploitation of domain knowledge in multimedia content filtering. It is also remarkable that the MPEG-7 user preference descriptions are a special case of the MP7QL user preferences.

12.9 Conclusions

We have presented in this chapter a formal model that allows the systematic representation and exploitation of domain knowledge using MPEG-7 constructs. The formal model for domain knowledge representation using MPEG-7 constructs proposed here presents clearly and unambiguously a way to integrate domain knowledge in MPEG-7 using exclusively MPEG-7 constructs. Therefore, all the descriptions produced are completely within the MPEG-7 standard.

The proposed model describes clearly and formally the axioms that hold (a subset of the semantics of OWL), and therefore it allows reasoning to be performed by distributed applications that utilize these axioms. This allows advanced functionality for multimedia applications to be implemented and exploited in distributed environments.

References

[1] Salembier, P. (2001) MPEG-7 multimedia description schemes. *IEEE Transactions on Circuits and Systems for Video Technology*, **11** (6), 748–759.

[2] Hammiche, S., Benbernou, S., and Vakali, A. (2005) A logic based approach for the multimedia data representation and retrieval. Proceedings of the IEEE International Symposium on Multimedia (ISM 2005), 12–14, December, Irvine, CA, pp. 241–248.

[3] The DELOS Network of Excellence in Digital Libraries (Project Number IST-2000-29243). Online http://www.delos.info (accessed June 2010).

[4] The OntoWeb Thematic Network (IST – Project Record No 26059). Online, http://cordis.europa.eu/ist/ka3/iaf/projects/ontoweb.htm (accessed June 2010).

[5] W3C OWL Working Group (2009) *OWL 2 Web Ontology Language Document Overview*. W3C Recommendation. Online, http://www.w3.org/TR/owl2-overview/ (accessed June 2010).

[6] Hunter, J. (2001) Adding multimedia to the semantic web: building an MPEG-7 ontology. Proceedings of the 1st Semantic Web Working Symposium (SWWS 2001), Stanford University, July 30-August 1, 2001, California, pp. 261–283.

[7] Tsinaraki, C., Polydoros, P., and Christodoulakis, S. (2004) Interoperability support for ontology-based video retrieval applications. Proceedings of the Conference on Image and Video Retrieval (CIVR) 2004, July, 2004, Dublin, Ireland, pp. 582–591.

[8] García, R. and Celma, O. (2006) Semantic integration and retrieval of multimedia metadata. Presented at the Knowledge Markup and Semantic Annotation Workshop, Semannot'05, November, 2005, Galway, Ireland, CEUR Workshop Proceedings, vol. 185, pp. 69–80, ISSN 1613-0073.

[9] Arndt, R., Troncy, R., Staab, S. *et al*. (2007) COMM: designing a well-founded multimedia ontology for the web. Proceedings of the ISWC/ASWC 2007, pp. 30–43.

[10] Tsinaraki, C., Polydoros, P., and Christodoulakis, S. (2004) Integration of OWL ontologies in MPEG-7 and TV-Anytime compliant Semantic Indexing. Proceedings of the 16th International Conference on Advanced Information Systems Engineering (CAISE), June, 2004, Riga, Latvia, pp. 398–413.

[11] Tsinaraki, C., Polydoros, P., and Christodoulakis, S. (2007) Interoperability support between MPEG-7/21 and OWL in DS-MIRF. *IEEE Transactions on Knowledge and Data Engineering (IEEE TKDE)*, Special Issue on the Semantic Web Era, **19** (2), 219–232.

[12] Tsinaraki, C., Fatourou, E., and Christodoulakis, S. (2003) An ontology-driven framework for the management of semantic metadata describing audiovisual information. Proceedings of the 15th International Conference on Advanced Information Systems Engineering (CAISE), June, 2003, Klagenfurt/Velden, Austria, pp. 340–356.

[13] Tsinaraki, C., Polydoros, P., Kazasis, F., and Christodoulakis, S. (2005) Ontology-based semantic indexing for MPEG-7 and TV-anytime audiovisual content. *Multimedia Tools and Application Journal (MTAP)*, Special Issue of on Video Segmentation for Semantic Annotation and Transcoding, **26**, pp. 299–325.

[14] Tsinaraki, C. and Christodoulakis, S. (2007) An MPEG-7 query language and a user preference model that allow semantic retrieval and filtering of multimedia content. *ACM Multimedia Systems Journal*, Special Issue on Semantic Multimedia Adaptation and Personalization, **13** (2), 131–153.

[15] Agius, H. and Angelides, M.C. (2009) From MPEG-7 user interaction tools to hanging basket models: bridging the gap. *Multimedia Tools and Applications*, **41** (3), 375–406.

[16] Tsinaraki, C. and Christodoulakis, S. (2006) A multimedia user preference model that supports semantics and its application to MPEG 7/21. Proceedings of the IEEE Multimedia Modeling 2006 Conference (IEEE MMM 2006), January, 2006, Beijing, China, pp. 35–42.

[17] Tsinaraki, C. and Christodoulakis, S. (2006) A user preference model and a query language that allow semantic retrieval and filtering of multimedia content. Proceedings of the Semantic Media Adaptation and Personalization Workshop (SMAP 2006), December, 2006, Athens, Greece, pp. 121–128.

13

Survey of MPEG-7 Applications in the Multimedia Lifecycle

Florian Stegmaier, Mario Döller, and Harald Kosch

Department of Informatics and Mathematics, University of Passau, Passau, Germany

In 1996, the first specification of requirements and call for proposals for the standardization of MPEG-7 were initiated. Since then, a large amount of work in terms of research articles, books, software tools and frameworks, seminars, conferences, and so on has been carried out. This culminated in the standardization of the first version of MPEG-7 in 2001, and has been finalized in the second version published in 2006.

While briefly navigating through the history of MPEG-7, a legitimate question emerges. Why is metadata and metadata format in general so essential? Why should one choose standardized solutions?

In order to elaborate on these important questions, we will focus on an everyday scenario. Let us assume someone, let us call him John Doe (a hobby photographer), wants to maintain his archive of holiday pictures in a more sophisticated way than he has done so far (annotation was done on a filename basis). Based on his experience with the current annotated information, the search for images was frustrating. In this context, one can briefly summarize his advanced requirements as follows: The extracted information should allow search based on traditional technical information (such as file size, width, height, etc.), common descriptive information about the content, as well as the possibility to look for specific regions or objects that are visible in the picture. In addition, as John often travels, his archive should be accessible over mobile devices in order to browse through the repository and display the latest additions.

It is clear that the annotation on a filename basis is not able to support retrieval based on these requirements. Here, metadata and especially rich metadata formats come into play. They provide tools to describe information about the multimedia asset and its content in a structured and expressive manner. In particular, MPEG-7 facilitates many application domains and is probably the richest multimedia metadata set available today. Therefore, the outlined requirements can be expressed by the use of the standardized format.

The Handbook of MPEG Applications: Standards in Practice   Edited by Marios C. Angelides and Harry Agius
© 2011 John Wiley & Sons, Ltd

Related to the introduced example scenario, the following main important components of an MPEG-7-based multimedia retrieval architecture can be identified (Figure 13.1).

A very important point in metadata production and consumption life cycle is the ability to extract the desired information in an efficient way. Therefore, good tools, techniques, and frameworks for extracting low- and high-level information in an automated (or semi-automated) manner are essential. Next, as presented in Figure 13.1 a central component of every retrieval architecture is the retrieval engine. A basis for every retrieval engine is an adequate query language supporting a sufficient list of multimedia search paradigms (e.g., Query-By-Example). Here, the combination of exact match and fuzzy retrieval is desirable. Based on this, middleware concepts can be used in order to address multiple repositories at the same time during search. Finally, access to the stored information needs to be accomplished in a user-friendly graphical user interface (GUI). This is valid for an easy request construction as well as the visualization and preparation of results. Here, the use of mobile devices increasingly comes into play.

The second issue becomes an important one whenever components of various vendors need to be combined. The interplay of all the different tools and applications can be guaranteed by the use of standardized technologies. This is one of the key points in order to support interoperability among multiple frameworks.

Based on the introduced example architecture, developed solutions and approaches of the presented areas are introduced in the following sections. In this context, the remainder of this chapter is as follows: First of all in Section 13.1, tools and frameworks supporting a user during the annotation process of multimedia data are introduced. This is followed

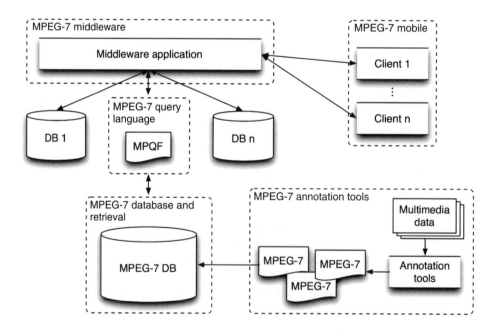

Figure 13.1 Example of MPEG-7-based multimedia retrieval architecture.

by storage and retrieval approaches for MPEG-7 documents (Section 13.1). A very important feature for efficient multimedia retrieval is the supported query interface. In this context, Section 13.3 presents, among others, the latest achievement within MPEG-7 standardization, namely the MPEG query format. How various multimedia database and retrieval systems can successfully be combined is elaborated in the middleware section (Section 13.4). Client applications, especially for the currently important mobile domain, will be highlighted in Section 13.5. This chapter concludes with Section 13.6.

13.1   MPEG-7 Annotation Tools

Recent research topics deal with the automatic extraction of multimedia metadata. The automatic extraction of low-level features (e.g., color) is already well understood, but in contrast to that, the automatic extraction of high-level (semantic) features is still an open issue [1].

In this context, an evaluation of currently available MPEG-7 annotation tools and frameworks has been accomplished and can be found in [2]. In general, most of the participating tools are able to extract low-level features automatically. Furthermore, some also provide functionalities to describe high-level features in a manual way. In the following, a brief overview of evaluated tools and frameworks related to the visual domain is presented.

Caliph & Emir [3, 4] are two applications for the annotation and retrieval of images with MPEG-7 descriptors. This project has been initiated at the University of Graz.[1] The tool allows automatic extraction of low-level features of images and supports the user by manual annotation of semantic descriptions. The manual annotation is supported by the integrated *semantic annotation panel*. Furthermore, an automatic conversion of EXIF[2] and IPTC IIM[3] is provided. Caliph & Emir obtained the ACM Multimedia Open Source Software Competition award in 2009.

The M-Ontomat-Annotizer is part of the aceMedia project [1] for analyzing and annotating multimedia data. It is based on the creation of metadata (CREAM) framework [5] and is an extension of the OntoMat-Annotizer [6]. The tool uses ontologies for supporting the annotation process. These ontologies can be domain-specific such as visual description ontology (VDO) for videos or multimedia structure ontology (MSO), which is based on MPEG-7 multimedia database schema (MDS).

The IBM MPEG-7 Annotation Tool (short VideoAnnEX) [7] allows the annotation of videos with MPEG-7 descriptions. The granularity of the annotation focuses on shot and frame elements where shots are detected automatically during the load process. Objects within frames can be tagged by bounding boxes which allow a separate region-based annotation. The tool supports descriptions about static scenes, events, and key objects within shot sequences.

The VIZARD tool [8] is a video publishing tool, which targets novice users who wish to process their home videos. It facilitates the annotation of videos by introducing a novel video-book model that provides structuring in terms of chapters, sections, index, conclusion, and so forth.

---

[1] http://www.tugraz.at/
[2] http://www.exif.org/
[3] http://www.iptc.org/IIM/

MARVel[4] is an image and video retrieval tool that provides automatic indexing and categorizing of image and/or video collections based on integrated content analysis techniques. For instance, the tool assigns the concept *outdoor* when an airplane is detected, and so on. Furthermore, MARVel provides retrieval strategies based on feature descriptors or semantic concepts.

The MPEG-7 Library[5] is a C++ implementation of MPEG-7, freely provided by the *Joanneum Research Forschungsgesellschaft mbH* at Graz, Austria. The library focuses on manipulating, validating, and creating MPEG-7 descriptors. It does not contain feature extractors. Therefore, the library supports developers in XML-DOM programming of MPEG-7 documents.

The POLYSEMA MPEG-7 Video Annotator [9] provides the functionalities for annotating videos with *high-level* MPEG-7 descriptions (e.g., shot detection) by the use of a user-friendly user interface (UI).

An example for an audio annotation tool is MARS.[6] This application offers the possibility to generate, analyze, and annotate electroacoustic music in a distribution scenario.

Not every application deals with the extraction of metadata and the annotation process. There also exist projects having an interoperability issue between metadata formats. A substitute for these projects would be MEDINA [10], which is a semiautomatic converter from Dublin Core to MPEG-7.

Beside these applications and frameworks, several EU-supported projects exist (e.g., KSpace[7]), whose main goal is the research and development of tools for semiautomatic annotation and retrieval of multimedia content.

After this overview of MPEG-7 annotation tools and projects, the remaining part will demonstrate the design and workflow of such tools on the basis of the VAnalyzer[8] [11]; this supports the annotation of audiovisual data. The VAnalyzer is a Java-based application that produces valid MPEG-7 metadata descriptions based on video data. It performs an automatic extraction of visual MPEG-7 low-level features (e.g., dominant color) as well as object (e.g., face) recognition [12], and tracing [13].

Figure 13.2 highlights the conceptual design of the VAnalyzer that is divided into three main units. Here, continuous lines show direct exchange of information and dashed lines indicate dependencies.

The *UI* is built inside the NetBeans Platform,[9] which is a generic framework for Swing applications. The UI is the graphical representation of the VAnalyzer functionalities. A user is able to load a video file, use well-known video playback options (e.g., play or fast forward), and select an arbitrary amount of available processing algorithms. During playback of a video, the UI also supports the visual presentation of results of the annotation algorithms (e.g., face detection, object tracing, and so on).

The *core components* serve as a mediator between the UI and the core processing units. It receives the data from the UI and forwards it to the according unit and vice versa.

---

[4] http://www.alphaworks.ibm.com/tech/marvels/
[5] http://iiss039.joanneum.at/cms/index.php?id=84
[6] http://www-i5.informatik.rwth-aachen.de/i5new/staff/spaniol/MARS/index.html
[7] http://kspace.qmul.net/
[8] https://www.dimis.fim.uni-passau.de/iris/index.php?view=vanalyzer
[9] http://platform.netbeans.org/

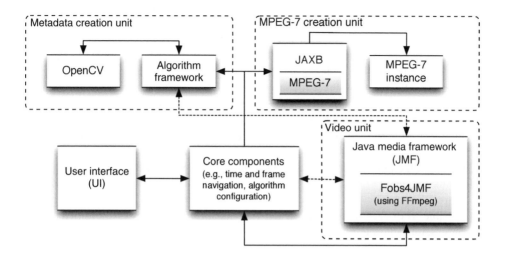

Figure 13.2   Architectural overview of the VAnalyzer.

As already mentioned, the conceptual design of the VAnalyzer is divided in three main units, which will be described next.

The *video unit* provides the access to the video data. For this purpose, the application makes use of the Java media framework (JMF).[10] Beside JMF, several other Java-based media processing frameworks exist; for example JVLC,[11] FMJ[12] or QTJava.[13] In contrast to JMF, these frameworks offer insufficient processing functionalities (e.g., frame access) or necessary documentation is missing (e.g., API). JMF at its core is able to process a certain set of media formats.[14] To enlarge this set, plug-ins for JMF exist, which permit the usage of media formats available in the underlying operating system or the integration of external libraries, like FFmpeg.[15] The VAnalyzer makes use of the Fobs4JMF[16] project to ensure a broad support of media formats (using FFmpeg).

The core objective of the VAnalyzer is the creation of valid MPEG-7 descriptions (XML instances) of video data. This functionality is encapsulated in the *MPEG-7 creation unit*. Here, JAXB[17] is used for XML processing. JAXB has been fully integrated into the Java runtime environment (JRE) since Version 1.6. It generates a Java class hierarchy on the basis of an XML Schema[18] and automatically performs the mapping between these classes and an XML instance. The procedure of writing the information saved in the classes to an XML instance is called *marshal* and unmarshal is the other way round.

---

[10] http://java.sun.com/javase/technologies/desktop/media/jmf/

[11] http://trac.videolan.org/jvlc/

[12] http://fmj-sf.net/

[13] http://sourceforge.net/projects/qtjava/

[14] http://java.sun.com/javase/technologies/desktop/media/jmf/2.1.1/formats.html

[15] http://ffmpeg.org/

[16] http://fobs.sourceforge.net/

[17] https://jaxb.dev.java.net/

[18] http://www.w3.org/XML/Schema/

The *metadata creation unit* is a container used to centralize the actual implementations of the extraction algorithms and the necessary external libraries. The input and output of these algorithms is the raw data of a video frame. If an algorithm recognizes or traces an object, it will be marked graphically by a *region of interest* (rectangle) in the output frame. This output will then be visualized at the UI. The VAnalyzer is able to extract the following MPEG-7 low-level features: *color layout*, *color structure*, *dominant color*, and *edge histogram*. In addition to these low-level features, the VAnalyzer offers two solutions for object recognition and tracing. The first solution makes use of the OpenCV project[19] [12]. This framework detects objects (e.g., faces) using Haar cascades. A second solution follows the approach issued by Marko Heikkilä and Matti Pietikäinen in [13]. In this article, the authors propose an object detection using background subtraction with background models.

The application overview and the showcase architecture of the VAnalyzer indicate that it is possible to extract reasonable MPEG-7 metadata descriptions of multimedia-related data in a (semi-)automatic way, but there are still open issues, for example the *semantic gap* [14] between low-level and high-level (semantic) features is still unsolved. Another issue is concluded in [2] that actually only a few applications are able to create valid MPEG-7 descriptions.

13.2   MPEG-7 Databases and Retrieval

Basically, MPEG-7 descriptions are XML documents that rely on a language extension of XML Schema, called *DDL*. Thus, the search for an efficient repository for MPEG-7 descriptions automatically leads us to the research field of XML databases. Two major research directions exist in this area. In the first, research concentrates on finding the most suitable platform for storing XML. Here, research mainly focuses on native XML solutions [15, 16] that develop XML storage solutions from scratch and database extensions such as those given in [17, 18] that use the extensibility services of modern databases. In the second case, research concentrates on how to map XML schema to an equivalent relational [19–21], object-relational [17, 22] or object-oriented [23] database model.

In this context, a good and still-valid overview of the usability of XML databases for MPEG-7 is provided by Westermann and Klas in [24]. The authors investigated the following main criteria: *representation of media descriptions* and *access to media descriptions*. To summarize their findings, neither native XML databases (e.g., Tamino [25], Xindice [15]) nor XML database extensions (e.g., Oracle XML DB [17, 26], Monet XML [20]) provide full support for managing MPEG-7 descriptions with respect to their given requirements. Based on identified limitations (e.g., supported indexing facilities for high-dimensional data), the retrieval capabilities for multimedia data are restrictive.

Current research also concentrates on semantic multimedia retrieval and annotation. Although, MPEG-7 is probably the richest multimedia metadata set, it is lacking in its ability to express semantic information [27–29]. As mentioned earlier, MPEG-7 relies on XML schema, which are mainly used for providing structure to documents and do not impose any interpretation on the data contained [27] and therefore, it does not express

---

[19] http://sourceforge.net/projects/opencv/

the meaning of the structure. Hence, the authors in [29] identified open issues related to semantic multimedia annotation and introduced a three-layer abstraction of the problem, indicating as the top-most level, the use of semantic web technology (e.g., RDF, OWL).

Therefore, many authors presented approaches in order to move the MPEG-7 description of multimedia data closer to those ontology-related languages [30, 31]. Related to this issue, the authors in [32] present a user preference model for supporting semantic information.

In the past, some MPEG-7 retrieval systems have been demonstrated [33, 34]. These systems implement low-level image retrieval based on color, texture, and shape descriptors. A deep analysis regarding the image retrieval topic can be found in [35]. The user can choose among different descriptors (and combinations of these) to be employed in the retrieval and therefore, optimize the search. However, these systems provide no indexing framework for querying large image data sets. Moreover, no query language support is given, nor are query optimization methods supplied. Similar approaches for other domains (e.g., cultural heritage [36, 37]) have recently emerged, which also investigate the use of MPEG-7.

In the following, a short overview of currently available full-fledged MPEG-7 databases and frameworks is presented.

IXMDB [38] is a storage approach for MPEG-7 documents integrating the advantages of both, the schema-conscious method and the schema-oblivious method. The design of IXMDB concentrates on multimedia information exchange and multimedia data manipulation. The database features a translation mechanism for converting XQuery to SQL requests. However, common multimedia query paradigms, such as query by example, spatial or temporal retrieval are not supported.

Another MPEG-7-based database is PTDOM [39]. PTDOM (persistent-type document object model) is a schema-aware XML (and therefore MPEG-7) database system supporting document validation, typed storage of elements and attribute values, structural indexing facilities, and optimizations of query plans. Nevertheless, their system focuses on datacentric retrieval and neglects multimedia retrieval features (e.g., QBE, spatial-temporal queries).

A unified query framework for multimedia repositories based on MPEG-7 has been introduced in [40]. The framework, called L7, consists of a query language (supporting a relational-like algebra, an expression language, an input query structure, and the output response format) and a service interface. The service interface acts as a set of views over the query language and is based on two different bindings (SOAP or REST-like interface).

Another framework for MPEG-7 has been developed by the authors in [41]. They proposed a framework that aims at high-level semantic retrieval and builds on three modules (the multimedia analysis module, the multimedia database module, and the retrieval module). Furthermore, the framework provides a rich set of automatic feature extraction components and an independent retrieval interface.

The authors in [42] evaluated existing RDBMS-based XML storage approaches for MPEG-7 documents and elaborated their advantages. Their findings resulted in a new storage approach called SM3+.

An embedded multimedia database management system for mobile devices (such as PDA) has been introduced by the authors in [43]. An approach highlighting the design and implementation of a DBMS-driven MPEG-7 layer on top of a content-based music retrieval system has been introduced in [44].

As mentioned before, many different approaches exist and provide the means for storing, managing, and retrieving MPEG-7 documents. In this context, the architecture of one system is demonstrated exemplarily. The *MPEG-7 MMDB*[20] [45] is an extension of the Oracle DBMS based on its *data cartridge technology*.[21] Oracle databases are built according to a modular architecture with *extensible services*. These extensible services enable database designers and programmers to extend for example, the type system, the query processing or the data indexing. Each extensible service offers an extensibility interface which can be used to enhance and modify the database for the user's needs.

Currently, the system consists of four main parts (Figure 13.3) which are introduced below:

Core Management System. The *core management system* (Figure 13.3, 1) is composed of a *MDS* based on MPEG-7, the *multimedia query optimizer* and the *index processing* module. The MDS relies on the *extensible type system* of the cartridge environment. For this purpose, the MPEG-7 schema is mapped to a database schema, that is, to respective object types and tables.

The indexing processing module provides the interface for the index types available in the schema. Its main task is to parse, control, and convert the input of the access operators (in PL/SQL) and to call the implementation routines (C++) in the multimedia indexing framework (MIF).

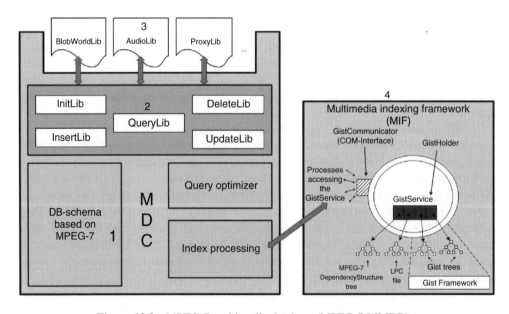

Figure 13.3 MPEG-7 multimedia database (MPEG-7 MMDB).

[20] https://www.dimis.fim.uni-passau.de/iris/index.php?view=mpeg7
[21] http://www.oracle.com/technology/documentation/database10g.html

The query optimizer implements a cost model for the similarity search, based on an estimation of the number of disk page accesses (see [46] for more details).

Multimedia Indexing Framework (MIF). The indexing facility of the core management system is supported by our *MIF* (Figure 13.3, 2). MIF provides various index structures: among others, balanced index trees such as SR- and SS-trees and a non-tree index such as LPC-files, for fast execution of similarity and exact search. The main part is the GistService which is located in an external address space. It manages all available access methods and relies partially on the generalized search tree (GiST) framework [47].

Internal Libraries. Above the core system reside several *internal libraries* (Figure 13.3, 3). These libraries provide basic functionalities such as insertion/deletion/updation of MPEG-7 documents in the database schema, as well as a query library which simplifies the query for product-specific application libraries. Currently, the internal libraries covers the following parts:

- *InitLib*: This library is used for creating new instances of the multimedia data types. It knows the complete multimedia schema with all essential rights and libraries.
- *InsertLib*: With the help of the insert-library, one can insert MPEG-7 descriptions into the database. The MPEG-7 description is inserted twice. First, the complete description is inserted into a database table which enables coarse-grained XPath queries. Second, it is broken down according to the MPEG-7-based database schema in order to allow fine-grained queries. The association between the complete and split documents is maintained by the assigned DOC_ID which denotes the membership of a table row to a specific MPEG-7 document.
- *DeleteLib*: The delete-library offers functionality for deleting MPEG-7 descriptions. Update operations are only possible as delete and reinsert.
- *QueryLib*: Besides the possibility of setting up SQL queries, we have the following query services: The first service allows one to query the database with the help of XPath expressions and produces XML-based output. The main disadvantage of the first approach is the complexity and size of the query statements. Therefore, alternatively, one may use the QueryLib, where the user can create individual select-statements with the help of a modular construction system. This modular construction enables users to specify the select-part as well as the where-part, according to their needs.

Application Libraries. The *application libraries* (Figure 13.3, 4) serve as interfaces between applications and the MPEG-7 MMDB. In general, these libraries use the underlying internal libraries for their specific needs. For instance, QueryLib is used to create application-specific queries. At the moment, libraries for the following applications have been implemented (Figure 13.4): BlobworldLib for a content-based image retrieval application, AudioLib for an audio recognition tool, and ProxyLib for supporting the video adaptation process in a mobile devices environment.

13.3 MPEG-7 Query Language

The previous consideration of MPEG-7 annotation tools as well as of MPEG-7 databases shows that it is possible to build database systems on the basis of MPEG-7 metadata. In general, retrieval engines use different (proprietary) query languages. This issue prevents

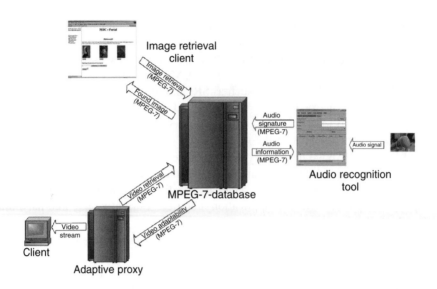

Figure 13.4   Multimedia applications on MPEG-7 MMDB.

users from experiencing a broad and unified access to different multimedia collections. This fact leads to the need for a unified query language in order to address multimedia data. The current landscape of query languages specially designed for multimedia applications includes many approaches. In the literature, there are, for example, extensions of SQL (e.g., SQL/MM) and OQL (e.g., $POQL^{MM}$ [48]), languages bound to a specific metadata model (e.g., MMDOC_QL [49]), languages concentrating on temporal or timeline retrieval (e.g., MQuery [50]) or languages that integrate weighting capabilities for expressing user preferences (e.g., WS-QBE [51]).

As demonstrated, the landscape for multimedia query languages is very diverse and provides several niche solutions. In the following, a deeper investigation of query languages for MPEG-7-related XML documents is provided.

XPath [52] (XML Path Language) is a recommendation of the W3C consortium that enables access to individual parts of data elements in an XML document. In general, an XPath expression consists of a path (where the main difference to filenames or uniform resource identifier (URI) is that each step selects a set of nodes and not just a single node) and a possible condition that restricts the solution set. The main disadvantage of XPath expressions is their limited usability in querying XML documents. For instance, it does not provide means for grouping or joins. In addition, XPath on its own provides no means for querying multimedia data in MPEG-7 descriptions based on the presented criteria.

XQuery [53] is a declarative query language and consists of the following primary areas that find their counterparts in SQL. For instance, the *for/let* clauses represent the SQL SELECT and SET statements and are used for defining variables iterating over a sequence of values. The *where* clause complies to the SQL WHERE statement by filtering the selection of the *for* clause. A main part of XQuery is the integration of XPath 2.0 and their functions, and an axis model which enables navigation over XML structures. Additional parts provide the ability to define own functions analogous to SQL stored procedures and the handling of namespaces. With reference to our requirements, XQuery does not provide means for querying multiple databases in one request and does not support multimodal or spatial/temporal queries. Nevertheless, there is ongoing work in this direction. For instance, the authors in [54] describe an XQuery extension for MPEG-7 vector-based feature queries. Furthermore, the authors in Refs [55, 56] adapted XQuery for the retrieval of MPEG-7 descriptions based on semantic views. Its adaptation, called itsemantic views query language (SVQL) is specialized for retrieving MPEG-7 descriptions in TV news retrieval applications and is not indented to be a general query language. Another adaptation of XQuery is presented in [57].

The authors in [49] propose an XML query language with multimedia query constructs called *MMDOC-QL*. MMDOC-QL bases on a logical formalism path predicate calculus [58] which supports multimedia content retrieval based on described spatial, temporal, and visual data types and relationships. The query language defines four main clauses: OPERATION (e.g., generate, insert) which is used to describe logical conclusions. The PATTERN clause describes domain constraints (e.g., address). Finally, there exist a FROM and CONTEXT clause which are paired together and can occur multiple times. The FROM clause specifies the MPEG-7 document and the CONTEXT is used to describe logical assertions about MPEG-7 descriptions in path predicate calculus. The query language is suitable for multimedia retrieval. Nevertheless, there are some drawbacks such as simultaneous searches in multiple databases or the integration of user preferences and usage history which are not considered in MMDOC-QL.

In order to enrich the list of presented solutions for XML, one has to also consider query languages such as XIRQL [59], XQL [60] or TQL [61]. However, one of the main drawbacks of XML is its limitation in expressing semantic meaning of the content information. This led to the development of the resource description framework (RDF) [62]. In contrast to XML, which provides a syntax to encode data, RDF supports a mechanism to express the semantics and relationships between and about data. Recent work uses RDF for *representing, reconciling, and semantically tagging multimedia resources* [63] in order to improve multimedia retrieval by semantic means. This development logically led to the need for domain query languages; representative solutions are XsRQL[22] and the newest recommendation from the W3C and SPARQL [64].

Most of the abovementioned solutions have several drawbacks. Either they do not support adequate multimedia retrieval paradigm (e.g., query by example, spatial) or they are rarely used and not standardized solutions, which prevents interoperability.

In this context, ISO/IEC SC29WG11 (more commonly known as MPEG) established the MPEG query format (MPQF)[23] standardization to create a standard interface for media repositories. MPQF [65] was issued as part 12 of the MPEG-7 standard in early 2009. The main intention of MPQF is to formulate queries in order to address and retrieve multimedia data, like audio, images, video, text or a combination of these. At its core, MPQF is an XML-based query language and intended to be used in a distributed multiplicity of multimedia retrieval systems (MMRS). Besides the standardization of the query language, MPQF specifies the service discovery and the service capability description. Here, a service is a particular system offering search and retrieval abilities (e.g., image retrieval).

---

[22] http://www.fatdog.com/xsrql.html
[23] http://www.mpegqueryformat.org

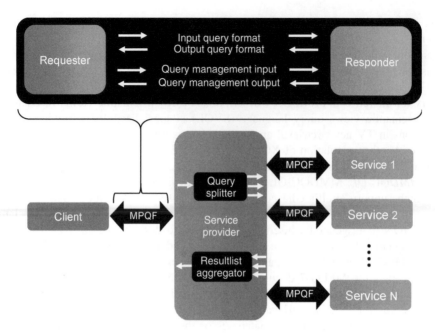

Figure 13.5 Possible scenario for the use of MPQF.

Figure 13.5 shows a possible retrieval scenario in a distributed MMRS environment. The *input query format (IQF)* provides means for describing query requests from a client to an MMRS. The *output query format (OQF)* specifies a message container for MMRS responses and finally the *query management tools (QMTs)* offer functionalities such as service discovery, service aggregation, and service capability description.

In particular, the IQF (Figure 13.6) defines the syntax of messages sent by the client to the multimedia service, which specifies the client's search criteria. The two main components allow specification of a filter condition tree (by using the *QueryCondition* element) and definition of the structure and desired content of the service output (by the *OutputDescription* element). The IQF also allows declaration of reusable resource definitions and metadata paths (fields) within the *QFDeclaration* element and the set of services where the query should be evaluated (the *ServiceSelection* element) in case of communication with an aggregation service. Finally, MPQF is able to combine fuzzy retrieval and exact retrieval abilities in a single condition tree.

In contrast to the IQF, the OQF (see Figure 13.7) deals with the specification of a standardized format for multimedia query responses. The two main components cover paging functionality and the definition of individual result items. The *ResultItem* element of the OQF holds a single record of a query result. In the MPQF schema, the element is based on an abstract type which is targeted at future extensibility and allows more concrete instantiations. Besides, the OQF provides a means for communicating global comments (by the *GlobalComment* element) and status or error information (by the *SystemMessage* element). Using a global comment, the responder can send general messages such as the service subscription expiration notice or a message from a sponsor,

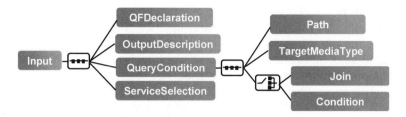

Figure 13.6 Structure of the input query format.

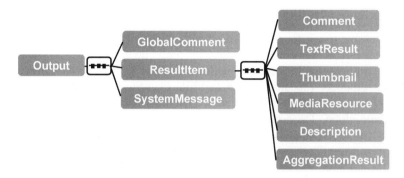

Figure 13.7 Structure of the output query format.

which is valid for the whole result set. When a proper result set cannot be composed, or when a special message regarding the system behavior should be communicated with the client, the multimedia service can use the *SystemMessage* element. This element provides three different levels for signaling problems, namely *Status*, *Warning*, and *Exception*. The codes and descriptions for the individual elements are defined in annex A of the standard specification. Finally, the validity period of a result set is indicated by the *expirationDate* attribute.

The management part of MPQF copes with the task of searching and choosing desired multimedia services. This includes service discovery, querying for service capabilities, and service capability descriptions. The MPQF consists of either the input or output element, depending on the direction of the communication (request or response). A management request can be used to find suitable services (e.g., by interacting with a registry service) which supports the intended queries or to scan individual services for their capabilities. The capability of every service is described by its service capability description which determines the supported query format, metadata, media formats, query types, expressions, and usage conditions.

The MPEG query format has been explicitly designed for its use in a distributed heterogeneous retrieval scenario. Therefore, the standard is open for any XML-based metadata description format (e.g., MPEG-7 or Dublin Core [66]) and supports, as already mentioned, service discovery functionalities. First steps in this direction have been taken by Döller *et al.* in [67] (processing and validating), [68 and 69]. The last two approaches address the retrieval in a multimodal scenario and introduce an MPQF-aware Web-Service-based middleware. Besides, MPQF adds support for asynchronous search requests as well. In contrast to a synchronous request (where the result is allocated as fast as possible), in an asynchronous scenario the user is able to define a time period after which the result will be cached. Such a retrieval paradigm might be of interest, for instance, to users of mobile devices with limited hardware/software capabilities. The results of requests (triggered by the mobile device) such as "Show me some videos containing information about the castle visible on the example image that has been taken with the digital camera" can then be gathered and viewed at a later point in time, from a different location (e.g., the home office), and a different device (e.g., a PC).

13.4 MPEG-7 Middleware

Owing to intensive research conducted over the last decade, many MMRS have emerged. Some concentrate on a specific domain (e.g., only image data is considered), while others are trying to provide access to multimodal data. Veltkamp and Tanase compared 43 available products (updated in 2004) [70]. Constitutively, latest work has been evaluated by Kosch *et al.* in [71]. These collections and retrieval systems are spread over the whole globe. The concatenation of those distributed databases and systems is a well-known research area. In the following, a brief overview of existing middleware systems is presented. Then, systems especially developed for MPEG-7 are introduced. MOCHA (Middleware based On a Code sHipping Architecture) was presented by Rodryguez-Martynez and Roussopoulos [72] as a self-extensible database middleware system, designed to interconnect a large number of distributed data sources. Its principle is to provide an (as far as possible) automatic deployment of user-defined functionality by the middleware itself, to the target databases.

Instant-X [73] is a novel OSGi[24]-based middleware for a generic multimedia API. It provides standard multimedia components and supports a dynamic deployment. For instance, unavailable components are automatically discovered and loaded in a peer-to-peer network on demand. The Instant-X middleware features a generic API which serves as an abstraction layer for supporting the replacement of specific protocol implementations at runtime.

The network-integrated multimedia middleware (NMM) [74] offers a multimedia architecture, which considers the network as an integral part and enables the use of devices distributed across a network. The system is available for multiple platforms and operating systems. Its novelty is the supported access to all kinds of networked and distributed multimedia systems, ranging from embedded and mobile systems to large-scale computing clusters.

As the short introduction above to middleware systems shows, these do not consider a particular (standardized) multimedia metadata format. In contrast to that, the following approaches introduce solutions taking metadata formats (e.g., MPEG-7) into account.

In 2004, the ISO/IEC SC29 WG 11 (known as MPEG) working group began an initiative. The goal of the MPEG Multimedia Middleware [75] (M3W) was to improve application portability and interoperability through the specification of a set of APIs dedicated to multimedia. The main aims of this project can be summarized as follows: (i) to allow application software to execute multimedia functions with a minimum

---

[24] http://www.osgi.org

knowledge of the inner workings of the multimedia middleware and (ii) to allow the triggering of updates to the multimedia middleware to extend the API. A successor of the M3W project has been implemented by the MPEG consortium and is called the MPEG eXtensible Middleware (MXM) [76] project. The result shall be a collection of MPEG and non-MPEG technologies organized in a middleware and supporting applications for different purposes (e.g., video/audio decoding, rights management, retrieval, and navigation among MM repositories).

Cao *et al.* proposed in [77], a middleware for MPEG-7-based multimedia services on the basis of Web Services especially designed for the integration of mobile devices. The middleware is based on service-oriented application servers, called *lightweight application server (LAS)*. The introduced architecture supports two different integration concepts for mobile devices. The first offers the possibility to connect via mobile web services using a Mobile Host. The second realizes the integration of LAS into an enterprise service bus middleware platform. Both concepts use MPEG-7 for exchanging multimedia-related metadata information.

Another approach that takes metadata formats into account was issued in [69]. The proposed system is based on a service-oriented architecture (SOA) and makes use of the aforementioned MPQF. The main purpose is to forward an MPQF query to an arbitrary amount of MMRS. One of its central, novel features is the distribution of an MPQF request to multiple multimedia services and the aggregation of individual result sets.

Figure 13.8 illustrates the implemented framework, that relies on Web Service technologies and consists of three main components: *service management*, *retrieval management*,

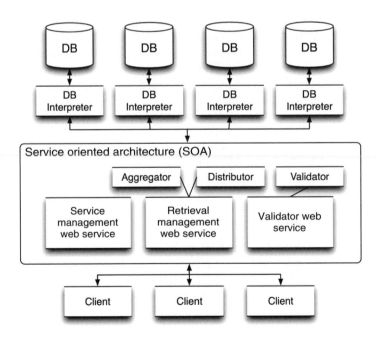

Figure 13.8 Architecture of the proposed MPQF web service framework.

and *validator* web service. Web services have many advantages. They are, for example, very flexible, powerful, and can be combined easily with each other. Using the Apache Axis[25] environment and its WSDL2Java command, the types of the MPQF XML Schema are transformed into Java classes which supersedes XML/String parsing.

The *service management web service* realizes service discovery and offers registry functionality. It provides two methods for MMRSs and clients. A MMRS can register (by calling the *registerService* method) at the service management. The method receives as input, an instance of the MPQF *AvailableCapabilityType* type which is a coverage for the service capability description. Clients are able to search (by calling the *searchService* method) for particular MMRSs at this registry. The method requires as input a valid MPQF input management query and results in a list of matching and available services delivered as a valid MPQF management output.

The *retrieval management web service* realizes service selection and result aggregation. This web service provides one method (*search*) in order to query multiple MMRSs at a particular time. The method requests an MPQF input query and responses with the merged result sets of the selected MMRS. The selection of MMRSs is realized by using the *ServiceSelection* element in the input query multiple times.

The two principal components of this web service are the aggregator and the distributor (Figure 13.8). For each incoming query, the retrieval management instantiates one *aggregator* and as many *distributors* as MMRS are specified inside the query. The task of the distributors is to forward the query to the respective MMRS and to wait for the query result. After all query results are returned to the distributors, the aggregator merges them into one single result using the Round Robin algorithm [78].

The *validator* web service provides a means for syntactic verification of an MPQF query. As MPQF bases on XML schema, the validator has to deal with XML instance documents. For this purpose, the current implementation embeds the XSV[26] XML validator. Ongoing implementations will also consider a rule-based verification of semantic relationships and conditions within an MPQF query.

After this consideration, the key features of using standardized metadata formats or query languages in middleware architectures are evident. The integration of standardized technologies provides means for interoperability among distributed multimedia search and retrieval services and makes intelligent content navigation possible for instance, in MPEG-7-enabled multimedia repositories that are loosely connected via distributed heterogeneous networks. The introduced framework served as a foundation for the recently issued AIR multimedia middleware framework[27] [79].

13.5 MPEG-7 Mobile

Recent studies[28] report that 60% of today's mobile multimedia devices, equipped with an image sensor, audio support, and video playback, have basic multimedia functionalities and this will hold true for almost nine out of ten devices in the year 2011. These studies show that there is a need for supporting multimedia services on mobile devices.

---

[25] http://ws.apache.org/axis/

[26] http://www.w3.org/2001/03/webdata/xsv

[27] https://www.dimis.fim.uni-passau.de/iris/index.php?view=air

[28] http://www.multimediaintelligence.com/

To underline this observation, two use cases will be presented for the importance of multimedia support in mobile devices.

The first use case is settled in the tourism domain. Multimedia devices may support users in tourism-related topics, like route-planning (e.g., find the nearest restaurant) and information on points of interest (e.g., find information about a building). Also virtual guided tours are conceivable. Several research projects address exactly these topics:

The George Square[29] project focuses on enabling collaboration as a port of leisure [80]. The goal is to enable two users to share their traveling experiences with each another. Mobile users carry a tablet PC, which is connected to the Internet and is equipped with a GPS receiver, camera, and headset used for voice-over-IP communication. A special software keeps track of the user's location and the user's activities.

In order to improve tourist experience, the city of Regensburg (Germany) has begun the campaign *REX* – shorthand for *Regensburg experience* – into life. A part of this project is the game *REXplorer*[30] [81], which has been in use since early 2007. As the name indicates, the goal of REXplorer is to explore Regensburg in a playful manner (e.g., solving puzzles), focusing on the cultural and historic sights of the medieval city center. The smartphone in use operates with a GPS receiver and a built-in camera. A similar project has been realized in the context of *In the Footsteps of Hans Christian Andersen*[31] which gives tourists an understanding of the author's life in Copenhagen, during the 19th century.

Another system supporting object recognition is PhoneGuide [82, 83]. It is a museum guidance system running on the user's cellular phone. The goal is to provide museum visitors with additional multimedia information on the exhibit they are currently watching, without interfering with the exhibition (e.g., by installing presentation boards or attaching tags to the objects). In order to reliably identify the current exhibit, PhoneGuide employs object recognition as well as location information. Object recognition employs artificial neural networks (NN) [84]. According to [83], PhoneGuide reaches a recognition rate of 95%. However, this approach depends heavily on well-defined lighting conditions and therefore, is limited to indoor settings.

This overview combined with the conclusion arrived at in [85] indicates that there is a lack of use of standards, reusability, and interoperability. Sending the raw multimedia data of an image to the retrieval engine is also an issue in the resource-limited mobile domain (e.g., bandwidth).

MoidEx [86] is a location-aware mobile tourism (mTourism) system for mobile devices. It depends on the recognition of buildings in a point-of-interest scenario. As the analysis and survey in [85] shows, the two key features of this approach are the integration of MPEG-7 metadata descriptions and transferring only this metadata to the retrieval system.

Figure 13.9 presents the overall architecture of the MoidEx system. The main goal of the system is to support tourists in identifying unknown buildings in foreign cities and to provide additional information (e.g., history). The system builds on the Moides framework [87] and adds the implementation of additional MPEG-7 visual feature extraction algorithms (e.g., edge histogram descriptor, dominant color descriptor), location detection, and the consistent line cluster algorithm [88] for building recognition.

---

[29] George Square is the central square in the city of Glasgow, Scotland.
[30] http://www.rex-regensburg.de/stadtspiel/rexplorer/
[31] http://www.goldendays.dk/

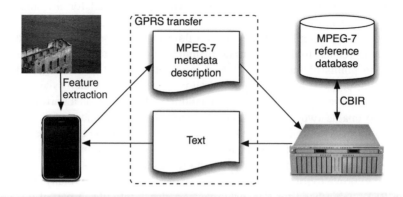

Figure 13.9   Workflow of MoidEx.

The extracted information is coded as an MPEG-7 document and sent to an mTourism library which has been developed on top of the MPEG-7 MMDB, which was introduced in Section 13.2. The information on the identified building is returned to the mobile phone and displayed to the user.

The second use case deals with the ability of multimedia retrieval and browsing. This topic was already addressed in several research projects and also in commercial approaches.

The personal video retrieval and browsing platform Candela [89] is an example of research projects that are especially designed for mobile users. As *"an infrastructure that allows the creation, storage and retrieval of home videos with special consideration of mobile terminals"*, it covers many parts of the lifecycle of digital videos. Metadata are available for all videos and represented by means of MPEG-7 media description schemes. Low-level (e.g., color histograms) as well as midlevel metadata (e.g., structural data such as video segments) are automatically generated. High-level metadata describe the semantic content and are partly provided using personal ontologies, annotated by the user. As UI, an Apache COCOON-based[32] web application is available for both, mobile and stationary (PC) users. For improving the usability to mobile users, the layout is split into three windows. The web interface lets users browse through ontology catalogs and search videos. Summarizing all these features, Candela focuses on the infrastructure as a whole. However, with regard to retrieval of videos, it provides only limited search functionalities (full-text keyword search).

Another research project in this area has been completed by Kamvar *et al.* [90]; it aims specifically at the UI. In this context, the MiniMedia Surfer is presented, a software for searching and browsing video segments of interest on small displays. The basic interface principle are transparent layers to support browsing tasks such as keyword queries, browsing through keyframes of search results, and video playback. Separated layers shall clearly present information while the (adjustable) transparency creates a connection between them.

---

[32] http://cocoon.apache.org

Figure 13.10 From left to right: home screen, popular videos menu, recently featured (Java applications). (*Source:* allaboutsymbian.com)

An example of commerce-driven approaches was issued by YouTube.[33] It is a website which needs no introduction and has been available to mobile users since June 2007. Last year, the mobile website[34] was completely revamped to allow access via 3G or WiFi to most of YouTube's regular video catalog, which contains tens of millions of videos. Another option which is currently still under beta testing is the YouTube for Mobile Java application which offers YouTube with a UI designed for mobile devices without relying on a mobile web browser Figure 13.10.

To accommodate mobile devices, YouTube for Mobile streams videos in 3GP format using the H.263/AMR codecs [91] instead of using the Flash video format. Most mobile devices do not have Adobe Flash installed, which means they cannot play the videos from the desktop version of YouTube without prior conversion. This conversion problem explains why YouTube for Mobile offers only a subset of the videos available on the main website.

A contribution toward approaching a standardized MMRS is the mobile multimedia query composer [92], which communicates with the inViPla video search framework (details below). This framework, with its client/server architecture, has been extended by MPQF functionalities. At the client-side the mobile query composer is responsible for generating MPQF queries being sent to the server as well as handling MPQF query results. Its architecture supports the retrieval in video collections that have been annotated by MPEG-7 [93]. The application domain of the test data, its annotation, and the used ontology has been tailored to soccer movies. However, the concepts and tools are open and adaptable for any topic. An overview of the current overall system architecture is presented in Figure 13.11.

Due to the use of the MPQF standard [65], the individual components can be exchanged and developed independently. Furthermore, an additional abstraction layer can be introduced by the integration of MPQF-aware middleware layers such as those described in [69]. In the following, the components will be described. The system

---

[33] http://www.youtube.com
[34] http://m.youtube.com

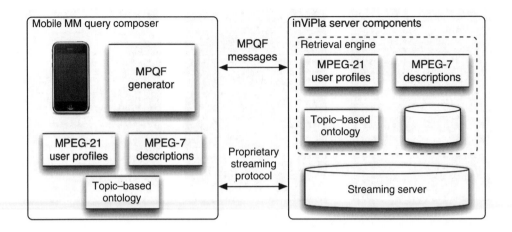

Figure 13.11 System architecture.

architecture of inViPla, shown in Figure 13.11, consist of two major components, the retrieval engine and a streaming server. These are separated applications, thus they can be deployed on different machines. The streaming server contains all videos in a database with streaming accessibility through real-time streaming protocol (RTSP) [94]. The retrieval engine provides search functionalities for those videos via MPQF queries. Based on metadata descriptions (MPEG-7) and a topic-based ontology, common queries (full-text search, criteria mapping etc.) as well as semantic ones are possible. Furthermore, the retrieval engine contains a component for handling user profiles to realize personalized queries. The Mobile Query Composer features a UI to create and/or edit queries, which afterwards are formulated as MPQF requests. These are sent to the inViPla server that performs the actual search and delivers the results in MPQF format as well, containing a subset of MPEG-7 descriptions. A user can load a profile from the server for more personalized queries. Therefore, MPEG-21 user profiles [95] are used; these contain information about digital item history, user rights, personal information such as needs and preferences (language, video length, codec etc.). The usage of standards such as MPEG-7 and MPEG-21 is a common approach to personalizing mobile multimedia queries and can be found in many works such as [96–98].

Developers are facing several limitations and challenges in the mobile devices domain, as shown in [86]. The overview of available MPEG-7 and multimedia-aware mobile applications shows that this topic is well but not completely investigated. As shown in [92], ease of use was one of the key issues while developing the Mobile Multimedia Query Composer. The *look & feel* of such applications could be improved by using, for instance, rich Internet application (RIA) technologies, which are able to build very appealing and comfortable UIs.

13.6 Summarization and Outlook

This chapter introduced standpoints on the practical use of the MPEG-7 standard. In general, the chapter investigated the use of MPEG-7 in the application domain of an end-to-end scenario. In detail, an overview of current state-of-the-art metadata annotation tools and frameworks for various domains (e.g., image, video) has been given. This was followed by approaches supporting the storage of MPEG-7 documents. Here, a closer look at current XML-based solutions and more sophisticated pure MPEG-7 repositories was presented. In the terms of retrieval engines, a deeper look into yet available retrieval interfaces and query languages has been provided. In this context, the newly standardized MPEG query format has been introduced. As a large number of retrieval systems based on MPEG-7 and multimedia in general have emerged, an outlook of existing and promising middleware systems has been given. Some of these middleware systems promise to unify access to heterogeneous retrieval systems and ease their use for the client. Finally, in the end-to-end scenario, the use of MPEG-7 for mobile devices has been elaborated. The chapter closes with an investigation of current standardization efforts in developing interoperability approaches among multiple metadata formats.

By summarizing the efforts that have been put into developing standardized solutions based on MPEG-7, one can find satisfying results. However, such developments have been driven mainly by research projects and institutes, and have not found their way into the industry. One of the reasons is that the extraction tools for low- and high-level features have been missing. Furthermore, as MPEG-7 is probably the richest metadata set available, many different ways can be found to describe the same information. A breakthrough for the MPEG-7 standard can only be obtained if the added value is recognized by global players in the multimedia production and consumption chain such as Google, YouTube or the broadcasting companies. A first step in this direction is the use of MPEG-7 in the TV-Anytime[35] project.

Finally, starting points for further reading can be found at the MPEG-7 community web page[36] or at the web page of the convener[37] of MPEG. Furthermore, several research projects supported by the European Union have been established in the recent past (e.g., KSpace[38] or SAPIR[39]). In the context of SAPIR, the content-based photo image retrieval (CoPhIR[40]) test collection has been established, which has realized MPEG-7 annotations of Flickr[41] images. A very good introduction of MPEG-7 can be found in [99 and 100].

References

[1] Hare, J.S., Sinclair, P.A.S., Lewis, P.H. *et al.* (2006) Bridging the semantic gap in multimedia information retrieval: top-down and bottom-up approaches. Proceedings of the 1st International Workshop on Semantic Web Annotations for Multimedia (SWAMM), Edinburgh, Scotland.

[2] Döller, M. and Lefin, N. (2007) Evaluation of available MPEG-7 Annotation Tools. Proceedings of I-MEDIA /I-SEMANTICS '07, 1st International Conference on New Media Technology, Graz, Austria, September.

[3] Lux, M., Klieber, W. and Granitzer, M. (2004) Caliph and Emir: semantics in multimedia retrieval and annotation. Proceedings of the 19th International CODATA Conference 2004: The Information Society: New Horizons for Science, Berlin, Germany, pp. 64–75.

---

[35] http://www.tv-anytime.org/

[36] http://www.multimedia-metadata.info/

[37] http://www.chiariglione.org/mpeg/working_documents.htm

[38] http://kspace.qmul.net:8080/kspace/kspaceabout.jsp

[39] http://www.sapir.eu/

[40] http://cophir.isti.cnr.it/

[41] http://www.flickr.com/

[4] Lux, M., Klieber, W., and Granitzer, M. (2006) On the complexity of annotation with the high level metadata. *Journal of Universal Knowledge Management*, **1** (1), 54–58.

[5] Handschuh, S., Staab, S., and Ciravegna, F. (2002) S-CREAM – semi-automatic CREAtion of metadata. Proceedings of SAAKM 2002 – Semantic Authoring, Annotation and Knowledge Markup, ECAI 2002 Workshop, Lyon, France, pp. 27–34.

[6] Handschuh, S. and Staab, S. (2003) CREAM – Creating metadata for the semantic web. *Computer Networks*, **42**, 579–598.

[7] Tseng, B.L., Lin, C.-Y., and Smith, J.R. (2002) Video personalization and summarization system. Proceedings of the SPIE Photonics East 2002 – Internet Multimedia Management Systems, Boston, USA.

[8] Rehatschek, H. and Kienast, G. (2001) Vizard – an innovative tool for video navigation, retrieval, annotation and editing. Proceedings of the 23rd Workshop of PVA Multimedia and Middleware, Vienna, Austria.

[9] Valkanas, G., Tsetsos, V., and Hadjiefthymiades, S. (2007) The polysema MPEG-7 video annotator. Poster and Demo Proceedings of the 2nd International Conference on Semantic and Digital Media Technologies, vol. 300, Genoa, Italy, December 5–7, 2007.

[10] Spaniol, M. and Klamma, R. (2005) MEDINA: a semi-automatic Dublin core to MPEG-7 converter for collaboration and knowledge management in multimedia repositories, in *Proceedings of I-KNOW '05, 5th International Conference on Knowledge Management, Graz, Austria, June 29–July 1, 2005, J.UCS (Journal of Universal Computer Science) Proceedings, LNCS 1590* (eds K. Tochtermann and H. Maurer), Springer, Graz, Austria, pp. 136–144.

[11] Stegmaier, F., Döller, M., Coquil, D. *et al.* (2010) VAnalyzer: a MPEG-7 based semantic video annotation tool. Proceedings of the Workshop on Interoperable Social Multimedia Applications (WISMA), Barcelona, Spain, to appear.

[12] Bradski, G. and Kaehler, A. (2008) *Learning OpenCV – Computer Vision with the OpenCV Library*, 1st edn, O'Reilly, Sebastopol, CA, United States of America.

[13] Heikkilä, M. and Pietikäinen, M. (2006) A texture-based method for modeling the background and detecting moving objects. *IEEE Transactions on Pattern Analysis and Machine Intelligence*, **28**, 657–662.

[14] Smeulders, A.W., Worring, M., Santini, S. *et al.* (2000) Content-based image retrieval at the end of the early years. *IEEE Transactions on Pattern Analysis and Machine Intelligence*, **22** (12), 1349–1380.

[15] Staken, K. and Viner, D. (2007) *Xindice Developers Guide 1.1. The Apache Foundation*, http://www.apache.org (accessed April 2010).

[16] Jagadish, H.V., Al-Khalifa, S., and Chapman, A. *et al.* (2002) TIMBER: a native XML database. *VLDB Journal*, **11** (4), 274–291.

[17] Murthy, R. and Banerjee, S. (2003) XML schema in oracle XML DB, Proceedings of the 29th VLDB Conference, Morgan Kaufmann, Berlin, Germany, pp. 1009–1018.

[18] Suciu, D. (2001) On database theory and XML. *ACM SIGMOD Record, Special Section on Advanced XML Data Processing*, **30**, 39–45.

[19] Shanmugasundaram, J., Shekita, E.J., Kiernan, J. *et al.* (2001) A general technique for querying XML documents using a relational database system. *SIGMOD Record*, **30** (3), 20–26.

[20] Schmidt, A., Kersten, M., Windhouwer, M., and Waas, F. (2001) Efficient relational storage and retrieval of XML documents. *Lecture Notes in Computer Science*, **1997**, 137+.

[21] Lee, D., Mani, M., and Chu, W.W. (2002) Effective schema conversions between XML and relational models. European Conference on Artificial Intelligence (ECAI), Knowledge Transformation Workshop (ECAI-OT), Lyon, France, July, 2002, pp. 3–11.

[22] Banerjee, S. (1994) Implementing XML schema inside a 'Relational' database. Proceedings of ACM SIGMOD International Conference on Management of Data, Minneapolis, MN, May, 1994, pp. 313–324.

[23] Christophides, V., Abiteboul, S., Cluet, S., and Scholl, M. (1994) From structured documents to novel query facilities. Proceedings of the 1994 ACM SIGMOD International Conference on Management of Data, Minneapolis, MN, May, 1994, pp. 313–324.

[24] Westermann, U. and Klas, W. (2003) An analysis of XML database solutions for the management of MPEG-7 media descriptions. *ACM Computing Surveys*, **35**, 331–373.

[25] Schöning, H. (2001) Tamino – a DBMS designed for XML. Proceedings of the 17th International Conference on Data Engineering (ICDE), April, pp. 149–154.

[26] Oracle (2006) *Oracle Database 10G Release 2. XML DB*, http://download-uk.oracle.com/otndocs/tech/xml/xmldb/TWP_XML_DB_10gR2_1%ong.pdf (accessed April 2010).

[27] Hammiche, S., Benbernou, S., Hacid, M.-S., and Vakali, A. (2004) Semantic retrieval of multimedia data, Proceedings of the 2nd ACM International Workshop on Multimedia Databases, ACM-MMDB 2004, ACM Press, Washington, DC, USA, pp. 36–44.

[28] Garcia, R. and Celma, O. (2005) Semantic integration and retrieval of multimedia metadata. Proceedings of the 5th International Workshop on Knowledge Markup and Semantic Annotation (SemAnnot 2005), Galway, Ireland, CEUR Workshop Proceedings, November 2005.

[29] van Ossenbruggen, J., Stamou, G., and Pan, J.Z. (2005) Multimedia annotations and the semantic Web. Proccedings of the ISWC Workshop on Semantic Web Case Studies and Best Practices for eBusiness, SWCASE05, Galway, Ireland.

[30] Tsinaraki, C., Polydoro, P., Moumoutzis, N., and Christodoulakis, S. (2004) Coupling OWL with MPEG-7 and TV-anytime for domain-specific multimedia information integration and retrieval. Proceedings of RIAO 2004, Avignon, France, April, 2004.

[31] Vembu, S., Kiesel, M., Sintek, M., and Baumann, S. (2006) Towards bridging the semantic gap in multimedia annotation and retrieval. Proceedings of the 1st International Workshop on Semantic Web Annotations for Multimedia, SWAMM 2006, Edinburgh, Scotland, May, 2006.

[32] Tsinaraki, C. and Christodoulakis, S. (2006) A multimedia user preference model that supports semantics and its application to MPEG 7/21. Proceedings of the 1st International Workshop on Semantic Media Adaptation and Personalization, Athens, Greece, December 2006.

[33] Mezaris, V., Doulaverakis, H., de Otalora, R.M.B. *et al.* (2004) Combining multiple segmentation algorithms and the MPEG-7 experimentation model in the schema reference system. Proceedings of the 8th International Conference on Information Visualisation (IV 2004), IEEE CS Proceedings, London, UK, July, 2004, pp. 253–258.

[34] Po, L.-M. and Wong, K.-M. (2004) A new palette histogram similarity measure for MPEG-7 dominant color descriptor. Proceedings of the 2004 International Conference on Image Processing (ICIP 2004), IEEE CS Proceedings, Singapore, October, 2004, pp. 1533–1536.

[35] Datta, R., Joshi, D., Li, J., and Wang, J.Z. (2008) Image retrieval: ideas, influences, and trends of the new age. *ACM Computing Surveys*, **40** (2), 1–60.

[36] Xu1, H. and Xiang, H. (2006) An image retrieval system based on MPEG-7 and XMLDB query for digital museum. *Lecture Notes in Computer Science: Technologies for E-Learning and Digital Entertainment*, **3942**, 1303–1311.

[37] Klamma, R., Spaniol, M., Jarke, M. *et al.* (2005) ACIS: intergenerational community learning supported by a hypermedia sites and monuments database, in Proceedings of the 5th International Conference on Advanced Learning Technologies (ICALT 2005), July 5–8, Kaohsiung, Taiwan (eds P. Goodyear, D.G. Sampson, D.J.-T. Yang, *et al.*), IEEE Computer Society, Los Alamitos, CA, pp. 108–112.

[38] Chu, Y., Chia, L.-T., and Bhowmick, S.S. (2007) Mapping, indexing and querying of MPEG-7 descriptors in RDBMS with IXMDB. *Journal of Data and Knowledge Engineering (DEK)*, **63** (2), 224–257.

[39] Westermann, U. and Klas, W. (2006) PTDOM: a schema-aware XML database system for MPEG-7 media descriptions. *Software: Practice and Experience*, **36** (8), 785–834.

[40] Tous, R. and Delgado, J. (2007) L7, an MPEG-7 query framework, Proceedings of the 3rd International Conference on Automated Production of Cross Media Content for Multi-channel Distribution, IEEE Computer Society, Washington, DC, pp. 256–263.

[41] Ma, Y., Fang, Z., Liu, J. *et al.* (2008) A content-based multimedia retrieval system base on MPEG-7 metadata schema, Proceedings of the 5th International Conference on Information Technology: New Generations, IEEE Computer Society, Las Vegas, Nevada, USA, pp. 1200–1201.

[42] Chu, Y., Chia, L.-T., and Bhowmick, S.S. (2005) SM3+: an XML database solution for the management of MPEG-7 descriptions, Proceedings of the 16th International Conference on Database and Expert Systems Applications (DEXA), Springer, Copenhagen, Denmark, pp. 134–144.

[43] Anh, B.-T. (2007) MPEG-7 scheme based embedded multimedia database management system, Proceedings of the 2007 International Conference on Convergence Information Technology, IEEE Computer Society, Gaithersburg, MD, pp. 1678–1686.

[44] Wust, O. and Celma, O. (2004) An MPEG-7 database system and application for content-based management and retrieval of music. ISMIR 2004, 5th International Conference on Music Information Retrieval, Barcelona, Spain, October 10–14, 2004, Proceedings 2004.

[45] Döller, M. and Kosch, H. (2008) The MPEG-7 Multimedia Database System (MPEG-7 MMDB). *Journal of Systems and Software*, **81** (9), 1559–1580.

[46] Kosch, H. and Döller, M. (2005) Approximating the selectivity of multimedia range queries. Proceedings of the IEEE International Conference on Multimedia and Expo, Amsterdam, The Netherlands.

[47] Hellerstein, J.M., Naughton, J.F., and Pfeffer, A. (1995) Generalized search trees for database systems. 21st International Conference of Very Large Databases VLDB, Zurich, Switzerland, pp. 562–573.

[48] Henrich, A. and Robbert, G. (2001) $POQL^{MM}$: a query language for structured multimedia documents. Proceedings 1st International Workshop on Multimedia Data and Document Engineering (MDDE'01), July 2001, pp. 17–26.

[49] Lui, P., Charkraborty, A., and Hsu, L.H. (2001) A logic approach for MPEG-7 XML document queries. Proceedings of the Extreme Markup Languages, Montreal, Canada.

[50] Dionisio, J.D.N. and Cardenas, A.F. (1996) MQuery: a visual query language for multimedia, time line and simulation data. *Journal of Visual Languages and Computing*, **7** (4), 377–401.

[51] Ingo Schmitt, T.H. and Schulz, N. (2005) WS-QBE: a QBE-like query language for complex multimedia queries. Proceedings of the 11th International Multi-media Modelling Conference (MMM), Melbourne, Australia, pp. 222–229.

[52] Clark, J. and DeRose, S. (1999) XML Path Language (XPath). W3C Recommendation, http://www.w3.org/TR/xpath (accessed April 2010).

[53] W3C (2007) XQuery 1.0: An XML Query Language. W3C, http://www.w3.org/TR/2007/REC-xquery-20070123/ (accessed April 2010).

[54] Xue, L., Li, C., Wu, Y., and Xiong, Z. (2006) VeXQuery: an XQuery extension for MPEG-7 vector-based feature query. Proceedings of the International Conference on Signal-image Technology and Internet–based Systems (IEEE/ACM SITIS'2006), Hammamet, Tunisia, pp. 176–185.

[55] Fatemi, N., Khaled, O.A., and Coray, G. (2003) An XQuery adaptation for MPEG-7 documents retrieval. Proceedings of the XML Conference and Exposition, Philadelphia, PA.

[56] Fatemi, N., Lalmas, M., and Rölleke, T. (2004) How to retrieve multimedia documents described by MPEG-7, Proceedings of the 2nd ACM SIGIR Semantic Web and Information Retrieval Workshop, ACM Press, New York, NY.

[57] Fatemi, N., Khaled, O.A., and Coray, G. (2003) An XQuery adaptation for MPEG-7 documents retrieval. XML Conference and Exposition, Philadelphia, PA, December 2003.

[58] Lui, P., Charkraborty, A., and Hsu, L.H. (2000) Path predicate calculus: towards a logic formalism for multimedia XML query language. Proceedings of the Extreme Markup Languages, Montreal, Canada.

[59] Furh, N. and Grossjohann, K. (2001) XIRQL: a query language for information retrieval in XML documents, Proceedings of the 24th ACM-SIGIR Conference on Research and Development in Information Retrieval, ACM Press, New Orleans, LA, pp. 172–180.

[60] Robie, J. (1999) *XQL (XML Query Language)*, http://www.ibiblio.org/xql/xql-proposal.html (accessed April 2010).

[61] Conforti, G., Ghelli, G., Albano, A. *et al.* (2002) The Query Language TQL. Proceedings of the 5th International Workshop on Web and Data Bases (WebDB02).

[62] Manola, F. and Miller, E. (2004) *RDF Primer*. W3C Recommendation, http://www.w3.org/TR/2004/REC-rdf-primer-20040210/ (accessed April 2010).

[63] Bonino, D., Corno, F., and Pellegrino, P. (2002) RQL: a declarative query language for RDF, Proceedings of the 11th International World Wide Web Conference (WWW 2002), ACM Press, Honolulu, HI, pp. 592–603.

[64] Hommeaux, E.P. and Seaborne, A. (2008) *SPARQL query language for RDF*, W3C Recommendation, http://www.w3.org/TR/rdf-sparql-query/.

[65] Döller, M., Tous, R., Gruhne, M. *et al.* (2008) The MPEG Query Format: on the way to unify the access to Multimedia Retrieval Systems. *IEEE Multimedia*, **15** (4), 82–95.

[66] Initiative, D.C.M. (2008) *Dublin Core Metadata Element Set – Version 1.1: Reference Description*, http://dublincore.org/documents/dces/ (accessed April 2010).

[67] Döller, M., Tous, R., Gruhne, M. *et al.* (2009) Semantic MPEG Query Format Validation and Processing, *IEEE Multimedia*, **16** (4), 22–33.

[68] Gruhne, M., Dunker, P., Tous, R., and Döller, M. (2008) Distributed cross-modal search with the MPEG query format, 9th International Workshop on Image Analysis for Multimedia Interactive Services, IEEE Computer Society, Klagenfurt, Austria, pp. 211–124.

[69] Döller, M., Bauer, K., Kosch, H., and Gruhne, M. (2008) Standardized multimedia retrieval based on web service technologies and the MPEG query format. *Journal of Digital Information*, **6** (4), 315–331.

[70] Veltkamp, R.C. and Tanase, M. (2001) Content-based Image Retrieval Systems: A Survey. *Tech. Rep. No. UU-CS-2000-34*. Department of Computing Science, Utrecht University, The Netherlands.

[71] Kosch, H. and Maier, P. (2009) Content-based image retrieval systems – reviewing and benchmarking. Proceedings of the 9th Workshop on Multimedia Metadata (WMM'09), Toulouse, France.

[72] Rodryguez-Martynez, M. and Roussopoulos, N. (2000) Mocha: a self-extensible database middleware system for distributed data sources. Proceedings of the 2000 ACM SIGMOD International Conference on Management of Data (SIGMOD00), Dallas, TX, pp. 213–224.

[73] Schmidt, H., Elsholz, J.-P., and Hauck, F.J. (2008) Instant-X: a component-based middleware architecture for a generic multimedia API, Proceedings of the ACM/IFIP/USENIX Middleware, (Leuven, Belgium), ACM, New York, NY, pp. 90–92.

[74] Lohse, M., Winter, F., Repplinger, M., and Slusallek, P. (2008) Network-integrated Multimedia Middleware (NMM), Proceedings of ACM Multimedia, IEEE Computer Society, Vancouver, Canada.

[75] ISO/IEC (2004) JTC1/SC29/WG11/N6835 MPEG Multimedia Middleware Requirements v.2.0, N6835, Palma de Mallorca, Spain, http://www.chiariglione.org/.

[76] MPEG (2008) ISO/IEC JTC1/SC29 WG11N9893 Requirements for MPEG eXtensible Middleware (MXM), Leonardo Chiariglione, Archamps, FR.

[77] Cao, Y., Jarke, M., Klamma, R. *et al.* (2009) Mobile access to MPEG-7 based multimedia services, MDM '09: Proceedings of the 2009 10th International Conference on Mobile Data Management: Systems, Services and Middleware, IEEE Computer Society, Washington, DC, pp. 102–111.

[78] Berretti, S., Bimbo, A.D., and Pala, P. (2003) Merging results of distributed image libraries. Proceedings of the 2003 International Conference on Multimedia and Expo (ICME03), Baltimore, Maryland, pp. 33–36.

[79] Stegmaier, F., Döller, M., Kosch, H. *et al.* (2010) AIR: architecture for interoperable retrieval on distributed and heterogeneous multimedia repositories. Proceedings of the 11th International Workshop on Image Analysis for Multimedia Interactive Services (WIAMIS), Desenzano del Garda, Italy, to appear.

[80] Brown, B., Chalmers, M., Bell, M. *et al.* (2005) Sharing the square: collaborative leisure in the city streets, Proceedings of the 9th conference on European Conference on Computer Supported Cooperative Work (ESCW), Springer, New York, NY, pp. 427–447.

[81] Walz, S.P., Ballagas, R., Borchers, J. *et al.* (2006) Cell spell-casting: designing a locative and gesture recognition multiplayer smartphone game for tourists, Proceedings of PERGAMES, 3rd International Workshop on Pervasive Gaming Applications at PERVASIVE, Springer, Dublin, Ireland.

[82] Föckler, P., Zeidler, T., Brombach, B. *et al.* (2005) Phoneguide: museum guidance supported by on-device object recognition on mobile phones, Proceedings of the 4th International Conference on Mobile and Ubiquitous Multimedia (MUM), ACM Press, New York, NY, pp. 3–10.

[83] Bruns, E., Brombach, B., Zeidler, T., and Bimber, O. (2007) Enabling mobile phones to support large-scale museum guidance. *IEEE MultiMedia*, **14** (2), 16–25.

[84] Jain, A.K., Duin, R.P.W., and Mao, J. (2000) Statistical pattern recognition: A review. *IEEE Transactions on Pattern Analysis and Machine Intelligence*, **22** (1), 4–37.

[85] Schwinger, W., Grün, C., Pröll, B. *et al.* (2005) Context-awareness in Mobile Tourism Guides – A Comprehensive Survey. *Tech. Rep.* Johannes Kepler Universität Linz, Austria.

[86] Döller, M., Köckerandl, G., Jans, S., and Limam, L. (2009) MoidEx: location-based mTourism system on mobile devices. Proceedings of International Conference on Multimedia Computing and Systems.

[87] Döller, M., Kosch, H., and Jun, J.H. (2006) Moides – mobile image description. Proceedings of 6th International Conference on Knowledge Management (I-KNOW 06).

[88] Li, Y. and Shapiro, L.G. (2002) Consistent line clusters for building recognition in CBIR, Proceedings of the 16th International Conference on Pattern Recognition (ICPR), IEEE Computer Society, Washington, DC, pp. 952–956.

[89] Sachinopoulou, A., Mäkelä, S.-M., Järvinen, S. *et al.* (2005) Personal video retrieval and browsing for mobile users. Multimedia on Mobile Devices, Proceedings of SPIE-IS&T Electronic Imaging, vol. 5684, pp. 219–230.

[90] Kamvar, M., Chiu, P., Wilcox, L. *et al.* (2004) MiniMedia surfer: browsing video segments on small displays, CHI '04: CHI '04 Extended Abstracts on Human Factors in Computing Systems, ACM, New York, NY, pp. 1371–1374.

[91] Cote, G., Erol, B., Gallant, M., and Kossentini, F. (1998) H.263+: video coding at low bit rates. *IEEE Transactions on Circuits and Systems for Video Technology*, **8**, 849–866.

[92] Döller, M., Mayer, T., Fong, K.L. *et al.* (2009) Standardized mobile multimedia query composer. *New Directions in Intelligent Interactive Multimedia Systems and Services – 2*, **226**, 87–101.

[93] Martinez, J.M., Koenen, R., and Pereira, F. (2002) MPEG-7. *IEEE Multimedia*, **9**, 78–87.

[94] Schulzrinne, H., Rao, A., and Lanphier, R. (1998) RFC 2326: real time streaming protocol (RTSP) April. Status: PROPOSED STANDARD.

[95] Burnett, I.S., Pereira, F., Van de Walle, R., and Koenen, R. (2006) The MPEG-21 Book, John Wiley and Sons, Ltd, Chichester.

[96] Andreou, G., Karpouzis, K., Maglogiannis, I., and KolliasAthens, S. (2006) MPEG-21 concepts for personalized consumption of heterogeneous multimedia, SMAP '06: Proceedings of the 1st International Workshop on Semantic Media Adaptation and Personalization, IEEE Computer Society, Washington, DC, pp. 141–145.

[97] Tseng, B., Lin, C.-Y., and Smith, J. (2004) Using MPEG-7 and MPEG-21 for personalizing video. *IEEE MultiMedia*, **11** (1), 42–53.

[98] Vlachogiannis, E., Gavalas, D., Anagnostopoulos, C., and Tsekouras, G. (2008) Towards iTV accessibility: the MPEG-21 case, PETRA '08: Proceedings of the 1st International Conference on PErvasive Technologies Related to Assistive Environments, ACM, New York, NY, pp. 1–6.

[99] Kosch, H. (2003) Distributed Multimedia Database Technologies Supported by MPEG-7 and MPEG-21, CRC Press, Boca Raton, FL, 248, ISBN: 0-849-31854-8.

[100] Manjunath, T.S.B.S. and Salembier, P. (2002) Introduction to MPEG-7: Multimedia Content Description Interface, Wiley, Chichester, England, ISBN: 978-0-471-48678-7.

14

Using MPEG Standards for Content-Based Indexing of Broadcast Television, Web, and Enterprise Content

David Gibbon, Zhu Liu, Andrea Basso, and Behzad Shahraray
Video and Multimedia Technologies and Services Research Department,
AT&T Labs – Research, NJ, USA

14.1 Background on Content-Based Indexing and Retrieval

MPEG-2 has been very successful in delivering high-quality video content to users. Its use in DVDs, Direct Broadcast Satellites (DBSs), cable, Digital Video Broadcast (DVB) systems as well as the recent US transition to digital TV using the Advanced Television Systems Committee (ATSC) specifications ensures that MPEG-2 will remain in use for many years given the large installed base of MPEG-2 decoders.

The emergence of IPTV systems, which promise to offer several hundred channels to consumers, has accelerated the deployment of H.264/MPEG-4 Advanced Video Coding (AVC) in set top applications, while it had already been gaining ground on the Internet and personal media player applications. IPTV as well as next generation IP-enabled cable and DBS set top boxes and televisions have motivated the establishment of home networks that allow users to view personal media on a wide range of consumer electronics devices. Widely adopted standards are essential for these systems and devices to function seamlessly, not only at the video codec and transport level, but also with respect to metadata for program descriptions so that users can find the content they want. MPEG standards play a key role in meeting this need not only for coding and transport, but also at the metadata level through embodiment in standards such as the Digital Living Network Alliance (DLNA), which adopts the Universal Plug and Play (UPnP) Forum's

The Handbook of MPEG Applications: Standards in Practice Edited by Marios C. Angelides and Harry Agius
© 2011 John Wiley & Sons, Ltd

[1] Digital Item Declaration Language-Lite (DIDL-Lite) built from elements defined by MPEG-21 [2]. Similarly, for broadcast television, MPEG-7 [3] and MPEG-21 elements are employed in standards such as European Telecommunications Standards Institute (ETSI) TV-Anytime (TVA), and the emerging Alliance for Telecommunications Industry Solutions (ATIS) Internet Protocol Television Interoperability Forum (IIF) specifications.

The capability of today's IPTV systems to deliver nearly unlimited content choices to users brings with it a challenge: users may become overwhelmed and frustrated as they attempt to find what they want to watch. To meet this challenge, MPEG-7 provides tools to represent user's content preferences as well as their usage history to support recommendation engines and content filtering systems. To increase the specificity and accuracy of these systems, it is advantageous to include as much detail in the program description as possible, beyond the typical bibliographic title, genre, and description tags found in an electronic program guide (EPG) or as represented by Dublin Core metadata. MPEG-7 allows for extremely detailed content descriptions, annotations, and can even represent low-level media features such as audio pitch. Populating these metadata elements with valuable semantic descriptions of the media can be a labor-intensive manual process, and while strides have been made in the area of automated metadata extraction, automated and efficient generation of reliable metadata remains an open research challenge.

Several specifications have been developed to address the need for content discovery, selection, and delivery for a range of applications. The following sections focus on the use of MPEG standards in television services and media sharing specifications for home networks. Next we discuss how content processing using MPEG standards for media and metadata representation can enable systems to provide better navigation and content selection mechanisms. Section 14.7 focuses on audio processing and representing results in MPEG-7.

The use of MPEG-7 and MPEG-21 for content personalization and other applications is addressed in [4, 5]. An introduction to MPEG-21 with an in-depth treatment of several aspects of the specification including the notion of a digital item, dealing with intellectual property and its use (specifically via intellectual property management and protection (IPMP), and rights expression language (REL)) as well as content adaptation is given in [6]. Several academic and industrial research groups have developed MPEG-7 annotation tools that operate on video and audio media. A good survey is available in [7]. C++ tools for interfacing to MPEG-7 XML are available, for instance, [8, 9] list several research and development projects using MPEG-7 and their MPEG-7 library in particular. On-line audio feature extraction and representation of results in MPEG-7 is available [10]. This architecture is an interesting model for using HTTP protocols to exchange MPEG media and content descriptions.

14.2 MPEG-7 and MPEG-21 in ETSI TV-Anytime

The goal of the ETSI TVA is to provide specifications for interoperability of services and consumer devices for content referencing, content description, and the rightful use of recorded television content [11]. TVA not only defines elements that represent the content referencing identifier (CRID), but also uses metadata elements defined by MPEG-7 for other purposes such as content description and user preferences for content selection that relate to the scope defined by the objectives of the specification. In many cases, base MPEG-7 types are extended to support TVA requirements. It should be noted that MPEG-7 includes many other elements and description schemes that support a range of applications with broader scope than TVA.

Phase 2 of TVA [12] extends Phase 1 to support content management and extended user information and usage context data models. For example, the "UserInformationType" defined by MPEG-7 and incorporated into TVA Phase 1 is extended to include "BiographicInformation" and "AccessibilityInformation" data types. These allow for services to be customized based on the user's language, age, and so on, and serve to make video services accessible to users with auditory or visual impairments. In addition, the "UsageEnvironmentType" can be used to convey the natural environment under which the content was consumed using a TVA Phase 2 defined type and the network conditions represented using the MPEG-21 "NetworkCharacteristicBase" type. Device or terminal information makes use of the MPEG-21 defined DisplayCapability and CodecCapability data types.

In summary, we can see how MPEG standards have been used as building blocks within the ETSI TVA specifications. This model has been followed in other cases as well, such as in the ATIS/IIF specifications, which are described in the next section.

14.3   MPEG-7 and MPEG-21 in ATIS IPTV Specifications

The ATIS/IIF is developing a suite of specifications to promote interoperability among telecommunications service providers, content providers, equipment vendors, and consumer electronics manufactures for delivery of next-generation television services. Specific service feature requirements are supported by high-level and detailed architecture specifications with well-defined logical domains including the IPTV service provider domain, the network provider domain, the content provider domain, and the consumer domain. Exchange of information among service elements across domain boundaries and within domains is achieved using specified transactions involving data models articulated via XML schemas.

The metadata for the consumer domain is specified by the Terminal Metadata document [13] and its primary model is based on the physical entities in the domain consisting of devices capable of receiving and rendering IPTV services as well as the users of those devices and services. This is a broad scope that encompasses a range of service requirements and implies the need to express device capabilities and user preferences for service consumption. Other ATIS/IIF metadata specifications cover device attachment, service discovery, EPG, and emergency alerting aspects of the IPTV service [14].

Figure 14.1 shows the ATIS/IIF Terminal Metadata data model for an IPTV user as an XML schema fragment. Here, the namespaces are as follows: "cons" – ATIS/IIF Terminal metadata for the consumer domain, "gt" – ATIS/IIF Global Types, "tva2" – TVA Phase II, "mpeg7" – MPEG-7. It can be seen that types such as "UserIdentifier" and "BrowsingPreferences" are taken directly from MPEG-7, while "cons" types such as "FilteringAndSearchPreferences" are related to their MPEG-7 namesakes but are extended for this application (in this case, to meet North American content rating requirements involving geographic regions).

Delving further into one particular element, namely, the "UserInformation" table of TVA, it can be seen from Figure 14.2 how it is possible for information about users'

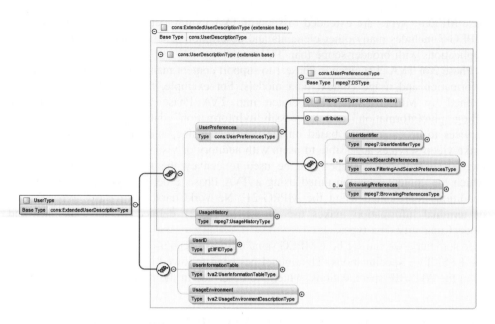

Figure 14.1 ATIS/IIF User metadata is related to TVA, MPEG-7 and 21.

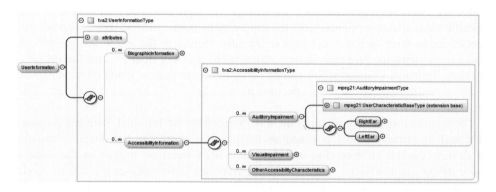

Figure 14.2 MPEG metadata related to creating accessible services.

impairments to be represented in MPEG-21 data types so that this data can be used to make content navigation and consumption more accessible to a wider audience. It should be pointed out that most of the elements in these data models are optional, and that any exchange or storage of personal information would be at the discretion of the user.

Moving beyond users, the other class of metadata in the ATIS/IIF consumer domain relates to devices. In fact, it is not required that users identify themselves prior to consuming IPTV services (as is the current paradigm with TV watching); therefore, consumers may simply specify their content preferences on the terminal device such as a set top box or firmware client integrated into a flat panel TV. This would be useful, for example, for preventing metadata and content intended for mature audiences from appearing on a user's family room TV. The IIF specification allows for the use of elements such as MPEG-7 preferences for filtering and search to apply to a device or set of devices. Furthermore, device capabilities, device settings, and DVR scheduling requests, as well as metadata about recorded programs can be expressed and exchanged to simplify service configuration and enable new services.

These examples demonstrate how MPEG-7, MPEG-21, TVA, and ATIS/IIF are harmonized so that, for instance, the MPEG-defined description schemes can be used by content creators with the assurance that these encodings will be supported to at least some measure by a broad range of television services. IPTV services require home networking, which enables new capabilities for users such as personal media sharing among connected devices. In the next section, we show how MPEG standards play a role in this area as well.

14.4 MEPG-21 in the Digital Living Network Alliance (DLNA)

The DLNA was created in response to a need within the consumer market for a common set of design guidelines for the interoperability of content-based services and networked devices in the home. The DLNA Home Networked Device Interoperability Guidelines is a combined effort that involves over 100 Consumer Electronics and PC and Mobile Device companies. It provides a long-term architectural view, as well as specific guidance for IP-networked devices, applications, and media services in the home.

The DLNA interoperability guidelines were defined in less than a year thanks to the pioneering work of the UPnP Forum, which was established in 1999 with the mission to ensure interoperability between networked IP devices. Specifications such as HTTP, HTML, XML, and SOAP provided UPnP the infrastructure to define basic key services such as device discovery, device and services description, control, and presentation. One of the most significant UPnP efforts was the UPnP AV specification. It became the basis for DLNA, which was formed in 2003 with the charter of facilitating the development of interoperable digital media devices for the home.

The DLNA Content Directory Service provides a mechanism for each DLNA-enabled networked content server to provide unified content directory information to any DLNA device. This service can be used to advertise various forms of content including MP3 audio, images, video, as well as EPG information for live or stored TV shows. Given the flexibility of the representation, nearly any type and any kind of mix of content can be listed via the Content Directory Service. The metadata returned by the Content Directory Service includes properties such as name, artist, creation date, size, and so on. In addition, the metadata also indicates for every piece of content listed the transfer protocols and media formats that are supported. This information is used by the Control Point to determine if a given Media Renderer is capable of rendering the content in its current format or if some type of transcoding is required. Content Directory Services are represented by means of a "lite" version of the MPEG-21 DIDL called DIDL-Lite [15].

DIDL is part of the MPEG-21 multimedia framework and defines a W3C XML Schema that provides broad flexibility and extensibility for object representation. In DIDL-lite, a digital item consists of a combination of resources (video, audio, tracks . . .), metadata, and relations among such resources. This representation is very flexible: For example, to represent a content source the same schema can be used and is able to cover all the relevant metadata for a single radio station.

Box 14.1 DLNA DIDL-Lite item with UPnP and Dublin Core metadata elements

```
<DIDL-Lite xmlns="urn:schemas-upnp-org:metadata-1-0/DIDL-Lite"
xmlns:dc="http://purl.org/dc/elements/1.1/" xmlns:upnp="urn:schemas-upnp-
org:metadata-1-0/upnp">
    <item>
        <upnp:class>object.item.audioItem.audioBroadcast</upnp:class>
        <dc:creator>Bill Smith</dc:creator>
        <dc:title>Internet Radio</dc:title>
        <upnp:genre>Rock</upnp:genre>
        <dc:description>Rock for anytime of the day</dc:description>
        <upnp:region>US - Northern California</upnp:region>
        <dc:language>English</dc:language>
        <dc:relation>http://www.host.com</dc:relation>
        <upnp:radioBand>Internet</upnp:radioBand>
        <res protocolInfo="http-get:*:audio/mpegurl:*"
bitrate="16384">http://www.host.com/assets/high_quality.m3u</res>
        <res protocolInfo="http-get:*:audio/mpegurl:*"
bitrate="8192">http://www.host.com/assets/good_qualtity.m3u</res>
    </item>
</DIDL-Lite>
```

Box 14.1 shows an item description for an internet radio station in the DIDL-Lite format (adapted from [16]). As can be seen, the UPnP and Dublin Core (dc) metadata elements are incorporated as appropriate through the use of XML namespaces.

DIDL is used whenever metadata is exchanged between DLNA media server and DLNA control point. For example if a DLNA control point needs to browse or to search via a DLNA Content Directory Service, the response will be provided as a DIDL XML document.

In addition, resources that are managed by a DLNA media server are stored in a logical hierarchy that it is represented by means of a DIDL class hierarchy, which is characterized by simple inheritance. The root class is Object. Each class can contain optional and required properties. Properties are inherited from a class to its subclasses. If properties have multiple values, they are serialized as XML elements, otherwise XML attributes are used. Object allows only two subclasses: Item and Container. A Container may contain Items or another Container. Further classes have to extend either Item or Container elements. DIDL instances are organized in a logical hierarchy, since each instance has to reference to a parent container using property "parentID". For example, MusicTrack, PlaylistItem, and Movie are Items. Album, Genre, and PlaylistContainer are Container elements. Class hierarchy can be extended by self-defined classes.

14.5 Content Analysis for MPEG-7 Metadata Generation

Most of the content descriptions that we have been considering above are high level and refer to the content as a whole. To obtain more detailed content descriptions, researchers have been developing systems for automated media analysis, and have employed MPEG-7 to represent the attributes extracted by this analysis. For example, Kim *et al.* describe a multimedia mining system using MPEG-7 [17]. Automated metadata extraction involves operating on video and audio content to derive low-level features, followed by higher-level processing to derive semantic information based on the media features. Given the large amount of data required to represent high-quality video, attention must be paid to data reduction, and to optimizing data movement, storage, and indexing. Applications ranging from broadcast television archiving to enterprise content management differ widely in their feature requirements, but share a basic data flow paradigm where content is acquired, analyzed, and archived. Some systems for broadcast monitoring also include an event generation or alerting capability.

Figure 14.3 depicts a number of metadata, video encoding, and transport formats used in several typical applications. As the figure indicates, MPEG standards play a major role in these applications. In video production, digital asset management (DAM) systems are used, and video is typically maintained in a mezzanine, or lightly compressed format such as JPEG 2000 to support a range of distribution options. For video on demand, the CableLabs Asset Distribution Interface (ADI) specification is typically used for managing and describing the content, which is often in MPEG-2 format. Over-the-air (OTA) broadcasts in North America use the ATSC specifications, which include the Program and System Information Protocol (PSIP) and MPEG-2 video and audio carried in multiprogram transport streams (MPTS) to enable multiple virtual channels in a single RF channel. Some IPTV systems use proprietary formats for EPG such as Microsoft's Global Listings Format (GLF) and use H.264 in an MPEG-2 single program transport

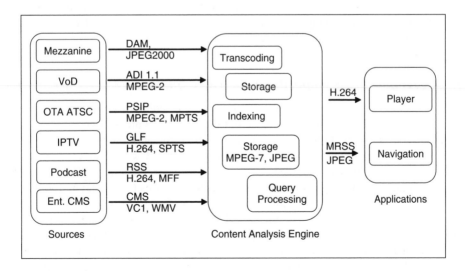

Figure 14.3 Use of MPEG standards in content analysis and retrieval systems.

stream (SPTS) that facilitates delivery and synchronization of the elementary streams. Internet content in the form of Podcasts is encoded in H.264 (MPEG-4 AVC) and stored in the MPEG file format. Really Simple Syndication (RSS) metadata with namespace extensions describes the media and manages distribution. In the enterprise domain, content management systems (CMSs) are often used to handle publishing, access, and description of videos that may be encoded in any of various formats such as VC1 or H.264.

These content sources are analyzed, and the descriptions are augmented with the results maintained in XML, ideally in MPEG-7 for maximum interoperability. For high-level metadata, in most cases, MPEG-7 is more expressive than the source metadata formats so that transformation does not result in information loss. However, systems may choose to maintain a copy of the source content description for preservation and archiving. On the delivery side, users interact with large content archives through navigation using implicit or explicit queries. The figure shows H.264 for content, MediaRSS for metadata and JPEG for thumbnails, which is common for internet applications; however, for other applications, different encodings may be used.

14.6   Representing Content Analysis Results Using MPEG-7

14.6.1   Temporal Decompositions

Much of the role of automated content analysis can be characterized as generating semantics related to segments of a video program, such as video shots, story boundaries, speaker changes derived from the audio. MPEG-7 contains rich tools for describing segmentations or decompositions with semantics that allow for overlapping decompositions or decompositions with gaps. The precision with which time is represented is specifiable. Applications that rely on automated content analysis for their metadata often use millisecond time stamps to ease application development, even though frame accurate representations are available within MPEG-7 and are more accurate for some of the media processing operations. In addition to the temporal decompositions, spatial decompositions are used to describe regions of images and video.

14.6.2   Temporal Decompositions for Video Shots

MPEG-7 defines a complex hierarchy for representing edited video content at various levels of segmentation using the "AnalyticEditedVideoSegment" description scheme. Fine-grained structure including subshots, and inserted image regions such as picture-in-picture can be detected and included in the description, but Box 14.2 shows a single-level nonoverlapping, nongapped segmentation indicating shot transitions. (Note that long lines of text have been wrapped in this and subsequent figures for display purposes only.) The segmentation refers to the entire shot, while the "GlobalTransition" indicates the type of transition such as a cut (BeginNormalShot) or gradual (e.g., FadeIn) transition.

This particular example shows what was used for evaluation of shot boundary detection algorithms against manually annotated video and follows certain specifications imposed by TRECVID [18] at the National Institute of Standards and Technologies (NIST). Here MPEG-7 is also used for representing the video segmentation, but it is interesting to

Box 14.2 MPEG-7 description of detected video shot transitions

```
<Description xsi:type="ContentEntityType">
    <MultimediaContent xsi:type="AnalyticEditedVideoType">
      <AnalyticEditedVideo xsi:type="EditedVideoType">
        <MediaLocator>
         <MediaUri>
         http://video.research.att.com/assets/NewsatNoon/2009/07/
         15/video.mp4
         </MediaUri>
        </MediaLocator>
        <MediaTime>
          <MediaRelIncrTimePoint mediaTimeBase="../
          MediaLocator[1]" mediaTimeUnit="PT1N1000F">0
          </MediaRelIncrTimePoint>
          <MediaIncrDuration>2097946</MediaIncrDuration>
        </MediaTime>
        <AnalyticEditingTemporalDecomposition gap="false"
         overlap="false" mediaTimeBase="../MediaLocator[1]"
         mediaTimeUnit="PT1N1000F">
          <GlobalTransition>
              <TextAnnotation>
                <StructuredAnnotation><WhatAction>
                  <Name>FadeIn</Name>
                </WhatAction></StructuredAnnotation>
              </TextAnnotation>
          </GlobalTransition>
          <Shot id="v24">
            <Relation type="urn:mpeg:mpeg7:cs:SemanticRelationCS:
            2001:key" target="http://thumnailserver.att.com/
            assets/NewsatNoon/2009/07/15/img24.jpg">
            </Relation>
            <MediaTime>
              <MediaRelIncrTimePoint>86353
              </MediaRelIncrTimePoint>
            </MediaTime>
          </Shot>
          <GlobalTransition>
              <TextAnnotation> <StructuredAnnotation>
              <WhatAction>
                <Name>BeginNormalShot</Name>
              </WhatAction> </StructuredAnnotation>
              </TextAnnotation>
          </GlobalTransition>
        </AnalyticEditingTemporalDecomposition>
      </AnalyticEditedVideo>
   </MultimediaContent>
</Description>
```

contrast this representation (Box 14.3) with that of Box 14.2. In this case, a second level of `TemporalDecomposition` is used to indicate the location of a representative key frame (RKF) within the shot. Also, the more generic `MultimediaContent` type of `VideoType` is used instead of the more specific `AnalyticEditedVideoType`. This latter type is more appropriate in this case since it is consistent with the MPEG definition "the description is made a posteriori automatically or manually based on the final video content" [2].

Box 14.3 Alternative representation of video segmentation

```
<Description xsi:type="ContentEntityType">
        <MultimediaContent xsi:type="VideoType">
            <Video id="TRECVID2003_1">
                <MediaLocator>
                  <MediaUri>19980104_ABC.mpg</MediaUri>
                </MediaLocator>
                <MediaTime>
                    <MediaTimePoint>
                    T00:00:00:0F30000</MediaTimePoint>
                    <MediaDuration>
                    PT28M28S16205N30000F</MediaDuration>
                </MediaTime>
                <TemporalDecomposition gap="false"
                overlap="false">
                    <VideoSegment id="shot1_1">
                      <MediaTime>
                        <MediaTimePoint>T00:00:00:0F30000
                        </MediaTimePoint>
                        <MediaDuration>
                        PT8S21261N30000F</MediaDuration>
                      </MediaTime>
                      <TemporalDecomposition>
                          <VideoSegment id="shot1_1_RKF">
                              <MediaTime>
                                <MediaTimePoint>
                                T00:00:04:14134F30000
                                </MediaTimePoint>
                              </MediaTime>
                          </VideoSegment>
                      </TemporalDecomposition>
                    </VideoSegment>
                    <!-- more VideoSegment elements here -->
                </TemporalDecomposition>
            </Video>
        </MultimediaContent>
</Description>
```

14.6.3 Spatial Decompositions

MPEG-7 allows for regions of interest in images and video to be referenced via a spatial decomposition. For example, face detection data may be represented using `SpatialDecompostion/StillRegion/SpatialLocator` as shown in Box 14.4 where a polygonal region containing the face is represented in pixel coordinates. The frame is indicated by a MediaUri reference to a JPEG encoded image corresponding to a temporal offset relative to the beginning of the video.

Box 14.4 MPEG-7 description of an image from a video sequence with two regions containing faces

```
<Description xsi:type="ContentEntityType">
    <MultimediaContent xsi:type="ImageType">
        <Image>
          <MediaLocator>
            <MediaUri>
              http://thumbnailserver.att.com/assets/NewsatNoon/
              2009/07/15/img4.jpg
            </MediaUri>
          </MediaLocator>
          <TextAnnotation>
            <StructuredAnnotation>
              <WhatObject>
                <Name>face</Name>
              </WhatObject>
            </StructuredAnnotation>
          </TextAnnotation>
          <MediaRelIncrTimePoint>154621</MediaRelIncrTimePoint>
          <SpatialDecomposition>
            <StillRegion id="v33i0">
              <SpatialLocator>
                <Polygon>
                  <Coords mpeg7:dim="4 1">101 49 82 82</Coords>
                </Polygon>
              </SpatialLocator>
            </StillRegion>
            <StillRegion id="v33i1">
              <SpatialLocator>
                <Polygon>
                  <Coords mpeg7:dim="4 1">202 171 54 54</Coords>
                </Polygon>
              </SpatialLocator>
            </StillRegion>
          </SpatialDecomposition>
        </Image>
    </MultimediaContent>
</Description>
```

14.6.4   Textual Content

Closed captions, aligned transcripts, and speech recognition results may also be represented in MPEG-7. In Box 14.5, we have chosen to use the `SummaryDescription-Type` since it is compact and easily readable. The ATSC closed captions for the beginning of a broadcast news program are shown.

Box 14.5 MPEG-7 representation of processed closed captions

```
<Description xsi:type="SummaryDescriptionType">
    <Summarization>
      <Summary xsi:type="SequentialSummaryType">
        <TextualSummaryComponent>
          <FreeText>Thanks for joining us.</FreeText>
          <SyncTime>
            <MediaRelIncrTimePoint>95943</MediaRelIncrTimePoint>
            <MediaIncrDuration>3474</MediaIncrDuration>
          </SyncTime>
        </TextualSummaryComponent>
        <TextualSummaryComponent>
          <FreeText>We begin with breaking news.</FreeText>
          <SyncTime>
            <MediaRelIncrTimePoint>99417</MediaRelIncrTimePoint>
            <MediaIncrDuration>1052</MediaIncrDuration>
          </SyncTime>
        </TextualSummaryComponent>
        <TextualSummaryComponent>
          <FreeText>
              Police made an arrest outside a restaurant.
          </FreeText>
          <SyncTime>
            <MediaRelIncrTimePoint>100470</MediaRelIncrTimePoint>
            <MediaIncrDuration>4400</MediaIncrDuration>
          </SyncTime>
        </TextualSummaryComponent>
        <TextualSummaryComponent>
          <FreeText>Our street reporter has details.</FreeText>
          <SyncTime>
            <MediaRelIncrTimePoint>109670</MediaRelIncrTimePoint>
            <MediaIncrDuration>600</MediaIncrDuration>
          </SyncTime>
        </TextualSummaryComponent>
      </Summary>
    </Summarization>
  </Description>
```

Additional metadata may be extracted through the application of a number of audio processing algorithms, such as speaker segmentation, speaker identification, voice activity detection, and used to create a richer MPEG-7 representation of the content. Box 14.6 shows a representation of detected speaker boundaries using Audio TemporalDecomposition elements. Segments are annotated to indicate if the speaker plays a major role in the program such as an anchorperson.

Box 14.6 MPEG-7 audio temporal decomposition indicating speaker segmentation

```
<Description xsi:type="ContentEntityType">
  <MultimediaContent xsi:type="AudioType">
    <Audio>
      <MediaTime>
        <MediaRelIncrTimePoint>0</MediaRelIncrTimePoint>
        <MediaIncrDuration>2097946</MediaIncrDuration>
      </MediaTime>
      <TemporalDecomposition overlap="false">
        <AudioSegment>
          <TextAnnotation>
            <FreeTextAnnotation>Speaker 1</FreeTextAnnotation>
            <FreeTextAnnotation>Major Speaker
</FreeTextAnnotation>
          </TextAnnotation>
          <MediaTime>
            <MediaRelIncrTimePoint>99426
</MediaRelIncrTimePoint>
            <MediaIncrDuration>7280</MediaIncrDuration>
          </MediaTime>
        </AudioSegment>
        <AudioSegment>
          <TextAnnotation>
            <FreeTextAnnotation>Speaker 0</FreeTextAnnotation>
          </TextAnnotation>
          <MediaTime>
            <MediaRelIncrTimePoint>106856
</MediaRelIncrTimePoint>
            <MediaIncrDuration>48160</MediaIncrDuration>
          </MediaTime>
        </AudioSegment>
      </TemporalDecomposition>
    </Audio>
  </MultimediaContent>
</Description>
```

In the following section, we explore audio feature representation in MPEG-7 in greater detail to give the reader an introduction to the expressive power provided by the specification.

14.7 Extraction of Audio Features and Representation in MPEG-7

14.7.1 Brief Introduction to MPEG-7 Audio

MPEG-7 audio provides structures, in conjunction with the part of the standard that is related to the Multimedia Description Schemes, for describing audio content. The set of standards in MPEG 7 audio descriptors makes it possible to develop content retrieval tools, and interoperable systems that are able to access diverse audio archives in a unified way. These descriptors are also useful to content creators for content editing, and for content distributors in selecting and filtering purposes. Some typical applications of MPEG-7 audio include large-scale audio content (e.g., radio, TV broadcast, movie, music) archives and retrieval, audio content distribution, education, and surveillance. The MPEG-7 audio standard comprises a set of descriptors that can be divided roughly into two classes: low-level audio descriptors (LLDs) and high-level audio description tools.

The LLDs include a set of simple and low-complexity audio features that can be used in a variety of applications. The foundation layer of the standard consists of 18 generic LLDs – 1 silence descriptor and 17 temporal and spectral LLDs in the following six groups:

- Basic Audio Descriptors include the Audio Waveform (AWF) Descriptor, which describes the audio waveform envelope, and the Audio Power (AP) Descriptor, which depicts the temporally smoothed instantaneous power.
- Basic Spectral Descriptors are derived from a single time-frequency analysis of audio signal. Among this group are the Audio Spectrum Envelope (ASE) Descriptor, which is a log-frequency spectrum; the Audio Spectrum Centroid (ASC) Descriptor, which describes the center of gravity of the log-frequency power spectrum; the Audio Spectrum Spread (ASS) Descriptor, which represents the second moment of thez log-frequency power spectrum; and the Audio Spectrum Flatness (ASF) Descriptor, which indicates the flatness of the spectrum within a number of frequency bands.
- Signal Parameter Descriptors consist of two descriptors. the Audio Fundamental Frequency (AFF) descriptor describes the fundamental frequency of an audio signal, and the Audio Harmonicity (AH) Descriptor represents the harmonicity of a signal.
- There are two Descriptors in Timbral Temporal Descriptors group. The Log Attack Time (LAT) Descriptor characterizes the attack of a sound, and the Temporal Centroid (TC) Descriptor represents where in time the energy of a signal is focused.
- Timbral Spectral Descriptors have five components. The Harmonic Spectral Centroid (HSC) Descriptor is the power-weighted average of the frequency of the bins in the linear power spectrum, the Harmonic Spectral Deviation (HSD) Descriptor indicates the spectral deviation of log-amplitude components from a global spectral envelop, the Harmonic Spectral Spread (HSS) Descriptor represents the amplitude-weighted standard deviation of the harmonic peaks of the spectrum, and finally the Harmonic Spectral Variation (HSV) Descriptor is the normalized correlation between the amplitude of the harmonic peaks between two subsequent time-slices of the signal.

- The last group of low-level descriptors is Spectral Basis Descriptors. It includes the Audio Spectrum Basis (ASB) Descriptor, which is a series of basis functions that are derived from the singular value decomposition of a normalized power spectrum, and the Audio Spectrum Projection (ASP) Descriptor, which represents low-dimensional features of a spectrum after projection upon a reduced rank basis.

High-level audio description tools are specialized for domain-specific applications. There are five sets of high-level tools that roughly correspond to the application areas that are integrated in the standard.

- Audio Signature Description Scheme statistically summarizes the Spectral Flatness Descriptor as a condensed representation of an audio signal. It provides a unique content identifier for robust automatic identification of audio signals.
- Musical Instrument Timbre Description Tools describe perceptual features of instrument sounds with a reduced set of Descriptors. They are related to notions such as "attack", "brightness", and "richness" of a sound.
- Melody Description Tools include a rich representation for monophonic melodic information to facilitate efficient, robust, and expressive melodic similarity matching. The scheme includes a Melody Contour Description Scheme for extremely terse and efficient melody contour representation, and a Melody Sequence Description Scheme for a more verbose, complete, and expressive melody representation.
- General Sound Recognition and Indexing Description Tools are a collection of tools for indexing and categorization of general sounds, with immediate application to sound effects.
- Spoken Content Description Tools allow detailed description of words spoken within an audio stream.

14.7.2 Content Processing Using MPEG-7 Audio

In this section, we present two content processing applications within the MPEG-7 audio framework. They are audio scene description and speaker annotation.

Audio scenes are segments with homogeneous content in an audio stream. Segmenting the audio into individual scenes serves many purposes including the extraction of the content structure, content indexing and search, and so on. For example, broadcast news programs generally consist of two different audio scenes: news reporting and commercials. Discriminating these two audio scenes is useful for indexing news content and compiling personalized playlists for the end user. Huang, Liu, and Wang [19] studied the problem of classifying TV broadcast into five different categories: news reporting, commercial, weather forecast, basketball game, and football game. Audio is first segmented into overlapped frames that are 20 ms long. Adjacent frames are then grouped into clips that are about 2 s long based on energy. Relying on a set of 14 audio features extracted for each audio clip, a hidden Markov model (HMM) classifier achieves an accuracy of 84.5%. In the following, we briefly describe the audio features, which can be categorized in four groups: volume-based, zero crossing rate (ZCR)-based, pitch-based, and frequency-based.

Volume-based features:

- The volume standard deviation (VSTD) is the standard deviation of the volume over a clip, normalized by the maximum volume in the clip.
- The volume dynamic range (VDR) is defined as $(max(v) - min(v))/max(v)$, where $min(v)$ and $max(v)$ are the minimum and maximum volume within an audio clip.
- The volume undulation (VU) is the accumulation of the difference of neighboring peaks and valleys of the volume contour within a clip.
- The nonsilence ratio (NSR) is the ratio of the number of nonsilent frames to the total number of frames in a clip.
- The 4 Hz modulation energy (4ME) is the normalized frequency component of volume contour in the neighborhood of 4 Hz.

ZCR-based features:

- The standard deviation of zero crossing rate (ZSTD) is the standard deviation of ZCR within a clip.

Pitch-based features:

- The standard deviation of pitch (PSTD) is the standard deviation of pitch over a clip.
- The smooth pitch ratio (SPR) is the percentage of frames in a clip that have similar pitch as the previous frames.
- The nonpitch ratio (NPR) is the percentage of frames without pitch.

Frequency-based features:

- The frequency centroid (FC) is the energy weighted frequency centroid of all frames within a clip.
- The frequency bandwidth (BW) is the energy weighted frequency bandwidth of all frames within a clip.
- The energy ratio of subband (ERSB) is the ratios of the energy in frequency subband. Three ERSB are computed for subbands 0–630 Hz, 630–1720 Hz, and 1720–4400 Hz.

Interested readers can find more details about these features in [17].

Speaker segmentation and identification is important for many audio applications. For example, speaker adaptation methods can significantly improve the accuracy of speech recognition, and speaker information provides useful cues for indexing audio content.

Gibbon *et al.* reported an iterative approach for speaker segmentation and clustering algorithm in [20]. They use Mel-frequency cepstral coefficients (MFCC) and Gaussian mixture model (GMM) to model the acoustic characteristics of speakers. The Bayesian information criteria (BIC) are adopted to locate the speaker boundaries and determine the number of speakers. The kernel proceeds iteratively, where during each iteration, speaker boundaries and speaker models are refined, allowing speaker segment splitting and merging at the same time. On the basis of the low-level speaker clustering information, higher level semantics can be derived. For example, by measuring the total duration and the temporal distribution of the speech of each speaker, the major speakers (e.g., the host of a news program or the organizer of a conference meeting) can be easily identified.

The authors also built a speaker segmentation evaluation tool, shown in Figure 14.4. This figure shows the result of speaker segmentation on 10 min (600 s) of audio recording from a television broadcast news program. Each row represents 2 min of audio. Each row

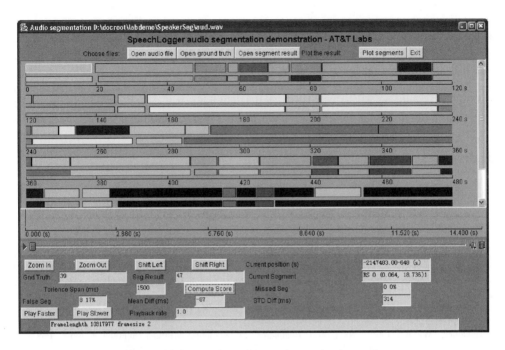

Figure 14.4   Speaker segmentation evaluation tool.

has two layers. The top layer shows the output of the speaker segmentation algorithm, and the bottom layer is the manually labeled ground truth. Each color (or grayscale) represents a different speaker. As the figure indicates, the results of the speaker segmentation algorithm are consistent with the ground truth in most cases. The differences between the two are caused by conditions such as the two speakers overlapping, or the presence of noise or background music. The bottom part of the interface displays the summary of the speaker segmentation results, including the number of detected segments, the probability of miss, the probability of false alarm, and so on.

Eisenberg, Batke *et al*. built two interesting audio query systems using MPEG-7 descriptors. One is query by tapping [21], and the other is query by humming [22]. In the query by tapping system, the user can formulate a query by tapping the melody line's rhythm on a MIDI keyboard or an e-drum. The music search relies on the MPEG-7 Beat Description Scheme. In the query by humming system, a hummed audio input is taken by a microphone, and an MPEG-7 AFF descriptor is extracted. The transcription module segments the input stream (AFF) into single notes, and forms an MPEG-7 Melody Contour Descriptor. Audio search is then carried out by comparing the Melody Contour Descriptor of the query to those in the music database.

14.8   Summary

The influence of the MPEG-7 and MPEG-21 metadata standards for content description and management is widespread in a range of applications from home networking to television services. Other standards bodies and industry forums have adopted components from the MPEG description languages to meet their specific application needs. Many research groups have created tools and systems that extract features, allow for annotation, and provide programmer's interfaces to MPEG-7 and MPEG-21 XML. Moving forward, we have begun to see these specifications used in conjunction with automated media processing systems to create standardized, detailed content descriptions with the promise of allowing users greater control over their content consumption experience.

References

[1] UPnP Forum (2006) ContentDirectory:2 Service Template Version 1.01 For UPnP™ Version 1.0. Approved Standard, May 31, 2006.
[2] ISO/IEC (2001) International Standard 21000-2:2001. *Information technology – Multimedia Framework (MPEG-21) – Part 2: Digital Item Declaration*, Switzerland.
[3] ISO/IEC (2003) International Standard 1538-5:2003. *Information Technology – Multimedia Content Description Interface – Part 5: Multimedia Description Schemes*, Switzerland.
[4] Sofokleous, A. and Angelides, M. (2008) Multimedia Content Personalisation on mobile devices using MPEG 7 and MPEG 21, *Encyclopedia of Multimedia*, 2nd edn (ed. B. Furht), Springer, New York.
[5] Agius, H. (2008) MPEG-7 applications, *Encyclopedia of Multimedia*, 2nd edn (ed. B. Furht), Springer, New York.
[6] Burnett, I., Pereira, F., Can de Walle, R. and Koenen, R. (2006) *The MPEG-21 Book*, John Wiley & Sons, Ltd, Chichester.
[7] Doller, M. and Lefin, N. (2007) Evaluation of available MPEG-7 annotation tools. Proceedings of the I-MEDIA '07 and I-SEMANTICS '07, September 5–7, 2007, Graz, Austria. Online, http://i-know.tugraz.at/wp-content/uploads/2008/11/3_evaluation-of-available-mpeg-7-annotation-tools.pdf (accessed 2010).
[8] Fürntratt, H., Neuschmied, H. and Bailer, W. (2009) *MPEG-7 Library – MPEG-7 C++ API Implementation*. Online, http://iiss039.joanneum.at/cms/fileadmin/mpeg7/files/Mp7Jrs2.4.1.pdf (accessed 2010).
[9] Joanneum Research – Institute of Information Systems & Information Management (2009) *MPEG-7: References*. Online, http://iiss039.joanneum.at/cms/index.php?id=194 (accessed 2010).
[10] The Technical University of Berlin (2003) *TU-Berlin: MPEG-7 Audio Analyzer – Low Level Descriptors (LLD) Extractor*. Online, http://mpeg7lld.nue.tu-berlin.de/ (accessed 2010).
[11] ETSI (2007) 102 822-3-1 V1.4.1. *Broadcast and On-line Services: Search, Select and Rightful Use of Content on Personal Storage Systems ("TV-Anytime"); Part 3: Metadata; Sub-part 1: Phase 1 – Metadata schemas," Technical Specification*, European Telecommunications Standards Institute (ETSI), Sophia Antipolis Cedex, France.
[12] ETSI (2006) 102 822-3-3 V1.2.1. *Broadcast and On-line Services: Search, Select and Rightful Use of Content on Personal Storage Systems ("TV-Anytime"); Part 3: Metadata, Sub-part 3: Phase 2 – Extended Metadata Schema," Technical Specification*, European Telecommunications Standards Institute (ETSI), Sophia Antipolis Cedex, France.
[13] ATIS (2009) International Standard ATIS-0800029. *IPTV Terminal Metadata Specification*, Alliance for Telecommunications Industry Solutions (ATIS), Washington, DC.
[14] ATIS (2008) International Standard ATIS-0800020. *IPTV Electronic Program Guide Metadata Specification*, Alliance for Telecommunications Industry Solutions (ATIS), Washington, DC.
[15] [DIDL-LITE-XSD] (2006) XML Schema for ContentDirectory:2 Structure and Metadata (DIDL-Lite), UPnP Forum, May 31.
[16] Cidero. *Software Solutions for the Digital Home*. Online, http://www.cidero.com/radioServer.html (accessed 2010).
[17] Kim, H.G., Moreau, N. and Sikora, T. (2005) *MPEG-7 Audio and Beyond: Audio Content Indexing and Retrieval*, John Wiley & Sons, Ltd, West Sussex.
[18] Smeaton, A.F., Over, P. and Doherty, A. (2009) Video shot boundary detection: seven years of TRECVid activity. *Computer Vision and Image Understanding*, **114** (4), 411–418.

[19] Huang, J., Liu, Z. and Wang, Y. (2005) Joint segmentation and classification of video based on HMM. *IEEE Transactions on Multimedia*, **7** (3), 538–550.

[20] Gibbon, D. and Liu, Z. (2008) *Introduction to Video Search Engines*, Springer, Berlin.

[21] Eisenberg, G., Batke, J. and Sikora, T. (2004) BeatBank – an MPEG-7 compliant query by tapping system. Proceedings of the 116th AES Convention, May 8–11, 2004, Berlin, Germany.

[22] Batke, J., Eisenberg, G., Weishaupt, P. and Sikora, T. (2004) A query by humming system using MPEG-7 descriptors. Proceedings of the 116th AES Convention, May 8–11, 2004, Berlin, Germany.

15

MPEG-7/21: Structured Metadata for Handling and Personalizing Multimedia Content

Benjamin Köhncke[1] and Wolf-Tilo Balke[1,2]
[1]L3S Research Center, Hannover, Germany
[2]IFIS, University of Braunschweig, Braunschweig, Germany

15.1 Introduction

In the digital age, the idea of universal multimedia access (UMA) is paramount. The knowledge society demands that everybody should have access to every kind of media anytime, anywhere independent of the technical device he/she uses. This evolution is also pushed by the hardware producers for entertainment devices. In recent years, a number of different kinds of portable devices have been developed that embrace the idea of UMA, for example, Netbooks, Smartphones, or the iPhone. The market for these devices is constantly growing: manufacturers actually had problems to accommodate the demand of popular devices, for example, the iPhone or the Eee PC. Since every device is used in different environmental settings and has different technical limitations, personalization aspects regarding individual content adaptation are essential. In this chapter we describe in detail the current personalization features of MPEG-7/21, apply them on real world scenarios, and investigate novel techniques to extend the personalization capabilities.

Besides the number of multimedia devices, the number of available audiovisual media also continues to increase rapidly. Owing to faster internet connections, users have (mobile) access to a plethora of different multimedia content. To make the actual resources searchable and accessible, basic features, for example, title or file type, together with a textual content description (metadata) of each resource are necessary. MPEG-21 includes all aspects regarding access and transmission of multimedia resources and thus offers excellent prospects for sufficiently describing multimedia resources for supporting personalized media access.

The Handbook of MPEG Applications: Standards in Practice   Edited by Marios C. Angelides and Harry Agius
© 2011 John Wiley & Sons, Ltd

During the recent years, with the idea of universal multimedia experience (UME), a more user-centric perspective has prevailed. The aim is to increase the quality of service (QoS) and thus the overall user experience by better controlling actions across the network layers [1]. Especially, if we consider a wireless network scenario where a direct reaction on changing network conditions (e.g., bandwidth or packet loss) is necessary. Therefore, a model is needed to measure the QoS by exploiting metrics from different layers. In [2], a public survey was conducted where each person watched at least 10 movies and rated the quality of each videostream. From this evaluation a QoS model has been derived. This model includes four direct impact factors: packet loss, bandwidth, frame rate, and delay. Please note that the delay is only required if the user directly interacts with the videostream, for example, in a videoconference. In classic streaming scenarios, the delay can be regulated by varying the buffer size on the client device. MPEG-21 Digital Item Adaptation (DIA) is used to describe the functional dependencies between the different layers. Besides QoS constraints, another important aspect considering user experience is security. Chalouf *et al.* [3] describes an approach where MPEG-21 is used to guarantee the tight management of QoS and security in an IPTV scenario. The MPEG-21 Usage Environment description has been enhanced with security parameters to enable an adequate description. But still, QoS is difficult to maintain especially in mobile scenarios with frequently changing network conditions.

Besides description for usage environment conditions, MPEG-21 also offers physical descriptions of the actual stream data within the generic Bitstream Syntax Description (gBSD) tool. This tool can be used to describe multimedia streams independent of their actual coding format. An adaptation of scalable content is decomposed in two steps: the first step includes the adaptation of the metadata document. The gBSD that describes the bitstream is adapted by removing the appropriate parts from the description. There are several ways to accomplish such a metadata adaptation, for example, using XSLT. The second step is the adaptation of the actual bitstream according to the transformed gBSD. In a streaming scenario, this adaptation is not performed on the whole bitstream at once, but on smaller units like single packets or pictures. This kind of adaptations can be done without a decoding or re-encoding phase by a simple removal of the corresponding video layers. Moreover, in addition to purely technical information about the multimedia content or the user's client device, information about content preferences, for example, regarding movie genres, actors, or creators, are useful to make individual recommendations. Such preferences therefore offer the chance for better customer-centered services.

Owing to its extensive description possibilities MPEG-21 is not only focused on one specific domain. Multimedia content is omnipresent in almost every part of our daily life.

15.1.1 Application Scenarios

In medicine, the offer of powerful mobile devices has posed the basis for integrating them into health-care application workflows. There are many useful scenarios where intelligent information can support doctors and their assistants at their work, for example, education, assistance of medical personnel during emergency intervention, or immediate access to patient data. The content types in medical applications are typically of several kinds, ranging from documents, audio and video files to even more complex data types like slide shows with synchronized audio and interactive guided workflows. MPEG-21 can help to inject certain intelligence into these content types by offering a semantic model [4]. The medical domain has some strict requirements for applications, for example, that the data has to be accessible from different devices, mobiles as well as stationary desktop PCs. The synchronization between these devices must happen automatically without any user interaction. Furthermore, access to certain content requires a reliable authorization method, especially if patient data is concerned. Moreover, even personalization aspects are useful to make the applications more user friendly.

Another application scenario that has been developing during the last few years is the area of Internet TV (e.g. see [5], or [6]. Here, metadata descriptions are useful to build interactive user interfaces, for example, known from DVD movies where images, texts, audio tracks, and audiovisual sequences are combined. Thus, the user is able to directly interact with the streamed video content. The collected metadata about the user interactions and the watched movies can be stored and used to make further recommendations. Furthermore, metadata is also necessary for copyright management, for example, to restrict content usage to a particular user or user group. Another important aspect are QoS requirements especially when considering streaming of a live event where a minimum delay is desirable.

Closely related applications can be found in the area of video-on-demand (VoD) providers [7]. The difference from Internet TV is that VoD architectures allow each client to receive a separate adapted bitstream, whereas in Internet TV, usually, multicast streaming is used. VoD providers usually provide a huge amount of different movies from all imaginable genres. However, today many providers still do not really offer device-specific personalization. Instead, they provide two to three different possible video formats, ranging from low quality to high quality. But from the users point of view a device specific adaptation is still desirable. Imagine a user who wants to watch a video stream on his/her iPhone. The provider might offer some different video formats, but let us assume that none of them suits the iPhone's display resolution. If the user chooses a stream in higher quality, the video resolution will surpass the actual display resolution. Thus, although the user cannot enjoy the advantages of the high-quality video stream, he/she has to pay for additional bandwidth consumption, because more data has to be transferred. On the other hand, if the user chooses a lower-quality stream, the video play-back looks grainy. From the users point of view, it would be great to get a personalized stream adapted to the special needs of his/her technical device. But for content providers there is always a trade-off between storage and on-line adaptation costs.

All different domains have in common the need to solve the problem of the vast variety of different client devices and the increasing amount of available multimedia content. To face this problem, MPEG-21 allocates appropriate description schemes in *Part 7 – Digital Item Adaptation (DIA)* of the framework, enabling the creation of suitable personalization workflows.

15.2   The Digital Item Adaptation Framework for Personalization

Part 7 of the MPEG-21 multimedia framework (DIA) is responsible for assisting the user with the adaptation of multimedia content. The DIA tools cover all necessary aspects concerning adaptation support, such as information about the content, the user, and the environment. In the following text we will shortly introduce the key aspects of the *Usage Environment* tool.

15.2.1 Usage Environment

The *Usage Environment* offers several opportunities to define user- specific information and is essential when considering personalization aspects. It includes two different information types: on one hand there are three description schemes containing static context information, that is, the *Terminal Capabilities*, *Network Characteristics*, and profile information about the *Natural Environment*. On the other hand user-specific preferences can be specified in the *User Characteristics* scheme, which also includes the *Usage Preference* part from MPEG-7.

15.2.1.1 User Characteristics

The *User Characteristics* tools offer possibilities to capture the preferences of the user. In contrast to the other description schemes these tools are bound only to the user, as opposed to multimedia content or specific terminals. Besides typical user-specific context preferences, like favorite locations for media consumptions or accessibility characteristics, the major focus of this part lies on the content preferences, described in the *User Preferences* scheme. This scheme includes a set of *Filtering and Search Preferences*, which capture individual user preferences regarding the retrieval and selection of desired multimedia content. Of course, preference hierarchies are allowed by nesting several Filtering and Search Preference elements. The following enumeration shows the most important elements:

- Attributes, such as language, production format, or country of origin can be stored in the *Classification Preference* element.
- The *Creation Preference* elements include information regarding the preferred creation of content, such as title, creator, or creation date.
- In addition, preferred repositories where multimedia content should be retrieved from for example, media servers can be defined within the *Source Preference* scheme.
- Finally, the *Browsing Preferences* schemes specify user's preferences regarding multimedia content navigation and browsing.

Since each user generally has more than one preference, a weighting factor, called *Preference Value*, can be specified to express the relative importance of each preference. The preference value is a simple numerical value ranging from -100 to 100. The value indicates the degree of users preference or nonpreference. The zero value indicates that the user is neutral in terms of preference. A default (positive) value of 10 corresponds to a nominal preference. By choosing a negative weighting the user can express negative preferences, that is, dislikes.

Figure 15.1 shows the typical interaction scenario of a content adaptation engine with a media database and the end user, his/her client device, respectively. The adaptation and delivery process needs two basic components: one for selecting content and deciding how

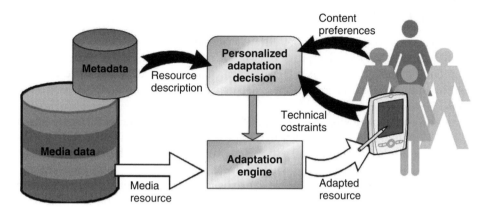

Figure 15.1 Content adaptation scenario.

it should be adapted, the other one for performing the actual adaptation. The *adaptation decision engine* analyzes the user's preference statements and searches the metadata descriptions at the content provider for matching multimedia files. User preferences include the actual query, general content preferences, and information about the technical capabilities of the client device. Besides general details like title, actors, or creator, the metadata files of the videos also often contain so-called *Transcoding Hints*. These hints are provided by the authors of the multimedia content and form lower bounds for the quality of multimedia material, like for example, the minimum possible resolution. If the technical capabilities of the user device and the transcoding hints do not overlap, a sensible media adaptation without changing the modality is not possible (Figure 15.2). Please note that in such a case it still may be viable to apply the InfoPyramid approach [8] to offer multimedia content in alternative modalities and/or fidelities.

After selecting the desired content and determining an optimal adaptation workflow, the decision is handed on to the *adaptation engine*. The adaptation engine retrieves the requested media resources from the content database, adapts it according to the adaptation decision and eventually delivers the adapted file to the end user.

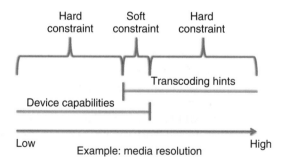

Figure 15.2 Transcoding hints versus technical capabilities.

15.3   Use Case Scenario

As a running example for illustrating different personalization techniques in this chapter we will assume a VoD service provider, who offers multiple kinds of video content in high definition quality. Of course, the provider's business model is to serve costumers according to their needs. Therefore, the video content has to be offered in a personalized fashion.

Imagine a user named Nina. Nina has an iPhone and wants to watch a "King of Queens" episode while sitting on a park bench in Central Park on a sunny summer day. Since the iPhone has a display resolution of 480×320 pixels, she cannot benefit from the high definition quality of the provider's video content. Moreover, streaming high-definition content to a mobile device is not sensible due to bandwidth consumption. When registering with her VoD provider Nina might configure a profile including information about her content preferences. Let us say she reveals details about her favorite actors (which are "Kevin James", "Brad Pitt", and "George Clooney") and her favorite genre "Comedy". Her preferred language is English, but she also understands German. All these preferences can be stored within a MPEG-21 metadata file using the value-based preference model. The following code snippet shows the corresponding section from her profile.

```
<UserPreference>
 <UserIdentifier userName="Nina"/>
 <UsagePreference>
  <FilteringAndSearchPreferences>
   <ClassificationPreference>
    <Genre>Comedy</Genre>
    <Language preferenceValue="68">english</Language>
    <Language preferenceValue="55">german</Language>
   </ClassificationPreference>
   <CreationPreference>
    <Actor preferenceValue="63">James</Actor>
    <Actor preferenceValue="50">Clooney</Actor>
    <Actor preferenceValue="27">Pitt</Actor>
   </CreationPreference>
  </FilteringAndSearchPreference>
 </UsagePreference>
</UserPreference>
```

But for an optimal adaptation process, information about Nina's client device are required too. Again they can be stored in a MPEG-21 metadata file within the *Terminal Capabilities* section. Nina's iPhone supports the following video formats: H.264, MPEG-4, and mov. Furthermore, details about Nina's physical surroundings are specified in the *Natural Environment* description scheme: "outside" and "sunny day".

During the login process, the MPEG-21 file plus the actual query for the "King of Queens" episode are transmitted to the VoD service provider. The adaptation decision engine analyzes Nina's specifications, builds a personalized adaptation workflow suiting her preferences, and hands it on to the adaptation engine, which is in turn responsible for the actual adaptation of the video content (Figure 15.3). Figure 15.3 visualizes the

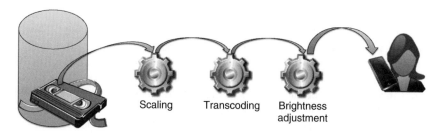

Figure 15.3   Use Case: Nina's adaptation workflow.

necessary adaptation steps. First, the video content has to be scaled down to the iPhone's display resolution. Afterwards it is transcoded to a compatible format. Finally, since it is a sunny day, the video's brightness value is suitably adjusted.

15.3.1   A Deeper Look at the MPEG-7/21 Preference Model

To perform a content selection, an adaptation decision engine matches the resource descriptions from a provider's metadata directory with the user-provided information. If no resource exactly matches the user's query or an adaptation is not possible due to constraint violations, the user preferences have to be examined in more detail.

For Nina's query, the workflow finding process might appear as follows:

(i) Nina starts the VoD application on her iPhone.
(ii) Nina's query, her content profile, and the iPhone's technical capabilities are transmitted to the service provider.
(iii) The decision engine gets the request.
    (a) If the "King of Queens" episode is available and all constraints are satisfied: deliver the content.
    (b) If the "King of Queens" episode is available, but some constraints are violated: find a suitable adaptation workflow.
    (c) If the "King of Queens" episode is not available or some constraints can not be fulfilled: choose the highest ranking preference(s) to adapt to other formats, resolutions, and so on, or to choose new content.

Let us assume the desired "King of Queens" episode is not available. As a consequence, the adaptation decision engine has to analyze all information stated in the user preferences to offer alternative video content. To decide between preferences, all the preference values within each attribute are compared separately: the higher the value, the more important the respective preference. Since, the MPEG-7/21 standard just defines the syntax and semantics of the user preference description scheme, but not the extraction method of the preference value, cf. [9], this is handled by the service provider's application. But, can semantically incomparable attributes (like preferences on actors and language settings) be compared in a quantitative way? It hardly makes sense to state something like: I prefer movies with "Kevin James" to movies in "German". Furthermore, all users must assign their preference values manually. However, from the users point of view it is entirely unintuitive, what an individual preference value (like 63 or 55) actually means.

In our use case example above, we have two preferences on different attributes: language and actors, but the attributes are basically incomparable. Thus, some combinations for media objects might also become incomparable (i.e., it actually might not be possible to rank them in a total order). For instance, consider an English "George Clooney" movie and a German movie with "Kevin James". Intuitively the two could be considered incomparable, because one is better with respect to the language preference, whereas the other better fulfills the actor preference.

In any case, a simple matching of preference values will rarely lead to an effective trade-off management. This is because preferences generally distinguish between hard and soft constraints. Hard constraints have to be adhered to, no matter how (un-)important the respective preference is. Consider for example *Transcoding Hints*, where the original author of multimedia material can define how the properties of the content can be changed without compromising the content's semantics. For instance, an author might state that the resolution of a movie can only be reduced up to 50% of the original resolution. A further reduction simply does not make sense, since to many details would be missed. This constraint remains valid, even if the content is exactly what a user requested using content preferences with high preference values. On the other hand, a user might express a preference for a preferred or best possible resolution for his/her device. Such a preference can be considered as a soft constraint, which can always be relaxed, if necessary.

As a conclusion from our use case scenario we can state that by using MPEG-21's simple value-based preference scheme, no adaptation engine can handle more complex trade-offs. Moreover, there is no way to that a high-ranked, but violated preference is compensated for by satisfying a set of lower-ranked preferences. Therefore, in the following section we will present current proposals of extensions of the MPEG-7/21 preference management, and discuss their specific advantages.

15.4   Extensions of MPEG-7/21 Preference Management

MPEG-7/21 annotations are based on XML schema definitions. The question is how to handle preference information with respect to media in a semantically meaningful ways beyond using simple numerical preference values. Generally speaking, today there are three major research directions aiming to extend MPEG-7/21 preference management. The first approach focuses on capturing information about media within a specialized ontology. This ontology can be used to classify multimedia content, as well as relax constraints, and moreover allows for easy integration into other domains. The second approach considers metadata description as simple attributes in an XML database model. To enable personalized retrieval, specialized XML query languages, like X-Path or XQuery, can be extended. The last approach directly targets the MPEG-7/21 preference model by extending its expressiveness, for example, with partial-order preference structures and the Pareto semantics. In the following sections we will discuss each of these three approaches.

15.4.1   Using Semantic Web Languages and Ontologies
           for Media Retrieval

For evaluating complex preference trade-offs it is necessary to derive a common understanding of semantic relationships between different MPEG-21 description schemes.

By building an MPEG-7/21 ontology several such schemes can be integrated and also a taxonomical, that is, hierarchically ordered, understanding of the concepts contained in a media description can be gained. It is this taxonomy, which allows node-based preference relaxations in case a user-defined soft constraint cannot be fulfilled [10]. If there is no leaf node exactly matching the user's preference, the semantically closest concept can be found in the corresponding parent class, thus slightly generalizing the preference constraint. Please note that the device and service descriptions in user environments are not bound to a special format. Besides MPEG-7/21, other XML-based standards, for example, UPnP [11], can be used, leading to a mapping process to the respective MPEG-7/21 ontology. A general overview of the area of semantic multimedia is given in [12].

Let us reconsider our use case scenario and assume that Nina is looking for a movie starring the actor "George Clooney". Unfortunately, the service provider is not able to deliver a matching movie and Nina's preference is relaxed by stepping up one level in the ontological order (Figure 15.4 for a hierarchical view of the user preferences part of the domain ontology). Instead of a movie with the actor "George Clooney" movies with "George Clooney" as director or producer are available and the user can be offered a choice between them.

Since multimedia content is ubiquitous in almost every domain, an MPEG-7/21 ontology would also foster the common semantic understanding and the integration of metadata standards from different communities. Each community has domain-specific requirements and, therefore, own metadata standards to enable simple resource discovery, for example, GEM[1] in the educational domain or CIDOC[2] in the area of museums.

In general, ontologies add a layer of semantics that provides a common and formal understanding of domain concepts on top of the syntax modeling provided by existing

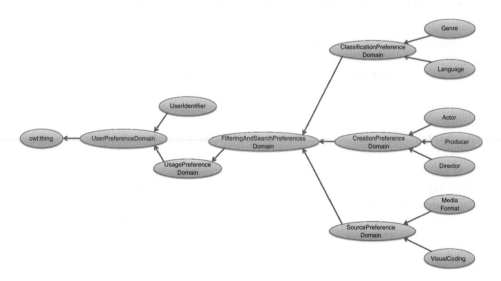

Figure 15.4   Example: preference ontology.

---

[1] The Gateway to Educational Materials: http://www.thegateway.org.
[2] International Committee for Documentation, provides the museum community with advice on good practice and developments in museum documentation: http://cidoc.mediahost.org.

schema languages, like XML. The ontology defines commonly agreed vocabulary for all participating nodes in the delivery workflow and can be used to infer any knowledge supporting suitable adaptation steps. Nevertheless, since within the MPEG-7 XML schemes 1182 elements, 417 attributes, and 377 complex types are defined, such a standard is difficult to manage. Please note that in the original schemes, the largest part of the semantics remains implicit. The same semantics can be expressed using different syntactic variations. But this syntax variability causes serious interoperability issues for multimedia processing and exchange. Since Semantic Web languages, currently, still lack the structural advantages of the XML-based approach, a combination of the existing standards within a common ontology framework, indeed, seems to be a promising path for multimedia annotations. Semantic Web languages such as resource description framework (RDF) or OWL promise to make the implicit knowledge of the multimedia content description explicit. Reasoning over the content descriptions would derive new knowledge that is not explicitly present in the individual descriptions.

Following this approach, MPEG-7 ontologies represented in OWL have already been investigated in trying to cover the entire standard [13–16]. Building expressive OWL representations is still, mostly, a manual process. In particular, there are no fixed rules guiding a manual transformation from XML schemes into OWL ontologies. A manual conversion, thus, has to analyze all elements and their attributes, evaluate their semantics, and find translations into suitable OWL constructs. However, given the plethora of different description schemes a manual creation of ontological relationships is not a sensible option, but relationships should be derived automatically from the XML schema.

15.4.1.1 Automatic Transformation of XML Document Structures

A first approach to do this is by means of simple XSLT transformations, for instance, following the rules in [13]. Building on a manual core subset of MPEG-7 to RDF schema mappings, the idea is to recognize patterns that allow for generating compatible RDF schema definitions for the remaining set of MPEG-7 descriptions automatically. The first step is to generate a DOM (Document Object Model) of the MPEG-7 XML schema to determine the class and properties hierarchies. Now, the basic multimedia entities and their hierarchies from the basic Multimedia Description Schemes (MDSs) are identified. Within MPEG-7 the multimedia content is classified into five types: Image, Video, Audio, Audiovisual, and Multimedia. Each of these types has special properties and thus has its own segment subclasses. The temporal decomposition of a *VideoSegment* into either smaller *VideoSegments* or *StillRegions* must be constrained. However, within the RDF schema this is not possible due to the inability to specify multiple range constraints on a single property (see [13] or [17]). To express this in the RDF schema it is necessary to define a new superclass, which merges the range classes into a single common class. An alternative to overcome this limitation is to use DAML-OIL extensions to the RDF schema. This extensions can include multiple range constraints, Boolean combination of classes and class-specific constraints on properties.

Providing domain-specific knowledge using a machine-processable RDF schema, thus enables to integrate knowledge from different domains, respectively metadata-repositories into a single encompassing ontology expressed using DAML+OIL. A version of such an ontology, the so-called MetaNet ontology was developed using the ABC vocabulary [18].

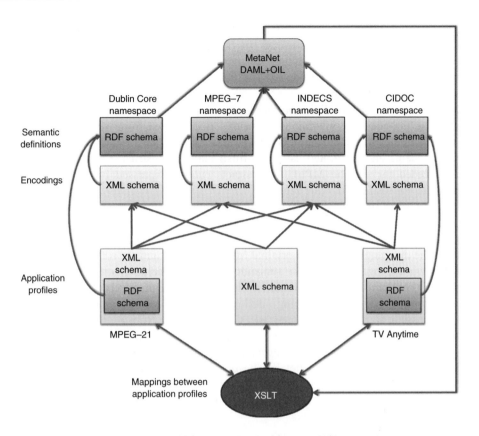

Figure 15.5   MetaNet Architecture [13].

The semantic knowledge provided by MetaNet is linked to metadata descriptions from different domains using XSLT (Figure 15.5). For each domain-specific namespace, which expresses the domain's metadata model and vocabulary, both an XML and an RDF schema are used. The application profiles combine, restrict, extend, and redefine elements from multiple existing namespaces and can also include RDF schema definitions of new classes or properties. An remaining open issue is the development of tools capable of automatically processing MPEG-7 schema descriptions and converting them to their respective DAML+OIL ontology.

Still, a general problem with converting the XML tree structure automatically is that the obtained ontology only describes the relationship between types of the tree elements and not their implicit semantics. Therefore, although this simple approach already expresses XML-based relationships in OWL, it does not add meaningful semantic expressiveness.

15.4.1.2   Creation of Upper Ontologies

A second approach is based on the definition of an OWL upper ontology, which fully captures the MPEG-7 description schemes [15]. Upper ontologies describe very general concepts that are identical across different domains. Therefore, they guarantee semantic interoperability at least for a restricted set of important concepts. An example of an upper ontology for the area of multimedia is the so-called DS-MIRF ontology [15]. This ontology builds a basis for interoperability between OWL and MPEG-7 and has been conceptualized manually.

MPEG-7 includes many different data types within its description schemes. A major challenge is the adequate integration of strictly typed nodes from MPEG-7 description schemes into semantic languages like OWL. Basically all such types can be defined in an XML schema and integrated using the rdfs:Datatype construct. For example, feature vectors needed for specific MPEG-7 constructs can be expressed by basic data types restricted to the respective value range.

All simple data types from the MPEG-7 description schemes are stored in one XML schema file, which is represented by the *&datatypes* XML entity. In addition, for each simple data type appearing in the ontology definition files, an rdfs:Datatype construct is defined. The mapping between the original MPEG-7 names and the rdf:IDs is represented in an OWL mapping ontology. The semantics of XML schema elements that cannot be mapped to OWL entities, like the sequence element order or the attribute's default values, are also captured within the mapping ontology. Therefore, using this mapping ontology it is also possible to return an original MPEG-7 description from RDF metadata content.

MPEG-7 complex types are mapped to OWL classes grouping entities with respect to the properties they share. Thus, for every complex type defined in MPEG-7, an OWL class using the owl:Class construct can be defined. The name of the complex type is stored within the corresponding rdf:ID. The following example shows the definition of the *FilteringAndSearchPreferenceType* as an OWL class and as an MPEG-7 complex type definition [15].

```
<complexType name="FilteringAndSearchPreferencesType">
 <complexContent>
  <extension base="mpeg7:DSType">
   <sequence>
    <element name="ActorPreferences"
     type="ActorPreferencesType" minOccurs="0"
     maxOccurs="unbounded"/>
   </sequence>
   <attribute name="protected" type="userChoiceType"
    use="optional"/>
  </extension>
 </complexContent>
</complexType>
```

```
<owl:Class rdf:ID="FilteringAndSearchPreferencesType">
 <rdfs:subClassOf rdf:resource="#DSType"/>
</owl:Class>
<owl:ObjectProperty rdf:ID="ActorPreferences">
```

```
<rdfs:domain rdf:resource="#FilteringAndSearchPreferencesType"/>
<rdfs:range rdf:resource="#ActorPreferencesType"/>
</owl:ObjectProperty>
<owl:DatatypeProperty rdf:ID="protected">
 <rdfs:domain rdf:resource="#FilteringAndSearchPreferencesType"/>
 <rdfs:range rdf:resource="&datatypes;userChoiceType"/>
 <rdf:type rdf:resource="&owl;FunctionalProperty"/>
</owl:DatatypeProperty>
```

This upper ontology includes simple and complex data types as well as their relationships. Now all data types used within specific applications can be mapped to these general concepts. Thus, an upper ontology enables an easy integration of knowledge from different domains using domain-specific ontologies (lower ontologies).

15.4.1.3 Building Specialized Topic-Centered Ontologies

Since ontology approaches covering the whole standard are still difficult to generate, there are also approaches that focus on building smaller ontologies for special parts of MPEG-7/21. A systematic approach for designing such a topic-centered ontology based on MPEG-7 descriptions and domain-specific vocabularies is presented in [19]. First, a set of suitable description schemes for the considered media types, for example soccer videos, are selected. These description schemes are usually used to model structure and low-level aspects. For instance, for soccer videos the focus would lie on structural aspects, like spatial, temporal, or spatio-temporal concepts, and also on certain low-level features, like shape or texture. All high-level semantics are captured using domain-specific ontologies instead of using the semantic part of MPEG-7. This is because all required semantic relationships between the domain-specific concepts are usually already available in custom-made ontologies widely used within the community. Therefore, it is not necessary to remodel these concepts in MPEG-7 and risk interoperability issues.

An example scenario is described in [19], where an ontology for soccer games is designed representing high-level semantics. First of all a sports event ontology is developed that uses concepts and properties introduced in SmartSUMO, which is a combination of the DOLCE foundational ontology [20] and the SUMO upper ontology [21]. By using this combined ontology, properties such as person names or birth dates need not be remodeled. Besides the sports event ontology, a multimedia ontology is created based on MPEG-7. Finally, both ontologies are integrated. Since the semantic descriptors from multimedia documents are inferred manually, again the major challenge is to automate this process considering approaches from various research areas like machine learning or audio and image processing.

15.4.2 XML Databases and Query Languages for Semantic Multimedia Retrieval

A crucial task for multimedia applications is basic content retrieval. And indeed, many groups are working on MPEG-7-based multimedia retrieval and filtering (see [22, 23] or [24]). Actually, for this purpose MPEG-7 offers the *Semantic Description Scheme* for building retrieval and filtering approaches using semantic metadata [25, 26]. However, none of them provides a uniform and transparent MPEG-7 retrieval and filtering framework. Since MPEG-7 metadata descriptions are based on XML schema definitions using MPEG-7 DDL, it is a straightforward idea to employ XML database solutions for retrieval tasks.

15.4.2.1 XML Database Solutions

There are many different XML database approaches on the market with different maturity and capabilities. This includes native XML database solutions, as well as XML extensions for traditional database systems, and commercial products, as well as open source approaches or research prototypes. To be able to decide whether existing database solutions are useful for MPEG-7/21 metadata retrieval, an overview of existing approaches is needed. Therefore, it is necessary to analyze requirements that should be fulfilled by an XML database allowing for satisfying MPEG-7/21 support. The requirements comprise the representation of MPEG-7/21 descriptions, the access to media descriptions, the ability to process description schemes, extensibility, and classic database management functionalities like transactions and concurrency control.

Currently available database approaches can be distinguished into native XML database solutions and XML database extensions (for a complete survey see [27]). A native XML database solution is expected to allow for the modeling of data only by means of XML documents. Therefore, it is not really necessary that a native solution has been specifically developed for XML data management, but as long as the data model of the underlying system is entirely hidden, it might also be based on conventional database technology. On the other hand, approaches using XML database extensions only have to offer modeling primitives of the extended DBMS's data model to the various applications.

Native Database Solutions. recently a variety of native XML database approaches appeared on the market. Several vendors developed entire DBMSs, specialized on the management of XML metadata, because conventional DBMSs are not able to efficiently handle XML documents due to their hierarchical and semistructured nature. A famous approach of an XML database management system completely designed for XML is Software AG's *Tamino*. In contrast to solutions of other DBMS vendors, *Tamino* is not just another layer on top of a database system designed to support the relational or an object-oriented data model [28]. Another solution, *Infonyte-DB*, constitutes a lightweight in-process storage solution for XML documents, but does not provide a database server with all functionality needed for transaction management and concurrency control. Furthermore, even vendors of object-oriented database systems extended their existing approaches to native XML database solutions. A representative of this area is *eXcelon XIS*,[3] which internally uses the object-oriented DBMS *ObjectStore*.

Besides these commercial approaches, open-source solutions are also available. The Apache XML Project implemented a native system called *Xindice*.[4] Another approach

---

[3] http://xml.coverpages.org/ExcelonXIS-Lite.html.

[4] http://xml.apache.org/xindice.

called *eXist*[5] is built on top of a relational database system, like MySQL or PostgreSQL, which internally serves as the persistent storage backend. Of course, there are also considerable research approaches, like the *Lore*[6] prototype. Here, the idea is to exploit *Lore's* ability to represent irregular graph structures including hierarchies.

Database Extensions. In the area of conventional database systems for XML document storage one can distinguish three different kinds of approaches. In the first an XML document is stored in its textual format in a character large object (CLOB). Today, almost all relational DBMSs support the unstructured storage of XML documents. They have been extended with CLOB-based data types and offer more or less sophisticated functions for querying XML repositories using SQL. Prominent examples from this area are *Oracle XML DB*, *IBM DB2 XML Extender*, and *Microsoft SQLXML*.

Other approaches offer the possibility of a structured storage of XML documents by developing a fine-grained metamodel. This metamodel is able to represent the node trees of XML documents and is built by employing the modeling primitives of the underlying conventional DBMS. Thus, the structure and the content can be used by DBMS-specific querying facilities. Many research prototypes for the storage of structured XML data have been developed (mostly for relational DBMSs). Examples are *XML Cartridge* [29] or *Monet XML* [30].

Finally, a third area of approaches use mappings of XML documents to database schemes specifically designed for that content. There are many tools and formalisms for the specification of the mapping between XML formats and database schemes, but the design of a database schema and the specification of an appropriate mapping of XML content are elaborate manual tasks. Since MPEG-7 allows the extension of the set of predefined description schemes, the effort necessary to cope with a media description following a previously unknown description scheme would be prohibitive. Current research activities focus on an automatic derivation of relational database schema definitions for XML metadata and the automatic mapping between them. Nevertheless, since they are based on Document Type Definitions (DTDs) instead of the far more complex MPEG-7 DDL they are not readily applicable for managing MPEG-7 description schemes.

A detailed analysis of all above-mentioned approaches (see [27] for more details) has shown that almost all examined solutions store and treat simple element content and the content of attribute values of MPEG-7 descriptions largely as text, regardless of the actual content type. This is inappropriate because in MPEG-7 many description schemes consist of nontextual data like numbers, vectors, and matrices. It is desirable that applications can access and process these schemes according to their real type and not as text. The problem of the inspected solutions is that they do not sufficiently make use of schema and type information offered within MPEG-7 descriptions. The majority of these approaches totally ignore schema definitions for the storage of XML documents, and use them for validating XML documents only. None of them fully support MPEG-7 DDL.

In addition to the limited support of nontextual data, there is another aspect that constrain the applicability of existing database solutions for the management of MPEG-7 multimedia descriptions. The value indexing support offered by these systems is

---

[5] http://www.exist-db.org.

[6] http://infolab.stanford.edu/lore/home/index.html.

generally not sufficient. They only offer one-dimensional, B-Tree-based index structures for indexing of the basic elements of XML documents. For implementing efficient multimedia applications on large collections of MPEG-7 descriptions, a system that supports multidimensional index structures, such as R-Trees, for the indexing of document content is needed.

Finally, we can state that the analysis of current approaches exposes significant deficiencies seriously affecting their eligibility for the management of MPEG-7 metadata descriptions. Neither native XML databases nor XML database extensions provide full support for managing MPEG-7 descriptions with respect to their requirements.

15.4.2.2   Semantic Query Languages

The main aspect regarding MPEG-7 database retrieval is the definition of a suitable query language. The obvious approach of trying to accomplish a system for MPEG-7-based multimedia content retrieval is to use standard database query languages like XQuery or XPath [31]. One limitation when using XQuery is that it is not possible to fully exploit the special features of the MPEG-7 description elements. For example, it is not possible to directly extract the entity with the highest preference value. To decide which entry is the most preferred, it is necessary to analyze all available entities of the corresponding categories. The reason is that the MPEG-7 semantic model and the domain knowledge integrated in the semantic MPEG-7 descriptions are expressed in an integrated way. To overcome these limitations, the MPEG standardization committee decided to work on a query format based on MPEG-7, called MP7QF. The aim of this framework is to provide a standardized interface to databases containing MPEG-7 metadata content.

For the special requirements of personalized multimedia retrieval it is also necessary to develop a compatible *Filtering and Search Preferences* model.

In [32, 33] an ontology-based methodology to open up the MPEG-7/21 usage environment for enriching user preferences by more complex semantics as expressed by domain ontologies is provided. The approach supports the complete functionality offered by the MPEG-7 semantic description scheme for multimedia content descriptions and respects all the MPEG-7/21 conventions. It is based on OWL and has been prototypically implemented in the DS-MIRF framework. The query language for MPEG-7 descriptions (called MP7QL [34]) differentiates between three query types:

- The *WeighedMPEG7QueryType* represents queries with explicit preference values ranging from −100 to 100.
- The *BooleanMPEG7QueryType* represents queries with explicit Boolean operators.
- The *BooleanWeighedMPEG7QueryType* represents queries with explicit preference values and Boolean operators.

For each of these query categories an abstract type defined in XML is provided allowing to express constraints on every aspect of a multimedia object described with MPEG-7. The following example shows the usage of the *BooleanMPEG7QueryType* based on our use case scenario.

Use case (cont.): Assume our user Nina states the following query: "I want all multimedia objects, where Kevin James plays a fireman". This query can be expressed in the frameworks formal syntax as follows:

```
BQS1 = (EventType AND (exemplifies, Fireman) AND (agent, $james)
    AND (($james, AgentObjectType)
    AND (exemplifies, ActorObject, $james)
    AND (Agent(Name(FamilyName 'James')))))
```

The abstract semantic entity "ActorObject" represents the class of all actors. The entity "Fireman" refers to the class of all actors who played the part of a fireman in some movie. Furthermore, the actor "Kevin James" is bound to the $james variable. The same query in XML reads:

```
<Mpeg7Query xsi:type="BooleanMpeg7QueryType">
 <QuerySpecification ANDOROperator="AND"
 xsi:type="BooleanContextQuerySpecificationType">
  <SemanticPreferences ANDOROperator="AND">
   <SemanticBase xsi:type="BooleanEventType" ANDOROperator="AND"
   NOTOperator="false">
    <Relation ANDOROperator="AND"
    type="urn:mpeg:mpeg7:cs:SemanticRelationCS:2001:exemplifies"
    target="actorRoles#Fireman"/>
    <Relation ANDOROperator="AND"
    type="urn:mpeg:mpeg7:cs:SemanticRelationCS:2001:agent"
    target="$james"/>
   </SemanticBase>
   <SemanticBase ANDOROperator="AND" xsi:type=
   "BooleanAgentObjectType" id="$james" NOTOperator="false">
    <Relation ANDOROperator="AND" target=" actoragents#
    ActorObject"type="urn:mpeg:mpeg7:cs:SemanticRelationCS:
    2001:exemplifies"/>
    <Agent xsi:type="BooleanPersonType">
     <Name>
      <FamilyName>James</FamilyName>
     </Name>
    </Agent>
   </SemanticBase>
  </SemanticPreferences>
 </QuerySpecification>
</Mpeg7Query>
```

Moreover, for building an effective query language the *Filtering and Search* description schemes originally offered by the standard still lack expressiveness. In [33], a complete model is proposed allowing to express preferences on every aspect of the MPEG-7 multimedia object descriptions.

15.4.3 Exploiting More Expressive Preference Models

The existence of multiple and often conflicting user preferences demands an efficient framework to resolve conflicts in a fair and meaningful way. The need for an effective trade-off management with complex user preferences has already been discussed in other communities, for example, in databases and information systems. Here, recent work in [35, 36] considers preferences in a *qualitative* way as partial orders of preferred values that can be relaxed should the need arise. To combine multiple preferences and derive a fair compromise usually, the concept of Pareto optimality is used.

The Pareto set (also known as *efficient frontier*) consists of all nondominated objects, that is, for each object no other object in the set has better or at least equal attribute values with respect to all attributes. Analyzing Nina's language preferences for English, and actor preferences for "Kevin James", an English "George Clooney" movie and a German "Kevin James" movie are incomparable, because one is better with respect to the language preference, whereas the other is better with respect to the actor preference. However, both options dominate a German "Brad Pitt" movie, which accordingly would not be part of the Pareto set. The use of the Pareto semantics is also advocated in [37, 38] providing decision-making frameworks where hard and soft constraints are represented as variables as input for the optimization problem.

If all preferences on different attributes are considered to be of equal importance, the suboptimal solutions can be automatically removed. Then, the adaptation decision engine can build a suitable adaptation workflow considering the remaining pool of possible solutions. Of course, if no fair relaxation scheme is desired, more discriminating combination methods (e.g., the ordering on the attributes in preference values in MPEG-7/21) can be used on qualitative partial-order preferences.

Use Case (cont.): Let us consider our user Nina who wants to get a video streamed to her iPhone. Owing to complexity reasons only two preferences are analyzed here: one about her preferred actors, stated in the *User Preferences*, and the other about preferred codecs available on her iPhone, defined in the *Terminal Capabilities*. Instead of describing the preferences using numerical values they are visualized as preference graphs (Figure 15.6).

To combine several preferences, the combination semantics has to be stated. For our example, let us assume a fair relaxation scheme between the two preferences. Figure 15.7 shows the first three layers of the product preference graph following the Pareto semantics. The graph is already quite complex for combining only the two preferences.

Please note that due to the qualitative nature of the preferences some combinations are incomparable. The best possible choice is a "Kevin James" movie in MPEG-4 format. If it is not available or adaptable, the adaptation decision engine can explore several other options that are all equally preferable according to Nina's preferences. In Figure 15.7,

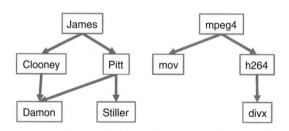

Figure 15.6 Example: preference graphs.

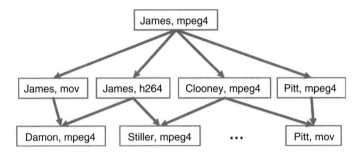

Figure 15.7   Example: combined preference graph.

these are all options on the second layer, like a "Kevin James" movie in H.264 format or a "Brad Pitt" movie in MPEG-4 format. These Pareto preferences are expressed in XML following the respective preference algebra. Interested readers may take a look at [36] for details on the evaluation of complex constraints.

```
<UserPreference>
 <UserIdentifier userName="Nina"/>
 <UsagePreference>
  <Preference>
   <Pareto>
    <EXP att="actor">
     <EXPSet>
      <Value val1="James" val2="Clooney">
      <Value val1="James" val2="Pitt">
      <Value val1="Clooney" val2="Damon">
      <Value val1="Pitt" val2="Damon">
      <Value val1="Pitt" val2="Stiller">
     </EXPSet>
    </EXP>
    <EXP att="codec">
     <EXPSet>
      <Value val1="mpeg4" val2="mov">
      <Value val1="mpeg4" val2="h264">
      <Value val1="h264" val2="divx">
     </EXPSet>
    </EXP>
   </Pareto>
  </Preference>
 </UsagePreference>
</UserPreference>
```

As we have seen, the more the preferences are specified, the more complex the mesh of the Pareto product order gets. Thus, for an efficient evaluation of complex preferences specially adapted algorithms are needed. In the field of databases, concepts for retrieving Pareto optimal sets arose with the so-called skyline queries [39, 40]. In skyline queries, all attributes are considered to be independent and equally important. Hence, for the combination of individual attribute scores no weighting function can be used, like it is usually done in top-k retrieval. Instead, all possibly optimal objects, based on the notion of Pareto optimality are returned to the user. Within skyline frameworks, users are also offered the possibility to declare several hard constraints on attributes. This is usually facilitated as a simple selection condition for filtering [39]. For the domain of adaptation frameworks, hard constraints have to be further distinguished. Some hard constraints can still be met by adapting the content (like a codec or resolution constraint), whereas others, mostly user preferences like preferences on actors or genres, can never be satisfied by content adaptation. We call hard constraints of the first type adaptation-sensitive hard constraints, whereas we refer to the second type as strict hard constraints.

Moreover, in traditional skyline scenarios each dimension has a total order. In contrast, in the adaptation domain all preferences are based on partial orders. Therefore, standard skyline query evaluation is not readily applicable. Actually it is possible to render a total order from partial order preferences, but we have to accept some inaccuracies by object incomparability. As a simple transformation rule one can consider for example, the "level" of each object in the preference graph. The "level" is defined as the longest path to any maximum value in the graph.

Use Case (cont.): Imagine our user Nina wants to watch a movie on her iPhone and states the preferences shown in Figure 15.6. If we transform the actor preference into a total order, "James" is the most important value (level 1), followed by "Clooney" and "Pitt" (both on level 2) and finally "Damon" and "Stiller" as least preferred actors on level 3. However, in the resulting total order of the actor preference, we can state that "Clooney" is preferred over "Stiller" whereas these actors are incomparable in the original partial order preference.

From this total order induced by the tree levels, it is simple to derive a numerical assignment of score values for objects by using an adequate utility function, translating the level information into simple scores. The score value is usually normalized to a numerical value between 0 (least preferred) and 1 (best object) [38].

Now assume Nina's content provider only offers the following five videos: a "Ben Stiller" movie in DivX format, a "Matt Damon" movie in H264 format, a "Brad Pitt" movie in mov format, a "George Clooney" movie in MPEG-4 format, and a "Kevin James" movie in H264 format. The resulting tuples are visualized in Figure 15.8.

The black point in the upper right corner of the figure would be the optimal solution. The skyline contains only two objects: the "Kevin James" movie in H264 format and the "George Clooney" movie in MPEG-4 format, since they dominate all other available movies in the database (visualized with the dotted lines). The adaptation decision engine does not need to consider any other movie from the database (light shaded) since they are definitely dominated by the two skyline objects (dark shaded). For example, a "Ben Stiller" movie in DivX format will never be taken into account since it is always dominated by a "George Clooney" movie in MPEG-4 format with respect to both dimensions. Considering the resulting skyline objects, we recognize that the optimal solution (dark point) is not included. One object has the highest possible value in the actors preference, the other one in the codec preference. The adaptation engine needs to check whether an adequate adaptation is available. Since the actors preference is marked as a strict hard constraint,

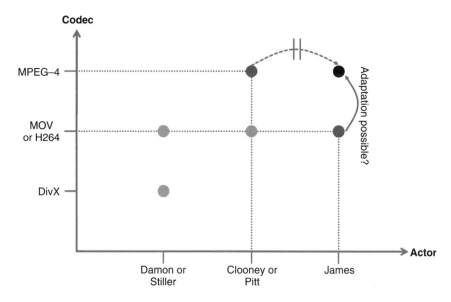

Figure 15.8   Example: skyline objects for Nina's preferences.

the adaptation engine knows that it is not possible to convert a "George Clooney" movie in MPEG-4 format to a "Kevin James" movie in MPEG-4 format (even though it would be really funny to replace "George Clooney" with "Kevin James"). On the other hand, the codec preference is an adaptation-sensitive hard constraint and, therefore, it is indeed possible to adapt a James/H264 movie to a James/MPEG-4 movie if a suitable transcoder is available.

Let us summarize the different delivery possibilities:

- retrieve a James/H264 movie and deliver the adapted James/MPEG-4 version;
- deliver a James/H264 movie;
- deliver a Clooney/MPEG-4 movie;
- retrieve a Pitt/MOV movie, transcode it to Pitt/MPEG-4 and deliver the adapted movie;
- deliver a Pitt/MOV movie and so on.

Now we have to take a closer look at how to compute a ranking for the best adaptation decision based on the movies available in the database. The objects must be ranked under consideration of their levels in the Pareto tree. An efficient ranking scheme for deriving the final preference order is given in [10, 38].

15.5   Example Application

Let us reconsider our use case scenario by designing a system for the VoD provider considering all advantages of the different preference extensions. The service provider has a database containing all movies and an XML database with their respective metadata descriptions in MPEG-7/21 format. For accessing the content, an interactive user interface

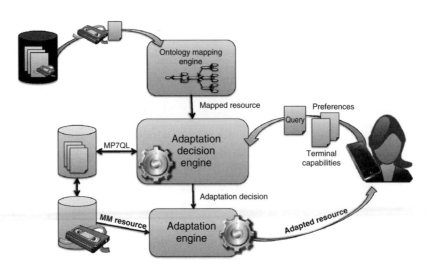

Figure 15.9   Example application.

is offered where users can state their preferences, for example, for actors or movie genres. Furthermore, a query field is available where users can formulate queries for example, "I want all movies where Kevin Costner plays a postman". The preferences are internally handled as partial-order preferences described in an enhanced MPEG-21 format (see Section 15.4.3). The query is expressed using semantically enriched query languages, for example, MP7QL (see Section 15.4.2). Finally, the user preferences, terminal capabilities, and the query are transmitted to the service provider and analyzed by its personalized adaptation decision engine (Figure 15.9).

This engine is responsible for finding the most appropriate multimedia content according to the user query and provide a suitable adaptation workflow. This workflow template is handed on to the adaptation engine that is responsible for finding adequate adaptation services. The actual adaptation of the multimedia content is done on-the-fly while streaming the content through the network to the end user. In case the desired movie is not available, the service provider's decision engine evaluates the user's preferences to find alternative multimedia content. Thus, it analyzes the combined preference graph (Figure 15.7) and retrieves the best matching multimedia content querying its metadata description database using for example, MP7QL. If the service provider could not find a matching movie at all it uses an MPEG-21 ontology to easily integrate content from third-party providers, respectively from other domains. Every community has its own domain-specific knowledge and often its own metadata standards. An upper ontology eases the integration of domain knowledge and allows for overall multimedia content retrieval. On the other hand, such an ontology allows users to use their specified preferences from other VoD providers. After transmitting the preferences to the service provider, they are mapped to the respective nodes in the ontology. Thus, the service provider can offer plenty of possibilities for multimedia retrieval delivering highly personalized content.

15.6 Summary

The MPEG-7/21 metadata standard was created to semantically annotate multimedia data in a standardized way. The basic unit of interaction in later applications is called a *digital item encapsulating multimedia content*. But since the search for content and the actual handling of digital items usually relies heavily on the application context, an essential feature of the standard is in the area of personalization. For this, MPEG-7/21 offers a variety of possibilities to describe user preferences, terminal capabilities, and transcoding hints within its Digital Item Adaptation part.

However, for many multimedia applications the standard itself is not enough. Researchers are working on enriching the semantic power of the basic standard by building ontologies. Since every community has domain-specific requirements and therefore, own metadata standards, it is necessary to get a common understanding of the semantic relationship between metadata standards from different domains. This integration of domain-specific knowledge in MPEG-7/21 is an ongoing research area for both representing the entire standard and modeling specific usage scenarios.

Since MPEG-7/21 is based on XML, XML databases can be used for retrieval tasks. But, languages like XQuery that have been proposed for XML document retrieval are not yet able to support MPEG-7/21 queries. For instance, no support for specific query types typically used in multimedia content retrieval is provided. Research in this area thus focuses on finding appropriate query languages for multimedia descriptions. The MPEG standardization committee already decided to provide a MPEG-7 query format (MP7QF), which defines input parameters for describing search criteria and a set of output parameters describing the result sets. However, query languages offering more semantic expressiveness are also being currently developed.

Moreover, the current preference model in the MPEG-7/21 standard is limited to the simple matching of numerical values representing the importance of each constraint. To enable more complex queries on multimedia content also more sophisticated preference models can be utilized. We have given the example of a model building on partial-order preferences and evaluating complex preference constraints using Pareto semantics, as currently explored by the database community. These efforts promise to handle trade-offs in a semantically more meaningful way.

Future research challenges embrace the idea of combining the Semantic and the Social Web – Web 3.0. Today, the world wide web is made up of all kinds of social communities. Each of them produce metadata content, for example, in terms of tags. The idea is to integrate community-generated metadata with other metadata standards. It will be necessary to develop appropriate weighting schemes and quality measures, respectively, to mark how trustful the metadata content is. Furthermore, the user needs the ability to choose which kind of metadata content is most reliable for his/her aims. Thus, the weighting is user specific and result ranking is dependent on the chosen metadata domain. One major challenge coming with this idea is the identification of relationships between resources in the Web. How to crawl user-generated content and identify discussions about particular videos, for example, in blogs? How to extract and structure this information? To summarize these ideas, it will be necessary to develop structured, weighted, semantically rich metadata descriptions that are automatically processable by machines.

References

[1] Kofler, I., Seidl, J., Timmerer, C. *et al.* (2008) Using MPEG-21 for cross-layer multimedia content adaptation. *Signal Image and Video Processing*, **2** (4), 355–370.

[2] Timmerer, C., Ortega, V.H., Calabozo, J.M.G., and León, A. (2008) Measuring quality of experience for MPEG-21-based cross-layer multimedia content adaptation. *AICCSA*, pp. 969–974.

[3] Chalouf, M.A., Djama, I., Ahmed, T., and Krief, F. (2009) On tightly managing end-to-end QOS and security for IPTV service delivery. *IWCMC*, pp. 1030–1034.

[4] Bellini, P., Bruno, I., Cenni, D. *et al.* (2009) Personal content management on PDA for health care applications. Proceedings of the International Conference on Semantic Computing (ICSC), IEEE Computer Society: Berkeley, CA, USA, pp. 601–605.

[5] Anagnostopoulos, C.-N., Vlachogiannis, E., Psoroulas, I. *et al.* (2008) Intelligent content personalisation in internet TV using MPEG-21. *International Journal of Internet Protocol Technology (IJIPT)*, **3** (3), 159–169.

[6] Vlachogiannis, E., Gavalas, D., Anagnostopoulos, C., and Tsekouras, G.E. (2008) Towards ITV accessibility: the MPEG-21 case, PETRA '08: Proceedings of the 1st International Conference on PErvasive Technologies Related to Assistive Environments, ACM, New York, pp. 1–6.

[7] Eberhard, M., Celetto, L., Timmerer, C. *et al.* (2008) An interoperable multimedia delivery framework for scalable video coding based on MPEG-21 digital item adaptation. *ICME*, pp. 1607–1608.

[8] Chung-Sheng, L., Mohan, R., and Smith, J. (1998) Multimedia content description in the infopyramid. Proceedings of the 1998 IEEE International Conference on Acoustics, Speech and Signal Processing.

[9] Lee, H.-K., Nam, J., Bae, B. *et al.* (2002) Personalized contents guide and browsing based on user preference. Proceedings of the 2nd International Conference on Adaptive Hypermedia and Adaptive Web Based Systems: Workshop on Personalization in Future TV.

[10] Balke, W.-T. and Wagner, M. (2004) Through different eyes: assessing multiple conceptual views for querying web services. Proceedings of the International World Wide Web Conference (WWW) (Alternate Track Papers & Posters), pp. 196–205.

[11] Li, N., Attou, A., De, S., and Moessner, K. (2008) Device and service descriptions for ontology-based ubiquitous multimedia services, MoMM '08: Proceedings of the 6th International Conference on Advances in Mobile Computing and Multimedia, ACM, New York, pp. 370–375.

[12] Staab, S., Scherp, A., Arndt, R. *et al.* (2008) Semantic multimedia. *Reasoning Web*, pp. 125–170.

[13] Hunter, J. (2001) Adding multimedia to the semantic web: building an MPEG-7 ontology. Proceedings of the International Conference on Semantic Web and Web Services (SWWS), pp. 261–283.

[14] Troncy, R. (2003) Integrating structure and semantics into audio-visual documents. Proceedings of the International Semantic Web Conference, pp. 566–581.

[15] Tsinaraki, C., Polydoros, P., and Christodoulakis, S. (2004) Interoperability support for ontology-based video retrieval applications. Proceedings of 3rd International Conference on Image and Video Retrieval (CIVR), pp. 582–591.

[16] Tsinaraki, C., Polydoros, P., and Christodoulakis, S. (2007) Interoperability support between MPEG-7/21 and owl in DS-MIRF. *IEEE Transactions on Knowledge and Data Engineering*, **19** (2), 219–232.

[17] Hunter, J. and Armstrong, L. (1999) A comparison of schemas for video metadata representation. *Computer Networks*, **31** (11–16), 1431–1451.

[18] Lagoze, C. and Hunter, J. (2001) The ABC ontology and model, Proceedings of the International Conference on Dublin Core and Metadata Applications (DCMI '01), National Institute of Informatics, Tokyo, Japan, pp. 160–176.

[19] Vembu, S., Kiesel, M., Sintek, M., and Baumann, S. (2006) Towards bridging the semantic gap in multimedia annotation and retrieval. Proceedings of the 1st International Workshop on Semantic Web Annotations for Multimedia.

[20] Gangemi, A., Guarino, N., Masolo, C. *et al.* (2002) Sweetening ontologies with dolce, Proceedings of the 13th International Conference on Knowledge Engineering and Knowledge Management. Ontologies and the Semantic Web (EKAW), Springer-Verlag, London, pp. 166–181.

[21] Adam, I.N. and Pease, A. (2001) Origins of the IEEE standard upper ontology. Working Notes of the IJCAI-2001 Workshop on the IEEE Standard Upper Ontology, pp. 4–10.

[22] Graves, A. and Lalmas, M. (2002) Video retrieval using an MPEG-7 based inference network, Proceedings of the 25th Annual International ACM SIGIR Conference on Research and Development in Information Retrieval (SIGIR), ACM, New York, pp. 339–346.

[23] Tseng, B.L., Lin, C.-Y., and Smith, J.R. (2004) Using MPEG-7 and MPEG-21 for personalizing video. *IEEE MultiMedia*, **11** (1), 42–53.

[24] Wang, Q., Balke, W.-T., Kießling, W., and Huhn, A. (2004) P-news: deeply personalized news dissemination for MPEG-7 based digital libraries. European Conference on Research and Advanced Technology for Digital Libraries (ECDL), pp. 256–268.

[25] Agius, H. and Angelides, M.C. (2004) Modelling and filtering of MPEG-7-compliant metadata for digital video, Proceedings of the 2004 ACM Symposium on Applied Computing (SAC), ACM, New York, pp. 1248–1252.

[26] Tsinaraki, C. and Christodoulakis, S. (2006) A multimedia user preference model that supports semantics and its application to MPEG-7/21. Proceedings of the 12th International Conference on Multi Media Modeling (MMM).

[27] Westermann, U. and Klas, W. (2003) An analysis of XML database solutions for the management of MPEG-7 media descriptions. *ACM Computer Surveys*, **35** (4), 331–373.

[28] Schöning, H. (2001) Tamino – a DBMS designed for XML. Proceedings of the 16th International Conference on Data Engineering, 0149.

[29] Gardarin, G., Sha, F., and Dang-Ngoc, T.-T. (1999) XML-based components for federating multiple heterogeneous data sources. Proceedings of the 18th International Conference on Conceptual Modeling (ER '99). Springer-Verlag, London, pp. 506–519.

[30] Schmidt, A., Kersten, M., Windhouwer, M., and Waas, F. (2000) Efficient relational storage and retrieval of XML documents. Proceedings of the ACM SIGMOD Workshop on the Web and Databases (WebDB), pp. 47–52.

[31] Lee, M.-H., Kang, J.-H., Myaeng, S.-H. *et al.* A multimedia digital library system based on MPEG-7 and XQUERY. Proceedings of the International Conference on Asian Digital Libraries (ICADL), 2003.

[32] Tsinaraki, C. and Christodoulakis, S. (2005) Semantic user preference descriptions in MPEG-7/21. Proceedings of Hellenic Data Management Symposium.

[33] Tsinaraki, C. and Christodoulakis, S. (2006) A user preference model and a query language that allow semantic retrieval and filtering of multimedia content. Proceedings of the 1st International Workshop on Semantic Media Adaptation and Personalization (SMAP), IEEE Computer Society, Washington, DC, pp. 121–128.

[34] Tsinaraki, C. and Christodoulakis, S. (2007) An MPEG-7 query language and a user preference model that allow semantic retrieval and filtering of multimedia content. *Multimedia Systems*, **13** (2), 131–153.

[35] Chomicki, J. (2003) Preference formulas in relational queries. *ACM Transactions on Database Systems*, **28** (4), 427–466.

[36] Kiessling, W. (2002) Foundations of preferences in database systems. Proceedings of the 28th International Conference on Very Large Data Bases (VLDB), VLDB Endowment: Hong Kong, China, pp. 311–322.

[37] Mukherjee, D., Delfosse, E., Jae-Gon, K., and Yong, W. (2005) Optimal adaptation decision-taking for terminal and network quality-of-service. *IEEE Transactions on Multimedia*, **7** (3), 454–462.

[38] Köhncke, B. and Balke, W.-T. (2007) Preference-driven personalization for flexible digital item adaptation. *Multimedia Systems*, **13** (2), 119–130.

[39] Börzsönyi, S., Kossmann, D., and Stocker, K. (2001) The skyline operator. Proceedings of the IEEE International Conference on Data Engineering (ICDE), pp. 421–430.

[40] Papadias, D., Tao, Y., Fu, G., and Seeger, B. (2003) An optimal and progressive algorithm for skyline queries. Proceedings of the 2003 ACM SIGMOD International Conference on Management of Data (SIGMOD), ACM, New York, pp. 467–478.

16

A Game Approach to Integrating MPEG-7 in MPEG-21 for Dynamic Bandwidth Dealing

Anastasis A. Sofokleous and Marios C. Angelides
Electronic and Computer Engineering, School of Engineering and Design, Brunel University, UK

16.1 Introduction

This chapter uses a game-based approach to fair bandwidth allocation in a game where all users are selfish and are only interested in maximizing their own Quality of Service (QoS) rather than settling for the average QoS. Such users have no or limited knowledge of one another and collaboration is never or seldom pursued. The resulting model assumes a fixed price per bandwidth unit, for example Mega Byte (MB), and no price fluctuations over time. The fixed cost per bandwidth unit prevents the users from using more bandwidth than they actually need and at the same time enables the use of pragmatic factors, such as waiting time and serve order, as pay off. Hence, neither is bandwidth allocated to users who wish to pay more, nor do users aim to buy bandwidth at the cheapest price. Noncooperative clients aim to satisfy their selfish objectives by getting the bandwidth they need and be served in the shortest possible time.

The proposed game approach integrates the multimedia standards MPEG-7 and MPEG-21 for describing the content and the usage environment, respectively. Furthermore, MPEG-21 is used to describe constraints that steer user strategy development and content variation selection. With the use of MPEG-7 and MPEG-21, the proposed approach addresses the interoperability between the clients and the server. Using game theory, policies and rules that ensure fairness and efficiency, the suggested approach allows the clients to develop their own strategies and compete for the bandwidth. Clients send their requirements using MPEG-21 and the video streaming server serves content by considering the client requirements and additional data extracted from other resources

The Handbook of MPEG Applications: Standards in Practice   Edited by Marios C. Angelides and Harry Agius
© 2011 John Wiley & Sons, Ltd

such as server-side requirements, also encoded in the MPEG-21, and video semantic and syntactic information encoded in the MPEG-7. The objective of bandwidth allocation mechanisms is not simply to avoid bandwidth bottlenecks but most importantly to optimize the overall network utility and to satisfy objectives and constraints, such as the QoS. In this case, user preferences and characteristics are expressed using MPEG-21 [1].

The rest of this chapter is organized as follows. The next section discusses the bandwidth allocation problem and existing approaches addressing this problem, followed by a section on game theory, where our approach is sourced from, and its application to bandwidth allocation. This section discusses our gaming approach to bandwidth allocation. The penultimate section discusses the model implementation and the final section concludes the article.

16.2   Related Work

This paper addresses the challenge of sharing bandwidth fairly among selfish clients who are requesting video streaming services and uses game theory to model the problem of server-centric bandwidth allocation [2] and to guarantee both, satisfaction of end-user experience and optimization of usage of shared resources.

Game theory was initially developed to analyze scenarios where individuals are competitive and each individual's success may be at the cost of others. Usually, a game consists of more than one player allowed to make moves or strategies, and each move or combination of moves has a payoff. Game theory's applications attempt to find equilibrium, a state in which game players are unlike to change their strategies [3]. The most famous equilibrium concept is the Nash Equilibrium (NE), according to which each player is assumed to know the final strategies of the rest of the players, and there is nothing to gain by changing only his own strategy. NE is not Pareto Optimal, that is, it does not necessarily imply that all the players will get the best cumulative payoff, as a better payoff could be gained in a cooperative environment, where players can agree on their strategies. NE is established by players following either pure-strategies or mixed-strategies. A pure-strategy defines exactly the player's move for each situation that a player meets, whereas in a mixed-strategy the player selects a pure-strategy randomly, according to the probability assigned to each pure-strategy. Furthermore, an equilibrium is said to be stable (stability) if by changing slightly the probabilities of a player's pure-strategies, the latter player is now playing with a worse strategy, while the rest of the players cannot improve their strategies. Stability will make the player of the changed mixed-strategy come back to NE. To guarantee NE, a set of conditions must be assumed including the assumption that the players are dedicated to doing everything in their power for maximizing their payoff. Games can be of perfect information, if the players know the moves previously made by other players, or imperfect information, if not every player knows the actions of the others. An example of the former is a sequential game which allows the players to observe the game, whereas the latter can occur in cases where players make their moves concurrently.

Game theory has been used with mixed success in bandwidth allocation. Auctioning is the most common approach for allocating resources to the clients. In an auction, players bid for bandwidth and therefore, each player aims to get a certain bandwidth capacity without any serving latency, both of which are guaranteed according to the player's bid, of which its amount may vary based on the demand. A central agent is responsible for allocating the resources and usually the highest bidder gets the resources as requested and pays the bid. Thus, each player must evaluate the cost of the resources to determine if it is a good offer (or optimum) for bidding it; where the player does not get the resources, it may have to wait until the next auction; for example, until there are available resources. Thus, the cost is the main payoff of this game. It is also assumed that players hold a constrained budget. The main problem with this strategy, however, is that the players can lie and the winner may have to pay more than the true value of the resources [4]. In such a case, NE cannot guarantee a social optimum, that is, that we can maximize the net benefits for everyone in society, irrespective of who enjoys the benefits or pays the cost. According to economic theory, in their attempt to maximize their private benefits, if players pay for any benefits they receive and bear only the corresponding costs (hence there are no externalities), then the social net benefits are maximized, that is, they are Pareto Optimal. If such externalities exist, then the decision-maker should not take into account the cost during its decision process.

In [5], the authors use game theory to model selfish and altruistic user behaviors in multihop relay networks. Their game uses four types of players who represent four types of elements in a multihop network. Despite the fact that the game utility involves end-user satisfaction, bandwidth and price are used to establish NE. A problem with resource allocation approaches that use only the cost is that the fairness of the game does not take into account the player waiting time in a queue. This may cause a problem as some players that keep losing may wait indefinitely in the queue. To address the problem, in this paper we use both the queue length and arrival time to prioritize the players and allow them to adapt their strategy accordingly. Likewise, users in [6] negotiate not only for the bandwidth, but also for the user waiting time in the queue. Their approach addresses the bandwidth bottleneck on a node that serves multiple decentralized users. The users who use only local information and feedback from the remote node need to go to NE to be served.

Some researchers classify the game players either as cooperative or noncooperative. Cooperative players can form binding commitments and communication between each other is allowed. However, the noncooperative player model is usually more representative of real problems. Examples of both types of players are presented in [7]. The authors apply a game theory in a Digital Video Broadcasting (DVB) network of users, who can be either cooperative or noncooperative. Motivated by environment problems that affect the reliability and performance of satellite streaming, they apply game theory in a distributed satellite resource allocation problem. Game theory is the most appropriate in distributed and scalable models in which conflict objectives exist. The behavior of noncooperative players is studied in [8]. Specifically, the authors use game theory to model mobile wireless clients in a noncooperative dynamic self-organized environment. The objective is to allocate bandwidth to network clients, which share only limited knowledge for each other. In our approach, we use noncooperative players as players are not allowed either to cooperative or communication with each other.

Game theory has been also used for solving a variety of other problems, such as service differentiation and data replication. In service differentiation, the objective is to provide QoS according to a user's class rather than according to a user's bid. In [9, 10], the authors present a game-based approach for providing service differentiation to p2p network users according to the service each user is providing to the network. The resource allocation process is modeled as a competition game between the nodes where NE is achieved and a resource distribution mechanism works between the nodes of the p2p network that share content. The main idea, which is to encourage users to share files and provide good p2p service differentiation, is that nodes earn higher contribution by sharing popular files and allowing uploading, and the higher the contribution a node makes, the higher the priority the node will have when downloading files. The authors report that their approach promotes fairness in resource sharing, avoids wastage of resources and takes into account the congestion level of the network link. They also argue that it is scalable and can adapt to the conditions of the environment, and can guarantee optimal allocation while maximizing the network utility value. [11] discusses the use of game theory in spectrum sharing for more flexible, efficient, and fair spectrum usage and provides an overview of this area by exploiting the behavior of users and analyzing the design and optimality of distributed access networks. Their model defines two types of players: the wireless users whose set of strategies include the choice of a license channel, the price, transmission power, and transmission time duration and the spectrum holders, whose strategies include charging for among other the usage and selection of unused channels. The authors provide an overview of current modeling approaches on spectrum sharing and describe an auction-based spectrum sharing game.

Game theory has been also applied for the data replication problem in data grids where the objective is to maximize the objectives of each provider participating in the grid [12]. In [13], game theory has been used for allocating network resources while consuming the minimum energy of battery-based stations of wireless networks. In a noncooperative environment, a variety of power control game approaches are presented where the utility is modeled as a function of data transmitted over consumed energy. The following section discusses our gaming approach to dealing bandwidth to mobile clients.

16.3   Dealing Bandwidth Using Game Theory

This chapter addresses bandwidth allocation where multiple users of different characteristics, preferences, and devices request content from a remote video streaming server. Using game theory to model this allows players to develop strategies using rules that set possible moves and payoffs. Players act selfishly based on their own objectives and constraints and are not interested in achieving an Average Quality of Service (AQoS) in collaboration with other players. Players pay for the bandwidth they are allocated; this constraints players from asking for more bandwidth than they actually need. If the server allocates more bandwidth than needed, initially, players may give back to the server the surplus, which in turn can be used to serve those players who may need more. The cost of bandwidth remains fixed, from the start of the game. Players formulate their strategy based on their arrival time and resulting order in the game, which is implemented as a queue, and decisions made during previous rounds of the same game.

Players are invited to make a decision based on their order in the queue. Furthermore, their strategy is developed based on constraints and objectives which are defined in relation to a variety of characteristics, such as the required bandwidth and the estimated time of service. We use both MPEG-7 and MPEG-21, the former to describe semantically and syntactically the video content, the latter to describe the characteristics of usage environment (device, natural environment, and network), the characteristics and preferences of users and the constraints which steer the strategies of the players. The following section describes the integration of the two MPEG standards 7 and 21 into the game approach. Section 16.3.2 describes the main game approach and Section 16.3.3 describes the implementation model.

16.3.1 Integration of MPEG-7 and MPEG-21 into the Game Approach

The proposed approach uses the MPEG-7 MDS (Multimedia Description Schemes) for describing the semantic and syntactic (low-level) features of the original video content. The MDS descriptions of video content is used during the validation of selected content variations against constraints specified as thresholds by the user and/or the server. For example, when watching a game of soccer, a user may ask for higher quality for the goals scored and the free kicks given. This assumes analysis of the video content and specification of these user preferences, rather than analyzing content in real-time and asking users to change options. MPEG-7 MDS enable content semantics, such as, objects, and spatio-temporal segments, to be described and user content preferences and constraints to be set in relation to these. For instance, it allows the user to set quality constraints based on specific events occurring or the presence of physical objects. An example of an MPEG-7 content description is shown in Figure 16.1.

```
<Mpeg7 ...>
  <Description xsi:type="ContentEntityType">
   <MultimediaContent xsi:type="VideoType">
    <Video>...</Video></MultimediaContent>
  </Description>
  <Description xsi:type="CreationDescriptionType">
   <CreationInformation>
        ...
     <Classification>
     <Genre href="urn:mpeg:mpeg7:cs:GenreCS:2001:1.6">
         <Name>Sports</Name>
     </Genre>
     <Target><Age max="35" min="15"/></Target>
     <MediaReview>
        <RatingValue>3.0</RatingValue>
      ...
   </CreationInformation>
  </Description>
  ...
</Mpeg7>
```

Figure 16.1 MPEG-7 content description.

The proposed approach uses the UCD (Universal Constraints Description), UED (Usage Environment Description) and AQoS parts of the MPEG-21 standard. The MPEG-21 UCD is used by the clients to describe their individual optimization and limit constraints. The optimization constraints and part of the limit constraints are used by the client to develop their own strategies during the main game progress. For example, let us consider the case where a client aims to get served in less than 2 min at the highest quality. The former is described as a limit constraint and the latter as an optimization constraint in the UCD. Information on these two constraints neither is forwarded to the server, nor is revealed to other players. If other players or the server knew of these constraints, these could be used to change the outcome of the game. The MPEG-21 UCD may also contain limit constraints which do not affect the strategy of the player, as they refer to the content itself. For example, the video codec supported by the client, desirable resolution, supported resolution. Limit constraints that do not affect the strategy development, are forwarded to the server, which uses them to filter the content variations that do not match the requirements; for instance, unsupported video codecs. The MPEG-21 UCD is also used statically by the server to describe global constraints, such as the total available bandwidth and the maximum total streaming sessions, which are validated against the aggregated totals of streaming requests during each game. An example of MPEG-21 UCD is shown in Figure 16.2a.

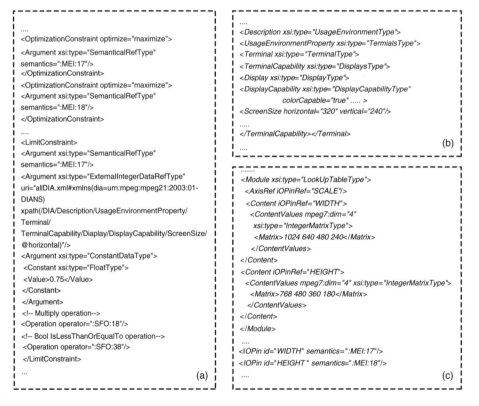

Figure 16.2 (a) MPEG-21 UCD, (b) MPEG-21 UED and (c) MPEG-21 AQoS.

The MPEG-21 UED is used to describe the usage environment characteristics, such as those of the client, network, and natural environment at the client location. Furthermore, the proposed approach uses the MPEG-21 UED to describe the characteristics of the user, which are used along with the MPEG-21 UCD constraints to filter suitable content variations and assist in strategy development. The MPEG-21 UED is generated from multiple sources, such as the client, proxies or server, either manually, automatically or as a mixture of both. Individual MPEG-21 UEDs are merged by the server to create the complete UED that will be used for filtering out unsuitable content variations and for determining the minimum bandwidth that will be offered to the client. An example of MPEG-21 UED is shown in Figure 16.2b.

Finally, the proposed game approach uses the MPEG-21 AQoS to describe all possible content variations. Each video is linked to an MPEG-21 AQoS which describes all its possible variations, which differ in terms of bandwidth, quality, resolution, and other encoding characteristics. The MPEG-21 AQoS is stored on the server along with the video and its MPEG-7 file. For example, when a server considers a video request, it uses its MPEG-21 AQoS to set minimum bandwidth values. An example of an MPEG-21 AQoS is shown in Figure 16.2c. Integration of MPEG-21 and MPEG-7 descriptors is shown in Figure 16.3.

16.3.2   The Bandwidth Dealing Game Approach

In this chapter, we assume that a server streams video over the internet and can serve multiple users concurrently. However, it is constrained by the limited available bandwidth which may vary over time and the cost per bandwidth unit. To serve the maximum number of users within the given bandwidth and to guarantee quality and fairness, the server employs a game algorithm. This algorithm iterates through a cycle of three phases: *Seat Arrangement*, *Main Game*, and *Seat Reallocation*. Figure 16.4 depicts the three phases.

The algorithm uses game theory and, therefore, every three-phase cycle is a new game where video streaming requests are modeled as players. A player refers to a video request made by a user and holds information that can help satisfying the request. For example, information about the video request, user characteristics and preferences, device, and constraints that can steer personalization of video streaming.

New players have to enter a FIFO queue, which is called *outerQueue*. This queue is used as a waiting place, where the players can wait until they are invited to participate in the game. Players that exit the *outerQueue*, enter the *gameQueue*, a queue that holds the players playing the actual game (Seat Arrangement Phase). While the size of *outerQueue* is not fixed, the size of *gameQueue*, is set dynamically by the server prior to the beginning of each game. At the end of each game, the server deals the bandwidth to the players participating in the game and starts a new game. Those players that have declined the server offer will rejoin the gameQueue (Seat Reallocation Phase). Each main game phase consists of three rounds, that is Minimum Bandwidth Dealing (MBD) (round 0), Dynamic Bandwidth Dealing (DBD) (round 1) and Remainder Bandwidth Dealing (RBD) (round 2).

Phase 1: Seat Arrangement. During this phase, the size of *gameQueue*, that is number of players that will be moved from *outerQueue* to *gameQueue* and will participate in the main game, is calculated. The number of seats is calculated as the maximum

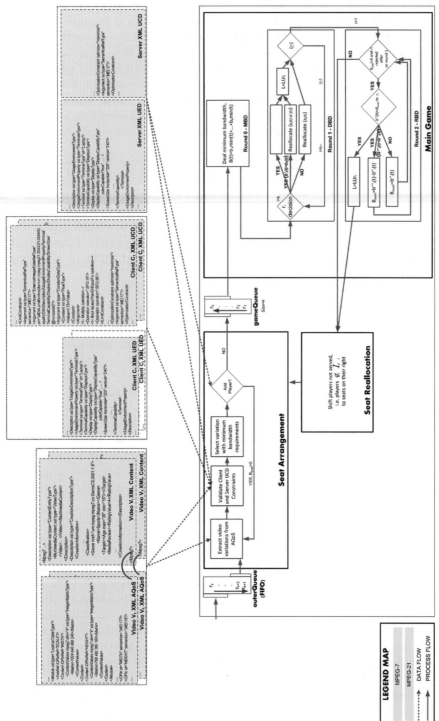

Figure 16.3 Implementation of the game approach.

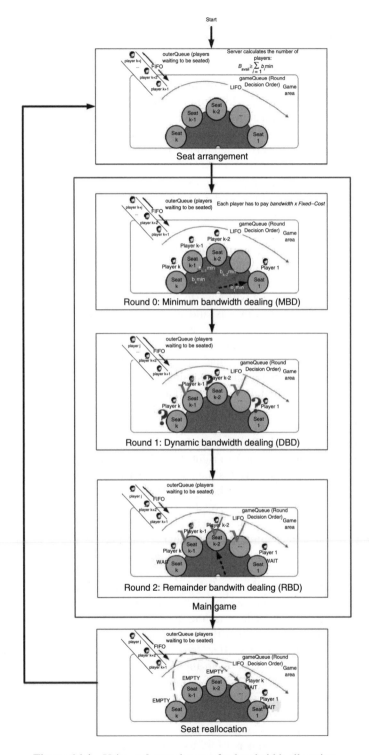

Figure 16.4 Using a 3-round game for bandwidth allocation.

players that can be served from the server's available bandwidth. The server makes an initial offer that matches the minimum acceptable quality, which however, may not meet the expectations of the user. The minimum bandwidth for each content variation of the video requested by the user is described in the MPEG-21 AQoS. The server scans the MPEG-21 AQoS in search of the content variations that satisfy the UCD limit constraints and optimize the UCD optimization constraints, and selects the minimum bandwidth value [14, 15]. The server's objective is to satisfy a maximum number of players in each game without compromising the quality of service. The server estimates how many players can be served and allows them to enter the *gameQueue*. The server uses FIFO to move a player from *outerQueue* to *gameQueue*.

Phase 2: Main Game. The phase consists of three rounds: round 0 deals a minimum amount of bandwidth, round 1 considers the players' decision in FIFO order and adjusts dynamically the bandwidth offer, and round 2 deals the unallocated bandwidth to players not served yet in FIFO.

Phase 2, Round 0: Minimum Bandwidth Dealing (MBD). In this round, the server announces its initial bandwidth allocation to the players participating in the current game, that is to the players of *gameQueue*. The server allocates the amount of bandwidth to the players and the players will have to make a decision in the next round whether to accept or not. The bandwidth is allocated to the players along with description on how the content will be served so the players will know what they will receive, that is video quality, video format, and so on. What may influence players to accept a solution depends on their individual game strategy, which in turn may depend on personal objectives and some limit constraints (e.g., minimum acceptable quality) that may not have been revealed to the server. The player may choose not to reveal all to the server (e.g., minimum acceptable video quality) if they believe that it may result in better bandwidth offer.

Phase 2, Round 1: Dynamic Bandwidth Dealing (DBD). At this round, following a LIFO order and starting from left to right, the players need to make an initial decision: either accept the server's offer as it is (i.e., a YES decision) or part of the initial allocated bandwidth if less is required than what is initially offered (i.e., a YES decision but with variation on the amount), or pass over the offer (i.e., a NO decision). With the latter decision, the server deals a NO player's bandwidth to the rest of the players still waiting in the game to make their initial decision; that is, the players sitting to the right of the NO player. Also, with this decision, the player knows she/he may not get another offer during this game and as a result she/he may have to wait for the next game. However, the payoff of this player is that in the next game she/he is guaranteed a better offer and also that they may be moved to a better seat in the game. Since using the LIFO order only one decision is made at a time, those players that get to decide last can get additional bandwidth from players that do not accept the server's initial offer. Thus, if a player declines the server's offer, the server takes their bandwidth and allocates it to the rest of the players waiting in the queue. If player j declined the offer, then bandwidth b_j must be reallocated before moving to the next player. In this case, the server offers the declined bandwidth equally to players $j - 1, j - 2, \ldots, 1$. A player will not get more bandwidth than they actually need, otherwise they will have to pay for bandwidth not consumed. A player may decide to decline an offer if the offer was not good enough or if she/he can afford to wait for the next game to get a better offer.

The former is calculated from the objectives and constraints set by the player, whereas the latter is the payoff of the game to players that give up their bandwidth during a game. The server records their decision and in the next game, these players will get better offers. During this round, all players must make their initial decision. At the end of the round, some "Yes" players will be satisfied and some will choose to wait.

Phase 2, Round 2: Remainder Bandwidth Dealing (RBD). This round will go ahead only if there is enough bandwidth to satisfy at least one more player. For example, consider the case where the last player declined the server's offer. In Figure 16.4, player 1, who decides last in round 1, declines the offer of the server. If b_1, which is the bandwidth offered to player 1, is also the available bandwidth at the end of round 1, in round 2 the objective is to use this bandwidth to make a new offer to unsatisfied players. If at the end of round 1, $B_{avail} > 0$ is the remaining bandwidth, the server offers this bandwidth to those players that declined its earlier offer following a FIFO order on *gameQueue*. If a player chooses to accept part of the offered bandwidth, then the server recalculates the available bandwidth and continues with the remaining players. However, if a player takes up the whole bandwidth (i.e., YES decision) then the game ends. At the end of round 2, the server satisfies players who accept the offer, for example in Figure 16.4, player $k - 1$ accepts the offer. Players not accepting the server's offer, such as in Figure 16.4 players k and l, will play again in the next game and will not be allocated any bandwidth in the current game.

Phase 3: Seat Reallocation. Figure 16.4 shows the final phase of the game, where players are either served, if they accept an offer, or move to a better seat, if one is available, in order to participate in the next game. A new seat arrangement for those players who have decided to wait, such as player k in Figure 16.4, will result in a better offer. This is the payoff for choosing to be served in a future game. For example, if the current game is game t, player j is a player of game t waiting to be served in the next game, then $b_j(t + 1) = b_j(t) + e$, where e is a small additional amount of bandwidth given to these players, for example $e = \frac{(B - b_j(t))}{k}$, and $b_n(m)$ is the bandwidth offered to player n during game m. The next section describes the implementation of our game-based bandwidth allocation.

16.3.3 *Implementing the Bandwidth Allocation Model*

This section describes the implementation of the proposed game-based approach to serving bandwidth to users. Figure 16.2 shows the complete architecture that accommodates the game model. The server uses user and server data in order to define game policies and constraints. Players develop strategies based on their objectives and constraints, described in the MPEG-21 UED, and on information collected by the server during the game.

The usage environment of the user, network, natural environment, device and user itself, is described in the XML UED, which is part of the MPEG-21 standard. As shown in Figure 16.2, the information is used during the seat arrangement phase, when the server selects, validates, and optimizes the possible content variation solutions to be offered to the user. The limit constraints and the objectives of the users are expressed in the XML UCD, which is also part of the MPEG-21. The limit constraints of the XML UCD are used by the server for filtering the solutions that meet the constraints defined by the user.

The optimization constraints defined in the XML UCD, are used to assist players with their moves, that is to develop their strategy. In addition to the UCD sent by the user, the server uses a Global Server XML UCD that describes the server constraints, for example total available bandwidth and maximum concurrent requests, which are taken into account when validating global constraints derived from the decision on each individual streaming request. The server maintains an XML AQoS for each video, which describes the possible content variations as shown in Figure 16.3. The XML AQoS is used during the seat arrangement phase to enable new players to enter the game.

The players participating in the game enter gameQueue, which is initially used as a LIFO. As in Figure 16.3, players are informed during round 0 of the server's initial offer, then they make their decision during round 1, and during round 2, some of the players may be made improved offers by the server. During the seat reallocation phase, those players in the current game who have not accepted the server's offer, may be moved to better seats if available, for improved bandwidth offers. The figure shows which parts of the algorithm use which data. It also shows the phases during which the players interact with the server, or enter and exit the main game. The approach develops an abstract decision layer that allows decision making without knowledge of the actual content encoding and/or the content encryption.

16.4   An Application Example

This section presents the game approach from the user point of view and discusses the user choices as they evolved during game play. When one or more users request video streaming, their requests enter a FIFO queue, that is the *outerQueue*. The queue is hosted on the server since not all requests may be served concurrently due to bandwidth limitations as seen in Figure 16.5.

The game approach incorporated in the server is transparent to the user, and the user needs only to send additional data describing his/her characteristics and preferences. Apart from personal information such as the age and gender, the user may communicate, for example, that the preferred option for presentation is video followed by audio, and that she/he likes sports more than she/he likes movies, and that she/he would prefer to have the video converted to other video formats. This information can be communicated automatically by an agent that keeps monitoring the user, by using information collected on the user (or in the user profile). Some browsers collect such information over time about a user and can submit such information when needed. In addition, a server collects information about the user device, such as supported video formats and maximum acceptable resolution. This information is crucial for the server, as it may use it to select the appropriate video variation and hence, optimize bandwidth. The server also collects information about the network link between the user and the server, such as the available bandwidth and the packet loss. The natural environment characteristics, such as location of the user and the environment noise, could also be collected, manually or automatically, as such information may be of great assistance to server decisions, such as in the case of selecting the appropriate content variation. The user, network, device, and natural environment are described as four individual XML UEDs and are merged at the server-side, to create the XML UED that will be used by the server during decision making. On the server-side, all possible video variations may be modeled in AQoS;

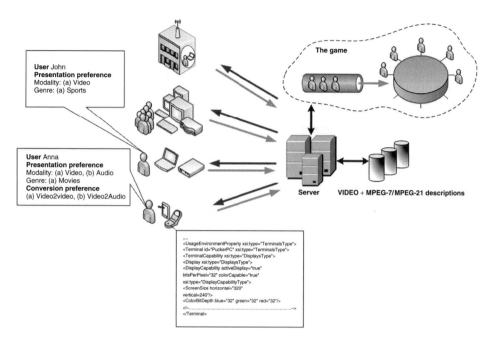

Figure 16.5   A usage case scenario.

for example, resolution, video bit rate, and color reduction. The server may also host MPEG-7 files describing the video content. The server considers this information during selection of the most appropriate video variation that satisfies the minimum requirements and selects variations that consume the minimum bandwidth, in order to allow the first users to enter the *gameQueue*, until the bandwidth is allocated.

In this problem model, the user has the chance to set and play an important role in game progress. When users enter the *gameQueue*, they will be offered a bandwidth amount in relation to how the content will be served (e.g., codec, resolution, quality). Before the user is asked to make a decision, the server may update its offer. During round 0 the server reallocates the bandwidth of users that declined the bandwidth offer (NO decision) to players that have not been asked yet for their decision. The user, before the end of round 1, is asked to choose either to accept (YES) or to decline (NO) the bandwidth offer. The user may request less bandwidth than the amount offered. At this point, the user starts to develop their game strategy. If this is their first game, the user knows that one is probably in a disadvantaged position compared to players who are already in their second or third game or in a better seat because of their order of arrival. The user does not know how many other players are participating in the current game, but knows that if the server has updated j-times its initial offer, then there are at least j-players who have already made their move (i.e., j-players are in a worse position in the game) and that j-players have decided NO (or have proposed to accept the smallest amount of bandwidth) to the server's initial offer. The user does not know how many more players are ahead in the game, but knows that if there is at least one player who has not yet been offered, then the user may be offered again more bandwidth before the next game, if that user declines. The user also knows that if one chooses not to accept the server's offer, in the worst-case scenario, one would have to wait until the next game where the server will pay back by offering better bandwidth and probably by moving them to a better seat in the game. Based on this knowledge, users may adapt their strategy and either decide NO, YES, or YES with a smallest amount of bandwidth to each server offer.

16.5 Concluding Discussion

This paper describes a game approach to dealing with bandwidth. It proposes the modeling of bandwidth allocation based on game theory, where players are users waiting to be served sufficient bandwidth. Each player participates in the game under a number of rules for gaining the desired bandwidth resources. Players have priorities according to the time of arrival. One of the differences with our approach is that it takes into account the length of the queue and the time that a player may need to wait before getting served. Thus, in some cases, the players can sacrifice the quality of the video in order to be served faster, or may choose to wait more in exchange for more bandwidth. Our approach uses cost to constrain players to use only the bandwidth that they actually need, and thus achieves a fair(er) allocation of bandwidth. We are currently extending our algorithm to incorporate content adaptation.

References

[1] Vetro, A., Timmerer, C., and Devillers, S. (2006) Digital item adaptation – tools for universal multimedia access, in *The MPEG-21 Book*, (eds I.S. Burnett, F. Pereira, R. Van de Walle, and R. Koenen), John Wiley & Sons, Inc, Hoboken, NJ, pp. 282–331.

[2] Prangl, M., Szkaliczki, T., and Hellwagner, H. (2007) A framework for utility-based multimedia adaptation. *IEEE Transactions on Circuits and Systems for Video Technology*, **17** (6), 719–728.

[3] Fotakis, D., Kontogiannis, S., Koutsoupias, E., Mavronicolas, M., and Spirakis, P. (2009) The structure and complexity of Nash equilibria for a selfish routing game. *Theoretical Computer Science*, **410** (36), 3305–3326.

[4] Sahasrabudhe, A. and Kar, K. (2008) Bandwidth allocation games under budget and access constraints. Proceedings of the 42nd Annual Conference on Information Sciences and Systems (CISS'08), Princeton, NJ, pp. 761–769.

[5] Chao, S.L., Lin, G.Y., and Wei, H.Y. (2008) Mixed altruistic and selfish users in wireless mesh networks: a game theoretic model for multihop bandwidth sharing. Proceedings of the 9th ACM International Symposium on Mobile Ad Hoc Networking and Computing, pp. 461–462.

[6] Maheswaran, R.T. and Basar, T. (1998) Multi-user flow control as a Nash game: performance of various algorithms. Proceedings of the 37th IEEE Conference on Decision and Control, Tampa, FL, pp. 1990–1995.

[7] Del Re, E., Gorni, G., Ronga, L.S., and Vazquez Castro, M.A. (2008) A game theory approach for DVB-RCS resource allocation. Proceedings of the IEEE Vehicular Technology Conference (VTC'08), Marina Bay, Singapore, pp. 2937–2941.

[8] Fang, Z. and Bensaou, B. (2004) Fair bandwidth sharing algorithms based on game theory frameworks for wireless ad-hoc networks. Proceedings of the 23rd Annual Joint Conference of the IEEE Computer and Communications Societies (INFOCOM'04), Hong Kong, China, pp. 1284–1295.

[9] Ma, R.T.B., Lee, S.C.M., Lui, J.C.S., and Yau, D.K.Y. (2004) A game theoretic approach to provide incentive and service differentiation in P2P networks. Proceedings of the Joint International Conference on Measurement and Modeling of Computer Systems, pp. 189–198.

[10] Ma, R.T.B., Lee, S.C.M., Lui, J.C.S., and Yau, D.K.Y. (2006) Incentive and service differentiation in P2P networks: a game theoretic approach. *IEEE/ACM Transactions on Networking (TON)*, **14** (5), 978–991.

[11] Ji, Z. and Liu, K.J.R. (2007) Dynamic spectrum sharing: a game theoretical overview. *IEEE Communications Magazine*, **45** (5), 88.

[12] Elghirani, A.H., Subrata, R., and Zomaya, A.Y. (2008) A proactive non-cooperative game-theoretic framework for data replication in data grids. Proceedings of the 8th IEEE International Symposium on Cluster Computing and the Grid (CCGRID'08), Lyon, France, pp. 433–440.

[13] Meshkati, F., Poor, H.V., and Schwartz, S.C. (2007) Energy-efficient resource allocation in wireless networks: an overview of game-theoretic approaches. *IEEE Signal Processing Magazine*, **24**, 58–68.

[14] Sofokleous, A.A. and Angelides, M.C. (2008) An MPEG-21 dynamic content adaptation framework. *Multimedia Tools and Applications*, **40** (2), 151–182.

[15] Sofokleous, A.A. and Angelides, M.C. (2008) Dynamic selection of a video content adaptation strategy from a pareto front. *The Computer Journal*, **52** (4), 413–428.

17

The Usage of MPEG-21 Digital Items in Research and Practice

Hermann Hellwagner and Christian Timmerer
Institute of Information Technology, Klagenfurt University, Klagenfurt, Austria

17.1 Introduction

The aim of the MPEG-21 standard, the so-called Multimedia Framework, is to enable transparent and augmented use of multimedia resources across a wide range of networks, devices, user preferences, and communities, notably for trading (of bits). As such, it provides an important step in the evolution of MPEG's standards; that is, the transaction of Digital Items (DIs) among Users [1, 2].

This chapter provides an overview of applications making use of MPEG-21 DIs and a more in-depth presentation of a few selected applications and use cases.

A brief overview of MPEG-21 DI applications is given in Section 17.2. In Section 17.3, we present one of the first adoptions of DIs, namely, Universal Plug and Play (UPnP)'s DIDL (Digital Item Declaration Language)-Lite [3], which is derived from a subset of MPEG-21 DIDL. It is basically used as a container format within UPnP's content directory and enhanced with UPnP-specific data (e.g., media resource attributes such as bit rate, resolution, and size) and Dublin Core (DC) metadata. We provide a brief description and a critical review thereof, in particular, whether and how interoperability between DIDL-Lite and DIDL can be achieved.

The abstract DI model has been adopted within Microsoft's Interactive Media Manager (IMM) [4] and implemented using the Web Ontology Language (OWL) [5]. This implementation is described in Section 17.4. It uses DC but also allows for the inclusion of domain-specific metadata (e.g., IPTC, EXIF, XMP, and SMPTE) or custom ontology predicates. Interestingly, IMM also adopts Part 3 of MPEG-21 – Digital Item Identification (DII) – which allows for uniquely identifying DIs and parts thereof [6].

Several EC-funded projects (e.g., DANAE [7], AXMEDIS [8], and ENTHRONE [9]) have adopted a wide range of MPEG-21 technologies and, in addition, provided reference

The Handbook of MPEG Applications: Standards in Practice Edited by Marios C. Angelides and Harry Agius
© 2011 John Wiley & Sons, Ltd

applications. In Sections 17.5 and 17.6, we describe these adoptions from an application's point of view.

Section 17.7 reviews a significant application of MPEG-21 core concepts, namely, of Digital Item Declaration (DID), DII, and Digital Item Processing (DIP), which interestingly is not in the core multimedia area. Rather, the use of MPEG-21 technology for representing, storing, managing, and disseminating complex information assets in a digital library has been reported in the literature and is described in this chapter [10, 11]. Finally, Section 17.8 concludes the chapter.

17.2 Overview of the Usage of MPEG-21 Digital Items

The core MPEG-21 specifications have been available for many years. However, apparently their wide scope and complexity seem to make it difficult for enterprises to exploit MPEG-21 technologies for their business directly.

To the best of our knowledge, only a few companies exist that provide MPEG-21 tools or base their products on MPEG-21. Two companies that seem to use a wide range of MPEG-21 standards are *Adactus* (www.adactus.no) and *Enikos* (www.enikos.com). *Adactus*, with their *Mobilize* platform, offers a content packaging, adaptation, and delivery system mainly targeting mobile devices. Several media resources can be packaged into a DI: during distribution, for example, commercials can be added as metadata; the content can be adapted (transcoded) to the end user device; and the commercials can be personalized to the end user or based on his/her current location, according to the Adactus website. Apparently, this application is mainly based on DID constructs, but also Digital Item Adaptation (DIA) descriptions seem to be made use of. *Enikos* provides the *Enhanced Media Platform (EMP)*, a solution by which content creators and distributors can bundle their digital audio and video media, metadata, and other digital assets, for example, comments, links to dynamic content, and advertising, to form a rich and partially interactive multimedia experience for the end user. The content can also be contextualized and repurposed (adapted) for the user and his/her device, respectively. Apparently, again DID and DIA constructs seem to be utilized in the EMP.

More intense use is being made of the MPEG-21 parts that can be deployed for Digital Rights Management (DRM) purposes, mainly the Rights Expression Language (REL) and the Rights Data Dictionary (RDD). Companies like *ContentGuard* (www.contentguard.com) and *Rightscom* (www.rightscom.com), which already contributed their technology and their personnel's expertise to the standards' development, now offer MPEG-21-based products or consulting services. Several European projects, such as the ones addressed in Sections 17.5 and 17.6, and non-European projects, for example, DigitalCopyright.hk, utilized particularly MPEG-21 REL for DRM solutions.

Interestingly, in the digital library field, the DID abstract model and DIDL have been adopted probably more widely than in the multimedia field. Apart from the effort reported in Section 17.7, similar work is reported in [12]. The requirement to clearly structure and combine information assets and associated metadata into complex digital objects for storage in digital repositories seems to be well addressed by the MPEG-21 DID concepts.

Finally, it must be noted that MPEG-21 technologies, mainly DID-, rights-, and file format-related ones, are being deployed in the specifications of *Multimedia Application Formats* (MAFs; see [13, 14]).

17.3   Universal Plug and Play (UPnP): DIDL-Lite

One of the first adoptions of MPEG-21 concepts was within the UPnP Forum where DIDL-Lite [3] has been proposed shortly after the specification of the abstract DID model and its implementation, namely, DIDL [15]. In fact, the DIDL-Lite schema [16] aims to be an implementation of the abstract DID model using XML Schema, but with a slightly different syntax compared to the DIDL schema [17].

In the following, we review the abstract DID model and compare its XML Schema-based implementation MPEG-21 DIDL with UPnP DIDL-Lite. The abstract DID model is defined using the Extended Backus–Naur Form (EBNF) [18] and shown in Listing 17.1.

Listing 17.1 Abstract DID model

```
container   ::= descriptor* container* item*
item        ::= condition* descriptor* choice* (item|component)*
                annotation
component   ::= condition* descriptor* resource anchor
anchor      ::= condition* descriptor* fragment
descriptor  ::= condition* descriptor* (component|statement)*
condition   ::= predicate+
choice      ::= condition* descriptor* selection+
selection   ::= condition* descriptor* predicate
annotation  ::= assertion* descriptor* anchor*
assertion   ::= predicate*
```

We give only a brief description of the elements required for the following sections; for the exact semantics, the interested reader is referred to [15].

In practice, a DI is referred to as a collection of *items* and *containers*, respectively, which may comprise further *items* and *containers* in a hierarchical way. The *container* allows for defining groups of items and/or containers which may form logical packages or shelves, whereas the *item* is primarily used as a collection of *components* bound to a set of relevant *descriptors*. However, an item may contain subitems, which is then considered as a compilation of items.

A *component* is the binding of a *resource* (i.e., assets such as a movie, video/audio clip, image, and text) to a set of *descriptors*. These descriptors contain usually structural information (e.g., bit rate, frame rate, and resolution) about the resource, but do not describe its content.

A *descriptor* associates information (i.e., metadata) with the enclosing element (e.g., item, container, and component). Interestingly, a descriptor may contain a component including a resource that provides descriptive information about the enclosing element such as a thumbnail of an image, summary of a video/audio clip, or text in the form of a PDF document.

The combination of *choice*, *condition*, *predicate*, and *selection* enables a so-called *choice/selection* mechanism, which may be used to make the static declaration of a DI configurable. That is, parts of a DI can be declared in a way that they are only conditionally available depending on a predefined context. For example, a DI could be declared such as to deliver a high-/medium-/low-quality version depending on the user's subscription type (e.g., high-quality for paying customers vs low-quality free of charge) and/or end

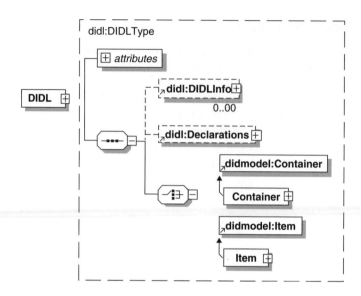

Figure 17.1   Top-level DIDL elements.

device capabilities (e.g., flat screen vs smart phone). Thus, these elements provide a very powerful mechanism for introducing flexibility within the media value delivery chain including associated networks.

The abstract DID model has been implemented using XML Schema resulting in the DIDL. The top-level elements of DIDL are depicted in Figure 17.1; for the full schema, the interested reader is referred to [17].

There is one noticeable difference between the abstract DID model and DIDL, which is the DIDL root element. The DIDL root element provides the entry point for DID, which may be either a Container or an Item and possibly prefixed by DIDLInfo and/or Declarations. The former is used to convey application domain–specific information about the DID and the latter for declaring a set of DIDL elements without instantiating them; for example, for later use within this document through a well-defined referencing/ inclusion mechanism. Container and Item are more or less an implementation of the abstract DID model as shown in Listing 17.1 without noticeable differences.

Finally, it is important to note that MPEG deliberately has not defined which kind of resources or metadata shall be included within a DI and how. It is expected that this should be specified within the respective application domains. An example of such a specification is UPnP's ContentDirectory Service Template [3], which defines DIDL-Lite that has been derived from MPEG-21 DIDL. The metadata model of UPnP DIDL-Lite is shown in Figure 17.2.

The base class from which all other classes are derived is called *object* which is an abstract class and, thus, cannot be instantiated similar to DIDBaseType as defined within urn:mpeg:mpeg21:2002:02-DIDMODEL-NS. Direct subclasses of *object* are *item* and *container*, which can be instantiated through the corresponding DIDL-Lite schema elements item and container, respectively. *Item* and *container* classes can be further refined as shown in Figure 17.2 and are indicated by the upnp:class element, which is a child element of item and container. That is, the nature of the *item* or *container*

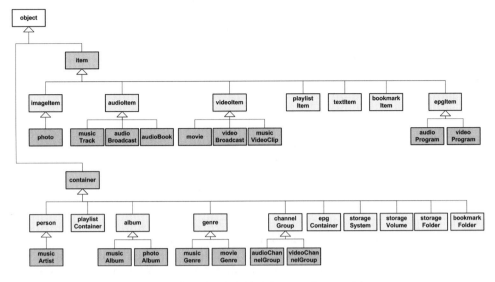

Figure 17.2   UPnP DIDL-Lite metadata model.

can be specified, for example, a photo, music track, movie, and photo album. Note that only leaf nodes as shown in Figure 17.2 are allowed within the upnp:class element. This functionality provides an extension of the DID model with respect to the application domain within which UPnP operates.

Further extensions of UPnP DIDL-Lite compared to the original MPEG-21 DID model are the adoption of DC metadata [19], various properties (*upnp:forContainer*), and certain attributes for the actual resources (*res-attributes*). A simplified EBNF syntax for UPnP DIDL-Lite is shown in Listing 17.2.

Listing 17.2 Simplified EBNF for UPnP DIDL-Lite

```
upnp:forContainer ::= <some properties>
upnp:forItem ::= upnp:forContainer
allowed-under-container ::= upnp:forContainer | dc | desc | item |
                            container | res
allowed-under-item ::= upnp:forItem | dc | desc | res
upnp:class ::= [object.item] [object.item.imageItem] ...
               [object.container] [object.container.person] ...
               [object.container.bookmarkFolder]

container ::= dc:title allowed-under-container* upnp:class
              allowed-under-container*
item ::= dc:title allowed-under-item* upnp:class
         allowed-under-item*

res-attributes ::= protocolInfo [importUri] [size] [duration]
                   [bitrate] [sampleFrequency] [bitsPerSample]
                   [nrAudioChannels] [resolution] [colorDepth]
```

```
                        [tspec] [allowedUse] [validityStart]
                        [validityEnd] [remainingTime] [usageInfo]
                        [rightsInfoURI] [contentInfoURI]
                        [recordQuality] [protection]
res ::= anyURI res-attributes

desc ::= any

DIDL-Lite ::= ( item | container | desc )*
```

While the `DIDL-Lite` root element has some similarities with the `DIDL` root element, it becomes apparent that the `container` and `item` elements, although present in both models, are quite different from their MPEG-21 DIDL counterparts. In particular, a `container` may equally include resources and a nested structure of further `containers` and/or `items` while an `item` may contain only resources (i.e., descriptive information is excluded for the moment). That is, the UPnP DIDL-Lite `item` element comes close to an MPEG-21 DIDL `Component` element and the UPnP DIDL-Lite `container` represents a combination or mixture of MPEG-21 DIDL `Container` and `Item` elements.

The UPnP `res` element has additional attributes providing structural information about the resource which is similar to MPEG-21's `Descriptor` within a `Component`. Thus, the UPnP `res` element can be seen as equivalent to the MPEG-21 `Component`, but with a restricted number of attributes, which are shown in Listing 17.2.

UPnP `DIDL-Lite`, `item`, and `container` may have a `desc` element which is equivalent to the MPEG-21 `Descriptor` element except that the UPnP version can only convey XML data, whereas MPEG-21 offers more possibilities (e.g., a `Component` with a `Resource`).

Finally, each UPnP `item` or `container` may include a set of properties providing descriptive information about the enclosing element – maybe a reason why `desc` is not used in practice. These properties include information related to the contributor (e.g., artist and actor), affiliation (e.g., genre and album), associated resources (e.g., album cover art and lyrics), general description (e.g., playback count and last playback position), and so on.

An example UPnP DIDL-Lite instance is shown in Listing 17.3, which provides the result of browsing a single soundtrack music album. In particular, three `items` are returned each characterized by `title`, `creator`, `class`, and information on how to access the actual resource (i.e., `res` element).

Listing 17.3 UPnP DIDL-Lite result of browsing a single soundtrack music album [3]

```
1 <?xml version="1.0" encoding="UTF-8"?>
2 <DIDL-Lite xmlns:dc="http://purl.org/dc/elements/1.1/"
   xmlns="urn:schemas-upnp-org:metadata-1-0/DIDL-Lite/"
   xmlns:upnp="urn:schemas-upnp-org:metadata-1-0/upnp/"
   xmlns:xsi="http://www.w3.org/2001/XMLSchema-instance"
   xsi:schemaLocation="
   urn:schemas-upnp-org:metadata-1-0/DIDL-Lite/
```

```
     http://www.upnp.org/schemas/av/didl-lite-v2-20060531.xsd
     urn:schemas-upnp-org:metadata-1-0/upnp/
     http://www.upnp.org/schemas/av/upnp-v2-20060531.xsd">

 3   <item id="6" parentID="3" restricted="0">
 4     <dc:title>Chloe Dancer</dc:title>
 5     <dc:creator>Mother Love Bone</dc:creator>
 6     <upnp:class>object.item.audioItem.musicTrack</upnp:class>
 7     <res protocolInfo="http-get:*:audio/x-ms-wma:*"
           size="200000">http://10.0.0.1/getcontent.asp?id=6</res>
 8   </item>
 9   <item id="8" parentID="3" restricted="0">
10     <dc:title>Drown</dc:title>
11     <dc:creator>Smashing Pumpkins</dc:creator>
12     <upnp:class>object.item.audioItem.musicTrack</upnp:class>
13     <res protocolInfo="http-get:*:audio/mpeg:*"
           size="140000">http://10.0.0.1/getcontent.asp?id=8</res>
14   </item>
15   <item id="7" parentID="3" restricted="0">
16     <dc:title>State Of Love And Trust</dc:title>
17     <dc:creator>Pearl Jam</dc:creator>
18     <upnp:class>object.item.audioItem.musicTrack</upnp:class>
19     <res protocolInfo="http-get:*:audio/x-ms-wma:*"
           size="70000">http://10.0.0.1/getcontent.asp?id=7</res>
20   </item>
21</DIDL-Lite>
```

Each item has title and creator information as defined by DC (see lines 4–5, 10–11, and 16–17). The upnp:class element classifies these items as music tracks according to the metadata model as shown in Figure 17.2 (see lines 6, 12, and 18). Finally, the res elements (cf. lines 7, 13, and 19) provide the URIs of the actual music tracks including information concerning the protocol information (i.e., transport and content encoding formats) and the sizes in bytes.

17.4 Microsoft's Interactive Media Manager (IMM)

IMM follows a similar approach as UPnP DIDL-Lite, but claims full compliance to the abstract DID model. For the implementation of the abstract DID model, OWL has been used. The metadata model is depicted in Figure 17.3. The metadata model is quite similar to the one of UPnP DIDL-Lite (cf. Figure 17.2), with fewer specializations, though.

The base class is called *Object* – as in UPnP DIDL-Lite – and forms the root item that all classes in the model inherit from. Classes directly derived from *Object* are *Item* and *Container*, which correspond to their counterparts within the MPEG-21 abstract DID model. The *Item* can be further refined to a *MediaItem*, which can be instantiated as *VideoItem*, *AudioItem*, or *ImageItem*. A *Container* might be instantiated as *Folder*. These subclasses define their own predicates partly adopted from MPEG-21 DIDL and DC, but also including predicates from the IMM namespace (Figure 17.4).

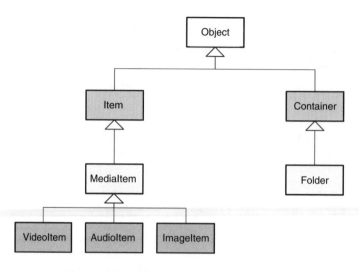

Figure 17.3 IMM top-level metadata model.

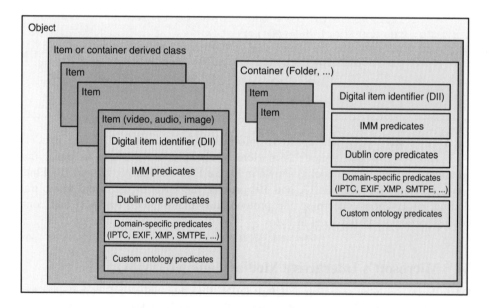

Figure 17.4 IMM detailed metadata model.

The `Object` class has predicates such as `created` and `modified` coming from DC and `hasVersion` and `modifiedBy` defined within the IMM namespace. It is the starting point for all other classes and, thus, they inherit the predicates provided by `Object`, but cannot be instantiated directly.

The `Item` class is derived from `Object` and corresponds to the MPEG-21 `Item` element. However, the IMM `Item` class does not implement the *choice/selection* mechanism and the IMM `Resource` merely reflects the component as shown in Figure 17.5.

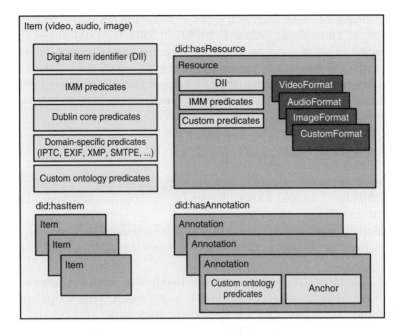

Figure 17.5 IMM metadata model: instance example.

The `Item` – instantiated as `VideoItem`, `AudioItem`, or `ImageItem` – comprises the following predicates:

- A *DII* – adopted from MPEG-21 Part 3 [6] – that uniquely identifies the item by making use of existing identification schemes, for example, the International Standard Audiovisual Number (ISAN) [20].
- Predicates defined within IMM are referred to as *IMM predicates* and include information that indicates whether this item has further subitems (`hasItem`), resources (`hasResource`), or annotations (`hasAnnotation`). Furthermore, `workflowState` indicates the current workflow state for the asset and `ingestDate` is the date that this item (or container) was ingested into the system including its accompanying essence files.
- The DC [19] predicates comprise the following properties as defined within the DC namespace: `title`, `subject`, `description`, `publisher`, `contributor`, `date`, `type`, `format`, `identifier`, `source`, `language`, `relation`, `coverage`, and `rights`. For further information about their semantics, the interested reader is referred to [19].
- Additionally, the item allows for the inclusion of *domain-specific predicates* such as IPTC [21], EXIF [22], XMP [23], and SMTPE [24].
- Finally, *custom ontology predicates* can be added to any *Item* (or *Container*) by simply creating a new OWL ontology file and adding it to the main IMM ontology as an import.

As mentioned earlier, the IMM `Resource` merely reflects the MPEG-21 `Component` that binds a set of descriptors – in this case DII, IMM, and custom predicates – to an individually identifiable asset such as a video or audio clip, an image, or a textual asset. In addition to the attributes as defined in MPEG-21 DID, the IMM `Resource` provides the total runtime of the resource in seconds (`durationSeconds`), the size (in bytes) of the physical data this resource is pointing to (`sizeInBytes`), and a link to an instance of a *Hash* class containing the hash type and value predicates (`hasHash`).

Depending on the type of the `Item`, additional predicates might be included as described in the following. For a `MetaItem`, predicates such as:

- subtitle (`subtitle`);
- production studio and network (`productionCompany`);
- licensor information (`licensorID`, `licensorType`);
- combined bit rate of the media item, for example, for both the audio and video resources in the item (`bitRate`);
- a flag indicating whether the `Item` is digital rights managed (`isDRM`);
- Web 2.0 style keyword tags associated with this media item (`tag`) and so on.

are defined. The `VideoItem` might include information regarding the video format (`videoFormat`), aspect ratio (`aspectRatio`), resolution (`resolution`), encoding format (`encoding`), frame rate (`frameRate`), color space (`colorspace`), carrier format (`carrierFormat`), and so on. The `AudioItem` has additional predicates for the encoding format (`encoding`), channel information – mono or stereo – (`channel`), and sampling rate in hertz (`samplingRate`). Finally, the `ImageItem` defines the format of the image (`format`) as well as the height and width of the image (`pixelWidth`, `pixelHeight`). Additional metadata for images might be added through domain-specific predicates (e.g., IPTC and EXIF).

A `Container` is also directly derived from `Object` and represents a collection of objects. In particular, it can represent the physical organization of objects (i.e., storage containers) or logical collections with formal definitions of their contents. Furthermore, `Containers` can be either homogeneous (i.e., containing objects that are all of the same class, e.g., video) or heterogeneous (i.e., containing objects from different classes, e.g., audio and image). Finally, `Containers` may contain other `Containers` and, thus, form a hierarchy of collections. A `Container` may have the same predicates as an `Item`.

Listing 17.4 shows an example DI describing a `VideoItem`.

Listing 17.4 `VideoItem` example [25]

```
1  <imm:VideoItem rdf:about="guid:testItem001">
2    <dc:creator rdf:datatype="http://www.w3.org/2001/XMLSchema#string">
       ericscho@medemo.com</dc:creator>
3    <dc:description rdf:datatype="http://www.w3.org/2001/XMLSchema#string">
       This is Test Item 001</dc:description>
4    <dc:identifier rdf:datatype="http://www.w3.org/2001/XMLSchema#string">
       ISAN code here</dc:identifier>
5    <dc:source rdf:datatype="http://www.w3.org/2001/XMLSchema#string">
       http://somepath</dc:source>
```

```
 6  <dc:title rdf:datatype="http://www.w3.org/2001/XMLSchema#string">
       Test Item 001</dc:title>
 7  <imm:creationDate rdf:datatype="http://www.w3.org/2001/XMLSchema#string">
       10/10/2005</imm:creationDate>
 8  <imm:hasProxy rdf:resource="guid:testProxy001"/>
 9  <imm:hasProxy rdf:resource="guid:testProxy002"/>
10  <imm:modifiedBy rdf:datatype="http://www.w3.org/2001/XMLSchema#string">
       administrator@medemo.com</imm:modifiedBy>
11  <imm:modifiedDate rdf:datatype="http://www.w3.org/2001/XMLSchema#string">
       10/10/2005</imm:modifiedDate>
12  <imm:startTimecode
       rdf:datatype="http://www.w3.org/2001/XMLSchema#string">
       00:00:00.00</imm:startTimecode>
13  <imm:thumbnail rdf:datatype="http://www.w3.org/2001/XMLSchema#string">
       http://somepath</imm:thumbnail>
14  <imm:versionNumber
       rdf:datatype="http://www.w3.org/2001/XMLSchema#string">
       0</imm:versionNumber>
15  <rdf:type
       rdf:resource="http://schemas.microsoft.com/imm/2006/3#VideoItem"/>
16</imm:VideoItem>
```

The `VideoItem` uses DC metadata for the `creator`, `description`, `identifier`, `source`, and `title` elements (lines 2–6). Lines 7–14 contain IMM predicates for indicating the creation date, whether it has a proxy (i.e., a link to another nested `Item` contained within this `Item`), who has modified the `Item` and when, the start time, a link to a thumbnail image, and the version number. Finally, line 15 provides information about the actual type of this `Item`, that is, `VideoItem`.

In order to query a database of `Items` and `Containers`, the SPARQL Protocol and RDF Query Language (SPARQL) [26] can be used. An example query is shown in Listing 17.5. This query requests all distinct production companies within `VideoItems`.

Listing 17.5 SELECT distinct production companies within VideoItems

```
PREFIX rdf:   <http://www.w3.org/1999/02/22-rdf-syntax-ns#>
PREFIX imm:   <http://schemas.microsoft.com/imm/2006/3#>
PREFIX imm:   <http://schemas.microsoft.com/imm#>
PREFIX dc:    <http://purl.org/dc/elements/1.1#>
PREFIX dii:   <urn:mpeg:mpeg21:2002:01-DII-NS#>
PREFIX did:   <urn:mpeg:mpeg21:2002:02-DIDMODEL-NS#>


SELECT DISTINCT ?companyName
WHERE
{
    ?subject imm:productionCompany ?companyName
    ?videoItem rdf:type <http://schemas.microsoft.com/imm/2006/3#VideoItem>

}
```

17.5   The DANAE Advanced MPEG-21 Infrastructure

In a project called *DANAE* (*D*ynamic and distributed *a*daptation of scalable multimedia co*n*tent in a context-*a*ware *e*nvironment), funded by the European Commission in the 6th Framework Programme in the time frame 2004–2006, the consortium developed an advanced MPEG-21 infrastructure for offering, delivering, personalizing, and adapting multimedia content in an interoperable way [7]. DID, DIP, and DIA play key roles in this architecture, and implementations of various MPEG-21 peers (server, proxy, and client) have been completed. In addition, the project contributed to the development of the recent Scalable Video Coding standard *H.264/SVC*; that is, the scalable extension of the widely used H.264/AVC coding scheme (ITU-T Rec. H.264 | ISO/IEC 14496-10 Advanced Video Coding).

17.5.1   Objectives

The major application of the DANAE MPEG-21 infrastructure was envisaged to be in a museum context. The main objective in this scenario is that museum visitors carrying MPEG-21-enabled mobile devices are delivered multimedia content (i) pertaining to the section of the exhibition they are currently in, (ii) personalized to their preferences and needs, and (iii) adapted to the capabilities of their device and the network they are connected to. It was further envisaged that the museum will have installed special presentation devices, for example, large flat screens, which visitors might at times prefer over their device and migrate their active multimedia session onto (a session mobility case addressed by MPEG-21). Although a full installation of this scenario in the museum that was among the project partners could not be realized due to practical and financial constraints, on a technical level the objectives have been fully achieved and demonstrated.

Interoperability of the entities and processes involved in this application is of utmost importance and was one of the driving forces behind the DANAE project. Consider the case that a visitor enters the museum with just an MPEG-21 conformant device, that is, without the device being specially configured or otherwise prepared for the museum environment. Vice versa, the museum's media server may not be familiar with this specific device type; in particular, the proper media format(s) for the device may not be stored at the museum server. The following major question arises from this scenario: How can the client device and the museum server interoperate in this setting such that the user will receive high-quality content adapted to his/her usage environment and preferences? The approach of the DANAE project was to develop and employ an advanced MPEG-21 infrastructure enabling this very scenario.

The key to ensure that the entities of such a multimedia infrastructure can interoperate *at the application level* is the consistent use of MPEG-21 DIDs (for application-layer content and context representation, content selection, and message exchange), DIP (for application-level processing), and DIA (for usage environment description and content adaptation purposes). Also, REL plays a role in that REL licenses can be accepted and validated by a terminal before content consumption.

Content mainly consists of advanced MPEG-4-based scenes; for example, a virtual character introducing a theme of the exhibition in the museum. The content at times provides interaction options for the user, for example, the choice of an exhibit object from a catalog scene about which he/she wants to receive further information. A consequence of this goal was that MPEG-4 content-level and MPEG-21 DID-level processing would have to coexist and, even more, invoke each other for tailored user information and experience. These interaction mechanisms had to be developed as well.

17.5.2 Architecture

In the sequel, the architecture of the MPEG-21 terminal and the adaptation/streaming server, as developed in the DANAE project for the above application scenario, are discussed. The DANAE terminal and server can be seen as typical MPEG-21 peers. The experiences gained from this design and implementation effort as well as from the deployment of the DANAE MPEG-21 infrastructure can be a valuable input for the development of MPEG-21 systems.

It must be noted that, apart from terminal and server, a third type of MPEG-21 conformant node has been developed within DANAE; namely, an adaptation node/ gateway that can be incorporated into a distributed adaptation system. A scenario in which distributed adaptation is important is an extra (proxy) server for a highly popular museum section that relieves the central adaptation/streaming server from servicing clients in that section (load balancing). Since most of the components and functionality of the separate adaptation node are in common with the central server, this extra node is not discussed here. Additional issues that have to be considered, though, are how to partition and stream metadata to the adaptation node, synchronized with the media data, and how the client devices get to know about and contact the extra server, for instance. Additional information can be found in [27].

17.5.2.1 MPEG-21 Terminal

The MPEG-21 terminal consists of the components depicted in the simplified block diagram of Figure 17.6 and described in the following text.

The *multimedia player* decodes and visualizes MPEG-4 multimedia content, including video (MPEG-4 Visual, scalable video), audio (AAC), scenes (2D/3D BIFS, LASeR), and synthetic content (procedural textures, 2D/3D face, and body animation). It also handles the interaction with the user on the *content* (MPEG-4) level, for example, when the user clicks an item in the multimedia content scene.

The *DRM engine* inspects and validates REL licenses as well as user rights and actually decrypts the content (if protected).

The *client context collection tool* collects all the context parameters required for proper customization and adaptation of the museum catalog and content to be delivered to the user of the device. The context comprises the location, device and network characteristics, and user preferences. The context is acquired from a localization module, read from device and user profile settings, delivered by a network quality estimation tool, or read from specific sensors on a DANAE device. The context information is communicated to the client DIP engine; whenever significant context changes occur, the DIP engine is notified as well.

A consequence of the design of the DANAE MPEG-21 infrastructure is that DIP and particularly the *client DIP engine* play a crucial role in ensuring interoperability and orchestrating processes required to realize the applications. In other words, the client DIP

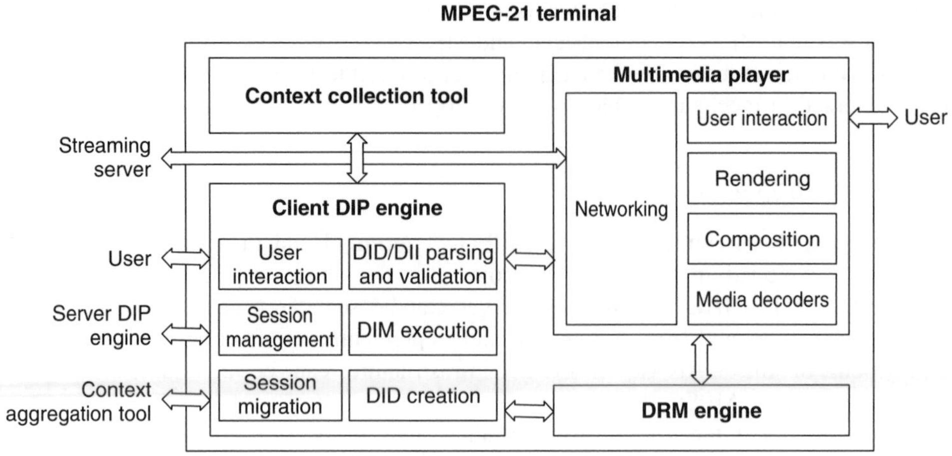

MPEG-21 terminal

Figure 17.6   DANAE MPEG-21 terminal architecture.

engine acts as an application controller and session manager at the MPEG-21 terminal. More specifically, the responsibilities of the DIP engine are as follows:

- Loading, controlling, triggering, unloading other modules in the terminal.
- Bootstrapping and initial configuration of the device.
- Parsing and validating DIDs and DIIs.
- Executing Digital Item Methods (DIMs).
- Managing the client's context and creating/updating context DIDs (from the context parameters received, including DIA descriptions).
- Managing the session, which includes receiving and sending DIDs.
- Managing session migration and generating DIDs for session transfer.
- Managing user access and user rights, with the help of the DRM engine.
- Interacting with the user on the *application* (MPEG-21) level, for example, when the user clicks a specific button during the device's configuration phase.

17.5.2.2   MPEG-21 Adaptation and Streaming Server

The MPEG-21 adaptation and streaming server is depicted in simplified form in Figure 17.7. The components and functionality of the server are briefly described as follows.

The *streaming server*, based on the open source Darwin server, delivers media data to its counterpart on the terminal side, the multimedia player, using the RTP/RTCP, RTSP, and UDP protocols. Media data has to be packetized and depacketized as well and, in the distributed adaptation case when the metadata must be delivered to the separate adaptation node, also metadata has to be (de-)packetized. Metadata here comprises descriptions as defined within MPEG-21 DIA, including generic Bitstream Syntax Descriptions (gBSDs), Adaptation Quality of Service (AQoS) information, and Universal Constraints Descriptions (UCDs).

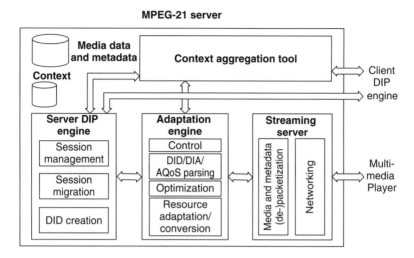

Figure 17.7   DANAE MPEG-21 server architecture.

The *context aggregation tool* is responsible for receiving, aggregating, and storing context as well as forwarding context information to server modules requesting it, mainly to the adaptation engine. The context aggregation tool receives context DIDs or fragments (updates) thereof from the client DIP engine, extracts the relevant parameters, and maintains a database of context information, specific for each user, terminal, and session.

The *adaptation engine* is at the core of the MPEG-21 server. It is designed to perform three types of adaptation: gBSD-based media resource adaptation, scene adaptation, and modality conversion. The adaptation component basically consists of the *optimizer* and the *resource adaptor* proper. The optimizer is a decision-taking engine that accepts content and context DIDs (including DIA descriptions, specifically AQoS information, from the context aggregation tool) as an input, in order to come up with appropriate adaptation decisions. The resource adaptor actually performs the types of adaptation listed above. The adaptation engine is supported by parsers and validators for the XML documents involved.

The *server DIP engine* is in control of the application on the server side, very much like its counterpart on the client side. The DIP engine basically manages the open sessions, retrieves or generates and customizes museum catalog and content DIDs according to the context of a user, delivers the DIDs, and invokes the adaptation engine if required. Clearly, the server side DIP engine is also involved in session migration activities.

17.5.3   Interaction of Content- and Application-Level Processing

An important element of the DANAE infrastructure is the interaction of content- and application-level processing, that is, between the MPEG-4 "world" (multimedia player) and the MPEG-21 "world" (predominantly, the DIP engines). As pointed out in the description of the application scenario, it is a requirement that, for example, a context-specific catalog of exhibit objects on which multimedia content is available or the navigation options available to the user, be presented in a graphical way and integrated into the MPEG-4 multimedia scenes.

In other words, when the client DIP engine receives, for example, a *catalog DID*, it should not present a simple textual list of objects (and thus content) that the user may choose from, but should rather invoke the MPEG-4 player to show an attractive graphical representation of this content catalog. This "call" of the MPEG-4 player from the MPEG-21 domain (in this case, the client DIP engine) is performed by a special DIM (akin to "show content") that hands over the specific MPEG-4 content, for example, a reference to an MP4 file, to be loaded by the player.

The visitor may subsequently interact with the scene content and potentially modify what is being presented to him/her merely on the MPEG-4 content level; for example, move fast-forward to the audiovisual content of the next exhibit object by pressing a navigation button in a visual scene. As long as such an interaction can be satisfied on the scene level, the MPEG-4 player remains in control.

However, there may be cases when a user takes an action or makes a choice that cannot be handled by the current scene and interaction control, that is, by the MPEG-4 player. For instance, the visitor may move on to another theme, jumping to a completely different section of the multimedia content catalog, or he/she may decide to transfer the active session to a more appealing display device provided in the museum by clicking on a *Transfer Session* button in a visual scene (the session migration use case). In such a case, the MPEG-4 player has to invoke the MPEG-21 "world" again, such that the DIP engine can select the correct resource from the current *catalog DID* or invoke the session management/mobility module. Such a "callback" from the MPEG-4 player to the MPEG-21 domain (here, again the client DIP engine) is effected by activating (loading) a specific DIM that takes further action on the application layer.

17.6 MPEG-21 in the European Projects ENTHRONE and AXMEDIS

17.6.1 Introduction

Various other projects funded by the European Commission have adopted and tested MPEG-21 concepts until now. Two such projects, namely AXMEDIS [8] and ENTHRONE [9], used MPEG-21 technology in the context of production, delivery, and consumption of DIs in heterogeneous and distributed environments. The work of each of these projects was basically oriented along a specific application scenario. The scenarios, which are described in the next section, mandated the DIs to be tailored to these specific use cases, with a subset of the functionalities/elements of the MPEG-21 DID standard being supported by, and proprietary metadata being included in, each of the DIs.

The question of interoperability thus arises. The members of these two projects cooperated to conduct experiments, in particular, to exchange the DIs of each project and have the DIs consumed by players implemented in both projects. The different data models are described and discussed below, in an attempt to assess their interoperability and conformance to the MPEG-21 standard.

17.6.2   Use Case Scenarios

In this section, two use case scenarios (UCSs) are described: *automated production of cross-media DIs (UCS-1)*, from the AXMEDIS project, and the *provisioning of end-to-end quality of service (QoS) for DIs across heterogeneous terminals and networks (UCS-2)*, from the ENTHRONE project.

Automated DI creation (UCS-1) aims to realize complete DI creation workflows: DIs are created, integrated, and finally delivered to the end users. These workflows can include automatic creation/processing of DIs, which can embed presentation logic, in order to be flexibly rendered on the end user devices. DI manipulation involves different actors:

- The content provider (CP) inserts into the value chain new DIs containing raw media files, encoded in any format.
- More content integrators, in different steps, annotate DIs, compose them to create new ones, and embed presentation logic in composed DIs in order to define layout, formatting, and behavior.

At each step, the DIs can be protected.

In order to enable the *provisioning of end-to-end QoS for DIs across heterogeneous environments (UCS-2)*, several actors along the delivery path are involved and play crucial roles, which are briefly highlighted in the following (Figure 17.8):

- The CP prepares the actual multimedia content as MPEG-21 DIs facilitating scalable coding formats and metadata formats.
- The service provider (SP) provisions and offers multimedia services to the end users and enriches the multimedia content with additional metadata with respect to service level

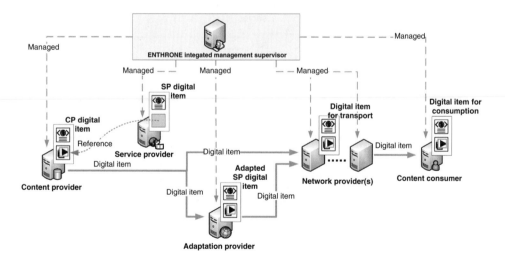

Figure 17.8   End-to-end QoS for Digital Items across heterogeneous environments.

agreements (SLAs) [28], taking into account constraints imposed by access networks for service provisioning toward the content consumer (CC).

- The adaptation provider (AP) operates in close relationship with the SP and the NPs (network providers). Its goal is to provide improved QoS of content delivery while optimizing available system and network resources across the end-to-end chain. It takes content adaptation decisions according to the *a priori* known as well as dynamically received context information. Note that the actual content adaptation is done by the CPs/SPs/NPs.
- The NP offers QoS-based network connectivity services at its autonomous domain level. Cooperation is needed among NPs for providing interdomain QoS-based network connectivity services.
- The CC requests the services provided by the SP and consumes them on his/her end device. The actual end device functions depend on the business model.

17.6.3   Data Model in Use Case Scenario 1

UCS-1 targets the delivery of a unique package along the value chain of content production, distribution, and consumption. The "cross-media" package is created as a result of different composition/integration steps from existing DIs and it has to be consumed at the end user site by a specific player. The player is able to coordinate the different resources included inside the DI by reading one or more presentation-specific resources, for example, LASeR [29], HTML [30], and SMIL [31].

Figure 17.9 depicts an example value chain for automated cross-media production in a governed environment. In this particular example, the producer creates the initial DI, in a

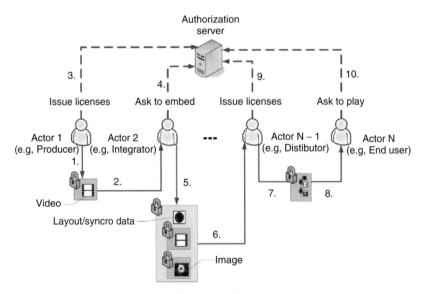

Figure 17.9   Digital Item workflow for a cross-media content value chain [2]. Reproduced with permission from © Association for Computing Machinery, Inc.

protected form, including a video resource and associated metadata. An integrator selects the producer's DI to create a new one, putting it together with an image; the integrator adds to the DI an HTML presentation layout, which refers to the video and the image resources. The integrator also adds protection (information) to the DI. The integrator could perform the required manipulation on the DI on the basis of a specific license issued by the producer. Further in the value chain, the distributor selects the composed DI to be distributed to her/his customers. The distributor needs to issue licenses that grant the customers the right to play the composed DI. Actually she/he could issue these licenses on the basis of a specific license issued by the previous actors in the value chain. The last actor that is involved in the value chain is the end user: she/he plays the DI provided by the distributor, her/his player accesses and renders the HTML presentation and the related resources. Also the end user is allowed to play the DI on the basis of the license issued by the distributor.

This data model has been developed in the context of the AXMEDIS project [8] and differentiates between composite and basic objects. A composite object is structured as follows:

```
DIDL
  Item
    OBJECT_AXOID
    OBJECT_METADATA
    ITEM [0]
    ...
    ITEM [n]
```

In this structure,

- OBJECT_AXOID is a `Descriptor/Statement` combination containing a DII;
- OBJECT_METADATA is a sequence of `Descriptor` elements containing the metadata of the object; and
- each ITEM describes a basic object which is structured as follows:

```
DIDL
  Item
    OBJECT_AXOID
    OBJECT_METADATA
    CONTENT
```

OBJECT_AXOID and OBJECT_METADATA are defined in a similar way as above. CONTENT is a sequence of `Component` elements containing a resource or a reference to a resource without additional metadata.

The metadata defined within the OBJECT_METADATA can be clustered into domain-specific and domain-independent metadata. The former is defined in a proprietary way and allows for predefined usage within the framework where this structure has been specified. The latter comprises metadata assets based on open standards such as MPEG-7 or DC in order to allow MPEG-21 terminals to access these metadata even if they are not compliant with this framework.

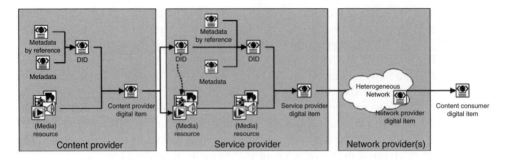

Figure 17.10 Provisioning of end-to-end quality of service (QoS) for Digital Items [2]. Reproduced with permission from © Association for Computing Machinery, Inc.

17.6.4 Data Model in Use Case Scenario 2

As UCS-2 addresses end-to-end QoS (across heterogeneous terminals and networks), various requirements from all actors within the end-to-end delivery chain need to be taken into account. The actors involved can be categorized into CP, SP, NP, and CC. Thus, the DI may undergo various – sometimes significant – changes while being delivered from the CP toward the CC as illustrated in Figure 17.10. However, the main changes will happen within the CP/SP domain. Hence, we focus on the requirements coming from CP and SP: for example, system-wide identification, temporal availability, encoding characteristics, adaptation possibilities and expected resulting qualities, and constraints to be considered.

As shown in Figure 17.10, the CP creates the initial DI including the actual media resource and associated metadata. In this context, this DI is referred to as the *CP DI*. An SP may enrich this CP DI with additional information pertaining to a particular service offered to the CC. This may, for example, include further metadata or an adapted version of the original DI which fits the *a priori* known requirements of certain CCs. The NPs are responsible for appropriate transfer of the so-called SP DIs, which may undergo well-defined modifications that optimize the transmission over heterogeneous networking infrastructures. Finally, the CC receives the desired DI appropriate to her/his context, that is, anywhere, anytime, and on any device.

This data model has been developed in the course of the ENTHRONE project [9] and differentiates between composed and final items. A composed item comprises subitems which can be themselves composed or final, whereas a final item does not contain any further subitems but components. This differentiation is similar to the data model from UCS-1 from a semantic point of view, but not from a syntactic point of view. DIs according to UCS-2 are structured as follows:

```
DIDL
  Declaration(s)   (referable descriptors)
  Container
  Descriptor(s)    (top-level container descriptors)
    Item           (composed item)
```

```
   Descriptor(s) (top-level item descriptors)
   Item            (final item)
    Descriptor(s) (item-level descriptors)
    Component(s)
     Descriptor(s) (component-level descriptors)
     Resource

  Item(s)   (further composed or final items)
  Item(s)   (further composed or final items)
```

In this structure,

- `Declaration` elements may include `Descriptors` that are used by reference (instead of duplicating them);
- `Descriptor` elements provide the metadata for the DI at different levels (i.e., `Container`, Composed `Item`, Final `Item`, `Component`); and
- one or more `Component` elements each represent a variation of semantically equal media resources (but with, e.g., different bit rates, resolutions, and qualities).

The `Descriptor` elements may contain not only standardized metadata (e.g., MPEG-7, TV-Anytime, and MPEG-21) but also proprietary data, mainly required for the delivery as defined within this framework. This proprietary metadata is used for the coordination of various entities within the delivery chain (e.g., servers, proxies, and adaptation gateways) in order to provide an agreed level of quality to the end user. It is important to note that this proprietary metadata does not hamper the consumption of media resources or open standards–based metadata at the receiving terminal.

17.6.5 Evaluation and Discussion

In this section, we evaluate and discuss the two UCSs and their data models regarding their interoperability and conformance to MPEG-21.

The two data models conform both to the abstract DI model and its declaration language (i.e., DIDL). The latter has been tested with XML tools and the available reference software [32]. Additionally, DIs composed according to the two data models can be consumed (i.e., displayed) by both players; that is, a DI according to UCS-1 can be consumed by the player from UCS-2 and vice versa. Nonetheless, (meta-)data not understood by the respective player are ignored, which means that in some cases only the media resources are displayed to the user, even if not in the intended manner. This is due to the fact that the player is not aware of the format (i.e., it is faced with proprietary metadata) or does not have installed the tools required for proper presentation of this data (i.e., for standardized metadata).

Interestingly, both data models do not make use of the *choice/selection* mechanism. This might be due to the fact that this functionality is either not required or is provided through additional semantics defined on top of the MPEG-21 standard, for example, within the data model or even the application logic. For example, UCS-2 describes multiple variations of semantically equal media resources through multiple `Component` elements. It is assumed that a single but most appropriate component is delivered to the terminal, that is, the one that is suitable given the available context (e.g., terminal and network conditions). However, for UCS-1 this would mean that only the first component (as defined in the hierarchy of the DID) is displayed to the user because in such a scenario – if multiple components are declared – a presentation logic must be present that describes how these components shall be presented to the user. Furthermore, both data models require the existence of an identifier for each item or subitem. Thus, it becomes apparent that, for example, MPEG-21 DII is required for each application running on top of these data models. This has an impact on the semantics but still allows for consumption of DIs in an interoperable way, with the restriction that this may not be performed as originally intended.

Another evaluation mainly concerns issues on whether appropriate processing tools (i.e., decoder, parser, and interpreter) for media resources and metadata have been installed on the targeted terminal. For media resources, solutions are already available that install appropriate decoders – if necessary – on demand. However, although parsers for metadata are very easy to provide, the interpretation of the metadata is not (yet) possible in an unambiguous way. This can be explained by the lack of a "decoder" specification for metadata, that is, the counterpart of a decoder for the media resources. Furthermore, as already mentioned above, (meta-)data not recognizable by the receiving terminal are ignored, for example, due to unknown namespace definitions. Thus, it is advisable to use proprietary formats only for information that does not hamper the play-out of a DI; in other words, only for information that is not necessarily required or that provides only auxiliary information.

Finally, regarding the consumption of DIs as a whole, we investigated the usage of presentation logic embedded in the DI versus the implementation thereof within the specification of the application logic as part of the framework definition. For example, the existence of multiple Component elements calls for the need of a presentation logic, which unambiguously defines how the various media resources – associated with these components – are presented to the end user. Examples of such presentation logics are HTML, SMIL, or LASeR. However, this requires the inclusion of this logic into the DI (e.g., as a separate Resource) and its appropriate tagging for unique identification by the receiving terminal. Furthermore, in case multiple presentation logics of the same type are available, another discrimination is required either as part of the DI (e.g., priorities) or as part of the application parsing the DI (e.g., depending on the platform where the DI is consumed).

17.7 Information Asset Management in a Digital Library

Digital libraries today must host, and make accessible, a vast amount of material that is usually structured as complex digital objects. Such objects aggregate the information assets proper, which may be of a wide variety of media types, as well as metadata that describe the information assets and support their identification, retrieval, dissemination, and the management of the digital rights associated with them. The format to represent, store, manage, and disseminate the complex digital objects is therefore of significant importance for the flexibility and success of a digital library architecture.

Interestingly, researchers of the Los Alamos National Laboratory (LANL) Research Library have chosen the following MPEG-21 concepts as important building blocks in one of their projects, the aDORe repository effort [33]:

- DID as one of the formats for representing (and serializing) complex digital library objects.
- DII for the identification of DIDs and assets therein [10, 11, 33].
- DIP to dynamically add processing information to DIDs when disseminating digital objects [11].

The LANL Research Library mainly accommodates scholarly data, locally stores Terabytes of raw material, and deals with tens of millions of digital assets to be managed by the digital library. (As of 2008, the aDORe Archive repository contained more than 100 million digital objects [34].)

The main reasons for adopting MPEG-21 concepts were as follows:

- The ability of DIDs to represent media data of any type together with metadata in a structured way, based on a well-defined abstract model.
- The applicability of the open, modular MPEG-21 multimedia framework to the requirements of digital libraries. This mainly pertains to DID and DII for the representation of digital objects and the inclusion of digital library–specific metadata. Moreover, this also holds, for example, for DIP and DIA for associating functionality with objects and adapting them according to the delivery context. (According to [10], concepts remarkably similar to DIP and DIA have been proposed by digital library projects.) Finally, Bekaert *et al.* [11] show how MPEG-21 and other standards, such as OAI-PMH (Open Archives Initiative Protocol for Metadata Harvesting) and NISO OpenURL, are integrated in the repository architecture.
- The potential impact of an MPEG standard.

Given the many possibilities to structure and nest DIDs, a fundamental design decision of the LANL researchers was how to map the complex digital library objects onto DIDs.

It was decided to use a simple three-level hierarchy comprising *Container*, *Item*, and *Component*. A DID may hold a *Container* or one or more *Items* directly. Each *Container* or *Item* entity can contain one or more subordinate entities. Each *Component* contains references and/or one or multiple *Resources*. A DID of this type can grow only in breadth, and not in depth.

A second important design aspect is to treat descriptive metadata and media data alike. This choice is mainly motivated by digital preservation concerns: both media data and descriptive metadata need to be preserved and hence deserve to be treated equally.

A fragment of an LANL DID illustrating the basic DID structure is given in Listing 17.6. The DID packages a PDF document and the library-specific MARC (Machine Readable Cataloging) XML metadata that describes the PDF, as peer entities. It must be noted that the DID structure has evolved since the work of Bekaert *et al.* [10, 11], but the simple structure illustrated by this example is still valid.

Listing 17.6 Basic LANL DID structure. Reproduced with the permission of the authors of the article: J. Bekaert, L. Balakireva, P. Hochstenbach, and H. Van de Sompel, 'Using MPEG-21 DIP and NISO OpenURL for the Dynamic Dissemination of Complex Digital Objects in the Los Alamos National Laboratory Digital Library.' *D-Lib Magazine* [Online]. **10** (2), Feb. 2004.

```xml
<?xml version="1.0" encoding="UTF-8"?>
<didl:DIDL xmlns:didl="urn:mpeg:mpeg21:2002:02-DIDL-NS">
<didl:Container>
   ...
   <!-- Item containing a MARCXML metadata record -->
   <didl:Item>
      ...
      <!-- Component containing the MARCXML datastream -->
      <didl:Component>
         ...
         <!-- The actual MARCXML datastream -->
         <didl:Resource mimeType="text/xml; charset=UTF-8">
            <record xmlns="http://www.loc.gov/MARC21/slim">
               <leader>01142cam 2200301 a 4500</leader>
               <controlfield tag="005">19930521155141.9</controlfield>
               <datafield tag="010" ind1=" " ind2=" ">
                  <subfield code="a">92005291</subfield>
               </datafield>
               ...
         </didl:Resource>
      </didl:Component>
   </didl:Item>
   <!-- Item containing a full-text document -->
   <didl:Item>
      ...
      <!-- Component containing the full-text datastream -->
      <didl:Component>
         ...
         <!-- The actual full-text (PDF) datastream -->
         <didl:Resource encoding="base64" mimeType="application/pdf">
            Ij5jMTk5My48L3N1YmZpZWxkPg0KICAgIDw9uIHhtbG5zSJodHgK...
         <didl:Resource>
      </didl:Component>
   </didl:Item>
   ...
</didl:Container>
</didl:DIDL>
```

Owing to their importance in digital library applications, identifiers became a core element in the design of DIDs at LANL. Two types of identifiers are used.

- *DID identifiers* for the identification of the DID XML documents as well as of the contained XML elements that represent core DID entities.
- *Content identifiers* for the identification of assets contained in the DIDs.

DID identifiers are introduced for the identification of the DID XML documents themselves; they are dynamically assigned when a DID is created and ingested into the repository. A DID identifier is conveyed as an attribute from an LANL-defined namespace at the DID root element. Also during the ingestion process, DID *Container*, *Item*, and *Component* entities receive XML IDs that are attached as attributes to the corresponding XML elements. Also, the *Descriptor/Statement* constructs containing MPEG-21 DII can be used to integrate community-specific identification schemes smoothly into the DIDs.

Content identifiers identify the information assets contained in DIDs, usually within *Item*s, and they are conveyed using *Descriptor/Statement* and *Identifier* constructs. Content identifiers are typically derived from the information assets proper. In many cases, the identifier naturally attached to an asset during its creation or publication is adopted as the content identifier [10, 11].

The same approach, that is, the use of *descriptor/statement*, is heavily used to provide further information pertaining to the content. For example, relationships between entities contained in DIDs are conveyed by special-purpose *Descriptor*s containing RDF statements expressing relationships like "is member of" or "is translation of". Creation date and time, datastream format information, and W3C XML Signatures, which are used to verify (e.g., authenticate) the DID itself and the information assets, can be embedded in this manner as well. More details are available in [33].

Finally, the LANL library researchers proposed to make specific use of DIP in their repository architecture [11]. In general, DIMs are embedded in a DID with the intent to provide specific functionality or services when the DID is retrieved from the repository and disseminated to the requester(s). However, at LANL, it was felt that static DIMs in DIDs would overly restrict the flexibility of the retrieval and dissemination process. After all, while content is of rather static, archival nature, the requirements or services of content dissemination will likely evolve over time. Freezing the functionality by embedding DIMs into DIDs already upon their ingestion into the repository would make it necessary to touch every DID and exchange the embedded DIMs whenever new dissemination services are devised and implemented as DIMs. This was felt as too much overhead, given the existence of tens of millions of DIDs in the repository.

Instead, a level of indirection and a late, dynamic binding mechanism for DIMs was introduced. Rather than placing DIMs directly into a DID, the so-called *PlaceHolder* elements from an LANL-defined namespace are embedded initially. Upon retrieval of a DID from the repository, a specific module of the DIP framework (the *DIM Inserter*) performs a matching of *PlaceHolder* values with DIMs conveyed in a special-purpose registry of services (the *DIP Table*) and dynamically adds actual DIMs to the DID before delivering it to the requester.

Since this matching and dynamic DIM insertion process is beyond the scope of MPEG-21, it is not further dealt with in this chapter. The interested reader is referred to [11], which describes the operation of the DIP engine in the LANL repository architecture in more detail. However, at the time of writing, it is unclear whether or not this proposal was pursued further; in more recent publications [33, 34], this specific use of DIP is not mentioned anymore.

It should be noted finally that the LANL aDORe team released a Java toolkit for constructing, validating, serializing, and deserializing MPEG-21 DIDs [35].

17.8   Conclusions

MPEG had far-reaching visions and goals when standardizing MPEG-21. The applications and experiences so far seem to indicate that the vision of providing *the* multimedia framework for wide-spread end-to-end use has not become reality so far. There seem to be several reasons behind this.

First, interoperability on a large scale in practical settings is difficult, if not impossible, to achieve. The DID abstract model and DIDL are well thought out; however, they are comprehensive and too flexible such that adopters tend to define subsets of DID functionalities and structures tailored to their specific applications and to integrate community-specific or even proprietary metadata into DIDs. While this substantiates the versatility of the DID concepts, it hampers the use of such DIDs beyond the specific application (domain).

Second, the experience from the DANAE MPEG-21 infrastructure development has shown that MPEG-21 support results in complex middleware and intricate interplay between the content level (e.g., MPEG-4 presentations) and the application level (e.g., MPEG-21 DIDs and metadata therein). A consequence of this seems to be that "MPEG-21 conformant devices" have not become available so far.

Third, it seems to be difficult to identify clear benefits for a *single* stakeholder in the multimedia value chain (*User* in MPEG-21 terminology) of adopting MPEG-21 concepts as compared to using proprietary technologies. Thus, there seems to be the need to work out viable and attractive strategies to MPEG-21 deployment on a large, end-to-end scale.

Finally, potential users might still be insufficiently aware of the MPEG-21 family of standards. We believe that this chapter has pointed out interesting MPEG-21 technologies and applications for these users.

References

[1] Timmerer, C. and Hellwagner, H. (2008) MPEG-21 multimedia framework, *Encyclopedia of Multimedia*, 2nd edn (ed. B. Furht), Springer, New York, NY, USA, pp. 463–469.

[2] Timmerer, C., Andrade, M.T., Carvalho, P. *et al*. (2008) The semantics of MPEG-21 digital items revisited. Proceedings of the ACM Multimedia 2008, 2nd International Workshop on the Many Faces of Multimedia Semantics, October 27 – November 1, 2008, Vancouver, Canada.

[3] UPnP Forum (2006) *ContentDirectory:2Service Template version 1.01*. Online, http://www.upnp.org /specs/av/UPnP-av-ContentDirectory-v2-Service-20060531.pdf (accessed June 2010).

[4] Microsoft Interactive Media Manager (IMM). Online, http://blogs.msdn.com/imm/ (accessed June 2010).

[5] McGuinness, D.L. and van Harmelen, F. (2004) *OWL Web Ontology Language Overview*. W3C Recommendation. Online, http://www.w3.org/TR/owl-features/ (accessed June 2010).

[6] Burnett, I.S., Davis, S.J., and Drury, G.M. (2005) MPEG-21 digital item declaration and identification – principles and compression. *IEEE Transactions on Multimedia*, **7** (3), 400–407.

[7] DANAE Website. Online, http://danae.rd.francetelecom.com/ (accessed June 2010).

[8] AXMEDIS Website. Online, http://www.axmedis.org/ (accessed June 2010).

[9] ENTHRONE Website. Online, http://www.ist-enthrone.org/ (accessed June 2010).

[10] Bekaert, J., Hochstenbach, P., and Van de Sompel, H. (2003) Using MPEG-21 DIDL to represent complex digital objects in the Los Alamos national laboratory digital library. *D-Lib Magazine*, **9** (11), http://www.dlib.org/dlib/november03/bekaert/11bekaert. html (accessed June 2010).

[11] Bekaert, J., Balakireva, L., Hochstenbach, P., and Van de Sompel, H. (2004) Using MPEG-21 DIP and NISO OpenURL for the dynamic dissemination of complex digital objects in the Los Alamos national laboratory digital library. *D-Lib Magazine*, **10** (2), http://www.dlib.org/dlib/february04/bekaert/02bekaert.html (accessed June 2010)

[12] MPEG21 DIDL Application Profile for Institutional Repositories. Online, http://www.surffoundation.nl /wiki/display/standards/MPEG21+DIDL+Application+Profile+for+Institutional+Repositories (accessed June 2010).

[13] Diepold, K., Pereira, F., and Chang, W. (2005) MPEG-A: multimedia application formats. *IEEE Multimedia*, **12** (4), 34–41.

[14] Kim, K., Schreiner, F., and Diepold, K. (2008) MAF Overview, ISO/IEC JTC1/SC29/WG11 N10233, Busan, Korea, October 2008.

[15] ISO/IEC (2005) 21000-2:2005. *InformationTechnology – Multimedia Framework (MPEG-21) – Part 2: Digital Item Declaration*, 2nd edn. Online, http://standards.iso.org/ittf/ PubliclyAvailable-Standards/index.html (accessed June 2010).

[16] (2006) *DIDL-Lite Schema for UPnP A/V ContentDirectory Services, version 2.0*. Online, http://www.upnp.org/schemas/av/didl-lite-v2.xsd (accessed June 2010).

[17] ISO/IEC 21000. *MPEG-21 Schema Files*. Online, http://standards.iso.org/ittf/PubliclyAvailableStandards /index.html (accessed June 2010).

[18] ISO/IEC (2001) 14977:1996. *Information Technology – Syntactic Metalanguage – Extended BNF*.

[19] Kunze, J. and Baker, T. (eds) (2007) *The Dublin Core Metadata Element Set, IETF RFC 5013*. Online, http://www.ietf.org/rfc/ rfc5013.txt (accessed June 2010).

[20] ISO (2008) 15706-1:2002. *Information and Documentation – International Standard Audiovisual Number (ISAN) – Part 1: Audiovisual Work Identifier*.

[21] International Press Telecommunications Council. (2009) Photo Metadata. Online, http://www.iptc.org (accessed June 2010).

[22] Japan Electronics and Information Technology Industries Association (2002) *Exchangeable Image File Format for Digital Still Cameras: Exif Version 2.2*. Online, http://www.exif.org/specifications.html (accessed June 2010).

[23] Adobe Extensible Metadata Platform (XMP) Specification (2005). Online, http://www.adobe.com/ products/xmp/ (accessed June 2010).

[24] Society of Motion Picture and Television Engineers (SMTPE) Website. Online, http://www.smpte.org/ (accessed June 2010).

[25] Deutscher, J., Sullivan, G., and Tescher, A. (2008) Information Regarding Microsoft IMM Metadata Model and Ontology, ISO/IEC JTC 1/SC 29/WG 11 M15481, Archamps, France.

[26] Prud'hommeaux, E. and Seaborne, A. (2008) *SPARQL query language for RDF*. W3C Recommendation. Online, http://www.w3.org/TR/2008/REC-rdf-sparql-query-20080115/ (accessed June 2010).

[27] Hutter, A., Amon, P., Panis, G. *et al.* (2005) Automatic adaptation of streaming multimedia content in a dynamic and distributed environment. Proceedings of the International Conference on Image Processing (ICIP 2005), September 2005, Genova, Italy.

[28] Verma, D.C. (2004) Service level agreements on IP networks. *Proceedings of the IEEE*, **92** (9), 1382–1388.

[29] Dufourd, J.-C., Avaro, O., and Concolato, C. (2005) An MPEG standard for rich media services. *IEEE Multimedia*, **12** (4), 60–68.

[30] Raggett, D., Le Hors, A., and Jacobs, I. (1999) *HTML 4.01 Specification*. W3C Recommendation. Online, http://www.w3.org/TR/ html401/ (accessed June 2010).

[31] Bulterman, D. *et al.* (eds) (2005) *Synchronized Multimedia Integration Language (SMIL 2.1)*. W3C Recommendation. Online, http://www.w3.org/TR/SMIL2/ (accessed June 2010).

[32] ISO/IEC (2008) 21000-8:2008. *Information Technology – Multimedia Framework (MPEG-21) – Part 8: Reference Software*. Online, http://standards.iso.org/ittf/PubliclyAvailableStandards/index.html (accessed June 2010).

[33] Bekaert, J., De Kooning, E., and Van de Sompel, H. (2006) Representing digital assets using MPEG-21 digital item declaration. *International Journal on Digital Libraries*, **6** (2), 159–173.

[34] Van de Sompel, H., Chute, R., and Hochstenbach, P. (2008) The aDORe federation architecture: digital repositories at scale. *International Journal on Digital Libraries*, **9** (2), 83–100.

[35] LANL aDORe DIDL Tools. Online, http://african.lanl.gov/ aDORe/projects/DIDLTools/ (accessed June 2010).

18

Distributing Sensitive Information in the MPEG-21 Multimedia Framework

Nicholas Paul Sheppard

Library eServices, Queensland University of Technology, Australia

18.1 Introduction

Computer networks, together with digital encoding of multimedia works, have greatly facilitated the distribution of art and information. Compression algorithms and high-capacity networks have enabled multimedia to be transmitted and shared over great distances at high speeds, and without the loss of quality associated with older forms of exchange. The growing popularity of the Internet over the past two decades has consequently promoted an explosion in the amount of art and information exchanged across the world.

Creators and owners of digital information, however, frequently have reason to limit the use and distribution of that art and information. Copyright owners wish to profit by licensing multimedia such as books, music and videos; governments, corporations and other organisations make use of sensitive documents that contain information that might disadvantage the organisation or its customers if it were revealed to an outsider; and individuals wish to protect the privacy of their health records, financial records and other personal information.

The MPEG-21 Multimedia Framework (ISO/IEC 21000) provides a set of specifications for organising, manipulating, distributing and using multimedia works in the form of *digital items*. A digital item is a complex multimedia document describing a hierarchy of atomic multimedia resources and metadata.

The Handbook of MPEG Applications: Standards in Practice   Edited by Marios C. Angelides and Harry Agius
© 2011 John Wiley & Sons, Ltd

Several parts of the multimedia framework are designed to support the needs of the owners of sensitive information:

- *Part 4: Intellectual Property Management and Protection Components* ("IPMP components") describes a mechanism by which access to the components of an MPEG-21 digital item may be controlled by one or more *IPMP tools*.
- *Part 5: Rights Expression Language* ("MPEG REL") specifies a language in which information owners can describe the terms and conditions under which their information may be distributed and used.
- *Part 6: Rights Data Dictionary* ("MPEG RDD") supports a dictionary of terms for describing rights-sensitive scenarios.
- *Part 11: Evaluation Tools for Persistent Association Technologies* describes tests by which the efficacy of digital watermarks can be evaluated.
- *Part 15: Event Reporting* describes a mechanism by which the use of digital items can be monitored.

This chapter discusses how the IPMP Components and REL, in particular, can be used to implement a *digital rights management (DRM) system*. A DRM system allows information owners to distribute their information under a *licence* that sets out the terms and conditions under which the information may be disseminated, used and can be enforced by a machine.

DRM was originally developed in the 1990s for copyright protection applications, in which a copyright owner wishes to restrict the use of some commercial multimedia to those who have paid to access it. The MPEG-21 Committee presumably had this application in mind when it developed the IPMP components and REL, and [1, 2], for example, describe applications of this kind for MPEG-21. More recently, however, DRM has also emerged as a technology for protecting sensitive corporate information [3] and private personal information [4]. This chapter shows how the IPMP components and REL can be applied in all of these contexts.

This chapter and the applications described in it are based on a particular DRM platform known as "SITDRM", which was developed at the Cooperative Research Centre for Smart Internet Technology in Australia. As well as providing an implementation of the IPMP components and REL themselves, SITDRM provides a software and security architecture suitable for all the applications described in this chapter.

Section 18.2 of the chapter gives an overview of the IPMP components and REL. The section then gives an overview of the SITDRM system, on which all the applications described in this chapter are based.

Section 18.3 describes a version of the classic copyright protection application. Users may purchase licences for multimedia works made available by some seller, and DRM prevents users from violating the terms of their licences.

Section 18.4 describes a DRM system that allows corporations to prevent sensitive documents from being accessed outside the corporation's premises. Employees may load sensitive documents onto mobile devices, and access the documents while they remain in a trusted area, but may not access the documents when the device moves out of the trusted area.

Section 18.5 describes a prototype in which SITDRM was used to protect personal information submitted to an organisation by its customers. Upon supplying personal information through an organisation's web site, customers are able to create a licence that controls what the organisation can and cannot do with that information.

Finally, Section 18.6 concludes the chapter with a summary of our observations on the applicability of MPEG-21 in DRM, and the decisions that must be made by developers of MPEG-21-based DRM systems.

18.2 Digital Rights Management in MPEG-21

Figure 18.1 shows our reference model for a DRM system [5]. In this model, some *provider* supplies information in a protected form. Most DRM systems use encryption for this purpose, as does SITDRM, though other methods are at least theoretically possible. The information may be distributed in its protected form through an arbitrary insecure distribution channel, such as a direct network connection, a file-sharing network, or physical media.

In order to use the protected information, a *user* must obtain a *licence* from the *licence issuer*. A licence is a document written in a machine-readable *REL* that sets out the conditions under which the information may be accessed, and is generally issued according to some policy desired by the information provider. Licences in most DRM systems, including SITDRM, also include the secret information required to access the protected information to which the licence refers.

The security of a DRM system depends on the inability of the user to access the information using anything but a special *DRM agent* that is guaranteed by its manufacturer to obey the conditions imposed by licences that have been issued by a recognised licence issuer. The licence issuer must be able to authenticate the DRM agents prior to issuing licences to them, and DRM agents must be able to verify the integrity of licences once they have been issued.

DRM agents may be implemented as tamper-resistant hardware devices or software applications using trusted computing techniques. The present chapter will not cover the construction of such devices and applications, nor the methods by which they are authenticated, but techniques include code obfuscation [6], trusted virtual machines [7] and use of a trusted platform module [8].

Throughout this chapter, the MPEG-21 terminal is assumed to be a DRM agent that cannot be internally inspected or modified by its user, as described above. We shall use

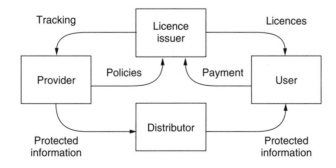

Figure 18.1 The components of a DRM system.

the word *terminal* to refer to a DRM agent including its user interface, MPEG REL interpreter, renderer and any secret cryptographic set-up required by the DRM system.

The MPEG-21 multimedia framework provides two fundamental components of the model shown in Figure 18.1, which will be described presently:

- The IPMP components (ISO/IEC 21000-4) provide a mechanism for marking certain components of a digital item as being protected, and for indicating the method by which they are protected.
- The MPEG REL (ISO/IEC 21000-5) provides a language in which licences can be written.

18.2.1 Intellectual Property Management and Protection

Unlike other specifications for DRM systems, such as those promulgated by the Open Mobile Alliance [9] and Marlin Developer Community [10], MPEG-21 does not specify a particular method by which individual multimedia resources should be protected. Instead, it provides a method of associating the protected components of a digital item with one or more vendor-specific *IPMP tools* that implement a particular method of protection. This approach, known as *configuration-driven interoperability* [11], allows MPEG-21 terminals to support DRM regimes promulgated by a multitude of vendors, and also allows security mechanisms to be renewed in the event that a mechanism is compromised by crackers.

According to ISO/IEC 21000-4, an IPMP tool "has the granularity that it can be a single protection module, for example, a single decryption tool, and can also be a collection of tools; that is, a complete IPMP system". All of the tools discussed in this chapter, however, come from the former end of this spectrum.

To understand the IPMP components, it is first necessary to understand the digital item declaration language (DIDL) (ISO/IEC 21000-2), in which MPEG-21 digital items are described. The DIDL is an XML-based language that arranges multimedia resources and metadata into a hierarchical document. This chapter will use the XML namespace prefix `didl` for elements of DIDL.

For the purposes of this chapter, the most important elements of DIDL are as follows:

Resources. Atomic multimedia objects such as images, sounds and videos.

Descriptors. Elements containing metadata about a resource, such as identifiers, abstracts, MPEG-7 descriptors and so on.

Components. Resources together with their descriptors.

Items. Complex multimedia objects, made up of sub-items and/or components.

An album of music, for example, might consist of an item that contains one component for each song. Each component might contain a descriptor with the title of the song, and a resource that contains the song itself.

The IPMP components define a parallel language called "IPMP DIDL" in which protected components may be expressed. For every element of DIDL, IPMP DIDL defines an equivalent element that contains:

- an optional identifier;
- an *IPMP information descriptor* that associates the element with the IPMP tools and licences required to access the element;
- the element itself in its protected form.

This chapter will use the XML namespace prefix `ipmpdidl` for elements of IPMP DIDL, so that the IPMP DIDL element `ipmpdidl:Statement`, for example, represents a protected form of the DIDL element `didl:Statement`.

Box 18.1 shows a simple MPEG-21 digital item in an unprotected and a protected form. (The resource itself – an XML document delimited by the `myxml:MyXML` tags – has been omitted for brevity). In the protected item, the `didl:Resource` element from the DIDL namespace has been replaced by the `ipmpdidl:Resource` element from the IPMP DIDL namespace. We have made the protected item slightly more concise by moving the resource's identifier – expressed as a digital item identifier as defined in ISO/IEC 21000-3 – from the component descriptor to the IPMP resource identifier. We could also, however, have kept the descriptor in its original form.

Box 18.1 (a) An MPEG-21 digital item and (b) its protected form

```
                              <didl:DIDL>
                               <didl:Item>
                                <didl:Component>
                                 <ipmpdidl:Resource
<didl:DIDL>                        mimeType="text/xml">
 <didl:Item>                       <ipmpdidl:Identifier>
  <didl:Component>                  <dii:Identifier>
   <didl:Descriptor>                 urn:org:doc:1
    <didl:Statement>                </dii:Identifier>
     <dii:Identifier>              </ipmpdidl:Identifier>
      urn:org:doc:1                <ipmpdidl:Info>
     </dii:Identifier>              <ipmpinfo:IPMPInfoDescriptor>
    </didl:Statement>                See Box 18.2
   </didl:Descriptor>               </ipmpinfo:IPMPInfoDescriptor>
   <didl:Resource                  </ipmpdidl:Info>
    mimeType="text/xml">           <ipmpdidl:Contents>
    <myxml:MyXML>                    <xenc:EncryptedData>
     . . .                           . . .
    </myxml:MyXML>                   </xenc:EncryptedData>
   </didl:Resource>                </ipmpdidl:Contents>
  </didl:Component>                </ipmpdidl:Resource>
 </didl:Item>                     </didl:Component>
</didl:DIDL>                      </didl:Item>
                                 </didl:DIDL>

         (a)                               (b)
```

The `ipmpdidl:Contents` element contains the protected resource itself. In this instance, the protected resource takes the form of an encrypted XML document contained in the `xenc:EncryptedData` element, whose form is defined by the XML Security Working Group [12]. The resource need not be protected in this particular way, and we will see some other possibilities later in the chapter, but XML encryption happens to be convenient for protecting XML documents.

The `ipmpdidl:Info` element contains an `ipmpinfo:IPMPInfoDescriptor` element that provides the information necessary for the MPEG-21 terminal to access the protected resource. The elements used in IPMP information descriptors belong to the *IPMP Information Descriptor and General Information Descriptor Namespace* defined by ISO/IEC 21000-4, which is represented by the namespace prefix `ipmpinfo` in this chapter. The IPMP information descriptor provides (up to) three pieces of information, as shown in Box 18.2:

- A series of `ipmpinfo:Tool` elements that describe the IPMP tools required to access the data inside the `ipmpdidl:Contents` element.
- A series of `ipmpinfo:RightsDescriptor` elements that describe the rights that exist over the data inside the `ipmpdidl:Contents` element.
- A `ds:Signature` element that contains a digital signature on the IPMP information, as defined by the XML Security Working Group [12].

Box 18.2 An IPMP information descriptor

```
<ipmpinfo:IPMPInfoDescriptor>
  <ipmpinfo:Tool>
    <ipmpinfo:ToolBaseDescription>
      <ipmpinfo:IPMPToolID>
        urn:mpegRA:mpeg21:IPMP:xmlenc
      </ipmpinfo:IPMPToolID>
    </ipmpinfo:ToolBaseDescription>
  </ipmpinfo:Tool>
  <ipmpinfo:RightsDescriptor>
    <ipmpinfo:License>
      ...
    </ipmpinfo:License>
  </ipmpinfo:RightsDescriptor>
  <ds:Signature>
    ...
  </ds:Signature>
</ipmpinfo:IPMPInfoDescriptor>
```

The `ipmpinfo:Tool` element may contain the base description of a tool (as in Box 18.2), or a reference to a tool description elsewhere in the digital item. Every tool must have a unique identifier assigned to it by some registration authority. The identifier in Box 18.2, for example, refers to a fictional tool that is able to decrypt `xenc:EncryptedData` elements. The `ipmpinfo:ToolBaseDescription` element may also contain parameters for the tool, instructions on where to obtain the tool, or even an inline binary of the tool itself, but only the identifier is essential and only the identifier will be used in this chapter.

The `ipmpinfo:RightsDescriptor` element may contain an inline licence to access the resource (as in Box 18.2), a reference to an external licence, or a reference to an on-line service that provides licences. This chapter uses a method similar to (but not the same as) the last one, since in the applications described here, it is not generally possible to know in advance which licences should be included when creating the digital item.

If a digital item contains many components that have been protected using the same IPMP tools and/or licences, the common information can be collected in an `ipmp-info:IPMPGeneralInfoDescriptor` element that describes the IPMP information for the digital item as a whole. Individual IPMP descriptors may then refer to this descriptor instead of copying the whole descriptor for each protected component. The digital items used in this chapter, however, are very simple and we will not need to use the `ipmpinfo:IPMPGeneralInfoDescriptor` element.

Though IPMP DIDL can describe the IPMP tools required to access a protected resource, MPEG-21 does not describe a method by which the MPEG-21 terminal communicates with tools, or by which the terminals and tool perform mutual authentication. The MPEG committee did (some years after first introducing IPMP) introduce "IPMP extensions" as Part 13 of the older MPEG-4 standard (ISO/IEC 14496) that provides just such an interface for MPEG-4 terminals [13], but MPEG-21 does not (yet) contain any equivalent part. Serrão *et al.* [14] and Fan *et al.* [15] describe implementations of the MPEG-4 IPMP system. Fan *et al.* make their implementation part of an MPEG-21 system, but their paper describes only the MPEG-4 interface to IPMP tools. The specification for an interoperable DRM platform promulgated by the Digital Media Project [16], which closely resembles MPEG-21's specficiation, also proposes a protocol suite by which the terminal may communicate with tools. For the applications described in this chapter, we developed our own interface that will be outlined in Section 18.2.4.

18.2.2 Rights Expression Language

Though MPEG-21 does not define a full DRM system, it does define a complete REL known as "MPEG REL". MPEG REL is closely based on the eXtensible Rights Markup Language ("XrML") promulgated by ContentGuard [17], which is itself based on the Digital Rights Property Language developed by Mark Stefik in the early days of DRM [18].

MPEG REL is defined as a collection of three XML schemata, called the *core schema* (denoted by the XML namespace prefix `r` in this chapter), the *standard extension schema* (prefix `sx`) and the *multimedia extension schema* (prefix `mx`). These schemata define the fundamental elements of the language, some widely useful conditions and elements useful in copyright protection applications, respectively.

An MPEG REL licence is structured as a collection of *grants* issued by some licence issuer. Each grant awards some *right* over some specified *resource* to a specified *principal*, that is, user of a resource. Each grant may be subject to a *condition*, such that the right contained in the grant may not be exercised unless the condition is satisfied.

Every application must define a set of *root grants* that have been granted by the system. A typical root grant, for example, might grant a certain entity the right to issue licences. In order to perform some action on a resource, a user (principal) must then possess a set of additional grants, known as an *authorisation proof*, that forms a proof that this principal may perform this action on that resource, given the root grants. A simple authorisation proof, for example, might consist of a licence that has been issued by the licence issuer authorised by a root grant.

Authorisation proofs may be quite complex, and the MPEG-21 Book [19] gives some fairly elaborate examples. All but one of the authorisation proofs used in this chapter, however, follow the simple pattern exemplified above.

Each of the four components of an MPEG REL grant is associated with an abstract XML schema type defined in the core schema. In any actual licence, each of these abstract types must be instantiated by a concrete type representing a particular principal, right, resource or condition. The `r:Principal` abstract type, for example, might be instantiated by the `r:KeyHolder` concrete type to identify a principal by a cryptographic key, and the `r:Right` abstract type might be instantiated by concrete types such as `mx:Play`, `mx:Print`, `mx:Copy` and so on. Note that the type names begin with upper-case letters, while the tags that have these types begin with lower-case letters, so that the `mx:play` tag has type `mx:Play` and so on.

The precise meanings of terms used to define MPEG REL are themselves defined in another part of the MPEG-21 multimedia framework, called the *RDD* (ISO/IEC 21000-6). The RDD defines a format for a dictionary of terms with formal definitions, then defines around 2000 such terms in an appendix. More terms can be added to the dictionary by applying to a registration authority. This chapter does not make specific use of the RDD, but we will give an informal definition of language elements as and when necessary.

18.2.3 Other Parts

Besides the IPMP components and REL, the MPEG-21 multimedia framework contains several other parts that may be of interest to developers of DRM and other security systems. None of the applications described in this chapter make any use of these parts, but we will give a short summary of each part presently.

The *Evaluation Tools for Persistent Association Technologies* (ISO/IEC 21000-11) define a methodology for testing the efficacy of techniques for associating information with a multimedia resource such that the information and resource cannot be separated. Persistent association technologies include file headers, digital signatures, digital watermarks and fingerprints (also known as "content hashes" or similar phrases in academic literature), but the specification does not mandate any particular technology to be used with MPEG-21. The version of the standard available at the time of writing considers only audio technologies, but anticipates that other kinds of media will be added in the future.

Event Reporting (ISO/IEC 21000-15) defines a mechanism by which players in a distribution chain can insert an *event report request* into a digital item. A terminal making use of the item obeys the request by sending an *event report* to the entity that created it. Event reporting has obvious applications in monitoring the use and distribution of information, but none of the applications described in this chapter attempt to monitor information. (If they did, they could also use the `sx:TrackReport` condition of MPEG REL to force the terminal to record its actions on some web service.)

18.2.4 SITDRM

The applications described in this chapter were implemented using a DRM platform known as "SITDRM", developed at the University of Wollongong and sponsored by the Cooperative Research Centre for Smart Internet Technology. SITDRM introduces an interface by which IPMP tools and MPEG-21 terminal communicate and a particular cryptographic architecture by which resources are protected; the present author has described this in detail in [20].

18.2.4.1 Cryptographic Architecture

SITDRM's cryptographic architecture is similar to that of other DRM systems, notably the "Scuba" key distribution system employed by Marlin [21]. In SITDRM, every resource is encrypted by a unique *resource encryption key*, which may be a symmetric key or an asymmetric key. In addition to the principal, resource, right and condition described above, every licence must contain the resource encryption key for its resource, itself encrypted by the public key of the terminal for which the licence is intended. This scheme ensures that only the target terminal is able to access the resource, and will be secure if licences are issued only to terminals that are trusted to comply with licences.

18.2.4.2 Terminal and Tool Authentication

SITDRM does not provide a public key infrastructure by which licence issuers may authenticate terminals, or by which terminals and IPMP tools may perform mutual authentication. (Our licence issuers simply accepted all public keys as valid.) Such an infrastructure would be necessary to ensure the security of a real DRM system, since terminals and tools have access to secret information that may compromise the system if it were revealed. We discuss how licence issuers can authenticate terminals based on specifications promulgated by the Trusted Computing Group in [22]. A similar scheme could be used by IPMP tools, though our implementation has tools simply trusting the terminal without question.

18.2.4.3 IPMP Tools

SITDRM's view of IPMP tools is unusual – and probably not anticipated by MPEG-21 – in that SITDRM requires a vendor to supply a tool that implements the logic of every element of MPEG REL that that vendor wishes to support. Thus vendors must supply tools that authenticate principals and check conditions, as well as decrypt resources. The present chapter, however, considers only tools for decrypting digital items and resources (called "IPMP navigation tools" and "resource access tools", respectively, in [20]), as is probably intended by MPEG-21.

IPMP tools in SITDRM are Java class files that conform to an interface defined by SITDRM. The present version of SITDRM requires that all of the necessary tools have been manually installed in the terminal prior to accessing any protected digital items. In an ideal system of the kind envisioned by the IPMP components, however, the terminal would also be able to locate and install tools as necessary, perhaps similar to the way in which existing web browsers offer to install unfamiliar plug-ins when they encounter a web site that requires them. The infrastructure required to support such activity, however, does not yet exist.

The IPMP components say that every tool must have a unique uniform resource identifier ("URI") registered with some suitable authority. SITDRM, however, identifies IPMP tools by their Java class names and in the absence of an actual registrar, this chapter will follow this convention.

18.2.4.4 Licences

None of the applications described in this chapter use the `ipmpinfo:RightsDescriptor` element to pass licences as part of a digital item. Instead, every terminal maintains a single logical pool of licences to which it has access, and which may consist of an arbitrary number of physical databases. A SITDRM-based application must provide some mechanism by which licences are added to the pool, and we will describe the mechanism individually for each application described in this chapter.

When a user requests permission to perform an action on a protected object, the terminal attempts to construct an authorisation proof from the licences in its pool, using a depth-first search algorithm similar to those used in theorem provers. In this way, an information provider is able to create a usable protected digital item without needing to know what licences will be used to access it, and we will see that this is very useful in the applications described in the remainder of this chapter.

18.3 MPEG-21 in Copyright Protection

SITDRM was originally developed for a classical copyright protection scenario of the kind for which the MPEG-21 IPMP components were devised. In this application, some multimedia seller has resources (images, in the demonstration application) that he or she wishes to license to customers in return for payment. The customers may view or print the images on their own computer for a fixed period of time according to the rights that they have licensed, but they may not use the images on another computer, or after the licence has expired.

Figure 18.2 shows the architecture of the application, which is very similar to that of the reference model described in Section 18.2. The seller creates an image as usual, then uses an application on his or her own computer to encrypt the image. The encrypted image becomes the resource of an MPEG-21 digital item of the form shown in Box 18.3, which refers to the encrypted file using the `ipmpdidl:ProtectedAsset` element.[1] The `ipmpdidl:ProtectedAsset` element has the same components as the other elements of IPMP DIDL described in Section 18.2.1, but forms a resource in its own right rather than replacing the `didl:Resource` element.

---

[1] Our implementation actually used a format somewhat different from this, as it was made before the final version of the IPMP components was available. The idea is the same, however.

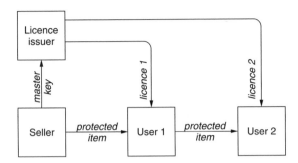

Figure 18.2 A simple image licensing application with super-distribution.

Box 18.3 A digital item referencing a protected image

```
<didl:DIDL>
  <didl:Item>
    <didl:Component>
      <didl:Resource mimeType="application/ipmp">
        <ipmpdidl:ProtectedAsset mimeType="image/jpeg">
          <ipmpdidl:Identifier>
            <dii:Identifier>urn:seller:picture1</dii:Identfier>
          </ipmpdidl:Indentifier>
          <ipmpdidl:Info>...</ipmpdidl:Info>
          <ipmpdidl:Contents ref="picture1.jpg.enc"/>
        </ipmpdidl:ProtectedAsset>
      </didl:Resource>
    </didl:Component>
  </didl:Item>
</didl:DIDL>
```

The seller may distribute the digital item shown in Box 18.3, together with the encrypted file, using any means available to him or her. In particular, DRM systems support *super-distribution*, in which a user who already has a copy of some protected multimedia may create a new copy and pass it on directly to another user. The second user does not need to download an "official" copy from the original seller, as would be the case for an ordinary store or a conditional access system. In this way, multimedia may be distributed through file-sharing networks and social networks, for example, without interfering with the seller's ability to earn money from the multimedia.

In order to make use of the image, however, individual users must purchase individual licences from a web site that plays the role of the licence issuer in the reference model. Users must fill in a web form that identifies the image that they want to license and the rights that they want to purchase. The web site then computes an appropriate payment. The web site verifies that the user's terminal is a trusted one and, if so, issues it with a licence similar to the one shown in Box 18.4. The terminal then installs the new licence in its licence pool. (Note that MPEG REL employs US spelling conventions for tag names such as `r:license`.)

Box 18.4 A licence for viewing the image of Box 18.3

```
<r:license>
  <r:grant>
    <r:keyHolder>
      <r:info>
        <ds:KeyValue>...</ds:KeyValue>
      </r:info>
    </r:keyHolder>
    <mx:play/>
    <mx:diReference>
      <mx:identifier>urn:seller:picture1</mx:identifier>
    </mx:diReference>
    <r:validityInterval>
      <r:notBefore>2010-01-01T00:00:00</r:notBefore>
      <r:notAfter>2010-12-31T23:59:59</r:notAfter>
    </r:validityInterval>
    <ds:KeyInfo>
      <xenc:EncryptedKey>...</xenc:EncryptedKey>
    </ds:KeyInfo>
  </r:grant>
  <r:issuer>
    <ds:Signature>...</ds:Signature>
  </r:issuer>
</r:license>
```

The grant of the licence shown in Box 18.4 consists of six parts:

- An r:keyHolder principal that identifies the person to whom the licence is granted by his or her public key.
- An mx:play right, indicating that the principal is permitted to view the image (users may also purchase licences containing an mx:print right that permits them to make a hard copy of the image).
- An mx:diReference resource that identifies the image that has been licensed by its digital item identifier (as defined in MPEG-21 Part 3: Digital Item Identifiers).
- An r:validityInterval condition that limits the term of the licence to a particular time period.
- A ds:KeyInfo element that contains the resource encryption key, itself encrypted by the public key of the terminal for which the licence was created.
- An r:issuer element that contains the digital signature of the licence issuer on the licence.

Since the licence must contain the resource encryption key for its resource, and this key was chosen by the seller during the encryption process, the seller must share this key with the licence issuer. SITDRM does this by having the seller and the licence issuer share a *master key* from which a the resource encryption key for any image can be generated using the image's identifier and a cryptographic hash function. They share the master key during some set-up phase, and afterwards use the hash function to generate resource encryption keys as necessary.

A user may exercise the rights that he or she has purchased using a special MPEG-21 terminal that is able to execute IPMP tools, and is trusted to obey the dictates of licences. Before permitting a user to view or print an image, the terminal must:

1. Locate a licence that grants the `mx:play` or `mx:print` right over that image.
2. Check that the licence is correctly signed by a recognised licence issuer.
3. Check that its current user is the holder of the public key identified in the `r:keyHolder` element (i.e., check that this user possesses the secret key that corresponds to this public key).
4. Check that the validity interval of the licence has not expired.

The second step requires that the terminal somehow possess a trusted copy of the public key of the system licence issuer. For the present, we suppose that this key has been installed in the terminal at its time of manufacture. This installation effectively represents a root grant that permits the system licence issuer to issue licences. If a suitable public key infrastructure were available, however, it would be possible for the set of recognised licence issuers to change over time, or for existing ones to change their keys should their current keys be retired.

If all of these steps are satisfied, the terminal may instantiate the IPMP tool identified in the IPMP descriptor of the resource, and request that this tool decrypt the image. The terminal is then able to display or print the image as usual.

Since every licence issued in Figure 18.2 contains the resource encryption key encrypted by the public key of the terminal that requested it, only that terminal may use that licence. Thus users must obtain an individual licence for every terminal on which they wish to use the image. This is obviously very inconvenient for users with more than one terminal, and may also be unreasonably expensive if the licence issuer charges a new payment for each terminal. Modern DRM systems overcome this limitation by use of an *authorised domain* of which multiple terminals may become members, and to which licences can be issued [23]. We will see how authorised domains can be implemented within the MPEG-21 framework in Section 18.5.

18.4   MPEG-21 in Enterprise Digital Rights Management

It is relatively straightforward to adapt the DRM system described in the previous section to a scenario in which the multimedia seller is replaced by an organisation with trade secrets, and the user is replaced by an employee of the organisation (or, indeed, an employee of a partner organisation with whom the first organisation shares information).

In the project described in this section, we implemented a system by which employees of an organisation could load sensitive documents onto mobile terminals, but were not permitted to access the documents unless they were physically present in (for example)

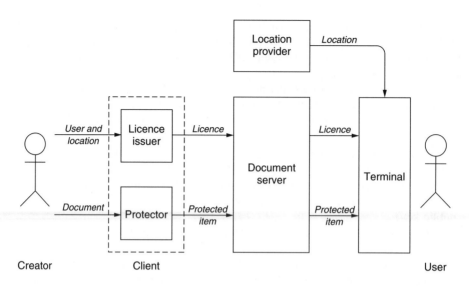

Figure 18.3   A location-based digital rights management system.

the organisation's offices. This scheme prevents access to information if the terminal is misplaced or stolen, if an employee attempts to access a document in a location in which the information may be vulnerable to "shoulder surfing", or if a dishonest employee attempts to leak documents to a competitor. The architecture described in this section, however, seems suitable for many other kinds of policies.

Figure 18.3 shows the architecture of the system used for the new scenario. The multimedia seller of Section 18.3 has been replaced by an "information creator" (an employee) who creates arbitrary XML documents that contain some sensitive information. Employees may upload their documents to a server using a client that converts the document into a protected resource of a digital item, and creates a suitable licence for it. Other employees may then download protected documents and the licences to use them from the document server.

In order for this system to operate securely, it must be possible for the terminal to verify its physical location. Verifying the location of a terminal requires significant effort in its own right if users are to be prevented from faking their locations, and this technology is beyond the scope of the present chapter. In our scenario, we assumed that the terminal had access to a trusted location provider from which it could obtain its location using the HTTP-enabled location delivery protocol ("HELD") [24].

The digital items used in Figure 18.3 have the same form as the one shown earlier in Box 18.1. The licences have the same form as those used in Section 18.3, except that the r:validityInterval condition has been replaced by an sx:territory condition, as shown in Box 18.5.[2]

---

[2] For ease of implementation, the software on which this section is based actually uses the "PIDF-LO" location format supported by HELD instead of the sx:location element specified by MPEG REL. The former format is also more flexible than MPEG REL's.

Box 18.5 An MPEG REL licence that binds a right to a physical location

```
<r:license>
  <r:grant>
    <r:keyHolder>
      <r:info>
        <ds:KeyValue>...</ds:KeyValue>
      </r:info>
    </r:keyHolder>
    <mx:play/>
    <mx:diReference>
      <mx:identifier>urn:company:doc:1</mx:identifier>
    </mx:diReference>
    <sx:territory>
      <sx:location>
        <sx:country>AU</sx:country>
        <sx:state>NSW</sx:state>
        <sx:city>Wollongong</sx:city>
        <sx:postalCode>2500</sx:postalCode>
        <sx:street>Crown St</sx:street>
      </sx:location>
    </sx:territory>
    <ds:KeyInfo>
      <xenc:EncryptedKey>...</xenc:EncryptedKey>
    </ds:KeyInfo>
  </r:grant>
  <r:issuer>
    <ds:Signature>...</ds:Signature>
  </r:issuer>
</r:license>
```

When a user attempts to view a protected document, the terminal must go through all of the same steps as it did in Section 18.3, except that it must now check the physical location of the terminal rather than the validity period of the licence. The terminal of Figure 18.3 does this by establishing an authenticated connection to the location provider using the transport layer security ("TLS") protocol [25], and requesting its own location from the server. The details of our implementation are given in [26].

In order to prevent dishonest users from faking licences or location information, the terminal in Figure 18.3 must verify the authenticity of both the licence and the location provider. If we suppose that the terminal is provided with the public keys of the document server and the location provider during some set-up phase, the terminal can authenticate licences that have been signed by the document server (but not the upload client – so the server must re-sign the licences it receives), and authenticate the location provider as part of the TLS handshake. Section 18.5.3 discusses more complex methods by which the terminal can authenticate licences that have been signed directly by the upload client.

Similar to the system described in Section 18.3, this simple system has a severe drawback in that the information creator must nominate a particular terminal and a particular user for which a licence will be used at the time he or she creates the licence. The next section describes how this can be overcome by implementing a form of role-based access control in which licences are issued to "properties" (roles, in this context) rather than individuals.

18.5 MPEG-21 in Privacy Protection

The use of DRM in privacy protection is a somewhat more recent concept than its use in copyright protection and in enterprises, and it is unlikely that the MPEG-21 committee had privacy protection in mind when it designed the IPMP components or adopted XrML for its REL.

Nonetheless, it is easy to see the parallels between copyright and privacy [27], and how DRM might therefore be adapted to the protection of privacy [4]. The multimedia seller of Section 18.3 is now an individual *data subject* who needs to reveal some personal information to an organisation (called the *data controller*) in order to receive some service. Various *data users* within the organisation may need access to the individual's information in order to provide the service but must not use it for any other purpose or pass it on to any other people. Thus, the data user here corresponds to the multimedia user of Section 18.3.

Brox [28] and, very recently, Fragopoulos *et al.* [29] and Leister *et al.* [30] have, in fact, observed that the MPEG-21 IPMP components may be useful in protecting medical information. The architecture proposed by Fragopoulos *et al.* is similar to the architecture described in this chapter, which we developed for a general privacy protection system [31]. Leister *et al.* focus more on the low-level security properties of the IPMP tools, and do not consider licences in any detail.

Figure 18.4 shows the architecture. Data subjects interact with an organisation via its web site, and submit information by filling in web forms. We used the XForms specification [32] because it is convenient for manipulating XML documents such as

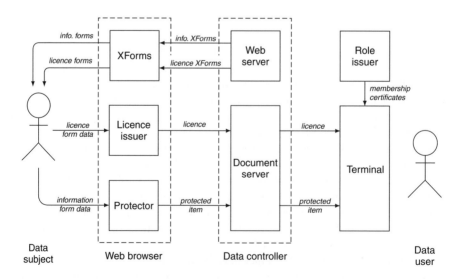

Figure 18.4 Submitting personal information to a web site.

digital items and MPEG REL licences. Prior to submitting the form, however, a browser plug-in transforms the information into a protected MPEG-21 digital item and creates a licence that describes what the organisation can and cannot do with the information. The organisation receives only the protected form and the licence. As in Section 18.4, protected documents and licence are stored on a document server, from which they may be downloaded and used by employees of the organisation according to the licences.

18.5.1   Roles and Authorised Domains in MPEG REL

As we noted in the previous two sections, binding licences to a single terminal is frequently inconvenient to users who use more than one terminal. The problem is particularly acute in Figure 18.4 since the data subject's web browser does not, in general, know the identity of the individuals who may be working on the information, or the identities of the terminals that they will be using.

The solution to these problems is to use *properties* to represent groups of individuals and groups of terminals. A property in MPEG REL is simply a URI. A licence issuer can assign a property to a principal by issuing it with a *membership certificate* that awards the r:possessProperty right over that URI, as shown in Box 18.6.

Box 18.6 A membership certificate

```
<r:license>
  <r:grant>
    <r:keyHolder>
      <r:info>
        <ds:KeyValue>...</ds:KeyValue>
      </r:info>
    </r:keyHolder>
    <r:possessProperty/>
    <sx:propertyUri definition="urn:roles:accounting"/>
    <ds:KeyInfo>
      <xenc:EncryptedKey>...</xenc:EncryptedKey>
    </ds:KeyInfo>
  </r:grant>
  <r:issuer>
    <ds:Signature>...</ds:Signature>
  </r:issuer>
</r:license>
```

In Figure 18.4, properties represent the roles of a role-based access control system [33]. An employee who is a member of a role may apply to the *role issuer* for a membership certificate for that role (that is, property), for each of the terminals that he or she uses. The role issuer checks that the requester is a member of the role for which he or she is applying, and that the terminal that he or she is using is a trusted one. If successful, it issues a membership certificate for the role, for that combination of individual and terminal. The terminal installs the certificate in its local licence pool.

In SITDRM, every property is associated with an asymmetric key pair. The secret key of this pair occupies the place of the resource encryption key (that is, the `xenc:EncryptedKey` element) in a membership certificate. This secret key is encrypted by the public key of the terminal to which the certificate has been issued. In this way, only that terminal is able to access the property's secret key.

Using properties, the original data subject can now issue licences to properties that represent roles of the organisation using the `r:propertyPossessor` principal, as shown in Box 18.7. This licence permits any principal who possesses the urn:roles:accounting property to view (`mx:play`) the resource. Note that, according to SITDRM's cryptographic architecture, the resource encryption key in this licence is encrypted with the public key of the urn:role:accounting property, and not the public key of a terminal, as for earlier licences in this chapter.

Box 18.7 A licence awarded to a property

```
<r:license>
  <r:grant>
    <r:propertyPossessor>
      <sx:propertyUri definition="urn:roles:accounting"/>
    </r:propertyPossessor>
    <mx:play/>
    <mx:diReference>
      <mx:identifier>urn:accounts:customer1</mx:identifier>
    </mx:diReference>
    <ds:KeyInfo>
      <xenc:EncryptedKey>...</xenc:EncryptedKey>
    </ds:KeyInfo>
  </r:grant>
  <r:issuer>
    <ds:Signature>...</ds:Signature>
  </r:issuer>
</r:license>
```

Determining whether or not an individual has permission to perform an action becomes somewhat more complex in the presence of properties. The terminal begins by locating a licence that permits the desired action on the selected resource, as before. Where the licence is awarded to a `r:propertyPossessor` principal, however, the terminal must find and validate a second licence (a membership certificate) that awards that property to the terminal. In SITDRM, the terminal may then use its own private key to extract the property's secret key from the membership certificate. It may then use the property's secret key to extract the resource encryption key from the first licence.

18.5.2 Extending MPEG REL for Privacy

Since MPEG REL (and the MPEG RDD) was not designed with privacy applications in mind, it lacks the means to express a number of concepts frequently used in privacy policies. Privacy policies frequently refer to the "purpose" of an action, for example, and MPEG REL has no obvious way of expressing this. For this reason, we developed a small *privacy extension scheme* in the style of the existing standard extension and media extension schemata. Elements of the privacy extensions are denoted by the namespace prefix px in this chapter.

We developed prelimary schema by examining the vocabulary of existing privacy policies expressed in the Platform for Privacy Preferences [34] and Enterprise Privacy Authorisation Language [35], and then drafting licences for a variety of simple scenarios until we were satisfied that our the syntax was convenient and unambiguous. Our extension included new rights such as px:contact (the right to contact a person identified in the resource) and conditions such as px:dealing that restricted the use of information to a particular session or transaction. Our observations are discussed in greater detail in [31].

Of course, adding new elements to MPEG REL (or any standardised language) may result in the creation of licences that cannot be understood by a standard terminal. SIT-DRM avoids this to some degree by allowing REL elements to be implemented by IPMP tools, but, nonetheless, it seems likely that MPEG or another suitable body would need to standardise privacy extension schema (and possibly also extensions to the RDD) before MPEG REL sees widespread use in privacy protection.

18.5.3   Verifying Licences without a Central Licence Issuer

In Sections 18.3 and 18.4, it was reasonable to assume that all licences were issued by some central licence issuer recognised by all of the terminals in the system. Supposing that the terminals had this licence issuer's public key installed in them during some set-up phase, the terminals were able to verify that licences had not been tampered with by validating the signature on the licence with this public key. Membership certificates can be treated similarly here, since the role issuer is well-known to the terminals.

In Figure 18.4, however, every data subject issues licences for his or her own data, and it would be unreasonable to require all of the data terminals to possess the public keys of all of the data subjects. In fact, the system may be insecure if this were permitted, since a naïve implementation would allow one data subject to create and issue an apparently valid licence for someone else's data.

One solution to this problem is to have licences issued by the data controller according to a policy supplied by the data subject, as described in [36]. An auditor can verify that the data controller correctly translates policies into licences, and terminals can verify licences by using the public key of the data controller.

Another solution is for data subjects to include a unique random nonce in both, the protected data and the signature on the licence that they issue for it. Since each data subject is the only person who possesses the nonce for his or her data, a terminal can check that the data and the licence were issued by the same person by comparing the nonce. The cryptographic details are discussed in an appendix of [31].

Finally, we could introduce a registrar who is responsible for recording which issuers may issue licences for which documents. In this regime, each data subject must register his or her public key with the registrar, and thereafter also register every document that he

or she creates. Upon receiving a document and a purported licence for it, a terminal must
then ask the registrar for the public key of the correct licence issuer for that document.

18.6 Conclusion

DRM has several uses beyond its original application to copyright protection. The
MPEG-21 IPMP components and REL were designed for the classical copyright
protection application, but can also be applied – possibly with some relatively minor
extensions – to the protection of sensitive documents and personal information.

MPEG-21 does not, however, fully specify all of the components of a DRM system.
Aside from its explicit decision to leave the cryptographic architecture of the system in the
hands of vendor-supplied IPMP tools, MPEG-21 also does not specify the means by which
terminals communicate with IPMP tools, or by which terminals and tools authenticate
each other. The MPEG-4 IPMP Extensions and Digital Media Project's specifications,
however, may provide some guidance.

Designers of DRM systems based on the MPEG-21 multimedia framework also need
to make a number of decisions about:

- How terminals establish trust in the system's licence issuers.
- How licence issuers establish trust in terminals.
- How cryptographic keys are securely transmitted to terminals.
- How users and terminals acquire licences to perform actions.
- How terminals acquire IPMP tools required to access protected resources.

Acknowledgments

This work was partly funded by the Cooperative Research Centre for Smart Internet
Technology, Australia, and carried out at the University of Wollongong. Numerous people
contributed to the projects described in this chapter, including Hartono Kurnio, Qiong Liu,
Adam Muhlbauer, Rei Safavi-Naini, Farzad Salim, Sid Stamm and Martin Surminen.

References

[1] Karpouzis, K., Maglogiannis, I., Pappaioannou, E. *et al.* (2007) MPEG-21 digital items to support integration of heterogeneous multimedia content. *Computer Communications*, **30**, 592–607.
[2] Lux, M., Granitzer, M., Klieber, W. *et al.* (2005) Digital rights management for distributed multimedia
e-learning content. Interactive Computer Aided Learning Conference.
[3] Arnab, A. and Hutchison, A. (2005) Requirement analysis of enterprise DRM systems. Proceedings of
Information Security South Africa.
[4] Kenny, S. and Korba, L. (2002) Applying digital rights management systems to privacy rights. *Computers
& Security*, **21**, 648–664.
[5] Liu, Q., Safavi-Naini, R. and Sheppard, N.P. (2003) Digital rights management for content distribution.
Australasian Information Security Workshop, Adelaide, Australia, pp. 49–58.
[6] Collberg, C.S. and Thomborson, C. (2002) Watermarking, tamper-proofing and obfuscation – tools for
software protection. *IEEE Transactions on Software Engineering*, **28** (8), 735–746.
[7] Garfinkel, T., Pfaff, B., Chow, J. *et al.* (2003) Terra: a virtual machine-based platform for trusted computing. *ACM SIGOPS Operating Systems Review*, **37** (5), 193–206.

[8] Marchesini, J., Smith, S.W., Wild, O. *et al.* (2004) Open-source applications of TCPA hardware. *Annual Computer Security Applications Conference, Tucson, USA.*

[9] Open Mobile Alliance (2009) *Digital Rights Management (DRM) Working Group*, http://www.openmobilealliance.org/Technical/DRM.aspx (accessed 2009).

[10] Marlin Developer Community (2009) *Marlin – The Content Sharing Platform for Consumer Devices and Multimedia Services*, http://www.marlin-community.com (accessed 2009).

[11] Koenen, R.H., Lacy, J., Mackay, M. and Mitchell, S. (2004) The long march to interoperable digital rights management. *Proceedings of the IEEE*, **92**, 883–897.

[12] XML Security Working Group (2008) *XML Security Working Group*, http://www.w3.org/2008/xmlsec (accessed 2009).

[13] Ji, M., Shen, S.M., Zeng, W. *et al.* (2004) MPEG-4 IPMP extension for interoperable protection of multimedia content. *EURASIP Journal on Applied Signal Processing*, **2004** (14), 2201–2213.

[14] Serrão, C., Dias, J.M.S. and Kudamakis, P. (2005) From OPIMA to MPEG IPMP-X: a standard's history across R&D projects. *Signal Processing-Image Communication*, **20**, 972–994.

[15] Fan, C.-W., Chang, F.-C. and Hang, H.-M. (2005) An MPEG-4 IPMPX design and implementation on MPEG-21 test bed. *IEEE International Symposium on Circuits and Systems*, 4550–4553.

[16] Digital Media Project (2008) Interoperable Digital Rights Management Platform. Technical Specification Version 3.2.

[17] ContentGuard (2004) *Extensible Rights Markup Language*, http://www.xrml.org (accessed 2009).

[18] Xerox Corporation (1998) *The Digital Rights Property Language: Manual and Tutorial – XML Edition*, http://www.oasis-open.org/cover/DPRLmanual-XML2.html (accessed 2009).

[19] DeMartini, T., Kalter, J., Nguyen, M. *et al.* (2006) Rights expression language, in *The MPEG-21 Book* (eds I.S. Burnett, P. Fernando, R. Van de Walle and R. Koenen), Wiley, Hoboken, NJ.

[20] Sheppard, N.P. (2007) On implementing MPEG-21 intellectual property management and protection. ACM Workshop on Digital Rights Management, Alexandria, Virginia, USA, pp. 10–22.

[21] Marlin Developer Community (2006) *The Role of Octopus in Marlin, Marlin Developer Community. White paper*, http://www.marlin-community.com/public/RoleofOctopusinMarlin.pdf (accessed 2009).

[22] Stamm, S., Sheppard, N.P. and Safavi-Naini, R. (2007) Implementing trusted terminals with a TPM and SITDRM. International Workshop on Run-Time Enforcement for Mobile and Distributed Systems, Dresden, Germany.

[23] Messerges, T.S. and Dabbish, E.A. (2003) Digital rights management in a 3G mobile phone and beyond. ACM Workshop on Digital Rights Management, Washington, DC, pp. 27–38.

[24] Barnes, M., Winterbottom, J., Thompson, M. and Stark, B. (2009) HTTP Enabled Location Delivery (HELD), Internet Engineering Taskforce, Internet Draft.

[25] Dierks, T. and Allen, C. (1999) The TLS Protocol: Version 1.0, Internet Engineering Taskforce, RFC 2246.

[26] Muhlbauer, A., Safavi-Naini, R., Salim, F. *et al.* (2008) Location constraints in digital rights management. *Computer Communications*, **31** (6), 1173–1180.

[27] Zittrain, J. (2000) What the publisher can teach the patient: Property and privacy in an era of trusted privication. *Stanford Law Review*, **52**, 1201–1250.

[28] Brox, G.A. (2005) MPEG-21 as an access control tool for the National Health Service care records service. *Journal of Telemedicine and Telecare*, **11**, 23–25.

[29] Fragopoulos, A., Gialelis, J. and Serpanos, D. (2009) Security framework for pervasive healthcare architectures utilizing MPEG-21 IPMP components. *International Journal of Telemedicine and Applications*, vol. 2009, Article ID 461560, http://www.hindawi.com/journals/ijta/2009/461560.html.

[30] Leister, W., Fretland, T. and Balasingham, I. (2009) Security and authentication architecture using MPEG-21 for wireless patient monitoring systems. *International Journal on Advances in Security*, **2** (1), 16–29.

[31] Sheppard, N.P. and Safavi-Naini, R. (2006) Protecting privacy with the MPEG-21 IPMP framework. International Workshop on Privacy Enhancing Technologies, Cambridge, UK, pp. 152–171.

[32] W3C (2007) *The Forms Working Group*, http://www.w3.org/MarkUp/Forms/ (accessed 2009).

[33] Sandhu, R.S., Coyne, E.J., Feinstein, H.L. and Youman, C.E. (1996) Role-based access control models. *IEEE Computer*, **29**, 38–47.

[34] Cranor, L. and Wenning, R. (2007) *P3P: The Platform for Privacy Preferences*, http://www.w3.org/P3P (accessed 2009).

[35] Powers, C., Adler, S. and Wishart, B. (2004) *EPAL Translation of the Freedom of Information and Protection of Privacy Act, Ontario Information and Privacy Commissioner, White Paper*, http://www.ipc.on.ca/docs/EPAL%20FI1.pdf (accessed 2009).

[36] Salim, F., Sheppard, N.P. and Safavi-Naini, R. (2007) Enforcing P3P policies using a digital rights management system. International Workshop on Privacy Enhancing Technologies, Ottawa, Ontario, Canada, pp. 200–217.

19

Designing Intelligent Content Delivery Frameworks Using MPEG-21

Samir Amir, Ioan Marius Bilasco, Thierry Urruty, Jean Martinet, and Chabane Djeraba
University Lille1, Télécom Lille1, Villeneuve d'Ascq, France

19.1 Introduction

Digital home systems are a reality. The possibility of switching between access devices while accessing online and multimedia contents is becoming common usage [1, 2]. Deploying the content regardless of the heterogeneity of devices capable of accessing multimedia contents is a key factor for producers. Once created, the contents should be deployable on various configurations without subsequent transformation performed manually by content creators, or completely redesigned by authors to make them deployable on new access devices. With regard to the current state of the art, the variety of devices as well as deployed technologies, it is *naive* to consider that a content can be transmitted anywhere as it is.

Automatic transformations are necessary to modify the encoding, the structure, or the content itself to make it accessible in constraint contexts. Among these transformations, we can mention *transrating* (i.e., changing the bitrate of the content), *transmoding* (i.e., changing the modality to convey the content), and *transcoding* (i.e., changing the encoding format). These three operations are closely linked to the encoding of the content. Basically, they are characterized by a set of parameters describing, respectively, the expected output rate, the output format (video, audio, etc.), and the output codec. They do not need any explicit knowledge about the content itself. The obtained output is a degraded version of the initial content.

More intelligent transformations like summarization, filtering, or reorganization of the content require specific resources and information. Such techniques need a deep access to

The Handbook of MPEG Applications: Standards in Practice   Edited by Marios C. Angelides and Harry Agius
© 2011 John Wiley & Sons, Ltd

the knowledge embedded within the content and to the characteristics of the broadcasting context. The broadcasting context is composed of access devices, networks, environmental configurations (indoor/outdoor, noisiness, visibility, etc.), user and community interests and preferences, as well as available adaptation services deployed on intermediate proxies. The description of all this content-related and context-related knowledge must be made following a standard format that can be accepted by all the devices and services involved in the delivery and adaptation process.

Owing to multimedia popularity and the wideness of its application domain, the amount of information describing the multimedia content and context has become essential. Information serves to describe all entities involved in multimedia systems in order to facilitate multimedia delivery and consumption. It starts with the description of the content itself (size, type, etc.), its semantics (objects appearing in a picture, place where a picture was taken, etc.), the characteristics of the devices transmitting or consuming the content (TV, networks, etc.), and finally the consumer profile (preferences, interests, etc.).

Currently, several standards just cover some part of the information. MPEG-7 [3, 4] and MPEG-21 DID (digital item declaration) [5], for instance, deal with the description of the structure and semantics of a media object. MPEG-21 DIA (digital item adaptation) [6], CC/PP [7], or device independent activity[1] offers tools for modeling the utilization context. WSDL [8] and OWL-S [9] standards deal with the characterization of Web services that might be involved in some adaptation process on the network. However, up to now, no integrated solution has clearly emerged. The MPEG-21 [10] set of tools (namely, DID [11] and DIA [6]) seems to be the most prolific candidate as it proposes tools to describe the content, the context, and the transformation to be applied to a given media by using BSDL [12, 13]. But still, the difficulty in acquiring a deep knowledge on these tools might not encourage the designers, who try to find friendly solutions for specific applications. We underline here that, as far as we know today, there is no off-the-shelf solutions concealing the complexity of standards from the designers (in particular in terms of encoding and retrieving information) like the one proposed above.

In this chapter, we report on the creation of a new metadata framework that embeds information related to the content, context, and adaptation services. This is part of the CAM4Home ITEA2 project.[2] A group of 20 multimedia academic and industrial practitioners from TV, 3G, and Internet application fields defined a restricted set of metadata requirements in order to support the convergence of multimedia content in digital home environments. A unified model, called *CAM* (*collaborative aggregated multimedia*) *metadata model* [14, 15], has been designed to cover the categories of information introduced above, making no reference to the effective type of metadata encoding used to represent information. In the following, we explore first an alternative encoding by using multimedia native standards, like MPEG-7 and MPEG-21, in order to illustrate how the mapping of application-specific requirements can be projected to existing descriptors of MPEG standards. We show also some other specific requirements that cannot be described natively by MPEG standards. They have been encoded using specific constructs developed by CAM4Home project partners. These requirements enrich the semantic and the context of information in order to allow the development of

---

[1] http://http://www.w3.org/2001/di/
[2] http://www.cam4home-itea.org.

a rich multimedia experience. However, the original MPEG21/7 constructs lay the basis of the semantic, structure, and the context descriptions.

This chapter is organized as follows. Section 19.2 is dedicated to the presentation of metadata requirements. Section 19.3 presents the abstraction of the requirements by means of a metamodel organizing metadata information by nature and usage. An overview about XML multimedia metadata standards for encoding content description is given in Section 19.4; we show here the lack of existing techniques with regard to the identified requirements. Section 19.5 illustrates how this metamodel can be mapped to the descriptors existing in MPEG-7 and MPEG-21. We have chosen MPEG as it covers most of our requirements. We provide also a series of new description needed to meet the requirements related to Web 2.0 specificities such as social tags and services. We conclude by discussing our encoding choices.

19.2   CAM Metadata Framework Requirements

In this section, we present the delivery architecture that we have selected in the frame of the CAM4Home ITEA2 project, and we expose the requirements in terms of metadata for the proposed framework.

19.2.1   CAM4Home Framework Overview

The purpose of the CAM4Home project is to create a metadata-enabled content delivery framework that allows end users and commercial content providers to create and deliver rich multimedia experiences. They are based on a novel concept of CAM, which is the main contribution of the CAM4Home project. CAM refers to the aggregation and composition of individual multimedia contents (called *objects*) into a content bundle that may include references to content-based services and can be delivered as a semantically coherent set of contents and related services over various communication channels.

In this project, one common metadata framework for CAM content is under development, which can be applied to both personal and commercial applications, and is interoperable with relevant standard metadata and content representation technologies. In order to better illustrate the role of the metadata framework within the project, the general architecture is presented in Figure 19.1.

This CAM metadata framework enables a novel way of content provisioning by bundling different types of multimedia objects and services into bundles on the level of metadata. The CAM metadata framework is able to encapsulate existing metadata technologies for multiple types of contents and to incorporate references to content-related services. These content bundles are delivered into the digital home environment over multiple communication channels and mediums in a controlled (e.g., time synchronized) and adaptive (e.g., adaptation to environment capabilities and user preferences) manner.

The functional aspects of the metadata framework are performed by the CAM4Home service architecture. The service architecture defines the necessary service components to support the content life cycle of CAM from content bundle creation to distribution, and finally interpretation and playback of the content bundles.

As explained previously, the metadata framework serves two purposes: providing metadata representation format for CAM content and enabling the processing of such

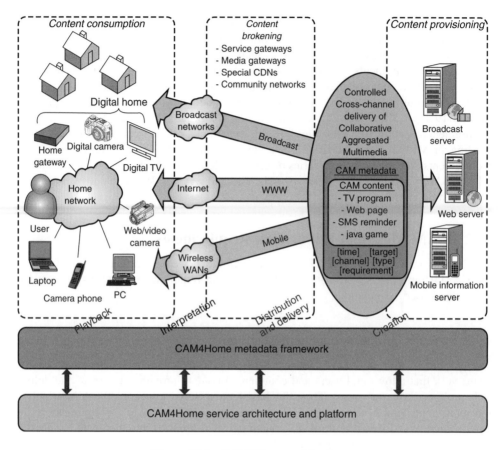

Figure 19.1   CAM4Home architecture.

metadata. However, the focus of this chapter is to represent the metadata model of the metadata framework, which constitutes the specification of the data format providing a medium for the applications and services to distribute and deliver the aggregated content. The description of the service platform is out of the scope of this chapter.

19.2.2   Metadata Requirements

In the following, we discuss some requirements that we observed while constructing the metadata framework. The requirements are related to content adaptation, content aggregation, and metadata extensibility topics that have been gathered in the project.

19.2.3   Content Adaptation Requirements

In the process of content adaptation, the framework selects the most suitable content according to the consumer profile and respective device characteristics; this operation is done through a content delivery step. In order to achieve such an operation, all elements included in this process must be well described. For instance, if a given content is not suitable for playback by the consumer's device, it needs to be adapted to the discovered content adaptation services that analyze the consumer's device characteristics via the interpretation of its metadata. The conceived metadata framework ensures a proper description of the user profile, preference, and usage context. This description covers the following:

- *Devices* and their audio capabilities, embedded decoding system, display capabilities, installed software and hardware description, and so on.
- *Network* and its QoS (quality of service) characteristics (e.g., maximum and minimum of data throughput and reported packet lost).
- *Services* deployed within the framework and their QoS characteristics.
- *Users* and their personal information (e.g., name and date of birth), environment, and preferences descriptions.
- *Communities* and their common denominators with regard to user interests.

19.2.4 Content Aggregation Requirements

The CAM metadata framework enables a novel way of content provisioning by bundling different types of content and content services into content bundles on the level of metadata. The framework describes the relationship between different types of contents; several relationships have been defined in order to help the consumers to select the related contents. For instance, we have defined a relationship named *thematic relationship* which links all the contents sharing the same theme. A user watching a video on a given subject has the ability to display all the contents on this subject (e.g., all videos on football). Many metadata relationships have been defined in the project, and the following are some of them:

- Part-of relationship.
- Aggregation-type relationship, showing why different types of contents are aggregated in the same bundle (e.g., same event and same date).
- Derivative-of relationship, when the content is a derivative work of another one (e.g., content#1 is a remix of content#2).
- Alternative relationship, when the content is an alternative representation of another one.
- Rendering relationship, when a multimedia content embeds the representation of another one (e.g., a web page with a video rendered with a plug-in).

19.2.5 Extensibility

In order to make the framework extensible and allow CAM4Home users to enrich the contents with other metadata, the designed metadata framework contains specific properties defined so as to link the metadata framework to other standards (e.g., users can upload a video and add metadata on the date of creation and the subject, for instance; or they may also add metadata that is encoded in an already existing format like MPEG-7).

19.3   CAM Metadata Model

The metadata requirements collected and detailed in the previous section have been organized into three main categories: metadata on the content – addressed as *core metadata*; metadata on the context – addressed as *supplementary metadata*; and metadata defined in the existing standards – addressed as *external metadata* (external with regard to the current metadata framework). The design of the CAM metadata model [14] is illustrated in Figure 19.2.

The CAM metadata model provides the core concepts and required metadata level information for collaborative distribution of multimedia and software contents as a structured model which can be partially or fully instantiated as metadata, and used in the system. In addition, the CAM metadata model is designed to allow an easy encapsulation of existing metadata formats into the structures of the instantiated metadata. Furthermore, the abstract from the CAM metadata model enables to define new structures and associations that a system might need in its operations. The CAM abstract metamodel defines a generic categorization of concrete metadata entities and associations between them on an abstract level. In the following, we ignore the presentation of the metamodel's abstract part. We focus our attention on the concrete part as we will study how the concrete set of metadata selected to cover the requirements can be mapped to MPEG-7 and MPEG-21 structures.

We briefly describe the role of the core, supplementary, and external metadata. Then, we present in more detail the simple and structured metadata belonging to each category. The *core* part of the metamodel is structured around two notions: the CAM object and the

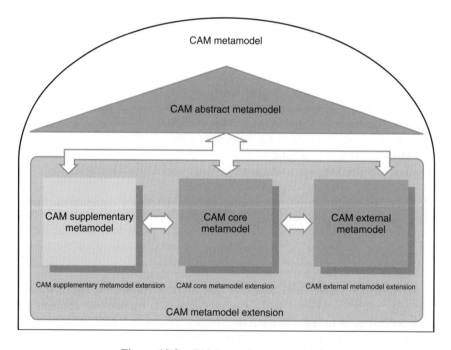

Figure 19.2   CAM metadata metamodel.

CAM bundle. A CAM object corresponds to a set of metadata describing an atomic media object regardless of its precise type. A CAM bundle is a metadata container representing information about the aggregation of several atomic media objects. These two concepts are the main deployment units within the framework.

The *supplementary* part of the metamodel introduces five entities: the access device, the network, the services available on the network, the user, and its communities. For each of these entities, several profiles can be associated in order to support time-dependent (in the morning, in the afternoon) and usage-dependent (at home, at work) characteristics.

The *external* part defines the structures in the CAM metadata model, which acts as an interface toward the external metadata formats (e.g., TV-Anytime [16], WSDL [17], and CC/PP [7]) and encapsulates them into the CAM metadata model.

19.3.1 CAM Core Metamodel

Constructed around CAM object and CAM bundle notions, the core metamodel supports the representation of a wide variety of multimedia contents: downloadable applications, software services, images, videos, and so on. The metadata describes both the content file (the *essence* of the content) and the actual content that is provided.

A CAM object or CAM bundle contains simple or structured metadata organized in six categories:

- *Content feature metadata* which describes the content itself. They are split into simple metadata (author, creator, copyright, description, legal notice, target domains, thumbnail, title, etc.) and complex metadata (access restrictions, appearing concepts, content genre, creation context metadata, cue tones, etc.).
- *Community-created metadata* [15]: social tags, user comments, and user ratings.
- *Essence of the content* (applying only to CAM objects): content location, nature of the deployment (streaming or downloadable content), essence file metadata, etc.
- *Aggregation metadata* (applying only to CAM bundles): semantic, spatial, and temporal relationships between composing objects within a bundle.
- *System metadata*, which is used to manage the instances of a CAM object and CAM bundle: UID, version number, and creation date time.
- *Supplementary reference metadata*, which is used to specify the deployment contexts for which the content was initially designed: target community reference, target device reference, and target domains.

A partial view of the CAM object and CAM bundle classes containing only the complex metadata is illustrated in Figure 19.3. The community-created metadata is attached to both object and bundles. The other complex metadata are directly associated only to CAM objects, but there can be an inference for bundles by considering the association between bundles and composing objects.

19.3.2 CAM Supplementary Metamodel

The supplementary part of the metamodel is built on three main concepts: the entity, profiles, and supplementary metadata. An entity can be described by several profiles. Each

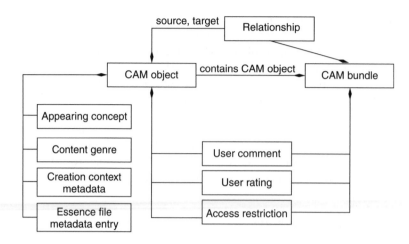

Figure 19.3 Partial view of CAM object and CAM bundle structured metadata.

profile gathers a predefined set of supplementary metadata. For instance, devices physical capacities, browser capabilities, display capabilities, audio capabilities, available software, decoding systems, embedded decoders are some examples of structured metadata used to describe an access device. Preference description, environment description, and personal descriptions are structured metadata to describe the users of the systems. Figure 19.4 reflects the organization of the supplementary metamodel.

The entities are also linked to each other. A user entity can belong to a community entity. A user entity uses a given device entity on a given network entity. A device entity uses, at a given time, a network entity. These relations are represented in Figure 19.5. The dashed lines indicate that the links are implemented by means of references.

19.3.3   CAM External Metamodel

This part of the abstract model provides the basic structures that allow the integration of existing standards within the CAM metadata framework. The possibility to include external metadata description in CAM metadata framework is a key feature as it permits CAM4Home practitioners to benefit from the existing metadata standards.

Two categories of external metadata descriptions are considered: external core metadata and external supplementary metadata. The external core metadata descriptions are related to the core aspects of a CAM object or a CAM bundle. The external supplementary metadata descriptions are related to the characterization of supplementary entities. In order to underline the type of external metadata classes that can be considered for integration within the CAM metadata framework, we have defined several subclasses for each type of external metadata. Hence, we have core-related external metadata classes that support the integration of content feature metadata or content aggregative metadata. With regard to the supplementary-related external metadata classes, we have considered external metadata classes that address the community, device, user, and so on.

In this section, we have presented an abstraction of CAM4Home delivery framework requirements. Effective instances of the abstraction have to be represented and encoded.

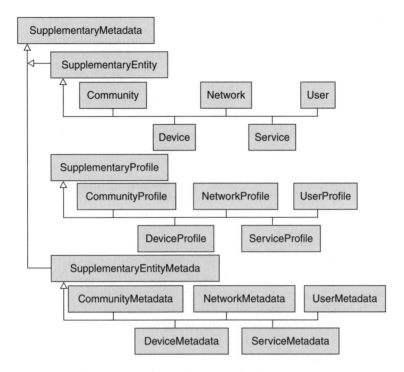

Figure 19.4   CAM abstract supplementary metamodel.

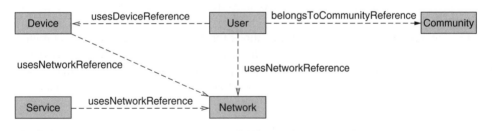

Figure 19.5   Relationships between supplementary entities.

We naturally look for XML-based multimedia standards. In the next section, we discuss some existing standards that seem suitable for encoding CAM4Home metadata requirements.

19.4   Study of the Existing Multimedia Standards

The ubiquitous presence of multimedia data requires an extensive use of metadata for multimedia content retrieval, filtering, and adaptation. The main metadata specification efforts are focused on the description of the multimedia content and context [18]. The MPEG-7 standard represents the most successful result in this field. It standardizes the description format (syntax and semantics) and decoding of a broad set of features

of the multimedia assets at many different levels of abstraction. MPEG-21 DIA and
TV-Anytime take MPEG-7-controlled terms to extend the metadata description to some
more specific purposes. MPEG-21 DIA standardizes the description of multimedia
adaptation procedures in a generic way, whereas TV-Anytime targets applications of
digital TV, such as electronic program guides (EPG). Content structure is also another
information that metadata takes into account. A multimedia presentation is a structured
collection of elements, such as video and audio clips, images, and documents. The
bundling of these elements is also described by multimedia metadata. Among the existing
metadata standards used for the structural description, we can note METS [19], IMS
Content Packaging [20], and SCORM [17]. But, the most generic approach for this
purpose is proposed by the MPEG-21 DID standard.

Another field of application of multimedia metadata is the description of the multimedia
life cycle. This information about content creation, modification, search, delivery, and
consumption is also described by the metadata. MPEG-7, for instance, is one of the
standards that include tools for the description of the user interaction with contents.

Multimedia content adaptation is also an interesting field of application of metadata.
The adaptation is made according to the context: where and by whom these resources will
be used. The context includes information about devices consuming or transmitting these
contents (e.g., networks, TV, and mobile) and user characteristics (e.g., user profile and
user preference). MPEG-21 DIA allows the description of device and network profiles.
W3C for device descriptions for web content adaptation uses CC/PP.

Several content-related standards exist, but none allow the homogenous description of
multimedia content, services, and use context (as illustrated in Table 19.1).

MPEG-7 standardizes the description of content features and aggregation, but does
not cover other information type such as user-created metadata (comment) or network
characteristics.

TV-Anytime standard encloses specifications for the controlled delivery of multimedia
content to a user's digital video recorder. It seeks to exploit the evolution in convenient,
high capacity storage of digital information to provide consumers with a highly personalized TV experience. Users will have access to content from a wide variety of sources,

Table 19.1 Metadata standards and the information they cover

	Standards information	MPEG-7	MPEG-21	TV-Anytime	METS
Content	Essence	Yes	Yes	Yes	Yes
	Feature	Yes	Yes	Yes	Yes
	User-created metadata	–	Yes	–	–
	Content aggregation	Yes	Yes	Yes	Yes
	Service aggregation	–	–	–	–
Context	User	Yes	Yes	Yes	
	Devices	–	Yes	–	–
	Services	–	–	–	–
	Networks	–	Yes	–	–
	Communities	Yes	Yes	–	

tailored to their needs and personal preferences. TV-Anytime does not cover all the required information related to content and context description. For instance, information describing device, service, and network characteristics are not covered by TV-Anytime.

METS is a metadata standard designed to encode metadata for electronic texts, still images, digitized video, sound files, and other digital materials within electronic library collections. In doing so, it attempts to address the lack of standardization in digital library metadata practices which is currently inhibiting the growth of coherent digital collections. METS offers a coherent overall structure for encoding all relevant types of metadata (descriptive, administrative, and structural). However, this standard does not offer a description of the use context. Besides this lack, the semantic description of this standard is very limited.

The MPEG-21 standard deals with most of the issues that we have enumerated above. Still, it only concerns multimedia content and context description, and does not allow the description of several other information. For instance, it does not provide native support for user-created metadata (such as comments), for the aggregation of content and services, and so on. Still, it can be extended using its DIDL part.

In the next section, we consider in detail the classes of the metadata metamodel, and we propose an MPEG-7/21 encoding. We believe that these two standards are pertinent for encoding, as we can find intuitively the resemblances between the MPEG-21 digital item and CAM objects and CAM bundles. Besides, the supplementary part of the metamodel can be reflected into the environment description tools included into the MPEG-21 DIA standard.

19.5 CAM Metadata Encoding Using MPEG-21/7

As we have mentioned earlier, the core metamodel regroups all properties describing metadata structures and semantics. In this section, we show how the structural and semantic information can be encoded using MPEG-21/7 standards. Sine MPEG-21/7 do not cover some requirement (e.g., complex relationships between CAM object, physiological state of a user, community-created metadata, and services seen as content), we show how to enrich MPEG-21/7 by adding some other information embedded from CAM4Home standard.

Before describing the encoding for the CAM metadata model, we recall briefly some features of the MPEG-21 tools we use. MPEG-21 is based on two essential concepts: the definition of a fundamental distribution and transaction unit (digital item) and the concept of users interacting with digital items. The composition, structure, and organization of a digital item are specified by a DID.

Figure 19.6a shows a DID, which encloses a set of abstract terms and concepts to form a useful model for defining digital items. A digital item is described by a container that aggregates descriptors and items. Items are defined as a collection of descriptors, components, or other items. The expressive power of MPEG-21 has already been proven [21]. The structure of the CAM metadata model fits the MPEG-21 DID specification properly (Figure 19.6b). In CAM4Home, CAM bundles are described by metadata (descriptor) and they aggregate several CAM objects (item). Furthermore, CAM objects enclose CAM elements (resources) and metadata (descriptor).

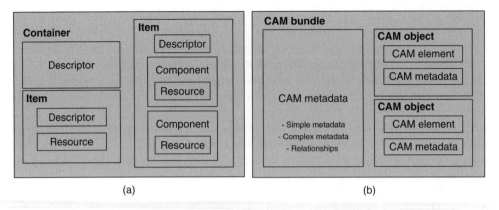

(a)   (b)

Figure 19.6   DID structures and C4H structures.

We detail the encoding of the main classes from the CAM metadata core model: CAM object and CAM bundle. We also present part of the encoding of CAM metadata supplementary classes modeling the context by using MPEG-21 DIA constructs. The code fragments that we present in the following sections include – besides standard MPEG namespaces (DII [11], DIDL [5], DIA [6], MPEG-7 [3]) – the following C4H specific namespaces: *core*, *suppl*, and *inst* – introducing respectively core and supplementary schema elements and default instances namespace.

In general, metadata are introduced by appropriate MPEG-21/7 constructs or specific didl:Statement attached to didl:Descriptor, or DIDL extensions (for metadata not existing natively in MPEG-21/7) describing either CAM objects or CAM bundles. For instance, in order to define the creator of a content, we can reuse the mpeg7:Creator element. To encode the display characteristics of a device, we can reuse the dia:Display element.

In the following section, we first describe how the two main metamodel classes, CAM object and CAM bundles, are encoded. Then, we present some examples illustrating how object or bundle properties (simple or complex) can be encoded directly or by proposing specific extensions.

19.5.1   CAM Object Encoding

Box 19.1 presents an MPEG-21 fragment describing a CAM object. The CAM object is encoded by the didl:Item element (lines 2-15).

Box 19.1 MPEG-21 fragment describing a CAM object instance

```
01: <didl:DIDL xmlns:didl="urn:mpeg:mpeg21:2002:01-DIDL-NS">
02:  <didl:Item> ...
03:    <didl:Descriptor>
04:      <didl:Statement mimeType="text/xml; charset=UTF-8">
05:        <dii:Identifier>urn:c4h:inst:0-39-36-1</dii:Identifier>
```

```
06:                           <!-- encodes core:camObjectUID -->
07:       </didl:Statement>
08:      </didl:Descriptor>
09:      <didl:Component>
10:       <didl:Resource mimeType="image/jpg"
11:            ref="http://www.cam4home-itea.org/graphics/logos
             /cam4home.png"/>
12:            <!-- encodes core:essenceFileIdentifier -->
13:      </didl:Component> ...
14:     </didl:Item>
15:    </didl:DIDL>
```

It contains a first descriptor to define the identifier of the CAM object (line 5). This descriptor corresponds to the *camObjectUID* metadata of a CAM object. Since the CAM object describes a physical content (multimedia file or service), the corresponding `didl:Item` element encloses a `didl:Component` definition (lines 09–13) which introduces a `didl:Reference` to the essence of the content (line 11).

19.5.2 CAM Bundle Encoding

Box 19.2 shows a part of the CAM bundle specification using MPEG-21. CAM bundles are encoded by means of `didl:Container` elements (lines 02–16) as they aggregate several descriptions of physical contents: the CAM Objects.

Regular metadata properties of CAM bundles are encoded in a similar way to CAM objects. However, special properties must describe the aggregation of CAM objects into CAM bundles. We distinguish between a CAM object whose life cycle is completely controlled by the CAM bundle and a CAM object that is shared between several CAM Bundles, having its own life cycle. The latter case is modeled by the `didl:Descriptor` (lines 03–08). This descriptor introduces, through a sentence, a *core*-specific property (`containsCAMObject` – lines 05-06) that retains the identifier of the (*freely*) aggregated CAM object. The inclusion of (*hard*) bound CAM objects is done through the inclusion of the `didl:Item` elements (line 10) defining the CAM objects within the `didl:container` structure.

Box 19.2 MPEG-21 fragment describing CAM bundle and CAM bundle metadata

```
01: <didl:DIDL ...>
02:    <didl:Container>
03:     <didl:Descriptor> <!-- referred CAM Objects -->
04:      <didl:Statement mimeType="text/xml"
          xmlns:core="urn:c4h:core:2009">
05:       <core:containsCAMObject>urn:c4h:inst:0-39-36-1
          </core:containsCAMObject>
06:       <core:containsCAMObject>urn:c4h:inst:0-24-47-5
          </core:containsCAMObject>...
```

```
07:     </didl:Statement>
08:     </didl:Descriptor>
09:    ...
10:    <didl:Item> ... </didl:Item> <!-enclosed CAM
       Object definition -->
11:    ...
12:   </didl:Container>
13: </didl:DIDL>
```

19.5.3   Core Metadata Encoding

In the remaining of this section, we illustrate first some common CAM4Home properties that can be mapped straightforward onto MPEG21/7 constructs. Then, we illustrate the mechanism that we have employed for encoding metamodel concepts not included natively in MPEG-21.

Owing to the number of requirements defined under the project, we have selected a few concepts that cover several multimedia metadata domain (e.g., creation information and semantic relationships).

19.5.3.1   Common Metadata

CAM object and CAM bundle descriptions are composed of some common metadata such as title, description, creation date and time, and creator. Some of this metadata are already enclosed in the `mpeg7:CreationInformationType` element. Box 19.3 illustrates the encoding of some common metadata. For instance, the `core:creationDateTime` metadata is encoded (lines 17–21) by the `CreationCoordinate/CreationDate/Time Point` element. The `core:description` metadata is encoded (lines 14–16) by the `Abstract/FreeTextAnnotation` text element. Information about the creator is brought by the `mpeg7:Creator` element (lines 04–12).

Box 19.3 Common metadata encoding using MPEG-21/7

```
01:<didl:Descriptor>
02: <didl:Statement mimeType="text/xml; charset=UTF-8" >
03:  <mpeg7:Creation xmlns:core="urn:c4h:core:2009">
04:   <mpeg7:Creator>                    <!-- encodes core:Creator -->
05:   <mpeg7:Role href="urn:mpeg:mpeg7:cs:RoleCS:AUTHOR">
06:    <mpeg7:Agent xsi:type="PersonType">
07:     <mpeg7:Name>
08:      <mpeg7:GivenName>Rob</mpeg7:GivenName>
09:      <mpeg7:FamilyName>Koenen< mpeg7:FamilyName>
10:     </mpeg7:Name>
11:    </mpeg7:Agent>
12:   </mpeg7:Creator>
```

```
13:    <mpeg7:Title xml:lang="en"> CAN 2010 football</mpeg7:Title>
14:    <mpeg7:Abstract>              <!-- encodes core:description -->
15:       <mpeg7:FreeTextAnnotation> All matches played in CAN 2010
             </mpeg7:FreeTextAnnotation>
16:    </mpeg7:Abstract>
17:    <mpeg7:CreationCoordinates>          <!-- encodes
                                        core:creationDateTime -->
18:       <mpeg7:CreationDate>
19:         <mpeg7:TimePoint>2008-07-13T14:10:00</mpeg7:TimePoint>
20:       </mpeg7:CreationDate>
21:    </mpeg7:CreationCoordinates>
22:       . . . . .
23: <mpeg7:Creation>
24:</didl:Descriptor>
```

19.5.3.2   Relationships Inside the Bundle

Within a CAM bundle, we can express simple-qualitative or complex-quantitative relationships that apply for some of the contained CAM object. A simple-qualitative relation (*relationship*) indicates only its nature. The complex-quantitative relation introduced has some specific attributes in order to better characterize the relation between two CAM objects. The simple *relationship* instances can be represented by a special-purpose didl:Descriptor that expresses the relationships between CAM objects by using the predefined mpeg7:relation element.

Box 19.4 illustrates the encoding of the *"SameEvent"* relationship between two CAM objects referenced by the mpeg7:source (which corresponds to core:sourceReference) and mpeg7:target (which corresponds to core: targetReference) elements. The mpeg7:typelist attribute indicates the nature of the relation between the source and target CAM objects (core:relationType).

Box 19.4 Relationship encoding between two CAM objects within a CAM bundle

```
01:<didl:DIDL xmlns:didl="urn:mpeg:mpeg21:2002:01-DIDL-NS">
02:    <didl:Container> ...
03:      <didl:Descriptor>
04:        <didl:Statement mimeType="text/xml; charset=UTF-8" >
05:          <mpeg7:relation typelist="urn:c4h:rel:SameEvent"
             source="#CAMObject1"
06:               target="#CAMObject2"/>
07:        </didl:Statement>
08:      </didl:Descriptor>
09:    </didl:Container>
10:   </didl:DIDL>
```

The concepts defined by MPEG-7 standard to describe the relationships between multimedia elements do not allow the description of complex relationships. Hence, we have

defined a new extension of mpeg7:RelationType element in order to support additional
descriptive parameters. Box 19.5 shows the XML Schema definition of this new element
(ExtendedRelationship). This new specification allows defining new parameters for
the relationships by introducing (name,value) pairs through the Param element.

Box 19.5 XML Schema for ExtendedRelationship element definition

```
01:<complexType name="ExtendedRelationship">
        <!-- encodes subclasses of core:Relationship-->
02: <complexContent>
03:  <extension base="mpeg7:RelationType">
04:   <element name="Param" minOccurs="0" maxOccurs="unbounded">
05:      <complexType>
06:       <attribute name="name" type="string" use="optional"/>
07:       <attribute name="value" type="anySimpleType"
           use="optional"/>
08:      </complexType>
09:   </element>
10:  </extension>
11: </complexContent>
12:</complexType>
```

In Box 19.6, we illustrate the encoding of the AdvertiseRelationship, which is
one of the relationships we have defined under CAM4Home project. It describes the fact
that an object referenced by #CAMObject1 includes some advertisement section that is
seen as an independent piece of content referenced by #CAMObject2 (for instance, a
movie trailer advertises the whole movie). AdvertiseRelationship contains attributes
describing the advertisement characteristics (its position, duration, size, a direct buying
link, etc.).

Box 19.6 Encoding of quantitative ExtendedRelationship instances

```
01:<didl:DIDL xmlns:didl="urn:mpeg:mpeg21:2002:01-DIDL-NS">
02: <didl:Container> ...
03:  <didl:Descriptor>
04:   <didl:Statement mimeType="text/xml; charset=UTF-8">
05:    <core:ExtendedRelationship xmlns:core="urn:c4h:core:2009"
             source="#CAMObject1" target="#CAMObject2"
             typelist="urn:c4h:rel:AdvertiseRelationship">
06:      <core:Param>
07:        <core:name>rapidBuyURL</core:name>
08:        <core:value>http://store.apple.com/us</core:value>
09:      <core:Param>
10:    </core:ExtendedRelationship>
11:   </didl:Statement>
12:  </didl:Descriptor>
13: </didl:Container>
14:</didl:DIDL>
```

For the community-created metadata that is not directly supported by MPEG-21/7, we make extensive use of the `didl:Statement` construct in order to embed in MPEG-21 description-specific metadata properties defined in CAM4Home.

19.5.3.3 Community-Created Metadada

Community-created metadata concept regroups all metadata created by users consuming the content (user comments, user ratings, or social tags). Since there is no MPEG-21/7 concepts allowing the description of such data, we have created new concepts for user feedbacks description. Box 19.7 illustrates the encoding of such metadata.

Box 19.7 A fragment of community-created metadata instance encoding

```
01:<didl:DIDL xmlns:didl="urn:mpeg:mpeg21:2002:01-DIDL-NS">
02: <didl:Container>
03:  <didl:Descriptor>
04:   <didl:Statement mimeType="text/xml; charset=UTF-8" >
05:    <core:CommunityCreatedMetadata
     xmlns:core="urn:c4h:core:2009">
06:       . . . . .
07:     <core:SocialTag>
08:      <core:tagValue>foot, match, zidane<core:tagValue>
09:     </core:SocialTag>
10:     <core:UserComment>
11:      <mpeg7:CreationTime>2003-04-20T13:20:25+09:00
        </mpeg7:CreationTime>
12:      <core:Comment> your video is null<core:Comment>
13:     </core:UserComment>
14:     <core:UserRating>
15:      <mpeg7:CreationTime>2003-04-20T13:20:25+09:00
        </mpeg7:CreationTime>
16:      <core:Rate>1/5<core:Rate>
17:     </core:UserRating>
18:       . . . . .
19:    </core:CommunityCreatedMetadata >
20:   </didl:Statement>
21:  </didl:Descriptor>
22: </didl:Container> ...
23:</didl:DIDL>
```

Even though in MPEG-7 some elements (such as `mepg7:KeywordAnnotation`) might have been used to encode social tag values, we have preferred to introduce new constructs in order to clearly state that such metadata are created by community lambda users and not necessarily by a clearly defined annotator. So, we found it ambiguous to have homonymous elements carrying information with very different levels of confidence.

In the following section, we discuss how the supplementary metadata can be encoded using MPEG-21 native constructs (such as DIA elements) or some extensions that we have designed.

19.5.4 Supplementary Metadata Encoding

The CAM4Home supplementary metadata model provides information about the context in order to enable the interoperability of various platform and content delivery services. The CAM4Home supplementary metadata provides the structures to profile users, communities, devices, networks, and platform services. The MPEG-21 DIA natively covers a part of the CAM4Home supplementary metadata model, so, naturally, we have tried to identify adequate mappings. MPEG-21 deals with most of the issues that we have defined under CAM4Home project. In this section, we show only a part of CAM4Home supplementary user-related metadata specification using MPEG-21.

19.5.4.1 Native Constructs for User Profile Encoding

Box 19.8 illustrates the use of MPEG-21 standard for encoding user profile. The example represents the encoding of metadata concerning user personal description (lines 04–09) which is a part of user profile.

Box 19.8 MPEG-21 fragment describing user profile

```
01:<dia:Description xsi:type="UsageEnvironmentType">
              <!-- encodes suppl:C4HUserPersonalDescription -->

02: <dia:UsageEnvironment xsi:type="UserCharacteristicsType">
03:   <dia:UserCharacteristics xsi:type="UserInfoType">
04:    <dia:UserInfo xsi:type="mpeg7:PersonType">
05:      <mpeg7:Name>
06:        <mpeg7:GivenName>John</mpeg7:GivenName>
07:        <mpeg7:FamilyName>Doe</mpeg7:FamilyName>
08:      </mpeg7:Name>
09:    </dia:UserInfo>
10:   </dia:UserCharacteristics>
11:  </dia:UsageEnvironment>
12: </dia:Description>
```

19.5.4.2 New Constructs for User Profile Encoding

In Box 19.9, we present some user-related metadata (about the user physiological state – lines 04–08) that is not enclosed in the MPEG-21/7. We have specialized the dia:UserCharacteristicsBaseType into suppl:PhysiologicalStateType in order to introduce specific information such as (blood pressure, fatigue level, etc.).

Box 19.9 PhysiologicalState instance encoding

```
01:<dia:Description xsi:type="UsageEnvironmentType">
              <!-- encodes suppl:C4HUserPersonalDescription -->
```

```
02: <dia:UsageEnvironment xsi:type="UserCharacteristicsType">
03:   <dia:UserCharacteristics xsi:
      type="suppl:PhysiologicalStateType">
04:     <suppl:PhysiologicalState
        xmlns:suppl="urn:c4h:suppl:2009">
05:       <suppl:bloodPressure> 12 cmHg</suppl:bloodPressure>
06:       <suppl:fatigue>false</suppl:fatigue>
07:       ......
08:     </suppl:PhysiologicalState>
09:   </dia:UserCharacteristics>
10:   </dia:UsageEnvironment>
11: </dia:Description>
```

19.6   Discussion

In this section, we discussed some of our choices to encode the metadata model. We have adopted an XML-based approach to encode it, as the processing of XML files is rather simple and widely spread. The data overhead resulting from the XML encoding is compensated by the flexibility of interpreting XML documents. In order to acquire significant compression rates and reduce the structure overhead, generic solutions exist [22, 23], and they can be applied directly to encodings before the transmission as well as the interpretation.

If our proposed metadata model had been made using plain XML (i.e., encoding based on XML Schema [24] only) it would have contained smaller data overhead. All the metadata related to a given element would have to be encoded together within the given element. However, we considered the extension of existing comprehensive multimedia description standards such as MPEG-21, as a well-established standard gives more visibility to our solution. The MPEG-21 covers similar topics as CAM4Home regarding the content (core part of CAM4Home) and the deployment context and environment (supplementary part of CAM4Home) descriptions. The main inconvenience of this solution is that the client would need to be capable of interpreting a very large set of encoding structures.

For covering parts of the metadata metamodel, which are not fully supported by MPEG-21/7, we have applied two different methods. The first one consists in introducing specific metadata by means of `didl:Statement` elements. This is applied when no similar concepts exist in MPEG-21/7. The second one corresponds to the extension of the existing description schemes and constructs of MPEG-21/7. This is applied when the existing MPEG-21/7 offers only restricted encoding possibilities (such as the `mpeg7:Relation` element or the `dia:UserCharacteristics`). We made this choice in order to keep the description as compatible as possible with the native MPEG-21/7 structures. Effectively, in this way, even applications that are not able to fully interpret the extended versions can still use the information in a restricted manner. One can rely on the fact that a given structure (like a complex relationship) is basically an extension of a well-known structure and treat it as such.

19.7   Conclusion and Perspectives

In this chapter, we have exposed an MPEG-21 encoding of a metadata model that we have designed collaboratively within the CAM4Home project. In future, new needs and new use contexts (intelligent networks, more powerful devices, etc.) will emerge. It is important to be able to respond to these two challenges by providing on the one hand means for extending the descriptions and, on the other hand, tools and encodings for adapting the descriptions to the interpretation capabilities of new devices or new networks.

The first part is ensured by the flexibility features of the encoding, as we have presented them in the previous section. The second part might require the automatic mapping between actual encodings (in MPEG-21) and future encodings. This work, in some way similar to ontology matching techniques, is currently explored in our research project [18, 25]. In future, we expect to free the client from any consideration related to a specific encoding. The client's queries are formulated using model terms, and the results are provided in terms of model instances without any reference to a specific encoding used to represent and transfer the information from one end to the other within the system.

References

[1] Gustafsson, E. and Jonsson, A. (2003) Always best connected. *Wireless Communications IEEE*, **10** (1), 49–55.
[2] Schulzrinne, H. and Wedlund, E. (2000) Application-layer mobility using SIP. *ACM SIGMOBILE Mobile Computing and Communications Review*, **4** (3), 1–9.
[3] International Organization for Standardization (2003) ISO/IEC 15938-5:2003. *Information Technology – Multimedia Content Description Interface – Part 5: Multimedia Description Schemes*, 1st edn, Geneva, Switzerland.
[4] Hunter, J. (2001) An overview of the MPEG-7 Description Definition Language (DDL). *IEEE Transactions on Circuits and Systems for Video Technology*, **11** (6), 765–772.
[5] International Organization for Standardization (2004) ISO/IEC 21000-2:2003. *Information Technology – Multimedia Framework (MPEG-21) – Part 2: Digital Item Declaration*, 1st edn, Geneva, Switzerland.
[6] International Organization for Standardization (2004) ISO/IEC 21000-7:2004. *Information Technology – Multimedia Framework (MPEG-21) – Part 7: Digital Item Adaptation*, 1st edn, Geneva, Switzerland.
[7] Klyne, G., Reynolds, F., Woodrow, C., and Ohto, H. *Composite Capability/Preference Profiles (CC/PP): Structure and Vocabularies*. W3C Recommandation, http://www.w3.org/TR/CCPP-struct-vocab/ (accessed 2004).
[8] Christensen, E., Curbera, F., Meredith, G., and Weerawarana, S. *Web Services Description Language (WSDL) 1.1*, http://www.w3.org/TR/wsdl (accessed 2001).
[9] Martin, D., Burstein, M., Hobbs, J., *et al.* (2004) (ed.) *OWL-S Semantic Markup for Web Services*, Member Submission. W3C, November, http://www.w3.org/Submission/OWL-S (accessed 2004).
[10] Burnett, I., Van de Walle, R., Hill, K. *et al.* (2003) MPEG-21: goals and achievements. *IEEE Multimedia*, **10** (4), 60–70.
[11] International Organization for Standardization (2003) ISO/IEC 21000-3:2003. *Information Technology – Multimedia Framework (MPEG-21) – Part 3: Digital Item Identification*, 1st edn, Geneva, Switzerland.
[12] Amielh, M. and Devillers, S. (2002) Bitstream syntax description language: application of XML schema to multimedia content adaptation. Proceedings of the 11th International World Wide Web Conference (WWW2002), May 7–11, 2002, Honolulu, HI.
[13] Amielh, M. and Devillers, S. (2001) Multimedia content adaptation with XML. Proceedings International Conference on Multimedia Modeling.

[14] Bilasco, I.M., Amir, S., Blandin, P. *et al*. (2010) Semantics for intelligent delivery of multimedia content. Proceedings of the 25th ACM Symposium on Applied Computing, March 22–26, 2010, Sierre, Switzerland.

[15] Zhou, J., Rautiainen, M., Ylianttila, M. *et al*. Metamodeling for community coordinated multimedia and experience on metamodel-driven content annotation service prototype. Proceedings of IEEE Congress on Services Part II, September 23–26, 2008, Beijing, China, pp. 88–95.

[16] TV-Anytime Metadata Specification. Online, http://www.tv-anytime.org.

[17] Sharable Content Object Reference Model (SCORM). *Advanced Distributed Learning*. Online, http://www.adlnet.org/ (accessed 1997).

[18] Amir, S., Bilasco, I.M., Sharif, M.H., and Djeraba, C. (2010) Towards a unified multimedia metadata management solution. *Intelligent Multimedia Databases and Information Retrieval: Advancing Applications and Technologiesl*, IGI Global.

[19] Metadata Encoding & Transmission Standard. *The Library of Contress*. Online, http://www.loc.gov/standards/mets (accessed 2002).

[20] IMS Content Packaging XML Binding. *IMS Global Learning Consortium*. Online, http://www.imsproject.org/ (accessed 2000).

[21] Bekaert, J., De Kooning, E., and de Sompel, H. (2006) Representing digital assets using MPEG-21 Digital Item Declaration. *International Journal on Digital Libraries*, **6** (2), 159–173.

[22] Pereira, F., Vetro, A., and Sikora, T. (2008) Multimedia retrieval and delivery: essential metadata challenges and standards. *Proceedings of the IEEE*, **96** (4), 721–744.

[23] Schneider, J. and Kamiya, T. *Efficient XML Interchange (EXI) Format*, http://www.w3.org/TR/exi/ (accessed 2007).

[24] Fallside, D.C. (ed.) (2002) *XML Schema Part0: Primer (W3C Recommendation*, http://www.w3.org/TR/xmlschema-0/ (accessed 2004).

[25] Amir, S. (2009) Un système d'intégration de métadonnées dédiées au multimédia. INFORSID'2009, May 26–29, 2009, Toulouse, France.

20

NinSuna: a Platform for Format-Independent Media Resource Adaptation and Delivery

Davy Van Deursen, Wim Van Lancker, Chris Poppe, and Rik Van de Walle

Ghent University – IBBT, Department of Electronics and Information Systems – Multimedia Lab, Belgium

20.1 Introduction

Recent years have witnessed an increasing heterogeneity in the multimedia landscape on different fronts. First, there is a growing diversity in end user devices that are able to consume multimedia content. In particular, these devices may vary in terms of screen size, processing power, and battery life. Next, network technologies, used to transport the multimedia content to the end user, may differ in terms of bandwidth, jitter, and error robustness. Furthermore, the number of multimedia coding standards has grown significantly over the last few years, especially with the introduction of new coding formats such as H.264/AVC [1], scalable video coding (SVC) [2], AAC [3], and JPEG XR [4]. At the same time, older standards such as H.262/MPEG-2 Video and MPEG-1 Audio are still present. Next to coding formats, there also exist a wide variety of delivery formats, that is, formats encapsulating encoded multimedia streams (e.g., the MP4 file format [5] or the real-time transport protocol (RTP) [6]). Finally, end users with specific preferences often want to obtain a personalized version of multimedia content (e.g., an end user only requesting scenes satisfying his/her interests). Therefore, metadata have an increasingly important role in multimedia search, adaptation, and delivery processes because they enable the effective organization, access, and interpretation of multimedia content.

This chapter introduces the design and functioning of NinSuna,[1] which is a fully integrated platform for multimedia adaptation and delivery based on MPEG and W3C

---

[1] NinSuna is short for "The NinSuna INtelligent Search framework for UNiversal multimedia Access".

The Handbook of MPEG Applications: Standards in Practice   Edited by Marios C. Angelides and Harry Agius
© 2011 John Wiley & Sons, Ltd

technologies. The platform is able to efficiently deal with the heterogeneity in the current and future multimedia landscape in terms of coding and delivery formats, usage environments, and user preferences. To satisfy these requirements and to obtain universal multimedia access (UMA) [7], NinSuna relies on format-agnostic adaptation engines (i.e., engines independent of the underlying coding format) and format-agnostic packaging engines (i.e., engines independent of the underlying delivery format). Moreover, the platform enables a seamless integration between metadata standards and adaptation processes.

NinSuna's basic design is inspired by the above described principles of XML-driven content adaptation techniques, while its final design consists of a hybrid architecture using both XML and Semantic Web technologies such as the resource description framework (RDF[2]), the Web ontology language (OWL[3]), and the SPARQL Protocol And RDF Query Language (SPARQL[4]). Furthermore, a tight coupling exists between NinSuna's design and a model for describing the structural, semantic, and scalability properties of media bitstreams. This model, implemented using OWL, provides support for a seamless integration of adaptation operations and semantic metadata. Furthermore, it allows format-independent packaging and delivery of multimedia content.

A various number of MPEG technologies are used to implement, support, or inspire the design of our NinSuna platform and its corresponding format-independent adaptation and packaging algorithms. A first category of MPEG technologies is the MPEG-21 digital item adaptation (DIA) tools [8]. More specifically, two format-agnostic content adaptation techniques were standardized within MPEG: the bitstream syntax description language (MPEG-B BSDL) and generic bitstream syntax schema (MPEG-21 gBS Schema). These techniques are based on automatically generated XML descriptions of the high-level structure of media resources. The XML descriptions, further denoted as bitstream syntax descriptions (BSDs), typically contain high-level syntax elements and pointers to data ranges in the original bitstream. BSDs are used to realize simple, high-level adaptation operations on compressed bitstreams. Examples are the removal of particular data blocks or the modification of the value of certain syntax elements. The actual adaptation takes place in the XML domain by transforming the BSDs using XML filters. A transformed BSD and its corresponding (original) bitstream are then used to create an adapted bitstream. Further, tools such as MPEG-21 usage environment description (UED), terminal and network quality of service (TNQoS) description, and universal constraints description (UCD) are used to determine well-fitted versions and adaptation parameters of requested resources. Also, the annotations of our media resources are based on the MPEG-7 specification. Finally, coding and container formats, which are specified in the MPEG-4 specification, are used to evaluate our platform (i.e., H.264/AVC, AAC, and MP4).

The organization of this chapter is as follows. The format-independent adaptation and delivery techniques used inside the NinSuna platform are outlined in Section 20.2. The global architecture and functioning of our adaptation and delivery platform are elaborated in Section 20.3; performance results are provided as well. Directions for future research are discussed in Section 20.4, while discussion and conclusions are provided in Section 20.5.

---

[2] http://www.w3.org/TR/rdf-concepts/
[3] http://www.w3.org/TR/owl-features/
[4] http://www.w3.org/TR/rdf-sparql-query/

20.2   Model-Driven Content Adaptation and Packaging

In this section, a new media resource adaptation and packaging technique, called *model-driven content adaptation and packaging*, is presented. Its design is inspired by the principles of XML-driven content adaptation techniques and is based on Semantic Web technologies and a model for media bitstreams covering the structural, semantic, and scalability properties of these media bitstreams [9].

20.2.1   Motivation

As discussed in the introduction, current format-independent content adaptation techniques are based on automatically generated XML descriptions (BSDs), that is, *structural metadata*. Despite its format-independent nature, XML-driven content adaptation has a number of disadvantages. The XML filters are dependent on the structure of the metadata and underlying coding formats. Furthermore, due to interoperability problems between XML-based metadata standards [10–12], integration with *semantic metadata* occurs in an *ad hoc* manner. Mappings between different XML-based metadata formats need to be implemented in different XML filters. Hence, creators of these XML filters cannot think in terms of high-level adaptation operations, but have to be aware of the underlying coding and metadata formats. For example, expressing the semantic adaptation operation (such as *select sport fragments*) in a scenario where two different content metadata standards are used (e.g., annotations are provided in both MPEG-7 and TV-Anytime) requires the development of two different XML filters (i.e., one that can interpret MPEG-7 and one that can interpret TV-Anytime).

The interoperability problems between XML-based metadata standards are due to the fact that XML Schema just describes grammars. There is no way to recognize a semantic unit from a particular domain because XML aims at document structure and imposes no common interpretation of the data contained in the document. For instance, taking into account different metadata standards, the same tags can have a different meaning, while tags with the same meaning can occur in different structures. Therefore, as is illustrated further in this section, Semantic Web technologies such as RDF and OWL can be used to enhance the interoperability among different metadata standards for multimedia content; thanks to the natural representation of objects and relationships [10, 11].

A logical step after the adaptation of multimedia content is multimedia delivery. Multimedia content is usually not delivered as elementary bitstreams but packed in a particular delivery format. Today, a significant number of delivery or packaging formats exists; examples are MPEG-4 Part 14 (MP4 file format) [5], MPEG-21 Part 2 (digital item declaration) [13], and RTP [6]. Since we have to deal with different coding formats on the one hand, and different delivery formats on the other hand, our goal is to develop a format-independent multimedia packager; that is, a generic software module that is independent of the incoming coding format and the outgoing delivery format. An additional challenge in this context is the coupling of format-independent multimedia adaptation with format-independent multimedia packaging. Therefore, we use MPEG-B BSDL to abstract the packed media bitstream and to enable the use of format-agnostic delivery modules. This way, we obtain a hybrid content adaptation and packaging technique using both XML and Semantic Web technologies.

20.2.2 Model for Media Bitstreams

The model for media bitstreams provides support for a seamless integration of adaptation operations and semantic metadata. As such, it enables the definition of adaptation operations on a higher level (i.e., based on the model), on the condition that current and future coding formats can be mapped to this model. The model for media bitstreams is implemented as an OWL DL ontology. The instances of the model (i.e., the structural metadata or BSDs) are expressed in RDF. The transformation of the structural metadata is implemented by using SPARQL queries, which are independent of the coding format. A visualization of an excerpt of our model is given in Figure 20.1.

The structural metadata part of the model (Figure 20.1a) describes information regarding the high-level structure of a compressed *MediaBitstream*. Such a *MediaBitstream* points to the physical location of the media bitstream by means of the *bitstreamSource* property. Further, it also provides the MIME (multipurpose Internet mail extensions) type of the underlying coding format by means of the *format* property. Also, delivery parameters (to assist in the packetization process) can be present by means of the *deliveryParameter* property. An example of a delivery parameter is the sampling frequency when the underlying coding format is AAC. The sampling frequency is a delivery parameter that is

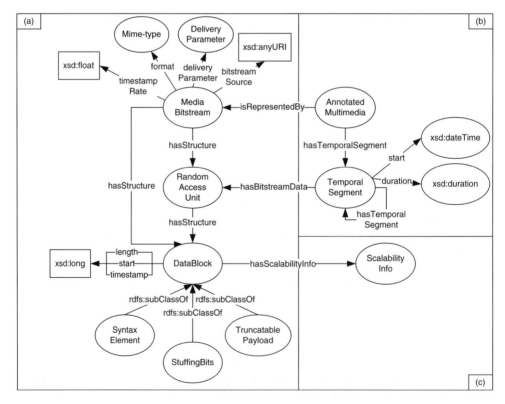

Figure 20.1 Excerpt of the model for media bitstreams. Ellipses and arrows represent OWL classes and properties, respectively.

needed by the packetization process of AAC streams, since the value of this parameter may be needed in the headers of a particular delivery format.

A *MediaBitstream* points to a list of *RandomAccessUnit*s by means of the *hasStructure* property. Random access refers to the ability of the decoder to start decoding at a point in a compressed media bitstream other than at the beginning and to recover an exact representation of the decoded bitstream [14]. Note that *RandomAccessUnit*s cannot overlap with each other.

Each random access unit points to a list of *DataBlock*s by means of the *hasStructure* property. Note that this property is transitive in order to express that *DataBlock*s are always contained in *MediaBitstream*s (even if they are located within a *RandomAccessUnit*). A *DataBlock* points to a particular segment of the compressed media bitstream by means of a bitstream position and a bitstream length in terms of bits. *DataBlock*s that must be available in every resulting media bitstream (e.g., sequence or picture parameter sets in H.264/AVC) are data blocks that do not belong to any random access unit. More specifically, the media bitstream points directly to these data blocks by means of the *hasStructure* property. Note that a *DataBlock* does not necessarily represent a well-defined structure in a coding format (such as a frame or slice); it just represents a single byte range pointer. Further, each *DataBlock* has a *time stamp*, which represents a number related to the display time of the data block. In order to actually calculate the display time, the *timestampRate* property of the *MediaBitstream* class is used. The latter contains a number indicating the amount of time stamps that are contained in 1 s. Additionally, a data block can contain *ScalabilityInformation* (Figure 20.1c), indicating to which scalability layers the data block belongs (in the assumption that the underlying bitstream is a scalable bitstream [15]).

The semantic metadata part of the model (Figure 20.1b) contains a content description of the media bitstream (i.e., *AnnotatedMultimedia*). *MediaBitstream*s are linked to an *AnnotatedMultimedia* instance by means of the *isRepresentedBy* property. *AnnotatedMultimedia* points to a list of *TemporalSegment*s by means of the *hasTemporalSegment* property. *TemporalSegment*s can be decomposed further into other *TemporalSegment*s by means of the *hasTemporalSegment* property. Note that different *TemporalSegment*s can overlap with each other. Each *TemporalSegment* points to a specific segment of the multimedia content by means of time stamps (i.e., *start* and *duration*). The connection between the semantic and structural metadata is realized by linking temporal segments (i.e., time stamps) to random access units (i.e., bits) by means of the *hasBitstreamData* property. Furthermore, already existing (domain-specific) ontologies can be linked to the semantic part of the model to create detailed semantic descriptions of the multimedia content.

Support for existing coding formats is provided by mapping them to the structural part of the model. When coding formats are mapped to the model and (domain-specific) ontologies are linked, instances of the model can be generated, resulting in a collection of RDF triples describing a particular media bitstream. Several possibilities exist to generate metadata compatible with the model. For instance, the semantic metadata could be obtained using feature extraction algorithms or by (manual) annotation. The resulting semantic metadata will consist of instances of *AnnotatedMultimedia* and *TemporalSegment*s. The structural metadata could be generated during the encoding of a media bitstream or by using generic software similar to the BSDL approach. As a result, a *MediaBitstream* instance is created accompanied by instances of *RandomAccessUnit*s,

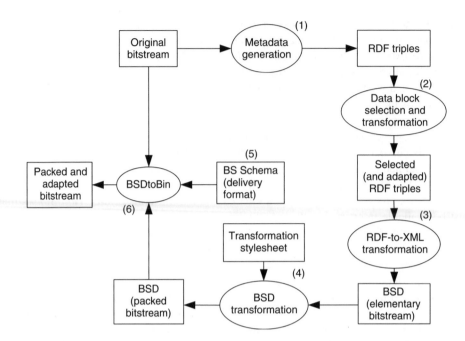

Figure 20.2   The general workflow of model-driven content adaptation and packaging.

*DataBlock*s, and so on. Note that the structural metadata generation process can take the semantic metadata as an input in order to connect the structural metadata with the seman- tic metadata (i.e., to link the bits of the encoded bitstream to the time stamps available in the semantic metadata). As previously discussed in this section, this is realized by linking *RandomAccessUnit*s to *TemporalSegment*s by using the *hasBitstreamData* property.

20.2.3 Adaptation and Packaging Workflow

The general workflow of model-driven content adaptation and packaging is depicted in Figure 20.2. Explanatory notes are given below.

1. *Metadata Generation.* Media bitstreams that need to be adapted and packaged in our framework have to be equipped with metadata compliant with our model for media bitstreams. Hence, the result of the metadata generation process is a collection of RDF triples compliant with the model for media bitstreams.
2. *Data Block Selection and Transformation.* RDF graphs describing data blocks are queried during the data block selection step. These data blocks, corresponding to the requested multimedia content, are selected using a SPARQL query. An example of such a query is shown in Listing 20.1. Evaluating this query results in the construction of a list of data blocks corresponding to the requested content. Hence, RDF graphs describing these data blocks are selected, constructed, and further processed.
   The primary goal of the data block transformation step is to make changes inside the selected RDF graphs describing a data block. For instance, the value of a *SyntaxElement* can be changed or the length of a *TruncatablePayload* can be shortened. A second use

case for data block transformation is the support for dynamic adaptations, that is, when the multimedia content is delivered during varying usage environment conditions. This way, each time an adaptation property changes, the initialization and evaluation of a new query can be avoided.

Listing 20.1 SPARQL query selecting data blocks based on user preferences

```
1    PREFIX mmo: <multimedia_model.owl#>
     CONSTRUCT {
         # triples to describe a datablock:
         ?db rdf:type mmo:DataBlock.
5        # ...
     }
     WHERE   {
         # select multimedia content based on a keyword:
         ?annoMM rdf:type mmo:AnnotatedMultimedia.
10       ?annoMM mmo:hasTemporalSegment ?segment.
         ?segment dc:creator 'John Smith'.

         # select the corresponding datablocks:
         ?annoMM mmo:isRepresentedBy ?bitstream.
15       ?bitstream rdf:type mmo:MediaBitstream.
         ?bitstream mmo:format 'video/H264'.
         ?bitstream mmo:hasStructure ?rau.
         ?segment mmo:hasBitstreamData ?rau.
         ?rau mmo:hasStructure ?db.
20       ?db rdf:type mmo:DataBlock.
         # ...
     }
```

3. *RDF-to-XML Transformation.* On the basis of the selected (and transformed) data blocks, a simple RDF-to-XML transformation is performed. The result of this transformation is a BSD (Section 20.1), which can be used to create a packaged version of the adapted media bitstream. An example of such a BSD is shown on the left-hand side of Figure 20.3. The classes and properties defined in our model, needed for the packaging process, are mapped to XML elements and attributes, respectively. Note that the time stamps are represented in terms of seconds and milliseconds.

4. *BSD Transformation.* The actual packaging process starts with the transformation of the BSD representing the adapted, elementary media bitstream. The resulting BSD represents an adapted and packaged media bitstream. The left-hand side of Figure 20.3 illustrates the BSD transformation for the RTP packaging of an AAC bitstream. The obtained BSD is compliant with MPEG-B BSDL, which implies that the BSDL framework can be used for further processing. The BSD transformation can be implemented using XSLT or STX, which enables the use of a format-independent transformation engine. However, it is important to note that the transformation stylesheets are not only dependent on the target delivery format, but also on the incoming coding format since each coding format requires a different packaging (i.e., fragmentation and packetization) strategy.

5. *BS Schema Creation*. A bitstream syntax (BS) Schema describes the high-level structures and syntax elements of a particular format. In this case, a BS Schema for the target delivery format needs to be created. The BSD obtained in the previous step needs to be compliant with this BS Schema. The right-hand side of Figure 20.3 shows an excerpt of the BS Schema for RTP.
6. *Adapted and Packed Bitstream Generation*. Finally, an adapted and packaged media bitstream can be created using BSDL's format-independent BSDtoBin parser, based on the BSD representing the adapted and packaged media bitstream, the BS Schema for the target delivery format, and the original media bitstream.

Packaging media bitstreams typically consists of two main processes: fragmentation and packetization. It is not trivial to see where these two processes actually occur in the above discussed workflow for model-driven content adaptation and packaging. Fragmentation is realized during the BSD transformation process, where the data blocks are mapped to fragments. Packetization is spread across multiple steps. One aspect is the assignment of time stamps to fragments. During the metadata generation step, the data blocks are labeled with initial time stamps (i.e., time stamps of the original media bitstreams). However, since the adaptation process can cause gaps in the initial time stamps (e.g., a particular scene is deleted during the adaptation), these time stamps need to be recalculated (i.e., the gaps need to be detected and corrected). The latter is performed during the

```
<MediaBitstream
    source="http://foo.foo/example.aac">
  <DeliveryParameters>
    <samplingFreq>48000</samplingFreq>
  </DeliveryParameters>
  <DataBlock start="665279" length="475"
             sec="0" msec="0"/>
  <DataBlock start="665754" length="447"
             sec="0" msec="21"/>
  <!-- ... -->
</MediaBitstream>
```

```
<RTP_stream
  bs1:bitstreamURI="http://foo.foo/example.aac">
  <rtp_packet>
    <rtp_header>
      <V>2</V>
      <P>0</P>
      <X>0</X>
      <CC>0</CC>
      <M>1</M>
      <PT>96</PT>
      <SN>0</SN>
      <TS>0</TS>
      <SSRC>0</SSRC>
      <!-- ... -->
    </rtp_header>
    <rtp_payload>665279 475</rtp_payload>
  </rtp_packet>
  <!-- ... -->
</RTP_stream>
```

BS Schema for RTP

```
<xsd:schema>
  <xsd:complexType name="RTP_header">
    <xsd:sequence>
      <xsd:element name="V" type="rtp:b2" fixed="2"/>
      <xsd:element name="P" type="rtp:b1"/>
      <xsd:element name="X" type="rtp:b1"/>
      <xsd:element name="CC" type="rtp:b4"/>
      <xsd:element name="M" type="rtp:b1"/>
      <xsd:element name="PT" type="rtp:b7"/>
      <xsd:element name="SN" type="xsd:unsignedShort"/>
      <xsd:element name="TS" type="xsd:unsignedInt"/>
      <xsd:element name="SSRC" type="xsd:unsignedInt"/>
      <!-- ... -->
    </xsd:sequence>
  </xsd:complexType>
  <xsd:complexType name="RTP_packet">
    <xsd:sequence>
      <xsd:element name="rtp_header" type="rtp:RTP_header"/>
      <xsd:element name="rtp_payload" type="bs1:byteRange"/>
    </xsd:sequence>
  </xsd:complexType>
  <xsd:element name="RTP_stream">
    <xsd:complexType>
      <xsd:sequence maxOccurs="unbounded">
        <xsd:element name="rtp_packet" type="rtp:RTP_packet"/>
      </xsd:sequence>
      <xsd:attribute ref="bs1:bitstreamURI"/>
    </xsd:complexType>
  </xsd:element>
</xsd:schema>
```

Figure 20.3 BSD-driven RTP packaging of AAC media bitstreams.

RDF-to-XML transformation. The packetization process also includes the addition of syntactical structures such as packet headers. This is done during the BSD transformation.

The choice to go back from RDF to XML during the packaging process can be justified as follows. We introduced Semantic Web technologies such as RDF to enhance the interoperability between different metadata standards. However, the latter is mainly an adaptation issue. More specifically, semantic adaptations such as scene selection, based on semantic metadata, are suffering from these interoperability problems (in case the adaptation is performed in the XML domain). In order to obtain packaging of media bitstreams in a format-independent way, a description of headers and syntax elements of the target delivery format is needed, together with pointers to data segments in the original bitstream, which is exactly what XML-based technologies such as MPEG-B BSDL support.

Note that the SPARQL query shown in Listing 20.1 expresses the semantic adaptation operation *select data blocks corresponding to temporal segments created by John Smith*. To show why it is beneficial to make use of RDF instead of XML, we illustrate the selection of data blocks from media bitstreams that were annotated using two different metadata formats (i.e., MPEG-7 [16] and Dublin Core [17]). Suppose we only want to extract fragments created by a specific person. When making use of XML-driven content adaptation and when relying on XML-based metadata, we need to take into account the structure and syntax of both MPEG-7 and Dublin Core descriptions. More specifically, we need to match the MPEG-7 creator tag (located in mp7:CreationInformation/mp7:Creation/mp7:Creator) and the Dublin Core creator tag (i.e., dc:creator). However, when the metadata is expressed in terms of RDF, we can state that the properties *mp7:Creator* and *dc:creator* are equal by using the *owl:equivalentProperty* property. Therefore, the SPARQL query shown in Listing 20.1 will select data blocks that are annotated by both MPEG-7 and Dublin Core metadata. Hence, using Semantic Web technologies to represent metadata enhances the interoperability between different metadata standards and allows us to express semantic metadata operations independent of the different underlying semantic metadata standards such as MPEG-7 and Dublin Core.

20.3 The NinSuna Platform

In this section, we introduce NinSuna,[5] which is a fully integrated platform for multimedia adaptation and delivery in heterogeneous usage environments, relying on both MPEG and W3C technologies for the implementation of format-independent adaptation and packaging engines (APEs) [18]. Furthermore, it aims at being deployable in streaming environments. Its multimedia content adaptation and packaging technique rely on our model for media bitstreams, as discussed in Section 20.2. Apart from the delivery of multimedia content, NinSuna also provides support for uploading content with corresponding metadata.

20.3.1 Architecture

The NinSuna architecture is shown in Figure 20.4. Three layers can be distinguished: the storage layer, the processing layer, and the front-end layer. The storage layer consists of

---

[5] A website containing information regarding the NinSuna platform and an on-line demo is available at http://ninsuna.elis.ugent.be.

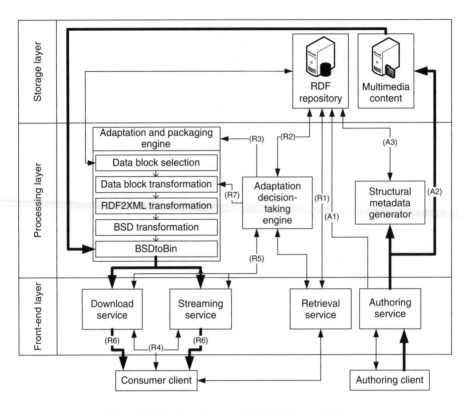

Figure 20.4   Architecture of the NinSuna platform.

a multimedia content server, containing the media bitstreams, and an RDF repository, containing all the necessary metadata (i.e., RDF triples compliant with our model for media bitstreams). The processing layer contains an APE (of which the working has been discussed in Section 20.2.3), a structural metadata generator (SMG) that enables the creation of triples compliant with the structural part of the model, and an adaptation decision-taking engine (ADTE). The ADTE calculates adaptation parameters [19], initializes the APE, and manages the different client sessions [20]. Note that its input is compliant with the UED, UCD, and TNQoS tools from MPEG-21 DIA. The front-end layer provides access points for clients of the NinSuna platform. New media bitstreams can be uploaded with their corresponding metadata using the authoring service. Information regarding media bitstreams can be obtained using the retrieval service. The adapted and packaged multimedia content is retrieved through the download or streaming service. The streaming service implements the RTSP (real-time streaming protocol), while the download service makes multimedia content available through (progressive) download-and-play scenarios (e.g., using MP4 as delivery format).

20.3.1.1   Workflow

Explanatory notes for the workflow within the NinSuna platform (Figure 20.4) are given below. The NinSuna platform allows authoring clients to communicate with the authoring service in order to extend the multimedia database. The workflow for uploading new multimedia content to the NinSuna platform is as follows:

A1. The authoring client sends semantic annotations for a particular media bitstream to the authoring service. These annotations, stored in the RDF repository, consist of RDF triples compliant with the semantic part of the model for media bitstreams.

A2. The authoring client uploads the actual multimedia content, encoded with a specific coding format, to the multimedia content repository.

A3. The SMG is used to generate the structural part of the metadata belonging to the uploaded media bitstream. It takes as input the encoded media bitstream and its semantic annotations and produces RDF triples compliant with the structural part of the multimedia model. The RDF triples are subsequently stored in the RDF repository. Note that the semantic metadata are needed by the SMG to create a mapping between the structural and semantic metadata (i.e., to connect random access units with temporal segments using the *hasBitstreamData* property, as discussed in Section 20.2.2).

Consumer clients of the NinSuna platform can make use of three services: retrieval, download, and streaming. The workflow for retrieving multimedia content is given below:

R1. The retrieval service makes it possible to query the RDF repository (by making use of SPARQL) in order to browse through the multimedia content, based on the available semantic metadata. Hence, the retrieval service can be compared to a SPARQL endpoint with a number of additional shortcuts to retrieve media bitstreams. Note that only the semantic metadata part can be browsed: the structural metadata are masked for the retrieval service since these metadata are irrelevant for the consumer client.

R2. The consumer client sends a SPARQL query in order to request a particular media bitstream (for an example of such a query, see Listing 20.1), together with a description of its usage environment (i.e., using the MPEG-21 DIA UED tools), to the retrieval service which passes this information to the ADTE. The latter creates a new session and selects coding and delivery formats based on the given usage environment characteristics. When the client desires both audio and video, two appropriate coding formats are selected. Next, the ADTE calculates the adaptation parameters for the selected coding formats by matching the scalability information of the requested content with the information about the usage environment (e.g., by comparing the video resolution with the screen size of the end user device).

R3. The ADTE initializes an APE with the received SPARQL query and the calculated adaptation parameters. Furthermore, it creates a URL for the consumer client, which indicates where the requested multimedia content can be found. This URL, which contains a session ID, is sent back to the consumer client.

R4. Depending on the received URL, the consumer client contacts the progressive download or streaming service to retrieve the desired content. When the streaming service is selected, the consumer client starts an RTP/RTSP session with the NinSuna platform.

R5. By using the session ID (included in the URL), the download or streaming service contacts the ADTE in order to obtain the proper session. Hence, based on the answer of the ADTE, the download or streaming service can determine which APE(s) will provide the requested content.

R6. The APE starts working (as described in Section 20.2.3) and provides the adapted and packaged media bitstream to the download or streaming service. When the streaming service is selected, the APE provides a stream of RTP packets. The latter are sent out by the streaming service to the consumer client according to the RTSP protocol.

R7. When the usage environment conditions change (e.g., the network connection changes from broadband to smallband), adaptation parameters can be dynamically adjusted. The consumer client uses the retrieval service to announce its new usage environment (i.e., using the MPEG-21 DIA UED tools). The ADTE recalculates and changes the adaptation parameters [20]. As discussed in Section 20.2.3, to avoid the initialization and evaluation of a new query each time an adaptation property changes, support for dynamic adaptations is provided in the data block transformation step.

20.3.1.2 Distributing NinSuna Across the Network

Communication within the NinSuna platform is realized using the HTTP protocol. Hence, the different components can be distributed across a network. First of all, the different layers (storage, processing, and front-end) can be divided across different machines. Furthermore, a pool of APEs and SMGs can be created to serve a large number of clients. These pools can also be divided across multiple machines. The management of the APEs can be done by the ADTE, which will choose the proper APE based on its current load. Management of the SMGs can be done by the authoring service. Note that such a distributed architecture increases the scalability of the platform, since it allows extending the platform with additional components in order to anticipate an increasing load.

20.3.1.3 Extensibility

One of the main features of the NinSuna platform is its format independency. Both the adaptation and packaging processes are format independent. Hence, it is rather straightforward to extend the platform with support for new coding, metadata, and delivery formats. Adding support for a new coding format consists of the following steps:

- A mapping needs to be created between the coding format and the model for media bitstreams. Note that this mapping is actually implemented and performed during the metadata generation step.
- XML transformation filters (implemented in STX or XSLT) need to be created for use during the BSD transformation step. More specifically, delivery formats that support the encapsulation of the new coding format and that are already available in the platform (i.e., a BS Schema exists for the delivery format) need to be taken into account. Hence, for each delivery format that needs to be supported for the new coding format, an XML transformation filter needs to be created.

New metadata formats are inherently supported, thanks to the use of our OWL-based model for media bitstreams: it is only necessary to align the new metadata format (i.e., ontology) with the semantic part of the model. Finally, a new delivery format is supported by the following steps:

- A BS Schema needs to be created, which describes the high-level syntax structures and syntax elements of the delivery format (as discussed in Section 20.2.3).
- XML transformation filters (implemented in STX or XSLT) need to be created for use during the BSD transformation step. More specifically, coding formats that are already supported by the platform and that are allowed to be encapsulated in the new delivery format need to be taken into account. Hence, for each coding format that needs to be supported for the new delivery format, an XML transformation filter needs to be created.

20.3.2   Implementation

The Java Platform, Enterprise Edition (Java EE) is used to implement NinSuna. Java EE enables the development of robust and scalable server-side Java applications; furthermore, complete Web services support is available. Sesame (version 2.1), which is an open source RDF database with support for RDF Schema inferencing and querying, is used as an RDF repository. The Sesame RDF API is used to access the repository and to evaluate the SPARQL queries. Within the APE, Saxon 6.5.5 and Joost v.2008-05-28 are used as XSLT and STX transformation engine, respectively. Also, an own Java implementation of the BSDtoBin parser is used. Note that we did not use the BSDL reference software due to the lack of support for multithreading. The SMG consists of parsers generated by Flavor [21], enhanced with support for the generation of RDF triples compliant with the structural part of the model for media bitstreams. Finally, the streaming service uses the RTSP implementation available in the C++ library of Live555 Streaming Media.

20.3.3   Performance Measurements

In this section, a number of performance measurements are presented to provide the reader with an impression of the performance of the NinSuna platform. First, a use case scenario is discussed, which is then followed by the experimental results.

20.3.3.1   Use Case Scenario

A number of news sequences were used to test our adaptation and delivery platform. Semiautomatic annotation was used for each news sequence; that is, shots were automatically detected after which each detected shot was manually annotated using the MPEG-7 specification. When mapping these metadata to our model for media bitstreams, each shot corresponds to a *TemporalSegment*, pointing to its MPEG-7 annotation.

The scenario to obtain (parts of) a news sequence is as follows. The user searches for news sequences containing news topics that are of his/her particular interest. Next, the user requests the selected news scenes and provides a description of the usage environment to the NinSuna platform. The latter selects the requested audio and video scenes, performs structural adaptations if needed (i.e., exploitation of scalability such as frame rate scaling), and packages the selected streams.

The multimedia content archive of NinSuna contained seven news sequences, each having a resolution of 720 × 432, a frame rate of 25 fps, and a length of approximately

22 min. The video streams of the news sequences were encoded using H.264/AVC. A hierarchical coding structure was used to obtain three layers of temporal scalability (i.e., the videos can be rescaled from 25 to 12.5 and 6.25 fps) [22]. Instantaneous decoding refresh (IDR) frames were inserted every 16 frames to obtain feasible random access. Further, the audio streams of the news sequences were encoded using AAC (with a sampling frequency equal to 48,000). Additional bitstream characteristics can be found in Table 20.1.

Two delivery formats are available in our scenario: RTP (streaming service) and MP4 (download service). Hence, three XML transformation stylesheets were developed: one STX stylesheet to guide the packaging of an H.264/AVC stream into RTP packets, one STX stylesheet to guide the packaging of an AAC stream into RTP packets, and one XSLT stylesheet to guide the packaging of an H.264/AVC and AAC stream into an MP4 container. We use STX for RTP because of its streaming capabilities. XSLT is used for MP4 because the format defines header values containing information related to the whole media bitstream, and these values need to be calculated at runtime (e.g., length of the resulting MP4 file and random access points in the media bitstreams). Note that we could have also used STX to implement the packaging process for MP4, but that would have introduced a significant overhead in terms of implementation effort because of the streaming character of STX.

Performance measurements were done on a PC having an Intel Pentium D 2.8 GHz CPU and 1 GB of system memory at its disposal. The operating system used was Windows XP Pro SP2, running Java 2 Runtime Environment (SE version 1.5.0_09). JProfiler 5.1.4 was used to profile our platform components. All time measurements were executed six times, whereupon an average was calculated over the last five runs to avoid start-up effects.

20.3.3.2 Structural Metadata Generation

As discussed in Section 20.3.1, the SMG enables the creation of triples compliant with the structural part of the model for media bitstreams. Enhanced Flavor-based [21] parsers are used to implement the SMG. For each of the seven news sequences, the SMG is used to generate their structural metadata. The memory usage of the SMG is low and constant (approximately 3 MB). Its execution times are provided in Table 20.2. For all

Table 20.1 Overview of the bitstream characteristics

Name	Length (s)	Video		Audio	
		Size (MB)	Bit rate (MBit/s)	Size (MB)	Bit rate (KBit/s)
news1	1302	217.5	1.34	19.7	124
news2	1301	198.7	1.22	19.4	122
news3	1274	184.7	1.16	19.9	128
news4	1284	196.9	1.23	20.0	128
news5	1460	198.2	1.09	22.3	125
news6	1269	187.3	1.18	19.2	124
news7	1305	174.4	1.07	20.4	128

Table 20.2 Execution times for the generation of structural metadata

Name	Video			Audio		
	Time (s)	Speed (MBit/s)	# Data blocks	Time (s)	Speed (KBit/s)	# Data blocks
news1	695.8	2.5	32,561	398.3	405.5	61,051
news2	753.0	2.1	32,538	381.8	417.0	61,008
news3	634.2	2.3	31,875	395.7	412.0	59,765
news4	625.1	2.5	32,111	396.2	413.4	60,207
news5	779.8	2.0	41,008	474.4	385.3	76,889
news6	736.6	2.0	31,729	403.0	391.3	59,491
news7	659.7	2.1	32,638	392.5	425.6	61,196

media bitstreams (audio and video streams), the SMG is able to generate the structural metadata in real time (i.e., the execution speed is higher than the bit rate of the media bitstream). The execution speed of the SMG is dependent on the following parameters:

- **# Parse Units per Second**. A higher number of parse units per second implies a lower execution speed for the SMG. Note that the number of parse units per second is dependent on the coding format (and its encoding parameters). For instance, a parse unit in H.264/AVC corresponds to an NALU. We have encoded the seven video news sequences in such a way that each NALU corresponds to one frame. Hence, the video streams are characterized by 25 parse units per second. Further, parse units for the audio news sequences correspond to AAC frames (containing 1024 samples), implying that the audio news sequences are characterized by 46.9 parse units per second.
- **# Skipped Bytes per Parse Unit**. A higher number of skipped bytes per parse unit implies a higher execution speed for the SMG. These skipped bytes correspond to the coded (audio or video) data (e.g., motion vectors and transform coefficients), because the SMG only parses high-level syntax structures of a media bitstream. In our example, the video news sequences have a higher bit rate than the audio news sequences (Table 20.1), implying that the video streams contain more coded data and hence that more bytes can be skipped by the SMG.

Table 20.2 also shows the number of data blocks that is generated for each media bitstream. In our case, a data block corresponds to a parse unit (i.e., an NALU for H.264/AVC and a frame for AAC). Since each data block is represented as an RDF graph, we can calculate the number of RDF triples that is necessary to represent the structural metadata. One RDF data block graph consists of five RDF triples. Further, one random access unit (RAU) (consisting of 3 RDF triples) points to 16 data blocks (for video) or 30 data blocks (for audio). For example, the total amount of RDF triples to represent the structural metadata for the *news1* video sequence is equal to $(32,561 * 5) + ((32,561/16) * 3) = 16,8910$.

20.3.3.3 Delivery of News Fragments

Three scenarios are considered to evaluate the delivery of (partial) media bitstreams. In the first scenario, a fragment of the media bitstream is selected occurring in the beginning of the media bitstream. The second scenario takes a fragment at the end of the media bitstream. The third scenario takes both fragments of scenarios 1 and 2. We distinguish these three scenarios in order to be able to investigate the impact of the temporal location of fragments in the original bitstream and the length of the selected fragments. More information regarding the resulting multimedia fragments of the *news2* audio and video sequences is provided in Table 20.3.

We have evaluated the media adaptation and delivery process within NinSuna in terms of peak memory consumption and execution times. Regarding the peak memory consumption, we do not consider the memory usage of the Java Virtual Machine and the Java Application Server, that is, only the memory usage is measured for the APE (i.e., data block selection and transformation, RDF-to-XML transformation, and BSD transformation and BSDtoBin). As shown in Table 20.3, RTP delivery is characterized by a low and constant memory usage (i.e., 10 MB). On the contrary, delivery using MP4 introduces memory usage that is dependent on the length (in terms of data blocks) of the multimedia fragments. This is due to the XSLT transformation that needs to store the full XML document, resulting from the RDF-to-SAX transformation, in memory. Note that this is necessary due to the presence of headers occurring in front of the MP4 file and covering information regarding the full bitstream (e.g., a list of random access points). In future developments, the XSLT stylesheet should be replaced by a more efficient streaming XML filter. Also, in Table 20.3, the time between the client's request and the first delivered byte (measured at server-side to avoid network delay) is provided (i.e., the latency). For RTP, the latency is low and independent of the length and position of the media fragment (i.e., 0.2 s). For MP4, the latency is dependent on the length of the requested media fragment. For instance, for scenario 3, the resulting MP4 file is available for (progressive) download after 8.2 s.

In Figure 20.5, the proportion between components of the APE are shown in terms of execution time percentages. RDF query, RDFtoSAX, and SAXtoBin correspond to data block selection, data block transformation and RDF-to-XML transformation, and BSD transformation and BSDtoBin, respectively. For RTP delivery, SAXtoBin takes most of the time with 65% on average. RDFtoSAX requires only a small proportion in terms of execution time (2%), while RDF query takes 33%. These proportions are independent of the length of the resulting media fragment; that is, they are only influenced by the resulting bit rate of the media fragment. For MP4 delivery, the proportions between the APE components are not independent of the length of the media fragment (the longer the fragment, the more the time spent by SAXtoBin). This is due to the

Table 20.3 Characteristics of the three delivery scenarios applied to the news2 sequence

	Original start offset (s)	Fragment length (s)	Fragment size (MB)		Peak memory usage (MB)		Latency (s)	
			MP4	RTP	MP4	RTP	MP4	RTP
Scenario 1	18	128	11.8	12.0	24	10	2.4	0.2
Scenario 2	810	139	18.5	18.0	25	10	2.5	0.2
Scenario 3	18	267	30.3	30.8	37	10	8.2	0.2

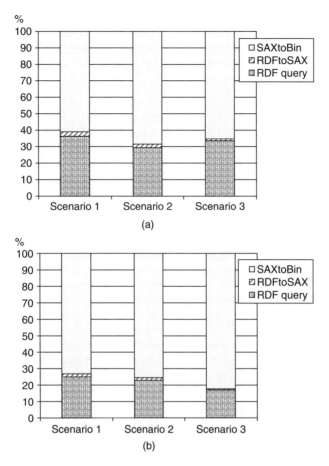

Figure 20.5 Proportion in terms of execution time percentages between components of the NinSuna platform: (a) news fragments delivered using RTP and (b) news fragments delivered using MP4.

decreasing performance of the BSD transformation when the size of the incoming XML document, which is dependent on the length of the media fragment, increases.

20.4 Directions for Future Research

Future work consists of the development of a more efficient MP4 packetizing filter. A SAX filter that is able to keep the header data of the MP4 file in memory could be created, while already writing the payload data to a temporary file. Note that the MP4 format also provides a solution in the form of *fragments*. More specifically, instead of one header covering the whole MP4 file, fragmented MP4 files contain multiple headers only covering parts of the MP4 file. This way, MP4 files can be created in an "on-the-fly" manner, making it no longer necessary to collect information regarding the full bitstream to create the header. Unfortunately, fragmented MP4 files are not supported yet by most media players.

Further, optimizations for the storage and retrieval of the structural metadata should be investigated. For example, one solution for this problem is to store the structural metadata and scalability information in an RDF store, which is specifically designed for the model for media bitstreams. In particular, the structural metadata and scalability information can be stored in a highly scalable relational database management system (RDBMS), using a database scheme based on the structural and scalability part of the model for media bitstreams. Hence, such an RDBMS can be seen as an efficient RDF store specifically designed for our model. RDBMSs should be capable of dealing with a large amount of structural metadata since they are mature, stable, and scalable, while also providing a high performance in terms of query execution speed.

Other future work consists of linking our model for media bitstreams to other multimedia ontologies. This will allow us to add fully detailed annotations to media bitstreams. Existing multimedia ontologies are listed by the MultiMedia SEMantics (MMSEM) W3C Incubator Group.[6] Following MMSEM, W3C has started a Media Annotation Working Group,[7] which has as mission to provide an ontology designed to facilitate cross-community data integration of information related to media objects in the Web, such as video, audio, and images.

20.5   Discussion and Conclusions

In this chapter, we presented a format-independent multimedia content adaptation and delivery platform, based on a model for media bitstreams. The platform combines MPEG and W3C technologies to get the benefits of both worlds. The model for media bitstreams covers the structural, semantic, and scalability properties of media bitstreams and is implemented by making use of OWL. Further, it provides support for a seamless integration of adaptation operations and semantic metadata, and supports format-independent packaging of multimedia content. Multimedia adaptation is performed by selecting and adapting portions of the structural metadata using SPARQL. Multimedia packaging is obtained by encapsulating the selected and transformed structural metadata within a specific delivery format. This packaging process is implemented using XML transformation filters and MPEG-B BSDL.

In an earlier work by the authors [23], a fully integrated multimedia adaptation platform relying on XML-driven content adaptation engines was presented. However, as discussed in Section 20.2.1, semantic adaptations introduce difficulties due to interoperability problems of XML between different metadata standards. Furthermore, the multimedia delivery in [23] is implemented by means of a dedicated and coding-format-specific streaming server. Hence, no generic solution for multimedia packaging is present. The NinSuna platform provides solutions for these problems by offering a seamless integration between adaptation processes and metadata standards, and by providing fully format-independent multimedia content APEs.

The continuous media markup language (CMML) [24] allows to annotate and index continuous media files. The presented architecture is able to extract temporal segments of media resources using a temporal URI scheme. A new file format is presented (i.e.,

---

[6] http://www.w3.org/2005/Incubator/mmsem/
[7] See http://www.w3.org/2008/01/media-annotations-wg.html for more information.

Annodex), which enables encapsulation of any type of streamable media resource (i.e., Annodex is coding-format independent). Annodex is based on the Ogg encapsulation format and is basically a bitstream consisting of media bitstreams combined with a CMML file. Comparing Annodex to our approach presented in this chapter, we can state that both solutions allow to extract temporal fragments from media resources in a format-independent manner. However, Annodex requires the use of a single delivery format (i.e., Ogg) while our approach is able to deliver media content using any delivery format, in a format-independent way. Further, in contrast to our approach, Annodex does not support structural adaptations of media resources (i.e., exploitation of scalability layers).

Digital item streaming (DIS) [25] is Part 18 of MPEG-21 and enables the incremental delivery of a digital item (covering both metadata and media resources) in a piece-wise fashion. DIS relies on the bitstream binding language (BBL) [26] for this purpose. BBL defines syntax and semantics to describe instructions on how a digital item can be fragmented and mapped onto one or more delivery channels. It uses the same principles for serializing the packed media bitstream as our proposed method; that is, MPEG-B BSDL is used to abstract the media bitstream and to enable the use of format-agnostic software modules. However, the BBL approach requires a new language to be used to specify the fragmentation and packetization process. Our proposed method to perform format-independent packaging requires knowledge of only commonly used XML transformation languages such as XSLT or STX. Furthermore, our model for media bitstreams provides support for the multimedia packaging process (i.e., time stamp support and coding-format-specific parameters). Hence, this information can already be calculated during the metadata generation step, which is in contrast to the BBL approach where this information needs to be calculated during the packaging process.

Ransburg *et al*. propose to use *media streaming instructions* within BSDs to implement a generic streaming server [27]. More specifically, access units (i.e., the smallest unit of data to which timing may be attached) are identified and time stamps are assigned to them. Note that these media streaming instructions have been adopted in the second amendment of the MPEG-21 DIA specification [28]. Using media streaming instructions, the fragmentation process and time stamp calculation are performed during the BSD generation step (i.e., during structural metadata generation). However, the fragmentation process is dependent on the delivery format (e.g., fragmentation of H.264/AVC streams is different for RTP and MP4 packetization). Also, BSDs including media streaming instructions are processed by delivery-format-specific software modules (e.g., an RTP packetizer).

López *et al*. present the CAIN-21 multimedia adaptation engine in [29]. It is an MPEG-21-compliant framework that facilitates the integration of pluggable multimedia adaptation modules, chooses the chain of adaptations to perform, and manages its execution. It is more focussed on the selection of adaptation tools and the adaptation parameters and less on format-independent delivery of (adapted) media resources.

Finally, the Darwin streaming server (DSS)[8] is an open source, cross-platform RTP/RTSP streaming server. It provides a coding-format agnostic design, that is, no codecs are present in the server. The streaming of media resources is guided by hint tracks, which contain all the information necessary to packetize and stream the media resource. Note that the creation of these hint tracks is coding-format specific (e.g.,

---

[8] http://developer.apple.com/opensource/server/streaming/

MP4Box[9] is a commonly used tool for the creation of hint tracks). Hint tracks can be compared to a part of our structural metadata (i.e., the mapping of time stamps to byte ranges of the media resource). However, support for adaptation operations is not available in DSS. Also, packing multimedia content with other delivery formats (other than RTP) is not possible.

Acknowledgments

The research activities as described in this chapter were funded by Ghent University, the Interdisciplinary Institute for Broadband Technology (IBBT), the Institute for the Promotion of Innovation by Science and Technology in Flanders (IWT), the Fund for Scientific Research-Flanders (FWO-Flanders), and the European Union.

References

[1] ITU-T and ISO/IEC (2003) 14496-10:2003. *Advanced Video Coding for Generic Audiovisual Services*.
[2] Schwarz, H., Marpe, D., and Wiegand, T. (2007) Overview of the scalable video coding extension of the H.264/AVC standard. *IEEE Transactions on Circuits and Systems for Video Technology*, **17** (9), 1103–1120.
[3] ISO/IEC (2005) 14496-3:2005. *Information Technology – Coding of Audio-visual Objects – Part 3: Audio*.
[4] Srinivasan, S., Tu, C., Regunathan, S.L., and Sullivan, G.J. (2007) HD photo: a new image coding technology for digital photography. Proceedings of the SPIE, vol. 6696, August, 2007, San Diego, CA.
[5] ISO/IEC (2004) 14496-14:2003. *Information Technology – Coding of Audio, Picture, Multimedia and Hypermedia Information – Part 14: MP4 File Format*.
[6] Schulzrinne, H., Casner, S., Frederick, R., and Jacobson, V. *RFC 3550: RTP: A Transport Protocol for Real-time Applications*. Online, http://www.ietf.org/rfc/rfc3550.txt (accessed 2003).
[7] Vetro, A., Christopoulos, C., and Ebrahimi, T. (2003) Universal multimedia access. *IEEE Signal Processing Magazine*, **20** (2), 16.
[8] ISO/IEC (2004) 21000-7:2004. *Information Technology – Multimedia Framework (MPEG-21) – Part 7: Digital Item Adaptation*.
[9] Van Deursen, D., Van Lancker, W., De Bruyne, S. *et al*. Format-independent and metadata-driven media resource adaptation using semantic web technologies. *Multimedia Systems*, **16** (2), 85–104.
[10] Arndt, R., Troncy, R., Staab, S. *et al*. (2007) COMM: designing a well-founded multimedia ontology for the web. Proceedings of the 6th International Semantic Web Conference, Busan, Korea.
[11] Decker, S., Melnik, S., van Harmelen, F. *et al*. (2000) The semantic web: the roles of XML and RDF. *IEEE Internet Computing*, **4** (5), 63–74.
[12] Stegmaier, F., Bailer, W., Bürger, T. *et al*. (2009) How to align media metadata schemas? Design and implementation of the media ontology. Workshop on Semantic Multimedia Database Technologies, December, 2009, Graz, Austria.
[13] Burnett, I., Pereira, F., Van de Walle, R., and Koenen, R. (eds) (2006) *The MPEG-21 Book*, John Wiley & Sons, Ltd, Chichester.
[14] Hannuksela, M.M., Wang, Y.-K., and Gabbouj, M. (2004) Isolated regions in video coding. *IEEE Transactions on Multimedia*, **6**, 259–267.
[15] Ohm, J.-R. (2005) Advances in scalable video coding. *Proceedings of the IEEE*, **93** (1), 42–56.
[16] ISO/IEC (2003) 15938-5:2003. *Information Technology – Multimedia Content Description Interface – Part 5: Multimedia Description Schemes*.
[17] Dublin Core Metadata Element Set, Version 1.1, ser. DCMI Recommendation. Dublin Core Metadata Initiative, January 2008. Online, http://www.dublincore.org/documents/dces/.
[18] Van Deursen, D., Van Lancker, W., De Neve, W. *et al*. (2010) NinSuna: a fully integrated platform for format-independent multimedia content adaptation and delivery using semantic web technologies. *Multimedia Tools and Applications – Special issue on Data Semantics for Multimedia Systems*, **46** (2–3), 371–398.

---

[9] http://gpac.sourceforge.net/packager.php.

[19] Sohn, H., Yoo, H., Lee, Y. *et al*. (2008) MPEG-21-based scalable bitstream adaptation using medium grain scalability. Proceedings of the TENCON 2008, November, 2008, Hyderabad, India.

[20] Mukherjee, D., Delfosse, E., Kim, J.-G., and Wang, Y. (2005) Optimal adaptation decision-taking for terminal and network quality of service. *IEEE Transactions on Multimedia*, **7** (3), 454–462.

[21] Eleftheriadis, A. (1997) Flavor: a language for media representation. Proceedings of the 5th ACM International Conference on Multimedia, November, 1997, Seattle, WA, pp. 1–9.

[22] De Neve, W., Van Deursen, D., De Schrijver, D. *et al*. (2005) Using bitstream structure descriptions for the exploitation of multi-layered temporal scalability in H.264/AVC's base specification. *Lecture Notes in Computer Science: Advances in Mulitmedia Information Processing – PCM 2005*, **3768**, 641–652.

[23] Van Deursen, D., De Bruyne, S., Van Lancker, W. *et al*. (2007) MuMiVA: a multimedia delivery platform using format-agnostic, XML-driven content adaptation. Proceedings of the 9th International Symposium on Multimedia, December, 2007, Taichung, Taiwan, pp. 131–138.

[24] Pfeiffer, S., Parker, C., and Schremmer, C. (2003) Annodex: a simple architecture to enable hyperlinking, search & retrieval of time continuous data on the web. Proceedings of the 5th ACM SIGMM International Workshop on Multimedia Information Retrieval, November, 2003, Berkeley, California, pp. 87–93.

[25] ISO/IEC (2007) 21000-18:2007. *Information Technology – Multimedia Framework (MPEG-21) – Part 18: Digital Item Streaming*.

[26] Thomas-Kerr, J., Burnett, I., and Ritz, C. (2008) Format-independent rich media delivery using the bitstream binding language. *IEEE Transactions on Multimedia*, **10** (3), 514–522.

[27] Ransburg, M., Devillers, S., Timmerer, C., and Hellwagner, H. (2007) Processing and delivery of multimedia metadata for multimedia content streaming. Proceedings of the 6th Workshop on Multimedia Semantics – The Role of Metadata, March, 2007, Aachen, Germany.

[28] ISO/IEC (2007) 21000-7:2007/Amd 2. *Information Technology – Multimedia Framework (MPEG-21) – Part 7: Digital Item Adaptation, Amendment 2: Dynamic and Distributed Adaptation*.

[29] López, F., Martínez, J., and García, N. (2009) CAIN-21: an extensible and metadata-driven multimedia adaptation engine in the MPEG-21 framework. *Lecture Notes in Computer Science: Semantic Multimedia*, **5887**, 114–125.

21

MPEG-A and its Open Access Application Format

Florian Schreiner and Klaus Diepold
Institute of Data Processing, Technische Universität München, Germany

21.1 Introduction

The MPEG group has developed several standards for the encoding and representation of audio, video, and metadata and designed these standards to match the needs of a range of anticipated applications. Other organizations outside of MPEG can choose from the list of MPEG-standards to create new specifications, which are tailor-made for industry-specific application scenarios. These specifications are a combination of the standardized technologies developed in MPEG. The DVD Forum and the Advanced Television Systems Committee are two prominent examples for such organizations: they developed the commercially successful DVD and the digital television system, respectively. The DVD has worldwide distribution and is commercially successful in the consumer electronic market and content creation industry. From a technical perspective, the product DVD consists of a data carrier from a factor that carries audiovisual media data which are coded using MPEG-2 video and audio as well as other non-MPEG technologies for the coding of the audio data. This successful combination of standardized technologies has been developed outside the realm of MPEG, because until recently, the MPEG group pursued a policy of creating generic and modular building blocks of standardized technologies, rather than complete systems which consist of combinations of different standard components, to arrive at a concise and application-specific solution. This has never been the mission of MPEG. More recently, the MPEG group initiated the family of MPEG-A standards [1] in order to fill this gap, developing application-driven formats for market-specific and industry-driven application scenarios. This modified modus operandi allows MPEG to create specifications which

The Handbook of MPEG Applications: Standards in Practice   Edited by Marios C. Angelides and Harry Agius
© Florian Schreiner and Klaus Diepold

consist of the best conceivable combinations of standard building blocks. This approach has become necessary because the task of picking technologies from the body of MPEG standards has become prohibitively difficult because of the increasing complexity and diversity of today's multimedia technologies.

MPEG-A standards are identified with ISO/IEC 23000 in the ISO/IEC numbering scheme and their goal is to ease the development and distribution for applications and services that require interoperability between different implementations. The standards in MPEG-A are also called *application formats* or AFs, which reflects their orientation toward specific application domains.

In previous standards MPEG has used the concept of "profiles", where a profile defines a subset of the syntax of a given standard to provide the technologies necessary to support a specific application scenario. For example, profiles have been instrumental in MPEG-2 video (e.g., main profile) or in MPEG-4 video (e.g., simple profile).

A profile may come in different levels, which define quantitative bounds on parameters associated with the contained tools to limit implementation complexity. Such bounded parameters can be, for example, the maximum allowed rate and memory. Thus, profiles offer a compromise to achieve a maximum of interoperability and functionality with respect to a limited overhead in the costs for the implementation and processing. However, profiles exist within one standard, such as MPEG-2 video, and do not allow combinations of subsets of two different parts of a standard; for example, it is not possible to have parts of MPEG-2 video and parts of MPEG-2 audio within one profile. Also, profiles do not provide mechanisms for combinations of technologies originating from totally different groups of standards, such as combining technologies from MPEG-4 [2, 3] with technologies from MPEG-7 [4].

Industry consortia like the digital video broadcasting project (DVB) or the 3rd Generation Partnership Project (3GPP) have created proprietary combinations of these technologies, matching the requirements of their respective application scenarios. However, this approach may also reduce the interoperability because the high amount of possible combinations can lead to significant differences between the resulting formats. These differences are incompatibilities that have to be incorporated in implementations that support multiple formats. As a consequence these implementations require intensive effort for development and result in more complex software or additional requirements to the hardware for the processing of the different formats.

21.2   The MPEG-A Standards

21.2.1   Concept

Each MPEG-A standard is designed for a specific application scenario and the components are chosen on the basis of this scenario. The components can originate from the whole set of standards in MPEG, which are tested and verified tools, capable of providing a suitable solution for a variety of application areas. The MPEG standards can be seen as a toolbox for the composition of an AF with the advantage that extensive investigation, implementation, and testing of the tools are not needed. An AF can also use non-MPEG standards if an application scenario needs particular tools that are not provided in MPEG. These tools from other organizations are added to an AF by reference. The goal is to

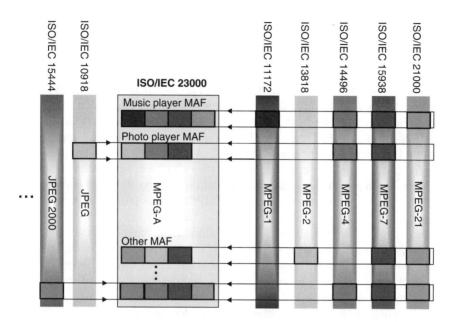

Figure 21.1   Concept of MPEG-A.

achieve a comprehensive and optimized solution for that particular application scenario so that companies can integrate and adopt tools effortlessly, for their product development.

Figure 21.1 shows the concept as an example with different standards from MPEG and outside of MPEG. The columns on the right represent MPEG standards and the boxes within the profiles in these standards (i.e., subsets of the standards). These profiles can be included in an AF to add the functionalities of the profile into the format. If an adequate profile does not exist in an MPEG standard, the AF can also select the required functionalities and technologies by itself. In this case, the AF contains a detailed description of the selected subset and the way of integration in the specification. The columns on the left side show examples for non-MPEG standards or other technologies. In this figure, the standards JPEG and JPEG2000 are depicted. An AF can also select a subset of these standards and combine them with chosen profiles from MPEG-standards. The resulting AFs with their different combinations are shown in the box with the headline ISO/IEC 23000. The way of combining is represented by the rows with the attached arrows and the components of an AF are shown as boxes.

For the utilization of the MPEG-A standards, it helps to understand their components and their structure. Each AF consists of two parts:

- The specification (textual description).
- The reference software (mostly as source code).

The specification contains the normative description of the AF, which comprises the components, their combination, and the usage. The components are explained in detail and references to standards outside of MPEG are added as required. The aim is to arrive at a comprehensive collection of technologies for the respective application scenario.

The reference software is an example of how to implement the standard and demonstrates the usage of the format. The software gives a company or any other implementer of products and services a technical basis to further develop and extend an application with additional functionalities. The reference software reduces the implementation effort and teaches how to apply the standard in order to achieve compliance. Companies can use this software to acquire an impression of the AF; they can accelerate their development process for new products and services. Furthermore, implementers of the standard spare the effort of searching, selecting, and implementing the appropriate ISO standards. The use of an MPEG-A standard facilitates the interoperability between products from different companies if they choose to support an AF as a whole. This leads to an improvement in acceptance and distribution of the related products.

At the beginning of the standardization of MPEG-A the individual parts were called "multimedia application formats", because the formats were mainly oriented toward multimedia content. However, this changed during the ongoing development of the standards and as further standards emerged, it became apparent that the specifications were not limited to dealing with multimedia content. These formats support multimedia content such as audio and video; they also support handling and management of other formats and data types. For this reason, the MPEG group decided to change the name to "application formats", so that the name does not restrict the standards to the multimedia area. Even if the original name is obsolete, the name can still be found in numerous documents created in this period. As of now, two AFs support multimedia and nonmultimedia content: the professional archival application format and the open access application format.

21.2.2 Components and Relations to Other Standards

To improve the understanding of MPEG-A, it is beneficial to understand the components of an MPEG-A standard and with it, the relations to the other standards. The MPEG group has specified several general standards for the compression of multimedia content, mainly for video, audio, speech, and graphics. These standards were specified in MPEG-1, MPEG-2, and MPEG-4 [2, 3, 5, 6]. In addition to the compression of multimedia content, MPEG also specified the MPEG-7 standard, which addresses the representation of metadata describing the content of media data. This voluminous standard also includes description schemes, system tools, and a description definition language [4]. The parts of MPEG-7 were the first standards that were generic and independent of the underlying content type and thus, also applicable in many areas of application. The same statement holds for the standards in MPEG-21 [7, 8]. MPEG-21 provides a framework for the creation, distribution, protection, and consumption of arbitrary digital content. Here, content is also called a *digital item*. A digital item comprises content and enriches it with standardized and machine-readable metadata, which can be used for the identification, description, and presentation of the content. The MPEG-21 framework also contains tools for rights management, protection, and adaptation of content, which form a basis for the creation of digital rights management systems with focus on interoperability between the systems.

All these MPEG standards will provide technically feasible solutions for specific application domains but the requirements vary widely, depending on the specific application domain. For most applications, it is desirable to have a high compression ratio to enable random access to the data and to provide high error tolerance. However, satisfying all these requirements may cause unacceptably high implementation costs or lead to prohibitive processing complexities. Compromising on those aspects and stripping down the standardized technologies to their bare necessities may cause a decrease in even the loss of interoperability for those implementations. Therefore, MPEG strives to find the most attractive trade-off between these factors for each application scenario, to arrive at lean and usable specifications.

In previous MPEG standards, the appropriate restriction of complexity for a standard to match the needs of a class of applications was done by specifying profiles and levels. This approach was sufficient for a long time but the ubiquity of multimedia content led to an explosion of different multimedia formats and implementations. For that reason it is insufficient to specify only profiles and levels within one standard without addressing the combination of individual components. To prevent the number of individual data formats from exploding, MPEG produces predefined and standardized superformats that package the appropriate tools in a complete solution. For example, by combining audio and video coding together with descriptive metadata, some rights management and protection tools can be the basis to build portable video players. MPEG-A provides these solutions as superformats, because they are designed to integrate the different elements of MPEG-1/2/4, MPEG-7, and MPEG-21 into concrete formats for specific application scenarios. The AFs contain standardized components that are required in their application domain; for example, only those elements of the MPEG-7 standard are integrated in an AF, which are needed for that specific metadata. MPEG-A increases interoperability at the application level and offers an optimized and tested basis for the subsequent development of sophisticated applications with proprietary extensions.

21.2.3 Advantages for the Industry and Organizations

The MPEG-7 and MPEG-21 standards contain an abundance of generic and broadly applicable technologies. While this is a positive thing per se, it forces implementers to invest significant efforts to pick and choose the building blocks which are appropriate for designing a particular product. The AFs offer a simplified access to these technologies, because they provide prepackaged standardized solutions and showcase the use of the numerous tools such as in MPEG-7 for metadata representation and the generic framework in MPEG-21.

MPEG-A allows companies to choose at a high level, the most appropriate AF for the targeted application scenario and with it, the required technologies to achieve a balanced format for the exchange and processing of content. The technologies in the AF are limited to the basics, so that only minimal efforts are needed to become familiar with the components and to support them in the implementation. The components are elaborated and tested tools that offer a solid and extensible solution. Companies and organization can use the AF as it is and go forward with the implementation, concentrating on further aspects for the development of a complete system. The standard offers interoperability, so that different implementations use the same basis, which increases the usability and acceptance in the market. The provided reference software demonstrates one way of implementing the AF. Typically, the reference software provides functions for the creation and processing of the files compliant to the standard, which can be used to reduce the training period and the development effort of new products. The software or parts of it can be flexibly integrated into new projects as a basic starting point for the initial development. In existing projects, parts of the software can be used to implement a standardized AF to achieve interoperability with other applications in the same domain.

The AFs can be understood as a treasure trove containing state-of-the-art technology, providing direct access to optimized solutions for specific application domains.

The concrete specification and the selected components of an AF depend on the chosen application scenario. The method of selecting the components and the resulting specification can be understood best with an example for a concrete application domain. In the following sections, the open access AF is shown as such an example of an AF to demonstrate the concept and the application of the MPEG-A standards.

21.3   The Open Access Application Format

21.3.1   Introduction

The open access AF [9, 10] is a basic interoperable format, to ease the exchange, management, and licensing of content material that shall be distributed free of charge. Today, there exists a variety of free content and the presence of such content has been increasing considerably over the last few years. Examples of such free content are user-generated content, teasers or publicly funded material. The open access AF is specified in the ISO/IEC family of standards that come with the identifier ISO/IEC 23000-7. It allows content creators to embed different content in a single file and to release it with additional metadata. This metadata can be some information about the content itself, the author of the content or a description of the license. The format and metadata are based on several components from MPEG-7 and MPEG-21. To sum up, the open access AF demonstrates the application of some standards in MPEG-7 and MPEG-21 and offers an insight into the concept and specification of an MPEG-A standard.

21.3.2   Concept

Content free of charge exists in many forms, depending on the content type and its origin. However, this type of content may consist of a collection of media content; each may be represented by different file formats, while all elements of the collection may be sharing metadata. For example, the content may come with a free-use license. This common information can be used to facilitate the distribution, sharing, and reuse of such content. Especially in the multimedia area, the distribution and availability of content that is free of charge is growing remarkably. The open access AF is a format which enables a content creator to attach appropriate metadata to this content. Consider the situation that a content creator wants to release his content to the public, but wants to inform the consumer about the licensing. For this purpose, the content creator can use the open access AF to publish his creative work in a single package, which contains the content itself, along with the metadata necessary to convey licensing information. This packaging is illustrated in Figure 21.2.

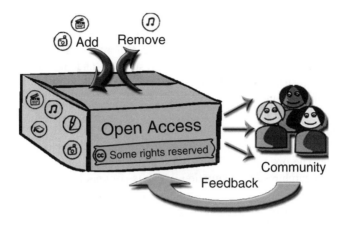

Figure 21.2   Overview of the open access AF.

The target audience for this type of content can be either the public or specific users. Furthermore, the author wants to promote his content with additional metadata describing the content. A part of the license information can be expressed in a machine-readable format, which supports the automatized management of licenses and eases the browsing and searching for content with a specific license. Additionally, in some cases, the content creator is interested in getting feedback about the usage of the content; that is, he/she wants to know about the spread and popularity of his/her content. The open access AF provides tools to implement a feedback mechanism that sends information about the usage of the content back to the creator.

21.3.3   Application Domains

The open access AF was designed for the publication and management of content. The standard with its features is specified in a generic way, to support a wide range of application domains which share similar properties. One example of publishing free content is open source software, which is promoted by the Open Source Initiative. Derived from this movement is "open content", which is not limited to software and source code. Open content can be any creative work independent of the content type, which allows the free distribution and modification of the work. The open access AF supports the distribution of this type of open software. The popularity of open content can be observed in the exchange of content within social networks such as sharing websites. One example of a sharing website is Wikimedia Commons, which provides already a large number of images, videos, and music. The licensing plays an important role for open content, because the terms of the license determine how the consumer may use the content. There are a variety of licenses available for open content allowing free distribution but differing in the terms of the utilization and the application of the content.

Creative Commons [11] developed a set of such licenses, each of them with different license terms. Some of these licenses are already used for many open content. All licenses defined by Creative Commons allow the free distribution of the content, but they contain different restrictions on its utilization. During the publishing process, the author can select one of these licenses, one which contains the terms in the license that he wants to apply to the content. The licenses defined by Creative Commons differentiate in their level of strictness; that is, some licenses are more restrictive and others contain very little restriction. Such a restriction can be for example, the prohibition of adaptation or the commercial use of the content.

Another initiative supported by the open access AF is "open access". The open access movement promotes free access to content in a way similar to the open content movement but the licenses in open access may contain more restrictive license constraints than for an open content one. The open access initiative supports and fosters the open publication of publicly funded research results, a situation which is commonly encountered in academia. These results shall be made publicly available and be distributed freely. However these results are not necessarily open content, for example, because the author may choose not to allow its commercial use. Therefore, content which is published according to open access can be understood also as open content, but it can also be published with more restrictions. In academia, open access became an international movement to enable the publication of scientific literature and documents without cost. This movement was confirmed with a declaration in 2003 [12], which was signed by 255 scientific institutions and organizations worldwide. This declaration demonstrates the importance of the open access movement and the gradual change in the way the academic domain intents to publish. As the publication process according to open access is not limited or tuned to one specific publisher or to one specific organization, the management, exchange, and referencing of publications across different systems turns out to be difficult and requires substantial organizational efforts.

The open access movement and the open content community already created a colossal amount of content available free of charge, but there are several problems that prevent their effective exchange and utilization. Some of these problems can be solved if all content comes with metadata using a common format. The legal license is one of these problems, for example, which needs to be connected to the content to inform the user. However, this connection is proprietary, so that each company or organization offers its own way or even several ways to assign a license to a piece of content. In many cases this connection is unclear and somewhat loose, because the license is kept in a separate file and is not directly connected with the content. This can be also observed on sharing websites for open content, where the license is shown on the site, but this information gets lost after the content has been downloaded. The license can also be embedded additionally in the content itself, but there is no common format to specify the license for all available content types. A machine-readable format for the legal license which is attached to the content can support automatic parsing, searching, and indexing of the different licenses assigned to content in a repository. In addition, search engines can be developed, which profit from this information and allow users to find content that matches specific license criteria. One of these criteria could be permission for the adaptation of the content. This allows users to know easily, if they are allowed to modify the content and publish the modification. This also helps the user to easily decide if the content is appropriate for him/her. The open access AF solves these problems and enables an interoperable exchange and identification of content and licenses. It also supports the licensing process in open access and hence eases the management of content in the repositories.

These are some dominant application domains for using the open access AF, but the format itself is not limited to them. It can also be used for document management within or between companies because the format also allows assignment of licenses only to specific users or to a group of users. The author can give a different set of permissions to the public and another set of permissions to specific users. This allows the author to distinguish between users and gives the author the possibility of describing in detail, the rights granted in the license. Furthermore, cryptographic digital signatures are used in the open access AF, to allow the verification of the authenticity and integrity of the exchanged content. The consumer can verify if the content really originates from the author and if the content and the license is unmodified. This enables companies or organizations to securely exchange content between users using this security attribute.

21.3.4 Components

Open content and open access are two concepts demonstrating that a machine-readable description attached to the exchanged content can improve the management, sharing, and promotion. The open access AF provides a general solution, which attaches human- and machine-readable metadata to the content. The open access AF provides a data packaging format that embeds the metadata along with the content, in a single file. Within the specification of the format, the content is also called a *resource*, which can be of any type of data; for example, a video file or a presentation, or images, or even software.

Figure 21.3 shows the basic scenario of the open access AF, which consists of three phases. In the first phase, the author of some content packages it in a file compliant with the open access AF standard, which is also called the "open access file". During the creation of this file, the author can specify the metadata, which comprises a description of the content, the author, and the license. As license he can choose to apply one of the Creative Commons licenses. In that case he adds the legal license text together with a machine-readable identification and representation of the license. The license information is attached to the content to inform the consumer about the license and the associated permissions granted by the license. In the second phase, the content is published and shared with the public or a community. The provided metadata can be used to present the content in the file to the users in a transparent way and to efficiently apply indexing and searching. This supports the distribution and promotion of the content, because the user does not need to open the file to find content that suits his/her needs. If the user finds appropriate content and he/she wants to consume it, then he/she enters the third phase.

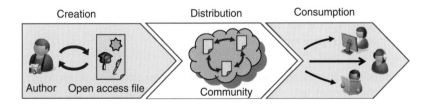

Figure 21.3 Basic scenario for the open access application format.

In this phase, the license is presented to the consumer before or during the consumption of the content, which informs his/her about the terms of the license.

The components of the open access AF are based on standards in MPEG-21 and MPEG-7. Most of the standards used in the open access AF originate from the MPEG-21 framework, which was specified for the delivery and consumption of content. One technological item comes from the MPEG-7 standards, which provides elements for the description of the content. The following standards are used in the open access AF:

1. MPEG-21 Part 2 – Digital item declaration (DID).
2. MPEG-21 Part 3 – Digital item identification (DII).
3. MPEG-21 Part 5 – Rights expression language (REL).
4. MPEG-21 Part 9 – File format.
5. MPEG-21 Part 15 – Event reporting.
6. MPEG-7 Part 5 – Multimedia description schemes (MDS).

These standards are structured hierarchically in the file format. The file format and its composition is depicted in Figure 21.4. The MPEG-21 file format is a generic format based on the ISO file format, which is already widespread. It frames the MPEG-21 DID [13] and the resources in a single file using a binary file structure. The resources represent the content as binary data, which are attached at the end of the file. The MPEG-21 DID specifies the metadata of the resources in XML format. Within the MPEG-21 DID, each resource is represented as an "Item", which comprises all metadata for the content in a single structure. This metadata consists of the standards MPEG-21 DII, REL, event reporting, and the MPEG-7 MDSs. The item is a superior structure that combines the metadata for a resource to a single re-identifiable object.

21.3.5 Realization of the Functionalities

The open access AF provides several functionalities derived from the support of the open content and open access. The open access AF provides the following functionalities:

- A standardized and open file format.
- Packaging of arbitrary data independent of content type.
- Global identification of the published content.
- Legal license information.
- Author and creation information.
- Machine-readable rights expressions.
- Adaptation and aggregation of content.
- Feedback mechanism for the author.
- Support for cryptographic signatures.

These functionalities are realized with subsets of several standards from MPEG-21 and MPEG-7. The file format and the packaging of the content in the file were shown in the previous section. The realization of the other features is explained in the following sections.

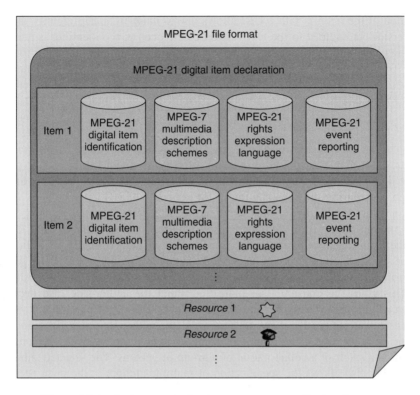

Figure 21.4   Basic scenario for the open access application format.

21.3.5.1   Global Identification of Content

The identification of the items is a vital part, which enables the management of the published content. The recognizability allows for example, the detection of duplicates and the synchronization between different content repositories. The MPEG-21 DII provides an identification scheme, which allows authors to assign globally unique identifiers to the content within the MPEG-21 DID. The values of the identifiers contain uniform resource identifiers (URIs), which are widely used and allow a hierarchical organization of the identifiers.

21.3.5.2   Legal License and Author Information

The license is a central aspect for publication according to the open content and open access initiative, because it informs the consumer about the conditions for the utilization of the content. Thus, it is also in the interest of the consumer to have a clear specification of the license regarding the license type and version. The open access AF supports three options to attach legal licenses: a text, a URI, and a link to a web page. In the text field, the author can embed the full text of a license so that the content and the license text are directly associated at the time of publication. However, this approach is inefficient, because the reader has to read the license text or to identify the license by himself. The specification of the license with a URI allows one to unambiguously identify the license and its version. In contrast to the text version of the license, the identifier is additionally machine-readable and globally unique, which allows indexing and searching for specific licenses. To achieve this, a registration authority is required that assigns unique URIs to licenses. As mentioned before, Creative Commons provides a set of different legal licenses, which can be used for the publication of free distributable content. Creative Commons provides a URI for its licenses which can be used for example, within the open access AF. One example of such a URI is http://creativecommons.org/licenses/by/3.0/. The third option, the specification of a web page, is an additional source of information for the consumer. It may provide more detailed information about the license or present it more intelligibly. However, this information is only available if the consumer has access to the web page during the consumption of the content.

In the open access AF the information about legal licenses is specified using MPEG-7 MDS. A minimal subset of this comprehensive standard is used in the open access AF to include the licensing information in the item as part of the MPEG-21 DID. In addition to that, the specification of information about the author and creation date is also supported. This information can be, for example, the name, address, e-mail, and website of the author. This gives the consumer an indication about the author and also declares the attribution of the creation of content to the author. This is also important for many legal licenses that require the clear declaration of the author to assign the rights for the attribution. In some cases, the author of some content is not a single person because the content is a result of a collaboration of a group of persons. The selected subset of the MPEG-7 MDS also allows the specification of multiple authors in the open access AF.

21.3.5.3 Rights Expressions

Rights expressions are declarations of rights assigned to content, written in a machine-readable syntax, and using semantics which are specified in the ISO/IEC 21000-5 REL. The specification of the open access AF does not contain instructions on how these rights can be applied in an implementation of the standard. Each implementation can utilize this information differently and decide how to process and present it to the user. One possibility for its application in an implementation of the open access AF is to use this language to allow the author to model the intentions of the legal license. This information can then be used to ease the management and utilization of the content. As the rights expressions are machine-readable, the application can inform the consumer if (s)he has the intention to perform an action that might infringe the license. This could happen if (s)he tries to adapt a piece of content that the license does not allow to be modified.

The open access AF references a predefined profile from the MPEG-21 REL [14, 15], which is specified as the ISO/IEC 21000-5/Amd3 REL OAC (open access content) profile [16]. This profile is based on the requirements of the open access AF. It combines elements from the MPEG-21 REL and additional elements in a profile to support this type of publication. A separate profile was created for the rights expressions to simplify the utilization in other applications. One of these applications is the MPEG-A media streaming AF [17], which also refers to the OAC profile in its specification and implementation.

The elements in the OAC profile support the licenses used for open content and the open access initiative. Some of these licenses are the ones defined by Creative Commons, which can also be modeled using the rights expressions in the OAC profile [18]. This allows the author to express the basic intentions of a Creative Commons license in a machine-readable way and to attach them to the content. As only the intentions can be modeled, the rights expressions are not legally related to the licenses defined by Creative Commons, because the model is not capable of representing the fine details and implications in a legal license. It also depends on the jurisdictional interpretation of the license because this can differ in many ways; for example, the country of issuance of specific license terms.

The rights expressions and their application in the open access AF are a capable mechanism to provide a variety of features. To acquire some idea about these features, some exemplary XML elements and their meaning in the OAC profile are explained. The names of the XML elements and attributes appear in **bold**.

Figure 21.5 shows the structure of the rights expressions compliant with the OAC profile. A license specifies the issuer and can contain several grants. A grant assigns one right to one principal for one resource under several conditions. The principal of a right can be either a person or a device, which can exercise the granted right.

Table 21.1 shows the rights and conditions included and defined in the MPEG-21 REL OAC profile. The elements marked in italics in the table are defined in the profile; the other elements are taken from other profiles of the MPEG-21 REL.

The rights **execute, play, print** allow the consumption of the content and are generally included in the licenses. With the right **adapt** an author can decide whether the released content can be adapted and published again. This informs the consumer that (s)he can either adapt the content or just use the content as it is. The right **governedAdapt** also allows the derivation of content, but only under the condition that the same rights and conditions are assigned to the adapted content as for the original content. With the right

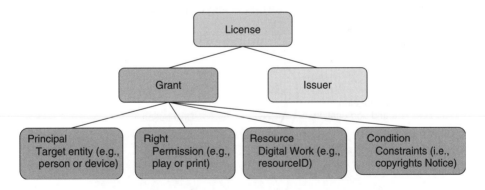

Figure 21.5 Rights expressions in the OAC profile.

Table 21.1 Rights and conditions in the MPEG-21 REL OAC profile

	Elements
Rights	execute, play, print, adapt, *governedAdapt*, governedCopy
Conditions	*copyrightNotice, nonCommercialUse, sourceCode*, territory

governedCopy the consumer can create copies of the items, whereas the license has to remain attached to the copy. The conditions in the OAC profile notify the consumer about the restrictions in the usage of the content. The element **copyrightNotice** requests the consumer to read a copyright text before (s)he can perform the associated right. For example, the consumer has to accept the license conditions before (s)he can adapt the content. If the author intends the content should not be used commercially, he can apply the condition **nonCommercialUse**. The condition **sourceCode** informs the consumer that adaptations shall contain the original resource or at least its accessible location within the derived content.

21.3.5.4 Adaptation and Aggregation of Content

Often, content is published as open content or as open access and it is supposed to be used and enhanced by the community. These collaborative enhancements are supported in the open access AF by allowing the authors to recombine freely created, adapted, and aggregated content and to publish it. In the open access AF, an aggregation is defined as the recombination of published items into a new open access file. An adaptation is performed by modifying an existing item and publishing the adapted item. Figure 21.6 shows an example for an adaptation and aggregation in the open access AF.

Adaptations and aggregations are often performed and even desired for free distributable content. The development and evolution of such content often relies on the collaboration of different authors. The open access AF supports aggregations as copying items as a whole between files from different authors. An item comprises the content and the metadata, so that the metadata remains attached to the content after copying. The author can explicitly allow aggregation by selecting the right **governedCopy** from the rights expression to declare that the consumer can freely distribute and copy the content.

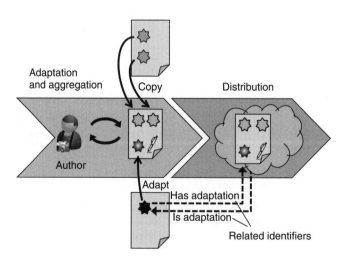

Figure 21.6 Example for adaptation and aggregation. The gray stars are aggregated, the black star was adapted. After publication, the related identifiers create a link between the original and the adapted star.

Adaptations are supported in the open access AF with two rights expressions and the related identifiers. The OAC profile provides the rights **adapt** and **governedAdapt** to grant the adaptation under chosen conditions. This information is machine-readable and can be used to notify the user before and after the adaptation. One example would be if an author intends to release an adapted content, where the original content does not allow adaptation. In this case, the software can inform the user that the adaptation is not permitted according to the rights expressions provided for the original content.

Adaptations are also enhanced with the related identifiers, which are specified in the MPEG-21 DII standard. After an adaptation, these identifiers specify a relationship between the adapted and the original item. The related identifiers are also depicted in the example shown in Figure 21.6. The related identifiers allow users to find the related content for a given item. This relation can be either the original content of a given derived content, or the available derivatives from a given content. Other content is referenced by URI, which allows identification of the content and possibly the retrieval of the content as well, from a central repository. This relationship also has a legal implication for adaptations because for the derived content, it specifies the attribution to the author of the original content. Some licenses require the specification of this attribution within the content, to declare the origin of the original content.

21.3.5.5   Feedback Mechanism

The feedback mechanism can be optionally activated for the content and allows the author to request a feedback from the published content. This feature is based on the MPEG-21 event reporting, which defines requests that can be attached to the items. These requests cause the creation and transmission of an event report on certain events. The open access AF supports the events "extraction" and "derivation" as possible events for the generation of a report. Thus, when a consumer wants to extract or adapt some content with an attached request, the report will be sent to the author. The full scenario with adaptations, aggregation, and the feedback mechanism is shown in Figure 21.7.

21.3.5.6   Cryptographic Signatures

For the exchange of content between different companies or organizations, verification of authenticity and integrity may be required. The open access AF optionally uses cryptographic signatures to allow the verification of content. This allows the detection

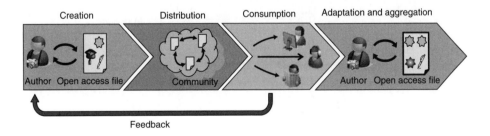

Figure 21.7   Full scenario of the open access AF.

of transmission errors or the malicious modification of content. The open access AF supports the embedding of signatures according to W3C XML Signature Syntax and Processing standard into the MPEG-21 DID. The application of the signature is optional so that an author may decide if the content shall be signed or not.

The signatures can be flexibly applied either on each item separately or on all items together. This allows authors to choose to sign only the content that requires a signature for the publication. Other content such as text files or images might not need to be signed. The signature algorithm and the trusted exchange of the public key are not specified in the standard. It is up to the implementation to choose a concrete algorithm and a public key infrastructure for the exchange and verification of the public key.

21.3.6 Implementation and Application of the Format

The implementation of a standard demonstrates its application and practical usage. In this section, two implementations of the open access AF are presented, that show the creation and application of the metadata provided in the standard.

21.3.6.1 Reference Software

The main features of the open access AF are demonstrated in the reference software, which is provided together with the textual specification. The software demonstrates the application of the standard and gives an idea of the advantages. The implementation is written in the Java programming language and is available on the website on-line [19] as open source software. This allows an ongoing development of the software within the community and the reuse of the source code in other projects. The reference software works as a basic file editor for the creation and consumption of open access files. It implements all parts of the standard and demonstrates the application of the metadata provided in the file. It can be used in other projects as a starting point or as a library for the creation, parsing, and modification of open access compliant files.

Architecture

In Figure 21.8, the main components and the structure of the software are shown. It also indicates the interfaces to external libraries and the operating system.

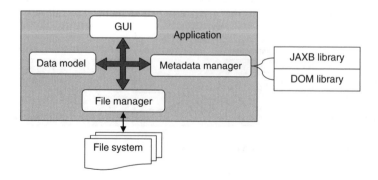

Figure 21.8   Architecture of the reference software.

The software is composed of four main components:

- The graphical user interface (GUI).
- The data model.
- The model manager.
- The file manager.

The GUI component contains functions for the creation of a user interface, which shows the content of an open access file in a user-friendly way and allows the user to modify the metadata. The GUI supports the user in the creation of an open access AF compliant file. All necessary information can be entered in text fields and the software checks the values for compliance. This information is then passed to the data model and data manager for the ongoing processing.

The data model is data storage for the required information, which consists of the content model and the user data model. The content model represents the resources and the metadata in the open access file. The metadata is the descriptive information for the content and license management. This model is aligned to the file format to ease the loading and storing of the metadata. The user data model contains the user information and the cryptographic keys assigned to the user. The user information identifies the user, for example with his/her name or his/her address, which is required for the release of open access files. The cryptographic keys are used for user authentication and are also applied for cryptographic signing operations.

The file and model manager contain the methods and operations for the data model. The file manager has access to the file system and allows opening and saving of open access files according to the MPEG-21 file format. The file manager can directly read and store open access files on the system. During the opening of a file, the file manager parses the file format and reads the XML metadata and resources as binary data. Similarly, the manager enables storage of the information from a data model into a file on the file system, which is standard-compliant and may contain verifiable signatures. The file manager is also used to add and save resources to a file or to delete resources.

While the file manager handles the file format and the resources, the model manager processes the XML metadata. It uses the JAXB and DOM library to parse and validate the XML metadata for standard compliance and verifies the embedded signatures. It converts the XML data into a content model and provides functions to extract data from the model and modify the model.

Functionalities

The software can be used for the creation and consumption of open access files. For each task, the software operates in a different mode. In the creation of an open access file, the user selects and enters all resources and metadata in the program. The user can save regularly his inputs in an editable file, called "package file". This file stores all metadata and resources in a certain point in time and can be reloaded later for further modifications. Once the editing is finished, the user can release the file and create a standard-compliant open access file. The released files cannot be modified any more. Their metadata is presented to the user and the resources packaged in the file can be consumed.

Initialization

The software has to be initialized on the first execution, because some information about the current user and mail system is required. During the initialization the software displays two dialogs. In the first dialog, the user enters his personal information, for example his/her name and address, which is required later on for the creation of open access files to identify the author. If there already exists an infrastructure to provide such personal information, such as a user directory, the dialog is not required because this information can be retrieved automatically from the infrastructure. In a second dialog, the software asks the user for the mail-server, which can be used to send e-mails. This is required for the transmission of event reports during the consumption of open access files. Other possibilities to determine the address of the mail-server is to read it from the operating system or to set the address statically to a specific host if the software is only deployed in selected networks. When the initialization is finished, the main window is shown and the user can use the software.

Main Window and File Browsing

The main window is shown in Figure 21.9. The software works in a manner similar to an archiving program, and allows the user to browse through directories or open files.

A menu and a tool bar in the upper part present the user with the operations that (s)he can execute in the current state. After startup, it allows the user to create a new editable package file or to open an existing file. The software uses two file extensions for the files: the extension ".oa" is used for a package file and ".m21" for a released open access file.

As soon as the user opens a package file, the software enters the creation mode and the user can continue to modify and prepare the file for the release. (S)He can add, delete items or alter the existing metadata. Furthermore the user can copy an existing item into the current file. This is explained more detailed in a following section. When the user finishes the modification of the file, (s)he can release the file and create a standard-compliant open access file which can be shared.

When the user opens a released open access file, the software changes into the consumption mode. In this mode the user can view the information in the file and (s)he can consume the items packaged in the file.

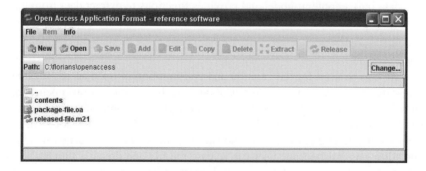

Figure 21.9 Main window of the software.

Creation Mode

The user can enter the creation mode by creating a new file or by opening a package file. The main window shows the items in the current file in a list. The user can modify the current package file in order to finalize it for the release. To add a new item, the user has to choose the resource, which can be any file containing arbitrary data. After that (s)he specifies the metadata for that resource in a dialog as shown in Figure 21.10.

The dialog shows the different metadata categories in the open access AF. The metadata categories are from top to bottom:

- Title and description of the image, as well as the author of the image.
- License information for the image, that is the copyright, license tags or the web page of the license.
- License properties described with rights expression from the MPEG-21 REL.
- Feedback information that will be retransmitted to the author on a chosen event.
- Relationship information to other items such as the adapted item of the current item.

All entered information is stored in the data model of the current file using the methods in the model manager. When the user has specified all items with the corresponding metadata, the user can release the file, which creates a standard-compliant open access file. If signatures are chosen, the application signs the selected items with a key pair assigned to the user. The file is then saved as an MPEG-21 file with the methods provided by the file manager. The user can then open the released file to enter the consumption mode.

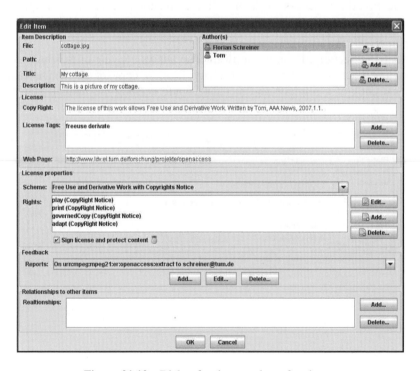

Figure 21.10   Dialog for the metadata of an item.

Relationships to Other Items

The function to set relationships between the items demonstrates the application of rights expressions provided in the standard. The relationship to another item can be one of two types showing the direction of the adaptation: either the other item is an adaptation of the current item or the current item is an adaptation of another item. To set a relationship to another item, the user first has to choose the other open access file containing the related item. The software opens the file and shows its items in a dialog as shown in Figure 21.11.

The user chooses one of the two relationships types and then selects the related item in the list. The figure shows the case that the selected item was adapted to create the current item. When the user selects the type of relationship with the radio boxes, the software reacts and automatically marks the items in the list to notify the consumer that the author of the selected item might not have allowed to set this kind of relationship. The software determines this information by examining the rights expressions of the other item. If the selected item does not grant the right "adapt" to the user, an adaptation might not be explicitly allowed by the author. In this example, the image "waterfall.jpg" grants the right "adapt" to the user, while the document "latex-doc.tex" shall not be adapted and is thus marked grey. If the user tries to set this relationship nevertheless, he is notified with another confirmation dialog that the author did not allow the adaptation of the item. Generally, the software only notifies the author that he might possibly act against the license. The user can still choose to ignore the notification and create and publish the derived content. It is the responsibility of the user to know if the adaptation is legally allowed or not. This functionality shows one way for the application of the rights expressions in the open access AF, which assists the user in the creation and release of adaptations.

Copying Items

As mentioned in Section 21.3.6, the software also allows copying of existing items from a released open access file into other package files. A copy of an item is defined as the identical copy of a resource and metadata while keeping the relation between both

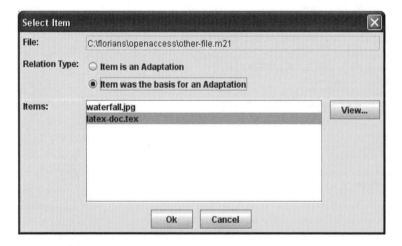

Figure 21.11 Specification of the relationship to another item.

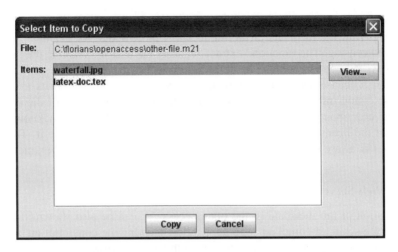

Figure 21.12   Selection of the item to copy.

parts intact. This function allows the user to create aggregations of existing items or combinations with his/her own items. When the user wants to copy an item out of another file, (s)he opens the other file and a dialog as is shown in Figure 21.12.

The software makes use of the rights expression to show the user the items which grant the right to copy and those that do not allow copies. This is done in a way similar to the one for the relationship between items. If the user intends to copy an item that does not allow this operation, the user is notified that there is no right granted for this action.

Consumption Mode

For the processing and presentation of open access files the software switches to the consumption mode. In this mode, the software shows the content of the file as shown in Figure 21.13.

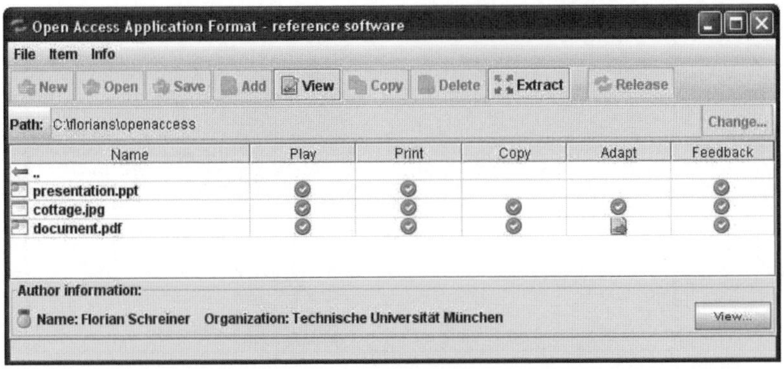

Figure 21.13   Content of an open access file in consumption mode.

The table contains the names of the items and the assigned rights for the item. The user can also view the metadata of the file to know more about, for example, the content itself or the licensing. The function "extract" enables the user to consume the item so that he can access the content and use it. Before the user can access the content, (s)he has to acknowledge a license dialog and eventually the event reports are sent back to the author. The license dialog informs the consumer about the license conditions of the content and informs the user about the rights expressions of the content. If the user acknowledges the reception of the license dialog, (s)he can save the file on a disk and use it. This ensures that the user is aware of the licensing before the software performs the extraction.

21.3.6.2 Web Server Scenario

The application of the metadata in the open access AF can be also shown in the implementation of a standard-compliant web application showing the content of an open access repository. The goal in this scenario is to enable the user to browse and search the content of the repository and to exchange the files. The software is implemented as a Java servlet, which is executed in a servlet container on the web server. The generated pages use the AJAX technology to create a client-side web application with asynchronous loading of data from the server. The servlet uses most components of the reference software as libraries for the file and metadata management; however, it replaces the GUI with the web interface and a different functionality. The software can parse open access files in the repository and allows the user to search or browse for content matching specific criteria. An example of such a web page for a repository of icons is shown in Figure 21.14.

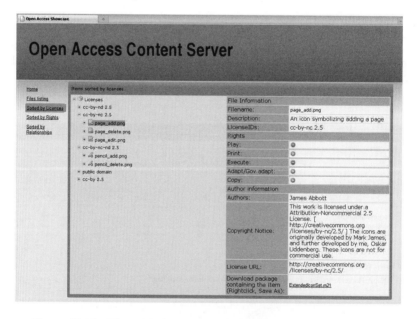

Figure 21.14   Hierarchical overview over the items in a web browser.

In this example the icons represent items, which are categorized according to their license. This allows the user to find items that have a specific license and thus grant the corresponding right in their license. The user can find items matching his/her requirements more efficiently, using the standardized metadata provided in the open access AF. Other categories implemented in the software are the rights expressions or the relationships between the items. When the user has found a suitable item, (s)he can download the resource and consume it on his/her computer.

21.3.7 Summary

The open access AF is a format that eases the management and exchange of free distributable content. It packages different content in a single file and includes metadata. This is beneficial in a multitude of application domains that deal with free distributable content. The file format and the metadata is based on standards from MPEG-21 and MPEG-7. The open access AF demonstrates the application of these standards and gives an example of the different elaborated standards in MPEG-A.

References

[1] Diepold, K., Pereira, F. and Chang, W. (2005) MPEG-A: multimedia application formats. *IEEE Multimedia*, **12** (4), 34–41.

[2] Pereira, F. and Ebrahimi, T. (2002) *The MPEG-4 Book*, Prentice Hall, Upper Saddle River, NJ, USA.

[3] Diepold, K. and Möritz, S. (2004) *Understanding MPEG-4: Technology and Business Insights*, Focal Press, Burlington, MA, USA.

[4] Manjunath, B.S., Salembier, P. and Sikora, T. (2002) *Introduction to MPEG-7: Multimedia Content Description Interface*, John Wiley & Sons, Inc, New York.

[5] Fogg, C., LeGall, D.J., Mitchell, J.L. and Pennebaker, W.B. (1996) *MPEG Video Compression Standard*, Chapman and Hall, London, GB.

[6] Haskell, B.G.H., Puri, A.P. and Netravali, A.N. (1997) *Digital Video: An Introduction to MPEG-2*, Chapman and Hall, London, GB.

[7] ISO/IEC (2004) 21000-1:2004. *Information Technology – Multimedia Framework (MPEG-21) – Part 1: Vision*, Technology and Strategy, Geneva, Switzerland.

[8] Burnett, I., Van de Walle, R., Hill, K. *et al.* (2003) MPEG-21: goals and achievements. *IEEE Multimedia*, **10** (4), 60–70.

[9] ISO/IEC (2008) 23000-7:2008. Information Technology – Multimedia Application Format (MPEG-A) – Part 7: Open Access Application Format, Geneva, Switzerland.

[10] Schreiner, F., Diepold, K., Abo El-Fotouh, M. and Kim, T. (2009) Standards: the MPEG open access application format. *IEEE Multimedia*, **16** (3), 8–12.

[11] Creative Commons. Online, http://creativecommons.org/ (accessed 28 January 2010).

[12] Berlin Declaration on Open Access to Knowledge in the Sciences and Humanities. Online, http://www.zim.mpg.de/openaccess-berlin/berlindeclaration.html (accessed 30 January 2010).

[13] Burnett, I.S., Davis, S.J. and Drury, G.M. (2005) MPEG-21 digital item declaration and Identification – principles and compression. *IEEE Transactions on Multimedia*, **7** (3), 400–407.

[14] ISO/IEC (2004) 21000-5:2004. *Information Technology – Multimedia Framework (MPEG-21) – Part 5: Rights Expression Language*, Geneva, Switzerland.

[15] Wang, X., DeMartini, T., Wragg, B. *et al.* (2005) The MPEG-21 rights expression language and rights data dictionary. *IEEE Transactions on Multimedia*, **7** (3), 408–417.

[16] ISO/IEC (2008) 21000-5/Amd3:2008. Information Technology – Multimedia Framework (MPEG-21) – Part 5: Rights Expression Language, AMENDMENT 3: OAC (Open Access Content) Profile, Geneva, Switzerland.

[17] ISO/IEC (2008) 23000-5:2008. *Information Technology – Multimedia Application Format (MPEG-A) – Part 5: Media streaming application Format*, Geneva, Switzerland.

[18] Rodriguez, E. and Delgado, J. (2006) Towards the interoperability between MPEG-21 REL and creative commons licenses. Proceedings of the 2nd International Conference on Automated Production of Cross Media Content for Multi-Channel Distribution, 2006. AXMEDIS '06, pp. 45–52.
[19] Open Access Reference Software (2009). Online, http://sourceforge.net/projects/openaccessaf (accessed 15 January 2010).

Index

1080i video, 38, 51, 54
2-D logarithmic (TDL) search, 183
720p video, 38, 56
802.11a/g, 47

AAC, 490
abstract DID model, 407–8, 411
access unit, 130
ActiveMovie, 37
adaptation, 512
adaptation and packaging engine, 485
adaptation decision taking, 140
adaptation decision-taking engine, 486
adaptation quality of service (AQoS), 140
advanced audio coding (AAC), 39, 56
advanced encryption standard (AES), 151
Advanced Media Workflow Association
    (AMWA), 71
Advanced Television Standards Committee
    (ATSC), 12, 343, 349, 354
Advanced Television Systems Committee, 499
advertising, 103–15, 117, 119–21
AFX, 11
    behavioural models, 11
    biomechanical models, 11
    cognitive models, 12
    geometric models, 11
    modelling models, 11
    physical models, 11
aggregation, 512
aggregation metadata, 461
AJAX, 520
Alliance for Telecommunications Industry
    Solutions (ATIS), 344–7
analysis, 269–70, 288
annotation, 263–9, 272, 276–7, 280–1, 283,
    285–9, 317–20, 322–3, 325, 335, 337,
    339

application format (AF), 499
application programming interface (API), 37
architecture, 514
arithmetic coding, 175
audio features, 356–7
authorisation proof, 439, 442
authorised domain, 445
AVC, 12
AVCHD, 12, 38
AXMEDIS, 405, 420–6, 430

bandwidth dealing, 395, 398–9
BIFS, 9–10
bit allocation, 177, 180, 186–95
bit fluctuations, 197
bitstream extraction, 129
bitstream syntax description (BSD), 129, 142
block-based gradient descent search (BBGDS),
    183
block matching motion estimation (BMME),
    182–3
blocking, 84
blocking artifacts, 39, 44
Blu-ray Disc, 12
B-pictures, 3–4, 8, 13
broadcast video servers, 63
BS Schema, 484
BSAC, 9
BSDtoBin, 484

C4H structures, 466
CAM, 456
CAM abstract supplementary metamodel, 463
CAM bundle, 461–2, 466–5
CAM external metamodel, 462
CAM metadata model, 460
CAM object, 461–2, 465–6

The Handbook of MPEG Applications: Standards in Practice   Edited by Marios C. Angelides and Harry Agius
© 2011 John Wiley & Sons, Ltd